W9-ANI-791

Multicultural
Writers
from Antiquity
to 1945

Multicultural Writers from Antiquity to 1945

A Bio-Bibliographical Sourcebook

Edited by
ALBA AMOIA and
BETTINA L. KNAPP

GREENWOOD PRESS
Westport, Connecticut • London

Library of Congress Cataloging-in-Publication Data

Multicultural writers from antiquity to 1945 : a bio-bibliographical sourcebook / edited
by Alba Amoia and Bettina L. Knapp.
    p. cm.
  Includes bibliographical references and index.
  ISBN 0–313–30687–7 (alk. paper)
  1. Authors—Biography. 2. Literature—Bio-Bibliography. 3. Multiculturalism in
literature. I. Amoia, Alba della Fazia. II. Knapp, Bettina Liebowitz, 1926–
PN452.M85   2002
809—dc21   00–069146
[B]

British Library Cataloguing in Publication Data is available.

Library of Congress Catalog Card Number: 00–69146
ISBN: 0–313–30687–7

First published in 2002

Greenwood Press, 88 Post Road West, Westport, CT 06881
An imprint of Greenwood Publishing Group, Inc.
www.greenwood.com

Printed in the United States of America

The paper used in this book complies with the
Permanent Paper Standard issued by the National
Information Standards Organization (Z39.48–1984).

10 9 8 7 6 5 4 3 2 1

Me tenant comme je suis, un pied dans un pays et l'autre en un autre, je trouve ma condition très heureuse en ce qu'elle est libre.

[In that I stand with one foot in one country and the other in another, I am a free man and find my situation to be a very happy one.]

—René Descartes,
Oeuvres et Lettres, p. 1305

Contents

Preface and
Acknowledgments

This reference volume attempts to summarize the life and work of a sampling from the host of writers who have contributed through the ages to the understanding and, in many cases, the enrichment of cultures other than their own. The Merriam-Webster dictionary definition of the word "multicultural" is "of, relating to, reflecting or adapted to diverse societies." Today, with the continuing growth of travel and migration and the intercontinental exchange of language and ideas, the word has taken on new and diverse overtones. To an extent undreamed of even a generation ago, we have all come to be largely "multicultural" in our lives and outlook. The thrust of the word in contemporary life encompasses a variety of tags and slogans that run the gamut from nationalism to universalism, from identity to "Otherness."

For the purposes of this volume, "multicultural authors" are those authors who lived, as children or adults, in a culture other than their own, and whose writings include works reflecting their experience of a different way of life, a different set of values, a different view of the world. Profiles of writers from antiquity to the watershed year of 1945 that closed World War II offer a selection of ancient, medieval, Renaissance, and modern authors, as well as a spectrum of linguistic, ethnic, and cultural diversities. Our choices were made with the aim of including as many names, eras, and nationalities as possible within the limitations of a single volume.

These original chapters focus specifically on the effects of multiculturalism and acculturation (or lack of acculturation) on the selected writers. The chapters, presented for easier reference in alphabetical rather than chronological or geographical order, generally include (1) an outline of the author's particular intercultural career and its repercussions on his or her works; (2) a discussion of multicultural themes in the works of the author; (3) a selective survey of criticism; and (4) a bibliography of and about the author, limited in most cases to those works that reflect a multicultural perspective. The volume concludes with a select bibliography featuring a selection of dictionaries and encyclopedias of world literature, as well as an index highlighting the writers' multicultural contacts, influences, and themes.

We are grateful to Professor Giorgio Amitrano, who offered general guidance through the field of Oriental literatures, and thank him and Professor Ikuko Sagiyama for their specialized knowledge of Japanese literature. Professor Robert Bird's expertise in the field of Russian literature was indispensable and of great profit to us. Professor Beatrice Stiglitz gave us invaluable aid throughout the course of preparation of this volume. A very special word of thanks is due to Professor Paul Archambault of Syracuse University, who orchestrated the volume's ancient and medieval Western components and himself contributed eight of the chapters.

The preparation of this book was made possible by the scholarship of the contributors, who are of various nationalities and who in themselves carry an adumbrated subtext of multiculturalism. We thank them for having responded so enthusiastically to our solicitations.

Introduction

Although the biblical myth of the Tower of Babel illustrates linguistic and cultural diversity, productive mutual influences marked the ancient civilizations of the Tigris-Euphrates and Nile valleys. China's 3,000-year-long uninterrupted literary history influenced the cultural traditions of other Asian countries. Ancient India extended itself into foreign countries under Emperor Asoka "of benevolent aspect," who served as an effective proselytizer of Buddhism in the third century B.C.E.

Powerfully forwarding the process of reintegration and consolidation in the West were the conquests of Alexander the Great and of successive Roman generals. They managed to impose a kind of unity on the entire Western world and thus made possible a proliferation of contact and cross-fertilization among what had hitherto been relatively isolated and self-sufficient ethnic and cultural groupings.

During the aftermath of Rome's decline, within a little more than a century after the prophet Muhammad's death in 632, Arabic control extended from Spain to the Indus River. The Arabic language, penetrating India, the Indies, and central Asia as well, became the language of law and culture even as the interplay between Islam and the West produced fascinating medieval artistic, architectonic, and scientific interactions.

The unity of Europe and parts of Asia, Africa, and later the Americas, consolidated by the influence of the Roman Church, was called in question by the Protestant Reformation and the rise of competing national states and ideologies from the sixteenth century onward, but these divisive tendencies in their turn triggered exploration, commerce, and technology. In Russia Czar Peter the Great (1682–1725), borrowing from the West, brought into his land multicultural mixtures that combined refusal and resentment with respect and admiration for the richness of other cultures. These paradoxes were reflected in Russian literature even as the migration of people, politics, art, and ideas between Russia,

Europe, and the United States spurred the development of Russian and Western cultural and intellectual history in the nineteenth and twentieth centuries. Correlations, juxtapositions, similarities, and antitheses among the world's civilizations ended in the twentieth century's creation for the first time of a unified global framework for the interplay of competing or cooperating national, ethnic, cultural, and economic interests.

Every civilization and every generation saw its own gifted individuals—Herodotus, Saint Augustine, Dante, Erasmus, Montaigne, Milton, Goethe, James Joyce, Rabindranath Tagore—who assimilated and transmuted the cultural riches of their time and who serve here as multicultural exemplars in the truest sense. The great majority of the authors treated in this volume, however, distinguished themselves rather by their mastery of a single or at most a pair of cultures in addition to the one into which they were born. Some experienced actual transplantation and a kind of rebirth in the new culture in which they found themselves. The Italian sojourns of the French novelist Stendhal (1783–1842), for example, served the author in his quest for identity and sustained his own myths and realities.

Though utterly diverse in their backgrounds and individualities, all of the writers are alike in that the challenge of the new environment awakened them to different values and ways of being. Seeking a view of the world as a whole, they became particularly aware of situations and events outside their own countries. Some writers even lost their native tongue as the language of their internal monologues and came to use an adopted language as their chief literary medium. One thinks, among many others, of Joseph Conrad, Jan Potocki, Guillaume Apollinaire, and Fernando Pessoa. Others enriched their own language and literature through the introduction of words, phrases, constructions, and ideas gained from intimacy with an alternative mode of speech and writing.

In this collection of multicultural writers from antiquity to 1945, chronologically the first authors are Herodotus, Xenophon, Terence, Flavius Josephus, and Tacitus, who set the scene for scores of other peripatetic writers. They represent an era when Graeco-Roman culture spread in the ancient world in the same measure that Chinese culture spread in Asia beginning in the Han period (202 B.C.E.–221 C.E.), and that Western culture has spread in modern times.

Our multicultural authors left their native lands for various and complex reasons. They underwent experiences of voluntary or forced religious conversion, exile, or education; or they set out in search of psychic or physical health; or they simply were eager to travel or reside abroad in order to know others. Their writings reveal the foreign influences that shaped their life and work. *Metamorphoses* (or *The Golden Ass*) by the trilingual Latin author Apuleius (second century C.E.), for example, discloses his knowledge of the various religious cults of his day and his own conversion to the Egyptian cult of Isis and Osiris. His contemporary Pausanias, from Asia Minor, if we read correctly his description of Greece, *Hellados Periegesis*, seemingly shed his "foreignness" when he was initiated into the Greek Eleusinian mysteries, a privilege granted only to citizens of Attica and especially of Athens.

"The plethora of ancient religions that [Gustave] Flaubert found in Syria astounded him, yet he felt at home among the followers of those religions," John Kneller writes. "The pages of the Bible came alive for him and took on new meaning in the Holy Land." In the desert regions of the Middle East Flaubert found the locus for his masterpieces *La Tentation de Saint Antoine*, *Salammbô*, *Hérodias*, and *Le Conte oriental*.

The French André Gide in the twentieth century discovered his own voice on the African continent, which gave him the freedom to write unconstrainedly on moral, ethical, and social questions. He felt that the conflicting faiths as well as the different geographical regions of his ancestors constituted a contradictory multicultural issue, which was resolved, in the words of Jeanine Plottel, only when he chose a life path devoted to the pursuit of art. Similarly, Gide's German contemporary Rainer Maria Rilke escaped from the sentimental and ostentatious Catholicism of his early years through liberating impressions in Russia and Italy. Russian culture was one of his most pervasive experiences and an influence on all his major works, Luanne Frank writes. Italy, where he laid the groundwork for his major poetic achievement that represented a departure from Western culture's 2,000-year-old modes of relating to the world, was another of his definitive cultural experiences.

CULTURES IN CONTACT AND HISTORICAL AND CULTURAL RELATIVISM

Itinerant writers brought their own literary or moral conditioning to be tried and tested in contact with intercultural realities. Contacts with peoples of different cultural backgrounds heightened their linguistic, literary, and sociopsychological experience. Contrasting the countries of their origin, they often found in the new land the occasion for philosophical reflection and for the questioning of the laws and customs of their homelands, or for pondering questions of universalism and relativism. They brought to their works dual or multiple perspectives on place, which in many cases influenced those who wrote after them. Lucian's fantastic *Alethes historia* (second century C.E.), for example, a mock narrative of travel describing a voyage that starts on the sea but continues in the skies and includes visits to the belly of a whale and to the Elysian Fields, may, together with the biblical account of Jonah, have influenced Rabelais's *Gargantua et Pantagruel* and Swift's *Gulliver's Travels*.

The Anglo-Saxon theologian and scholar Alcuin, in Parma in 781, encountered the emperor Charlemagne, who invited him to join the Frankish court and to assist him in his attempt to renovate the Frankish schools. Alcuin accepted, leaving for the Continent in 781 or 782, where he remained until the end of his life and attained notoriety as the "father" of the Carolingian Renaissance.

During the European Renaissance writers sought not only to commune more directly with the ancient Greeks and Romans in order to strengthen their connections with antiquity; they also considered it their conscious duty seriously to observe foreign countries, sometimes ultimately coming to realize that they did not belong to any nation, but to the world. The Dutch humanist Erasmus, author of *Encomium moriae* (*The Praise of Folly*, 1509), as well as of *Querela pacis* (1517) condemning war and expressing concern for Europe's impending fragmentation, "in his life, as in his work, . . . transcended nationality" and was a "high-profile citizen of the world," according to Beatrice Stiglitz. He lived, studied, and worked in several countries, always ready to move "anywhere, where the climate is healthy and kind." In his remarkable knowledge of Latin and Greek, coupled with a most comprehensive erudition, he reflected the Western world during the Northern Renaissance period.

The great sixteenth-century French philosopher and essayist Michel de Montaigne also received the careful and complete Renaissance education that included travel and instruction in languages. He had "a facility for looking at his own place and time as from the outside," Marcel Gutwirth writes. "He derided our tendency to think that the truth is lodged in our own bailiwick. He saw in the ways of the so-called savages of the New World less savagery than in the conduct of their conquerors." As an antidote to insularity, Montaigne prescribed foreign travel "to rub and polish our brains by contact with those of others."

The Italian philosopher and historian Giambattista Vico intuited that what Homer himself, and what Western humanism since the Renaissance, had called "antiquity," far from being ancient, was but the culmination of thousands of years of previous civilization. Vico, as Paul Archambault writes, "exploded the European sense of time and history, forcing historians to look back thousands of years to the roots of European thought," thereby giving impetus to fields such as Egyptology and the study of Near Eastern civilizations.

In the Orient Kublai Khan, whose thirteenth-century empire stretched from Korea to the Arabian desert and eastern Poland, "polished his brains" by patronizing Chinese literature and culture. He favored Lamaist Buddhism, to which he himself became a convert; and in trade, commerce, science, and medicine he gave a prominent role to Uighurs, Persians, Jews, and Syrians. Although he opposed the Chinese Sung dynasty, he felt himself as much a legitimate emperor of the Chinese as he was a descendant of Genghis Khan, his rule in China being characterized by a synthesis of traditional Chinese features and Mongol elements.

Just as Latin poetry had held sway in Europe during the Middle Ages, verse in Chinese dominated Japanese literature during the fifteenth century, while in Korean poetry some pearls continue even to this day to be written in Chinese. China's vast and successful civilization, however, was disastrously left behind by the early nineteenth century because of the development of the country's "bunker mentality." Thus the Chinese authors represented in this volume are all of the nineteenth and twentieth centuries.

The French philosopher and author Voltaire inveighed against neglecting the civilizations of the Chinese, the Japanese, the Hindus, and others. He stressed in his *Essai sur l'histoire générale et sur les moeurs et l'esprit des nations* (1756) the importance of studying world history, and not merely focusing on Europe alone. Even going beyond the borders of France and reducing the study of history to Western civilization represented a total distortion of the field of historiography. The *Essai*, for Richard Brooks, "is at one and the same time a broad sketch of philosophical history and an expansion of historiography to the study of humanity itself."

The contribution to nineteenth-century and contemporary European thought of the German philosopher and writer Johann Gottfried von Herder (1744–1803) lies in his historical and cultural relativism. In his revolutionary *Ideen zur Philosophie der Geschichte der Menschheit* (1784–1791) he insists on the immanent value and autonomy of each historical epoch and on the greatness, equality, and uniqueness of all cultures at all levels, thus making multiculturalism a condition to be sought and fostered, both in the past and the present.

Russian writers who traveled in Europe either were favorably disposed to Western literary influences and melded perfectly Russian thought and culture with that of the Occident or expressed their discomfort and distress at living in two different spiritual universes. Robert Bird demonstrates how Nikolai Karamzin, holding a "Russocentric" view of the West, furthered the cause of Russian cultural self-awareness by granting it a multivolume history worthy of a European power; that Nikolai Gogol did much to initiate a rich tradition of contemplations on the cultural and metaphysical identity of imperial Russia, caught between a lost spiritual heritage and an imperfectly assimilated Western civilization; that the preeminent Russian European, Ivan Turgenev, made efforts to synthesize Russian cultural energy and the forms of Western civilization; that Fedor Dostoevsky was both a modern observer of ancient Rus and a traditionalist chronicler of Europe and Europeanized Russia; and that Lev Tolstoy, whose European tour inspired him to social critique, relished the clash of human imperfections, which for him underscored a universal ideal of human brotherhood and self-abnegation.

The impact of Europe on the American visitor is a recurring theme in a literature whose writers were steeped in foreign culture. Some of America's greatest literary expatriates abandoned America's cultural establishment for Europe, choosing to become what Alex Zwerdling calls "improvised Europeans." Ralph Waldo Emerson's European tour in the early 1830s helped mend his health and set him on a new intellectual course. His *English Traits* (1856), a product of the confrontation between a self-reliant American Self and an independent, simultaneously foreign and familiar Other, demonstrates the important ways in which English and American life and thought both complemented and contradicted each other (Stowe, *Going Abroad*, 91–92).

The fiction of the multicultural literary lion Henry James often treats the late-nineteenth-century phenomenon of transatlantic marriages between newly rich

Americans and titled, though impoverished, Europeans—a theme that also addresses the contrast between, in Jane Benardete's words, "an immature American culture and a formalized, but desiccated European tradition." Benardete tells us too that Washington Irving was one of the postrevolutionary Americans who remained culturally attached to England, especially in arts and letters, but that borrowings from German legends and folktales provided the basis for some of his most enduring works, such as "Rip van Winkle," "The Legend of Sleepy Hollow," and "The Robber Bridegroom." In later works his romantic treatment of Spain, based upon seven years of Spanish residence, made the Alhambra an international attraction. As one of America's first cultural ambassadors to Europe, he helped to establish a cultivated, if sentimental, appreciation of America's European heritage.

The exploration of foreign cultures by the French author André Malraux reveals his curiosity about, and fascination with, the "Other" (illustrated in *La Tentation de l'Occident*, 1926) as he shifts from the "Other" back to the "Self" for reconsideration and reinterpretation of his own culture. He sought "to probe the specific means by which a given culture grasps the basic existential problem of the meaning of life and death and by which it leaves its trace in the world," Domnica Radulescu writes. His own participation in the Chinese and Spanish civil wars stimulated his social novels, *La Condition humaine* (1933) and *L'Espoir* (1937).

Western influence in its turn began to be felt on Indian writing in the early nineteenth century, when authors and the growing literary public were introduced to Western literary forms in English. Yet in the soul of Indians the omission of Graeco-Judaic elements in their cultural heritage made for tension in the presence of an extraneous spiritual force coming from the West. Gradually, however, translation of Western texts gave way to imitation, and from imitation arose original, creative writing. Rabindranath Tagore (1861–1941), a product of the confluence of three cultures, Hindu, Muhammadan, and British, acknowledged the mixed soil out of which his complex cultural identity had grown.

Some writers, like the French Paul Claudel, were so affected by the enormous divergence between the customs of the Orient and of their own culture that they altered their art and psyche. Because he found the mores, language, religion, and psyche in the Orient to be so different from what he had known, a sense of displacement and rejection of these overcame Claudel during his early years in government service in China, where he wrote verses expressing feelings of isolation. During his stay in Japan, however, becoming immersed in Japanese culture, he wrote in 1923 "Un Regard sur l'âme japonaise" and *L'Oiseau noir dans le soleil levant*, among other works inspired by Japanese iconography, art, drama, and music.

China, Japan, and Korea had closed their doors to Europeans in the seventeenth and eighteenth centuries and had become "hermit kingdoms." The wars of the 1930s and 1940s stifled most Japanese literary production, yet three multicultural Japanese authors find their place in this volume: Mori Ōgai, Horiguchi

Daigaku, whose translations of French literature offer, in the words of Ikuko Sagiyama, "a felicitous dialogue between the original and the Japanese version," and Nagai Kafū, whose European experience reinforced his scorn of Japan of the Meiji period, and whose role in introducing to Japan Western literature, and especially French Naturalism, is described by Luisa Bienati. Works focusing on cultural differences between East and West reveal how authors recognize their own foreignness most clearly when they are away from their native homelands. The elusiveness of meanings, as well as the difficulty of translation within as well as across different cultures and nationalities, underlies the writings of the Oriental authors featured in this volume. Yet M. Cristina Pisciotta demonstrates how Xu Zhimo succeeded in fusing West and East, the new and the conventional, the different and the familiar, in his adaptations of English models to modern Chinese romantic poetry, and how Jiang Guangci translated the ideals of Soviet Russia into fluid colloquial Chinese prose.

In Korea, side by side with the moderns represented in this volume by Kim Sowŏl (1902–1934), poets continued to write poetry and the traditional *sijo* (short polished poem to be sung to a lute accompaniment) in Chinese. The birth of modern Korean literature, Maurizio Riotto explains, was an unexpected, almost explosive phenomenon, caused by sudden contact between a closed cultural reality and literary tendencies of the West. Representing the break with his country's past is the young poet Kim Sowŏl, whose readings of Western literature so influenced him that he has been compared to a Yeats, a Robert Frost, a Verlaine, and a Baudelaire. Korea is represented in this volume also by the ninth-century literary figure Ch'oe Ch'iwŏn, whose long and rich experience as a young man in the highly cosmopolitan society of China in the Tang period allowed him to learn to live with diverse ethnic and religious realities. This multicultural experience stirred in him those feelings of tolerance and respect for the Other that would come to characterize his thought and his literary production.

NOMADISM AND EXILE

Many multicultural authors were governed by the nomadic imperative. Mobile, scattered, dislodged, and in a perpetual state of transience, they felt that the true condition of the human race was nomadism, not the sedentary life. Some writers used the metaphor of travel allegorically, and the connection between travel and construction of identity has a very long history indeed. Pausanias searched for his roots in ancient Hellas, described not as a physical place but rather as a spiritual landscape. In the genre of the pre-Islamic *qasidah* (ode) perfected by al-Mutanabbi, the poet, depicting himself on a journey marked by halts at deserted camping grounds, metamorphoses his horse or camel into some wild desert creature. In Japanese *jishō bungaku* (introspective travel literature), meditation (internal) is as important as observation and description (external) (Didier, 1897). "Childe Harold," or Lord Byron himself, is a man sated of the world, who roams from place to place in order to flee from himself. The despairing, still-unrecognized Henrik Ibsen left his native Norway in 1864 to live for twenty-seven years abroad, mainly in Italy and Germany—an expatriation that brought a change over his life and gave birth to his first dramatic success (*Brand*, 1866). In August Strindberg's 1898 drama *Till Damaskus* (*The Road to Damascus*), the author describes himself as "the Stranger," wandering and finally finding spiritual peace. He had earlier moved restlessly about the Continent for six years, perhaps nourishing his pessimism and realism on French Naturalism and the theories of Nietzsche. The frequent voyages of the twentieth-century Lebanese writer Ameen F. Rihani have been seen by Ameen Albert Rihani as giving origin to "Adab al-Mahjar" (emigrant literature) as well as to an Arab-American literature that is "Arab in its concerns, . . . English in language, and American in spirit and platform."

Writers in exile feed on "difference" in their new environment, shed some of their former ethnocentrism, and grow and change in a reciprocal expansion of knowledge. Max Noordhoorn illustrates how the German lyric poet, journalist, and critic Heinrich Heine, after the publication of his travel sketches, *Reisebilder* (1826–1831), left his native Germany to go into lifelong exile in Paris. He tried not merely to establish cultural, sociopolitical, and philosophical links between Germany and the rest of the Western world, but also to place these in a historical framework, relating them to the past and to the future—an all-embracing spirit that infused his travel sketches, his journalistic reports, and his literary-historical and philosophical writings. Noordhoorn writes also about Herman Hesse, the German-born novelist who lived in Switzerland during World War I. Although Hesse was firmly grounded in the literary heritage of German Romanticism, Swiss-German regionalism, and European culture, he was also conversant with Chinese Taoist, Indian Buddhist, and Japanese writings, which "blended into a truly individualistic perception and expression of cultural, sociopolitical, and philosophical constructs."

Some exiled authors became assimilated into their host society; others resisted acculturation, and the theme of loss is constant for some. Thomas Mann, in exile in the United States after 1938, longed for his beloved Europe, to which he returned to seek a home not in divided postwar Germany but in Switzerland, his previous place of exile. "In all of his works," Ingeborg Baumgartner writes, "he uses his multiculturalism not as access to a particular foreign culture, but as a mirror of his own personal experience."

The Irish writer James Joyce, the exiled artist par excellence who spent most of his life in Italy and France and possessed as well a wide appreciation of other cultures and languages, was, in Mary Hudson's words, "the very embodiment of multiculturalism at a time before it became perceived as a good." His Triestine friendship with Italo Svevo contributed to his fascination and love for Jewish culture, which became a distinguishing mark of *Ulysses* (1922).

EDUCATION

Multicultural educational experience inspired new views of the world. Goethe's turn toward multicultural themes must be seen within the context of his late work, which is underscored by the conviction that the highest creations of the human spirit are reflections of a complex inner order existing behind the appearance of things. Spiritual affinities between cultures, whatever their outward differences, underlay what Goethe came to refer to as "Weltliteratur." "Thus Italy, as depicted in *Italienische Reise* (1816)," Elizabeth Powers writes, "is revealed as a great organism, the product of immutable laws." Similarly, Goethe was attracted to the literature and cultures of the East not for their local color but rather for the eternal presence of the human element in them.

The purpose of Alexis de Tocqueville's trip to the United States in 1831 was to study democracy firsthand. The result was his well-known *De la démocratie en Amérique* (1835–1840). Through his absorption of knowledge of cultures other than his own, Melvin Richter demonstrates, he was able to see, for example, what was significant in French politics and history because of what he had learned about British and American institutions. The course of impersonal Japanese fiction might not have been altered in 1890 had Mori Ōgai not undertaken medical studies in Germany and recorded his personal experiences in *Maihime*, the first Japanese "I" novel (*shishosetsu*)—a story closely based on one's own experiences. Berlin and the German culture represented for Ōgai fascination and splendor but also, Matilde Mastrangelo explains, the possibility of moving away from cultural ties that inhibited his full self-realization.

Argentina's Jorge Luis Borges completed his secondary education in Switzerland, where he not only mastered English, French, and German, but also searched deeply into the European encyclopedias for the cultural components of the themes of his readings in those languages. In Spain he studied Latin and Arabic in a continuous process of storing knowledge in his fabulous memory. "His cultural world," James O. Pellicer writes, "is the universal library."

POWER OF PLACE AND THE SEARCH FOR HEALTH

The power of place affected the life and thought of many multicultural authors. The experience of Persia was a liberating factor for the French theorist of social and racial behavior Joseph Arthur Gobineau, author of *Souvenirs de voyage* (1872) and *Les Pléiades* (1874). Venice and its surroundings, where George Sand traveled with the poet Alfred de Musset, inspired her delightful series of semifictional narratives known as *Lettres d'un voyageur* (1830–1836). "Sand's German and Swedish ancestry, her English educational experience, [her French attachments,] . . . and [her] attraction to Spain and Italy produced a truly international frame of reference for all her works," Nadine Dormoy writes. The lush Mediterranean island of Majorca, where Sand spent the winter of 1838–39 with Frédéric Chopin, inspired both to produce some of their finest works.

Whereas some multicultural authors succeeded in buoying their morale or gaining a sense of cohesion in troubled times by traveling to foreign lands, others set out in search of health or catharsis. The sun and sea of Mediterranean lands—idealized as spring in midwinter—were the goal of many British writers. Tobias Smollett, who went to Italy in 1769 in search of health, was the author of a classic travel account, *Travels through France and Italy* (1766), which helped to produce Laurence Sterne's better-known *A Sentimental Journey through France and Italy* (1768). Sterne, too, had taken an extended trip to Italy in 1764 in search of sun and renewal of health, but died before the completion of *A Sentimental Journey*, a new kind of travel book in which he concentrated on the effects of his voyage on himself.

TRAVEL AND LITERARY EXOTICISM

Travel writers are an important subcategory within the multicultural multitude, and the place of the travel tale is firmly entrenched in literary tradition. Travel served to enlarge the sympathies and diminish the pessimism of many writers; it took others out of their bustling metropolises into the purer atmosphere of lush nature or the desert; and travel significantly liberated those who despised the provincial morality or social rigidity that characterized their own homeland.

William Beckford's (1760–1844) writings, Marie-Madeleine Martinet shows us, reveal how multicultural experience influences a traveler's sense of place and of chronology, expressing itself through "double-reading" motifs in the forms of travel literature and modes of artistic experience. They demonstrate the link between European cosmopolitanism and exoticism, since for Beckford the culture and language of other European countries create an imaginative world that provides a transition toward distant civilizations.

Far-off lands have always stirred the imagination of writers, from antiquity to our day. Love of travel and intellectual curiosity produced an Arabic literary genre known as the *rihla*, represented in this volume by Ibn Battuta (1304–1369?), who considered himself a citizen not only of his native Morocco but of Dar al-Islam, or the Abode of Islam—that is, the lands where Muslims predominated, where Muslim kings or princes ruled, and where the *shari'a*, or Sacred Law of Islam, was the foundation of the social order. His allegiance was to its universalist, spiritual, and social values. Ibn Battuta's *rihla* is the record not only of a vivid personal adventure but also a survey of the governments, personalities, rulers, and holy men of the Muslim world in the second quarter of the fourteenth century, making it a valuable historical source. In modern Arabic literature the writings of Lebanese author Ameen Rihani may be seen as an extension of the Ibn Battuta tradition.

Abdellatif Attafi describes the multicultural experiences of Ibn Khaldun, the Arab historian and sociologist born in Tunis, which are reflected in *Muqaddi-*

mah, a pluridisciplinary work based on a cause/effect chain of developmental stages reached in the history of human civilization. Ibn Khaldun moved from Granada to Cairo to Damascus in the fourteenth century, when the English poet Geoffrey Chaucer, himself a frequent traveler to France and Italy, acquired his knowledge of the Italian works of Dante and Boccaccio that was to become important for his poetry.

From the nineteenth century onward, India was narrated by European writers as a surrogate for the unreachable real object, even as authors persisted in describing India, Africa, and the Arab world from their ethnocentric vantage points and according to their Western imagination and literary fantasy. It was Rudyard Kipling who, as a journalist, had the opportunity to see the British Empire at work in India at all levels. Kipling translated, in the words of T.S. Eliot, "the imperial . . . into the historical imagination." He reported the life and customs in remote Indian villages, giving voice to the many facets of the complex relationships in Anglo-Indian society. His travel writings *From Sea to Sea* (1899) embrace the United States to New Zealand, South Africa to Japan, but "almost all of Kipling's art," Maria Antonietta Saracino writes, "fed on the memories of his early Indian years."

Other authors of fiction set in foreign lands (such as Pierre Loti's *Madame Chrysanthème*, 1887; Joseph Conrad's *Heart of Darkness*, 1902; and E.M. Forster's *A Passage to India*, 1924) helped contribute to the crumbling of barriers and the closing of gaps between cultures. Almost all of Pierre Loti's work, which derived from his extensive travel as a French naval officer, "plunges deep into the cultural identity of the other, of many others," and at the same time reveals "his own difference, a self ironically ever diverging from its avatars," in the words of Michael Bishop. Most of Joseph Conrad's narratives are set in distant and "exotic" areas outside Europe and deal, in various ways, with the interaction between human beings of different races, cultures, and languages against an often-inhospitable and hostile background. In his tales set in Malaya (*Almayer's Folly* and *An Outcast of the Islands*), for example, natural beauty does not overshadow racial differences and betrayals, Saracino demonstrates; and *Heart of Darkness*, unfolding deep in the African continent, becomes a real journey into humankind's innermost conscience.

For Conrad and for William Somerset Maugham, the exoticism of foreign places allowed for a heightened or different existence and for the illusion of liberation. Maugham turned his back temporarily on Europe and made a journey to the South Sea island groups, which proved a turning point in his career. Though he was generally pessimistic about the possibility of reconciling cultural differences, Marina MacKay writes, "his distaste for the missionary mindset rather unexpectedly anticipates a later, postcolonial, consciousness." The widely traveled Belgian author Georges Simenon rejected outright picturesque tropical-island literature, asserting that there was "no such thing as exoticism" (*La mauvaise étoile*, 31), or, in the words of Czesław Miłosz, that "the trappings of exoticism . . . [mask] the eternal man" (cited in Scammell, 36). Simenon discovered for himself, according to Lucille Frackman Becker, that "wherever one travels, one takes oneself along, and that always limits the possibilities for transcendence."

Whether we look at historical times or modern ones, at empires or at small nations, we notice a historical-geographical sweep that transforms cultures, firms up the uniqueness of each, and, above all, emphasizes their interdependency. The world's civilizations hang together and interact with each other. A multicultural world is unavoidable in the face of everyday encounters, trade, and literary contacts, which have an effect in recasting the identities as well as the political affinities of different civilizations. Our multicultural authors were shaped by the experience of their own societies, but they discerned in other environments differences that mattered and that found their keenest expression in the writings featured in this volume.

ALCUIN
(735–804)

Paul Archambault

BIOGRAPHY

Alcuin, whose baptismal name was Albinus Flaccus Alcoinus and whose Saxon name was Ealh-wine, was born in Northumbria, England, in 735. An anonymous and highly hagiographical *Vita*, written between 823 and 829, tells of Alcuin's coming from a family of the local nobility but being "handed over as a young child [*parvulus*] to the mystical breasts of the Church as soon as he was weaned from the carnal breasts of his mother" (Migne, 100:91). Alcuin's entire formal schooling took place at the cathedral school of York, where his teacher was Aelberht, the future bishop of York (767–82). Alcuin succeeded Aelberht as master of the York school in 767, the year of Aelberht's consecration. Although he was a man of extraordinary piety and learning, Alcuin never advanced beyond the diaconate, to which he was ordained at York, no doubt in his early twenties. He owed his outstanding reputation at York well into middle age less to his official position in the Church than to the obvious quality of his mind and the patronage of Aelberht and other friends (Godman, xxxvi).

The turning point in his life came in 781, when he was sent on a mission from York to Rome by Archbishop Eanbald, successor to Archbishop Egbert, to request from the Apostolic See the episcopal pallium for Eanbald. Returning from Rome, he encountered Charlemagne at Parma. Charlemagne, who had met Alcuin before, invited him to join the Frankish court and to assist him in his attempt to renovate the Frankish schools. Alcuin accepted Charlemagne's offer, returned briefly to York to finish his mission there, and left for the Continent in 781 or 782, to be welcomed by Charlemagne in a fatherly way. He remained on the Continent until the end of his life, with the exception of two visits to England, in 786 and 790–93.

At Aachen, where Charlemagne settled his court in 794, Alcuin was "at the centre of that international élite of scholars and poets in whose work is celebrated the first brilliant phase of the Carolingian *renovatio*" (Godman, xxxvii). During the first decade of his stay on the Continent he was named abbot of the monasteries of St-Loup at Troyes and of Ferrières, and in 796 he acquired the abbacy of St. Martin's at Tours. Although he traveled back to the Aachen court after that date, his last years were spent in increasing retirement at St. Martin's. Alcuin died on 19 May 804. His anonymous biographer well summarizes his lifetime achievement as the initiator of the cultural marriage between England and France. His career marks the final and most fertile point of contact between Anglo-Saxon and continental scholarship in the eighth century (Godman, xxxvii–xxxviii).

MAJOR MULTICULTURAL THEMES

In his *Vita Karoli* Eginhard (Einhard), Charlemagne's best-known biographer (775–840), describes Alcuin as the most influential of Charlemagne's preceptors: "He had as his preceptor Alcuin, otherwise called Albinus . . . , a man of the Saxon race who came from Britain, the most learned of all men whatever their origin. . . . With him he devoted much time and labor studying rhetoric, dialectics, and especially astronomy. He also learned calculus and devoted much studious attention to learning the course of the stars" (*Vita Karoli*, 25, my translation).

The exceptional nature of Alcuin's learning is thus linked, in Eginhard's mind, with the foreignness of his origins. That Alcuin was a Saxon from Britain is a fact Eginhard cites not with resentment but with pride: as a Rhinelander from the Mainz region who had met Alcuin at Charlemagne's court and could only be in awe of this great master forty years his senior, Eginhard realized that the Carolingian educational *renovatio* had been propelled and nourished by learned men who came from many different places (*undecumque*). The rebirth of culture in the Carolingian schools had been the result of Charlemagne's appeal to the best scholars of Europe. Eginhard knew that Anglo-Saxon humanism, centered around the prestigious school of York, had, since the time of the Venerable Bede (673–735), the master of Jarrow, a head start on Carolingian humanism; and in luring Alcuin to the Continent, Charlemagne realized that he was bringing a most sophisticated scholar, who represented a culture that Charlemagne could only find superior, to the Aachen court. One might compare Charlemagne's coup with Francis I's successful attempt, nearly eight centuries later, to bring to France the brilliant Leonardo da Vinci.

Had Alcuin remained at York and not been hired by Charlemagne in 781, he might never have attained his fame as the "father" of the Carolingian Renaissance. Yet he always remained conscious of being a Northumbrian Saxon, especially after making the Continent his permanent home. His longest poem, *Versus de patribus et sanctis Euboricensis Ecclesiae* (*The Bishops, Kings, and Saints of York*), is presumed to have been written on the Continent between 782 and 801 (Godman, xlii–xliii), and it perhaps would not glow with the same patriotic feeling had it been written at York itself. "My mind," writes Alcuin in his invocation, "is eager to speak in praise of my homeland / and swiftly to proclaim the ancient foundation / of York's famed city in rare verse!" (vv. 16–18). Showing unmistakable ethnic pride, he situates the Saxons "between the peoples of Germany and the outlying realms / . . . an ancient race, powerful in war, of splendid physique, / called by the name of 'rock' because of its toughness [*duritiam propter dicti cognomine saxi*]" (vv. 46–48).

If he was conscious of being a Saxon, however, he was careful never to represent himself as culturally superior. His mind was catholic; and though upon his arrival at the Aachen court, presided over by a king, soon to be emperor of the West, whose relative illiteracy was matched only by his thirst for culture, Alcuin must have exuded an air of gentle but brilliant sophistication, his magic seems to have resided in a supreme ability to make his students, including Charlemagne himself, feel intelligent. This led the young Eginhard, who might have resented him, to call him "the greatest of the preceptors."

If we rightly include Alcuin in this collection of "multicultural" writers, then, it is less because of his Saxon origins than because of his ability to fuse classical, Northumbrian, and Carolingian cultural traditions so ably in his own mind. Bishop Aelberht's great library at the York cathedral contained "the legacy of the ancient Fathers: / all the Roman possessed in the Latin world, / whatever famous Greece has transmitted to the Latins, / draughts of the Hebrew race from Heaven's showers, / and what Africa has spread abroad in streams of light" (vv. 1536–40). In spite of the multiple origins of his literary culture, Alcuin believed in the fundamental unity of all human knowledge, and in the ultimate ability of Christian doctrine to unite all specific cultures. There can be no true rhetoric without virtue, he says in his treatise on rhetoric, echoing Cicero's definition of the orator ("Vir bonus peritus dicendi"—a good man expert in speaking); and in his treatise on the Trinity he says to Charlemagne that Faith is the foundation of all things (Migne, 101:13). More, perhaps, than any other figure of the Carolingian Renaissance, he was masterful in his ability to fuse and reconcile classical and Christian learning.

SURVEY OF CRITICISM

The Alcuin bibliography, especially among English and German scholars of the Merovingian and Carolingian periods (A. Kleinclausz, R. Folz, L. Wallach, E.S. Duckett), is extensive but the basic texts on which they all seem to rely are the two volumes of Migne's complete works of Alcuin (*Patrologia Latina*, vols. 100–101, especially the anonymous *Vita* in 100:89–105, and Alcuin's letters, 100:135–514). For Eginhard, Louis Halphen's Latin-French Belles Lettres edition is indispensable, although Lewis Thorpe's *Two Lives of Charlemagne* in the Penguin edition is highly readable. Luitpold Wallach's article on Alcuin in the *New Catholic Encyclopedia* is very helpful, more so than his highly specialized work on *Alcuin and Charlemagne*. Luitpold Wallach remains, however, one of the most learned historians of the Carolingian period in our century. Peter Godman's excellent edition of *The Bishops, Kings, and Saints of York* has an indispensable introduction.

SELECTIVE BIBLIOGRAPHY

Works by Alcuin

B. Flacci seu Alcuini Opera Omnia. In *Patrologiae Latinae Cursus Completus.* Vols. 100–101. Ed. J.-P. Migne. Paris: Montrouge, 1863.
Alcuin of York, c. A.D. 732 to 804: His Life and Letters. Trans. Stephen Allott. York: William Sessions, 1974.
The Bishops, Kings, and Saints of York. Ed. and trans. Peter Godman. Oxford: Clarendon Press, 1982.

Selective Studies of Alcuin

Duckett, E.S. *Alcuin, Friend of Charlemagne: His World and His Work.* New York: Macmillan, 1951.
Eginhard. *Vie de Charlemagne.* Ed. Louis Halphen. Paris: Les Belles Lettres, 1947.
Einhard. *Two Lives of Charlemagne.* Trans. Lewis Thorpe. Harmondsworth: Penguin Books, 1969.
Folz, Robert. *Le Couronnement impérial de Charlemagne.* Paris: Gallimard, 1989.
Kleinclausz, Arthur. *Charlemagne.* Paris: Hachette, 1938.
Wallach, Luitpold. "Alcuin." In *New Catholic Encyclopedia*, vol. 1, 279–80. New York: McGraw-Hill, 1967.
———. *Alcuin and Charlemagne: Studies in Carolingian History and Literature.* Ithaca: Cornell University Press, 1959.

APULEIUS
(c. 125–after 170?)

Robert J. White

BIOGRAPHY

Although Apuleius's first name is unknown, it does appear in several manuscripts as Lucius, a praenomen derived no doubt from the name of the protagonist of his novel, the *Metamorphoses*. He was born of prosperous Roman parents in Madauros (now Mdaourouch in Algeria) in North Africa. His father was a *duovir iuri dicundo*, a title given to the two highest magistrates in the municipal towns. Apuleius received a superior education, first at Carthage and then at Athens, where he pursued his love of philosophy, and traveled throughout Greece, Asia Minor, the Aegean Islands, and to Rome. In 155–56, on his way to Alexandria in Egypt, he became ill and stopped at Oea (modern Tripoli in Libya). There he renewed his friendship with Sicinius Pontianus, his Athens schoolmate, who persuaded him to extend his visit in the family home. Apuleius eventually married Pontianus's widowed mother Pudentilla, seven years his senior. When Pontianus himself married and met with a sudden death, his father-in-law Herennius Rufus sought the support of Pontianus's younger brother, Pudens, to prevent Apuleius from acquiring the inheritance of his wife. Apuleius was accused of having won Pudentilla's affection through the use of love potions. The trial took place at Sabrata in 158–59, at a time when conviction of practicing magic was punishable by death. Apuleius defended himself and was acquitted. His speech in his own defense (*Apologia*, sometimes called *De magia* in the manuscripts) still survives. It is a bizarre but fascinating glimpse of both himself and the lives and preoccupations of superstitious provincials. He spent the last years of his life at Carthage, where he enjoyed great fame as a philosoper and orator. He was appointed chief priest of the province and was honored with public statues both in Carthage and Madauros. It is clear that Apuleius was still alive in the late 160s, but the date of his death is unknown.

Six of his works survive: the *Apologia*; the *Florida*, an anthology of twenty-three amusing, trivial excerpts on various themes taken from his lectures and public readings after he returned to Carthage; the *De dogmate Platonis*, an exposition of Plato's life, physics, and ethics that reveals a superficial grasp of his material; the flamboyant and spellbinding *De deo Socratis*, a systematic inquiry into the existence and nature of demons; the *De mundo*, a translation of the *Peri kosmou*, a treatise on cosmology and theology once erroneously attributed to Aristotle; and his most famous and influential work, the novel *Metamorphoses*, which has also been called, since the time of Augustine, *Asinus aureus* (*The Golden Ass*). It is the only Latin novel that survives in its entirety. A charming work, the novel is fast paced and exciting, erotic, imaginative, and witty, yet serious and deeply moral. A young man named Lucius, because of his excessive curiosity and his misuse of magic, is transformed into an ass but retains his human thought processes. After many adventures he is restored to his human form by eating roses provided by the Egyptian goddess Isis, into whose mysteries he is eventually initiated. Apuleius embellishes his tale with a series of incidents and episodes that flesh out the main narrative, the most important of which is the captivating story of Cupid and Psyche.

MAJOR MULTICULTURAL THEMES

The degree to which the *Metamorphoses* is autobiographical is uncertain. Most critics assume that Apuleius was trilingual: as a citizen of Madauros, in the Roman province of Africa, he would no doubt have spoken Punic, a Semitic language common to his native region; Latin, the official language of the colony; and Greek, as a result of his studies in Athens. In his opening address to the reader, Lucius, Apuleius's alter ego, states that he was brought to Athens as a child to learn Attic Greek and that later he went to Rome, where he learned Latin with excruciating difficulty since he had no regular schoolteachers. Lucius considers himself a novice in the foreign language, Latin, in use at the Roman bar and begs his readers' indulgence for the switch of language, comparing himself to a circus rider leaping from one horse to another. In being trilingual, Apuleius was not alone in the second century C.E. He was a typical Roman citizen living in the provinces and, indeed, an ideal Roman, since Rome was, from its very beginnings, a city of outsiders. Unlike the Athenians, who had created for themselves a myth of autochthony and took immense pride in their homogeneous citizenry, the Romans acknowledged that even the ancestor of the Roman people, Aeneas, was a foreigner from Troy (in Asia Minor) who waged bitter war to lay hold of the land of Italy. The Romans also admitted freely that Etruscans, Oscans, Umbrians, and Greeks had flourished in Italy long before Rome had grown from a small village to a vast empire. This recognition of their multicultural and pluralistic roots made Roman citizens more receptive than most to the many cultures—African, Semitic, Greek, Celtic, and Germanic, to name a few—that would eventually constitute the Roman Empire.

Apuleius reveals the multicultural influences that shaped his life and work in his knowledge of the various religious cults of his day and especially in his own conversion to the Egyptian cult of Isis and Osiris. In Book 8 of the *Metamorphoses* he describes the false ecstasy and masochistic excesses of the eunuch devotees of the Syrian goddess Atargatis, whose cult, widespread in Greece from the third century B.C.E. onward, had reached Rome by the first century C.E., numbering even the emperor Nero among its followers. Apuleius's unflattering portrait of the bald, greedy priests, "the meanest dregs of society" (*The Golden Ass*, trans. P.G. Walsh, 154), marching through the streets banging cymbals and shaking castanets is surpassed only by his depiction of the despicable woman who "possessed every conceivable wickedness in her mind . . . as in some filthy cesspool" (ibid., 170) and who believed in a divinity whom she proclaimed to be the only God. Here Lucius (or Apuleius) is attacking the adherents of either Judaism or Christianity. Given the relentless spread in North Africa of Christianity, a cult opposed to Apuleius's own religion of Isis and to the cult of Mithras, to which he alludes in Book 11, it is Christianity that seems the likelier target. Despite its author's obvious bias, the *Metamorphoses* is a testament to what Gwyn Griffiths called the "atmosphere of friendly syncretism" that characterized the second century.

SELECTIVE BIBLIOGRAPHY

Works by Apuleius

Apologie. Florides. Ed. Paul Vallette. Paris: Les Belles Lettres, 1924.

Metamorphoses. 3 vols. Ed. Donald S. Robertson. Paris: Les Belles Lettres, 1940–1945.

Metamorphoses. Ed. Rudolf Helm and Paul Thomas. Leipzig: Teubner, 1955.

Metamorphoses. Ed. and trans. J. Arthur Hanson. Cambridge, Mass.: Harvard University Press, 1989.

The Golden Ass. Trans. P.G. Walsh. Oxford and New York: Oxford University Press, 1995.

Selective Studies of Apuleius

Griffiths, J. Gwyn. *The Isis Book (Metamorphoses, Book XI).* Leiden: E.J. Brill, 1975.

Hijmans, B.L., and R.T. van der Paardt, eds. *Aspects of Apuleius' Golden Ass.* Groningen: Bouma's Boekhuis, 1978.

James, Paula. *Unity in Diversity: A Study of Apuleius' Metamorphoses.* Altertumswissenschaftliche Texte und Studien, vol. 16. Hildesheim: G. Olms, 1987.

Millar, Fergus. "The World of the Golden Ass." *Journal of Roman Studies* 71 (1981): 63–75.

Nock, Arthur Darby. *Conversion.* Oxford: Clarendon Press, 1933.

Schlam, Carl C. *The Metamorphoses of Apuleius: On Making an Ass of Oneself.* Chapel Hill: University of North Carolina Press, 1992.

Shumate, Nancy. *Crisis and Conversion in Apuleius' Metamorphoses.* Ann Arbor: University of Michigan Press, 1996.

Tatum, James. *Apuleius and the Golden Ass.* Ithaca: Cornell University Press, 1979.
von Franz, Marie-Louise. *A Psychological Interpretation of the Golden Ass of Apuleius.* Zürich: Spring Publications, 1970.
Walsh, P.G. "Was Lucius a Roman?" *Classical Journal* 63, no. 6 (March 1968): 264–65.
Winkler, John J. *Auctor & Actor: A Narratological Reading of Apuleius' Golden Ass.* Berkeley and Los Angeles: University of California Press, 1985.

ANTONIN ARTAUD
(1896–1948)

Bettina L. Knapp

BIOGRAPHY

Antonin Artaud was born in Marseille. His mother was of Greek origin; his father, in the shipfitting business, was French Provençal. The child developed meningitis at the age of five, and although he was cured, the head pains he suffered and the increasing doses of painkillers prescribed by the doctors resulted in his eventual drug addiction. At school he loved to read and draw and developed a passion for the works of Baudelaire, Poe, and other writers. In 1910 he founded a small literary magazine that lasted three years. A bent for the dramatic became noticeable with a stage set he arranged in his room, which was so grotesque that it frightened his cousin who was visiting him at the time.

Prior to his baccalaureate examination, Artaud became despondent, complained of "internal" discomfort, and refused to see people. He suffered an acute case of neurasthenia, tore up his poems and short stories, and gave his books away. After a period of convalescence his condition had so improved that he went to live in Paris (1920), where he composed poems, essays, and short stories that focused increasingly on the unseen, the unknown, the symbolic, and the metaphysical.

Wanting to devote his life to the dramatic arts, he became associated with Aurélien Marie Lugné-Poe's Théâtre de l'Oeuvre and joined Charles Dullin's Théâtre de l'Atelier, where he met Génica Athanasiou, a beautiful actress who was to be the only person with whom Artaud could, even for a short while, share some measure of warmth and love. After a year with Dullin's troupe divergencies of interpretation between master and student led to a break.

At the Colonial Exhibit in Marseille in 1922 Artaud was enthralled by the strange gestures, masks, stunning costumes, exotic atmosphere, and haunting lighting effects of the sacred Cambodian dancers performing before a reproduction of the Temple of Angkor Wat. He knew that the brand of theater he now had in mind would be different from anything anyone had ever seen.

In 1924 he joined the Surrealists, who sought to lay bare the treasures that the unconscious mind held buried within its folds. Two years later he broke relations with André Breton and many in his group over their political commitment to Communism and founded his Théâtre Alfred Jarry. Artaud had been drawn to Jarry (1873–1907) because of the spontaneous irrationality of his works, especially *Ubu roi*, and their satiric, grotesque, and mystical intents. Among the productions offered at the Théâtre Alfred Jarry were Artaud's own play *Jet de sang* amd Strindberg's *Drömspelet*. For lack of funds, Artaud's innovative theater aborted, and he branched out into films, creating such unforgettable roles as Marat in Abel Gance's *Napoleon* (1926) and Brother Massieu in Carl Dreyer's *Passion of Joan of Arc* (1928), but only one of his scenarios was turned into a film.

Artaud looked upon the theater as a curative agent—a means whereby an individual could come to the theater to be cut open, split, dissected, and then healed. After witnessing a production of the Balinese Theater at the 1931 Colonial Exhibition in Paris, his heretofore vaguely defined theatrical ideas suddenly coalesced. Gestures, words, sounds, and stage images were to be looked upon as types of hieroglyphs or symbols, thereby permitting the inner eye to become operative and to encapsulate the mythic elements in the dramatic unfoldings. Artaud's seminal essays, manifestos, and letters—"Alchemical Theater," "Theater and the Plague," "Oriental and Occidental Theater," "Theater of Cruelty," to mention but a few—were published under the title *Le Théâtre et son double* (1938). His unique brand of stage play was designed to activate people's "magnetic" nervous systems to such an extent as to enable them to project their feelings and sensations beyond the usual limits imposed by time and space. "I employ the word 'cruelty' in the sense of an appetite for life, a cosmic rigor, an implacable necessity" (*Le Théâtre et son double*, trans. Caroline Richards, 102).

Upon his return to Paris in 1937 after a trip to Mexico, a friend gave him a cane with three hooks and three knots that, Artaud asserted, had not only been mentioned in St. Patrick's prophecy, but had been used by Jesus to ward off the demons in the desert. He left Paris for Ireland to investigate traces of the ancient Druid tree worshipers who might have fashioned this magic weapon. So fearsome had his mental condition become that he was forcibly sent back to France, where he was incarcerated in several mental institutions. At Rodez he was subjected to electroshock and insulin therapy. The now half-starved Artaud, fully aware of what was happening to him, complained bitterly about what he considered to be inhuman treatment (see his *Lettres de Rodez*). By 1945, at the war's end, funds were raised to send him to a hospital in the suburbs of Paris. On one of his jaunts through the hospital grounds, he noticed a charming eighteenth-century pavilion set apart from the rest of the establishment, which had once been inhabited by Gérard de Nerval. He was permitted to move into it. Meanwhile, it was discovered that he was suffering from inoperable cancer. On March 4, 1948, the gardener who daily brought him his breakfast found him seated at the foot of his bed, dead.

MAJOR MULTICULTURAL THEMES

In Artaud's outline of his play *La Conquête du Mexique* (1933) he stressed humankind's drive to colonize, to brutalize others, and to insist on converting natives from the natural religion they professed to Christianity. In that he sought to create a theater of symbols and myths, he chose superhuman antagonists, conflicting civilizations and epochs to move above the scenic space and to collide with great force. The remote, mountainous, mythical land of the Tarahumaras in Mexico is described in *Les Tarahumaras* (published posthumously in 1963), both a record of his trip and a philosophical and metaphysical statement of the underpinnings of his "Theater of Cruelty." From the very outset of his trajectory up the mountains on horseback and on foot to reach the settlements of the Tarahumaras, he felt himself both electrified by the strange superhuman power inhabiting the area and bewitched by the shapes and forms of the region's topography. He declared that certain strange natural land and rock formations had been pressed out of the earth at its birth; that others had taken the shapes of men's tortured bodies; and that a selected few resembled the heads of gods peering from behind rock clusters. That he was living a "Theater of Cruelty" production became evident to him during his initiation into the peyotl rite. As Artaud observed the priest-sorcerers descending the highest peaks of the mountain, bearing the accessories needed for their religious (dramatic) ceremony (mirrors, baskets, crosses), he felt that he had been ushered into the heart of the Tarahumaras' cosmogony, that he had become one with the androgyne as manifested in the sacred hallucinatory and self-fertilizing peyotl plant. The intensity of the inner Light invading his inner world plunged him into the very "Mystery of Mysteries."

SURVEY OF CRITICISM

Paule Thévenin is responsible for the masterful twenty-six-volume edition of Artaud's *Oeuvres complètes*. Without her devotion, knowledge, and perseverance, Artaud's complete works would probably never have seen the light of day. In *The Theatre of Jean-Louis Barrault* (1961) Barrault, who knew Artaud well, gives valuable insights on his work and his character. A thorough study of Artaud's works by Bettina L. Knapp is *Antonin Artaud, Man of Vision* (1980), which also touches upon aspects of his multiculturalism.

SELECTIVE BIBLIOGRAPHY

Works by Artaud

Le Théâtre et son double (1938). [*The Theater and Its Double.*] Trans. Caroline Richards. New York: Grove Press, 1958.

Lettres de Rodez. Paris: Henri Parisot, 1946.

Oeuvres complètes. Ed. Paule Thévenin. 26 vols. Paris: Gallimard, 1956–1994.

Les Tarahumaras. Décines (Isère): L'Arbalète, 1963.

Selective Studies of Artaud

Barrault, Jean-Louis. *The Theatre of Jean-Louis Barrault.* New York: Hill and Wang, 1961.

Bouthors-Paillart, Catherine. *Antonin Artaud: L'énonciation ou l'épreuve de la cruauté.* Geneva: Droz, 1997.

Dumoulie, Camille. *Antonin Artaud.* Paris: Seuil, 1996.

Knapp, Bettina L. *Antonin Artaud, Man of Vision.* Chicago: Swallow Press, 1980.

SAINT AUGUSTINE OF HIPPO
(354–430)

Paul Archambault

BIOGRAPHY

To rely on Saint Augustine's *Confessiones* for the details of his life is to leave many questions unanswered. We must go to the *De beata vita* to know that he was born in Thagaste (present-day Souk-Ahras, in northeastern Algeria) "on the Ides [13th] of November," 354. His mother was a devout Christian; his father was a pagan and a "good husband" by the standards of the day, though an unfaithful and highly irascible one, served by his wife as her master (*Confessiones* 9.19). As a schoolboy Augustine nearly died of a serious stomach ailment. After three years of rhetorical studies in the neighboring city of Madaura (364–67), he pursued his university studies at Carthage (370). Sexually precocious and active, he was soon living with a young woman and by the summer of his eighteenth year had fathered a son whom he named Adeodatus, or "God-given."

Reading Cicero's *Hortensius* at age nineteen convinced him for the first time that the intellectual life was a serious matter. He had been a clever student of "rhetoric," that is, literary studies combined with the study of oratory. In his *Confessiones* he looked back with loathing on the "damnable and frivolous" literary pursuits of his youth (3.4). He found his weeping over Dido's suicide "sinful" because he disregarded the "death" in his own soul (1.13). Thirsting for a life of wisdom after reading the *Hortensius*, he studied the holy Scriptures "to see what they were like," but their mysterious wisdom appeared at the time "unworthy of comparing with the dignity of Cicero" (3.5).

For nine years, from 374 to about 382, he adhered to the dualistic metaphysics of the Manicheans while teaching at Thagaste and at Carthage. In 383 he secretly left for Rome, where he frequented other members of the Manichean sect and grew increasingly skeptical about Manichean teachings. He was appointed in 384 to a chair of rhetoric at Milan, where he met Bishop Ambrose, whose preaching was to have a profound impact on his thinking. Augustine grew increasingly attracted to Ambrose, to Scripture, and to the Catholic faith and decided to pursue his instruction in Catholic doctrine.

He rejected marriage in preference to celibacy that would free him for a life of philosophic research. The call came in August 386: while he was sitting in a garden in Milan, he heard a voice urging him to "take up and read" the book next to him. The words "put on the Lord Jesus Christ and make not provision for the flesh, to fulfill the lusts thereof" (Romans 13:14) were clearly the sign he had been looking for. He resigned his chair at Milan, was baptized a Catholic in March 387, and left for Africa in the autumn of 388.

Back at Hippo he led a life of monastic study, was ordained to the priesthood in 391, and was acclaimed bishop of Hippo in 395. During the next thirty-five years he became a leading figure of the Western Church and no doubt its most prestigious teacher. His preaching, his writing, and his tireless creation of new monastic communities all contributed to his shaping the doctrine of the Roman Catholic Church and becoming its most articulate defender against heresy, from Donatism to Manicheanism. At the time of his death in 430 he had more than a hundred philosophical, theological, and epistolary works to his credit, including the *Confessiones*, which appeared in 401, the *De Trinitate* (422), and the *Retractationes* (427). His greatest apologetic work, and in every way his magnum opus, was the *De civitate Dei* (*The City of God*), begun after the sack of Rome in 410 and written over a fifteen-year period. Against those who accused the Christian religion of being responsible for the fall of Rome, he argued for the coexistence in history of a temporal city of those who love themselves even unto the rejection of God, and a spiritual city of those who love God even unto the rejection of self. If the *Confessiones* arguably made Augustine the founder of modern autobiography, *De civitate Dei* surely made him the first writer to articulate a philosophy of history. He died at Hippo in 430, as Alaric and the Goths were besieging the city.

MAJOR MULTICULTURAL THEMES

It may seem arguable to include Augustine of Hippo, a Doctor of the Roman Catholic Church, in a sourcebook of "multicultural" writers. This forceful articulator of Catholic dogma, nearly one-fourth of whose books and treatises were written against (*Contra*) groups and individuals he considered heretical—Jews, Donatists, Academics, Manicheans, Priscillianists, Origenists, and others—hardly seems to qualify as a relativist. At the same time, however, he is an extraordinarily fertile point of encounter between several systems that he was the first to syncretize into a coherent whole. Among these systems were Greek political philosophy, Ciceronian rhetoric, Jewish collective history, and the Christian doctrine of individual salvation.

Nowhere is his multicultural syncretism better articulated than in *De civitate Dei*. Though he had balked at the learning of Greek since his Madaura years, he knew the main themes of Plato's *Republic* through Cicero and Varro; and he was largely allergic to the Platonic conviction that an ideal Republic is attainable in the earthly city. He knew that attempts had been made to approach this Platonic ideal, of which the *Pax romana* had by no means been the least successful; but he also realized that worldly empires do not last forever, and that the gods of the city ultimately prove ineffectual if one considers them as protectors of the city's good fortunes. He was convinced of the real presence of a spiritual God in history. *De civitate Dei* is not a refutation of Plato's *Republic*; it is not even an "answer" to Plato; it is a reconfiguration of Plato in Christian terms.

While he seems to reject his past pagan learning, Augustine in fact incorporated everything he learned in his youth and never really jettisoned any of his intellectual baggage. While he retracted many of his past positions, he never attempted to censure or outlaw the pagan classics in his later years as a Christian educator. Rather, he elaborated a Christian philosophy of education based on the best ideals of Greek *paideia* (instruction), chiefly on a responsible reading of the works of Plato and Cicero (Kevane, 93–112). He incorporated Jewish thinking into his own system because he knew that it was Jewish, not Greek, thought that had introduced the idea of history into European thinking. He appropriated for his own purposes, especially in *De civitate Dei*, a Jewish sense of history as a covenant initiated by Yahweh with Abraham and his descendants forever, but he extended the Jewish definition of Abraham's descendants to include the entire human race. Thus Augustine drew on a multiplicity of cultural strands to build what seems a monolithic, somewhat unbending structure of dogma; but on closer examination it reveals many open questions and an astonishing plasticity of structure.

SURVEY OF CRITICISM

There are literally tens of thousands of books and articles in the critical bibliography on Augustine, and so I have limited myself mainly to works that have influenced my interpretation of Augustine. These works are mainly centered in the French Catholic tradition, and I must confess to having read few Calvinist or Lutheran interpreters of his works. Rebecca West's 1933 biography is largely psychoanalytical and reductionist. I cite it as a highly readable example of a biography that chooses to reduce Augustine's conversion experience to naturalistic terms. Perhaps the best one-volume introduction to the reading of Augustine is John J. O'Meara's (1997). Whitney Oates's selections in the *Basic Writings* volumes are excellent and well translated. Ernest Fortin's essays (edited by J. Brian Benestad, 1996) are highly penetrating studies of Augustine as a political thinker, a dimension of Augustine's thought that has come to be taken seriously in the past three decades.

SELECTIVE BIBLIOGRAPHY

Works by Saint Augustine

Basic Writings of Saint Augustine. Ed. and trans. Whitney J. Oates. 2 vols. New York: Random House, 1948.

Les Confessions. Ed. M. Skutella. Intro. and notes A. Solignac. Trans. E. Tréhoul and G. Bouisson. Paris: Desclée de Brouwer, 1962.

Concerning the City of God against the Pagans. Trans. Henry Bettenson. Intro. David Knowles. Harmondsworth: Penguin Books, 1972.

La Cité de Dieu. 3 vols. Intro. Isabelle Bochet. Trans. Gustave Combès, rev. Goulven Madec. Paris: Etudes Augustiniennes, 1993–1995.

Political Writings. Trans. Michael W. Tkacz and Douglas Kries. Intro. Ernest L. Fortin. Indianapolis: Hackett Publishing Co., 1994.

Selective Studies of Saint Augustine

Courcelle, Pierre. *Les Confessions de Saint Augustin dans la tradition littéraire*. Paris: Etudes Augustiniennes, 1963.

Fortin, Ernest. *Collected Essays*. 3 vols. Vol. 1, *The Birth of Philosophic Christianity*. Ed. J. Brian Benestad. Lanham, Md.: Rowman and Littlefield, 1996.

Kevane, Eugene. *Augustine the Educator*. Westminster, Md.: Newman Press, 1964.

O'Meara, John J. *Understanding Augustine*. Dublin: Four Courts Press, 1997.

West, Rebecca. *St. Augustine* (1933). In *Rebecca West: A Celebration*. New York: Viking Press, 1977.

WILLIAM BECKFORD
(1760–1844)

Marie-Madeleine Martinet

BIOGRAPHY

William Beckford lived from childhood in social surroundings linked with distant countries. He was the son of a lord mayor of London whose family had interests in Jamaica as sugar planters and had been involved in the government of the island. His mother belonged to the aristocratic family of the Hamiltons. Anthony Hamilton, the late-seventeenth-century author of the *Mémoires du comte de Gramont* (in French), was a relative on his mother's side, whom Beckford said he hoped to meet in the afterlife. The Beckford family seat of Fonthill in Wiltshire contained numerous works of art and rooms decorated in the Oriental style, as well as a library including the *Arabian Nights*. In his family surroundings the usual classical imaginative world of the period was strongly mixed with exotic influences.

Beckford's father died when the boy was ten; he was educated at home by his mother (known as "the Begum," an Oriental title), guardians, and tutors, who offered the precocious child a cosmopolitan education including classical, modern, and Oriental languages. He is said to have received lessons in piano at the age of five from the nine-year-old Mozart. He took lessons in architecture from William Chambers, and his drawing master was Alexander Cozens, nicknamed "the Persian," who had been brought up at the Russian court, where his father was the czar's shipbuilder, and who developed his interests in Oriental cultures. Cozens had created a method of drawing called "blotting" in which the draughtsman allowed blots of paint to drop at random on the paper, forming unpredictable shapes that he then interpreted into landscapes: form preceded meaning, a mode of sensibility that corresponded to Beckford's atmospheric perception.

In 1777 Beckford traveled to Switzerland where he met Voltaire, became a member of the Jacques Necker circle—Necker's daughter was the future Madame de Staël—and visited the Grande Chartreuse, developing his taste for wild landscapes. In 1780 he made his Grand Tour, traveled to Italy, and in Naples became acquainted with the antiquarian and scientist Sir William Hamilton.

He traveled frequently, visiting Germany and Italy in 1782 with Cozens. He then traveled in Switzerland with his bride in 1783 and entered Parliament as a member for Wells in 1784, which seemed to be the beginning of a successful career but actually brought his downfall. From 1785 to 1796 he lived mostly abroad, being estranged from English society on account of rumors of an affair with a young man that were circulated by the political opponents he had just acquired when he entered public life. With occasional brief spells in England, he stayed in Switzerland, where his wife died in childbirth; there he was shunned by Edward Gibbon, whose library he later bought and locked up as a revenge. He then went to Portugal (1787), where he was well received in Lisbon society but failed to be presented at court because of the opposition of the British envoy. In Paris he bought works of art in the early stages of the French Revolution (1790–92), and he moved again to Portugal on the declaration of war in 1793. From 1796 he devoted his energies to Fonthill which, because of financial difficulties, he had to sell in 1822. He moved to Bath, where he died in 1844.

MAJOR MULTICULTURAL THEMES

Besides parodic tales and satirical texts, Beckford composed in French *Vathek* (1782–1786), first published as a pirated English translation. Narrating the story of Caliph Vathek, the grandson of Harun-al-Rashid of the *Arabian Nights*, it includes episodes of superlative sensuous indulgence alternating with scenes of treachery and cruelty, which take place in palaces and landscapes of barbaric splendor.

The use of the French language for *Vathek* is multicultural in more than one sense. In addition to cosmopolitan culture, it reveals Beckford's desire to place the novel in a literary tradition with exotic vistas. The French language in the eighteenth century may well have been felt to be the medium through which the *Arabian Nights* was first known in Europe, since the fairly recent French translation by the orientalist Antoine Galland (1704–1717) was the first in a European language. French was then the route to the culture of the East and to the Oriental literary form of the tales within the tale, which is the structure of the *Thousand and One Nights* (as they were known); it was used by non-French writers of the time for accounts of journeys (such as Gibbon's) or for extraordinary fictional works with the embedded effect of tales within tales (such as Jan Potocki's later texts). It is a frequent feature of multicultural writing that a neighboring foreign country is seen as a stepping-stone toward other more distant regions, and the aspects of its culture that attract foreigners are those that are of exotic origin.

The dream architecture of *Vathek* is an image of the self: it describes a palace with five wings, one for each of the senses, and the Caliph builds a tower so high that he can see the whole world, helped by genii, to discover the mysteries of Heaven. The Orient is a world where spatial immensity and echoing atmospheric effects are symbolic correlatives of moral excess.

Beckford's main travel narratives are highly original accounts of his visits to Mediterranean countries, especially to Italy and the Iberian Peninsula. In them the traveler's perception of a foreign country is emotional and expresses immediate and intuitive sympathy. Such a form of writing was so unusual that the 1783 edition of his account of his journey to Italy and other southern countries was suppressed, and only a handful of copies have survived. Its title, *Dreams, Waking Thoughts, and Incidents: In a Series of Letters from Various Parts of Europe*, is indicative of its emotional tone; the reason for the suppression may have been that Beckford's family meant him for a political career and thought that revealing his sensitive nature would disqualify him. An edition with a title more in the conventional descriptive tradition, *Italy, with Sketches of Spain and Portugal*, was published in Paris in 1834. Many of the more florid sentences have been cut, the phrases expressing passionate responses to the landscape and the atmospheric effects having been deleted. Beckford also published *Recollections of an Excursion to the Monasteries of Alcobaça and Batalha* in 1835, from notes in his travel diary of 1794, with the introductory remark that when he came by chance upon these notes, he "invoked the powers of memory—and, behold, up rose the whole series of recollections."

Beckford evokes countries by suggesting and then denying descriptions, in a game of shifting perspectives. His perception of a country is a blend of synesthetic sensations, in which sight is accompanied (and frequently preceded) by the other senses. The objects of sight, as caught in succession by the traveler's eye, may well be first a detail or an atmospheric effect, which leaves the nature and shape of the elements of the landscape in uncertainty until they are identified later in the sentence; the rhythm is that of discovery. His grammatical constructions frequently place the landscape as the subject of the sentence, while the narrator becomes the object. In *Dreams, Waking Thoughts, and Incidents* the moment of the approach to Venice is thus narrated impressionistically: "The softness and transparency of the air, soon told me I was arrived in happier climates; and I felt sensations of joy and novelty run through my veins, upon beholding the smiling land of groves and verdure which stretched before me" (82). His account of his entrance into Rome through the Porta del Popolo (a usual set piece for previous travelers) is a source of "sensations" and atmospheric indulgence: "Shall I ever forget the sensations I experienced, . . . when I . . . beheld the square, the domes, the obelisk; the long perspective of streets and palaces opening beyond, all glowing with the vivid red of sunset. You can imagine how I enjoyed my beloved tint, my favourite hour, surrounded by such objects" (199). In his *Recollections of an Excursion to the Monasteries of Alcobaça and Batalha* in Portugal, a sentence will begin with a notation such as "The soft air of the evening" (22), and the gradual revelation of the landscape may be reproduced in the word order: "Lights glimmering at the extremity of an avenue of orange-trees directed us to the house, a low picturesque building" (22), or "Sometimes I was enticed down a mysterious lane by the prospect of a crag and a Moorish castle which offered itself to view at its termination, and sometimes under ruined arches which crossed my path in the most picturesque manner" (66). Variations in scale are implicit in allusions to *Gulliver's Travels*, such as references to Brobdingnag (162), and the sense of endlessness in the landscape is apparent in phrases such as "the world was all before us" (44), a quotation from the end of *Paradise Lost*, XII, 646.

Understanding a foreign country also means adopting its rhythm. Beckford frequently describes how he feels enveloped by the midday atmosphere of Mediterranean countries, when life seems to stop: "I loitered away the sultry hours of midday most pleasantly under its deep, fragrant shade" (*Recollections*, 26), and later he refers to this moment of the day under its Mediterranean name "the hour of siesta" (62). When he attempts to define this atmosphere, the memories of several countries fuse. His works exemplify how the experience of a country considered as a fundamental reference can serve to illuminate later discoveries, since he interprets the Portuguese atmosphere with the help of an Italian phrase: "If ever a decent excuse could be offered for perfect laziness, it was to be found in the warm, enervating atmosphere, loaded with perfume, which universally invested this pleasant umbrageous region. No wonder my Lord of Aviz, the most consummate professor of 'il dolce far niente' in all Portugal, and Algarve to boot, could not be withdrawn from it without infinite reluctance" (32). While he is in Iberia, he introduces references to more exotic countries of the Far East, such as China, from the accounts of Padre Machado and Chambers—Sir William Chambers being one of the main exponents of Chinese architecture in Britain.

The traveler's imagination may open toward more distant versions of the culture of the country where he is staying (through the medium of sound, as usual). In Portugal he finds traces of Brazil: "At length, a faint musical murmur stole upon my ear: I advanced towards the spot whence it seemed to come. . . . Drawing nearer and nearer, my heart beating quickly all the while, I distinguished the thrilling cadences of a delightful Brasiliera (sinha che vem da Bahia—a lady who comes from Bahia)—well-known sounds. I looked up to a latticed window just thrown open by a lovely arm—a well-known arm" (66). As usual in multicultural writing, a foreign country serves to provide an interpretive paradigm though which the writer views third and fourth countries in a series of superimposed perceptions.

SURVEY OF CRITICISM

Mallarmé's (1865) tribute to *Vathek* is well known; he stresses the crescendo effects and the shifting architectural vistas, which he links to the vast echoing corridors of Beckford's childhood home. He comments on the use of a foreign language: "Le fait général du recours à un autre parler que le natal, pour se délivrer, par un écrit, de l'obsession régnant sur toute une jeunesse: renoncer à y voir mieux que l'espèce de solennité avec quoi il fallut s'asseoir à une tâche de caractère unique." (Generally speaking, resorting to a language other than the native tongue, to free onself, through a written text, from the obsession prevailing over one's whole youth; forbear to interpret it as anything higher than the solemn attitude of sitting down to a unique task.) Brian Fothergill's *Beckford of Fonthill* (1979) is the most up-to-date biography of the author.

SELECTIVE BIBLIOGRAPHY

Works by Beckford

Dreams, Waking Thoughts, and Incidents; In a Series of Letters from Various Parts of Europe. London: Johnson and Elmsly, 1783.
Excursion à Alcobaça et Batalha. Ed. André Parreaux. Paris: Société les Belles Lettres, 1956.
Vathek and Other Stories. Ed. Malcolm Jack. London: Penguin, 1995.

Selective Studies of Beckford

Chapman, Guy. *Beckford*. London: Hart-Davis, 1952.
Fothergill, Brian. *Beckford of Fonthill*. London: Faber, 1979.
Graham, Kenneth W., ed. *"Vathek" and the Escape from Time*. New York: AMS, 1990.
Mallarmé, Stéphane. "Préface à *Vathek*" (1865). In *Oeuvres complètes*. Ed. Henri Mondor et G. Jean-Aubry. Paris: Gallimard, 1945. 2nd ed., 1965.
Parreaux, André. *William Beckford, auteur de "Vathek." (1760–1844)*. Paris: Nizet, 1960.

MARÍA LUISA BOMBAL
(1910–1980)

Martha L. Rubí

BIOGRAPHY

Born on June 8, 1910, in Viña del Mar, Chile, María Luisa Bombal bears the French existential and Surrealist trademark of the twentieth-century writer. Her parents, Martín Bombal Videla and Blanca d'Anthes Precht, both of French ancestry—he from Limoges and she a direct descendant of French Huguenots—along with other rebellious European kindred, settled in Chile in the nineteenth century. They wielded enormous influence on her dramatic writing style and sentimental perception of reality, her ancestors sometimes appearing in her fiction as a reminder of her roots. In the novel *La amortajada* (1938) the male character, Antonio, is named after her grandfather Antonio Bombal Videla, whose father, Francisco Videla Gómez, hunted by the Argentine dictator Juan Manuel de Rosas, crossed the Andes and settled in Chile in the nineteenth century. Memories of her grandmother, María Luisa Videla, and her father, Martín, linger in images that nostalgically evoke the scent of her father's cologne and her grandmother's perfume—images forever lodged in the pages of *La amortajada*. Legends and stories of escape and exile filled the young mind of María Luisa. It is not surprising that her first language was French; that through French ancestry, culture, and, later, residence in Paris, she would be shaped and defined; and that her ambiguous symbolism and tragic vision of the world would become the essence of her nightmarish novel *La última niebla* (1935).

The birth in 1911 of her twin sisters Loreto and Blanca impacted on María Luisa. She looked frail and out of place next to her robust sisters. As her father's favorite child, the nine-year-old María Luisa was devastated at the news of his death in 1919 at the age of forty-one. This event brought the existence of death into her innocent concept of life, a theme always present in her stories. Her mother and the three daughters settled in Paris in 1923, where María Luisa attended the Ecole Notre Dame de l'Assomption. She was immediately drawn to the classics of the nineteenth century: Balzac, Mérimée, Flaubert, and Stendhal, as well as Goethe and Schiller among the German Romantics.

The future author attended the Lycée La Bruyere (1927–28), which prepared her for the French baccalaureate. During this period she formally studied Pascal's thinking in logic. Yet this formation seems almost absent from her works, where her characters move in anguish and in surreal time. At the age of eighteen she entered the Sorbonne, obtaining a degree in French literature with a thesis on Mérimée in April 1931, when she left France for Chile and soon joined Pablo Neruda's literary circle of Chilean poets and writers of the vanguard movement. Although she infused French Romantic ideas into the literary gatherings, she soon found that Surrealism, at its height during her Parisian years, predominated in her Chilean literary circle. She learned to fuse both aesthetic movements, resulting in her ambiguous style of writing.

In Buenos Aires she published her first novel, *La última niebla*, reworking in this and other writings the theme of love in its essential state, converting it into a literary creation, even while continuing to develop the recurrent theme of "loveless marriage." Influenced by Virginia Woolf's feminist stance and Victoria Ocampo's celebrated review *Sur*, Bombal wrote her second novel, *La amortajada*, published by Ocampo. The following year she wrote an extensive short story, "El arbol," followed by others: "Las islas nuevas," "Trenzas," "Lo secreto," and "La historia de María Griselda." In 1941 she left Chile definitively and settled in the United States, the Chilean Embassy having offered her a contract to work in the U.S. capital. There she wrote a chronicle about the city of Washington, D.C., which was published in Buenos Aires. Upon completion of her contract, she moved to New York City, married Count Raphael de Saint-Phalle (1944), and in the same year gave birth to her only child, Brigitte de Saint-Phalle. She died in Los Angeles in 1980.

MAJOR MULTICULTURAL THEMES

Bombal's multicultural contacts with Paris, Buenos Aires, and New York clearly mark the influences each country had on her literary formation. Her French years shaped her pronounced existential and Surrealist narrative and dramatic form. Although she did not come into direct contact with the French existentialists, the philosophy permeated the artistic milieu of that period, as witnessed by Jean-Paul Sartre's *La Nausée* (1938) and *L'Etre et le néant* (1943). Yet not only is the content of Bombal's work existential in nature, but her narrative style bears the pessimistic tone of existence that cannot transcend reality (*La última niebla*).

By contrast, Surrealism, created in 1916, imbued her work with its dreamscape quality. The irrational state implies a reaction against what is real. It is precisely this clash between reality and fantasy that causes desperation and the almost incomprehensible finale for which Bombal's writing is noted. What is surreal, therefore, causes disequilibrium in the conscious and subconscious state of her women characters, who seem to desire the love of which they are deprived. It is not surprising that magic and unreality fill the Surrealist landscape. This being-in-the-world therefore becomes laden with the conscious act of existing and the frustrated desire of becoming. The main thrust of Surrealist doctrine manifests itself in the tension between Bombal's women and the world they inhabit.

The richness, complexity, and vitality of her awakening women characters seem, at first glance, almost disguised, but the subjective self emerges from lethargy to become the central concern of her works. This theme of women's sexuality would become paramount to women's identity in 1945 when Simone de Beauvoir published *Le Deuxième Sexe*. But the seed of Bombal's ontological thinking was a product of both a European education and Hispanic breeding. It created the interaction she clearly anticipated in the emergence of a new form of writing that would become the heart of future Hispanic feminist writings. Both the existential and the Surrealist movements, along with Freud's theories on psychoanalysis and dreams, permeate Bombal's feminist discourse, making her brand of literature a precursor of literary feminist writings.

SURVEY OF CRITICISM

Agata Gligo captures Bombal's early years in Viña del Mar in her biography, *María Luisa: Sobre la vida de María Luisa Bombal* (1984). She reconstructs the author's life in a novel way, through the autobiographical component present in her fiction. The multidimensional life of the author and episodes of her elusive, at times conflicting, and rather fragmented life story are pieced together with personal interviews, letters, and other documentation.

In her critical analysis of Bombal's narrative, *Las desterradas del paraíso, protagonistas en la narrativa de María Luisa Bombal* (1983), Marjorie Agosín explores the importance of Bombal's heroines, leitmotifs, themes, and the mythic quality surrounding them. This invaluable book is organized in chronological order, tracing her texts and central themes of her works.

An enormous and impressive corpus of doctoral dissertations and articles in literary journals is dedicated to Bombal's narrative. Aside from Gligo's biography on Bombal, work still needs to be done to emphasize her multicultural experiences and perhaps rework in a novel way ideas that stemmed directly from the countries that influenced her writing.

SELECTIVE BIBLIOGRAPHY

Work by Bombal

Obras completas. Ed. Lucía Guerra-Cunningham. Santiago de Chile: Editorial Andrés Bello, 1996.

Selective Studies of Bombal

Agosín, Marjorie. *Las desterradas del paraíso, protagonistas en la narrativa de María Luisa Bombal.* New York: Senda Nueva, 1983.

Gligo, Agata. *María Luisa: Sobre la vida de María Luisa Bombal.* Santiago de Chile: Editorial Andrés Bello, 1984.

Méndez Rodenas, Adriana. "El lenguaje de los sueños en 'La última niebla' ": La metáfora del Eros." *Revista Iberoamericana* 168–169 (1994): 935–43.

Rabago, Alberto. "Elementos surrealistas en 'La última niebla.' " *Hispania* 64, no. 1 (1981): 31–40.

JORGE LUIS BORGES
(1899–1986)

James O. Pellicer

BIOGRAPHY

The boy who was to become the greatest Spanish-American writer of the twentieth century was born in the city of Buenos Aires. Jorge Luis Borges would boost Hispanic letters to their heights by means of a partly inherited and partly acquired multicultural wealth. English probably was his first language, since his father and his paternal grandmother used that language at home, and the latter was determined to have the child read English even before he knew the Spanish alphabet. His father taught psychology in English in Buenos Aires; his favorite authors were Swinburne, Keats, and Shelley, whose poetry became the preferred theme of family conversations. Later Borges recognized that "it was he [his father] who revealed the power of poetry to me—the fact that words are not only a means of communication but also magic symbols and music" (*Borges A/Z: La Biblioteca de Babel*, 214, my translation). His mother was also a literarily oriented woman, and the daily family conversations revolved around themes of art and poetry. Borges's only sister became a painter and married a Spanish critic of art and literature.

Borges finished elementary school in Argentina, but due to the outbreak of World War I, which caught his family in Geneva during a vacation trip, his father preferred to establish residence there. Young Borges excelled in French and German at Calvin College in Switzerland, where he completed his secondary education. With four languages perfectly mastered, a total dedication to art, and no financial need, he used his abundant time to read innumerable works written in all those languages and to begin writing himself in Spanish, English, and French. He accompanied his readings with an intense search for the cultural components of each theme, using the great German, English, and French encyclopedias. In his prologue, originally written in French, to the 1979 edition of the *Encyclopédie de Diderot et d'Alembert* in eighteen volumes, he wrote:

"The encyclopedia is possibly the most pleasurable literary genre, but not the ones published today, which are composed of simple statistical information not designed for reading but for fast consultation that the reader immediately forgets. The great old encyclopedias, such as Pliny's *Historia Naturalis* or *The Etymologies* by St. Isidore of Seville and *The Triple Mirror* by Vincent de Beauvais, attempt to give us the total sum of human knowledge. Diderot and D'Alembert complete this wonderful tradition, admirably enriching it, in addition, with the French language" (*Borges A/Z: La Biblioteca de Babel*, 81, trans. Antonio Fernández Ferrer). His own fabulous memory allowed him to keep at hand enormous quantities of information.

After spending five years in Switzerland, the Borgeses moved to Spain in 1919, where they lived for three years. Now twenty, young Borges dedicated his time to the study of Latin, making some room for Arabic. He became acquainted with the most important leaders of Spanish letters at a historical moment when the new Modern Art movement was publishing literary magazines such as *Grecia* and *Ultra*, which would be his models for those he created later in Buenos Aires: *Prisma* in 1921 and *Proa* in 1922. To all of them, the Spanish as well as the Argentinean ones, he contributed very original articles, many of them reprinted for the first time in 1997 in *Textos recobrados*.

In 1923 Borges returned to Europe for a year, while in Buenos Aires his first book of poems, *Fervor de Buenos Aires*, was published. In it he nostalgically sang the simple things of everyday life and places, exactly as he had lived them during his childhood: "the aroma of the jasmine and the honeysuckle / the silence of the sleeping bird" (in *Obras completas*, 1974, 19, my translation). In 1925 he published his second book of poetry, *Luna de enfrente*, and his first of essays, *Inquisiciones*, dealing with themes of international as well as national literature.

As he published work after work, mainly in prose with the exception of *Cuaderno San Martín* (1929), in which he continued the earlier evocation of his city, something interesting happened. Several essays subtly began to be narrative pieces and from that point entered the world of fiction and ended up as superlative masterworks. Thus appeared his first narrative, "Hombre de la esquina rosada," published in the *Historia Universal de la Infamia* (1935), as well as *Historia de la Eternidad* (1936). In 1941 he published in *Sur* the first of his short stories as such, "El jardín de los senderos que se bifurcan," which he presented in the competition for the National Award in Literature and later included in his first collection of short stories, *Ficciones* (1944).

Borges received his first official recognition, the Gran Premio de Honor de la Sociedad Argentina de Escritores, in 1944 and thereafter published every year, sometimes in collaboration with his friends, given progressive problems with his eyesight. *La cifra* (1981), dedicated to his future wife, María Kodama, ends with "Unas notas," in which Borges comments on a theme that probably summarizes completely the subject and form of his entire production: "Philosophy and theology are—I suspect—two species of fantastic literature. Two splendid species. As a matter of fact, what are the nights of Sharazad or the invisible man, compared with infinite substance endowed with infinite attributes of Baruch Spinoza or the Platonic archetypes?" (*La cifra*, "Unas notas," 105, my translation).

Numerous are the positions and honors Borges received throughout his lifetime, including the directorship of the National Library of Buenos Aires (1950), membership in the Argentine Academy of Letters (1950), and a professorship in English literature at the University of Buenos Aires (1956). He won the National Award of Literature in 1956, and from 1961 until his death many countries and universities bestowed on him honorary appointments and doctorates. He died in Geneva on June 14, 1986.

MAJOR MULTICULTURAL THEMES

Borges started his career multiculturally and progressed intentionally in the same manner. His cultural world is the universal library; his thematic world is rich and complex. Spain's minister of culture, Javier Solana Madariaga, on the occasion of the writer's death, declared that "speaking of Borges's work is dealing with a whole world because he deciphered history for us and upon doing it, he made the world more complex and suggestive" (Biblioteca Nacional, *Borges*, 7, my translation). Although multiplicity best describes Borges, his basic theme is always the same, very twentieth century, and Schopenhauer is always behind the multiple aspects of his complex world. The elusive and illusory character of reality is the essence of his vision of the world. When Umberto Eco was asked the question of why he had made Borges the protagonist of his best-selling novel *Il nome della rosa*, he answered, "Debts are to be paid" ("Postille a *Il nome della rosa*, 1983," 515, my translation), with which he recognized Borges as the master of the modern world, submerged in the anguish of the real frailty of an illusory fortress.

Borges materialized the universality of his distressing theme in the specific reality of various cultures; the more, the better, so as to return to the universal through the particular. Thus his anecdotes may take place in the Argentine countryside, where the characters are cowhands in the vast southern plains or brawlers in the outskirts of Buenos Aires ("El hombre de la esquina rosada"; "El Sur"; "La intrusa"); or in a medieval library that becomes fantastic ("La biblioteca de Babel"); or among British books in which the reader may appreciate every particular detail that truly characterized the culture of England (*Otras inquisiciones*, 1952). The history of Ireland with all its cultural aspects may be the mirror of the elusive character of reality ("El tema del traidor y del heroe," in *Artificios*, 1944). Every detail of the region of Central America, motherland of the Mayas—its supreme priest, the pyramid, the conquistador, even the discourse style—perfectly reflects that pre-Columbian culture ("La escritura del Dios," in *El Aleph*, 1949). Sometimes the place is Hindustan, or Persia and its old temples ("Ruinas circulares," in *Ficciones*), or Germany and the Nazis and the Jews ("El milagro secreto," in *Artificios*; "Deutsches Requiem," in *El Aleph*). On other occasions it is all about the Jews, but from Argentina ("Emma Zunz," in *El Aleph*). Elsewhere it is just a book that creates the anecdote ("Pierre Menard, autor del Quijote," in *Ficciones*). In all cases every cultural detail is always faithful to the particular reality it reflects, and, infallibly, that exact and definite reality brings a terrible universal truth—the incomprehensible chaos, the real inheritance of humankind.

SURVEY OF CRITICISM

The bibliography on Borges is as complex as his themes, but a small book, *Poética de la prosa de J.L. Borges*, by Alberto Julián Pérez, is one of the best studies. Basing his work on a Bakhtinian literary thesis, its author examines in detail Borges's complex themes. An excellent aid to visualizing the sources used by Borges is the book published by the Biblioteca Nacional of Madrid, *Borges*, in which eighty large-format pages with three compact columns each are dedicated to the authors cited by Borges in his rich list of publications. This work ends with a chronology of all Borges's works, which is very useful for the study of the different stages of his literary life. Very important is *Homenaje a Jorge Luis Borges*, which ends with an update of Borges's bibliography to 1991. Unpublished letters, pictures, old magazines, and journals supplied by Borges's widow, María Kodama, compose Jorge Luis Borges' *Textos recobrados, 1919–1929*, published in 1997. For a comprehensive interpretation of Borges and a good literary biography, the works of Emir Rodríguez Monegal are commendable.

SELECTIVE BIBLIOGRAPHY

Works by Borges

Obras completas, 1923–1972. Ed. Carlos V. Frías. Madrid: Ultramar, 1977.
Obras completas en colaboración. Buenos Aires: Emecé Editores, 1979.
La cifra. Buenos Aires: Emecé Editores, 1981.
Borges A/Z: La Biblioteca de Babel. Ed. Antonio Fernández Ferrer. Madrid: Ediciones Siruela, 1988.
Textos recobrados, 1919–1929. Buenos Aires: Emecé Editores, 1997.

Selective Studies of Borges

Biblioteca Nacional. *Borges*. Madrid: Dirección General de Libros y Biblioteca, 1986.
Eco, Umberto. "Postille a *Il nome della rosa*, 1983." In *Il nome della rosa*. Milano: Bompiani, 1986.
Homenaje a Jorge Luis Borges. Cuadernos Hispanoamericanos 505/507 (July–September 1992).
Pérez, Alberto Julián. *Poética de la prosa de J.L. Borges*. Madrid: Gredos, 1986.

————. *Realidad y suprarealidad de los cuentos fantásticos de Jorge Luis Borges*. Miami: Universal, 1971.

Rodríguez Monegal, Emir. *Borges: Hacia una interpretación*. Madrid: Guadarrama, 1976.

————. *Jorge Luis Borges: A Literary Biography*. New York: E.P. Dutton, 1978.

Stark, John Olsen. *The Literature of Exhaustion: Borges, Nabokov, and Barth*. Durham, N.C.: Duke University Press, 1974.

JAMES BOSWELL
(1740–1795)

Marlies K. Danziger

BIOGRAPHY

James Boswell was brought up in two cultures, the Scottish and the English, and became acquainted with still other cultures during his three-year stay on the European continent. After receiving a classical education and studying law in Scotland without enthusiasm, he greatly enjoyed London, where he was be-friended by Samuel Johnson. Not finding a suitable occupation, Boswell was pleased when his father, a prominent judge and Ayrshire landowner, allowed him to travel abroad.

In Holland (1763) he heard lectures on law but spent more time on learning French. He then chose to visit various German principalities, where he could "acquire French and polite manners" in societies closer to his own than the artificial society of France (Journal, 27 September 1764, *Boswell on the Grand Tour; Germany and Switzerland, 1764* [hereafter cited as *Germany and Switzerland*], 112–13). At every stage he cultivated interesting acquaintances, most notably Rousseau and Voltaire. He proceeded to Italy and then took the unusual step of visiting Corsica, which he found so interesting that he described its history and topography as well as his experiences there in his first major publication, *An Account of Corsica* (1768).

Back in Scotland (1766) he practiced law in Edinburgh. On his father's death in 1782 he inherited the family estate and took seriously his position as "laird of Auchinleck." Annual visits to London enabled him to continue his friendship with Johnson. On the latter's death in 1784 Boswell published the *Journal of a Tour to the Hebrides* (1785), based on the journals he had written while taking Johnson to Scotland in 1773. He then mined his other journals to complete his monumental *The Life of Samuel Johnson, LL.D.* (1791), his first claim to fame until his private papers (journals, letters, and verses) were discovered in modern times.

He tried to practice law in England, without much success, and was equally unsuccessful in his attempt to enter politics by attaching himself to a powerful patron. Later he hoped to go to America as secretary to Richard Penn, grandson of the founder of Pennsylvania, or to China as secretary to the first British ambassador to that country, but neither of these positions became available. Boswell also thought of writing a travel book based on his journals but got no further than enquiring about possible publishers. His health undermined by periodic episodes of gonorrhea and increasingly frequent bouts of drinking, he died in May 1795.

MAJOR MULTICULTURAL THEMES

On the Continent Boswell not only observed other societies but actively involved himself with their cultures. Since he could speak French and was a novelty as a Scot, he was welcomed at the courts of Brunswick, Dessau, Gotha, Baden-Durlach, and Baden-Baden. "I live with princes," he wrote exultantly in his journal (28 June 1764, *Germany and Switzerland*, 16). To ensure his social acceptance, he called himself baron, a title that was his due according to the standards of the German nobility.

He quickly became enthralled by the high culture of the courts—the palaces, art collections, operas, concerts, and theatrical performances. In Switzerland and Italy he took detailed notes about the works of artists ranging from Holbein to Raphael to Guercino, as well as about Roman antiquities—all good preparation for his later friendship with the painter Sir Joshua Reynolds.

He furthermore actively looked for new insights into religious questions that troubled him. He had been brought up by strict Presbyterians, had already briefly tried Methodism and Catholicism, and had entered the Anglican Church while he was in Holland. Now he discussed free will and Providence with the prominent Lutheran minister J.F.W. Jerusalem in Brunswick; considered religious conversions with a Huguenot in Kassel, who told him about the landgrave of Hessen-Kassel's startling change from Calvinism to Catholicism; and debated the eternity of punishments with a Jesuit in Mannheim. Without accepting their particular ideas, he was gaining new perspectives from clergymen of different denominations.

Boswell was eager to meet even more prominent people, "great men" who had made their mark in the world. He was thrilled by the sight of Frederick the Great striding among his officers, but was disappointed when no introduction could be arranged and, more seriously, disenchanted with Prussian militarism after witnessing the flogging of a soldier and seeing the wilful destruction of Dresden ordered during the Seven Years' War (Journal, 13 July and 9 October 1764, *Germany and Switzerland*, 24, 133). Fortunately, he found a more admirable ruler in Karl Friedrich, margrave of Baden-Durlach, a genuinely enlightened prince with whom he formed a bond of friendship while he was staying in Karlsruhe.

For Boswell, Rousseau and Voltaire were "great men" par excellence, representatives of an intellectual culture more radical than any he had known. Familiar with their unorthodox religious beliefs, Boswell asked both whether they still considered themselves Christians. Rousseau, whose works had just been banned by the French, Bernese, and Genevan authorities, firmly declared that indeed he was a Christian in that he believed in the Trinity and the teachings of the New Testament, though not in any additional teachings, including St. Paul's. Voltaire went even further. He could not affirm the immortality of the soul, and when he spoke eloquently about an all-wise Supreme Being in whom he believed, it was "not as a Christian but as a man" (letter to W.J. Temple, 28 December 1764, in *Germany and Switzerland*, 294). Boswell was fascinated by such extreme positions but recognized that he himself needed more structured forms of worship, including church services and the ministrations of the clergy. He had tested and clarified his ideas.

In Corsica, finally, he saw a culture far removed from his own. The islanders were rough, simple people, whom he idealized as intrepid fighters staunchly loyal to their leader. In Pasquale Paoli, the freedom fighter who was trying to liberate his country from the occupying forces of the Genoese and French, Boswell recognized another "great man," noble in bearing and stern but kindly in rule. Boswell gave particular attention to the Corsicans' system of justice, which relied on their sense of honor. Corsicans themselves refused to execute their criminals and had to engage a foreign hangman. Later, as a practicing lawyer, Boswell defended several lower-class clients whom he considered deserving.

His experiences with other cultures undoubtedly broadened his horizons and influenced his later life, but he retained the prejudices of his time. Most notably, he disapproved of the attempts to abolish the slave trade, regarding these as attacks on property and paternalistically believing that slaves had a better life with benevolent masters than on their own (*No Abolition of Slavery*, 1791, in verse). Throughout his life he remained conservative and patriarchal.

SURVEY OF CRITICISM

Little attention has been paid to Boswell's possible connection with multiculturalism. Still, Frederick A. Pottle's magisterial biography, *James Boswell: The Earlier Years* (1966), describes Boswell's experiences abroad, and Frank Brady's continuation, *James Boswell: The Later Years* (1984), traces Boswell's further aspirations. C.P. Courtney discusses Boswell in Dutch society and as suitor in *Isabelle de Charrière (Belle de Zuylen)* (1993). Marlies K. Danziger's "Boswell's Travels through the German, Swiss, and French Enlightenment" (1995) and "Young Boswell, Aspiring Cosmopolite" (1997) deal, respectively, with Boswell's intellectual and social experiences on the Continent. Joseph Foladare's *Boswell's Paoli* (1979) focuses on Boswell's relations with the Corsican general, including their later friendship in London, where Paoli lived in exile from 1769 to 1790.

SELECTIVE BIBLIOGRAPHY

Works by Boswell

Boswell in Holland, 1763–1764. Ed. F.A. Pottle. New York: McGraw-Hill, 1952.
Boswell on the Grand Tour: Germany and Switzerland, 1764. Ed. F.A. Pottle. New York: McGraw-Hill, 1953.
Boswell on the Grand Tour: Italy, Corsica, and France, 1765–1766. Ed. Frank Brady and F.A. Pottle. New York: McGraw-Hill, 1955.
An Account of Corsica. London: printed for Edward and Charles Dilly, 1768.
No Abolition of Slavery; or, the Empire of Love: A Poem. London: printed for R. Faulder, 1791.

Selective Studies of Boswell

Brady, Frank. *James Boswell: The Later Years, 1769–1795*. New York: McGraw-Hill, 1984.
Courtney, C.P. *Isabelle de Charrière (Belle de Zuylen)*. Oxford: Voltaire Foundation, 1993.
Danziger, Marlies K. "Boswell's Travels through the German, Swiss, and French Enlightenment." In *Boswell: Citizen of the World, Man of Letters*, 13–36. Ed. Irma S. Lustig. Lexington: University Press of Kentucky, 1995.
———. "Young Boswell, Aspiring Cosmopolite." In *Boswell in Scotland and Beyond*, 33–54. Ed. Thomas Crawford. Association for Scottish Literary Studies, Occasional Papers Number 12. Glasgow, 1997.
Foladare, Joseph. *Boswell's Paoli*. Hamden, Conn.: Archon Books, 1979.
Pottle, F.A. *James Boswell: The Earlier Years, 1740–1769*. New York: McGraw-Hill, 1966.

FREDRIKA BREMER
(1801–1865)

Brita Stendahl

On 18 August 1854, when the Crimean War was raging, on the front page of *The Times* of London appeared an appeal to all women to unite for peace by creating central committees in every country. If women united to take up this task, then war could be prevented in the future and the children of the world could be cared for. The author of the appeal was Fredrika Bremer, a widely known Swedish novelist and philanthropist. *The Times* wrote a respectful but critical editorial: there would be chaos if women did not stay at home and care for their children.

BIOGRAPHY

Fredrika Bremer was born in Finland, but her family moved to Sweden when she was only three years old. Her parents brought up their many children to study and memorize in order to become brilliant conversationalists. Tutors in English, German, and French were hired. The girls were expected to learn all social graces and were subjected to the regimented upbringing of their well-intentioned but authoritarian father, who took the family on a year-long European tour in horse-drawn, covered carriages. The effect of this education on the sensitive Fredrika was confusion. She loathed her patriarchally dominated home. Whereas her brothers left home to prepare themselves for their future professions, the frustrated girl was forced to carry on feminine pursuits at home and wait for marriage. Close to a serious breakdown, Fredrika was rescued by being allowed to spend two winters at the family's country home without parental supervision. There she discovered that she could be useful, visiting and helping the sick and the poor.

Bremer began writing short stories and in 1828 published, anonymously, her first collection. *Famillen H**** (1831), her first novel, was enthusiastically greeted by the public, who demanded to know who the authoress of this story was. It introduced something new in Swedish literature—the first bourgeois novel—and was awarded a medal by the Swedish Academy for its mix of realism and romanticism. Her early success coincided with her father's death, an event that set her free. Her brother was nominally her new legal guardian, but she went to court to win her own majority, promising herself to make women's lives visible in her work. She hired a tutor, Per Böklin, a philosopher and theologian, who instantly became interested in this unusual pupil and her quest for what the role of women should be in this world. Eventually he fell in love with her, but when he proposed, she withdrew. She was not ready to give up her freedom. She fled to Norway, and Böklin soon married someone else. In 1837 and 1839, respectively, Bremer published two of her widely read, entertaining family novels, *Grannarne* and *Hemmet*. She spent the years 1849–51 in the United States, traveled widely from 1856 to 1861, and died at Årsta, near Stockholm, in 1865.

Her fame in foreign countries was at its peak during the 1840s and 1850s but faded toward the end of the nineteenth century, whereas in Sweden she remained famous and revered, though not much read. That changed in the latter part of the twentieth century when feminist scholars rediscovered her genius and resurrected her life and work.

MAJOR MULTICULTURAL THEMES

Bremer's long stay in Norway taught her how different cultures behaved strangely toward each other. Norway at that time was united with Sweden, its bullying big brother. She wrote a novel and a reading play in 1840, both of which have as their main theme the danger of not understanding and empathizing with the Other. After studying Charles Fourier's ideas of socialistic communities and reading about American equalitarian phalansteries, she presented her idea of what such a community would look like in Sweden. The proceeds from the book (*Syskonlif*, 1848) helped her to buy the ticket to go and experience the real America. Before she sailed, she visited and went to readings by Hans Christian Andersen in Denmark, was received by the queen, was tutored in natural science by Hans Christian Ørsted, the discoverer of electromagnetism, and read galleys for Hans Lassen Martensen's textbook in systematic theology, *Den Christelige Dogmatik*. Everybody in Copenhagen spoke of Søren Kierkegaard, but he refused to meet her. Her impressions of Denmark were favorable, and she appreciated its old-fashioned, conservative society. When she finally arrived at the docks of New York, the noise and vulgarity of the crowd assembled to greet her—very different from refined Denmark—horrified her. The letters she wrote to her sister Agathe eventually became a book about the New World, *Hemmen i den Nya Verlden* (1853–1854). She met with powerful and influential people: President Zachary Taylor, senators, Dorothea Dix, the Longfellows, the Lowells, Emerson, Hawthorne, Lucretia Mott, and others. She had come to collect facts about how equality had changed the role of women, but Americans were occupied with debating the abolition of slavery. Abandoning her intention to write novels or articles, she became an excellent journalist. She realized that America was not at all what she had imagined, but she came to love those United States, on the brink of a civil war, as a fearful and potentially glorious experiment in democracy.

After almost two years she was ready to sail back to Europe, but before she returned to Sweden, she spent three months in England writing articles about the social conditions in the country for a Swedish newspaper. In these articles she deplored the disparity between the unbelievable riches and the wretched poverty that, she observed, had followed in the wake of rapid industrialization. Finally, back in Sweden, she published *Hertha* (1856), her book assailing patriarchy as holding women hostage. It aroused a storm of criticism, but she was already off to Belgium when it broke loose. Together with Florence Nightingale and Harriet Beecher Stowe, she was the featured speaker at the first international socialist congress in Brussels. From there she went on a five-year study tour through Switzerland to Italy, Palestine, Turkey, and Greece. We can follow her adventures week by week thanks to the entries in her diaries, published during 1860–1862 under the title *Lifvet i gamla verlden*. In each country she studied its people, its history, literature, art, and religion. She saw history as a constant unfolding toward something better and toward higher ideals. In Rome she interviewed the pope and spent a week in a monastery. In Greece, where she stayed the longest, she reported from a leper colony and wrote of sailing in the king's yacht and of a quarrel she had with the queen over women's education. In Palestine, where she felt herself to be a pilgrim, she detested the clutter and turmoil of the Church of the Holy Sepulchre in Jerusalem, while in Istanbul she adored the beauty of purity and light in Hagia Sophia. Upon her return to Sweden she was overjoyed to discover that many of the liberal causes that she had embraced and promoted—women's rights to education and work, the right of Jews to settle in any city of the country, the right to worship outside of the established church—were gaining support in the new, democratically reformed parliament.

SURVEY OF CRITICISM

Bremer was reviewed and much praised by her contemporary colleagues inside and outside of Sweden (in America, for instance, by Ralph Waldo Emerson and Walt Whitman). Her first biography did not appear until 1896, but since then there has been a steady trickle of Swedish books about her. An American scholar, Signe Rooth, wrote about Bremer's visit to North America in *Seeress of the Northland* (1955). The last two decades have seen a Fredrika Bremer renaissance that began with Birgitta Holm's *Fredrika Bremer och den borgerliga romanens födelse* (Fredrika Bremer and the birth of the bourgeois novel, 1981).

Holm's fresh interpretation of Bremer's first novel generated a flood of articles, symposia, and collections of essays by women who enthusiastically embraced the feminist perspective that Bremer always had had in mind.

SELECTIVE BIBLIOGRAPHY

Works by Bremer

Titles of translations into English by Mary Howitt are in parentheses.

Famillen H***. Uppsala: Palmblad & Co., 1831. (*The H--- Family*. New York: Harper, 1844.)

Grannarne. Christianstad: Schmidt & Co., 1837. (*The Neighbours*. Boston: James Munroe, 1843.)

Hemmen i den Nya Verlden. 3 vols. Stockholm: Norstedt & Söner, 1853–1854. (*Homes of the New World: Impressions of America*. 2 vols. New York: Harper, 1854.)

Hertha. Stockholm: Norstedt & Söner, 1856. (*Hertha*. New York: G.P. Putnam, 1856.)

Lifvet i gamla verlden. 6 vols. Stockholm: Norstedt & Söner, 1860–1862. (*Life in the Old World*. 3 vols. Philadelphia: T.B. Petersen, 1860–1865.)

Fredrika Bremer. Brev. Ny följd I 1821–1852. Ed. Carina Burman. Stockholm: Gidlunds förlag, 1996.

Fredrika Bremer. Brev. Ny följd II 1853–1865. Ed. Carina Burman. Stockholm: Gidlunds förlag, 1996.

Selective Studies of Bremer

Adlersparre, Sofie, and Sigrid Leijonhufvud. *Fredrika Bremer*, 2 vols. Stockholm: Norstedt, 1896.

Holm, Birgitta. *Fredrika Bremer och den borgerliga romanens födelse*. Stockholm: Gidlunds förlag, 1981.

Linnér, Sture. *Fredrika Bremer i Grekland*. Stockholm: Bonniers, 1965.

Rooth, Signe A. *Seeress of the Northland: Fredrika Bremer's American Journey, 1849–1851*. Philadelphia: American Swedish Historical Foundation, 1955.

Stendahl, Brita K. *The Education of a Self-made Woman: Fredrika Bremer, 1801–1865*. Lewiston, N.Y.: Edwin Mellen Press, 1994.

THE BROWNINGS:
ROBERT BROWNING
and ELIZABETH
BARRETT BROWNING
(1812–1889/1806–1861)

Marie-Madeleine Martinet

BIOGRAPHY

The Brownings differed in their education: whereas Elizabeth Barrett (Robert Browning's senior by six years) was born near Durham and was brought up rurally before moving to London in 1836, he was a Londoner who traveled abroad from his youth. They first met by reading each other's poetic works.

Elizabeth Barrett was an invalid from the age of fifteen. She lived almost as a recluse because of ill health, attendance on her aging father, and the impression caused by the death of her brother by drowning. She published poetry and read Browning's verse.

Born in London of a very religious Congregational mother, Robert Browning later read Shelley on atheism, but his thought remained imbued with religious concerns: this accounts for the philosophical questioning in his poetry. He visited Italy several times in his youth, and it became part of his culture. His early poetry was self-confessional and was criticized for being too personal; he then resorted to the device of literary personas, many of whom were Italian historical figures, such as the character of *Sordello* (1840, written after his first visit to Italy in 1838). He read Elizabeth Barrett's poetry in 1845 and wrote to her, "I love your verse."

They had to marry secretly in 1846 and escape to Italy since, though she had been advised by doctors to go to southern countries for her health, her father forbade her to leave him. For most of their stay in Italy they lived in Florence, in Casa Guidi in the Oltrarno, where their son was born in 1849. They made trips to various places (Vallombrosa, Rimini, Siena, Venice, Rome), as well as journeys to Paris and London. Browning pursued his interests in music and played on the organ in Vallombrosa, which Milton had played before. They were both interested in Italian politics since this was the period of unification, and they attempted to attract the interest of the British public to the Risorgimento. They went on publishing poetry: his *Poems* (1849) and *Men and Women* (1855); her *Sonnets from the Portuguese* (1850) and *Aurora Leigh* (1856).

Elizabeth Barrett died in 1861 (she is buried in the Cimitero degli Inglesi in Florence), and Browning returned to England with their son. His later work met with success: *Dramatis Personae* (1864), a series of dramatic monologues by historical characters, several of whom belong to the ancient, Italian, or Oriental world; *The Ring and the Book* (1868), which is the story of a trial in Italy; and *Asolando* (1889), with a title evoking a place of meditation in the Veneto of the Renaissance. He died in 1889 at his son's house in Venice, and his funeral took place on the island of San Michele (the usual burial place in Venice), followed by interment in the Poets' Corner in Westminster Abbey. An imaginative re-creation of the Brownings was written by Virginia Woolf from the point of view of Flush, Elizabeth Barrett's dog.

MAJOR MULTICULTURAL THEMES

The Brownings' poetry exemplifies the use of faraway settings to mediate self-expression. Using foreign themes to render feelings creates a double world of cross-references. Elizabeth Barrett presents her love poetry, at the moment of her engagement to Browning, under the form of an adaptation from poems in a Mediterranean language, *Sonnets from the Portuguese*. It also contains allusions to Italian settings as symbols of love tokens: "The soul's Rialto has its merchandise" (XIX), which refers to the lovers' exchange of hairlocks. Browning's "By the Fireside" stages this process of making the Italian landscape an objective correlative of mutual love: he imagines himself in old age, able to "slope to Italy . . . and youth" where he "follow[s] wherever [he is] led / Knowing so well the leader's hand" in an Alpine gorge.

The poetics of the two authors imply a certain distance between the narrative voice and the chief character; the use of an Italian setting serves to establish it. The square of the Santissima Annunziata in Florence is the major symbolic starting point both in Browning's "The Statue and the Bust" (*Men and Women*) and in Elizabeth Barrett's *Aurora Leigh*. In the two poems it is a place where a tragic love is born, but in distinct ways. In *Aurora Leigh* the beginning of the poem describes images of the self as a means "To hold together what he was and is" (I, 8). The "great square of the Santissima" is introduced for what it means in Florentine society: the entrance to a church that is the object of great devotion and the destination of religious processions. Staging there the encounter between a Catholic girl in a procession and an older Protestant Englishman makes it the setting for a union of opposites: "I write. My mother was a Florentine" (29), "I, Aurora Leigh" (45), "My father was an austere Englishman" (65). The father has been attracted to Italy by scientific interests ("Da Vinci's drains," 72), but the narrator represents his love in Catholic terms as a "sacramental gift" (90), with a musical metaphor suggesting surprise in itself (the cymbal) as well as because of its oxymoronic form ("silent clangour," 88). The cymbals later evoke exiles in a foreign land, in a conversation between Aurora and her cousin Romney about the sweatshop system of contemporary industry compared to the plight of Moses in Egypt (II, 176). The memorial to the dead mother is placed in Santa Croce since, as the burial place of famous men, it was the best-liked church of Victorian Englishmen. In a later stay in Florence (end of Book VII) the Santissima is the only church in which Aurora is recognized by an acquaintance.

The two poets explicitly dramatized the reciprocal visions of two countries. Browning wrote companion poems, "The Italian in England" and "The Englishman in Italy." They suggest opposed images: the Italian has fled to England as an exiled patriot fleeing the Austrians, and the political tone dominates the poem, whereas the Englishman has found in the Bay of Naples a way of escaping the public life of his country to enjoy an idyll.

In *Aurora Leigh* the episodes in which Aurora goes to England cause an interplay of reciprocal points of view figuring mutual images between countries: an English author living in Italy creates a first-person character brought up in Italy but partly of English descent and traveling to England, which is a position symmetrical to the author's. The descriptions of the contrast between Italian and English landscapes represent the feelings of a girl brought up in Italy, as expressed by an English writer. She notes the red houses and the fog; when she describes the hedges separating the fields, it is a social comment on the enclosures, which were a topic for debate in England, and this is in fact an English writer's critical distancing from her own country placed in the mouth of an Italian girl (second half of Book I). Comparisons between England and Italy are expressed in terms of artistic references; the English sunset is compared regretfully to "Giotto's background."

Both poets use motifs from Italian art to suggest the capacity of concrete appearances to evoke the spiritual world. Narratives about English characters in Italy—for instance, George Eliot's *Middlemarch*—frequently dramatized the questioning of people brought up in the Protestant belief that the sacred is above representation when they are faced with art mediating religious themes. Several of Browning's poems—"Andrea del Sarto," "Fra Lippo Lippi"—have painters as first-person characters expressing delight in their art's capacity to represent reality, as well as anguish over the gap between it and the hidden life. In *Aurora Leigh* the heroine visits a painter friend who argues that by painting the body he paints the soul, and he imagines that one could feel "The spiritual significance burn through / The hieroglyphic of material shows" (VII, 860–61). Works of art are used as images of the self, sometimes ironically: it is Lady Waldemar (the heroine's wicked rival) who (III, 513) symbolizes contradictions in Romney by comparing him to a combination of a perfect sculpture known as "the genius of the Vatican" (in the Belvedere) with the statue "dancing faun" (in the tribuna of the Uffizi); the suggestion is that such an incoherent view of men belongs to characters of limited vision, symbolized by composite art. The idea is applied to poetry: "More's felt than is perceived, / And more's perceived than can be interpreted, / And Love strikes higher with his lambent flame / Than Art can pile the faggots" (VII, 891–94). The phrasing includes an allusion to Milton's "more is meant than meets the ear" (*Il Penseroso*, 120), the classic expression of the superiority of suggestive meaning over formal explicitness. At this moment the Florentine landscape is given an emblematic value; it is Bellosguardo, an image of sight, and it is mentioned, not as an adequate image, but to suggest hyperbolically the incommensurability of spiritual meanings over the visible. But the issue is also the comparison between the limited self and the vaster universal soul:

> As well suppose my little handkerchief
> Would cover Sanminiato, church and all,
> If out I threw it past the cypresses,
> As, in this ragged, narrow life of mine,
> Contain my own conclusions.
>   But at least
> We'll shut up the persiani. (VII, 916–21)

The evocation of the panorama from San Miniato over Florence appears, only to be negated by the vignette of shutters interrupting it. The strikingly Italian feature of the shutters (to an English visitor) is the major image, one that conceals reality behind a veil.

Visual metaphors are also used in the sections of *Aurora Leigh* that include journeys to other countries to evoke their reciprocal images. At the beginning of Book VI the image of the cannon is used to suggest the English view of French levity and to question it since the cannonball is swift, not light. The parallelism between literary themes such as knight-errantry in different countries (Britain and Spain) is meant to suggest a woman's view by comparison with a man's: "And if Cervantes had been Shakespeare too, / He had made his Don a Donna" (VII, 226–27). The Brownings favored liberal movements in Mediterranean countries, and their poetry creates an image of these countries where art is associated with the struggle for freedom. One of the early poems of Elizabeth Barrett, "On a Picture of Riego's Widow," celebrates the Spanish constitutionalist Rafael del Riego by commenting on a portrait of his widow (Riego, an army officer, had led a rebellion in 1820 meant to restore the 1812 constitution under an absolutist regime and had been executed). Again the portrait is described only to be negated, since what the author praises is the widow's suppression of her feelings in public, and the poem denies the capacity of appearances to represent the inner life.

Her later poem "Casa Guidi's Windows," which deals with the Italian Risorgimento of 1848, again associates art and freedom, and so does Browning's "Old Painters in Florence." The latter poem starts from the author's quest for Old Master paintings, leading to a praise of allusiveness in art where the "roughhewn" character of the early painters is said to be more powerful than the more perfect and explicit art of later centuries; this incompleteness is then assimilated by the poet to Giotto's unfinished campanile, which stands for the equally incipient Italian freedom.

The position of the two poets in a multicultural setting becomes essential to their poetics. The allusive technique of the descriptive passages and their multiple ironical meanings also suggest the polysemy of literary landscapes when experienced by visitors of cosmopolitan culture, coming to serve as objective correlatives of moral questioning.

SELECTIVE BIBLIOGRAPHY

Works by the Brownings

Browning, Elizabeth Barrett. *Aurora Leigh*. Ed. Kerry McSweeney. The World's Classics. Oxford: Oxford University Press, 1993.

The Poetical Works of Robert Browning. Ed. Ian Jack, Margaret Smith, Rowena Fowler, Robert Inglesfield, Stefan Hawlin, and T.A.J. Burnett. 7 vols. Oxford: Clarendon Press, 1983–1998.

Browning, Robert. *Poems*. 2 vols. Ed. John Woolford and Daniel Karlin. Longman Annotated English Poets. London: Longman, 1991.

Selective Studies of the Brownings

Armstrong, Isobel, ed. *Robert Browning*. Writers and Their Background. London: Bell, 1974.

Cooper, Helen. *Elizabeth Barrett Browning: Woman and Artist*. Chapel Hill: University of North Carolina Press, 1988.

Korg, Jacob. *Browning in Italy*. Athens: Ohio University Press, 1983.

Markus, Julia. " 'Old Pictures in Florence' through *Casa Guidi's Windows*." *Browning Institute Studies* 6 (1978): 43–61.

Melchiori, Barbara. "Browning in Italy." In *Robert Browning*, 168–83. Ed. Isobel Armstrong. London: Bell, 1974.

Merwin, Dorothy. *Elizabeth Barrett Browning: The Origins of a New Poetry*. Chicago: University of Chicago Press, 1989.

Tracy, Clarence, ed. *Browning's Mind and Art*. Edinburgh: Oliver & Boyd, 1968.

Watson, J.R., ed. *Browning: Men and Women and Other Poems: A Casebook*. London: Macmillan, 1974.

Woolf, Virginia. *Flush: A Biography*. London: Hogarth Press, 1933.

GEORGE GORDON BYRON

(1788–1824)

Robert E. Clark

BIOGRAPHY

George Gordon, the sixth Baron Byron, was born in 1788, the son of Captain John "Mad Jack" Byron, a gold digger from a proud ancient family. Captain Byron squandered his first wife's fortune and after her early death married Catherine Gordon, a Scottish heiress. Captain Byron next briskly exhausted his second wife's funds and died in France away from wife, children, and creditors at age thirty-six. Catherine Gordon then took the future poet to Aberdeen. In 1798 Byron unexpectedly inherited the family title and privileges, and the household moved to crumbling Newstead Abbey, Nottingham, bestowed on the Byrons by Henry VIII (Marchand, 3–23).

Tutored at home before attending boarding school at Dulwich and then the famous public school Harrow, Byron distinguished himself in literature and languages, oratory, and athletics. At Trinity College, Cambridge, he lived the unharassed-by-study student life of noblemen of his day, even briefly keeping a formidable black bear in his digs (Marchand, 35–49). In 1809, a year after leaving Cambridge with a master's degree, Byron assumed his seat in the House of Lords, speaking against death sentences for weavers who destroyed looms to protest their replacement by machinery.

Byron's political career was siderailed by fame after the publication of *Childe Harold*; the poem's first cantos drew on earlier adventures in a two-year "eastern tour" of Iberia, Asia Minor, Greece, and Albania. That sojourn, wide reading, and a vogue for melodrama in lands exotic (to Britains) were also backdrops for his astoundingly popular Eastern Tales. One, *The Corsair* (1814), sold 10,000 copies on publication day.

A devil-may-care attitude seems to have pervaded Byron's private life as well. He was as in love with nations, cultures, and ethnic groups at odds with British mores as with particular women. His outlawed attachments (e.g., to his married half sister Augusta) and attachment to fellow outlaws (Lady Caroline Lamb, Shelley's half sister Claire Clairmont) give an appearance of intensity to what Northrop Frye acutely calls Byron's "impersonal and ritualistic" seducing and seduction (59). Equally notable is that Byron often chose lovers of literary and cultural sophistication; he admired the candid classic writers of Italy and France, continental sexual customs, and venturesome foreign souls who shared his interests. Byron's actual relations with women were rarely a credit to either party; some recompense is that his affairs deepened his understanding of other cultures, and his scandalous liaisons burnished his literary legend from London to St. Petersburg.

Byron anticipated such attention. His masterpiece *Don Juan*, his delightful *Beppo*, and his satire *The Vision of Judgment* mock hypocrisy worldwide; they coincide with his recorded conversation, superb letters, and forceful prose in extolling what he admitted were his only two unwavering values, the love of freedom and a detestation of "cant political, cant poetical, cant religious, cant moral" (*Byron's Letters and Journals*, 1:542).

Dying fighting for Greek freedom in 1824 at Missolonghi, Greece, from fever, other uncertain causes, and medical quackery, Byron may seem like one of his own fictional creations. By then, however, he had a real-world leader's awareness that the military forces he was charged to command were feuding, that attempts were being made to cheat him of a fortune he donated to the cause, and that Greek nationhood was distant. Yet with typical flair and bravery Byron persisted, as he had in protecting individuals from cruelty in the East, protesting British policy at home and Lord Elgin's rapacity in Athens, and giving arms and funds to the Italian Carbonari. Even among Romantic poets Byron is exceptional as a consistent inspiration to seekers of personal, political, and spiritual freedom (Marchand, 424–61).

MULTICULTURAL THEMES

Byron's reputation now rests on his satires, Don Juan crowning them and representing the poet's gift for raiding literature across the West for his purposes. A mock epic, *Don Juan* yet retains the classical epic's maturing and disillusioning of its hero by the story's end. *Don Juan* also borrows from Italian burlesque and romance poetry in ottava rima. (Byron translated part of Luigi Pulci's *Morgante Maggiore* after reading J.H. Frere's *Whistlecraft*, another derivative.)

Don Juan's story in Byron's telling draws on Spanish and British picaresque—disjointed comic episodes, serious digressions, and a flexible but always pointed tone. The tone derived from Byron's idol Alexander Pope, whose testing of secular truths against experience and common sense was among the reasons Byron called him "the moral poet of our civilisation" (Trueblood, *Flowering*, 60).

Byron intended for the protagonist of *Don Juan* to make a complete "tour of

Europe, with a mixture of siege, battle, adventure . . . finishing in the French Revolution" (*Byron's Letters and Journals* 6, 16 February 1821). But the poet died before completing his masterpiece. A "satire on *abuses*, not a eulogy of vice" (Trueblood, *Byron*, 150), the poem nonetheless delivers vivid episodes of human depravity in shipwreck, starvation, slavery, harem life, seduction, and warfare. Every canto contains digressions after Sterne, but each returns to the theme of castigating anyone hampering natural human freedom: a Spanish Doña, a Greek pirate, Catherine of Russia, military leaders, British squires. Greed, lust, and religious pretense are all ridiculed, but Byron's antiwar passages are among his most powerful. He notes, "War's a brain-spattering, windpipe-slitting art, / Unless the cause by Right be sanctified" (*Don Juan*, IX, 1).

SURVEY OF CRITICISM

Jerome J. McGann (1976) makes an enduring case for the interrelation of Byron's art and life (McGann is also a prominent editor of Byron). Byron's definitive biographer is Leslie Marchand (1970), also the editor of his letters and journals. Pietro Gamba (1825), the brother of Byron's last mistress, Countess Teresa Guiccioli, tells of the poet's last journey to Greece, while Iris Origo (1949) dwells on the Byron/Guiccioli attachment.

On Byron and other cultures, see Paul G. Trueblood's edited volume (1981), Daniel P. Watkins's study of Byron's Eastern Tales (1987), and Richard A. Cardwell's edited volume (1997) for Byron's reputation in France, Greece, Central Europe, and Italy and postmodern theories of his international appeal. Other authors of works focusing on Byron's travels and multicultural subjects include Allan Massie (1988); C.M. Woodhouse (1971); Peter Vassallo (1984); and E.R. Vincent (1949, revised 1972) for Byron's role in creating the modern vampire tale.

SELECTIVE BIBLIOGRAPHY

Works by Byron

The Works of Lord Byron: Poetry. Ed. Ernest Hartley Coleridge. 7 vols. London: John Murray, 1889–1904.

Lord Byron's Cain: Twelve Essays and Text with Variants and Annotations. Ed. T.G. Steffan. Austin: University of Texas Press, 1968.

Byron's Hebrew Melodies. Ed. Thomas L. Ashton. Austin: University of Texas Press, 1972.

Byron's Letters and Journals. Ed. Leslie A. Marchand. 12 vols. London: John Murray; Cambridge, Mass.: Belknap Press of Harvard University Press, 1973–1982.

Don Juan. Harmondsworth: Penguin, 1982.

The Complete Poetical Works. Ed. Jerome McGann. 7 vols. Oxford: Clarendon Press; New York: Oxford University Press, 1980–1993.

Selective Studies of Byron

Cardwell, Richard A., ed. *Lord Byron the European*. Lewiston, N.Y.: Edwin Mellen Press, 1997.

Frye, Northrop. "Lord Byron." In *George Gordon, Lord Byron*, 56–65. Ed. Harold Bloom. New York: Chelsea House, 1986.

Gamba, Pietro. *A Narrative of Lord Byron's Last Journey to Greece*. London: Murray, 1825.

McGann, Jerome J. *Don Juan in Context*. Chicago: University of Chicago Press, 1976.

Marchand, Leslie A. *Byron*. New York: Knopf, 1970.

Massie, Allan. *Byron's Travels*. London: Sidgwick and Jackson, 1988.

Nicolson, Harold. *Byron, the Last Journey, April 1823–April 1824*. London: Constable, 1924, rev. 1948.

Origo, Iris. *The Last Attachment*. New York: Scribner's, 1949.

Trueblood, Paul. *Byron*. Boston: Twayne, 1977.

———, ed. *Byron's Political and Cultural Influence in Nineteenth-Century Europe: A Symposium*. London: Macmillan, 1981.

———. *The Flowering of Byron's Genius*. New York: Russell & Russell, 1962.

Vassallo, Peter. *Byron: The Italian Literary Influence*. London: Macmillan, 1984.

Vincent, E.R. *Byron, Hobhouse, and Foscolo*. New York: Farrar, Straus, and Giroux, 1949, reprint, 1972.

Watkins, Daniel P. *Social Relations in Byron's Eastern Tales*. London: Associated University Presses, 1987.

Woodhouse, C.M. *The Philhellenes*. Rutherford, N.J.: Fairleigh Dickinson University Press, 1971.

LUÍS VAZ DE CAMÕES
(c. 1525–1580)

Valeria Tocco

BIOGRAPHY

Although Luís Vaz de Camões today is still considered "the prince of Portuguese poets," information about his life is scarce and contradictory. Seventeenth-century biographies present a confused picture of the ups and downs of what was undoubtedly a tormented life (Pedro de Mariz, Lisbon, 1613; Manuel Severim de Faria, Évora, 1624; the two versions by Manuel Faria e Sousa in the commentary to *Os Lusíadas*, Madrid, 1639, and to the *Rimas*, published posthumously between 1685 and 1689). In fact, very little documentation remains: only indirect testimony and the writing itself have been used by historians and critics to reconstruct and romanticize the poet's life.

Born around 1525, possibly in Lisbon, Camões may well have studied in Coimbra, where his uncle, the Augustinian Bento Camões, was prior at the Santa Cruz Monastery from 1539 to 1542 and subsequently chancellor of the university. No evidence exists of the nephew's enrollment, however. In Coimbra the more scholarly aspect of his education would have been cultivated. After this presumed interval he would have returned to Lisbon, where he frequented court circles. At court he came into contact with the new culture modeled on the Italian one assimilated through the Castilians, and with the Neoplatonic ideal that often emerges in his love poems.

During his years in Lisbon he probably suffered his first punishment in the form of exile in Ribatejo (though not all the biographies agree in seeing this period as exile); subsequently, around 1547, he sailed to the outpost of Ceuta in Morocco, where he lost an eye in battle. Here, then, he saw firsthand the Catholic-Islamic dualism that supported his ideal of the "expansion of the faith"—an ideal that is clearly apparent everywhere in *Os Lusíadas* and determined his scornful and negative characterization of nearly all the Muslim characters in this epic poem.

Back in Portugal he frequented the dregs of Lisbon society (on this point all the biographies agree) and was often involved in brawls. In one of these he wounded a court squire and was imprisoned and sentenced; he remained in prison from 16 June 1552 to 13 March 1553. The pardon signed by King João III mentions his imminent departure for India.

He remained in the East—India and China—for more than fifteen years, taking part in at least two military expeditions (one to the Red Sea) and working in public administration (he was probably property administrator for orphans and controller of assets of the deceased and the absent in Macao), but was always persecuted, it seems, by some *longa manus* (secret agent) who continued to block his every project. This was also the period of his supposed love affair with a Chinese damsel who drowned at sea, named in his poetry Dinamene (most likely a feminine ideal), and of his mythical rescue of the manuscript of his masterpiece *Os Lusíadas* when he was swimming to safety following a shipwreck at the mouth of the Mekong River.

In Macao he was again sent to prison, this time on a charge of misappropriation of property entrusted to him as an administrator. He was certainly back in Goa during the governorship of Francisco Coutinho (1561–64), who probably saved him from being imprisoned for debt, appointing him *provedor* of Chaul, a post he was never to occupy. On his way back to Portugal in 1569 he was imprisoned in Mozambique for a debt to the captain of the ship that had carried him there, but was able to continue on to Lisbon thanks to the help of a few friends. Tradition has it that the manuscript of his lyric poems *Parnaso* was stolen while he was in prison in Africa.

The final stage of his life seems to have been marked by poverty and hardship. He went regularly to the Church of San Domingos in Lisbon to read through *Os Lusíadas* with Bartolomeu Ferreira, the inquisitorial censor. The epic poem was finally published in 1572, and the king granted him a pension of 15,000 réis a year. Ignored by almost all the poets of his era, he ended his life in the most abject poverty, probably in 1580. His fame began to spread only after his death and has never dimmed since.

MAJOR MULTICULTURAL THEMES

The culture that emerges from Camões's lyric poems and the epic is an unusual one in which a classical tradition (beginning with Virgil) coexists with the Italian (Petrarch and Ariosto above all) and the Castilian (he also wrote in the Castilian language), and there is evidence of studies in historiography, philosophy, astronomy, and geography as well as literature. Specific textual comparisons show that Camões read and assimilated the most diverse writings from the late Middle Ages and the Renaissance, enabling him to bear witness to one of the most polyvalent of multicultural worlds. There are few references in the lyric poems to "multicultural" themes in the narrower sense, or to his interest in and adherence to the "Other," but an important example are the famous strophes in blank verse (*endechas*) of "A Bárbara escrava," in which he uses a play on the term "prisoner of love" (fashionable in late-fifteenth-century lyric poetry) to celebrate the beauty of a dark-skinned, raven-haired, and black-eyed slave girl.

Os Lusíadas, by contrast, contains numerous references to the "Other," given that it revolves around the story of Vasco da Gama's sea voyage from Lisbon to India (often interpreted as symbol or metaphor: see, for example, Jackson and Lucas). Thus we find the figure of the black African, rough, wild, and slow-witted, but at the same time occasionally immersed in a bucolic world; the Muslim (African or Indian), always idle and malicious, the enemy par excellence; the Indian, extravagant to Western eyes but always suspicious and greedy. Communication problems are always given prominence: central to almost every contact with outsiders is the role of the interpreter (Finazzi Agrò). The full and detailed description Thetis gives to Vasco da Gama (X, 92–141), which ranges from the Middle East to the Far East, is rich in ideas on customs and religious notions and information about flora, fauna, agricultural and mineral products, and atmospheric and astronomical phenomena.

SURVEY OF CRITICISM

Studies of *Os Lusíadas* have concentrated chiefly on relationships with the Muslim world—a "just war" against Islam being the ideological axis of the poem's structure. Oliveira (1975) believes that Thetis's narration to da Gama mirrors a journey Camões himself presumably took. The sea goddess's words, then, reflect his actual experience in the face of a reality that to a Westerner was foreign and strange. For this reason *Os Lusíadas* is valuable principally for its ethnographic content (Brasil, 1969).

Domingues (1972) and Didier (1998) examine the representation of the Islamic world. The former concentrates on the different designations used by Camões for the Muslims. The latter addresses the ambiguity of relations between the Portuguese and the Muslims (the Portuguese supposedly being descended from the son of Bacchus, who is identified with Mahomet as the poem proceeds, and hence with the "devil") and the related problems of reconciling Hinduism and Islam in India.

Janeira (1977) focuses on Camões's Oriental experience (accepting as true even the more fanciful side of the poet's life in the East), attempting to show that although the poet had no desire to understand the deep significance of Oriental culture, he was fascinated and attracted by it. But in effect what this scholar calls "pitorescas e alegras descrições" (153) in the African and Oriental scenes do not demonstrate any "admiração" for what is being recorded, but rather the skilled use of sources (mainly the chronicles of João de Barros and Fernão Lopes), in which these same scenes are described in detail. Jacqueline Kaye (1985) circumvents the issue and admits in the end that her chapter "is entitled 'Intercultural Relations in *Os Lusíadas*' because that is what is absent from it. What is missing is any real sense of intercultural encounters, of exchange or mutability" (140).

The main areas of interest in this epic are the chromatic, the decorative, and the picturesque, the poet showing an awareness of the superiority of his own Western and Christian values. Unlike his contemporary, Fernão Mendes Pinto, Camões does not attempt to understand or set up any constructive comparison with the culture with which he comes into contact. He describes it rather with the attention and pleasure of a poet and recorder. In short, Camões always demonstrates "a firmeza da sua consciência ocidental" (Janeira, 135), "a superioridade da civilização europeia" (Janeira, 156).

SELECTIVE BIBLIOGRAPHY

Works by Camões

Os Lusíadas (1572). Ed. Álvaro Júlio da Costa Pimpão. 3rd ed. Lisboa: Ministério da Educação, Instituto Camões, 1992. (*The Lusiads*. Trans. Landeg White. Oxford and New York: Oxford University Press, 1997.)

Rimas (1595). Ed. Álvaro Júlio da Costa Pimpão. Coimbra: Atlântida, 1973.

Selective Studies of Camões

Brasil, Reis. "Camões e os Povos do Oriente." *Estudos de Castelo Branco* 29 (1969): 7–18.

Didier, Hugues. "Luís de Camões et l'Islam." In *Chrétiens et Musulmans à la Renaissance: Actes du 37e colloque international du CESR (1994)*, 133–47. Paris: Honoré Champion, 1998.

Domingues, José D. Garcia. "A Concepção do Mundo Árabe-Islâmico n'*Os Lusíadas*." *Garcia da Orta*, special commemorative issue (1972): 201–26.

Finazzi Agrò, Ettore. "I Lusiadi e gli altri (contatti tra culture e tra lingue nell'epos camoniano: la figura dell'interprete)." In *Studi camoniani 80*, 17–45. Ed. Giulia Lanciani. Roma and L'Aquila: Japadre, 1980.

Jackson, K. David. "Utopia and Identity in the Voyages: Camões between India and Portugal." *Arquivos do Centro Cultural Português* 37 (1998): 185–94.

Janeira, Armando Martins. "O Oriente n'*Os Lusíadas*." *Arquivos do Centro Cultural Português* 11 (1977): 133–58.

Kaye, Jacqueline. "Intercultural Relations in Os Lusíadas." In *As Dimensões da Alteridade nas Culturas de Língua Portuguesa—O Outro: I Simpósio Interdisciplinar de Estudos Portugueses*, vol. 2, 133–43. Lisbon: Departamento de Estudos Portugueses, Faculdade de Ciências Sociais e Humanas da Universidade Nova, 1985.

Lucas, Maria Clara Almeida. "A Viagem de Vasco da Gama: Estrutura da Narrativa Mítica." In *A Viagem de "Os Lusíadas": Simbolo e Mito*, 55–102. Lisboa: Arcádia, 1981.

Oliveira, Isócrates de. "Itinerário de Camões no Extremo Oriente." *Boletim da Sociedade de Geografia de Lisboa* 1–12 (1975): 71–89.

Ruas, Henrique Barrilaro. "Camões e os Afraicanos." *Brotéria* 3, nos. 1–3 (1980): 160–63.

CH'OE CH'IWŎN
(857-?)

Maurizio Riotto

BIOGRAPHY

Ch'oe Ch'iwŏn, one of Korea's greatest scholars, wrote under the pseudonym Koun (Solitary cloud). (Signature under a pseudonym is still today a common practice among Korean men of letters.) The *Samguk sagi*, a historic work completed in 1145, provides some information about Ch'oe's life. Accordingly, we know that he probably came from Kyŏngju, the capital of the kingdom of Silla, and that he was undoubtedly a precocious child of exceptional versatility. At the young age of twelve he was sent by his parents to study in China, in accordance with the widespread custom among the Korean literati of the past. Apparently, before he left for China, his father, who had intuited his enormous talent, threatened to disown him as his son if he did not distinguish himself in his studies. After only eight years of instruction, he passed the Chinese state examinations and obtained an administrative post (even foreigners could do so at that time in China), but resigned after a year in order to devote himself to further study. After three years of hunger and hardship, he finally was helped by a government official named Gao Pian, who assigned him a job in his own office. At the age of twenty-eight, Ch'oe returned to his native land. Certainly those long years spent in China marked his entire life, implanting in him notions of multiculturalism that would render him one of the most productive and open-minded Korean writers.

Returning to his homeland, he immediately became immersed in the heavy political climate that would soon bring about the end of the dynasty and the dissolution of the kingdom of Silla. Nevertheless, he succeeded in holding several important public positions and in 893 was named ambassador to China, a post he was prevented from reaching by bands of brigands infesting the territory of Silla, which was now on the brink of collapse.

In 894 he sent a petition to the queen, Chinsŏng (887–897), in which he denounced the climate of corruption and the breakdown of institutions in the land. After this last known official act of his, he withdrew from the world to live on Mount Kaya, far from public life and leading an almost hermitlike existence. Voluntary exile or forced renunciation of involvement in political life on the part of intellectual government officials was, in fact, a commonplace among erudite Koreans of the past: in the quiet of their hermitages they drew comfort from the justness of their own ideals.

Ch'oe Ch'iwŏn wrote an impressive number of works, most of which are today lost or fragmentary. His extant writings are contained in the *Kyewŏn p'ilgyŏng-jip* in twenty books; a number of poems transmitted above all through the *Tongmunsŏn*, an anthology of Oriental literature that was a treasure trove of information in the fifteenth century; and declarations and fragments handed down through later works or from epigraphic documents. Ch'oe Ch'iwŏn wrote in Chinese, which was the literary language of Korea as well as the language used in official documents up to the end of the monarchy in 1910.

Ch'oe's long and rich experience as a young man in the highly cosmopolitan society of China in the Tang period allowed him to learn to live in diverse ethnic and religious situations. This stirred in him feelings of tolerance and respect for the "Other" that came to characterize both his thought and his literary production. He always declared himself to be fundamentally Confucian, and he certainly cherished a Confucian love for the past, as we read in the following passage from Book XVI of the *Kyewŏn p'ilgyŏng-jip*: "To follow the good teachings of Confucian thought does not mean to lose time but rather to set down, through recovery of the past, the rules of civility" (381). Nonetheless, he did not reject either Buddhism or Taoism, and he himself often repeated: "Tao is not removed from men, nor is it alien to them. And for this very reason one can follow either Buddhism or Confucianism" (627).

Recognizing his own eclecticism, he actually was frightened by it, triggering doubt as to his literary talent. His fear—the result of his deep modesty—that he had reached only a superficial level of knowledge and mastery of writing lingered in his mind, as may be deduced from the following:

As a youth, I made a name for myself in China, where I scarcely did more than taste the marvelous liqueur of phrases and verses. Now that I am mature and must drink from the bitter cup of my obligations, I am unable to become elated, floundering rather in life's mud. Of this, frankly, I am ashamed. (630)

Ch'oe's modesty probably developed in China as well, where, as a citizen of a small limitrophe country, he must have had feelings not only of deep solitude but also of inferiority. In spite of his own doubts, however, he sought always to focus on the slightest nuances of every problem, always lending himself willingly to critical consideration. Another quotation in this regard is revealing:

One reads in the *Shih Ching* that by underestimating the importance of small things one cannot attain to great virtue. If indeed men strive to live together, within the bounds of a civil society, how can one even think of transcending those bounds? A big mountain receives even the smallest speck of dust, and even the smallest stream reaches the vast sea. (709)

It is thus not surprising that in the exercise of his functions as a public official he distinguished himself for his honesty and correctness toward the citizenry, inspired as he was by a great sense of justice that, however, was inefficacious in preventing the dissolution of the kingdom of Silla.

With his self-exile, his life became a legend. Yet his choice must have appeared to him, too, as a defeat and a very poor epilogue to that fulminating and brilliant career begun so many years earlier in China. An author of great erudition and unusual talent, he certainly felt disappointed by human society and those universal principles of virtue on which he had always counted and had concentrated his efforts.

The year of his death is unknown. Certainly, in the final period of his life, in the hermitage of Haein Temple on Mount Kaya, he must have been weighed down with deep pessimism and heavily burdened by a sense of devastating loneliness, clearly echoed in these splendid verses entitled "Ch'uya ujung" that may indeed be read as his spiritual testament:

> In the autumn wind, no more than a bitter poem.
> To find a friend is rare on the roads of life.
> All night the rain outside the window:
> Before the oil-lamp, my thoughts fly ten thousand *li* [a measure of about one-third of a mile]. (511)

SELECTIVE BIBLIOGRAPHY

Works by Ch'oe Ch'iwŏn

Koun Ch'oe Ch'iwŏn sŏnsaeng munjip (Koun Ch'oe Ch'iwŏn sŏnsaeng munjip wiwŏnhoe, an edition of the collected writings of Master Ch'oe Ch'iwŏn, called Koun). Pusan: Cheil munhwasa, 1982.

Selective Studies of Ch'oe Ch'iwŏn

Cho Tong'il. *Han'guk munhak t'ongsa* (Complete history of Korean literature). 3rd ed. Vol. 1, 270–76. Seoul: Chisik sanŏpsa, 1996.

Kim, Injong, Yi Hyŏnt'aek, Han Chongman, Kim Nakp'il, Kim Yŏngdu, Yu Sŏngt'ae. *Koun Ch'oe Ch'iwŏn* (Ch'oe Ch'iwŏn, called Koun). Seoul: Minŭmsa, 1989.

PAUL CLAUDEL
(1868–1955)

Bettina L. Knapp

BIOGRAPHY

Writer, world traveler, and government official—vice-consul in Boston, consul suppléant in Shanghai, consul in Prague and Frankfurt, ambassador to the United States, Belgium, and Japan, chargé d'affaires in Rio de Janeiro—Paul Claudel was always stirred by a desire to engage in a life of excitement and mystery. He was born in the town of Villeneuve-sur-Fère in the Aisne region of France. "Nothing is more bitter, or more religious," he wrote in *Mémoires improvisés* (13), than Villeneuve. Its character is marked with duality: a "dramatic struggle" between serenity and a "terrible wind" that beats about violently, intransigently. Because his sister Camille, a talented sculptor, decided to pursue her studies in Paris, the family moved there in 1881. That the father remained behind was catastrophic for the lad, whose life was torn apart by his parents' separation. He attended the Lycée Louis-le-Grand in Paris, wrote a satire/farce, *L'Endormie*, received a law degree, and enrolled at the prestigious Ecole des Sciences Politiques, taking it for granted that he would eventually work for the government. But the intellectual atmosphere in Paris—the reign of Positivism, naturalism, scientism—corroded his spirit and crushed his enthusiasm for the future. The scientific determinism of Hippolyte Taine and the relativist historical works of Ernest Renan did nothing to relieve his anxiety. The year 1886 was momentous for Claudel: he discovered Arthur Rimbaud's *Illuminations*, poems that opened him up to "the supernatural world." In the same year he "converted" to the faith of his fathers, becoming deeply religious.

Drama seemed to him the most expressive of creative forms, allowing him to quell the antagonism breeding within him and to expel it in palpable creatures. The protagonist of *Tête d'or* (1889) was a conqueror—a rebellious, active being who rejected the status quo, fomented divisiveness, and aroused fresh ideas and ideals. *La Ville* (1890), a dramatic presentation set in the Sodom and Gomorrah atmosphere in which Claudel felt "plunged" at the time, catalyzed his need to wander about the earth. "Above all else, I had always had the desire to leave, absolutely, and see the world," he wrote in *Mémoires improvisés* (30–31). His first diplomatic post was French consul to the United States (1893–94), where he wrote *L'Echange* (1893). Although it is a poor play, it mirrored his feelings of entrapment. In China (1895), his next port of call, the disorientation he now felt caused him to increase his readings of religious works, thereby counterbalancing his fear of loss of Catholic values.

He was back in France in 1900, but returned to China the following year, traveling on the same ship as a beautiful Polish blond, Rose Vetch, a wife and a mother. Their liaison, which resulted in the birth of a child, lasted for several years. His grief and turmoil after the "breakup," however, were transmuted into his great dramatic work *Partage de midi* (1905).

Upon being named consul in Prague, he continued working on a trilogy: *L'Otage* (1908), *Le Pain dur* (1913), and *Le Père humilié* (1916). His many other works include *La jeune fille Violaine* (1892–1900); *L'Annonce faite à Marie* (1910–1911); *Le Soulier de Satin* (1919–1924); translations of Aeschylus's *Choephorae*, among other Greek tragedies; and *La Légende de prakriti* (1932). The music for his monumental *Le Livre de Christophe Colomb* (1927) was composed by Darius Milhaud, who combined stylized litanies with wild and passionate outbursts of energetic tonalities. *Jeanne au bûcher* (1934), with music by Arthur Honegger, followed, along with many other works, including essays, poems, and religious commentaries. He died in Paris in 1955.

MAJOR MULTICULTURAL THEMES

Claudel found the mores, language, religion, and psyche in the Orient to be very different from what he had known. "China is an ancient land, vertiginous, inextricable," he wrote in *Mémoires improvisés*. "It proliferates, dense, naïve, disorderly, emerging from the deepest instinctual resources and traditions" (153). Although he made an effort to open his mind to foreign ways and to accept the spiritual offerings of other peoples and lands, he failed. He completely rejected Buddhism, making his intolerance evident in his "intimate diary," *Connaissance de l'Est* (1895–1900). Although his prejudices were modified over the course of years, they never left him. For Claudel, Buddhism was a religion of "idolators," a "pagan blasphemy"; it taught a "monstrous communion," based on a "Nothingness" that he viewed as "Satanic."

During his stay in China he wrote *Vers d'exil* (1895), expressing his feelings of disquietude and isolation. *Le Repos du septième jour* (1896–1897), a complex theological drama, takes place in China, where the cult of the dead enjoys an important role. The play shows the dead invading the domain of the living, with the result that the living can neither eat, drink, nor sleep, so possessed are they by those hovering, invisible forces.

During his stay in Japan he became immersed in Japanese culture and wrote "Un Regard sur l'âme japonaise" (1923) and *L'Oiseau noir dans le soleil levant*

(1923), among other works inspired by the mysteries of Japanese iconography, art, drama, and music. He commented on the works of Kano, Korin, Hokusai, and others. The *haiku* poems of Basho inspired him to write *Cent phrases pour éventails* (1941), in which he took paintbrush in hand and drew the characters described—the rose, the camellia, the moon, and other forms, both abstract and concrete—in a panoply of exquisite delineations. It was in Tokyo that his short play *La Femme et son ombre* was performed at the Imperial Theatre to the accompaniment of Japanese music (1922).

Claudel considered Noh drama "one of the highest forms of lyric and dramatic art" and was astounded by the intensity that emerged from the characters as they stood immobile on stage, underscoring attitudes and moods by a shift of the arm, a cry of despair, an eye movement. *Bunraku*, the Japanese puppet theater, also fascinated him. He described it as the work of a "collective soul." *Bungaku*, Japanese dance, was viewed by him as something "inhuman," the interlocking of circuitous masked forces as living Elements and Passions, colliding, bruising, or harmonizing with each other.

While Claudel was ambassador to Brussels, his art criticisms appeared. They were extraordinary for their perceptions, depth, and breadth of understanding, as were his essays on Jan Steen (1937), Watteau (1939), Velázquez, Zurbarán, Goya, Ribera (1939), Rembrandt (1947), and others, which were gathered together in *L'Oeil écoute* (1946).

No matter the domain—theater, poetry, music, drama, or the pictorial arts— secret affinities existed for Claudel throughout the world and beyond, inviting him to absorb a tree, a flower, a word, an image, a rhythm, a sonority into himself. The world nourished him; the universe was his inspiration, the earth his food, the ocean his sustenance.

SURVEY OF CRITICISM

Gerald Antoine's *Paul Claudel ou l'enfer du génie* (1988) is fascinating for its insights on Claudel's years spent in China, Japan, the United States, Prague, Frankfurt, and Hamburg. Maurice Pinguet's study on Claudel's understanding of and reactions to Japan, "Paul Claudel exégète du Japon" (1969), is seminal. The lectures delivered at Cerisy-la-Sale edited by Georges Cattaui and Jacques Madaule and published as *Entretiens sur Paul Claudel* (1969) are particularly rewarding for the chapters devoted to his sojourns in China, Japan, England, Belgium, and Germany. Jean-Bertrand Barrère's *Claudel: Le destin et l'oeuvre* (1979) is significant for the specifics regarding Claudel's years in foreign service and how they impacted on his art and psyche.

SELECTIVE BIBLIOGRAPHY

Works by Claudel

Partage de midi (1905). Paris: Gallimard, 1949.
L'Oiseau noir dans le soleil levant (1923). Paris: Excelsior, 1927.

Le Soulier de Satin (1919–1924). Paris: Gallimard, 1953.

Oeuvres en prose (1928, 1934). Paris: Gallimard (Bibliothèque de la Pléiade), 1965.

Mémoires improvisés. Paris: Gallimard, 1954. 2nd ed., 1969.

Cahiers Paul Claudel. Vols. 1–12. Paris: Gallimard, 1959–1984.

Oeuvre poétique. Paris: Gallimard (Bibliothèque de la Pléiade), 1967.

Journal. Ed. François Varillon and Jacques Petit. 2 vols. Paris: Gallimard (Bibliothèque de la Pléiade), 1968–1969.

Selective Studies of Claudel

Antoine, Gérald. *Paul Claudel ou l'enfer du génie.* Paris: Robert Laffont, 1988.

Barrère, Jean-Bertrand. *Claudel: Le destin et l'oeuvre.* Paris: Sedes, 1979.

Cattaui, Georges, and Jacques Madaule, eds. *Entretiens sur Paul Claudel.* The Hague: Mouton, 1969.

Knapp, Bettina L. *Paul Claudel.* New York: Frederick Ungar, 1982.

Pinguet, Maurice. "Paul Claudel exégète du Japon." *Etudes de langue et littérature françaises* 14 (March 1969): 11.

Vachon, André. *Le Temps et l'espace dans l'oeuvre de Paul Claudel.* Paris: Editions du Seuil, 1965.

JOSEPH CONRAD
(1857–1924)

Maria Antonietta Saracino

BIOGRAPHY

Joseph Conrad was born Jozef Teodor Konrad Nalecz Korzeniowski on December 3, 1857, at Berdiczew, Podolia, one of the southern provinces of Poland, at that time under Russian czarist rule. He was the son of aristocratic political exiles who had been involved in national insurrection against Russian oppression. It was after the death of both his parents that young Jozef decided to follow one of his childhood dreams: to become a seaman and travel the world. In October 1874 Conrad, who by that time spoke French fluently, left Cracow for Marseille, determined "to follow the sea." His career as a seaman began in June 1875 when he sailed to Martinique and the West Indies, bound for Central America, and it came to an end on October 15, 1893, after which his new life as a writer began.

During Conrad's voyaging years he traveled the globe, noting impressions of places and peoples and details of his life as a mariner. For him, life and books were so tightly interwoven that often what passed for a story was in fact directly drawn from his biography. From a very early stage his life was deeply marked by his passionate love for geography and the lives of explorers such as Mungo Park, Sir Richard Francis Burton, John Hanning Speke, and David Livingstone: "the geography which I had discovered for myself was the geography of open spaces and wide horizons built up on men's devoted work in the open air, the geography still militant but already conscious of its approaching end with the death of the last great explorer," he wrote in 1923 in *Geography and Some Explorers* (cited in Hoppé, 255).

Life at sea had provided him with an infinite variety of ideas and themes for future narrations. His first novel, *Almayer's Folly*, appeared in 1895, followed by *An Outcast of the Islands* (1896), *The Nigger of the Narcissus* (1897), *Heart of Darkness* (written 1898, published 1902), *Lord Jim* (1900), and *Nostromo* (1904), to mention only the most important titles.

In 1886 he became a British subject and in 1896 married Jessie George, a London girl of twenty-two. The couple settled in England at a farmhouse near Ashford, in Kent. Later, in 1919, they moved to Oswalds, Bishopsbourne, near Canterbury, where Conrad died of a heart attack three months after having declined the offer of a knighthood.

MAJOR MULTICULTURAL THEMES

Multiculturalism is implicit in Joseph Conrad's life and literary experience from the moment he left Poland, adjusted to an entirely new language and environment, and chose a new name for himself. English was, among other things, the lingua franca that helped him to distance himself emotionally from his own experiences, even while allowing him to "translate" those very experiences into a totally different world: the world of literature. "My faculty to write in English," he wrote, "is as natural as any other aptitude with which I might have been born. . . . If I had not written in English I would not have written at all" (Author's Note to *A Personal Record*, v–vi).

With the exception of a few novels and some short stories, all of Conrad's major narratives are set in distant and "exotic" places, outside Europe. They deal, in various ways, with the interaction between human beings of different races, cultures, and languages against an often-inhospitable and hostile background. *Romance* (1903), written in collaboration with Ford Madox Ford, draws to the full on Conrad's early experiences in the Caribbean: the setting is the same, but the period he refers to is that of the early years of the nineteenth century.

Closely linked are *Almayer's Folly* and *An Outcast of the Islands*, both set in Malaya, and both stories of disintegration (*Almayer's Folly*) and betrayal (*Outcast*). Here his mastery in depicting the atmosphere of the islands of the East, where natural beauty does not overshadow racial differences and problems, is already evident. It is even more so in *Lord Jim* (1900), one of his first full-length novels, also set in Malaya and centered on the theme of redemption and, again, of betrayal.

Modeled on various places in South America that Conrad had visited in the course of his travels, *Nostromo: A Tale of the Seaboard* is a powerful work of fiction. Here he created an entire republic, with its own geography, topography, railways, and a silver mine, which he named Costaguana—a world of great wealth and extreme poverty, of political instability and strong human passions.

Directly drawn from his short but intensely traumatic experience of the Congo in 1890 (so painful that after this journey up the river Congo he decided not to go to sea again), the short novel *Heart of Darkness* is certainly the best known of all his writings as well as the most widely read English novel in the world. It has also been regarded as being "as near a perfect work of art as one can conceive [as] the heat of actuality is in it as well as the spirit of the place and the people, white and black, struggling with one another and with oppressive nature, killing and dying, all in the name of Progress—which stood for both the 'civilizing' and the exploitation of the blacks" (Hoppé, 10). Hence the Narrator's journey into a "God-forsaken wilderness," represented by the heart of the African continent at the time of Belgian colonial exploitation, becomes a real journey into humankind's innermost conscience.

SURVEY OF CRITICISM

The critics of his time were unanimous in praising Joseph Conrad's writings. For Virginia Woolf, "his books are full of moments of vision. They light up a whole character in a flash" ("Mr. Conrad: A Conversation," 302); they are "complete and still, very chaste and very beautiful, they rise in the memory as, on these hot summer nights, in their slow and stately way first one star comes out and then another" ("Joseph Conrad," 308). Even more enthusiastic about Conrad's writing was his friend and colleague Ford Madox Ford, in whose opinion "Conrad was Conrad because he was his books. It was not that he made literature: he was literature, the literature of the Elizabethan Gentleman Adventurer" (*A Personal Remembrance*, 19).

For Norman Sherry in *Conrad's Western World* (1971), the writer's concern in the novel *Heart of Darkness* is "with the extent to which, once he is in a situation of isolation and primitiveness, the disciplined white man is sustained by a code of behaviour evolved in his civilized society" (4). In recent times much multicultural criticism has been devoted to *Heart of Darkness*, generally regarded as the one in which such themes as the struggle between colonizer and colonized, between masters and servants, between Europeans and Africans, finds its highest as well as its most controversial literary expression. If, in the opinion of Caribbean writer Wilson Harris, "it is possible to view *Heart of Darkness* as a frontier novel" (in Kimbrough, *Heart of Darkness*, 263), for Nigerian novelist and critic Chinua Achebe "*Heart of Darkness* projects the image of Africa as 'the other world,' the antithesis of Europe and therefore of civilization, a place where man's vaunted intelligence and refinement are finally mocked by triumphant bestiality" (in Kimbrough, 252). In the opinion of Palestinian critic Edward Said (1993), Conrad is a master stylist who has rendered with extraordinary force the experience of empire as the main subject of his work.

SELECTIVE BIBLIOGRAPHY

Works by Conrad

Heart of Darkness (1902), with *An Outpost of Progress* (1897). Intro. Norman Sherry. London: J.M. Dent & Sons, 1973.
Lord Jim: A Tale. Edinburgh and London: W. Blackwood & Sons, 1900.
Nostromo: A Tale of the Seaboard. London: Harper & Brothers, 1904.
A Personal Record. New York: Harper & Brothers, 1912. Also in *The Mirror of the Sea*

& *A Personal Record*, 3–138. Ed. and intro. Zdzislaw Najder. Oxford: Oxford
    University Press, 1988.
Geography and Some Explorers (1923). Originally published as *The Romance of Travel*
    in *National Geographic Magazine*, March 1924. Also in *The Conrad Companion*,
    ed. A.J. Hoppé. London: Readers Union, 1945.
Congo Diary and Other Uncollected Pieces by Joseph Conrad. Ed. Zdzislaw Najder.
    Garden City, N.Y.: Doubleday & Co., 1978.

Selective Studies of Conrad

Baines, Jocelyn. *Joseph Conrad: A Critical Biography*. Harmondsworth: Penguin, 1971.
Ching-Liang Low, Gail. *White Skins/Black Masks: Representation and Colonialism*. Lon-
    don: Routledge, 1996.
Ford, Ford Madox. *Joseph Conrad: A Personal Remembrance* (1924). New York: Ecco
    Press, 1989.
Hoppé, A.J., ed. *The Conrad Companion*. London: Readers Union, 1945.
Kimbrough, Robert, ed. *Heart of Darkness: An Authoritative Text, Backgrounds and
    Sources, Criticism*. 3rd ed. New York: Norton, 1988.
Said, Edward. *Culture and Imperialism*. London: Chatto & Windus, 1993.
———. *Joseph Conrad and the Fiction of Autobiography*. Cambridge, Mass.: Harvard
    University Press, 1966.
Saracino, Maria Antonietta, trans. and ed. *Un avamposto del progresso* [*An Outpost of
    Progress*], *Cuore di tenebra* [*Heart of Darkness*], *Diario del Congo* [*The Congo
    Diary*], *Diario del viaggio a monte* [*Up-River Book*]. Milano: Frassinelli, 1996.
Sherry, Norman. *Conrad's Eastern World*. Cambridge: Cambridge University Press,
    1966.
———. *Conrad's Western World*. Cambridge: Cambridge University Press, 1971.
Woolf, Virginia. "Joseph Conrad" (1924). In *Collected Essays*, vol. 1, 302–8. Ed. Leon-
    ard Woolf. London: Chatto & Windus, 1966.
———. "Mr. Conrad: A Conversation." (1923). Ibid., 309–11.

STEPHEN CRANE
(1871–1900)

Bettina L. Knapp

BIOGRAPHY

Born on November 1, 1871, in Newark, New Jersey, Stephen Crane was brought up in an austere and religious home. His father was a revivalist Methodist minister; his mother, the daughter of a minister, was even more church oriented than her husband. One of eight children (six others did not survive), Crane was raised and educated in New Jersey, New York, and Pennsylvania. His earliest extant manuscript was stamped with an intense feeling for nature as well as vivid dialogue marked by various regional accents, which would become characteristics of his future prose. But he was also fascinated by the seamy side of life: two novels deal with existence in the slums, *Maggie: A Girl of the Streets* (1893) and *George's Mother* (1896). The novel for which he is perhaps best known, *The Red Badge of Courage* (1895), is about the pain and despair of the foot soldier fighting in the American Civil War and the terror of living out the transition from adolescence to manhood.

As a lad Crane had enjoyed mock battles and war games and had asked to be sent to the quasi-military Hudson River Institute in Claverack, New York. After the publication of *The Red Badge of Courage* and several short stories dealing with the military, he was determined to see some fighting. He set out for Cuba on an assignment to report on the Cuban insurrection against Spain, but the sinking of the *Commodore*, which was carrying weapons from the United States to the Cuban rebels, and his harrowing escape in a lifeboat thwarted that intention. He decided then to go to Greece, where a war with the Turks was imminent. There he witnessed the Yanina campaign in April 1897, as well as a battle at Velestino in May, which inspired the tale "An Episode of War." Crane was by now enriched by experiences that would serve as the background for his novel *Active Service* (1899).

After his Greek adventure he settled in England with his mistress Cora Taylor, another war correspondent. The couple entertained lavishly and frequented distinguished local writers. Crane continued his writing, enjoyed his fame, made friends with Joseph Conrad, Henry James, H.G. Wells, and Ford Madox Ford, and was much admired by the British, who in their turn enjoyed the company of the refreshing young American. In England he wrote stories of the American West. But when he learned of the blowing up of the American battleship *Maine* in Havana Harbor, he was determined to return to his homeland, to adventure, and to war. In New York he attempted to volunteer as a seaman in the Spanish-American War but was rejected for health reasons and, in fact, died of tuberculosis two years later. He filled those two years with writing first-rate dispatches and comporting himself heroically as a Cuban war correspondent for Joseph Pulitzer. He then sailed to Haiti, where he experienced exciting adventures later recounted in his semifictionalized "War Memories" (1899). Moving on to San Domingo, he learned that the French and German merchants on the island sided with the Spanish, and sent dispatches that stirred the hearts of his New York readers. Traveling in whatever tugboats were available, he neared the coast of Santiago on the way to Jamaica and circled around the island of Cuba in an attempt to ferret out the Spanish fleet. The landing of the American marines at Guantánamo Bay changed the pace of events and plunged him into "the vat of war," which he captured in the poignant short story "The Upturned Face." Subsequently, as a correspondent for William Randolph Hearst, he went to Puerto Rico for the final phase of the war, arriving in Havana prior to the Spanish surrender in 1898 and remaining there after the cessation of hostilities to write sketches—"Stephen Crane's Views of Havana"—for the *New York Journal*. His Spanish-American War tales appeared posthumously under the title *Wounds in the Rain* (1900).

A return to England in 1899 saw him cherish another dream: that of covering the Boer War as a correspondent. In ill health, he toyed with the idea of going to St. Helena to interview soldiers interned at the Boer prison camp there. Suffering repeated hemorrhages from his active tuberculosis, he was taken by stretcher and invalid carriage to a German spa in the Black Forest. Friends and admirers, including Andrew Carnegie, contributed to this futile undertaking, which was to be the prelude to his death in a sanatorium in Germany at the young age of twenty-eight.

MAJOR MULTICULTURAL THEMES

Crane personally lived the adventures he portrayed and wrote from observation of the foreign lands he visited. In *Active Service*, revolving around the Greco-Turkish War of 1897, the hero-journalist moves in scenes unfolding at the Hotel d'Angleterre in Athens, then travels to Patras by train, and continues on horseback through the danger zone. He notes with precision the bombings and the artillery duels and leads his guide astutely through the Greek lines. What

Crane had learned in Greece during his war experience had enriched him both intellectually and psychologically.

The thirteen short stories in *The Open Boat and Other Tales Of Adventure* (1898) deal with three periods in Crane's life: his New Jersey boyhood, his trip to the West and to Mexico in 1895, and his Cuban venture in 1897. A feeling for nature and for natural man is molded directly into his colorful landscapes and precise descriptions of people and things, which remain indelibly fixed in the mind's eye.

"One Dash—Horses" (1896) was the first of a group of tales he wrote about his trip to the western United States and to Mexico in early 1895. The story is based on a real incident in which he and his guide, riding into Mexican back country, experienced a confrontation with a drunken bandit in a local adobe tavern. The painting of the scene in foreboding reds and lambent hues builds up the protagonist's fear and the chaos of the unresolved situation.

"The Open Boat" (1898), one of America's finest short stories, describes the adventure that satisfied Crane most fully. He had once said that he wanted to go somewhere in the world where mail was uncertain, and he did just that when he accepted the offer to cover the Cuban rebellion against Spain. The well-known opening line of the story, "None of them knew the color of the sky," dramatizes the fierce struggle between finite man and the infinitude that engulfs him, as in Melville's *Moby-Dick*. The harrowing sea journey creates a new morality, a new "brotherhood of men." Comfort and feelings of well-being emerge as each helps the other assuage his growing terror. The poetry and rhythmic schemes of "The Open Boat" match those in Melville's "White Jacket" and the best of Jack London and Joseph Conrad.

The central figure in "Death and the Child" (1898), based in part on Crane's own experience as a war correspondent in Greece, is the correspondent Peza, whose own Greek heritage involves him emotionally with the people he was sent to write about. He immediately decides to join forces with the Greeks to fight against the Turks, believing that a Greek victory would preserve the fatherland. Crane supplies a frightening image of Greek peasants streaming down a mountain trail as they flee the enemy and presents a child as everyman at the beginning and at the end of the ordeal that is life.

Fascinated by the dichotomies of eastern and western landscapes, of wild and churning seas, Crane, like Melville, Poe, and Conrad, uses his painter's eye to reveal strikingly vast spaces and war-torn areas. He uses the detail to reveal the whole; he scrutinizes the isolated incident to explain the larger drama.

SURVEY OF CRITICISM

John Berryman's *Stephen Crane*, a classic-type biography and critical study, although written in 1950, is not only insightful in its empathetic approach to Crane's writings, but deeply moving as well. Thomas A. Gullason's extensive study of *Stephen Crane's Career* (1972) contains H.G. Wells's evaluation of Crane's work as "the first expression of the opening mind of a new period, or, at least, the early emphatic phase of a new initiative" (133), as well as Joseph Conrad's view of Crane's "passage on this earth [as] one of a horseman riding swiftly in the dawn of a day fated to be short and without sunshine" (136).

R.W. Stallman edited both the works (1952) and the letters (with Lilian Gilkes, 1960) of Crane and produced one of the most comprehensive studies of the author, *Stephen Crane: A Biography* (1968). Chester L. Wolford's *The Anger of Stephen Crane: Fiction and the Epic Tradition* (1983) is rewarding for the explanations offered concerning the impact of Crane's inner chaos on his writings. Wolford's *Stephen Crane: A Study of the Short Fiction* (1989) is especially significant for its explications of Crane's interviews and letters. Stanley Wertheim's *A Stephen Crane Encyclopedia* (1997) is a meticulously conceived and researched volume detailing biographical, literary, and bibliographical information.

SELECTIVE BIBLIOGRAPHY

Works by Crane

Stephen Crane: Letters. Ed. R.W. Stallman and Lilian Gilkes. New York: New York University Press, 1960.
The Works of Stephen Crane. Ed. Fredson Bowers. 10 vols. Charlottesville: University Press of Virginia, 1969–1975.

Selective Studies of Crane

Berryman, John. *Stephen Crane.* New York: William Sloane Associates, 1950.
Brown, Bill. *The Material Unconscious: American Amusement: Stephen Crane and the Economies of Play.* Cambridge, Mass.: Harvard University Press, 1996.
Chowder, Ken. "A Writer Who Lived the Adventures He Portrayed." *Smithsonian* (January 1995): 109–21.
Gullason, Thomas A., ed. *Stephen Crane's Career.* New York: New York University Press, 1972.
Halliburton, David. *The Color of the Sky: A Study of Stephen Crane.* Cambridge, England: Cambridge University Press, 1989.
Stallman, R.W. *Stephen Crane: A Biography.* New York: George Braziller, 1968.
———, ed. *Stephen Crane: An Omnibus.* New York: Alfred A. Knopf, 1952.
Wertheim, Stanley. *A Stephen Crane Encyclopedia.* Westport, Conn.: Greenwood Press, 1997.
Wolford, Chester L. *The Anger of Stephen Crane: Fiction and the Epic Tradition.* Lincoln: University of Nebraska Press, 1983.
———. *Stephen Crane: A Study of the Short Fiction.* Boston: Twayne, 1989.

RUBÉN DARÍO
(1867–1916)

James O. Pellicer

BIOGRAPHY

The boy who was born on January 18, 1867, in the little town of Metapa, Nicaragua, was named Félix Rubén García, but the world later would know him as Rubén Darío, the poet who would renew Hispanic letters on both sides of the Atlantic. Abandoned by his parents, the child was adopted and reared by his maternal grandfather, Colonel Félix Ramírez, and his wife, Bernarda Sarmiento. He lived through difficult times: the dissolution of the Central American Federation, increasing militarism, local and foreign dictatorships and invasions, growing U.S. intervention, aggressive rivalries between liberals and conservatives, failing economies, high unemployment, and official corruption.

The lad entered the world of culture through some forgotten books in Colonel Ramírez's closets: Cervantes's *Don Quixote*, plays of the Spanish Golden Age, and the Bible. At a very young age he discovered his gift as a poet; he published some verses in *El Termómetro* and read some in a local literary club, "El Ateneo," in León, where he met the pedagogue José Leonard Bertholet, whose pupil he became. Leonard Bertholet categorically opposed the Jesuits and optimistically adhered to a belief in the progressive perfectibility of humankind. Like many in his day, he had angrily reacted against Pope Pius IX's encyclical letter *Quanta cura* (1864) proclaiming that education was the domain of the Roman Church by divine mandate, and that any disagreement would be punished by excommunication. The Roman pontiff later put an end to all discussions and polemics on the subject by having the Vatican Council of 1870 declare as a dogma of faith the infallibility of the pope. Leonard Bertholet believed in a universal creator God and in science as a panacea for all evil; thus he preferred to become a Mason. The young Darío followed in his footsteps.

Later he traveled to the capital, Managua, where he read the Colección de Clásicos Españoles Ribadeneira, an anthology of the main classical Spanish authors, and French authors as well—the Goncourts, Catulle Mendès, Gustave Flaubert, and especially Théophile Gautier, whose style captivated him. By reciting one of his own poems at a public patriotic celebration, he obtained a job as a writer for the president of Nicaragua, Joaquín Zabala, and met General Juan J. Cañas, who convinced him to move to Chile, an ideal place, in his view, for writers. Darío arrived in Valparaiso on June 24, 1886. In Chile education had been an important matter since the days of the famous Venezuelan educator Andrés Bello, founder of the National University of Chile; of Domingo Faustino Sarmiento's creation of the Normal School for teachers; and of the rise of journalism. Innumerable periodicals circulated among the people of Santiago and Valparaiso, thirsty for debate and exchange of ideas. Here Darío found the opportunity to foster his talents as a poet and journalist and also to become acquainted with famous writers, such as the most prestigious Chilean scholar, José Victorino Lastarria. He befriended Pedro Balmaceda, son of the Chilean president, and this resulted in an appointment as Chilean correspondent for *La Nación*, Argentina's most important newspaper.

In Chile Darío published two books that would open many doors to him in the future: *Abrojos* (1887) and *Azul* (1888). The latter had great repercussions in the entire Hispanic world, especially in Spain, and marked the starting point for the artistic movement known as "Modernismo," derived in part from the French Symbolists and Parnassians.

Of capital importance was a trip to Spain, where he met the most important writers of the day: José Zorrilla y Moral, Gaspar Núñez de Arce, Ramón de Campoamor y Campoosorio, and Salvador Rueda. Rueda invited him to write a prologue in verse to his book *En tropel*; with his "Portico," Darío's name was affirmed in the mother country. The days of celebration were short, however. He had to return to Central America, jobless and in mourning for his wife. His ship, bound for Cuba, was detoured instead to Cartagena, Colombia, where, through Dr. Rafael Núñez, the country's former president, he gained an appointment as a general consul of Colombia in Argentina, with an immediate cash award of twenty-four hundred American dollars. He had never seen that much money together in his life; departing immediately for Buenos Aires, he took the longest route possible, via New York, where he met one of the most important poets of the Spanish world, José Martí, and via Paris, where he lost no time in seeking out Paul Verlaine and other French poets. He not only admired the French Symbolist and Parnassian poets; he felt that they coincided with him. Paris was the great occasion to find himself, and once he discovered his very essence, he became the unquestionable standard-bearer of "Modernismo," two examples of which, *Los raros* and *Prosas profanas*, were both published in Buenos Aires in 1896.

With the death of his protector, his position as general consul of Colombia in Argentina evaporated together with the salary that had allowed him to live comfortably in Buenos Aires. But luck returned in the form of an invitation from the director of *La Nación* to study in situ the psychological effects of the

Spanish-American War on the people of Spain. Thus in 1898 he returned to the mother country, where he was already famous; he traveled to Paris and, from 1900 to 1905, visited various European countries. His native Nicaragua remembered him and appointed him its representative in Spain in 1908. From there he attempted to travel to the United States but was thwarted by deteriorating health due to alcoholism. He died of liver cirrhosis in February 1916.

MAJOR MULTICULTURAL THEMES

Rubén Darío inherited old Spanish traditions and beliefs, but he opened his mind to new ideas through multiple exposures to friends, teachers, and great poets from Spain and France, and especially through voracious reading. Under the guidance of his teacher Leonard Bertholet, he took his first steps outside of fusty Spanish orthodoxy. The cultural contact that proved to be the strongest was Pythagoreanism, which he assimilated through his readings of the French writer Edouard Schuré's *The Great Initiates: A Study of the Secret History of Religions* (1889). The vision of universal harmony and music as the manifestation of God gave Darío the key to poetry as the rhythmic and musical expression of the inner beauty that resides in the spirit of the poet. The French Parnassians confirmed his conviction that formal perfection was of capital importance; the French Symbolists, that music and rhythm are the essence of poetry.

That Rubén Darío's life and works were a product of several cultural trends is corroborated by a letter from one of Spain's greatest poets and thinkers, Miguel de Unamuno: "I would like to write about you and your poetry, especially about your influence, which is enormous, on Spanish and Hispanic American letters" (cited in Torres Bodet, 333). Coming from Unamuno, who never indulged in vain flattery and even less recognized the influence of Spanish-American letters, this testimony of the "enormous influence" of Darío is of great value.

SURVEY OF CRITICISM

The quotation from Unamuno is drawn from Jaime Torres Bodet's now-classic *Rubén Darío, abismo y cima* (1966). The first critic to detect Darío's importance, dedicating an article to him in *El Imparcial*, was Juan Valera, in the same year that Darío became the standard-bearer of Latin American poetry with his publication of *Azul* (1888). Another critic who foresaw Darío's leading role in Spanish letters was Pedro Salinas in his 1948 work *La poesía de Rubén Darío*. The first scholar to study the importance of Pythagoreanism in the writings of the Modernists was Ricardo Gullón in a work entitled *Direcciones del Modernismo* (1971). Cathy Login Jrade, in *Rubén Darío and the Romantic Search for Unity* (1983), discovered the capital influence of Schuré on the poet's creative production. One of the first commentators to analyze Darío's multicultural wealth was Angel Rama in several works, especially *Rubén Darío y el Modernismo* (1970), in which he also studied the virtuosity of Darío's poetics in the "Prólogo" to his poems.

SELECTIVE BIBLIOGRAPHY

Works by Darío

Azul . . . ; Cantos de vida y esperanza. Ed. Alvaro Salvador. Madrid: Espasa Calpe (Colección Austral), 1994.
Paginas escogidas. Ed. Ricardo Gullón. Madrid: Cathedra, 1995.

Selective Studies of Darío

Gullón, Ricardo. *Direcciones del Modernismo*. 2nd ed. Madrid: Gredos, 1971.
———. "Pitagorismo y Modernismo." *Mundo Nuevo* 7 (1967): 22–32.
Login Jrade, Cathy. *Rubén Darío and the Romantic Search for Unity*. Austin: University of Texas Press, 1983.
Lorenz, Erika. *Rubén Darío: "Bajo el divino imperio de la musica."* Trans. Fidel Coloma González. Managua: Ediciones lengua, 1960.
Rama, Angel. *Rubén Darío y el Modernismo*. Caracas: Universidad Central de Venezuela, 1970.
Salinas, Pedro. *La poesía de Rubén Darío*. Buenos Aires: Editorial Losada, 1948.
Schuré, Edouard. *The Great Initiates: A Study of the Secret History of Religions*. Trans. Gloria Rasberry. Intro. Paul M. Allen. West Nyack, N.Y.: St. George Books, 1961.
Torres Bodet, Jaime. *Rubén Darío, abismo y cima*. Mexico: Universidad Nacional Autónoma, 1966.
Valera, Juan. "Cartas Americanas." In *Obras Completas*, 3rd ed., 284–98. Madrid: M. Aguilar, 1947.

ALEXANDRA DAVID-NEEL
(1868–1969)

Barbara Foster and Michael Foster

BIOGRAPHY

Lawrence Durrell called Alexandra David-Neel "the most astonishing French-woman of our time." Alan Watts praised her "wonderfully lucid" writing. Indeed, the Buddhist adventurer who lived over one hundred years merits superlatives. A Renaissance woman, she defied Victorian stereotypes operative in Belle Epoque Paris, refusing to be either a "nice girl" or a prostitute. Instead, she found her own identity on the snowcapped mountains of Tibet. Peter Hopkirk, the noted Asian expert, extolled her remarkable courage and determination in his preface to her classic travel yarn written in English, *My Journey to Lhasa*, a worldwide best-seller when it appeared in 1927: "At the age of fifty-four, Alexandra David-Neel became the first white woman to enter the holy city of Lhasa (Tibet). Disguised as a beggar, and with a revolver concealed beneath her rags, she made her bold dash for the forbidden Buddhist citadel in 1923."

Louise Eugénie Alexandrine Marie was born in Paris in 1868 and died at Digne, France, in 1969. Her radical father (Louis David) took the infant Alexandra to view the remnants of the Paris Commune in flames. Seeking adventure, the precocious child ran away from her wealthy home often. An introspective yet lovely young woman, she became a left-winger given to philosophical speculations. Trapped in a bourgeois family, she tried hashish, kept a revolver hidden in her drawer, and briefly contemplated suicide. Studying at the Sorbonne, where male students pushed females who dared intrude on their exclusive domain downstairs, she became a lifelong feminist. After her parents lost their fortune, she became an opera singer, but her voice eventually failed. She descended from Parisian opera to singing in a provincial nightclub in Tunisia.

In 1904 she married a staid railroad engineer, Philip Neel, who shared her Protestant background, if not her passion for adventure. The reluctant matron dabbled in journalism and wrote an inflammatory essay advocating that housewives be paid for their labor, and that unwed mothers be treated as worthy members of society. By 1911, off to India, she hit the right road both intellectually and spiritually. Her letters to her husband mix Buddhist wisdom and homey advice. At a distance the couple maintained their liberated "marriage of correspondence" for almost twenty years. The connection enriched both of them—particularly Alexandra, since Neel's contribution funded her travels. Alexandra, who knew English perfectly, explored India and settled in Benares to learn Sanskrit. Her research on Eastern themes resulted in the publication of twenty-five books—some scholarly, others for the general reader—that sold worldwide. In 1912 she met the Thirteenth Dalai Lama, who praised her Buddhist erudition. In 1913 she visited the prince of Sikkim in his capital, Gangtok. Smitten, the English-educated prince, soon to be maharaja, showered gifts on the French Buddhist informed enough to discuss the most abstruse philosophical points. His mysterious murder plunged David-Neel into despair: she secluded herself for two years with a local hermit-magician (Gomchen) who initiated her into the Tibetan mysteries. Earlier studies of the occult in London and Paris had made her suspicious of sham occultists; fortunately, her guru proved genuine. He taught her a range of "psychic sports," among them trance walking and breathing practices to keep warm in high altitudes. Her apprenticeship in Tantric Buddhism completed, the newly initiated lama plunged into mystical Tibet, an opportunity to practice the Gomchen's teachings. Her *Magie d'amour et magie noire*, written in 1931, related these experiences.

By 1923, determined to show "what the will of woman can do," she set out on her spine-chilling walk along the "roof of the world" to forbidden Lhasa, taking along a lad she met in Sikkim, Lama Yongden, whom she later adopted. She spent two months in Lhasa savoring her triumph, having proved that a clever woman could succeed where expensive expeditions headed by professional male explorers failed. Returning to acclaim in Paris, she briefly contemplated settling in America but instead bought a home in Digne, France. In 1937 the "sacred fire of adventure" flamed up, resulting in another trip to China. Back in Digne, Alexandra and Yongden lectured and synthesized years of data gathered in their rambles. Occasionally they were joined by Philip Neel, ever fond of his wife—devoted in her fashion—and of the well-heated Digne bedroom reserved for him. At his death Alexandra moaned that she had lost the best of husbands and her only friend. Yongden also predeceased her. She remained fecund with book projects till the end of her long, active life.

MAJOR MULTICULTURAL THEMES

David-Neel's books range among the political, sociological, historical, mystical, and philosophical. She also wrote two novels with Tibetan themes after having gathered data in the field rather than from an armchair, in contrast to other orientalists of her time. She spoke perfect Tibetan, lived among the natives, and was conversant with every aspect of Tibetan life. Her cohorts were gurus and magicians whose practices she mastered, then disseminated to her readers. Tibet was her spiritual homeland, unlike Paris, where she never fit in. Meanwhile, a relentless skepticism is evident in her studies of Buddhist philosophy— some for a scholarly audience, others for the general reader. A few examples of her large output are *Le Bouddhisme du Bouddha* (1960), *La Puissance du néant* (1954), and *Les enseignements secrets dans les sectes bouddhistes tibétaines* (1951).

Her works on India, where she lived on and off for several years, reveal ritual practices never before seen by Western eyes. Her *L'Inde où j'ai vécu* (1969) and *L'Inde hier, aujourd'hui, et demain* (1951), mixtures of reportage and philosophical speculation, are examples of her ability to cull information from gurus, politicians, and the common person. They include eyewitness accounts of Tantric sexual practices.

Her views on pre-Mao China were indulgent. Even during the height of Maoist excesses, she did not condemn the zealots. Perhaps she hoped that this revolution would usher in a more democratic China. While her earlier visits to China had been as a tourist or researcher, during the Sino-Japanese War (1937– 45) she found herself trapped—bombed on all sides. She turned this adversity into opportunity by gathering data that she later published in book form. Her books on China are a mixture of the political and sociological, unique documents that predict current Chinese expansionism over nearby territories. She experienced a supine China, but predicted its emergence as a world power. Her *Sous des nueés d'orage* (1940), *Quarante siècles d'expansion chinoise* (1964), and *Le vieux Tibet face à la Chine nouvelle* (1953) are unbiased studies that look at the age-old Tibet-China dispute from an informed perspective.

SURVEY OF CRITICISM

Luree Miller's collective biography (1976) contains original research done in the Digne archives. However, David-Neel is but one among many travelers whom Miller covers in a cursory fashion. China Galland's 1980 work concentrates on David-Neel as an explorer but fails to evaluate her intellectual accomplishments. Barbara and Michael Foster's *Forbidden Journey: The Life of Alexandra David-Neel* (1987) is the first full-length biography to take an objective view of the author, who purposely hid those episodes in her life that she deemed unfit for public consumption. The Fosters' *The Secret Lives of Alexandra David-Neel* (1998), a sequel to their earlier biography, employs new research from the British Library India Office in addition to unpublished letters from individuals who met David-Neel during her travels. Dea Birkett's collective biography (1989) includes a chapter on David-Neel. Ruth Middleton's brief study (1989) is based on research supplied by the curator of Digne's archives. Jeanne Denys (1972) made scandalous assertions without any concrete evidence to back them up. Jacques Brosse (1978) supplies a more balanced picture. Jean Chalon (1985) perpetuates the myth of "our lady of Tibet," a glorification that ignores the darker side of this complex woman's character.

SELECTIVE BIBLIOGRAPHY

Works by David-Neel

My Journey to Lhasa. New York: Harper & Brothers, 1927.
Grand Tibet. Paris: Plon, 1933.
Sous des nuées d'orage. Paris: Plon, 1940.
Au coeur des Himalayas: le Népal. Paris: Dessart, 1949.
L'Inde hier, aujourd'hui, et demain. Paris: Plon, 1951.
Le vieux Tibet face à la Chine nouvelle. Paris: Plon, 1953.
La Connaissance transcendante. Paris: Adyar, 1958.
Quarante siècles d'expansion chinoise. Paris: Plon, 1964.
L'Inde où j'ai vécu. Paris: Plon, 1969.
Textes tibétains inédits. Paris: Pygmalion, 1977.
Le Lama aux cinq sagesses. Paris: Plon, 1995.

Selective Studies of David-Neel

Birkett, Dea. *Spinsters Abroad.* London: Basil Blackwell, 1989.
Brosse, Jacques. *Alexandra David-Neel: L'aventure et la spiritualité.* Paris: Retz, 1978.
Chalon, Jean. *Le lumineux destin d'Alexandra David-Neel.* Paris: Perrin, 1985.
Champy, Huguette. "Quelques exploratrices." *Revue économique* 6 (1955): 32–35.
Dedman, Jane. "Walker in the Sky." *Quest* 78 (May–June 1978): 21–26, 90–92.
Denys, Jeanne. *Alexandra David-Neel au Tibet.* Paris: Pensée Universelle, 1972.
Foster, Barbara, and Michael Foster. *Forbidden Journey: The Life of Alexandra David-Neel.* San Francisco: Harper Collins, 1987.
———. *The Secret Lives of Alexandra David-Neel.* New York: Overlook Press, 1998.
Galland, China. *Women in the Wilderness.* New York: Harper & Row, 1980.
Guy, David. "Ancestors: Alexandra David-Neel." *Tricycle* 5 (Fall 1995): 12–17.
Middleton, Ruth. *Alexandra David-Neel: Portrait of an Adventurer.* Boston: Shambhala, 1989.
Miller, Luree. *On Top of the World.* New York: Paddington Press, 1976.

CHARLES DICKENS
(1812–1870)

A.L. Rogers II

BIOGRAPHY

In the nineteenth century, says novelist George Gissing, "Charles Dickens, in the world of literature, meant England" (*Charles Dickens*, 84). Today Dickens is still closely tied to that Victorian England his eccentric and supremely British characters bring to life for readers worldwide. Surprisingly, perhaps, the "eminently English" author spent much of his life abroad, traveling, living, and writing among other, non-English cultures.

After happy childhood years on England's southern coast, he was separated from his family at age twelve and put to work in a London shoe-blacking warehouse during his father's imprisonment for debt, an experience that scarred the sensitive boy deeply. Once family finances improved, he returned to school and became an apprentice law clerk, then a freelance reporter of court proceedings, later still a parliamentary and political reporter. After marrying Catherine Hogarth in 1836, he achieved instant fame with *The Pickwick Papers* (1837). *Oliver Twist* (1838), *Nicholas Nickleby* (1839), and *The Old Curiosity Shop* (1841) then established him as the preeminent English novelist of his day. In 1842 he toured the United States and Canada, experiences he related factually in *American Notes* (1842) and fictionalized in *Martin Chuzzlewit* (1844). Both books were critical of Americans, and a heated controversy between Dickens and the Americans ensued in the press. He learned Italian and in 1844 moved his now-growing family to Genoa, where at first he found it hard to work in unfamiliar surroundings. He soon mastered the difficulty, and his friend and biographer John Forster would later describe the year in Italy as the "turning-point of his career" (*Life of Charles Dickens*, 334). In addition to recording his Italian experiences in the travel book *Pictures from Italy* (1846), Dickens revisited the time in Italy, together with a seven-month 1846 stay in Lausanne, Switzerland, fictionally in *Little Dorrit* (1857). *Dombey and Son* (1848) was begun in Lausanne and continued in Paris, where Dickens fell in love with the French, admiring their elegance and sophistication so much that he rated them "the first people of the universe."

In all, Dickens made more than sixty crossings of the English Channel, and for his frequent and extended visits to France throughout the 1850s and 1860s he was considered almost a French resident. On the longer stays in Italy and France he dressed in the French fashions and grew a "continental" mustache and beard he rarely wore at home, which may suggest how he enjoyed escaping his English identity when he was on the Continent. Increasingly he found it easier to write in France than in England, and in his later stays in Paris and especially in the French village of Condette, France offered refuge from the pressures of his hectic life in London. Significant portions of *Bleak House* (1853), *Hard Times* (1854), and *Little Dorrit* (1857) were composed in Boulogne, the family's adopted summer home for several years. With novelist Wilkie Collins he toured Switzerland and Italy in 1853, and Collins became his regular companion in subsequent visits to Paris. In 1858 there was scandal when Dickens separated from his wife, with whom he had ten children, and pursued a relationship with the eighteen-year-old actress Ellen Ternan. The year 1859 saw the publication of *A Tale of Two Cities*, the novel set in England and France during the years of the French Revolution, and in 1860 *The Uncommercial Traveller* collected various essays, several among them imparting Dickens's most recent experiences abroad. Between 1862 and 1865 he traveled regularly to Condette, where he was able to spend time discreetly with Ellen Ternan. In his final years a series of exhausting public readings, including stops in Paris and a second tour of the United States, led to a fatal stroke in 1870.

MAJOR MULTICULTURAL THEMES

The confrontation of English and American cultures depicted in *Martin Chuzzlewit* may remind us of the disorientation and prejudice that sometimes beset a foreigner in a strange land. The unpleasantness of being treated as a spectacle by the American public in his 1842 visit was distressing for Dickens, and he came to see most Americans as coarse, boastful, disrespectful, frequently dishonest, and obsessed with money. He sympathized with the plight of American slaves and was profoundly disturbed by the failure of the United States to meet his expectations of enlightened liberty for all. As he wrote the actor William Macready, "This is not the Republic I came to see. This is not the Republic of my imagination" (*Letters*, 3, 156). But the disillusionment of this American trip confirmed his "Englishness" and effected his political maturation: the naïve idealism that had made him something of a radical before the U.S. tour was essentially transformed into the generally more moderate political beliefs he would hold for the remainder of his life. Also, the realization in America that his work was considered "important" outside of England encouraged him to approach his writing with greater artistic care.

In Europe, in lieu of the standard pleasures of the guidebook-toting tourist, he loved to prowl the streets in search of what gave each place its own unique character. He often avoided the society of the English abroad so that he might appreciate the life of the country as lived by the native residents: in *Little Dorrit* the insulated communities of expatriate British who keep to themselves are shown to suffer a form of cultural imprisonment. While stays in Italy, Switzerland, and France were certainly bright times for Dickens the man, his work always remains "eminently English," and the novels often play upon the worst English prejudices of his day. Following Victorian stage convention, his novels present conspicuously French villains: the French maid Hortense kills Mr. Tulkinghorn in *Bleak House* with only the thinnest motivation; "Monsieur Blandois of Paris" is the villainous blackmailing swindler in *Little Dorrit*. Eastern cultures are linked with moral decadence in *The Mystery of Edwin Drood*, and Neville Landless is there drawn as "naturally savage" from years living in Ceylon among "abject and servile dependents, of an inferior race." However, as George Orwell suggests, Dickens was not thoroughly anti-foreigner in the "vulgar nationalism" common in nineteenth-century England (431, 433).

The one Dickens novel that centers most on multicultural themes is *A Tale of Two Cities*. From the time of the French Revolution through much of the nineteenth century there was great prejudice and animosity between the English and the French. During the years of the French Revolution and for some time following, many English feared that the horrors of the French popular revolt might spread to England, and the two countries were opposed in several wars in the later 1700s and early 1800s. But *A Tale of Two Cities* is generally very fair to the French, showing sympathy and understanding for both the French masses and their oppressors in the Revolution. Ultimately, the English and French cultures are joined in this novel when Sydney Carton, an English scoundrel, is sacrificed to the guillotine in place of the French Charles Darnay so that Darnay is not lost to his wife, the naturalized English Lucie Manette.

In "Our French Watering Place" (from *Reprinted Pieces*) Dickens notes that there were always many English living in Boulogne, and here we see that his experiences abroad taught him that even traditionally and sometimes bitterly opposed peoples can learn to see past their differences: "it is not the least pleasant feature of our French watering-place that a long and constant fusion of the two great nations there has taught each to like the other, and to learn from the other, and to rise superior to the absurd prejudices that have lingered among the weak and ignorant in both countries equally" (412). The first American visit was integral in Dickens's coming of age as both man and author; in his maturity, his European experiences taught him that intercultural experiences bring knowledge and growth.

SURVEY OF CRITICISM

Jerome Meckier (1984) examines the first American tour's reaffirmation of Dickens's "Englishness" and softening of his radical politics; he discusses at greater length (1990) the disappointments of both American tours. Sidney Moss

(1984) revisits the antagonism between Dickens and the Americans as recorded in the press. Sylvère Monod (1979) collects papers presented at the 1978 Colloque International de Boulogne that examine such topics as Dickens's experiences in Boulogne and Paris, his depiction of "French Wickedness," and his treatment of French history in *A Tale of Two Cities* and of French characters in the other novels. Anny Sadrin (1999) has edited papers from the 1996 Dickens Project conference in Burgundy, where scholars from fourteen countries presented fifty papers on such matters as the difficulties in translating Dickens, his depiction of the colonial possessions, responses to Dickens in African and other cultures with former colonial connections to England, the American controversy, points of contact and difference between the English and Italian cultures in Dickens's works, and Dickens's explorations of rejection and acceptance of the "other" or "alien" in a variety of cultural forms.

SELECTIVE BIBLIOGRAPHY

Works by Dickens

American Notes and Pictures from Italy (1842 and 1846). Oxford: Oxford University Press, 1989.
Martin Chuzzlewit (1844). Oxford: Clarendon Press, 1982.
Little Dorrit (1857). Oxford: Clarendon Press, 1979.
A Tale of Two Cities (1859). Oxford: Oxford University Press, 1989.
The Uncommercial Traveller and Reprinted Pieces (1860 and 1868). Oxford: Oxford University Press, 1989.
The Letters of Charles Dickens. Vol. 3, Pilgrim Edition. Ed. Madeline House, Graham Storey, and Kathleen Tillotson. Oxford: Clarendon Press, 1974.

Selective Studies of Dickens

Forster, John. *The Life of Charles Dickens*. Vol. 1, 1812–1847. New York: Charles Scribner's Sons, 1900.
Gissing, George. *Charles Dickens: A Critical Study*. New York: Haskell House, 1974.
Hollington, Michael. "Dickens and Italy." *Journal of Anglo-Italian Studies* 1 (1991): 126–36.
Meckier, Jerome. "Dickens Discovers America, Dickens Discovers Dickens: The First Visit Reconsidered." *Modern Language Review* 79, no. 2 (1984): 266–77.
———. *Innocent Abroad: Charles Dickens' American Engagements*. Lexington: University Press of Kentucky, 1990.
Monod, Sylvère, ed. *Charles Dickens et la France*. Lille: Presses Universitaires de Lille, 1979.
Moss, Sidney P. *Charles Dickens' Quarrel with America*. Troy, N.Y.: Whitston, 1984.
Orwell, George. "Charles Dickens." In *The Collected Essays, Journalism and Letters of George Orwell*. Vol. 1: *An Age Like This, 1920–1940*, 413–60. Ed. Sonia Orwell and Ian Angus. New York: Harcourt, Brace & World, 1968.
Sadrin, Anny, ed. *Dickens, Europe, and the New Worlds*. New York: St. Martin's Press, 1999.

ISAK DINESEN
(KAREN BLIXEN)
(1885–1962)

Susan Brantly

BIOGRAPHY

Karen Christenze Dinesen was born in Denmark to a family related to, though not belonging to, nobility. Her mother, Ingeborg Westenholz, came from a well-to-do family of merchants. Her father, Captain Wilhelm Dinesen, fought in the Franco-Prussian War, lived in Wisconsin with the Chippewa Indian tribe for a time, and wrote his hunting memoirs under the pseudonym "Boganis." He committed suicide when his daughter was only ten. Many biographers have suggested that Dinesen's own biography echoes her father's wanderlust and authorial ambitions.

Dinesen married her Swedish cousin, the Baron Bror Blixen-Finecke, in 1914, and the two settled in Kenya with the intention of raising coffee. Bror Blixen showed a great aptitude for hunting, but little for farming, and before long Dinesen was charged by her family investors to take over the management of the coffee plantation. Shortly after her marriage she contracted syphilis and returned to Europe for treatment. The aftereffects of the disease plagued her for the rest of her life. After they had been separated for four years, the couple divorced in 1925. During her final years in Kenya the great love of her life became Denys Finch Hatton, a younger son of English nobility and a legendary Kenyan personality. Several years of bad harvests and a depressed coffee market forced her to sell the farm in 1931. Before leaving for Denmark, she attended to the collective resettling of the Africans who had lived on her farm, an act considered eccentric and unnecessary by the British authorities. Shortly before her departure Finch Hatton was killed in an airplane accident. Overall, Dinesen had spent nineteen years in Kenya.

Her return to her native Denmark was anything but triumphant, and she later claimed that if she had not lost the farm, she would have stayed in Africa forever and never have become an author. Previously, she had published a few stories in Danish periodicals under the pseudonym Osceola, but her major literary debut occurred when she was forty-nine with the publication of *Seven Gothic Tales* (1934) in the United States under the name Isak Dinesen. These fantastic tales, set in nineteenth-century Europe, received enthusiastic reviews; British and Danish editions soon followed. In Denmark she published under her own name, Karen Blixen. Two years later she produced *Out of Africa* (1937), which was even more widely acclaimed than her first effort.

When World War II broke out, wishing to become a foreign correspondent and intending to travel to Berlin, Paris, and London, she completed her trip to Berlin, but further plans were thwarted by the German invasion and occupation of Denmark on April 9, 1940. The occupation lasted until May 7, 1945, a period she compared to imprisonment, since her movements were restricted and no news came from the outside. Even as her health deteriorated, she produced during the occupation her *Winter's Tales* (1942), characterized as "more Danish" than her previous ones. She remained unaware until after the war that they had been successfully published in Britain and America. To amuse herself, she also penned a gothic thriller called *The Angelic Avengers* (1946), published under the French pseudonym Pierre Andrézel.

After the war she adopted an increasingly flamboyant aristocratic persona in opposition to the fairly homogeneous, Social-Democratic Danish society of the 1950s and early 1960s, which made her legendary and no doubt tested the Danish tolerance for difference. In 1959 she made her first and only trip to the United States, where the exotic persona of the baroness that evoked misgivings in Denmark was embraced with zeal. Although she published tales in periodicals during this time, she did not produce another collection until *Last Tales* (1957), which was followed closely by *Anecdotes of Destiny* (1958). *Shadows on the Grass* (1960), another African memoir, was the last work published during her lifetime. *Ehrengard* (1963), *Carnival* (1977), *Daguerreotypes and Other Essays* (1979), and *Letters from Africa: 1914–1931* (1981) were all published posthumously. She died at her Rungstedlund estate in Denmark in 1962. Her home is now a museum and a bird sanctuary.

MAJOR MULTICULTURAL THEMES

Dinesen has been described as an author who lived on the slash: Danish/ English, European/African, male/female. She generally wrote her fiction in English first and later recast it into Danish, the differences between the two versions being often slight but occasionally significant. The suggestion has been made, with good reason, that her Danish and English bodies of work be treated as two distinct, but highly intertextual, authorships by Karen Blixen and Isak Dinesen, respectively.

Her choice to write in English resulted in a wider audience, but, for the Danish press, she claimed that she chose English because she did not think that the Danish public would be interested in her fantastic stories. The prevalent literary mode in Denmark in the 1930s was social realism. The harshest critics of *Seven Gothic Tales* were, in fact, Danish; they accused her of snobbery and perversity. In the earliest reviews one can detect a modicum of resentment that Dinesen had won recognition abroad before presenting herself to the Danes for judgment. Although she clearly loved Denmark, the Danes, and their literary traditions, she frequently adopted a critical and provocative posture toward her native culture. In her tales set in Europe, the cold, restrained North is frequently contrasted with the passionate, voluptuous South. Her stories set in Denmark often deal with themes of confinement. The North becomes a site of restrictions; the South a locus of freedom.

Dinesen said that her meeting with the people of Africa was the most profound experience of her life. In an unpublished speech delivered to students at Lund University in Sweden, she described the experience as a progressive peeling back of layers: when confronted with people who do not care what your father did and do not notice whether you are well dressed, you discover that features of your personality you took to be a natural extension of your "self" are really only cultural constructs. Only in such encounters with different cultures can you begin to understand who you really are. In British East Africa she ran her own coffee farm and was able to act as "an honorary man" in ways that would not have been possible in Denmark. Thus her experience in Africa exposed the cultural construction not only of ethnicity, but also of gender.

Dinesen's *Out of Africa* is unusual as a settler memoir in that it foregrounds the African tribes and individuals she met rather than the white community. She disapproved of the behavior of the British settlers toward the Africans and in later years expressed her support of the Kikuyu during the Mau Mau rebellion (1952–58). A central theme in *Out of Africa* is a shift in perspective. Her attempts to reconstruct the African view of the European consistently destabilize the implied Eurocentric perspective of her readers. Even so, decades later, Dinesen remarked that *Out of Africa* had become as out-of-date as papyrus from a pyramid.

SURVEY OF CRITICISM

Much of the scholarship on Dinesen has consisted of close readings of her tales, and Robert Langbaum (1964) quite possibly provides the best of these. Else Brundbjerg (1985) offers a thorough survey of the author's major themes as well as a glimpse into the Danish view of her work, renewed interest in which has been sparked by Judith Thurman's standard biography (1982). Attention has turned to Dinesen's role as a colonial author. Perhaps her most outspoken critic has been Kenyan author Ngugi wa Thiong'o (1981), who cannot forgive her participation in the colonial enterprise. Rob Nixon (1986) has also expressed serious misgivings about her paternalistic attitude toward the Africans. Other critics have questioned whether she deserves to be lumped alongside all other colonial authors. Abdul JanMohamed (1983) calls her a "major exception."

Others, such as Susan Hardy Aiken (1990) and Dane Kennedy (1987), have argued along similar lines. Quite recently, Tove Hussein (1998) has provided more fuel for the discussion by tracking down and interviewing surviving inhabitants of the African farm. Those she interviewed expressed nothing but respect and affection for Karen Blixen. No doubt the issues of Dinesen's role as a colonial author will remain under negotiation for some time to come.

SELECTIVE BIBLIOGRAPHY

Works by Dinesen

Out of Africa. London: Putnam, 1937.
Shadows on the Grass. New York: Random House, 1960.
Letters from Africa: 1914–1931. Ed. Frans Lasson. Trans. Anne Born. Chicago: University of Chicago Press, 1981.

Selective Studies of Dinesen

Aiken, Susan Hardy. *Isak Dinesen and the Engendering of Narrative*. Chicago: University of Chicago Press, 1990.

Brundbjerg, Else. *Kvinden, kætteren, kunstneren Karen Blixen* (1985). Reprint, Charlottenlund: KnowWare, 1995.

Hannah, Donald. *Isak Dinesen and Karen Blixen: The Mask and the Reality*. New York: Random House, 1971.

Hussein, Tove. *Africa's Song of Karen Blixen*. Nairobi: Majestic Printing Works, 1998.

JanMohamed, Abdul. *Manichean Aesthetics: The Politics of Literature in Colonial Africa*. Amherst: University of Massachusetts Press, 1983.

Kennedy, Dane. "Isak Dinesen's African Recovery of a European Past." *Clio* 17, no. 1 (Fall 1987): 38–50.

Langbaum, Robert. *The Gayety of Vision. A Study in Isak Dinesen's Art*. New York: Random House, 1964.

Lee, Judith. "The Mask of Form in *Out of Africa*." *Prose Studies* 8, no. 2 (September 1985): 45–57.

Ngugi wa Thiong'o. "A Tremendous Service in Rectifying the Harm Done to Africa." *Bogens verden* 63, no. 10 (December 1981): 663–65.

Nixon, Rob. "*Out of Africa*." *Grand Street* 5, no. 4 (Summer 1986): 216–27.

Thurman, Judith. *Isak Dinesen: The Life of a Storyteller*. New York: St. Martin's Press, 1982.

FEDOR MIKHAILOVICH DOSTOEVSKY
(1821–1881)

Robert Bird

BIOGRAPHY

From his very birth Dostoevsky's life bore major contradictions that propelled his creative spirit toward a reconciling vision. Although his father was descended from the West-Russian nobility, he was a doctor of modest means. Raised in an atmosphere of Orthodox piety, Dostoevsky was influenced by numerous Western sources, particularly German pietism and authors from Schiller to Walter Scott and Ann Radcliffe. Lastly, though his life and works are inextricably linked to St. Petersburg, that most European of Russian cities, he was born and raised in traditional Moscow and at family properties in the country. In this way his intimations of nobility were belied by chronically severe financial straits and a tortured psychology, and his knowledge and advocacy of a traditional Russian identity were accompanied by a pained awareness of its dislocation in the reality of Europeanized Russia and in his own soul.

At the age of sixteen he traveled with his brother to St. Petersburg, where they were to enter the Engineering Institute. However, he later recalled, "We dreamt only of poetry and poets and I spent my time mentally composing a novel on Venetian life" (*Polnoe sobranie sochinenii*, 22:27, my translation). This idealism was tempered by the sordid aspects of Russian life, symbolized by Dostoevsky's witnessing the merciless beating of a horse by a drunken peasant. After graduating from the institute and serving in the army for two years, he devoted himself to literature, finding his main inspiration in Gogol and in French realists of a humanist bent such as Balzac, Hugo, and George Sand. In 1844 he published a translation of Balzac's *Eugénie Grandet* and that same year came to the notice of literary Petersburg through his short novel *Bednye liudi* (1845). The social thematics of this work accorded with the increasingly realist or naturalist orientation of Russian thought, and it was celebrated by radical critics. Dostoevsky entered into a series of political circles and groups, some of which pursued explicitly revolutionary aims. At the same time his prose took a Hoffmannesque turn, exemplified by the 1846 novel *Dvoinik*. In April 1849 he was arrested for his conspiratorial activities and received a death sentence, which, as he learned only minutes before the execution, was commuted to eight years of hard labor, followed by compulsory military service. He served four years in a prison camp and five more in Siberian exile.

The Dostoevsky who returned to Petersburg in 1859 was both profoundly different from and surprisingly similar to the man arrested ten years previous. His new religious faith dictated a view of society no less radical than his previous socialism. He began to focus on the human subject in all its manifestations (social, psychological, metaphysical), which made his original fantastic realism both more realistic and more fantastic. The dynamic of his great novels was already visible in his 1861–1862 *Zapiski iz mertvogo doma*, in which the Dantesque world of the labor camp offers glimpses of redemption through love for fellow man and faith in divine justice. The critical side of his new vision emerged through his 1863 *Zimnie zametki o letnikh vpechatleniiakh* (based on his 1862 trip to Western Europe) and 1864 *Zapiski iz podpol'ia*, the classic exploration of the contradictions and depravity of modern consciousness, which is trapped in the web of its own rationality. These basic themes were given broader exposition and development in his famous novels: *Prestuplenie i nakazanie* (1866), *Idiot* (1868), *Besy* (1870), *Podrostok* (1875), and *Brat'ia Karamazovy* (1879–1880). *Besy* and *Podrostok* were written at various locales in Europe, where he traveled with his second wife Anna to avoid his creditors and find some measure of solitude.

Like Dickens, alongside his fiction Dostoevsky worked extensively in more journalistic genres. Together with his brother Mikhail he published the journals *Vremia* (1861–63), and then *Epokha* (1864–65) that failed owing mostly to the death in 1864 of his brother and of Dostoevsky's first wife Maria. He intermittently published a monthly, *Dnevnik pisatelia*, devoted to a broad range of literary, social, or political issues and including short works of fiction woven into this confessional fabric. In these publications he advocated an eclectic mix of socialism and religious nationalism known as "native soil conservatism" (*pochvennichestvo*). By the time of his death Dostoevsky was a leading spokesman of conservative ideology in Russia and was gaining renown in the West as a critic of culture. Even in his final great work, *Brat'ia Karamazovy*, however, he finds the principle of reconciliation in what can only be termed an amalgam of Orthodox piety and a Schillerian vision of the beautiful man.

MAJOR MULTICULTURAL THEMES

Dostoevsky was both a modern observer of ancient Rus and a traditionalist chronicler of Europe and Europeanized Russia, both the poet of the "Petersburg period" and the prophet of a future, universalist Russia. His statements and images of non-Russian peoples and cultures must be viewed from this simultaneously critical and utopian vantage point and read in the context of his creative works.

The prisoners in his *Zapiski iz mertvogo doma* include Poles, Jews, and Tatars, and some of the narrator's comments about these non-Russian peoples might be seen as negative and stereotypical. In the context of the work, however, he is much more interested in investigating the common humanity of all different peoples, despite their shared baseness. *Zimnie zametki o letnikh vpechatleniiakh* follows the itinerary of Nikolai Karamzin's *Pis'ma russkogo puteshestvennika* and shares Karamzin's "Russocentric" view of the West. Dostoevsky's trip around Europe is transformed into an excursion around contemporary Western ideologies, none of which address humanity's most urgent needs, but which have unfortunately taken root in Russia. In *Zapiski iz podpol'ia* these very shortcomings are concentrated in a single (Russian) man, who is both culprit and victim of the spiritual debasement engendered by post-Christian ideology. *Dnevnik pisatelia* contains many passages on various foreign cultures, but almost always in connection to Russia; for example, the issue for July/August 1876 is almost wholly devoted to thoughts and observations from his trip to Bad Ems, but most of these refer to Russians abroad and to various Russian problems arising therefrom. Dostoevsky's critique of the West is more a critique of the rootlessness of modern Russia, which has superficially adopted Western forms but possesses the spiritual potential to overcome its inner disorder and lead the rest of the world out of the materialist morass.

Of all Dostoevsky's works, only *Igrok* is set outside of Russia; here he contrasts the calculating West to the passionate nature of the Russian hero and his lover, with the protagonist exclaiming, "I would rather live my whole life as a nomad in a Kirgiz tent . . . than worship the German idol . . . the German method of accumulating wealth" (*Polnoe sobranie sochinenii*, 5:225). The prominence of Western Europe in Dostoevsky's works increased during his four-year sojourn there in 1867–71: *Idiot* contains a vituperous critique of the West (especially of the Catholic Church), expressed by the otherwise mild-mannered Prince Myshkin, and similar views were often voiced by Dostoevsky in his *Dnevnik pisatelia*. The universal mission of Russia, and the idea of Russia giving rise to an "all-man," were first voiced by the character Versilov in *Podrostok*.

In Dostoevsky's major novels a prominent place is occupied by the collision of the centrifugal cultural energy of Western Europe with Russia's more centripetal spiritualism. Moreover, *Prestuplenie i nakazanie*, *Idiot*, and *Podrostok* all take place in St. Petersburg, on the very fault line of this cultural divide. Even when the action takes place in the heartland, as in *Besy* and *Brat'ia Karamazovy*, this merely demonstrates that the battle lines have receded into the heart of Russia. There is no physical citadel of Russian culture; Dostoevsky instead identifies specific character traits and types that are capable of engendering a future Russian "man" capable of withstanding the temptation of superficial Western enlightenment and extending the Orthodox principles of gathering and reconciliation to the West. This universalist ideal was also the message of his spiritual testament, his speech at the Pushkin celebration of 1880, when he discerned in the works of Pushkin and others (even Turgenev, with whom he often feuded) traces of this future Russian all-man. However, just as his "native soil conservatism" preserved his socialist beliefs, so his messianic search for a new Russian man remained inextricably linked to the Romantic and humanitarian ideals he gathered largely from Western literary models.

SURVEY OF CRITICISM

The best overall source on Dostoevsky is the multivolume biography by Joseph Frank (1976–1995), who has also analyzed (1963) his encounter with Europe in the context of his subsequent *Zapiski iz podpol'ia*. Dostoevsky's trips to Bad Ems, undertaken for medical purposes, are examined by N.A. Natova (1971), who concludes that *Dnevnik pisatelia* and Dostoevsky's letters disprove the stereotype about his "Germanophobia." On the other hand, Malcolm V. Jones in "Dostoyevsky and Europe" (1980), based on an analysis of Dostoevsky's sojourn abroad in 1867–71, compares the writer's "fascination" with Western Europe to the pathological conditions of his characters. Jones notes the Dostoevskys' isolation from their host nations, his circular and almost random peregrinations, and the lack of works set in the European locales he visited (*Igrok* is set at a fictional resort).

Western scholarship has been severely challenged by Dostoevsky's fundamental critique of Western ideals. Ward's *Dostoyevsky's Critique of the West: The Quest for the Earthly Paradise* (1986) provides a sensitive exploration of the writer's views in connection with his theology and metaphysics. Two of Waclaw Lednicki's essays in *Russia, Poland, and the West* (1954) are worthy of note: "Europe in Dostoevsky's Ideological Novel" examines the role of ideology in the peculiar kind of novel pioneered by Dostoevsky and concludes that Dostoevsky's ideological novel is based on the belief that "theologia est ancilla rei politicae" (theology is the servant of politics). "Dostoevsky and Poland" provides an incendiary portrait of Dostoevsky's simultaneous suspicion of and debt to Polish culture.

Several books have been devoted to Dostoevsky's debt to and influence upon foreign cultures. *Dostoevskii and Britain*, edited by W.J. Leatherbarrow (1995), collects studies by Russian and Western scholars on Dostoevsky's relationship to British figures from Shakespeare to D.H. Lawrence and Iris Murdoch. In *From Earthly Paradise to Hell on Earth* (1989) Jack Weiner presents an exaggerated but detailed account of Dostoevsky's interest in and indebtedness to Spanish culture. Robert Kenneth Schulz (1969) single-mindedly examines all the depictions of Germans and Germany in Dostoevsky's works, concluding that Dostoevsky may have secretly envied the Germans' efficiency and neatness. The controversial problem of Dostoevsky's attitude toward Jews is well summarized and analyzed in David Goldstein's *Dostoyevsky and the Jews* (1981) and Felix Ingold's *Dostojewskij und das Judentum* (1981). Ingold gives a sophisticated reading of Dostoevsky's texts, basing himself on a conception of Dostoevsky's emphasis on dialogism: "Dostoevsky's word *about* the Jews should not be interpreted as a monological authorial word *against* the Jews" (161). Ingold utilizes the terminology of Mikhail Bakhtin, whose book on Dostoevsky's "polyphonic" poetics has led to a widespread reassessment of Dostoevsky's divisive words in the context of his unifying art.

SELECTIVE BIBLIOGRAPHY

Works by Dostoevsky

Zimnie zametki o letnikh vpechatleniiakh (1863). *Winter Notes on Summer Impressions.* Trans. David Patterson. Evanston, Ill.: Northwestern University Press, 1988.

Podrostok (1875). *A Raw Youth.* Trans. Constance Garnett. London: Heinemann, 1979.

Dnevnik pisatelia (1873, 1876–1877, 1880). *A Writer's Diary.* Trans. Kenneth Lantz. 2 vols. Evanston, Ill.: Northwestern University Press, 1993–1994.

Polnoe sobranie sochinenii v tridtsati tomakh. 30 vols. Leningrad: Nauka, 1972–1990.

Selective Studies of Dostoevsky

Bakhtin, M.M. *Problems of Dostoevsky's Poetics.* Ed. and trans. Caryl Emerson. Intro. Wayne C. Booth. Minneapolis: University of Minnesota Press, 1984.

Briusovani, M.I., and R.G. Gal'perina. "Zagranichnye puteshestviia F.M. Dostoevskogo 1862 i 1863 gg." In *Dostoevskii: Materialy i issledovaniia,* Vol. 8, 272–92. Leningrad: Nauka, 1988.

Frank, Joseph. *Dostoevsky.* 4 vols. Princeton: Princeton University Press, 1976–1995.

———. "Dostoevsky: The Encounter with Europe." *Russian Review* 22 (1963): 237–52.

Goldstein, David I. *Dostoïevski et les Juifs.* Paris: Gallimard, 1976. *Dostoyevsky and the Jews.* Foreword by Joseph Frank. Austin: University of Texas Press, 1981.

Grossman, L.P. "Dostoevskii i Evropa." In *Tri sovremennika: Tiutchev-Dostoevskii–Ap. Grigoriev,* 63–224. Moscow: Knigoizdatel'stvo pisatelei v Moskve, 1922.

Ingold, Felix Philipp. *Dostojewskij und das Judentum.* Frankfurt am Main: Insel Verlag, 1981.

Jones, Malcolm V. "Dostoyevsky and Europe: Travels in the Mind." *Renaissance and Modern Studies* 24 (1980): 38–57.

Leatherbarrow, W.J., ed. *Dostoevskii and Britain.* Oxford and Providence, R.I.: Berg, 1995.

Lednicki, Waclaw. *Russia, Poland, and the West: Essays in Literary and Cultural History.* London: Hutchinson, 1954.

Milosz, Czeslaw. "Dostoevsky and Western Culture." *Cross Currents* 5, no. 5 (1986): 493–505.

Natova, N.A. *F.M. Dostoevskii v Bad Emse.* Frankfurt am Main: Possev-Verlag, 1971.

Schulz, Robert Kenneth. *The Portrayal of the German in Russian Novels: Goncarov, Turgenev, Dostoevskij, Tolstoj.* Slavistische Beiträge, Bd. 42. Munich: O. Sagner, 1969.

Ward, B.K. *Dostoyevsky's Critique of the West: The Quest for the Earthly Paradise.* Waterloo, Canada: Wilfrid Laurier University Press, 1986.

Weiner, Jack. *From Earthly Paradise to Hell on Earth: Spain in the Works of Dostoevsky.* Valencia: Albatros Hispanofila, 1989.

PIERRE DRIEU LA ROCHELLE
(1893–1945)

Valeria Pompejano

BIOGRAPHY

Multiculturalism underlay Pierre Drieu La Rochelle's life and writings. It took him out of his native Paris, to which he always remained organically attached, into the rest of France, then outside of France into the countries of Europe, and, from 1932 onwards, outside of the Europe that he thought should one day be joined in federation.

Of French descent (Breton grandparents, Norman mother, and father from Cotentin), of bourgeois extraction (his grandfather was an architect and his father a lawyer), and, as far as family "culture" went, the son of parents who never loved each other and whose furious altercations he continually witnessed, Drieu at age fourteen was captivated by reading Nietzsche's *Also sprach Zarathustra*, and at age fifteen by the Anglo-Saxon culture. His first vacation in Shrewsbury, England, convinced him that he had found a second homeland. Then, visiting Oxford, he loved the combination of sports and study at the university: he himself canoed and played tennis, after which he plunged into the reading of books in the Bodleian Library. There he came into contact with writers who, together with Nietzsche, would remain his idolized masters: Carlyle, Kipling, and Whitman. In that "paradise of virility" he discovered and cultivated the Oxonian dream of a hero model that perfectly synthesized athlete and aesthete. He assumed the dandy model for himself, in exterior appearance as much as in lifestyle and thought.

At age nineteen he returned to England—to London—where he befriended Roger Frey, Virginia Woolf's future friend. English would remain Drieu's second language, and Anglo-Saxon his literature of choice. Mobilized during World War I, after serving in the eastern campaign—two months in the Dardanelles that inspired the novella *Le Voyage des Dardanelles*—he served as interpreter for the American forces at Verdun in 1918.

For the publisher Gallimard he wrote the preface to Ernest Hemingway's *A Farewell to Arms* in 1931 and translated and introduced in 1934 *The Man Who Died* by D.H. Lawrence, the English author whom he particularly loved. His predilection for England led him to write in the preface to his own *Genève ou Moscou* (1928) that "what neither Italy nor Greece had been able to do, England has done" (14), asserting that it was only when French poets began reading English that they shed their rhetoric and learned to capture ideas in movement. His readings during the last years of his life, according to his *Journal 1939–1945*, were Shakespeare, Coleridge, and Byron. By contrast, the philo-Nazi and collaborator never learned German.

The years that followed World War I saw him as a rich traveler making international friendships: Aldous Huxley and José Ortega y Gasset, among others. The winter of 1921–22 took him to North Africa and then to Venice in the company of his friend Maurice Martin du Gard. The year 1925 again found him in Italy, where, in Florence, he made the acquaintance of a Roman noblewoman. Their relationship took him to Rome in 1926—two months of accumulated impressions that found their place in a long novella in which Rome is, in many ways, the subject matter, *L'Intermède romain* (1944, published posthumously in the collection *Histoires déplaisantes*, 1963).

April–May of 1928 found him in Greece, followed by the writing of the novel *Une femme à sa fenêtre*. *Genève ou Moscou* (1928) is perhaps a first expression of his theoretic elaboration of early European impressions, which already tended toward the political reflections consolidated in *L'Europe contre les patries* (1931).

In 1929 Drieu met Victoria Ocampo, Argentina's important literary figure and an "Amazon of liberty." He collaborated with her literary review, *Sur*, as well as with the Argentinean newspaper *La Nación*, from 1931 on. After delivering successful lectures in Argentina (1932), he traveled in South America until October, then returned to France to publish *Drôle de voyage*, dedicated to Victoria Ocampo.

In Germany the young flocked to his lectures; in Berlin (1934) he met with Otto Abetz, director of the Sohlbergkreis, an association for French-German rapprochement, under whose auspices Drieu delivered a lecture that encapsulated those elements of racism on which his choice of Fascism is based. A series of inquiries for the newspaper *Marianne* took him to Hungary, Czechoslovakia, and Italy (1934). He joined the Parti Populaire Français (PPF) in 1936, after having long vacillated between Fascism and Communism; from that moment on, his travels—to Berlin, Italy, North Africa, and Franco's Spain—were for strictly political purposes.

The German occupation of France and the Vichy governments followed. The Germans took control of the *Nouvelle revue française* (in exchange for the liberation of imprisoned intellectuals). Drieu undertook studies of religions and continued writing his dramatic *Journal 1939–1945* until his death by suicide in 1945.

MAJOR MULTICULTURAL THEMES

Drieu was deeply impressed by his encounter with the Argentinean writer Jorge Luis Borges and the dreamlike enchantment of his language. The tales of this bewitching prophetic author smoldered in his mind for twelve years, to be reborn, transformed, in Drieu's *L'Homme à cheval* (1943). In *Récit secret* (1951) he narrated the turning point in his life during the trip to South America, where he came to understand that the Western world would be rent by the "Fascism-Communism dilemma" and that he himself would "fall into a political destiny" (60). Two trips in 1935 held him in thrall both politically and aesthetically: Nuremberg, where he found the parading elite troops dressed in black "superb," rivaling the artistry and emotional impact of the Russian ballet; and Moscow, which he described as being bathed in a balmy atmosphere of youthfulness and freshness.

To gain objectivity for his bildungsroman, *Gilles*, written during 1937–38, he left Paris for Deauville and then went on to Cambridge, Biarritz, Cannes, Venice, and Annecy. England, after an eighteen-year absence, appeared provincial to him compared to the spectacular offerings of Nuremberg and Moscow. The unfolding sequences in *Gilles* reveal a personal story, a reflection in many ways of the history and culture of his own country. It was precisely his travels and the impressions he received from his contacts with "other" cultures that helped him to recognize his special brand of intellectuality, as well as to establish the basis and the aims of his complex and contradictory political project. As early as 1921 he had declared in *Etat civil* that it was through contact with others that he discovered his own inner self and his own deepest satisfactions (175). Drieu's modern cosmopolitanism may be understood as a cultural attitude designed to override nationalisms that were now reduced to obsolete particularisms and that were no longer functional in constructing a new "European" political system. The evolution of his political thought moves toward the making of a new Europe, as expressed in his essays *Mesure de la France* (1922) and *L'Europe contre les patries* (1931) or in studies such as *Etat civil* (1921) and *Le Jeune Européen* (1927), but also in novels like *Blèche* (1928) and *Une femme à sa fenêtre* (1930), where he seeks to give political resonance to his personal reflections.

In the short novel *Une femme à sa fenêtre* and in the long novella *L'Intermède romain* the protagonist-narrator records the emotions and reflections aroused by the ruins of great past civilizations. The hero of *Une femme à sa fenêtre*, Boutros, a Communist convinced of the collapse of Western civilization, finds himself in Greece in a moment of forced inactivity. As he looks at the ruins, which to his eyes represent the foundation of the outmoded values of an educated bourgeoisie, he has ambivalent feelings, vacillating between nostalgia for the past and fear of giving in to its seductions. The protagonist of *L'Intermède romain* is wont to withdraw in solitude to the Palatine, the hill on which Rome was founded. While the spot is perfectly in tune with the depths of his soul, the ruins of ancient Rome below depress him: the silence of the Forums remind him of "le calme d'un cimetière" (220).

Voyage as quest is the central theme of *Drôle de voyage*. Fearing decadence in his endless search for renewal, the protagonist refuses his society founded on dead values such as matrimony, social rules, and responsibility, or their opposites, adultery, hypocrisy, and disengagement. A "stranger" in every way, he is tempted by everything and by their opposites, representing the deep drama of the bourgeois class to which he belongs.

As Felipe, the guitarist-narrator in *L'Homme à cheval*, relates fragments of the memoirs of the nineteenth-century Bolivian dictator Jaime Torrijos, the two personages come to embody Drieu's double postulations: the desire to abandon himself to writing and intellectual reflection and, at the same time, yearning for action. The latter inspired him to write the play *Le Chef* (1944), in which the duce becomes the paradigm of his ideas.

SURVEY OF CRITICISM

Frédéric Grover, in *Drieu La Rochelle* (1962), the best biography of the author, sees Drieu as being ahead of his times, painfully living out the drama of the fall of nations and his dream of a federation of European countries (88–89). Grover illustrates how the English experience and his foreign travels revealed to the author what was missing in his own homeland (42). Victoria Ocampo, in "El caso de Drieu La Rochelle" (1949), bears witness to Drieu's difficult, tormented, and contradictory choice of political camp. Giuliano Compagno's *L'identità del nemico* (1993), analyzing Drieu's intellectual activity in France in the 1930s and his collaboration with the Nazis, seeks to separate the man from his works. Dominique Desanti, in *Drieu La Rochelle: Du dandy au nazi* (1978), considers *Le Jeune Européen*, of all of Drieu's books, one of the most singular and most relevant works of the twentieth century (235).

SELECTIVE BIBLIOGRAPHY

Works by Drieu La Rochelle

Etat civil. Paris: Editions de la Nouvelle Revue Française, 1921.
Mesure de la France. Paris: Grasset, 1922.
Le Jeune Européen. Paris: Gallimard, 1927.
Genève ou Moscou. Paris: Gallimard, 1928.
Blèche. Paris: Gallimard, 1928.
Une femme à sa fenêtre. Paris: Gallimard, 1930.
L'Europe contre les patries. Paris: Gallimard, 1931.
Drôle de voyage. Paris: Gallimard, 1933.
L'Homme à cheval. Paris: Gallimard, 1943.
Le Chef. Paris: Gallimard, 1944.

Récit secret (1951). In *Journal 1939–1945*. Annexe II, 475–95. Paris: Gallimard, 1992.
L'Intermède romain. In *Histoires déplaisantes*. Paris: Gallimard, 1963.
Journal 1939–1945. Ed. Julien Hervier. Paris: Gallimard, 1992.

Selective Studies of Drieu La Rochelle

Cadwallader, Barrie. *Crisis of the European Mind. A Study of A. Malraux and Drieu La Rochelle*. Cardiff: University of Wales Press, 1981.

Compagno, Giuliano. *L'identità del nemico: Drieu La Rochelle e il pensiero della collaborazione*. Napoli: Liguori, 1993.

Desanti, Dominique. *Drieu La Rochelle: Du dandy au nazi*. Paris: Flammarion, 1978.

Field, Frank. *The French Writers and the Great War. Barbusse, Drieu La Rochelle, Bernanos*. London: Cambridge University Press, 1975.

Grover, Frédéric. *Drieu La Rochelle and the Fiction of Testimony*. Berkeley: University of California Press, 1958.

———. *Drieu La Rochelle*. Paris: Gallimard, 1962, 2nd ed., 1979.

Leal, Robert Barry. *Drieu La Rochelle*. Boston: Twayne Publishers, 1982.

Ocampo, Victoria. "El caso de Drieu La Rochelle." *Sur* 180 (October 1949): 7–27.

GEORGE ELIOT (MARY ANNE, later MARY ANN and MARIAN, EVANS)
(1819–1880)

Marina MacKay

BIOGRAPHY

One of the many paradoxes surrounding the life of this woman with a man's name is that George Eliot should have been so immersed in European culture even while she was writing so memorably of her native Warwickshire. Many of her novels—*Adam Bede* (1859), *The Mill on the Floss* (1860), *Silas Marner* (1861), *Felix Holt, The Radical* (1866), and *Middlemarch* (1871–1872)—vividly evoke the life of the English Midlands, where she was born as Mary Anne Evans, the daughter of an estate agent, and where she spent her early years before she took her place in the lively, comparatively liberated, metropolitan milieu of literary London. The move to London in 1851 was prepared for by an eight-month, solitary stay in Geneva during 1849–50, itself a bold step for a single woman of her time. She arrived in Geneva with her friends, the Coventry freethinkers Charles and Caroline Bray, via Paris, Genoa, Milan, Como, and Vevey. It was the Brays who had earlier been responsible for obtaining Evans a publishing contract for her well-received 1846 translation of David Friedrich Strauss's *Das Leben Jesu*. Although this translation had appeared without Evans's name, when she consolidated her interests in the German language and the so-called higher criticism with her translation, in 1854, of Ludwig Feuerbach's *Das Wesen des Christenthums*, she received her due credit for the achievement. Her love of Germany was, by the early 1850s, shared by her new lover, the scholar and eminent Victorian George Henry Lewes. Together the couple traveled to Weimar to undertake research for Lewes's biography of Goethe, a journey recorded by Evans in "Recollections of Weimar 1854."

Throughout the 1850s she contributed articles to the *Westminster Review*, of which the publisher John Chapman had appointed her his managing editor. This was a journal with a proud liberal heritage: it had been founded by James Mill, assisted by Jeremy Bentham, in 1824, and had subsequently been edited by John

Stuart Mill. Although Eliot was always rather an uncertain feminist, she wrote admiringly in the *Westminster Review* of France's more emancipated stance on the education of women. In "Woman in France: Madame de Sablé" (1854) she argued that French women had been the beneficiaries of a national "laxity of opinion and practice with regard to the marriage-tie," a laxity that encouraged "more intelligent sympathy with men" (11). Unable to obtain a divorce from his wife because he had hitherto condoned her adultery by bringing up her illegitimate children, Lewes lived with Evans as her husband until his death in 1878. Their long "marriage" indeed allowed Evans the access to the "common fund of ideas" that was denied most English women. Together they worked closely on their shared projects on European themes and traveled widely around the Continent ("Woman in France: Madame de Sablé," 36). Although her unconventional domestic situation brought her a notoriety at odds with the widespread popularity of her novels, she courted controversy once more when, after Lewes's death, she married John Walter Cross. She had met Cross, a longtime admirer, in 1869, on her fourth trip to Italy, and the encounter was perhaps in her mind when she described in *Middlemarch* Dorothea's meeting with Ladislaw in Rome. Evans had been married to Cross, twenty years her junior, for only six months when she died in 1880, aged sixty-one.

MAJOR MULTICULTURAL THEMES

The Positivist doctrine of the French philosopher Auguste Comte is one of the most important multicultural influences in the moral flavor of Eliot's novels. Also known as the "religion of humanity," Comtean thought privileges the examination of observable psychological and physical laws over the more abstruse, unanswerable questions of God's purposes. We find Eliot and Lewes's shared interest in this Comtean "scientific" morality woven into the fabric of Eliot's fictions, or "experiments in life," as she described them. Her translations within the new, German-led, scholarly discipline of higher criticism (the application of the techniques of historical and literary research to the Bible, hitherto considered the self-contained product of divine inspiration) provided her with the painful impetus to renounce the Evangelical Christianity of her youth. Thus the higher criticism is synonymous with progressive thinking and clearsightedness in *Middlemarch*: the limitations of the blinkered Casaubon and his quest for a "key to all mythologies" are evident in his ignorance of the advanced state of German scholarship. In addition to her translations of Feuerbach, with whom she "everywhere agree[d]," and Strauss, Eliot had begun to translate Benedict de Spinoza's *Tractatus theologico-politicus* in 1843, although this translation was abandoned at an early stage. Her completed translation of Spinoza's *Ethics* was published only a century after the translator's death. Spinoza's conception of ethical action as a trade-off between natural egoism and altruism, a human capacity for imaginative sympathy, is central to the morality of Eliot's novels. Moral growth, for her, is the recognition that our native "moral stupidity" must be replaced by the awareness that other people have "an equivalent centre of self, whence the lights and shadows must always fall with a certain difference" (*Middlemarch*, 211).

However, Eliot's multicultural interests were not exclusively moral and religious, but also aesthetic. In an essay on Heinrich Heine, whom she praised for his light tread across the "ploughed clay" of German prose, she listed Germany's achievements: "[s]he has fought the hardest fight for freedom of thought, has produced the grandest inventions, has made magnificent contributions to science, has given us some of the divinest poetry, and quite the divinest music, in the world" ("German Wit: Heinrich Heine" [1856], 102, 74–75). Further thoughts on German artistic achievements are recorded in "Germany 1858," a journal notable for, among other things, the extraordinary sensuality of Eliot's description of Rubens. About Italy's virtues she was more ambivalent, and although her first trip to Italy in 1860 inspired *Romola* (1862–1863), a historical romance based on the life of the Dominican martyr Savonarola, her "Recollections of Italy, 1860" deals harshly with papal Rome and the "perverted appliance of money and labour." Her journey around Spain in 1867 contributed to the making of *The Spanish Gypsy* (1868), a long dramatic poem that places the typical Eliot conflict of duty and desire in the context of fifteenth-century, intolerantly Roman Catholic Spain. In 1876 she published her final novel, *Daniel Deronda*, which likewise looks far beyond the British national scene through its discussion of the destiny of European Jewry.

SURVEY OF CRITICISM

Harris and Johnston's edition (1998) of Eliot's journals provides detailed and lively glosses for her accounts of her European travels, and the editors usefully juxtapose Eliot's record with passages taken from Lewes's versions of the same journeys. Bellringer's chapter (1993) on *Romola* and *Daniel Deronda*, a mixture of close reading and historical contextualizing, offers a wide-ranging introductory overview of both novels. Couch's appendix to his book (1967) on the reception of Eliot's novels in France offers a concise account of her treatment of France and the French in her journals, novels, letters, and essays. He pays particular attention to how Eliot, despite her famous tolerance, shared many of the anti-French prejudices of her contemporaries. Ashton's critical biography (1996) provides detailed accounts of all the author's sojourns abroad and similarly ranges across the broad spectrum of Eliot's writings. Her earlier chapter on Eliot in *The German Idea* (1980) provides invaluable intellectual context for Eliot's lifelong passion for German culture and places her and Lewes alongside Coleridge and Carlyle as major English interpreters of German culture. Ashton shows how Eliot's role as a translator of Spinoza (whom she counts as German), Strauss, and Feuerbach informs her role as a writer of fiction. The emphasis of the essays in Rignall's edited volume (1997) is on a primarily literary discussion of Eliot's uses of European themes and tropes in her fictional works, and Mc-

Cormack's article (1992) uses the Rome section of *Middlemarch* as a starting point for her discussion of Eliot's conception of art.

SELECTIVE BIBLIOGRAPHY

Works by Eliot

Selected Essays, Poems, and Other Writings. Ed. A.S. Byatt and Nicholas Warren. Harmondsworth: Penguin, 1990. [Contains "Woman in France: Madame de Sablé"; "The Natural History of German Life"; "German Wit: Heinrich Heine"; and extracts from *The Spanish Gypsy*.]
Romola (1862–1863). Ed. Andrew Sanders. Harmondsworth: Penguin, 1980.
Middlemarch (1871–1872). Ed. Rosemary Ashton. Harmondsworth: Penguin, 1994.
Daniel Deronda (1876). Ed. Barbara Hardy. Harmondsworth: Penguin, 1967.
The Journals of George Eliot. Ed. Margaret Harris and Judith Johnston. Cambridge: Cambridge University Press, 1998.

Selective Studies of Eliot

Ashton, Rosemary. "George Eliot." In her *The German Idea: Four English Writers and the Reception of German Thought, 1800–1860*, 147–77. Cambridge: Cambridge University Press, 1980.
———. *George Eliot: A Life*. London: Hamish Hamilton, 1996.
Bellringer, Alan W. "Europe and Beyond: *Romola, Daniel Deronda*." In his *George Eliot*, 80–100. Basingstoke: Macmillan, 1993.
Couch, John Philip. "France and George Eliot." In his *George Eliot in France*, 184–90. Chapel Hill: University of North Carolina Press, 1967.
McCormack, Kathleen. "*Middlemarch*: Dorothea's Husbands in the Vatican Museums." *Victorians Institute Journal* 20 (1992): 75–91.
Rignall, John, ed. *George Eliot and Europe*. Aldershot: Scolar Press, 1997.

ERASMUS (DESIDERIUS ERASMUS ROTTERDAMUS)

(c. 1466–1536)

Beatrice Stiglitz

BIOGRAPHY

The dominant figure of the humanist period, the intellectual arbiter of the early years of Christian unity, Erasmus was then, and is still considered today, the greatest European scholar of the sixteenth century. Of this high-profile citizen of the world little is known; his early life offers meager available information and leaves us with the necessity of conjecture. Considering his own biography, written in middle age, we can surmise that he was born in Rotterdam, or possibly in the Dutch village of Gouda. His parents were Margaret, a physician's daughter, and a priest, probably named Roger Gerard. As a result of his illegitimacy he would endure both shame and legal problems. He would later add to his name Desiderius—meaning "beloved" in Latin—and thus give himself a more desirable identity. During his childhood he grew to despise the provinciality and social rigidity of his homeland. After his parents' death during a plague, he entered the Augustinian order at Steyn, near Gouda, was ordained a priest in 1492, and, while employed as Latin secretary by the bishop of Cambrai, studied Scholastic philosophy and Greek at the University of Paris.

Beginning in 1499, he moved from country to country, tutoring, lecturing, writing, and searching out ancient manuscripts. More than fifteen hundred of his letters to some of the most prominent figures of his time survive. During his six trips to England he befriended John Colet, founder of the Saint Paul School of London; Thomas Linacre, founder of the Royal College of Physicians; William Grocyn, lecturer in Greek at the University of Oxford; and especially Thomas More, author and lord chancellor of England, who became his lifelong friend. At the accession of Henry VIII Erasmus was called back to England and taught Greek at the University of Cambridge. He continued writing, using the spiritual interpretations favored by the "ancients" to make the Scriptures pertinent to modern and moral concerns. The *Enchiridion militis Christiani* (1501) was, in this respect, a manifesto of lay mysticism asserting that "monasticism is not piety."

In Italy he earned a doctorate at the University of Turin. In Venice he befriended Aldus Manutius, the first of the crucial links to publishing enterprises that would later secure his financial and professional independence. Back in England, disillusioned with the Church and its clergy, he wrote in 1509 *Encomium moriae* (*The Praise of Folly*), a satiric exposition of the obstacles restricting the fulfillment of Christ's teaching. Sadly, but wisely, he concludes that "even a wise man must play the fool, if he wishes to beget a child."

In the Swiss city of Basel he became a friend of, and editor for, publisher Johann Froben, whose press published Erasmus's *Novum instrumentum* (1516), an annotated edition of the New Testament containing a revised text of the Vulgate faced by the Greek original. It was the first printed Greek text of the New Testament to reach the market. A landmark for scholars and reformers, it paved the way for the literary and educational classics of the Christian humanists.

While Erasmus was a councillor to the future emperor Charles V, he wrote a guide for educating princes, *Institutio principis Christiani* (1516), and *Querela pacis* (1517), condemning war and expressing concern for Europe's impending fragmentation. After the famous exchange with Luther (1524–25) about the role of human will in salvation, and the publication of his *De libero arbitrio*, Erasmus disengaged from theological disputations and moved again, this time to Freiburg im Breisgau and then to Protestant Basel, where he lived until his death in 1536.

MAJOR MULTICULTURAL THEMES

Erasmus reflects the Western world during the Northern Renaissance period. This most famous man in Europe, frail and sickly most of his life, would often pack up his luggage and be ready to go "anywhere, where the climate is healthy and kind." His writings show us the life of monasteries and busy cities in the Low Countries, France, the England of London, Oxford, and Cambridge, northern Italy, Rome, and the cities of the Rhineland and Basel. His remarkable knowledge of Greek and Latin, coupled with a most comprehensive erudition, and his graceful and elegant Ciceronian prose (whose principles he set down in *De duplici copia verborum et rerum*, 1512) helped shape the character of European style; his gift of ridicule was dreaded throughout Europe. At Louvain he showed a keen interest and participated actively in the newly founded Trilingual College, especially the endowed chairs in Latin, Greek, and Hebrew. *Ratio verae theologiae* of 1518 provided the rationale for the new theological education based on the study of languages.

Erasmus wished that the Scriptures be translated into all languages and be accessible to all men. He also soon realized that after the invention of printing books would be circulated far and wide. He himself contributed to such diverse fields as linguistics, theology, social criticism, education, the art of translation, biblical exegesis, and literature. In view of the vast influence he exerted, he may well be called "the schoolmaster of Europe." The Swiss Protestant chronicler John Kessler wrote that whatever is artistic, finished, learned, and wise is called Erasmian, and today students on exchange under international programs in Europe are called Erasmians.

Erasmus's works fascinated readers as diverse as Marot, Rabelais, Montaigne, Calvin, Guillaume Budé, Lord Acton, and Marguerite de Navarre. Diderot referred to him as the most universal scholar of his age. Modern times owe much to his exegesis and to his ideas of progress. At the height of his fame, many potentates angled for his presence: Francis I of France invited him to the royal court; the cardinals of Rome offered their extensive libraries and hospitable palaces, and even the Vatican's red hat; Henry VIII promised his favors if Erasmus would return to England; Zürich begged him to visit and receive the freedom of the city. He respectfully declined these favors and told friends that they all made him feel like "the proverbial cat in court dress."

In his life, as in his work, Erasmus transcended nationality. After his death he was claimed by Holland, Switzerland, Germany, and France as their own. Ultimately, though, he does not belong to any nation, but to the world.

SURVEY OF CRITICISM

Modern Erasmus scholarship includes Huizinga's biography (1957), in which he portrays Erasmus as a man, scholar, and true personality of his times. The last chapter, showing him at war with humanists and reformers, is particularly pertinent. English-speaking readers have Preserved Smith's 1923 study that provides an in-depth study not only of the reformer's life, ideals, and place in history, but of his genius and influence on the international community through history. In France Augustin Renaudet published several volumes on the humanist, most notably *Erasme et l'Italie* (1954) and *Etudes Erasmiennes* (1939); on the basis of letters written in the 1520s, he depicts Erasmus's relationship to the reformers and to the defenders of the old Church and outlines his position independent both of Rome and of Wittenberg. Margaret Mann Phillips (1949) writes on the great man's significance in history as the one who truly took the lead in the most important movements of his day.

SELECTIVE BIBLIOGRAPHY

Works by Erasmus

Enchiridion militis Christiani [1501]: *An English Version*. Ed. Anne M. O'Donnell, S.N.D. Oxford: Oxford University Press, 1981.
Encomium moriae (1509). [*The Praise of Folly*. Trans. Clarence H. Miller. New Haven: Yale University Press, 1979.]

Institutio principis Christiani (1516). [*The Education of a Christian Prince*. Trans. Lester K. Born. New York: Columbia University Press, 1936.]

Querela Pacis (1517). [*The Complaint of Peace*. Intro. William Hirten. New York: Scholars' Facsimiles & Reprints, 1946 (facsimile edition of a 1559 English text).]

De libero arbitrio (1524). [*Discourse on Free Will* (Erasmus-Luther). Trans. and ed. Ernst F. Winter. New York: Ungar, 1961.]

Selective Studies of Erasmus

Godin, André. *Erasme, lecteur d'Origène*. Geneva: Droz, 1982.

Huizinga, Johan. *Erasmus & the Age of Reformation*. Trans. F. Hopman. New York: Harper and Row, 1957.

Kaiser, Walter. *Praisers of Folly: Erasmus, Rabelais, Shakespeare*. Cambridge, Mass.: Harvard University Press, 1963.

Kristeller, P.O. "Erasmus from an Italian Perspective." *Renaissance Quarterly* 23 (1970): 1–14.

Phillips, Margaret Mann. *Erasmus and the Northern Renaissance*. London: English Universities Press, 1949.

Renaudet, Augustin. *Etudes Erasmiennes 1521–1529*. Paris: Droz, 1939. (Reprint by Slatkine, 1981).

———. *Erasme et l'Italie*. Paris: Droz, 1954.

Smith, Preserved. *Erasmus: A Study of His Life, Ideals and Place in History* (1923). New York: Frederick Ungar, 1962.

Spitz, Lewis W. *The Religious Renaissance of the German Humanists*. Cambridge, Mass.: Harvard University Press, 1963.

Thompson, C.R. "Erasmus and Tudor England." In *Actes du Congrès Erasme*. Amsterdam, 1971.

GUSTAVE FLAUBERT
(1821–1880)

John W. Kneller

BIOGRAPHY

Gustave Flaubert's contemporaries never thought of him as a traveler. He lived most of his life in Normandy; his stays in Paris were short. Later, however, he did travel, and his notes and correspondence show the importance of his journeys, both in his life and in his works. Born in Rouen in 1821, he was not yet ten when he wrote a historical résumé entitled "Louis XIII," which he dedicated to his mother on her birthday. He founded and contributed to a journal, *Art et progrès*, at age fourteen. Steeped in the Romantic literature of Hugo, Dumas, George Sand, Byron, and others, he later lived Romanticism, falling in unreciprocated love with an older woman, Elisa Schlésinger. That love was to inspire the *Memoires d'un fou* (1838) and *Novembre* (1842) and, later, the memorable Madame Arnoux, Frédéric's unrequited love in the second version of *L'Education sentimentale*.

From the doctors who surrounded him during his entire childhood and youth he absorbed massive surgical and anatomical knowledge as if by osmosis. His own chronic illnesses—the most serious of which manifested itself in epileptiform convulsions—aggravated his implacable hatred of the bourgeoisie and their accepted ideas and, with the early exposure to anatomy and medicine, challenged his Romantic leanings. His most grievous attack occurred at the end of January 1844, but the episode had a beneficial outcome. It prompted a family decision to take him out of law school, where he had been languishing in boredom for the previous three years. He could now devote himself to writing.

He took his first trip in 1840, to the Pyrénées, the south of France, and Corsica, taking notes on the way and later writing them up in manuscript form. Subsequently he accompanied his newly married sister and her husband through France and to Italy. He was bored and wrote to a close friend, "By all that you hold sacred . . . never travel with anyone! (*Correspondance*, 1:223)—particularly with relatives.

His next liaison was again with an older woman, this time a bluestocking minor poet, Louise Colet, who clung to him for nine years. Their liaison informed the genesis of *Madame Bovary* (1857) and led to an extended and revealing correspondence.

From an early age Flaubert dreamed of a magnum opus, a French *Faust*. He had read Gérard de Nerval's translation of Goethe's masterwork and Byron's *Cain*. In 1839 he had written a philosophical story, *Smarh*, which depicted Satan tempting the eponymous hero. Then, while visiting the Balbi Senaraga Palace in Genoa during the family honeymoon trip, he came upon Pieter Brueghel's painting *The Temptations of Saint Anthony, the Hermit*. This painting gave a fillip to the work that would preoccupy him for more than thirty years. He completed what we now know as the first version of his *La Tentation de Saint Antoine* in 1849. In September of that year he holed himself up for days with two friends and read them the manuscript. Their reaction was devastating. The manuscript was not publishable, they said, and should be thrown into the fire. He would be better advised "to pick a down-to-earth subject, one of those happenings everywhere in bourgeois life." He reluctantly took their advice, but not right away. Something had to happen in his life that would make him write the down-to-earth book that he did not want to write, *Madame Bovary*, and abandon for a long time the book that he really wanted to write, *La Tentation de Saint Antoine*. That something was the now-famous Middle East journey in the company of Maxime Du Camp, one of the friends who had heard out his reading of the manuscript.

Arriving at Alexandria in Egypt in November 1849, they went on to Cairo, where they stayed until the following February, then sailed up the Nile across Upper Egypt and went north to Esna. From there they reached the second cataract, where, according to Du Camp, the idea for *Madame Bovary* was born. After visiting the temples of Luxor and the halls of Karnak at Thebes, they went by camel, almost dying of thirst, from Keneh to Al Qusair on the Red Sea, returning to Cairo before leaving Egypt. Stopping briefly in Beirut, Lebanon, they made Jerusalem their base for the month of August 1850 and visited the holy places. In early September they were in Damascus, Syria, and then in Baalbek, Lebanon. They returned to Beirut and proceeded to the island of Rhodes, where a quarantine held them up and gave Flaubert the time to make a fair copy of his travel notes. After Rhodes they went on to Constantinople and then to Athens and the Peloponnesus. Sailing from Patras to Brindisi, they reached Naples by coach. In Rome, in Florence, and in Venice Flaubert spent most of his time in museums. He returned to France after an absence of eighteen months.

His biography after that trip blends with his works. The first of these was his most famous, *Madame Bovary*, which cost him fifty-five months of hard labor.

Because this commonplace story of adultery angered the censors of the day, Flaubert was accused of immorality, but after a lengthy trial he was acquitted. He returned to his lifelong preoccupation, *La Tentation de Saint Antoine*. After deciding not to publish in its entirety a second version of the novel, he turned to the subject of the revolt of the mercenaries against Carthage toward the end of the First Punic War (264–241 B.C.E.). Against historical background provided by Polybius and Jules Michelet, he invented a fictitious heroine, Salammbô, who gave her name to the novel. Managing to finish no more than the first chapter, the normally sedentary Flaubert found that he could not rely on book learning alone. A visit to the places where the novel's action would take place was indispensable. After an inspiring two-month visit to Carthage he returned, cleaned up his notes, and completed the novel. Following the success of *Salammbô* (1862), he returned to his second version of *L'Education sentimentale*. During the last ten years of his life, generally failing health combined with serious financial difficulties to worsen his innate despondency. He died of cerebral hemorrhage in 1880.

MAJOR MULTICULTURAL THEMES

The plethora of ancient religions that Flaubert found in Syria astounded him, yet he felt at home among the followers of those religions. The pages of the Bible came alive for him and took on new meaning in the Holy Land. After a conversation with a Coptic bishop in Cairo, he wrote, "Soon I began to ask questions concerning the Virgin, the Gospels; the Eucharist . . . all my old erudition regarding Saint Anthony came rushing back to me" (*Correspondance*, 1: 559). Indeed, the erudition gathered for *La Tentation de Saint Antoine* found a new value in the desert where the hermit had lived. It is significant that *La Tentation de Saint Antoine*, *Salammbô*, *Hérodias*, and *Le Conte oriental* all take place for the most part in the desert.

Flaubert polished but did not publish his travel notes. He never wrote a "Voyage en Orient" because he scorned travel literature as an inferior genre. The travel notes and the letters he wrote while he was abroad—all available to us today—tell us far more than any single travel publication. By taking notes he sharpened his analytical eye; by writing letters home he transformed things seen into words written. By doing both he prepared himself to write *Madame Bovary* and *Salammbô* and to rewrite *La Tentation de Saint Antoine*.

Flaubert's entire oeuvre did not simply come after his foreign travel; it came because of it. Prior to the Middle Eastern journey the only publications that he could point to were two youthful short stories. His masterpieces all came after that. The journey was therefore a major turning point in his life.

SURVEY OF CRITICISM

In English Herbert Lottman's *Flaubert: A Biography* (1989) is a well-documented study of the author's life, with separate chapters on the Middle

Eastern journey, the trip to Carthage, and the major works. Francis Steegmuller's *Flaubert in Egypt: A Sensibility on Tour* (1972) is "a narrative drawn from Gustave Flaubert's travel notes and letters." It is also highly readable, thanks to Steegmuller's excellent translation of works previously unavailable in English. Victor Brombert's *The Novels of Flaubert* (1966) contains pertinent studies of *Salammbô*, *The Temptation of Saint Anthony*, *The Legend of Saint Julien the Hospitalier*, and *Hérodias*.

In French the most usable edition of the complete works is Flaubert, *Oeuvres complètes* (1964) in two volumes, edited by Bernard Masson and with a preface by Jean Bruneau, which includes a whole section devoted to Flaubert's travel notes, with up-to-date commentaries. Bruneau's edition of *Le Conte oriental* (1973) contains the text of this previously unpublished Oriental tale, with significant remarks on the influence of Middle Eastern travel on Flaubert's subsequent works.

SELECTIVE BIBLIOGRAPHY

Works by Flaubert

Lettres de Grèce. Ed. Jacques Heuzey. Paris: Editions du Péplos, 1948.

Voyages. 2 vols. Ed. René Dumesnil. Paris: Société Les Belles Lettres, 1948.

Oeuvres complètes. 2 vols. Ed. Bernard Masson. Pref. Jean Bruneau. Paris: Aux Editions du Seuil, 1964.

Les Lettres d'Egypte de Gustave Flaubert. Ed. Antoine Youssef Naaman. Paris: A.G. Nizet, 1965.

Le "Conte oriental" de Gustave Flaubert. Ed. Jean Bruneau. Paris: Les Lettres Nouvelles, 1973.

Correspondance. 4 vols. Ed. Jean Bruneau. Editions de la Pléiade, Paris: Gallimard, 1973–1998.

Voyage en Egypte. Ed. Pierre-Marc de Biasi. Paris: Grasset, 1991.

Selective Studies of Flaubert

Addison, Claire. *Where Flaubert Lies: Chronology, Mythology, and History*. Cambridge and New York: Cambridge University Press, 1996.

Biasi, Pierre-Marc de. *Flaubert: Les secrets de l'"homme-plume."* Paris: Hachette, 1995.

Brombert, Victor. *The Novels of Flaubert*. Princeton: Princeton University Press, 1966.

Carré, J.-M. *Voyageurs et écrivains français en Egypte*. 2 vols. 2nd ed. Cairo: Institut français d'archéologie orientale du Caire, 1956.

Chessex, Jacques. *Flaubert; ou, Le désert en abîme*. Paris: Grasset, 1991.

Lottman, Herbert. *Flaubert: A Biography*. Boston: Little, Brown, 1989.

Steegmuller, Francis. *Flaubert in Egypt: A Sensibility on Tour*. Boston: Little, Brown, 1972.

E.M. FORSTER

(1879–1970)

Maria Antonietta Saracino

BIOGRAPHY

Edward Morgan Forster was born in London on 1 January 1879. His father, an architect of Welsh origin, died of consumption about a year after his son's birth. Edward was brought up by his mother, Lily, who distinguished herself for her philanthropic activities, and by a paternal great-aunt, Marianne Thornton, whose biography he published in 1956. He was educated at Tonbridge School ("Sawston" in *The Longest Journey*) and King's College, Cambridge, and although his studies obviously made an impact on him, it was his travels that would later exert a true influence on his life. In 1906 he became a tutor to Syed Masood, an Indian Muslim patriot in whose company he traveled throughout India in 1912–13. He then revisited the country in 1921–22, working as a personal secretary for the maharajah of the native state of Dewas Senior. In *A Passage to India*, which was to be his last novel and remains one of the most widely read of English novels, the two communities confronting each other in India are the English and the Indians in the early 1920s.

An honorary fellow of King's College, Cambridge, he was also a member of the so-called Bloomsbury group, along with such writers as Virginia Woolf and Lytton Strachey, the art historians Clive Bell and Roger Fry, and the economist John Maynard Keynes. He is the author of six major novels, *Where Angels Fear to Tread* (1905), *The Longest Journey* (1907), *A Room with a View* (1908), *Howard's End* (1910), *A Passage to India* (1924), and *Maurice*, completed in 1914 but published posthumously in 1971; in addition to these, he published about fourteen other works, including two biographies; two books on Alexandria, the result of a period of time he spent there as a member of the Red Cross; a film script; and, together with Eric Crozier, the libretto for Benjamin Britten's opera *Billy Budd*. He is also the author of *Aspects of the Novel* (1927), a major contribution to literary theory. In spite of much acclaim for his creative achievements, it is paradoxical that a writer who during his lifetime sternly opposed the screen adaptation of his works should in recent days have become known to the general public through five film adaptations of his novels, which achieved great success.

In 1953 Queen Elizabeth II awarded Forster the Order of Companions of Honour, and on 1 January 1969, the day of his ninetieth birthday, he received the Order of Merit. He died in Coventry in June 1970.

MAJOR MULTICULTURAL THEMES

Forster traveled extensively, to Italy, Germany, Egypt, and India, among other places, and these experiences had a permanent influence on him. He visited Greece and spent some time in Italy in 1901, but it was India that he came to know best and in which he set the last and most famous of his novels, *A Passage to India* (1924), followed in 1953 by *The Hill of Devi*, a portrait of the country. He underlines how in most cases his way of writing "does indeed depend from an encounter with the genius loci," each of his stories being somehow the outcome and the gift of a particular place (but this would appear to apply to almost all his writings). Stories "rush to my mind" as a consequence of an encounter with a specific place, Forster writes, "as if they had waited for me there" (Introduction to *Collected Short Stories*, 5)—places and peoples, one is tempted to add, with all the bulk of their history, mythology, and art forms and beliefs, complexities, and distortions. His attention was focused simultaneously on relationships set against the background of a socially hostile or multifaceted world, on friendship and love, as well as on the abuses of the outside world; in short, on the contradictions of society at large, over which he cast a critical, suspicious eye.

Rather than confining himself to the complexities of British society, Forster devoted special attention to different, often very distant, cultures, as encounters that were to take narrative shape in most of his major writing. Italy and Greece are the two European countries in which his narrative finds its own multicultural themes. Greece is the setting for "The Road from Colonus," a short story that "hung ready for me in a hollow tree not far from Olympia" (ibid., 5) and that develops Greek tragic themes with a modern twist.

Italy provided him with the settings for short stories such as "The Story of a Panic," set in Ravello, on the coast near Naples, and for his first novel, *Where Angels Fear to Tread*, "a tragicomic projection of conflicts between . . . English gentility and . . . Italian vitality" (Abrams, 1976). In *A Room with a View* Italy in general and Florence in particular act as a liberating agent, offering Forster the opportunity to give narrative voice to love in connection with different views of social acceptability.

While Forster was rather critical of princely India, he was sympathetic to the country's democratic aspirations after World War I as expressed by Gandhi's revolutionary ideas. Dealing with love and misunderstanding of cultural differences, *A Passage to India* gives narrative voice to the whole range of Forster's views on India, while the richness and subtlety of the story line help to transform the novel into one of the most distinguished achievements in contemporary literature about India.

SURVEY OF CRITICISM

K. Natwar-Singh (1969) emphasizes how deeply engaging was the relationship between the writer and this far-off land, and how strong the influence of his Indian writings proved to be even on Indian readers during their years of national self-discovery. "His writings and his personal example have made some of his readers aware, if not capable, of higher things. He cured us of some of our baser ambitions and instincts: if, to adapt a familiar saying, we can't beat them we don't want to join them either" (37). This capacity seems to be mostly due, in Malcolm Bradbury's view (1969), to the fact that Forster "is indeed, to a remarkable degree, the representative of two kinds of mind, two versions of literary possibility. . . . He stands at the beginning of the age of the new, speaking through and against it. . . . In *A Passage to India* the final nullity of romanticism is exposed in the cave, where the worlds within us and without echo together the sound of *boum*" (125–27).

For Barbara Rosecrance too, Forster's Indian writing offers the reader an extraordinary example of structural coherence. Here Forster's narrative is at its best in moving "between polarities of exclusion and inclusion, separation and unity, discord and harmony, negation and affirmation, the emptiness of the caves and the fullness of a universe animated by divine presence, the reductive vision and the inclusive vision" (242). A master in bridging opposition and apparently irreconcilable cultural differences, Forster is a master, too, in bringing together elements common to distant cultures and weaving them into a coherent dialogue.

SELECTIVE BIBLIOGRAPHY

Works by Forster

Where Angels Fear to Tread. London: Edward Arnold, 1905.
A Room with a View. London: Edward Arnold, 1908.
A Passage to India. London: Edward Arnold, 1924.
Aspects of the Novel. London: Edward Arnold, 1927.
Collected Short Stories (1947). Intro. E.M. Forster. London: Penguin, 1976.
The Prince's Tale and Other Uncollected Writings. London: Andre Deutsch, 1998.

Selective Studies of Forster

Abrams, M.H., ed. *The Norton Anthology of English Literature*. 5th ed. Vol. 2. 1986. New York: Norton, 1986.

Bradbury, Malcolm. "Two Passages to India: Forster as Victorian and Modern." In *Aspects of E.M. Forster: Essays and Recollections Written for His Ninetieth Birthday, 1st January 1969*. Ed. J. Arlott, E. Bowen, M. Bradbury, et al. London: Edward Arnold, 1969.

Craft, Robert. *"The Prince's Tale and Other Uncollected Writings* by E.M. Forster." *New York Review of Books* (May 6, 1999): 39–40.

Das, G.K. *E.M. Forster's India*. London: Macmillan, 1977.

Gardner, P., ed. *E.M. Forster: The Critical Heritage*. London: Routledge, 1973.

Lane, Christopher. "Volatile Desire: Ambivalence and Distress in Forster's Colonial Narratives." In *Writing India, 1757–1990*, 188–212. Ed. Bart Moore-Gilbert. Manchester: Manchester University Press, 1996.

Natwar-Singh, K. "Only Connect . . . : Forster and India." In *Aspects of E.M. Forster: Essays and Recollections Written for His Ninetieth Birthday, 1st January 1969*. Ed. J. Arlott, E. Bowen, M. Bradbury, et al. London: Edward Arnold, 1969.

Rosecrance, Barbara. "A Passage to India: The Dominant Voice." In *E.M. Forster: Centenary Revaluations*. Ed. J. Scherer Herz and R.K. Martin. London: Macmillan, 1982.

Scherer Herz, Judith, and Robert K. Martin, eds. *E.M. Forster: Centenary Revaluations*. London: Macmillan, 1982.

Stape, J.H., ed. *E.M. Forster: Critical Assessments*. 4 vols. London: Helm, 1998.

Woolf, Virginia. "The Art of Fiction" (1927). In *A Woman's Essays*, 121–25. London: Penguin, 1992.

MARGARET FULLER
(1810–1850)

Joan von Mehren

BIOGRAPHY

Margaret Fuller, an American woman after whom a street on the Janiculum Hill in Rome has been named, and who was known as the Marchesa Ossoli in her last year of life, was born in Cambridge, Massachusetts, the eldest of eight children. Her father, a Harvard-educated lawyer who served in the U.S. Congress, was a liberal-minded but demanding parent who submitted his daughter from the age of three to a rigorous regimen in the classics and literature. She became a constant reader, admired for her familiarity with English, French, and Italian literature, and with respect for the English Romantics, even though she later credited Jean-Jacques Rousseau with having the greatest influence on her. In her early twenties she discovered German literature. She taught herself the language, translated Goethe's *Torquato Tasso* and several of his poems, and prepared to write his biography. Believing that her education would not be complete without a visit to Italy, which she honored for having given to posterity its love of beauty and art, she agreed to help with the education of her younger siblings to help earn the cost of the voyage, but her father's sudden death when she was twenty-five left the family in financial straits and dashed her hopes for a European journey.

While Fuller was teaching in Boston and Providence, Rhode Island, she published several book reviews and some occasional poetry and collected material for her Goethe biography. Although she never finished it, she became known as Goethe's most effective American publicist. By the time *Conversations with Goethe in the Last Years of His Life* (translated from the German of Eckermann) was published in 1839, she had a solid reputation as a literary critic and interpreter of foreign literature among the New England transcendentalists, of whom Ralph Waldo Emerson was the most prominent. With him she established a lifelong relationship in which the two were often at odds. However, when the transcendentalists established their journal, *The Dial*, he backed her to become its first editor. An extension of one of her articles, a partial translation of Bettina von Arnim's *Die Günderode*, appeared as a book under the title *Correspondence of Fräulein Günderode and Bettina von Arnim* (1842).

In 1843 Fuller turned over the editorship of *The Dial* to Emerson and set out with a group of friends on a trip west. Her third book, *Summer on the Lakes, in 1843* (1844), tells of encounters with Native Americans, including several days living among Native American women on Mackinac Island—experiences that forced her to articulate her thoughts on the relations between Anglo- and Native American culture. The book impressed Horace Greeley, editor of the *New York Daily Tribune*, who employed her as his first literary editor. He also published her *Woman in the Nineteenth Century* (1845), an extension of one of her *Dial* articles in which she argued, with an array of multicultural examples of feminine achievement and subjection, for a larger role for women in the emerging society.

While Fuller was working for the *Daily Tribune*, she developed a critical theory that viewed literature as a multicultural enterprise that facilitated communication and interpretation between all ranks and types of people. Although she promoted American writers, she kept her readers informed of contemporary European literature, making a practice of translating articles from New York's foreign-language newspapers. When a collection of her essays and reviews, *Papers on Literature and Art* (1846), was published, she fiercely objected to the publisher's last-minute decision to omit her reviews of continental literature on the grounds that they were too controversial.

Marcus and Rebecca Spring, Quaker activists in the abolition movement and backers of Brook Farm and the North American Phalanx in New Jersey, both Fourieristic communities, invited Fuller to join them in a year-long trip to Europe (1846). She convinced Greeley to send her as a foreign correspondent. The route that the Springs had planned was the standard Grand Tour for Americans at the time, to England, Scotland, France, Italy, and Germany. They combined sight-seeing in Britain with investigating British efforts at ameliorating the effects of industrialization on the working poor. Among the public figures they met were Harriet Martineau, William Wordsworth, and Jane and Thomas Carlyle, but it was the Italian political exile Giuseppe Mazzini, whom Fuller met in London, who was to play the greatest role in her future.

In France she befriended the socialist George Sand, the revolutionary Polish poet-in-exile Adam Mickiewicz, and several leading French utopian socialists. The socialist Pauline Roland translated an article of Fuller's on American literature in Pierre Leroux's *La Revue indépendante*. While Fuller took French lessons and was received at court, the dominating feature of her news was the misery on the streets of Paris during an especially cold winter after a failed harvest.

Fuller and the Springs reached Italy on March 1, 1847, just as the movement for Italian independence was gathering momentum. On arrival Fuller declared that Italy was her true home. She followed the political situation closely in her dispatches and became a firm partisan of the Italian revolutionists. After two months in Rome and a tour of northern Italy, she decided to remain when the Springs departed for Germany in July. She wanted to follow the outcome of the Italian struggle, and she had fallen in love with Marchese Giovanni Ossoli, a young Italian who shared her republican sympathies and limited means. In the fall of 1848 she bore his child. As the revolutionary fervor increased throughout much of Italy and many parts of Europe, she continued to cover the story from Rome. When the city came under siege in the spring of 1849, through her connections with Mazzini and other sympathizers with the Italian cause, she was put in charge of the Fate Bene Fratelli Hospital on the Tiber Island in Rome. Believing that progress and history were on the side of her adopted country's aspirations, she fell into despair when the short-lived Roman Republic was defeated in July 1849, but she prophesied that in the next century all European countries would be democratic republics. The Ossolis fled to Florence. On their return to the United States a year later, the family was lost in a shipwreck off Long Island, New York. The manuscript of Fuller's book was never found, but her thirty-seven European dispatches, especially the twenty-four from Italy, constitute an unfolding record of the 1848 revolutionary outburst in Europe from an American point of view.

MAJOR MULTICULTURAL THEMES

Fuller's dispatches from England often read like diary entries crammed with rich and busy days of tourism and stopovers with interesting personalities. The theme that began to intrude repeatedly into her observations was her shock at the condition of the urban poor in the industrial cities, and sometimes in the countryside as well. She was particularly mindful of the situation of women. While she shared with the Springs an interest in European industrial exploitation and especially in proposals and projects to improve the living conditions of the factory workers, it was not until after she arrived in France that she began to analyze the dislocations of industrialization in terms of power and to prophesy that the wave of the future was some form of social republicanism incorporating Fourieristic doctrine.

After Fuller arrived in Italy, her constant theme was the cause of Italian independence and the establishment of a Roman republic under the leadership of Mazzini. Although she continued to believe in America's special destiny in world history, she was full of praise for the courage and self-sacrifice of the Italian people in their battle for independence and urged Americans to show equal dedication in coming to grips with slavery and runaway capitalism, the two issues she considered were challenging America's democratic future at the time.

SURVEY OF CRITICISM

Margaret Vanderhaar Allen (1979) emphasizes Fuller's skill as a political analyst during her European years, while Paula Blanchard (1978) explains that Fuller identified with the cause of the Roman revolution because she was "an Italian in spirit and . . . a republican by birth" (268). Bell Gale Chevigny (1994) combines ample source material with her biographical analysis in explaining how Fuller's Italian experience fused her hunger for deep emotional experience and heroic action with her instinctive humane qualities and developing commitment to social and political action. Joseph Jay Deiss (1969), who sketches Fuller's life as transformative from Puritan to transcendentalist to gradualist liberal in her American years, views her as a nineteenth-century Romantic radical in her last years. Analyzing Fuller's political and social positions in regard to the revolutions of 1848, Julie Ellison (1990) stresses that Fuller was always well within the tradition of Romanticism. Larry Reynolds (1988), while examining the role ideology played in Fuller's depiction of Europe in the late 1840s and the effect of her total engagement on her writing style, compares her response to that of Emerson. In the introduction to their annotated edition (1991) of Fuller's European *Tribune* dispatches, Larry Reynolds and Susan Belasco Smith give a biographical sketch of Fuller with emphasis on her European years and explain her investment in the idea of democracy as the driving force behind her involvement in the chaotic situation in Europe. Joan von Mehren's biography (1994) follows the calendar of the unfolding story of Fuller's European life, showing the interaction of her personal life with the political developments of the tumultuous last years of the 1840s.

SELECTIVE BIBLIOGRAPHY

Works by Fuller

Summer on the Lakes, in 1843 (1844). Ed. Susan Belasco Smith. Reprint. Urbana: University of Illinois Press, 1991.
Woman in the Nineteenth Century. New York: Greeley and McElrath, 1845.
"These Sad But Glorious Days": Dispatches from Europe, 1846–1850 by Margaret Fuller. Ed. Larry J. Reynolds and Susan Belasco Smith. New Haven: Yale University Press, 1991.

Selective Studies of Fuller

Allen, Margaret Vanderhaar. *The Achievement of Margaret Fuller.* University Park: Pennsylvania State University Press, 1979.
Blanchard, Paula. *Margaret Fuller: From Transcendentalism to Revolution.* New York: Dell, 1978.

Capper, Charles. *Margaret Fuller: An American Romantic Life*. Vol. 1, *The Private Years*. New York: Oxford University Press, 1992.

Chevigny, Bell Gale. *The Woman and the Myth: Margaret Fuller's Life and Writings*. Rev. ed. Boston: Northeastern University Press, 1994.

Deiss, Joseph Jay. *The Roman Years of Margaret Fuller: A Biography*. New York: Thomas Y. Crowell, 1969.

Ellison, Julie. *Delicate Subjects: Romanticism, Gender, and the Ethics of Understanding*. Ithaca: Cornell University Press, 1990.

Reynolds, Larry J. *European Revolutions and the American Literary Renaissance*. New Haven: Yale University Press, 1988.

von Mehren, Joan. *Minerva and the Muse: A Life of Margaret Fuller*. Amherst: University of Massachusetts Press, 1994.

GEORGE GEMISTOS PLETHON
(c. 1355/60–1452)

Bruce Merry

BIOGRAPHY

George Gemistos (who late in life changed his surname to Plethon, another way of connoting "full" in Greek) was born, probably in Constantinople, sometime after 1355. He died at Sparta nearly a century later. As a young man he went to Adrianopolis, at that time the Turkish capital and a center of learning, for Sultan Murat, promoting the arts, followed the model of the caliphates of Cairo and Baghdad. Here one Judaeus Elissaeus initiated Gemistos into the mysteries of Zoroaster. After his teacher was burned at the stake for heresy, Gemistos left Adrianopolis and journeyed to Cyprus, Palestine, and other places, ending up at the Byzantine fortress of Mistra, just outside Sparta, in the Peloponnese. Here he began to teach and write philosophy. Among his pupils were the future Cardinal Bessarion and George Scholarios, eventually to be Patriarch Gennadios of Constantinople. Gemistos composed historical, geographical, and astronomical works and drafted digests (summaries) of many classical writers. Theodore, despot of Morea (i.e., the Peloponnese), made him chief magistrate. In 1415 he directed letters to Emperor Manuel Paleologus and to Theodore with ideas for political, legal, and economic reform. His reputation as a legal thinker spread. Some of his contemporaries claimed that he carried legal codes in his memory. His main work on laws, *Nómon singrafí*, was apparently carried in manuscript to Constantinople by the wife of the despot of Morea and burned at Scholarios's injunction after Gemistos's death. Only a few sections of *Nómon singrafí*, quoted or copied, survive. In them Gemistos appears to merge the teaching of the Stoics with the esoteric of Zoroaster, propounding mystical theories like astrology, the influence of demons, and the migration of human souls. His doctrinal enemy, Scholarios, apparently preserved certain fragments of this peripatetic masterpiece before destroying it.

Gemistos interpreted the gods of ancient Greece as metaphysical principles.

The lesser deities were planetary powers. He recommended classical religious rites for their salutary effect on students. He deplored monks as unproductive and idle. He saw a chance in the old Platonism for a reformed Byzantium. He constructed a political science of feudalism out of a lifetime of reading and experience. He held that Aristotle was wrong in his view that heaven is composed of a fifth element. He was capable of arguing from empirical data, just like Aristotle the field scientist, and he scoffed at Aristotle's disquisition on shellfish and embryos. Gemistos noted the organizational power of bees, the foresight of ants, and the dexterity of spiders. These animals' aptitude was not based on reasoning power, but was a manifestation of the soul of the universe, which governs all things. This governing principle explains the power of the vine to wrap, the magnet to attract, and mercury to amalgamate with gold. He saw Aristotle as wrong in holding that the first substance, the sensibly perceived thing, is prior to the second substance, which is the universal. He considered that Aristotle's description of contemplation as the most pleasurable activity meant that Aristotle was akin to Epicurus, who placed the supreme good in pleasures of the soul. This juxtaposition did not please clerical readers.

Gemistos regarded it as axiomatic that the universe has no beginning in time and will have no end. The universe was created in the perfect manner, and thus nothing may be added to it. Because man is related to the gods, all humans should deem the goal of life to be whatever is good. He expounded the role of the gods, how to revere them, how to effect social organization, how to create a community, the mixing of the sexes, and the institutions of marriage, family, class behavior, and etiquette. His axioms often seem to anticipate modern trends. The human soul is always attached to a mortal body, for it is sent by the gods from one body to another, in the interests of the harmony and coherence of the universe (Woodhouse, 319). When Gemistos took something as a self-evident truth, he called it "of divine origin." All men, he argued, believe in some deity, but since their beliefs differ, that belief that has always existed must be the best. Or again, because love is a sacred act (not because it is shameful), it should be kept private, like religious devotion. Gemistos believed that land should be shared, not owned by individuals. A third of agricultural produce should go back to the laborers; soldiers should be professionals. He invented a new calendar, based on "full" months and "hollow" months of twenty-nine days. Provocatively, he addressed hymns to pagan gods. Zeus is invoked as a "king," created from nothing. The most stable government occurs under a benevolent monarch. This sentiment was not lost on Sigismondo Malatesta, hereditary prince of Rimini, who revered Gemistos and later carried his bones back to Italy.

MAJOR MULTICULTURAL THEMES

Gemistos was consulted by the Byzantine emperor in 1428 about the paramount issue of the union of the Greek and Latin churches. His advice was that delegations from the Greek and the Latin churches should have exact parity in voting power. Some years later he was among the Greek delegates to the 1438–39 Council of Ferrara-Florence, held in Italy to debate union. While he was in Italy, he worked harder to establish Plato's primacy over Aristotle than for ecclesiastical unity. His treatise *Perì ôn Aristotélis pròs Plátona diaféretai* on the differences between Aristotle and Plato is thought to be the source of Cosimo de' Medici's sponsorship of learning, the creation of the Platonic Academy at Florence, and indirectly of the great Renaissance translations by Marsilio Ficino and of Neoplatonism *tout court*. Back in the Peloponnese, Gemistos founded a school at Sparta on the model of the Eleusinian mysteries. A few chosen pupils formed a closed philosophical coterie. Some of these scholars prayed to statues of the ancient divinities. Gemistos made a tactical choice, shunning monotheism at a time when monotheism was a matter of life (and death), since all European traditions of thought and power were imbued with it. Here was the last Hellene and the first modern theorist of the philosopher-king.

No lost book in world literature fascinates posterity with quite the poignancy of Gemistos's *Nómon singrafí*. Its magnificent final paragraph dismisses the notion that human affairs cannot change by themselves, but only with the whole universe. He rejects the presumption that the reign of evil will be short and will be followed by eternal happiness. Gemistos sees his cosmic doctrine as preferable because it ascribes absolute eternity to the soul, and he makes his formidable knowledge accessible to a universal readership.

SURVEY OF CRITICISM

When John Argyropoulos, a Byzantine refugee, lectured in Florence (1454–71), his classes on Aristotle fired listeners with enthusiasm for Plato. George Holmes (1992) considers this an index of the influence of Gemistos on Renaissance scholars and surmises that Gemistos prompted a mystical devotion in colleagues (264). Cardinal Bessarion speculated whether the soul of Plato was sent down to Earth to occupy the body of Gemistos. Indeed, Gemistos and Italian humanism had a vivifying effect on each other. D.P. Walker (1972) suggests that Gemistos is one of the origins of Marsilio Ficino's Orphic magic (13). M.J.B. Allen (1990) considers Gemistos a "great Byzantine controversialist and Platonist." He suggests that Ficino was induced by his encounter with Gemistos's thought between 1463 and 1469 to include the Persian Zoroaster in the list of inventors of writing, a series of "ancient theologians" that ran from Hermes to Plato (i.e., Hermes, Orpheus, Aglaophemus, Pythagoras, Philolaus—dropped to make room for Zoroaster—and Plato). According to J. Moreau (1976), Gemistos's real reason for debunking Aristotelianism was that it led to Averrhoism and subtended Christian Scholasticism. So Gemistos elevated Platonism because he saw it as a rationalist theology, the basis for a lay science (49). C.M. Woodhouse (1986) offers an indispensable selection of translations from Gemistos's works.

SELECTIVE BIBLIOGRAPHY

Works by Gemistos

Pléthon: Traité des Lois. Trans. Pierre-Augustin Pellissier. Paris: Firmin Didot, 1858.
Nómon singrafí. Ed. Charles Alexandre. Amsterdam: A.M. Hakkart, 1966.
Perì ôn Aristotélis pròs Plátona diaféretai. Ed. Bernadette Lagarde. *Byzantion* 43 (1973): 312–43.

Selective Studies of Gemistos

Allen, Michael J.B. "Ficino, Hermes, and the Corpus Hermeticum." In *New Perspectives on Renaissance Thought: Essays in the History of Science, Education, and Philosophy in Memory of Charles B. Schmitt*, 38–47. Ed. John Henry and Sarah Hutton. London: Duckworth, 1990.

Holmes, George. *The Florentine Enlightenment, 1400–1450.* Oxford: Clarendon Press, 1992.

Kretzmann, Norman, Anthony Kenny, and Jan Pinborg, eds. *The Cambridge History of Later Medieval Philosophy: From the Rediscovery of Aristotle to the Disintegration of Scholasticism, 1100–1600.* Cambridge: Cambridge University Press, 1982.

Moreau, Joseph. "Concordance d'Aristote et de Platon." In *Platon et Aristote à la Renaissance: XVIe Colloque International de Tours.* Paris: Librairie Philosophique, J. Vrin, 1976.

Walker, Daniel Pickering. *The Ancient Theology: Studies in Christian Platonism from the Fifteenth to the Eighteenth Century.* London: Duckworth, 1972.

Woodhouse, Christopher Montague. *George Gemistos Plethon: The Last of the Hellenes.* Oxford: Clarendon Press, 1986.

ANDRÉ GIDE
(1869–1951)

Jeanine Parisier Plottel

BIOGRAPHY

André Paul-Guillaume Gide was born in Paris, the only child of Paul Gide and Juliette Rondeaux. Paul stemmed from a long lineage of prominent Huguenot magistrates; Juliette's family was originally Catholic and had converted to Protestantism. By the time of André's birth some of its members had reverted to Catholicism, but Juliette herself remained a strict Protestant all her life. André's father, who held the prestigious chair of Roman law at the University of Paris, died just before his son's eleventh birthday. While his widow tried hard to improve herself and her child, her rigid standards and her desire for total control led to constant conflicts between them. André came to hate his lonely and constrained childhood spent indoors, often sick in bed. Except for some cousins, he had few friends, and most of his schooling took place at home.

His first work, *Les Cahiers d'André Walter*, was published anonymously and at his own expense in 1891. His friend Paul Valéry summarized the melancholic tones of this book as follows: "Art, love, faith, the poor self flounders among these huge specters that cause reality to grow pale. From your book soars the following: one must create, one must love, one must believe" (Gide and Valéry, *Correspondance*, 68, my translation). During this what may be called symbolist period of Gide's life, he published artificial and stilted works, *Le Traité du Narcisse* (1891), and *Le Voyage d'Urien* and *La Tentative amoureuse* (both 1893).

His many trips to Africa, beginning in 1893, were to play a capital role in his life. He visited North Africa also on his honeymoon in 1896, having married his first cousin Madeleine Rondeaux after his mother's death in 1895. By 1931–32 he was writing favorably about Communism and the Soviet Union. Together with other French writers he participated in the struggle against Nazism, and in 1933 he presided at a public meeting of the Association des écrivains et artistes

révolutionnaires convened to protest Hitler's coming to power. He himself refused to join this French section of a Soviet organization. Like Karl Marx, he
was not a Marxist. He considered the communist ideal to be a contemporary
version of life according to the Gospels.

He accepted the Soviet government's invitation to visit Russia in 1936. Unlike
many zealots whose fanaticism led them to bear false testimony about what was
known about the uses and abuses of Stalinist totalitarianism, Gide described
what he learned about political correctness, Leninist agitprop, social and moral
conformity, and the Stalinist cult. His 1936 books *Retour de l'U.R.S.S.* and
Retouches à mon Retour de l'U.R.S.S. were almost unanimously assailed by the
French left wing. Today they are counted among the most prescient and accurate
analyses of a failed, chimerical governing system. The elderly Gide retreated to
private spheres, yet in May 1937 he protested the arrest of Trotskyist militants
in Barcelona.

During World War II he refused to write for the *Nouvelle revue française*
and other journals financed by dubious sources and used as Vichy or Nazi
propaganda vehicles. He spent the years from 1942 to 1945 in Tunisia and
Algeria and supported General Charles de Gaulle, who invited him for lunch in
Algiers. He received a doctorate *honoris causa* from Oxford as well as the Nobel
Prize in Literature in 1947. After a short illness he died in Paris in 1951.

MAJOR MULTICULTURAL THEMES

Gide felt that the conflicting faiths and the different geographical regions of
his ancestors constituted a contradictory multicultural issue: "Nothing could be
more different than these two families," he wrote in his autobiography, "nothing
more different than the two provinces of France which combine their contradictory influences in me." These were resolved when he chose a life path
devoted to the pursuit of art: ". . . artists are, I imagine, produced when crossbreeding encourages the simultaneous growth and consequent neutralisation of
opposing elements" (Gide, *Si le Grain ne meurt*, trans. Bussy, 15).

The discovery of his own voice and the freedom to follow his own path and
write according to his own way are legacies the African continent bestowed
upon him. Consultation of the Bible for sustenance and advice had been a part
of young Gide's daily ritual. When he sailed from Marseille to North Africa for
the first time in 1893, he left behind the Holy Book. This act, which was meant
to wean him from the support of the Scriptures that had justified his strict
Protestant upbringing, symbolized his determination to unbind himself and to
live according to his nature (*Si le Grain ne meurt*, 253–57). Thrust into a strange
"Arabian Nights" world, he shed the rules of morality in favor of physical and
spiritual liberation. His lyrical gospel *Les Nourritures terrestres* (1897) and the
novel *L'Immoraliste* (1902) articulate how experience on the African continent
led to a transformation of his vision of life and his liberation from stifling social
and moral bonds. His already-cited autobiography, *Si le Grain ne meurt*, his

Corydon (1924), a defense of homosexuality, and his *Journal* covering the years 1889–1949 confirm that the easy encounters made possible by North African tolerance of adolescent sensuality allowed him to discover and satisfy his impulses.

His return to North Africa in 1895, when he met Oscar Wilde and Alfred Douglas at Blida, Algeria, strengthened his curiosity for Arab theater, music and mime, the Caracous, and especially the nomadic Ouled Naïl tribes who often figured in semiprofane, semireligious ceremonies (*Si le Grain ne meurt*, 275). Another voyage to Africa in 1923, to the Congo and Equatorial Africa, accounted for a change of intellectual pursuits. He shifted from moral and ethical questions to consider social issues. His accounts of the journey, *Voyage au Congo* (1927) and *Le Retour du Tchad* (1928), are dedicated to the memory of Joseph Conrad and his *Heart of Darkness*. Gide's journey retraced the elder writer's 1889 travels on the *Roi des Belges* to the center of the continent, the "blank space then representing the unsolved mystery of the continent" (Conrad, *A Personal Record*, 13).

Traveling through parts of countries today designated as Nigeria, Cameroon, Equatorial Guinea, Gabon, Republic of the Congo, Zaire, Central African Republic, and Chad, Gide made notations about rain and mountain forests, trees, flowers, bird and animal life—like Vladimir Nabokov, he was an expert on butterflies—lakes, and rivers; modes of transportation; and accounts of his readings—La Fontaine, Molière's *Le Misanthrope*, Robert Louis Stevenson's *The Master of Ballantrae*. Above all he involved himself in the lives and problems of the Africans he met, becoming more and more indignant as he learned about the concessionaire companies' exploitation of Africa and Africans and the petty tyranny of certain native chieftains over their powerless employees and dependents. He also maintained that, contrary to what was often assumed, most French colonial government authorities sought to curb these abuses and protect the powerless and often-destitute population.

Gide had long felt a special affinity for Russian masters—Chekhov, Dostoevsky, Tolstoy, Turgenev—and had stimulated French interest in their writings. It was natural, then, that he set foot on Russian soil with great enthusiasm, which was reciprocated by his hosts. As his plane landed in Moscow on June 18, 1936, his friend Maksim Gorky, the leader of Soviet writers, died suddenly, of natural or unnatural causes. It was a measure of Gide's renown that, along with Stalin and the well-known novelist and short story writer Aleksey Tolstoi, Gide was called upon to give a funeral oration at the Red Square memorial service.

SURVEY OF CRITICISM

The best biography of Gide in English remains the admirable *Portrait of André Gide* by Justin O'Brien (1953). A recent general biography by Pierre Lepape, *André Gide: Le Messager* (1997), gives an excellent synthesis of Gide's life. The early years and the North African journey have been closely examined in Jean Delay's *La Jeunesse d'André Gide (1869–1893)* (1956–1957). Claude Martin's *La Maturité d'André Gide* (1977) provides a remarkable sequel. Auguste Anglès's awesome *André Gide et le premier groupe de la Nouvelle Revue Française* (1978–1986) is an important historical examination of the intellectual movement and of Gide's role in promoting pluralism and diversity in French intellectual life.

SELECTIVE BIBLIOGRAPHY

Works by Gide

Si le Grain ne meurt (1920–1921). [*If It Die: An Autobiography*. Trans. Dorothy Bussy. New York: Random House, 1935.]

Voyage au Congo (1927). [*Travels in the Congo*. New York and London: Alfred A. Knopf, 1929–1930.]

Le Retour du Tchad (1928). In *Journal 1939–1949: Souvenirs*. Paris: Gallimard, Bibliothèque de la Pléiade, 1955.

Retour de l'U.R.S.S. [1936] *suivi de Retouches à mon retour de l'U.R.S.S.* [1937]. Paris: Gallimard, 1950. [*Return from the U.S.S.R.* New York: Alfred A. Knopf, 1937; London: Secker & Warburg, 1937. *Afterthoughts on the U.S.S.R.* New York: Dial Press, 1938; London: Secker & Warburg, 1938.]

Journal 1939–1949. Souvenirs. Paris: Gallimard, Bibliothèque de la Pléiade, 1955.

Gide, André, and Paul Valéry. *Correspondance, 1890–1942*. Paris: Gallimard, 1955.

Selective Studies of Gide

Anglès, Auguste. *André Gide et le premier groupe de la Nouvelle Revue Française*. 3 vols. Paris: Gallimard, 1978–1986.

Conrad, Joseph. *A Personal Record*. London: J.M. Dent & Sons, 1955.

Delay, Jean. *La Jeunesse d'André Gide*. 2 vols. Paris: Gallimard, 1956–1957.

Lepape, Pierre. *André Gide: Le Messager*. Paris: Seuil, 1997.

Martin, Claude. *La Maturité d'André Gide*. Paris: Klincksieck, 1977.

O'Brien, Justin. *Portrait of André Gide*. New York: Alfred A. Knopf, 1953.

JOHANN WOLFGANG VON GOETHE
(1749–1832)

Elizabeth Powers

BIOGRAPHY

Johann Wolfgang von Goethe, Germany's most famous poet, was born in Frankfurt, the son of Catharina Elisabeth (née Textor) and Johann Caspar, a cultured and prosperous gentleman who devoted himself to the education of his son and daughter. Under his watchful eye they received instruction at home from a variety of tutors. The young Goethe displayed a prodigious memory, particularly for foreign languages, his first being Italian, a reflection of his father's enthusiasms: in 1739 Johann Caspar had traveled to Italy and had penned an account of that journey. Italian was followed by Latin, French, English, and Greek; Goethe even learned Hebrew in order to read the Old Testament. There are indications that he began writing an epistolary novel in six languages at the age of twelve.

His voracious reading was nurtured by his father's enormous library. The letters he wrote home from Leipzig, where he went in 1766 to study law, are littered with references to his reading and show the importance of foreign literatures in his self-conception and in his artistic development. His poetry begins to resonate with literary and linguistic influences that he absorbed and continued to assimilate in his long and productive career.

Already in Leipzig Goethe was affected by the rebellion against the dominant French standards of poetic decorum and taste. His turn away from artificiality and toward naturalness in poetry was influenced by his encounter with Johann Gottfried von Herder in Strassburg, where he had gone in 1770 to continue his legal studies. He absorbed Herder's ideas concerning authentic poetry, which sprang from the *Volk*, and was introduced by him to the Koran, which, like the Bible, in which Goethe was well versed, became a rich store of poetic images. In 1773 he began a drama on the life of Muhammad that became the substance of the hymn "Mahomets Gesang."

In 1775 he went to Weimar, escaping the Europe-wide notoriety of his novel *Die Leiden des jungen Werthers* (1774). He remained there the rest of his life. The ducal court of his patron, Karl August, offered a lively cultural life, yet his literary output shrank. Charlotte von Stein, wife of the duke's chief equerry, replaced Herder as the guiding influence in Goethe's life. That relationship and his service at the Weimar court in several administrative posts tamed his Sturm und Drang attitudes. He underwent a deep personal reorientation that led him to seek aesthetic control and self-mastery.

In September 1786 he made another escape, to Italy, where he remained until April 1788, primarily in Rome. There he completed the drama *Egmont* and two dramas that are the first signs of "classicism," *Tasso* and *Iphigenia auf Tauris*. On his return to Weimar he wrote *Römische Elegien* (first published in 1795), but for a while it seemed that he would devote his life to science, including the attempt to refute Newton's theory of light. His friendship with Friedrich von Schiller, from 1794 until the latter's death in 1805, led Goethe back to his literary calling.

The period of his late work commenced in 1811 with the writing of his autobiography, *Dichtung und Wahrheit*. He moved even more decisively away from the individualism of *Werther*. High points of these years include *West-östlicher Divan* (1819), the novel *Wilhelm Meisters Wanderjahre* (1821), and "Die Trilogie der Leidenschaft" (1827)—each reflecting an acceptance of the limits on human understanding and action. The second part of his *Faust*, the final scenes of which were written in the year of his death, displays—like his childhood precocity with language—his astonishing ability to assimilate an encyclopedic range of literary forms.

MAJOR MULTICULTURAL THEMES

From the early 1790s until the end of his life, Goethe's diaries, letters, and records of conversations show his wide reading in Indian, Arabic, Chinese, and Persian literature and in the burgeoning European scholarship on non-European cultures. He wrote two ballads on Indian subjects: "Der Gott und die Bajadere" (1797) and "Die Paria" (1824); and he contemplated a stage adaptation of the *Shakuntala* by the fifth-century Indian poet Kalidasa, which, when it appeared in William Jones's English translation in 1789, created a sensation in Europe comparable to the earlier enthusiasm for Ossian. His idea for the "Vorspiel auf dem Theater" in *Faust* derived from a similar "Vorspiel" in that Indian drama.

His turn toward multicultural themes must be seen within the context of his late work, from 1811. Informing this work is the conviction that the highest creations of the human spirit offer a reflection of the superposing order that stands behind the multifarious appearance of things. In this connection a sense of spiritual affinities between cultures, whatever their outward differences, which had pervaded Herder's writings, underlay what Goethe now came to refer to as "Weltliteratur." The discoveries of family affinities among Indo-European languages, first posited by Sir William Jones in 1786 and explored by Friedrich von Schlegel in his 1808 treatise "Über die Sprache und Weisheit der Indier," may also have affected these conceptions.

Thus Italy, as depicted in *Italienische Reise* (1816), is not a repository of disconnected phenomena or an occasion for personal ecstasy, but is revealed as a great organism, the product of immutable laws. Weaving personal impressions, description, and commentaries on nature, man, and the arts, *Italienische Reise* also describes its author's genesis as an artist and the spiritual laws that guided that development.

In 1814 Goethe became acquainted with the work of the Persian lyric poet Hafiz (fl. fourteenth century) in the translation of the Austrian Oriental scholar Josef von Hammer. Hafiz's surviving poetry was collected in what is called a *Divan* (*divan* being a Persian word meaning "assembly," thus "assemblage," here a collection of songs). Inspired by this poetic encounter, Goethe wrote 40 poems of his own *Divan* in 1814, and by the end of the next year 140 more. The *West-östlicher Divan* (1819) represents a dialogue between poets that crosses cultural boundaries while affirming the values of both. The first two lines of Goethe's poem "Talismane" can be quoted in this connection: "Gottes ist der Orient! / Gottes ist der Okzident!" ("God is of the East possessed, God is ruler of the West"; E.A. Bowring translation, 390). The *Divan* was accompanied by an appendix that provided a sketch of Western conceptions of the East since Marco Polo and discussed Goethe's vast Oriental source reading, from Jean Chardin's *Voyage en Perse* in the original 1686 French edition to Sir John Malcolm's *The History of Persia from the Most Early Period to the Present Time* (published in London, 1815).

An 1821 essay, "Indische und chinesische Dichtung," revealing Goethe's decades-long admiration for the *Shakuntala*, stresses that it was not local color that attracted him to the literature and cultures of the East but rather the eternal presence of the human element. This essay also displays his wide reading of Chinese works in European translations, including Latin. "Chinesisch-deutsche Jahres- und Tageszeiten" (1830), a cycle of fourteen short lyric poems, like the *Divan*, seems to express in its title the spiritual affinities between cultures. The final poem of the cycle manages to sound Confucian while containing an aphoristic formulation of the ethics of renunciation that characterizes Goethe's late work, namely, that of renouncing the longing for infinitude and instead transforming that longing into useful activity in the finite world.

SURVEY OF CRITICISM

On its publication in 1816, *Italienische Reise* was criticized for its seeming lack of interest in Italy itself, particularly for the Christian or even picturesque attractions that were at that date of such consuming interest to Romantic travelers. Nicholas Boyle (1992) has noted that Goethe lived there in a German world, in its language, personalities, and interests. As Trevelyan (1942) has pointed out, it was as the heir of Winckelmann that Goethe experienced Rome, which was considered the repository of the legacy of ancient Greece. An idealized Hellas, a civilization of ideal creatures raised above the accidents of time and space, permeates *Italienische Reise*. Goethe's discovery of himself as an artist—which is revealed at the end of this work—was portrayed as guided by the eternal values that ancient Hellas symbolized. As Erich Jenisch (1932) has noted (91), Goethe glimpsed in the works of the ancients a gently exalted human nature, one nearing superhuman perfection without ever disturbing humanness of form.

In the Indian literature Goethe admired he was able to recognize sentiments and conditions that were thoroughly human, rendered more profound—as in Kalidasa's *Meghaduta*—by the semigodly nature of the hero. Goethe missed such balance in Indian plastic art. Despite his admiration for the *Shakuntala*, as Raymond Schwab (1984) has written, "Goethe was never able to put up with many-headed, many-armed gods" (60). Though Katharina Mommsen (1972) finds that the last book of the *Divan*, the "Book of Paradise," is an homage to the Koran (161), one of the *Divan*'s translators has written that Goethe does not "portray either the Orient or the Occident . . . but *mankind* which, by intuition, he uncovers in the one as well as in the other" (quoted in Schwab, with ellipses, 365). According to Christine Wagner-Dittmar (1971), the changes of season and the experience of nature that are the subject of Goethe's "Chinese" poems are not specifically Chinese, nor are the elements of Chinese landscape they contain (221–22).

SELECTIVE BIBLIOGRAPHY

Works by Goethe

Unless otherwise noted, references to Goethe's works are to the 14-volume Hamburg edition of the *Werke* (Munich: C.H. Beck, 1988).

Italienische Reise (1816). Vol. 11, 9–349.

West-östlicher Divan (1819). Vol. 2, 7–270.

"Indische und chinesische Dichtung" (1821). Vol. 12, 301–3.

"Chinesisches" (trans. of "Neun Gesänge über die Bilder hundert schöne Frauen" [1827]).
    In *Werke*, Weimar: H. Böhlau, 1887–1919, Vol. 41, 272–75; vol. 42, 230–35.

"Chinesisch-deutsche Jahres- und Tageszeiten" (1830). Vol. 1, 387–90.

Selective Studies of Goethe

Bowring, E.A. "Talismane." In *The Poems of Goethe Translated in the Original Metres*, 390. New York: Thomas Y. Crowell & Co., 1882.

Boyle, Nicholas. *Goethe: The Poet and the Age*. Vol. 1, *The Poetry of Desire (1749– 1790)*. Oxford: Oxford University Press, 1992.

Jenisch, Erich. "Goethe and the Far East." In *Goethe: A Symposium*, 90–104. Ed. Dagobert D. Runes. New York: Roerich Museum Press, 1932.

Klenze, Camillo von. "A Renaissance Vision: Goethe's Italy." In Camillo von Klenze, *From Goethe to Hauptmann: Studies in a Changing Culture* (1926), 3–64. Reprint. New York: Biblo & Tannen, 1966.

Lemmel, Monika. "Wechselwirkungen zwischen Goethes 'West-östlicher Divan' und der 'Italienische Reise.' " *Jahrbuch der deutschen Schillergesellschaft* 33 (1989): 281–98.

Mommsen, Katharina. "Die Bedeutung des Korans für Goethe: Vom Götz bis zum *Buch des Paradieses*." In *Goethe und die Tradition*, 138–62. Ed. Hans Reiss. Frankfurt: Athenäum, 1972.

Schwab, Raymond. *The Oriental Renaissance: Europe's Rediscovery of India and the East, 1680–1880*. New York: Columbia University Press, 1984.

Strich, Fritz. *Goethe und die Weltliteratur*, 2nd ed. Bern: Francke, 1957.

Trevelyan, Humphrey. *Goethe and the Greeks*. Cambridge: Cambridge University Press, 1942.

Wagner-Dittmar, Christine. "Goethe und die chinesische Literatur." In *Studien zu Goethes Alterswerken*, 122–228. Ed. Erich Trunz. Frankfurt: Athenäum, 1971.

NIKOLAI VASILIEVICH GOGOL
(1809–1852)

Robert Bird

BIOGRAPHY

Born and raised in an obscure corner of the Ukraine, Nikolai Gogol owed his masterpieces to the cosmopolitan centers of St. Petersburg and Rome, to which he made successive escapes in a life haunted by hardship and paranoia. Paradoxically, it was in Petersburg that he penned his early stories from Ukrainian life, and in Rome that he turned his attention to Petersburg and the generic Russia of his novel *Mertvye dushi*. He was educated at the gymnasium of Nezhin (1821–28); all of his education and writings were in Russian, except for one epigram and one letter in Ukrainian. Immediately after completing his course of study he set off for Petersburg in order to become a writer. In 1828 he published his first works: a poem, "Italiia," and a narrative poem entitled "Gants Kiukhel'garten," which was so unsuccessful that he bought up and burned all the copies he could find. After taking a short trip to Germany he turned his background to his advantage by exploiting the Romantic fashion for depictions of the "folky" Ukraine, together with its native manners and belief in supernatural forces. His first collection of short stories, *Vechera na khutore bliz Dikan'ki* (two volumes, 1831–1832), attracted the attention of the Petersburg literary elite, especially Pushkin, whose friendship and patronage were especially important for Gogol. He had an abortive stint as lecturer in history at the university (1834–35), publishing several historical articles and planning a history of the Ukraine. The disastrous outcome of this venture confirmed his aspiration to become a professional writer of fiction.

In 1835 he followed his debut with a "continuation" entitled *Mirgorod* (the region where he was born), which included more mature works such as "Taras Bul'ba" (a rousing depiction of Cossack life) and "Vii." In 1835 he also published a volume of essays, *Arabeski*, which included articles on Ukrainian culture. Thereafter he turned increasingly to Petersburg for inspiration, creating a series of famous tales that contributed to the myth of Petersburg as a phantom and vengeful city ("Nevskii Prospekt," "Nos," "Zapiski sumasshedshego," and others) and the classic drama *Revizor* (1836). In July 1836 he moved to Italy, where he remained (with two short periods of eight months each in Russia) for thirteen years. In Rome he established a close friendship with the expatriate painter Aleksandr Ivanov. Here he wrote his most famous Petersburg tale, "Shinel'," and the first part of a projected trilogy of novels entitled *Mertvye dushi* (1842). The last ten years of his life were filled with frustration and alienation. His abandonment of Rome for German sanatoria and then Naples can be taken to symbolize a turn away from the aesthetic realm in general. He burned the completed second part of *Mertvye dushi* in 1845, and his impassioned treatise *Vybrannye mesta iz perepiski s druz'iami* provoked a backlash against his perceived apostasy from the cause of social critique. In January 1848 Gogol continued his search for spiritual solace by undertaking a pilgrimage to the Holy Land, after which he began work on a new version of the second part of *Mertvye dushi*, which, however, he burned shortly before his death in 1852.

MAJOR MULTICULTURAL THEMES

Gogol's first works, in a poetic mode he soon abandoned, were both devoted to idealized foreign lands (Germany and Italy), betraying the influence of Romantic sources. His first success can be partly attributed to his application of Romantic schemes to the one foreign culture he knew well, that of the Ukraine, which in Russian writing of the time had begun to play a role analogous to that of Walter Scott's Scotland in Britain. In *Vechera na khutore bliz Dikan'ki* he mixed genuine folkloric and ethnographic themes with free fantasy and humor. Subsequent investigation has shown that much of the local color of these tales was either derived from inquiries made of his mother or simply the fruit of his imagination, but his narrative skill lent this potpourri the cumulative impression of verisimilitude. The stories of *Mirgorod* provide at once a more authentic and a more socially engaged treatment of Ukrainian life, although Gogol's usual love for the hyperbolic and grotesque is in clear evidence: for instance, "Starosvetskie pomeshchiki" betrays a clear mythological subtext, while "Taras Bul'ba" is notoriously resistant to any attempts to specify the time and place of its action. On the other hand, the horror story "Vii" has been shown to be dependent on non-Slavic folklore. "Taras Bul'ba" is also notable insofar as it depicts an inherently multicultural milieu, that of the Cossacks, and among its characters are a Polish woman and a Tatar maid (although the eponymous hero is an irrepressible chauvinist). In the early Gogol, however, national types often betray their origin as masks in the Ukrainian folk comedy that influenced him so heavily.

Most of his subsequent artistic works were set in Russia, mainly in the capital, St. Petersburg, but he did much to initiate a rich tradition of contemplations on the cultural and metaphysical identity of St. Petersburg, and by extension of

imperial Russia, caught between a lost spiritual heritage and imperfectly assimilated Western civilization. When the hero of "Zapiski sumasshedshego" identifies himself as the king of Spain, this might be seen as a logical extension of
Russia's phantasmagoric Europeanization. Typical of Gogol's ambivalent attitude toward St. Petersburg was his depiction of Germans, representative of all
Europeans. In "Nevskii Prospekt" the Germans combine calculating logic with
tight morals and a somewhat vulgar preoccupation with the petty side of life;
the fact that their surnames are Schiller and Hoffmann underscores their shortcomings, but also indicates Gogol's indebtedness to German models. This ambivalent attitude, combining respect for Europe's cultural achievements with
disgust at its mercantile and bourgeois vulgarity, was adopted also by Dostoevsky, Turgenev, Tolstoy, and many others. Much of Gogol's historical or cultural
interest in other countries was dictated by his view of the contemporary situation
in Russia. In his article "al-Mamun," for example, he really appears to be commenting on Peter the Great when he writes of the Islamic leader: "He neglected
the great truth that culture is derived from the nation itself, that superficial
enlightenment should be borrowed only to the degree that it can aid one's own
development, but that the nation should develop from its own national element"
(*Sobranie sochinenii*, 7:334). In "Al'fred," an unfinished drama of 1835, he
apparently intended to provide an Aesopic commentary on Russian life by depicting the rule of the Anglo-Saxon king Alfred the Great.

After his Ukrainian tales he became most enamored of the culture of Italy, a
love that is most brilliantly reflected in his sketch "Rim," in which he contrasts
soulless and superficial Paris (comparable to his image of St. Petersburg) with
the colorful and profound beauty of Rome. His idealization of Italy as an aesthetic paradise, home of beautiful people, reinforced and reinvigorated a strong
tradition in Russian culture, one that would be expanded especially by Turgenev
and the Symbolists. Lastly, the hero of the only partially surviving second part
of *Mertvye dushi* is a Russified Greek named Konstantin Kostanzhoglo, who
personifies a kind of Orthodox industriousness that Gogol preached in *Vybrannye mesta iz perepiski s druz'iami*.

SURVEY OF CRITICISM

Simon Karlinsky's book-length essay (1976) provides eloquent and insightful
discussion of Gogol's contacts with non-Russian cultures. Karlinsky argues for
the influence of Ukrainian folk theater (following Gippius) and opera in the
creation of the narrative mode of his early stories, and for the overwhelming
impression made on Gogol by Rome. Also of note is Vasily Gippius's book
(1924), which Karlinsky calls "the single most critical study of Gogol." Gippius
details the three utopias or "idylls" present in Gogol's works: the idealized
Germany of "Gants Kiukhel'garten," the pristine Ukraine of "Starosvetskie pomeshchiki," and the hierarchic and theocratic Russia of *Vybrannye mesta iz
perepiski s druz'iami*. He concludes that these utopias were the only places

Gogol really felt at home. Gippius, like Iu. Barabash (1999), stresses that even in his ethnographical and historical studies, Gogol was ever a poet, fashioning the facts to illustrate a primarily artistic vision. Kornblatt (1992) analyzes the image of the Cossack in Gogol's early prose.

The literary memoirs of Pavel Annenkov (1968) contain a vivid portrait of Gogol and Aleksandr Ivanov in Rome. Louis Pedrotti (1971) has analyzed Gogol's use of architectural images in "Rome," showing that the hero's love for his Annunziata parallels Gogol's love for the city, which in an 1838 letter he had called "the homeland of my soul, where my soul lived before I was born into this world." Lucy Vogel (1967) examines the role of "Rome" in Gogol's turn from an aesthetically based view of reality to an ethical view, after which "the pagan symbol of beauty must make room for Christian morality in accordance with eternal laws. Gogol's message of Rome must make room for Gogol's personal message of Christ to the world" (157). M.P. Alekseev's 1936 article on "Al'fred" demonstrates how this unfinished drama was intended as a commentary on Russian life.

SELECTIVE BIBLIOGRAPHY

Works by Gogol

The Complete Tales. Trans. Constance Garnett. Ed. Leonard J. Kent. 2 vols. Chicago: University of Chicago Press, 1985.
Sobranie sochinenii v deviati tomakh. 9 vols. Moscow: Russkaia kniga, 1994.

Selective Studies of Gogol

Alekseev, M.P. "Drama Gogolia iz anglo-saksonskoi istorii." In *N.V. Gogol': Materialy i issledovaniia*, vol. 2, 242–85. Ed. V. Gippius. Moscow and Leningrad: AN SSSR, 1936.
Annenkov, P.V. *The Extraordinary Decade: Literary Memoirs*. Ed. Arthur P. Mendel. Trans. Irwin R. Titunik. Ann Arbor: University of Michigan Press, 1968.
Barabash, Iu. " 'Litsa basurmanskoi national'nosti' u Gogolia i Shevchenko." *Voprosy literatury* (May–June 1999): 204–35.
Gippius, Vasily. *Gogol'*. Leningrad: Mysl', 1924.
Karlinsky, Simon. *The Sexual Labyrinth of Nikolai Gogol*. Cambridge, Mass.: Harvard University Press, 1976.
Kornblatt, Judith Deutsch. *The Cossack Hero in Russian Literature: A Study in Cultural Mythology*. Madison: University of Wisconsin Press, 1992.
Pedrotti, Louis. "The Architecture of Love in Gogol's Rome." *California Slavic Studies* 6 (1971): 17–27.
Richter, Sigrid. *Rom und Gogol': Gogol's Romerlebnis und sein Fragment "Rim."* Dissertation zur Erlangung der Doktorwürde der Philosophischen Fakultät der Universität Hamburg. Hamburg: n.p., 1964.
Vogel, Lucy. "Gogol's Rome." *Slavic and East European Journal* 11, no. 2 (1967): 145–58.

CARLO GOLDONI
(1707–1793)

Carla Scognamiglio

BIOGRAPHY

The life of the Venetian Carlo Goldoni—a good, peaceful man, truly enamored of art—was completely dominated by his passion for the theater. He wrote more than 120 witty, humoristic, rhythmic comedies marked by incisive characterization, of which the best known internationally are, perhaps, *La vedova scaltra* (1748), *La locandiera* (1752), *Il ventaglio* (1763), and, in Venetian dialect, *Le baruffe chiozzotte* (1762).

Goldoni's vivacious temperament inspired avid readings of comic authors, and he found "delightful amusement" in the puppets his father manipulated on the stage of their household theater. His peregrinations began early in life: though he was born in Venice, he lived with his family for three years in Perugia, where his father, a physician, played prima donna roles inasmuch as women were forbidden to perform in the Papal States. At Rimini, aged twelve, Carlo ran away from school and from his philosophy tutor, a certain Father Candini, in order to set out with a troupe of traveling actors, after which he returned to his family's home at Chioggia in the Veneto region. His parents wanted him to become a lawyer. To this end, they sent him first to Venice, then to the University of Pavia, from which he was expelled in his third year (1725) for having written a satirical dialogue ("Il colosso") that roused the townspeople's ire. Only his father's death and the need to think about his own future convinced him to obtain his degree in law at the University of Padua in 1731. He moved to Milan, then Verona, and finally Genoa, where he met and married the gentle Nicoletta Connio. After a year's wandering from Emilia to Romagna to Tuscany, he finally settled in Pisa and began practicing law even though he was ceaselessly haunted by the performing arts. His encounter with the producer Gerolamo Medebach marked his return to the uncertainties and hardships of the theater world, which gradually absorbed all of his energies. He triumphantly won the well-known wager that he could write sixteen plays in a single season (1750–51).

At the invitation of Cardinal Carlo Rezzonico in 1758, he settled in Rome for almost a year. In 1762 he accepted an invitation to Paris to write for the Comédie Italienne, where, most reluctantly, he had to adapt to Parisian public taste that was accustomed to extemporaneous comedy. He might have left Paris had he not been summoned to the French court as Italian-language instructor for the royal princesses. Well remunerated with a court pension, he frequented Paris's literary society and its theaters. He met many important personages, including Diderot and Rousseau, even while working on his comedies and librettos. For Louis XVI's wedding he wrote in French one of his best-known works, *Le Bourru bienfaisant* (1771).

In his old age and in poor health, he wrote in French his *Mémoires*, begun in 1784, published in 1787, and dedicated to Louis XVI. The brio of the *Mémoires* allows us to forgive its chronological inaccuracies, and they are a precious source for understanding humankind's components and Goldonian art. When nothing more was left him but to write the story of his theater, he seized the opportunity to create a completely new stage character: himself. He evokes his vagabond existence of times past in the style of a true playwright who often will move from place to place following the actors who bring his protagonists to life. Reduced to poverty once his pension was terminated, Goldoni died in Paris in 1793 as the Revolution raged and the Reign of Terror loomed large.

MAJOR MULTICULTURAL THEMES

What remain pertinent to today's audiences are not only Goldoni's works written in Italian, French, and Venetian dialect, but also the manner in which he captures the multiplicity of human shortcomings: "La vérité," he wrote, "a été toujours ma vertu favorite" (*Mémoires pour servir à l'histoire de sa vie et à celle de son théâtre*, in *Opere complete*, 36:224). His European dimension— his diplomatic appointments and his long period of productivity in Paris—is certainly one of the most significant aspects of his modernity. A man of the eighteenth century, he was illuminated by the clear, slightly ironic, light of reason, and, as was the case for all of his contemporary intellectuals—Vico, Metastasio, and Alfieri, for example—travel was a means for gaining knowledge of human typology, just as art was a representation of real life.

His temperament was more that of a spectator than of an actor: a sharp observation of human nature and of places seemed more significant than fanciful and frequently outlandish combinations. What Molière had done for France, Goldoni attempted to do for Italy. Living and working with his troupe, he effected his dramatic reform, embodying his theories in *Il teatro comico*, a manifesto of comic poetics in which he rejected both the erudite tradition of the previous century and the commedia dell'arte. He proposed instead a theater of civil dignity, of natural expression, plausible and simple, which, by relating to daily realities, could attract the new bourgeois public. Goldoni the bourgeois was born and raised in a Venice that was nearing the end of its economic and military Adriatic hegemony. Its languishing aristocratic class was incapable of restoring its old splendor; its commercial middle class was unable to elaborate an organic political scheme and impose itself as a ruling class. Against this background of crisis and decay, we may place his itineraries as an "honored adventurer" (Nicastro, 375).

SURVEY OF CRITICISM

A man ready for any adventure as long as it did not involve too much responsibility, a man drawn to the unstable life of a vagabond and lacking any authentic political or religious ideology—such is the figure that emerges from Guido Nicastro's chapter "Carlo Goldoni" (1974). Nicastro also sees his cultural commitment as limited to a vague, generic adherence to the Enlightenment, but does not ascribe this to superficiality. Goldoni may, in fact, be placed within a precise historical and social structure that defines his human and artistic components.

Worthy of note are the *Atti del convegno Goldoni all'estero* (1993) published for the bicentennial of Goldoni's death. The proceedings offer an original and exhaustive panorama of the fortune of Goldoni's literary and theatrical works in Europe and even on the international scene. Thus we learn that the "honored adventurer," albeit with different intensity, has been translated, read, and variously represented in the whole world, beginning as early as the turn of the nineteenth century.

SELECTIVE BIBLIOGRAPHY

Works by Goldoni

Opere complete di Carlo Goldoni. Ed. Giuseppe Ortolani, Edgardo Maddalena, and Cesare Musatti. Venezia: Edizioni del Municipio, 1907–1960.
Les Années françaises (posthumous). Paris: Imprimerie nationale, 1993.

Selective Studies of Goldoni

Atti del colloquio sul tema Goldoni in Francia. Roma: Accademia Nazionale dei Lincei, 1972.
Atti del convegno Goldoni all'estero: Vicenza 1993. Roma: Presidenza del Consiglio dei Ministri, Dipartimento per l'informazione e l'editoria, 1993.
Ferrone, Siro. *Carlo Goldoni: Vita, opere, critica, messinscena.* 2nd ed. Firenze: Sansoni, 1990.
Nicastro, Guido. "Carlo Goldoni." In *La letteratura italiana: Storia e testi*, vol. 6.2, 371–451. Roma and Bari: Laterza, 1974.

Weichmann, Birgit. *Eccomi finalmente a Parigi! Untersuchungen zu Goldonis Pariser Jahrer (1762–1793).* Bonn: Romanistischer Verlag, 1993.

Zorzi, A. *Monsieur Goldoni: Un veneziano a Parigi tra il declino di una Repubblica e la morte di un regno, 1762–1793.* Milano: Corbaccio, 1993.

KNUT PEDERSEN HAMSUN
(1859–1952)

Barry Jacobs

BIOGRAPHY

Though Knut Pedersen was born in Gudbrandsdal in the heart of Norway, his family moved to a small farm above the Arctic Circle in Nordland when he was only four years old. A dozen of his novels are set in this remote and exotic region of midnight summer sun and endless winter nights; part of the action takes place there in another seven of his works. In the late 1870s, when he published his first short novel, he added "Hamsund," the name of his uncle's farm, to his name, which a printer's error later shortened to "Hamsun," now the name of Norway's greatest novelist. Author of thirty-three books and winner of the Nobel Prize for Literature in 1920, Hamsun had little schooling; nor did his early odd jobs seem to point to a brilliant literary career. He was only eighteen when he published his first book, *Den Gaadefulde*, a naïve love story. His next novels met with little acclaim, although they do contain touches that adumbrate his later masterpieces.

In 1882 he borrowed some money and sailed to America, where he hoped that his fortunes would improve. He tried to earn money as a journalist and a public lecturer in Wisconsin and Minnesota, but he found that the Norwegian immigrant population had little interest in learning about their own literary contemporaries. Unlike his famous countryman Bjørnstjerne Bjørnson, who visited America's leading cultural centers and met intellectuals and writers, Hamsun's American experience convinced him that this raw, young country would never produce literature of any cultural or artistic value. The only American writer he admired was Mark Twain. In 1884 he fell ill with what was misdiagnosed as "galloping consumption" and returned to Norway to die. Two years later he returned to America in hope of earning enough to enable him to settle in Norway and pursue his literary career. In 1888 he established himself in Copenhagen, where he began to be recognized as a writer of great promise. Lectures he gave on American cultural life were published in 1889, and he made literary history with his novel *Sult* (1890).

Sult, which deals with a series of crises in a man's life, is a novel without plot or character in the conventional sense. It eliminates psychological realism altogether, and the time sequence is sometimes ungraspable. Now famous, he produced a steady stream of literary works, the best known being *Mysterier* (1892), *Pan* (1894), and *Victoria* (1898). Between 1904 and 1936 he published three groups of novels describing the progress of civilization as a disease passing through several stages. During this period his social theories became increasingly conservative; at the same time he became more conventional as a novelist. Although not his best novel, the most popular of the second group is *Markens grøde* (1917). Beginning in 1927, he wrote three novels about a wanderer named August: *Landstrykere* (1927), *August* (1930), and *Men livet lever* (1933). Ingenuity and industry, the protagonist's good qualities, are offset by his mendacious, ruthless nature; he has been called Hamsun's answer to Ibsen's Peer Gynt.

In 1906 Hamsun, a lifelong misogynist, divorced his wife of seven years. In 1909 he remarried and began to raise a family. Though he was always restless and given to vagabondage, in 1918 he purchased Nørholm, a working farm in southern Norway, and became a gentleman farmer. During the 1930s he became ever more identified with the forces of reaction. Owing perhaps to his Anglophobia and to the great popularity his books had enjoyed in Germany, he defended Hitler's Germany in 1934 and wrote in support of Norwegian Nazi leader Vidkun Quisling two years later. Shortly after the German invasion of Norway in 1940 he shocked and dismayed his countrymen by coming out in support of Germany. During the course of the war he wrote over a dozen more articles urging his countrymen to cooperate with the Germans. After the war he was arrested and subjected to examination by psychiatrists, who declared him to be "a person with permanently impaired mental faculties." He defended himself in a brilliantly written book *På gjengrodde stier* (1949). Although his Nazism made him very unpopular in the years immediately following the war, by proving that he had been unjustly declared incompetent, this book helped to rehabilitate him with the Norwegian public.

MAJOR MULTICULTURAL THEMES

Hamsun was strongly influenced by both the Swedish dramatist and novelist August Strindberg and the Russian novelist Fedor Dostoevsky. He particularly admired Strindberg's attempts to create complex characters who are full of inconsistencies and subject to the promptings of the unconscious mind. In *Sult* he pushed the exploration of irrational states of mind even further than Strindberg had done. The heroes of Hamsun's early novels tend to be richly imaginative outsiders who attempt to adapt to bourgeois life; their inability to do so usually results in flight or suicide. The unpredictable heroines of these novels often sacrifice love to their social ambitions. Hamsun was disturbed by the erosion of traditional cultural values, particularly in highly industrialized nations like America, and, inspired by Rousseauian ideas, he longed for the simplicity of agrarian life. By contrast, though he believed that the city corrupts and that renewal always comes from the country, he found it difficult to reject urban sophistication out of hand in favor of simple rural life. After he settled at Nørholm in 1918, his social theories took final form. Characters like Isak, the protagonist of *Markens grøde*, find happiness in farmwork because it makes them feel a part of the great cycle of nature, whereas men who leave the agrarian life to become industrial workers or petty civil servants cut themselves off from their roots. Harald Næss has observed that in this novel Hamsun suggests that the synthesis between city culture and wild nature, "or between Nature, Art, and the acquisitive instinct," was to be found in the patriarchal society of the traditional farm life (Næss, 1984, 116).

SURVEY OF CRITICISM

Though there is a considerable body of criticism of Hamsun's work in Norwegian, he has not received the attention in other countries that one might have expected for such an important writer. Næss's excellent introduction to Hamsun's life and works (1984) contains careful analyses of every aspect of his extensive oeuvre, while his 1969 study, in Norwegian, is the best work on Hamsun and America. Scattered articles by scholars like Kittang, McFarlane, and Næss give in-depth studies of various works by Hamsun. Appreciative essays by important writers like Paul Auster and John Updike indicate some of the ways in which Hamsun has shaped the modernist novel. The recent (and most authoritative) translation of *Sult* by Sverre Lyngstad (1998) contains an excellent introduction and very informative notes.

SELECTIVE BIBLIOGRAPHY

Work by Hamsun

Sult (1890). Trans. Sverre Lyngstad. New York: Penguin Books, 1998.

Selective Studies of Hamsun

Auster, Paul. "The Art of Hunger." *Shearsman* 3 (1981): 62–68.
Bolckmans, Alex. "Henry Miller's *Tropic of Cancer* and Knut Hamsun's *Sult*." *Scandinavica* 14 (1975): 115–26.
Ferguson, Robert. *Enigma: The Life of Knut Hamsun.* New York: Farrar, Straus & Giroux, 1987.
Gustafson, Alrik. "Man and the Soil." In *Six Scandinavian Novelists*, 226–85. New York: American-Scandinavian Foundation, 1940.
Heller, Erich. "Norway's Great Novelist." *New Republic* (August 2 and 9, 1980): 28–34.

Kittang, Atle. "Knut Hamsun's *Sult*: Psychological Deep Structures and Metapoetic Plot." In *Facets of European Modernism*, 295–308. Ed. J. Garton. Norwich, England: University of East Anglia, 1985.

McFarlane, James W. "Knut Hamsun." In *Ibsen and the Temper of Norwegian Literature*, 114–57. London: Oxford University Press, 1960.

Næss, Harald. *Knut Hamsun*. Boston: Twayne Publishers, 1984.

———. *Knut Hamsun og Amerika*. Oslo: Gydendal Norsk Forlag, 1969.

———. "Strindberg and Hamsun." In *Structures of Influence: A Comparative Approach to August Strindberg*, 121–36. Ed. M.J. Blackwell. University of North Carolina Studies in Germanic Languages and Literatures, vol. 98. Chapel Hill: University of North Carolina Press, 1981.

———. "Who Was Hamsun's Hero?" *In The Hero in Scandinavian Literature*, 63–86. Ed. J.M. Weinstock and R.T. Rovinsky. Austin: University of Texas Press, 1975.

Updike, John. "A Primal Modern." *New Yorker* (May 31, 1976): 116–18.

THE HAWTHORNES: NATHANIEL HAWTHORNE and SOPHIA PEABODY HAWTHORNE
(1804–1864/1809–1871)

Julie E. Hall

BIOGRAPHY

Often referred to as "America's Great Romancer" and best known for his fictions of Puritan New England, Nathaniel Hawthorne lived abroad from 1853 to 1860 and based his last novel, *The Marble Faun* (1860), and his last sustained work, *Our Old Home* (1863), on his European experiences. Native son of Salem, Massachusetts, he was born to a sea captain who died on a voyage when Nathaniel was only four years old. Although Salem was already declining as an important seaport, Nathaniel's earliest intimations of and curiosities about a world beyond his own were certainly owing to its influence. After attending Bowdoin College in Maine, he returned to Salem to enter upon a famous twelve-year period "under the eaves" of his mother's house, honing his craft, producing some of his finest tales, and, in 1837, publishing his first collection of short stories, *Twice-told Tales*. In 1842 he married Sophia Peabody, an artist, a life-long writer of letters and journals—genres that were culturally sanctioned for women in the nineteenth century—and, late in her life, a published author. Also born in Salem, Sophia had two sisters who, like herself, became prominent figures in nineteenth-century America (Elizabeth, the oldest, was part of the influential Transcendental group; Mary wed famous educator Horace Mann and wrote his biography after his death). The Hawthornes' three children, Una, Julian, and Rose, were born in 1844, 1846, and 1851.

A stint as surveyor at the Salem Custom House ended for Nathaniel in 1849 with what Hawthorne fans can consider a fortunate dismissal, for it initiated the most productive period of his life. *The Scarlet Letter* (1850), *The House of the Seven Gables* (1851), and *The Blithedale Romance* (1852) appeared in rapid succession, along with another volume of short stories. In 1853 he was appointed U.S. consul to Liverpool, England, by longtime friend and then President of the

United States Franklin Pierce. In England, where the family lived from 1853 to 1858, and then in Italy, where they sojourned for sixteen months, Sophia and Nathaniel both wrote letters and kept journals that would eventuate in literary productions. In Italy Nathaniel also began *The Marble Faun*, set against a rich Italian backdrop and revolving around the lives of three expatriate artists, two of them American. The Hawthornes returned to England in 1859, where Nathaniel revised his novel and saw it into the press, and in 1860 they returned to the United States. In the four years before his death Nathaniel produced only one more complete work, *Our Old Home*, based largely on his English journals. In 1868 Sophia, then widowed, moved with her children to Dresden, Germany, hoping to live more economically than was possible in the United States. Here she edited the letters she had written from England and the journals kept in Italy some ten years earlier to produce her travel book, *Notes in England and Italy* (1869). The family moved one last time to England, where Sophia died in 1871.

MAJOR MULTICULTURAL THEMES

While Hawthorne held the post of American consul to Liverpool, an office he said he "disliked . . . from the first" (*Our Old Home*, 37), he found it impossible to produce works of fiction. However, he wrote extensively in notebooks of his impressions of Great Britain and its people, maintaining that he also "grew better acquainted with many of our national characteristics, during those four years, than in all my preceding life" (10). When he returned to the United States, he drew on the journals to produce essays published in the *Atlantic*; these essays and others that he wrote expressly for the purpose were collected and shaped into *Our Old Home*. One of Hawthorne's responses to the motherland is communicated in his title and reiterated throughout the volume. "I was often conscious of a fervent hereditary attachment to the native soil of our forefathers," he writes, "and felt it to be our own Old Home" (40). This affinity, however, did not extend to the English people, whom Nathaniel found "as a whole . . . beset by a curious and inevitable infelicity, which compels them . . . to keep up . . . a wholesome bitterness of feeling between themselves and all other nationalities, especially that of America" (64). He was, perhaps inevitably, led to make comparisons. The "sluggishness and decay" of Old Boston, or St. Botolph's Town, calls to his mind "the mighty and populous activity of our own Boston, which was once the feeble infant of this old English town" (156); "the dirt of a poverty-stricken English street" is "a monstrosity unknown on our side of the Atlantic" (277). Nevertheless, when he left for Italy, he wrote, "I should be well content to spend the remainder of my days in England" (Woodson, "Historical Commentary," 909).

In February 1858 the Hawthornes arrived in Rome. Nathaniel's first impressions of the Eternal City were dominated by his own discomfort, occasioned by a feverish cold, and the chill winter climate. As he exclaimed in his first journal entry, "I have seldom or never spent so wretched a time anywhere" (*The French and Italian Notebooks*, 53). In the coming months, however, Rome began to lay claim to his mind, heart, and imagination. His journalizing during this period was "the most sustained and detailed . . . of [his] life" (Woodson, 903); it tapered off in July, when, living in Florence to escape the Roman summer, he began "sketching out" a new romance. That romance, *The Marble Faun*, drew heavily not only on Hawthorne's knowledge of the streets and sites of Rome and Florence, but also on his own experiences and reactions, as he recorded them in his notebooks. He walked, as his characters would, on the Pincian Hill; he gazed upon the *Beatrice Cenci* and the *Faun* of Praxiteles; and he met the American artists who served as models for the fictional Kenyon and Hilda. Perhaps even more important, though, Rome itself embodied one of Hawthorne's thematic preoccupations, the burden of the past. The "state of feeling which is experienced oftenest at Rome," he writes in his novel, is "a vague sense of ponderous remembrances; a perception of such weight and density in a by-gone life" (*The Marble Faun*, 6). When Hawthorne returned to Rome after his residence in Florence, he felt a "quiet, gentle, comfortable pleasure, as if, after many wanderings, I was drawing near home" (*The French and Italian Notebooks*, 488). His last words on Rome, though, were not wholly positive. After living through another Roman winter and enduring the protracted and nearly fatal illness of his daughter, Una, Nathaniel bid farewell to Rome with characteristic ambivalence, writing that "no place ever took so strong a hold of my being," but that he desired "never to set eyes on it again" (524).

Sophia, who had trained with some of the most prominent figures in the nineteenth-century American art world, saw England and Italy through an artist's eyes. Her aim is announced in her "Preface" to the *Notes in England and Italy*. "If," she writes, "these [Notes] will aid any one in the least to enjoy . . . the illustrious works of the Great Masters . . . , I shall be well repaid for the pain it has cost me to appear before the public." In England, although she sketches characters with skill, her gaze is almost wholly fixed upon great architectural works—York Minster, Lincoln and Peterboro cathedrals—which she describes in illuminating, often highly technical detail. Italy, though, the great land of art, receives the majority of her attention and 352 of her book's 549 pages. As she writes when she visits the Pitti Palace in Florence, "To-day I saw . . . Michel Angelo's Three Fates; and I needed more than one pair of eyes to gaze, for I had all my life wished to see it" (360). Accounts of individual works often occupy two to three pages of text; and some, like the following description of the campanile, or bell tower, in Florence, are pure poetry: "Giotto must have diffused his spirit through the stones and lines. One of its bells sang out as we passed—a deep, round, liquid sound. . . . It was music, dropped through water . . . It was as if the great dome itself had rolled from the soul of its artist, a pure globe of melody, and dropped singing into the sea of space" (341). During her European travels in the 1850s Sophia found her subject; in 1868, when she returned, she found the will to bring her vision, and her voice, before the public.

SURVEY OF CRITICISM

Frederick Newberry (1987) examines Nathaniel's attitudes toward England in his early fiction and then in *The English Notebooks* and *Our Old Home*. Alba Amoia (1998) compares Rome as Hawthorne describes it in his *Notebooks* and *The Marble Faun* to what one might see today. In the only published study to date of Sophia Hawthorne's *Notes to England and Italy*, Mary Schriber (1997) argues that *Notes*, read as autobiography, provides an example of "writing as self-destruction" (93).

SELECTIVE BIBLIOGRAPHY

Works by the Hawthornes

Hawthorne, Nathaniel. *The English Notebooks, 1853–1856*, and *The English Notebooks, 1856–1860*. *The Centenary Edition of the Works of Nathaniel Hawthorne*, vols. 21 and 22. Ed. Thomas Woodson and Bill Ellis. Columbus: Ohio State University Press, 1997.

———. *The French and Italian Notebooks* (1858–1859). *The Centenary Edition*, vol. 14. Ed. by Thomas Woodson. Columbus: Ohio State University Press, 1980.

———. *The Marble Faun* (1860). *The Centenary Edition*, vol. 4. Ed. William Charvat, Roy Harvey Pearce, Claude Simpson, Matthew J. Bruccoli, Fredson Bowers, and L. Neal Smith. Columbus: Ohio State University Press, 1968.

———. *Our Old Home: A Series of English Sketches* (1863). Textual ed. Fredson Bowers. Columbus: Ohio State University Press, 1970.

Hawthorne, Sophia. *Notes in England and Italy*. New York: G.P. Putnam and Son, 1869.

Selective Studies of the Hawthornes

Amoia, Alba. "Hawthorne's Rome: Then and Now." *Nathaniel Hawthorne Review* 24 (Spring 1998): 1–35.

Hull, Raymona E. *Nathaniel Hawthorne: The English Experience, 1853–1864*. Pittsburgh: University of Pittsburgh Press, 1980.

Newberry, Frederick. *Hawthorne's Divided Loyalties: England and America in His Works*. London and Toronto: Associated University Presses, 1987.

Schriber, Mary Suzanne. *Writing Home: American Women Abroad, 1830–1920*. Charlottesville: University Press of Virginia, 1997.

Woodson, Thomas. "Historical Commentary." In *The French and Italian Notebooks*, by Nathaniel Hawthorne. *The Centenary Edition*, vol. 14. Ed. Thomas Woodson. Columbus: Ohio State University Press, 1980.

HEINRICH HEINE

(1797–1856)

Max E. Noordhoom

BIOGRAPHY

Heinrich Heine was born in Düsseldorf, the eldest son of Jewish parents. He received some Jewish education as a child, but his mother, Betty van Gelderen, influenced by the French Revolution and ambitious for her son's future, had him educated by freethinking Jesuits at the Düsseldorf Lyceum. Not surprisingly, he became a liberal and was for many years an ardent admirer of Napoleon. He took his law degree in Göttingen in 1825, but never practiced law. He began to establish a name as a poet and journalist in the 1820s and was among the first Germans successfully to make a living as a man of letters. As a young man he had apparently conceived an unrequited passion for one, if not both, of his uncle Solomon's daughters. The emotional impact of the experiences colored the cycles of poems that were eventually collected in *Buch der Lieder* (1827), which established his fame in Germany and abroad.

Unable to find a permanent position in Germany, he left in 1831 for Paris, where he spent the rest of his life, undertaking but two trips to his native land. Saint-Simonism, which he dreamt of as his "new religion" with its social order fit for an industrial and scientific age, was the magnet that drew him to France. Heine hoped that it could effect a reconciliation between "Nazarism," spirituality in the Judeo-Christian tradition, and Hellenism, life-affirming sensualism, in order to attain the synthesis that he had long yearned for. The greater political freedom and the new social order under the citizen-king Louis Philippe also spurred his interest. He wrote many articles for German newspapers and French journals, interpreting the cultural and political scene within the larger framework of sociopolitical, historic trends. These political essays appeared in *Französische Zustände* (1832). His letters from Paris appeared later as part of a four-volume set, *Der Salon* (1834–1840). To acquaint his French readership with German literary and philosophical developments, while simultaneously counteracting the idealized notions about German Romanticism that Madame de Staël had disseminated in her famous *De l'Allemagne* (1810), he published *Die romantische Schule* (1833–1835) and *Zur Geschichte der Religion und Philosophie in Deutschland* (1834–1835) in French and German.

Der Salon contained an essay on French poetry, a collection of poems, *Frühlingslieder*, and a humorous prose work in the first volume. The second consisted of a synopsis of his history of German religion and philosophy; the third featured two prose pieces, *Elementargeister* and *Florentinische Nächte*, the introductory chapters of an unfinished novel *Der Rabbi von Baccharach*, and a piece that caused a literary furor, *Ludwig Börne, ein Denkschrift*, a memorial essay on the recently deceased Ludwig Börne, another multicultural German writer who had settled in Paris in 1830 and mediated French liberal ideas through his *Briefe aus Paris* (1830–1834). The two were personally at odds, and Heine depicted him as a fanatical ideologue and political activist, while showing himself as an autonomous artist. Heine then tried his hand at a new genre, the mock epic. *Deutschland: Ein Wintermärchen* (1844), a satiric verse travelogue, written after a return from his native land, is an attack on Prussia's militarism, its backward economic conditions, and the prevailing apathy and servility of its residents.

Heine's later years were characterized by continuing financial squabbles with his relatives and above all by his ill health. He died in Paris and was buried in Montmartre Cemetery.

MAJOR MULTICULTURAL THEMES

Heine is truly a multicultural author, for, like few before or after him, he was a genuinely European poet and writer. He tried not merely to establish cultural, sociopolitical, and philosophical links between Germany and the rest of the Western world, but also to place these in a historical framework, relating them to the past and to the future. This all-embracing spirit infused not only his travel sketches but also his journalistic reports and his literary-historical and philosophical writings. Occupying himself with contemporary social and political issues, he began with *Briefe aus Berlin* (1821) and a report on Poland that became part of his *Reisebilder* (1826–1831). These sketches, a popular genre at the time, became in his hands a novel narrative mélange of nature description, anecdotes, wit, poetry, and social criticism. The first volume, containing *Die Harzreise*, contrasts the philistinism of Göttingen's academics with the natural harmony of the miners' lives of Claustal. A lyric cycle, *Die Heimkehr*, and a free-verse cycle of North Sea poems, *Die Nordsee I*, are also included. The second volume features the poems of *Nordsee II* and *Nordsee III*, a prose piece whose theme shows the conflict between the primitive contentment of the local inhabitants and the sense of "Zerrissenheit" (inner strife) and "Weltschmerz" of the visitors. However, Heine also realizes that greater intellectual joy can be experienced by the latter than is afforded to the folk of Norderney by their blind faith. The last two volumes feature Heine's trip to Italy, *Die Bäder von Lucca* (volume 3), and *Die englischen Fragmente* (volume 4). Again he touches upon the inner division of modern man and in particular that of the poet who cannot flee to a separate realm but must take part in the political struggle. He maintains that the task of his age is the emancipation not only of European peoples but of all humankind. *Die englischen Fragmente* consists primarily of a denunciation of the churchgoing, materialistic, and prosaic nature of the British people, although Heine did admire some features of English political life.

He unwaveringly believed in the Enlightenment and the perfectibility of the world through education. *Ideen: Das Buch Le Grand* (1827) unveils his conviction that humans should seek fulfillment in life rather than in religious belief. Through the figure of the simple drummer Le Grand, Heine expresses veneration for Napoleon, which resulted in the banning of the volume in 1835, together with all the *Reisebilder* sketches.

SURVEY OF CRITICISM

Chief among the biographies of Heine is Jeffrey L. Sammons's *Heinrich Heine: A Modern Biography* (1979). The same author's *Heinrich Heine: The Elusive Poet* (1969) ranks among the best literary studies for its sensitive look at Heine's prose and late poetry. Heine's social and political attitudes as well as his "Jewish feeling" are explored with insight by Willam Rose in *Heinrich Heine: Two Studies of His Thought and Feeling* (1956). E.M. Butler provides an analysis of Saint-Simonism in *The Saint-Simonian Religion in Germany: A Study of the Young German Movement* (1926).

SELECTIVE BIBLIOGRAPHY

Works by Heine

Briefe. 6 vols. Ed. Friedrich Hirth. Mainz: Florian Kupferberg, 1948–1951.
Werke. 27 vols. Ed. Fritz Mende et al. Berlin: Akademie-Verlag; Paris: Editions du Centre National de la Recherche Scientifique (CNRS), 1979–1984.
The Complete Poems of Heinrich Heine. Trans. Hal Draper. Oxford: Oxford University Press, 1982.
Poetry and Prose. Trans. Jost Hermand and Robert C. Holub. New York: Continuum, 1982.

Selective Studies of Heine

Butler, E.M. *The Saint-Simonian Religion in Germany: A Study of the Young German Movement*. Cambridge: University Press, 1926.
Fairley, Barker. *Heinrich Heine: An Interpretation*. Oxford: Clarendon Press, 1954.
Hofrichter, Laura. *Heinrich Heine*. Oxford: Clarendon Press, 1963.
Pawel, Ernst. *The Poet Dying*. New York: Farrar, Straus and Giroux, 1995.

Rose, William. *Heinrich Heine: Two Studies of His Thought and Feeling*. Oxford: Clarendon Press, 1956.

———. *The Early Love Poetry of Heinrich Heine: An Inquiry into Poetic Inspiration*. Oxford: Clarendon Press, 1962.

Sammons, Jeffrey L. *Heinrich Heine: A Modern Biography*. Princeton: Princeton University Press, 1979.

———. *Heinrich Heine: The Elusive Poet*. New Haven: Yale University Press, 1969.

Spencer, Hanna. *Heinrich Heine*. Boston: Twayne Publishers, 1982.

ERNEST HEMINGWAY
(1899–1961)

Lucille Frackman Becker

BIOGRAPHY

Ernest Hemingway, novelist, short-story writer, and essayist, winner of the Nobel Prize for Literature in 1954, was born in 1899 in Oak Park, Illinois, an upper-middle-class, predominantly Protestant suburb of Chicago. He was the second of the six children of Dr. Clarence and Grace Hall Hemingway. His mother, an accomplished singer who had given up a professional career for marriage, fostered his love of art and music; his father, who took him hunting and fishing, imparted to him a love of nature and of the outdoors that remained with him throughout his life.

Hemingway attended the public schools in Oak Park. When he graduated in 1917, he went to work as a cub reporter for the *Kansas City Star*, where he learned the rules of concision and clarity that would characterize his writing style. Because his poor vision prevented him from enlisting in the army, he joined the American Red Cross ambulance corps in Italy, where he received serious leg wounds from shrapnel; he was subsequently decorated by the Italian government. His recovery at a hospital in Milan and his affair with his nurse, Agnes von Kurowsky, inspired his novel *A Farewell to Arms* (1929). His inability to readjust to civilian life after his war experiences, not uncommon among men returning from the front, is the subject of the short story "Soldier's Home."

After the war he worked as a journalist in Toronto and then in Chicago, where he met and married Hadley Richardson in 1921. They soon left for Paris, where Hemingway took up his position as European correspondent for the *Toronto Star*. *A Moveable Feast* (1964, posthumous) is made up of twenty sketches that constitute a memoir of his years in Paris (1921–26). His reporting covered the most important events of the time, including the Greco-Turkish War. At the same time, under the guidance of writers like Gertrude Stein and F. Scott Fitzgerald, he was working on his own fiction. During his years in Paris he traveled widely for the skiing, bullfighting, hunting, and fishing that would be at the heart of much of his work.

His first collection of short stories, *In Our Time* (1925), as well as a short comic novel, *The Torrents of Spring* (1926), were followed by *The Sun Also Rises* (1926), a novel set in France and Spain that deals with a group of aimless expatriates, members of the so-called postwar lost generation. Hemingway and Hadley divorced in 1927, and, with his second wife, Pauline Pfeiffer, the mother of his second and third sons, he returned to the United States. *A Farewell to Arms* was published in 1929 and, in 1932, *Death in the Afternoon*, a comprehensive study of the art of bullfighting, interspersed with observations on Spanish history, culture, and customs.

The Hemingways went to Africa on safari in 1931 and spent three months there hunting and gathering material for the writer's account of big-game hunting, *Green Hills of Africa* (1935). In March 1937 he went as a correspondent to Spain to cover the Spanish Civil War; he transcribed his experiences there into a play, *The Fifth Column*, several short stories, and the novel considered to be his finest, *For Whom the Bell Tolls* (1940). He divorced Pauline and, in 1940, married Martha Gellhorn, also a war correspondent, who, unlike Pauline, shared his Republican sympathies. Motivated by his fascination with Spanish culture, Hemingway moved to Havana, Cuba, with Martha. In 1941 the couple covered the Chinese-Japanese War, and in 1942, after their return to Cuba, Hemingway participated in a futile search for German submarines off the coast of Cuba. He returned to Europe two years later, first to London, where he met Mary Welsh, who became his fourth wife, and then to France, where he participated in the liberation of Paris. *Across the River and into the Trees* (1950) is his only novel about World War II.

After the war Hemingway returned to Cuba to write. He also continued to travel extensively. An account of his African safari of 1954, in the course of which he was severely injured in a plane crash, was edited and published posthumously in 1999 as *True at First Light*. In 1953 he received the Pulitzer Prize in Fiction for *The Old Man and the Sea* (1952), a short novel about a Cuban fisherman, and, in 1954, the Nobel Prize for Literature. Despite these honors, physically debilitated, suffering from paranoia and depression, Hemingway, as had his father in 1928, shot himself in the head in 1961.

MAJOR MULTICULTURAL THEMES

All of Hemingway's work must of necessity be considered in terms of multiculturalism, since, with the exception of the novel *To Have and Have Not* and several short stories—his only works with an American background—all others are illustrative of a literary career of worldwide dimensions. Like many American artists of the nineteenth and twentieth centuries, Hemingway fled the provincial constraints of his milieu in search of different cultural and religious attitudes to enlarge his own horizons and those of his protagonists. His years in Paris expanded his literary and artistic development by providing direct contact with the new literature and art that were being created by writers like Gertrude Stein and Ezra Pound and artists like Pablo Picasso and Joan Miró. But France and the French served only as background in his fiction, a source of local color in the first third of *The Sun Also Rises* and in the memoirs of *A Moveable Feast*; they did not have the emotional and psychological impact on him of Spanish culture, which he assimilated completely. In Spain he discovered certain rituals, codes of behavior, and religious attitudes that were to offer new dimensions to his fictional protagonists and greatly transform his own life. His celebration of Spanish culture, *Death in the Afternoon*, centers on the tragedy and ritual of the bullfight, with the matador as the embodiment of Hemingway's prototypal stoical hero who faces deadly opposition while still performing his duties with professionalism and skill. The disciplined heroism of the bullfighter in the face of violent death, for Hemingway, gave a true sense of man's dignity and of the tragedy of life.

SURVEY OF CRITICISM

In his introduction to *Hemingway and His Critics: An International Anthology* (1961), Carlos Baker writes that for years before he won the Nobel Prize for Literature at the age of fifty-five, Hemingway had been a citizen of the world, a natural expatriate, belonging everywhere or nowhere. The four subjects that always fascinated Hemingway, fishing, hunting, bullfighting, and war, he adds, all show certain international aspects, while the people and events in his works, though remaining in their time and their space, become universal symbols of the story of man. In his personal reminiscences of Hemingway's years in Spain, José-Luis Castillo Puche (1974) points out that Hemingway was the most outstanding observer of that country in the modern era. Angel Capellán (1985) illustrates the way in which Spanish landscapes, heroes, rituals, moral codes, religious attitudes, and literary traditions pervade all of Hemingway's works. Michael Reynolds (1986) considers Hemingway's wounding on the Italian front during World War I as the single major event of his life and the most influential on his writing career. It was his experience then of death and resurrection that would explain the psyche of his protagonists. Reynolds discusses (1989 and 1997) the decisive influence on Hemingway's work of his European experiences.

SELECTIVE BIBLIOGRAPHY

Works by Hemingway

All of Hemingway's works were published in New York by Scribner's.
The Sun Also Rises, 1926.
The Torrents of Spring, 1926.

A Farewell to Arms, 1929.
Death in the Afternoon, 1932.
Green Hills of Africa, 1935.
The Fifth Column and the First Forty-nine Stories, 1938.
For Whom the Bell Tolls, 1940.
Across the River and into the Trees, 1950.
The Old Man and the Sea, 1952.
A Moveable Feast, 1964.
Islands in the Stream, 1970.
The Dangerous Summer, 1985.
The Complete Short Stories of Ernest Hemingway, 1987.
True at First Light, 1999.

Selective Studies of Hemingway

Baker, Carlos. *Ernest Hemingway, a Life Story*. New York: Scribner's, 1969 (reissued 1988).

———, ed. *Hemingway and His Critics: An International Anthology*. New York: Hill and Wang, 1961.

Capellán, Angel. *Hemingway and the Hispanic World*. Ann Arbor: University of Michigan Research Press, 1985.

Castillo Puche, José Luis. *Hemingway in Spain: A Personal Reminiscence of Hemingway's Years in Spain by His Friend*. Garden City, N.Y.: Doubleday, 1974. Translation of *Hemingway: Entre la vida y la muerte* of 1968.

Griffin, Peter. *Less Than a Treason: Hemingway in Paris*. New York: Oxford University Press, 1990.

Reynolds, Michael. *The Young Hemingway*. New York: W.W. Norton, 1986.

———. *The Paris Years*. New York: W.W. Norton, 1989.

———. *Hemingway: The 1930s*. New York: W.W. Norton, 1997.

JOHANN GOTTFRIED VON HERDER

(1744–1803)

Luanne Frank

BIOGRAPHY

Johann Gottfried von Herder, the German philosopher-historian, literary critic, theologian, and educator whose works inhabit innumerable cultures worldwide— "cultures" to be understood in two senses, linguistic-geographical (as in French, German, and Hindi), and epocal (as in Homeric, Greco-Roman versus medieval)—was born in Mohrungen, East Prussia (now Morag, Poland), the only son of a poor, Pietistic family. His father was stern and undemonstrative; his mother was warmer by nature and close to her son. Herder, shy and studious, began and completed his early education in the local Latin school. Placed at sixteen in the service of his father's superior, he was permitted to read in his "employer's" substantial library and did so voraciously until he was offered a free medical education at Königsberg University by the surgeon of a Russian regiment stationed in the area, then under Russian rule. Fainting on witnessing his first dissection, Herder shifted to theology and supported himself by teaching. He studied under and became a friend of Immanuel Kant, not yet the philosopher of the three great critiques, whose thought Herder would eventually challenge. He also befriended Johann Georg Hamann, the "Magus of the North," a philosopher-mystic who, along with Herder, would inspire the Sturm und Drang (storm and stress) movement and German Romanticism. Assisted by Hamann, Herder went to teach and preach in the Hanseatic city of Riga, then (1764) in Russian hands, but notably occupied by German Rationalist burghers. There he experienced his "Golden Age," admired and respected by the city's leaders and lionized socially. He swiftly emerged as Germany's foremost critic after G.E. Lessing via numerous essays and reviews in the learned regional and national press and via publication of *Über die neuere deutsche Literatur: Fragmente* (1766–67) and *Kritische Wälder* (1769).

He embarked after five years in Riga on an extended, recuperative sea journey to Nantes (1769), where for four months he devoted himself to absorbing French language and customs and to an account of his journey and his anticipated destiny: to show humankind the way to realization of its potential by educating it across the fullnesses (the depths and varieties) of its cultural pasts. He then traveled to Paris, met Diderot, and worked further on his travel journal, *Journal meiner Reise im Jahre 1769*, published posthumously. He gave up plans to return to Riga, taking the post of traveling tutor and psychological counselor to the son of the prince-bishop of Oldenburg-Eutin. After weeks of mandatory state visits en route to Italy with the prince of Eutin, he gave up his charge in Strassburg to undergo (in vain) an eye operation by a university surgeon. A young law student, Johann Wolfgang von Goethe, visiting Herder's inn, introduced himself and soon became his "satellite." The views Herder unfolded for Goethe were grounded in a historical relativism traceable in his thought to 1764–65. The winter of this encounter, 1770–1771, became one of the most momentous in Western literary and critical history when Herder presented to an eager Goethe what would become Herder's great reversal of the fortunes of individual national cultures and levels of culture (seen by the age as inferior to classical/aristocratic ones and measurable in their terms); of national literatures similarly presumed subordinate and often unworthy; and of cultural epochs misapprehended as nonautonomous and insignificant. He turned the young Goethe's interests, as he later would the Occident's, to indigenous cultural forms validated by his relativism—particularly the sturdy forms evolved by folk cultures and supposed "primitives" (i.e., "Ossian") and possessed of their strength, vitality, and authenticity. The same winter also produced the *Abhandlung über den Ursprung der Sprache*, which, identifying thought with language and observing the rich linguistic uniqueness of various cultures, such as the Arabic, won the 1770 essay competition of the Berlin Academy and marked Herder as Europe's foremost language theorist.

Herder accepted the post of court preacher, superintendent of schools, and consistory president in the diminutive principality of Schaumburg-Lippe in 1770. Socially and intellectually isolated, he nonetheless remained characteristically inspired, completing, among other major projects, the groundbreaking *Von deutscher Art und Kunst* (1773), lauding Germany's native art forms and Shakespeare's native Englishness, and thus forwarding the Sturm und Drang, and the equally revolutionary *Auch eine Philosophie der Geschichte Zur Bildung der Menschheit* (1774), which insists on the immanent value and autonomy of each historical epoch and culture. Through the offices of Goethe, now minister of state in the Duchy of Sachsen-Weimar, he became superintendent of schools and head ecclesiastical administrator there (1776). With his appointment, Duke Karl August's principality became Germany's most illustrious.

Among the works that brought Herder to the pinnacle of his career were the essay paving the way for the folk songs he had collected for twenty years, *Von Ähnlichkeit der mittleren englischen und deutschen Dichtkunst* (1777), which argues the fundamental uniqueness, irreplaceability, and equality of historical-geographical cultures, and *Lieder der Liebe*, which applies his relativism and critical acumen to the songs of Solomon. *Vom Geist der ebräischen Poesie* (1782–1783) demonstrated the literary artistry of Hebrew culture and founded his delayed fame in England and America.

Entering into regular and productive exchanges with Goethe, he brought to near completion his greatest work, the monumental *Ideen zur Philosophie der Geschichte der Menschheit* (1784–1791). To extend his forty-year advocacy of cultural relativism, he founded a journal, *Adrastea*, one volume of which is dedicated to the supreme moments in Spanish folk culture that are the stories of *El Cid*. Herder's translation-adaptation became, literally, a textbook of multiculturalism of the nineteenth century. Death interrupted this project on December 18, 1803.

MAJOR MULTICULTURAL THEMES

Much of Herder's contribution as a thinker suffused the nineteenth century and continues to exert often-unacknowledged influence. Contemporary sociological, anthropological, historical, and culture-critical (most notably poststructuralist) thought rests on his historical and cultural relativism, which grounds his insistence, not on the devaluing of cultures traditionally considered great, but rather on the greatness, equality, and uniqueness of all cultures at all levels, making them worthy of understanding and inhabiting, physically and imaginatively, and thus making multiculturalism a condition to be sought and fostered, both in the past and present. His vehement arguments in favor of such ideas ground his more muted *Ebräische Poesie* and the magnificent *Ideen*, during the long course of which Herder applies few nonpositive judgments to the cultures in which he situates himself. This has made him beloved of dwellers in the so-called developing countries (a term he would deplore), such as Islamic and Hindu peoples, to whose cultures and others' (including neglected Eastern Europe's) he brought a regard equal to that he voiced for those Western European and Near Eastern folk cultures he first celebrated, and in all of which he immersed himself, "swimming up and down in their stream" (Herder, *Zweites Wäldchen*, quoted in Clark, 84).

SURVEY OF CRITICISM

Robert T. Clark, Jr.,'s *Herder: His Life and Thought* (1955) is the most complete biography of Herder in English. Pierre Birnbaum's "From Multiculturalism to Nationalism" (1996) and Daniel Chirot's "Herder's Multicultural Theory of Nationalism and Its Consequences" (1996) review Herder's ideas that culture is the soul of a people, and that all cultures are valid, to comment on the growth of European nationalism. The following, except Dobbek, treat his multiculturalism by nationality: Wilhelm Dobbek, *Herders Humanitätsidee als Ausdruck seines Weltbild und seiner Persönlichkeit* (1949); Alfred Fischel, *Der Pansla-*

wismus bis zum Weltkrieg (1919); Ruth Frank, "Herders Frankreich-Erlebnis" (1933); Paul Theodor Hoffmann, *Der indische und der deutsche Geist von Herder bis zur Romantik* (1915); Wolfgang Kayser, *Die iberische Welt im Denken J.G. Herders* (1945); and Lubov Keefer, "Herder's Russian Utopia" (1936).

SELECTIVE BIBLIOGRAPHY

Works by Herder

Vom Geist der ebräischen Poesie (1782–1783). [*The Spirit of Hebrew Poetry*. Trans. James Marsh. Naperville, Ill.: R. Allenson, 1971 (reprint).]

Ideen zur Philosophie der Geschichte der Menschheit (1784–1791). [*Reflections on the Philosophy of the History of Mankind*. Ed. Frank Manuel. Chicago: University of Chicago Press, 1968. A truncated version of the preferable T. Churchill translation, *Outlines of a Philosophy of the History of Man*. London: Johnson, 1800.]

Journal meiner Reise im Jahre 1769 (posthumous). Ed. Alexander Gillies. Oxford: Blackwell, 1947.

Selective Studies of Herder

Birnbaum, Pierre. "From Multiculturalism to Nationalism." *Political Theory* 24 (February 1996): 33–45.

Chirot, Daniel. "Herder's Multicultural Theory of Nationalism and Its Consequences." *East European Politics and Societies* 10 (Winter 1996): 1–15.

Clark, Robert T., Jr. *Herder: His Life and Thought*. Berkeley: University of California Press, 1955.

Dobbek, Wilhelm. *J.G. Herders Humanitätsidee als Ausdruck seines Weltbild und seiner Persönlichkeit*. Braunschweig: Westermann, 1949.

Fischel, Alfred. *Der Panslawismus bis zum Weltkrieg*. Stuttgart: Cotta, 1919.

Frank, Ruth. "Herders Frankreich-Erlebnis." Inaugural Dissertation. Hamburg, 1933.

Hoffmann, Paul Theodor. *Der indische und der deutsche Geist von Herder bis zur Romantik*. Tübingen: Laupp, 1915.

Kayser, Wolfgang. *Die iberische Welt im Denken J.G. Herders*. Hamburg: Behre, 1945.

Keefer, Lubov. "Herder's Russian Utopia." *Modern Language Notes* 51 (1936): 361–69.

HERODOTUS
(c. 480–c. 420)

Paul Archambault

BIOGRAPHY

Herodotus has been a subject of scholarly discussion for nearly two and a half millennia, yet nearly everything about his life and work is still open to scholarly debate. In the opening lines of Book 1 of his *Historiai* (*Inquiries*, in the root sense of the Greek *Historiai*), he identifies himself as "Herodotus of Halicarnassus," indicating that he came from Greek-speaking Ionia, in southwestern Asia Minor (now Bodrun, Turkey). He is believed to have been exiled from Halicarnassus in 457 B.C.E. for conspiring against Persian rule and to have exiled himself to the island of Samos. Around 447 he went to Athens, where he won the admiration of Pericles and other Athenian notables. In 444 or 443 he settled at the Panhellenic colony of Thurii in southern Italy, a migration that explains why some manuscripts refer to him as "Herodotus of Thurii." He seems to have spent the remaining twenty years or so of his life at Thurii, where he completed his *Historiai*.

MAJOR MULTICULTURAL THEMES

Herodotus's reputation as a "multicultural" writer is due especially to the extraordinary breadth of his geographical stage and to his talent as ethnographer as much as historian. The *Historiae*, which posterity has divided into nine books, might (somewhat artificially) be subdivided into books of "ethnography," in the modern sense, and books of "history." Herodotus surely intended no such divisions, even though the "ethnography" books deal with substance that today's reader might consider more ethnographic than historical: the customs, legends, and everyday life of peoples in an area stretching eastward from the Pillars of Hercules to the Indus River, and northward from the Indian Ocean to central Russia. The "history" books deal, in a clearly epic manner, with the Persian invasion of Greece and include epic narrations of the battles of Marathon (490), Thermopylae (480), Salamis (479), and Plataea (479). The books describe the customs and legends of peoples in Egypt, in the Black Sea region (among the Scythians), in southern Italy, and in mainland Greece. Many scholars have doubted that Herodotus journeyed to these countries, or they argue that he saw far less than he claims to have seen, or that he should be judged according to the criteria of historical fiction rather than of historical truth (see Survey of Criticism). Herodotus would surely have been puzzled by such an indirect incrimination posing as absolution. He does arguably use the resources of poetry "to present the truth," but he surely claims to be stating more than merely poetic truth when he insists repeatedly in his long inquiry on the Egyptians (Book 2) that he constantly attempted to verify his facts on the spot: "I heard this story from the priests of Hephaestos in Memphis. . . . Indeed it was because of this that I went to Thebes and Heliopolis: I wanted to know whether the people there would tell me the same story as those in Memphis" (2.2–3). "So I believe those who say these things about Egypt . . . for I have seen that Egypt projects into the sea beyond" (2.12). "So far it is my eyes, my judgment, and my searching that speak these words to you; from this on, it is the accounts of the Egyptians that I will tell to you as I heard them, though there will be, as a supplement to them, what I have seen myself" (2.99). "Throughout the entire history it is my underlying principle that it is what people severally have said to me, and what I have heard, that I must write down" (2.123).

These are but a few of the many passages, in his inquiry on the Egyptians, where Herodotus plainly states his physical "autopsy" of things Egyptian. Though he provides an equally fascinating ethnographic description of the Scythians in Book 4, he states explicitly that his information on the Scythians and other peoples of the Black Sea region depends on "hearsay evidence" (4.16). He claims "personal knowlege of Persian customs" (1.131) but never claims to have traveled extensively in the Persian empire. If Herodotus's claims to first-hand observation ("autopsy") are merely a poetic ploy in a work of historical fiction, as Detlev Fehling argues, one is allowed to wonder why he claimed so repeatedly that he was present in Egypt while he never made that claim about Scythia or the Black Sea region.

Herodotus may have brought Greek preconceptions to his ethnographic inquiries, but a careful reading of the *Historiai* makes it clear that it is not always the Greeks who end up looking superior. He saw the Egyptians as superior to the Greeks in their calculations of the yearly calendar (2.4). They were the first to build altars, images, temples, and carved statues of the gods (2.4), the first to organize religious assemblies, processions, and services, "and it was from them that the Greeks learned these things" (2.58). Herodotus's Egyptians are indisputably older and more sophisticated than the Greeks in everything, from science to religious sensitivity to meteorology to artistic creativity (2.19–20; 58–64). In sum, Egypt "has more wonders in it than any country in the world and more works that are beyond description than anywhere else" (2.35).

In Herodotus's symmetrically mirrored and inverted world, where every country and river in the southern "half" is a positive reflection of a country or river in the northern half, the Nile, which flows north, is the mirror of the Ister (or Danube), which flows south; and the wisdom and sophistication of the Egyptians are negatively reflected by the stupidity and ignorance of the nations around the Euxine Pontus, or Black Sea. Greece, one notices, is right in the middle of Herodotus's world, and one assumes that Greece has learned from the sophistication of the south and has avoided the stupidity of the north. Only the Scythians, to the north, are an exception to the law of northern benightedness. In Book 4 (2–82) Herodotus spends most of his ethnographic curiosity on the Scythians, who represent for him a radically Other culture. The Scythians inhabit the northernmost limits of the known and knowable world, and beyond them lie lands "uninhabited, as far as we know." Among the many curiosities about the Scythians, besides the baldness of both sexes from birth (4.23), is that they grow grain not for their own consumption but for sale to other peoples (4.17).

Of the roughly 200 uses of the word *bárbaros* in the *Historiai*, Herodotus uses the term about 170 times in Books 6–9, in reference to Xerxes and his Persian invaders. In these books, describing what even Thucydides acknowledged to be "the greatest war in the past" (*History of the Peloponnesian War* 1:22; trans. Warner, 25), Herodotus can be said to use the techniques of both poetry and history, for these Persian wars did have an epic dimension. This is clearly a war for Greek freedom against Asiatic enslavement; Herodotus presents it as a clash not only of two continents but of two ways of life (6.106; 7.8). His affirmation of Greek moral superiority is unequivocal, and it is the affirmation of the daring underdog against the tyrant and his enslaved hordes. When Xerxes' bridge over the Hellespont collapses under a strong wind, Xerxes, in a move "worthy of a barbarian," has the Hellespont whipped and branded, as if the tyrant could do to natural forces what he does to his slaves (7.35). Xerxes weeps over the brevity of life, like a barbarian unable to face its reality (7.45–46). In the epic manner of Homer, Herodotus catalogues Xerxes' gigantic army of more than five million (7.61–81). It is said of the barbarian army that when they shoot their arrows into the air, they obscure the sun. But it is a Greek, Dieneces the Spartan, who dares reply, "If the Medes hide the sun, we shall fight them in the shade" (7.226).

A great and curious surveyor and ethnographer, Herodotus told the story of the Persian invasion as a Greek. Over the graves of those Spartans who fell at Thermopylae was a special inscription: "Go tell the Spartans, stranger passing by / that here obedient to their words we lie" (7.228). Herodotus knew that in the Greek fight against Asiatic enslavement, there was no place for cultural relativism. The intellectual and visual excitement he conveys as both curious ethnographer and as committed historian makes reading him today as fresh an experience as it must have been to his Athenian audiences.

SURVEY OF CRITICISM

Criticism of Herodotus's *Historiae* has centered largely around the question of his historical veracity. The tradition of doubting Herodotus's work in spite of its charm seems to stem from his younger contemporary Thucydides (c. 465–c. 395) who, according to tradition, felt himself called to the writing of history after he heard a public reading (or *agonisma*) of Herodotus. But, without naming him explicitly, it is from Herodotus that Thucydides distances himself in the first book of the *History of the Peloponnesian War* when he writes: "It may well be that my history will seem less easy to read because of the absence in it of a romantic element. . . . My work is not a piece of writing designed to meet the taste of an immediate public [*agonisma*], but was done to last forever" (1.22; trans. Warner, 24–25).

In the modern period Voltaire provided a famous echo to Thucydides's critique of Herodotus, citing "the novelty of his undertaking, the charm of his diction and, above all, . . . the fables" (cited in Hartog, xviii). Voltaire's view that Herodotus was both the "father of history" and the "father of lies" became common in much German, English, and American scholarship in the nineteenth and twentieth centuries (Sayce, Panofsky; cf. Fehling, 2, nn. 5, 6). In recent years Detlev Fehling, a German critic, has offered perhaps the most radical critique of Herodotus's sources, arguing that most of his travels are imaginary or copied from other sources. "There is not a single passage," Fehling writes, "certainly none concerned with anywhere outside Greece, that we can treat as evidence [that Herodotus] went to a certain place," adding that any examination of Herodotus's veracity about his travels must be confined "to those of his statements about monuments that are capable of archeological verification; and then only the ones whose truth can be positively proved should be allowed to count" (240–41).

Having subjected Herodotus's veracity to such narrow criteria, Fehling seemingly absolves the author of the *Historiai* by arguing, in his conclusion, that he should not be judged according to the criteria of science but according to those of historical fiction. Rather than be judged as fraudulent, Fehling argues, "Herodotus did nothing less than found a new literary genre, and he had to hammer out the rules for himself" (11). Historiography, he concludes, should "use the resources of poetry to present the truth," and "in the hands of Herodotus the two are combined in a thoroughly methodical way" (253).

The best strain of current Herodotus scholarship seems to consider the question of Herodotus's "real" travels either moot or irrelevant. "The important thing [in reading the *Histories*]," writes François Hartog, a French structuralist, "is to concentrate on the major organizing procedures: the surveying, the classifying, the listing and the ordering; and to see how the *Histories* are constructed through the interplay of the operations" (340). What is truly important about the *Histories*, Hartog argues, is Herodotus's remarkable ability to see the Other as Other and not simply to judge him once and for all as "Barbarian." Herodotus's description of peoples beyond Greece was a mirror and a measuring stick wherewith the Greeks saw and measured themselves.

SELECTIVE BIBLIOGRAPHY

Work by Herodotus

The History. Trans. David Grene. Chicago: University of Chicago Press, 1987.

Selective Studies of Herodotus

Fehling, Detlev. *Herodotus and His Sources.* Trans. J.G. Howie. Trowbridge, G.B.: Francis Cairns, 1989. (First published as *Die Quellenangaben bei Herodot.* Berlin and New York: Walter de Gruyter & Co., 1971.)
Hartog, François. *The Mirror of Herodotus: The Representation of the Other in the Writing of History.* Trans. Janet Lloyd. Berkeley and Los Angeles: University of California Press, 1988.
Thucydides. *History of the Peloponnesian War.* Trans. Rex Warner. Harmondsworth: Penguin Books, 1954; rpt., 1956.

HERMANN HESSE
(1877–1962)

Max E. Noordhoorn

BIOGRAPHY

Hermann Hesse, the German-Swiss poet, novelist, and essayist known for his psychologically perceptive works, was born in Calw, Württemberg, to a family of missionaries. He studied theology at the Maulbronn Seminary, which he left after only six months in 1892, signaling the beginning of a three-year-long crisis. He became an apprentice mechanic in Calw and a bookseller in Tübingen and then worked in the book trade in Basel before turning to a career in writing. Not having enjoyed formal university training, he educated himself by reading voraciously in world and German literature, art history, and history, as well as in Eastern and Western philosophy. His family's Pietist tradition and scholarly Oriental background, as well as his introspective-analytical bent, shaped his thought and his work, which is strongly autobiographical in nature. His early writings are rooted in the German Romantic and regionalist traditions.

Hesse established himself with his wife, Maria Bernouilli, in Gaienhofen on Lake Constance in 1904. Here he enjoyed the company of artists, undertook lecture tours, and traveled often to Italy, which stimulated his interest in art. In 1912 he moved to Bern, where he lived until 1919, when he decided to leave his family (his wife was suffering from progressive mental illness) to settle in Montagnola (Ticino, Switzerland). *Rosshalde* (1914) is the setting for a novel depicting the illness and death of a boy, symbolic of the breakdown of a marriage. He lived in Montagnola from 1919 on, divorcing his wife in 1923. He was briefly married to Ruth Wenger (1924–27) before entering into a lasting marriage to Ninon Dolbin in 1931.

During World War I he worked in the German-Swiss Center for Prisoners of War in Bern and established a journal for internees. Being an ardent pacifist, he condemned chauvinism and militarism. He had possessed Swiss citizenship up to age fourteen and resumed it in 1923. Following the war, he made a plea for spiritual regeneration in *Zarathustras Wiederkehr: Ein Wort an die deutsche Jugend* (1919). The pressure of personal problems, the stress of war, and criticism of his pacifist stance led him to study psychoanalysis and to undergo treatment by J.B. Lang, a disciple of Carl Jung. This, together with the influence of Nietzsche and Dostoevsky, is reflected in the novel *Demian: Die Geschichte von Emil Sinclairs Jugend* (1919), written under the pseudonym Emil Sinclair after Isaak von Sinclair, a friend of Hölderlin. The investigation of the achievement of self-awareness by a troubled young man in *Demian* had a pervasive effect on a troubled postwar Europe and catapulted its author to international fame.

Hesse's next creative period began with the experimental novel *Der Steppenwolf* (1927), whose hero's inner strife reflects the opposing tendencies of the civilized and the barbarous, rendered by means of psychoanalytical and expressionistic imagery. The work grew in popularity among the young in the late 1960s and early 1970s. The theme of division recurs in his next novel, *Narziss und Goldmund* (1930). Here, however, the problematic nature of man's duality is presented through the two contrasting title characters, who are irresistibly drawn together, yet driven to express their individuality to its limit. The opposing claims of the father principle (the intellect) and the mother principle (the senses) combined with Indo-Chinese philosophical influences to occupy Hesse until his death.

His last great work, the utopian novel *Das Glasperlenspiel* (1943), set in the year 2400, relates the life story of Joseph Knecht, a former Magister Ludi or Game Master. An exceedingly complex work fraught with symbolic significance, *Das Glasperlenspiel* is a metaphor for the game of life, embracing the sensual and the spiritual.

In the same year as that of the publication of *Das Glasperlenspiel*, Hesse was accused of having betrayed German literature to Judaism and was blacklisted in Germany. This resulted from his criticism of Nazi ideology and the publication of literary reviews in the Swedish *Bonniers Litterära Magasin* (1935–1936). Throughout his life he had published literary reviews and essays in the most respected European newspapers and magazines, such as *Die neue zürcher Zeitung*, *Die neue Rundschau*, *Die frankfurter Allgemeine*, and *La Revue des deux mondes*. He was also the editor, not only of the anti-Wilhelminian magazine *März* that he cofounded in 1905 and to which he contributed many articles, but also of various German and foreign literary works. Numerous honors were bestowed on him, notably the Nobel and the Goethe prizes in 1946. He died in Montagnola in 1962.

MAJOR MULTICULTURAL THEMES

Although Hesse was firmly grounded in the literary heritage of German Romanticism and Swiss-German regionalism, he had studied European art, history, literature, and philosophy and was conversant with Chinese Taoist, Indian Buddhist, and Japanese writings as well. These diverse sources pervaded his writing and were blended into a truly individualistic perception and expression of cultural, sociopolitical, and philosophical constructs. His visit to India in 1911 was a flight from Europe and a disintegrating marriage, and *Aus Indien* (1913) anticipated his famous postwar works, while in *Die Morgenlandfahrt* (1932) the Orient is symbolic of a spiritual realm, encompassing all times and places. His insistence on moral values reflected in individual engagement and constant renewal, to the exclusion of ideological systematization, is the theme, in Oriental guise, of *Siddharta: Eine indische Dichtung* (1922). All certainties—family, religion, wealth, sensual enjoyment—have turned insipid and nauseating to the hero, who only in serving a sage ferryman achieves self-knowledge and integration into nature, the understanding of permanence in eternal flux.

Hesse's humanitarian attitude, identifiable with Goethe's *Weltbürgertum*, arises from a respect for Christian piety and a deep faith in mankind's spirituality, which he termed *Weltglaube*. It formed the basis for his pacifism as expressed not only in his periodical *Vivos Voco*, which he edited from 1919 to 1921, but also in his *Dank an Goethe* (1932), *Der Europäer* (1946, five essays written between 1918 and 1940), and *Krieg und Frieden* (1946, containing *Brief nach Deutschland* as its epilogue). His 1904 monograph *Boccaccio* grew out of his interest in the Italian Renaissance and his trips to Italy, while *Franz von Assisi* (monograph, 1904) arose from a deep veneration for Saint Francis of Assisi as a man in harmony with himself, the world, and God.

SURVEY OF CRITICISM

Chief among the studies of Hesse as a man and an artist are those by Mark Boulby (1967), Joseph Mileck (1978), Theodore Ziolkowski (1965), and Lewis W. Tusken (1998). Martin Pfeifer's edited work (1990) contains eleven chapters by leading Hesse scholars. Ernst Rose wrote a "spiritual biography" (1965) tracing the evolution of Hesse's romantic world view into his problematic religious faith.

SELECTIVE BIBLIOGRAPHY

Works by Hesse

Demian (1919). Trans. Michael Roloff and Michael Lebeck. New York: Harper & Row, 1965.

Siddharta (1922). Trans. Hilda Rosner. New York: New Directions, 1951.

Steppenwolf (1927). Trans. Basil Creighton. London: Secker, 1929.

Narcissus and Goldmund (1930). Trans. Ursule Molinaro. New York: Farrar, Straus & Giroux, 1968.

The Glass Bead Game (1943). Trans. Richard Winston and Clara Winston. New York: Holt, Rinehart & Winston, 1969.

Gesammelte Werke in Einzelausgaben. 26 vols. Berlin and Frankfurt am Main: Suhrkamp, 1956–1965.

Gesammelte Werke Werkausgabe. 12 vols. Frankfurt am Main: Suhrkamp, 1970–1973.

Selective Studies of Hesse

Boulby, Mark. *Hermann Hesse: His Mind and Art*. Ithaca: Cornell University Press, 1967.

Michels, Volker, ed. *Materialien zu Hermann Hesses "Siddharta."* 2 vols. Frankfurt am Main: Suhrkamp, 1975, 1976.

Mileck, Joseph. *Hermann Hesse: Life and Art*. Berkeley: University of California Press, 1978.

Pfeifer, Martin, ed. *Hermann Hesses weltweite Wirkung*. 2 vols. Frankfurt am Main: Suhrkamp, 1977–1979.

———, ed. *Hermann Hesse und die Religion*. Bad Liebenzell: Verlag B. Gengenbach, 1990.

Rose, Ernst. *Faith from the Abyss: Hermann Hesse's Way from Romanticism to Modernity*. New York: New York University Press, 1965.

Tusken, Lewis W. *Understanding Hermann Hesse: The Man, His Myth, His Metaphor*. Columbia: University of South Carolina Press, 1998.

Ziolkowski, Theodore. *The Novels of Hermann Hesse: A Study in Theme and Structure*. Princeton: Princeton University Press, 1965.

HUGO VON HOFMANNSTHAL
(1874–1929)

Luanne Frank

BIOGRAPHY

Hugo Laurenz August Hofmann Elder von Hofmannsthal was born into a cultivated Viennese family that attended the opera, dominated by Wagner, and kept a box at the Burgtheater, where the repertoire included ancient tragedy, Shakespeare, and Calderón. His father was a prominent bank director and prodigious reader; his mother, the daughter of a judge. He was educated privately to age ten, then entered the prestigious Vienna Academic Gymnasium, where he demonstrated a precocious intellect and read indefatigably. By age eighteen he had read Homer, Virgil, Dante, Voltaire, Shakespeare, Byron, and Browning in the original; he had also published his first poem, his first literary essay, and his first lyric play, *Gestern* (1891); and he had begun to move in a group of young writers including Felix Salten, Hermann Bahr, and Arthur Schnitzler. The elitist Stefan George, symbolist poet and arbiter of German poetic taste, sought Hofmannsthal out as a collaborator for a planned literary journal, *Blätter für die Kunst*. Its first issue (1892) featured Hofmannsthal's verse play *Der Tod des Tizian*.

Having entered Vienna University's law school at the behest of his father in 1892, he left in dissatisfaction and enlisted in the army in 1893, but returned to the university, where he completed his doctorate (1899) with a dissertation on language use among the French Pléiade poets. He married Gertrud Schlesinger in 1901 and fathered three children.

He achieved fame in an improbable range of literary genres and a similar range of forms within them. An already-accomplished lyric poet and literary critic, seen by some as a contender for Goethe's laurels, he turned to stage and narrative writing, producing as well over two hundred essays on a wide range of subjects—literature, art, music, drama, history, politics, and travel. Interest in reanimating Austria's performing arts led him, along with Max Reinhardt,

Richard Strauss, and others, to plan in 1918 an ongoing theater program for Salzburg, in Hofmannsthal's view both a center of Austrian culture and history and Europe's heart. The result was the Salzburg Festival, for which Hofmannsthal wrote some of his best-known works. He participated in a number of publishing projects (1922–27), chiefly anthologies designed to emphasize the German literary heritage, in balance with a pervasive multiculturalism. His travels took him to Italy, France, Greece, Copenhagen, and Brussels. Intermittently ill from 1920 on, he nonetheless remained immersed in writing and traveled frequently—to Italy, Paris, Morocco, London, and Oxford. His eldest son died a suicide on July 13, 1929, followed two days later by his father, struck by a cerebral hemorrhage while preparing to leave for the funeral.

MAJOR MULTICULTURAL THEMES

Hofmannsthal's conviction of art's essential role in human affairs and his insistence that life be lived broadly, with a sense of its unity and with indebtedness to what it encounters and what surrounds it, are at one with his multiculturalism. He was attracted to the entirety of European culture and was inspired by many of the great works of other traditions—English, French, Spanish, Italian, Persian, Arabian, and ancient Greek. His unprecedentedly deep-gazing criticism, much of which depends on his aspiration to an integrated, synthesized all-inclusiveness, treats writers and works from England, France, Italy, Russia, and America, as well as Germany, Switzerland, and Austria. His travels and travel commentary are counterparts to his allegiance to his homeland.

Italy provided him with lively and mysterious land-, village-, and cityscapes that served as the setting for *Der Tod des Tizian, Die Hochzeit der Sobeide* (premiere, 1899), *Der Abenteurer und die Sängerin* (premiere, 1899), and the unfinished novel *Andreas* (1932). For *Der Abenteurer*, the Venetian libertine Casanova served as the model for Baron Weidenstamm, the middle-aged man of the world, as he would for the young libertine, Florindo, of *Cristina's Heimreise* (1910). Casanova's memoirs also provided inspiration for the Baron in the comedy fragment *Sylvia im "Stern"* and for Jaromir in *Der Unbestechliche* (premiere, 1923). Venice perhaps attracted Hofmannsthal to Thomas Otway's 1682 English drama *Venice Preserved*, which he adapted as his own first five-act play, *Das gerettete Venedig* (1905). Bicycling in Italy for a month in 1897, he wrote over two thousand lines of poetic and dramatic lyric in Varese and completed his first staged theatrical work, *Die Frau im Fenster* (premiere, 1898). The setting for the short narrative *Reitergeschichte* (1898) is Milan and its rural environs.

England, in the thought of Roger Bacon, provided the promptings to Hofmannsthal's extraordinary literary-critical essay that came to be called the Chandos letter ("Ein Brief," 1902). England provided as well the morality play *Everyman*, which he adapted as the Salzburg festival drama *Jedermann* (1911, premiere, 1920), and the pervasive influence of Shakespeare: Hofmannsthal planned a Merovingian *Lear.*

Spain, via Calderón, occupied him: his major adaptation of *El gran teatro del mundo* was the festival drama *Das Salzburger grosse Welttheater* (premiere, 1922). Having first adapted Calderon's *La vida es sueño* in 1902 (*Das Leben ein Traum*), he read the Spanish dramatist intensively in 1918 and worked throughout the 1920s on three more versions of it, now called *Der Turm*, two of which saw production (1928). He adapted Molière's comedy in 1917 as *Der Bürger als Edelmann.*

The ancient world occupied him from his earliest years. With Reinhardt as a probable instigator, he adapted Sophocles' *Elektra* (premiere, 1903), his first popular success, forming the basis of a lifelong link with Reinhardt and marking the beginning of a similar collaboration with Strauss, for whom Hofmannsthal wrote librettos for six operas, three on classical themes. The success of the first, *Elektra* (premiere, 1909), overshadowed even that of the play. Librettos for two more successes followed, *Der Rosenkavalier* (premiere, 1911), and *Ariadne auf Naxos* (premiere, 1912). *Die Frau ohne Schatten* premiered in 1919, and *Die ägyptische Helena* in 1928. The sixth was *Arabella* (premiere, 1933), whose success rivaled *Rosenkavalier*'s. Other works on classical themes were *König Oedipus* (premiere, 1910), *Alkestis* (1911), and *Orestes im Delphi, Die Bacchae, Liebe der Danae,* and the *Prologue* to an *Antigone,* none of which was produced.

The Orient also captured Hofmannsthal's imagination. His first short narrative, *Das Märchen der 672. Nacht* (written in 1895), borrows from the *Thousand and One Nights.* He also wrote an essay on Buddhism, and he planned a Chinese tragedy in 1927.

A trip to Paris in 1912 and the Ballet Russe's performances there renewed his wish to write a ballet scenario: his *Josephslegende,* an Old Testament story with music by Strauss, premiered triumphantly in Paris (1914), and other ballet scenarios on ancient themes followed—*Achilles auf Skyros* (1925) and *Die Ruinen von Athen* (1925). He also labored on a major work on Semiramis for more than a decade.

Hofmannsthal had the ability not only to immerse himself in other traditions and their works and ways, but to become one with them or let them become one with him. The unity of the self with what appears to be merely outside it and other than it, in fact, becomes one of his works' controlling themes. His experience in North Africa in 1925 provides a late illustrative example. Rather than alienation there or mere curiosity, he felt an identification so strong that he was tempted to remain. His essays on the Italian actress Eleonora Duse likewise recorded his finding an "everything" in her. In these instances he encountered a single, complex variety of life that at the same time expressed all of it. In addition to other lands and actors, literary works and criticism had a similar potential for expressing life comprehensively, he felt, though critics seldom realized this. His multiculturalism, with its frequent embrace of the ancient world, is so multifarious, so multifaceted, so pervasive, so prodigious, and so complex that even exhaustive attention to it fails to account for it satisfactorily.

SURVEY OF CRITICISM

Richard Alewyn (1949 and 1958) treats Hofmannsthal's life and work. Useful brief overviews are by Lowell A. Bangerter (1977) and Werner Volke (1967). Among studies of specific national emphases, Walter Jens (1955) and Karl G. Esselborn (1969) study Hofmannsthal's relation to classical literature; Hanna B. Lewis (1969), to America; Michael Hamburger (1964) and Mary Enole Gilbert (1936), to England; F. Claudon (1979), Steven P. Sondrup (1976), and Karen E.S. Simone (1991), to France; Dean L. Castle (1972), to Italy; Nino Nodia (1999), to Russia; Egon Schwarz (1962), to Spain; Algot Werin (1972), to Sweden; Wolfgang Köhler (1972) and Freny Mistry (1971, 1972), to the Orient; and Ulrike Stamm (1997), to art.

SELECTIVE BIBLIOGRAPHY

Work by Hofmannsthal

Sämtliche Werke: Kritische Ausgabe. Frankfurt: S. Fischer, 1998.

Selective Studies of Hofmannsthal

Alewyn, Richard. *Hofmannsthals Wandlung.* Frankfurt: Klostermann, 1949.
———. *Über Hugo von Hofmannsthal.* Göttingen: Vandenhoeck und Ruprecht, 1958.
Altenhofer, Norbert. " 'Frei nach dem Molière': Zu Hofmannsthals Gesellschaftskomödie *Die Lastigen.*" In *Festschrift für Bernhard Blume: Aufsätze zur deutschen und europäischen Literatur*, 218–37. Ed. Hunter G. Hannum, Edgar Lohner, and Egon Schwarz. Göttingen: Vandenhoeck und Ruprecht, 1967.
Bangerter, Lowell A. *Hugo von Hofmannsthal.* New York: Ungar, 1977.
Billeter-Ziegler, Marianne. "Hofmannsthal und Claudel." *Hofmannsthal Blätter* 17 (1977): 311–25.
Castle, Dean L. "Italy in the Life and Work of Hugo von Hofmannsthal." Dissertation, University of Illinois, 1971.
Claudon, F. *Hofmannsthal et la France.* Bern: Lang, 1979.
Cohn, Dorrit. "The Misanthrope: Molière and Hofmannsthal." *Arcadia* 3 (1968): 292–98.
Ernst, Erhard. "Das Karma-Thema und der 'Turm'-Stoff bei Hugo von Hofmannsthal." *Wirkendes Wort* 21 (1971): 14–24.
Esselborn, Karl G. *Hofmannsthal und der antike Mythos.* Munich: Fink, 1969.
Gilbert, Mary Enole. "Hugo von Hofmannsthal and England." *German Life and Letters* OS [Old Series] 1 (1936): 182–93.
———. "Painter and Poet: Hogarth's 'Marriage à la Mode' and Hofmannsthal's *Der Rosenkavalier.*" *Modern Language Review* 64 (1969): 818–27.

Goff, Penrith. "Hugo von Hofmannsthal and Walter Pater." *Comparative Literature Studies* 7 (1970): 1–11.

Gray, Mary. "Hugo von Hofmannsthal and Nineteenth-Century French Symbolism." Dissertation, Trinity College, Dublin, 1951.

Hamburger, Michael. "Hofmannsthal und England." *Wort in der Zeit* 10, no. 11 (1964): 30–43.

Jens, Walter. *Hofmannsthal und die Griechen.* Tübingen: Niemeyer, 1955.

Klieneberger, H.R. "Otway's *Venice Preserved* and Hofmannsthal's *Das gerettete Venedig*." *Modern Language Review* 62 (1967): 292–99.

Köhler, Wolfgang. *Hugo von Hofmannsthal und "Tausend undeine Nacht."* Bern: Peter Lang, 1972.

Lewis, Hanna B. "Hofmannsthal and America." In *Studies in German: In Memory of Andrew Louis.* Houston: Rice University, 1969.

————. "Hofmannsthal and Browning." *Comparative Literature* 19 (1967): 142–59.

————. "Hofmannsthal and Milton." *Modern Language Notes* 87 (1972): 732–41.

————. "Molière and Hofmannsthal." In *Molière and the Commonwealth of Letters,* 345–51. Ed. Roger Johnson, Editha S. Neumann, and Guy T. Trail. Jackson: University Press of Mississippi, 1975.

Mauser, Wolfram, ed. *Hofmannsthal und Frankreich.* Freiburg: Die Hofmannsthal Gesellschaft, 1987.

————. "Hofmannsthal und Molière." *Innsbrucker Beiträge zu Kulturwissenschaft.* Sonderheft 20. 1964.

Mistry, Freny. "The Concept of Asia in Hofmannsthal's Prose Writings." *Seminar* 13 (1977): 227–56.

————. "Hofmannsthal's Oriental Library." *Journal of English and Germanic Philology* 71 (1972): 177–97.

————. "Hugo von Hofmannsthal: A Study of His Relation to East Asia and Its Significance for His Development." Dissertation, University of Toronto, 1971.

Nodia, Nino. *Das Fremde und das Eigene: Hugo von Hofmannsthal und die russische Kultur.* Frankfurt: Peter Lang, 1999.

Ritter, Ellen. "Die chinesische Quelle von Hofmannsthals Dramolett *Der weisse Fächer.*" *Arcadia* 3 (1968): 299–305.

Schwarz, Egon. *Hofmannsthal und Calderón.* Cambridge, Mass.: Harvard University Press, 1962.

Shuster, Ingrid. "Die 'chinesische' Quelle des *Weissen Fächers.*" *Hofmannsthal Blätter* 8/9 (1972): 168–72.

Simone, Karin E.S. "Hugo von Hofmannsthal and Molière." Dissertation, University of Colorado, 1991.

Sondrup, Steven P. *Hofmannsthal and the French Symbolist Tradition.* Bern: Peter Lang, 1976.

Stamm, Ulrike. *Ein Kritiker aus dem Willen der Natur: Hugo von Hofmannsthal und das Werk Walter Paters.* Würzburg: Königshausen & Neumann, 1997.

Volke, Werner. *Hugo von Hofmannsthal in Selbstzeugnissen und Bilddokumenten.* Reinbek bei Hamburg: Rowohlt, 1967.

Weiss, Winfried F. "Hofmannsthal's Early Essay über Moderne Englische Malerei." *Colloquia Germanica* 9 (1975): 305–9.

Werin, Algot. "Hofmannsthal und Schweden." *Nerthus: Nordisch-deutsche Beiträge* 3 (1972): 173–91.

Zelinsky, Hartmut. "Hugo von Hofmannsthal und Asien." In *Fin de Siècle: Zu Literatur und Kunst der Jahrhundert*, 508–66. Ed. Roger Bauer et al. Frankfurt: Klostermann, 1977.

HORIGUCHI DAIGAKU
(1892–1981)

Ikuko Sagiyama

BIOGRAPHY

The first child of Horiguchi Kumaichi and Masa was named Daigaku (literally, "University") because he was born when his father was still a law student at Tokyo's Imperial University and the family lived directly opposite its main entrance. Proficient in languages and a lover of literature, especially of his own poetry, Daigaku's father, a career diplomat, was a constant guide in his son's development. When he was assigned to Korea in 1893, the family moved to Nagaoka in the prefecture of Niigata (Japan), where Daigaku's mother died, leaving her three-year-old son in the care of his grandmother. His father remarried in 1899, taking a Belgian wife. Obtaining his high-school diploma in 1909, Daigaku returned to Tokyo, where his passion for literature prompted him to join the Shinshisha (New Poetry Society), the stronghold of Japanese Romantic poetry, headed by Yosano Tekkan and his wife, Akiko. Here Daigaku met Satō Haruo (1892–1964), another future poet and prose writer, with whom he formed a fast friendship that lasted until the latter's death. The following year Daigaku enrolled at the University of Keiō and began publishing his poems in *Subaru* and *Mita Bungaku*, reviews of decadent trend in reaction to the Naturalism then in vogue.

After joining his father in Mexico in 1911, he deepened his studies of French and, under his father's guidance, read the works of Maupassant, the Parnassian poets, and Verlaine. Depending on his father's diplomatic assignments, he lived in Belgium, Spain, Brazil, and Romania, with short stays in Switzerland and in Paris. His discovery of Remy de Gourmont's poetry in 1913 was decisive in fostering his "admiration for Symbolism": "I believe that the intellectual euphoria Gourmont produced in me will remain the greatest spiritual event of my life" (*Horiguchi Daigaku Zenshū*, 6:366–67). In Spain the following year he met the French painter Marie Laurencin, who introduced him to the poetry of Guillaume

Apollinaire. To Apollinaire he would dedicate an elegy, *Konjiki no Aporo* (Gilded Apollo). His interests henceforth were directed toward French contemporary poetry: "After Gourmont, my preference extended to Régnier, Laforgue, Samain, then moved toward Jammes, Paul Fort, and, through Guy-Charles Cros, finally grew close to contemporary poetry with Apollinaire, Cocteau, Salmon and Jacob. . . . In that period I also took great pleasure in becoming acquainted with Valéry's poetry" (ibid., 367). During Daigaku's physical and artistic peregrinations, which lasted until his definitive return to his native land in 1925, he not only met Paul Fort, André Salmon, and Paul Morand, but also produced his first collections of poetry. *Gekkō to Piero* was published in 1919, with a preface by the prominent novelist Nagai Kafū. His numerous translations of both French poetry (in the anthology *Gekka no Ichigun*, 1925) and short stories, including Morand's *Ouvert la Nuit* and *Fermé la nuit*, helped to foment the *Shinkankakuha* (New Sensation School), a literary avant-garde movement led by Yokomitsu Riichi and Kawabata Yasunari. In addition to Morand's works, Daigaku also translated Raymond Radiguet's *Le Bal du comte d'Orgel* and Jean Genet's *Notre-Dame-des-Fleurs* and *Le Miracle de la rose*, published in Japan in 1931, 1953, and 1956, respectively.

During World War II Daigaku's activities as poet and translator were suspended because of censorship, but were resumed at its conclusion. The collection *Ningen no Uta* (1947) contains verses composed during his enforced silence, and *Yū no Niji* (1957) won him the Yomiuri literary prize. His translations (including Baudelaire's *Fleurs du mal*) now ranged from anthologies of major French poets from Symbolism on, to the novels, short stories, and essays of Gide, Radiguet, Cocteau, Saint-Exupéry, Kessel, Cervantes, Jean Genet, and others. He also wrote essays on poetry, including a monograph on Verlaine, *Verlaine Kenkyū* (1948). In addition, he gained a reputation as a poet of traditional tanka in thirty-one syllables. After producing more than three hundred volumes of his own works and translations, he died in 1981.

MAJOR MULTICULTURAL THEMES

Daigaku's "excellent sampling of modern French poetry" (Preface to *Gekka no Ichigun no koro*, in *Horiguchi Daigaku Zenshū*, 2:7) appearing in translation in *Gekka no Ichigun* contains 340 poems by sixty-six authors, ranging from Baudelaire, Verlaine, and Mallarmé to Apollinaire, Cocteau, Soupault, and Pierre Reverdy. The translations (1913–1925) were done during Daigaku's "wanderings" in Belgium, Spain, Brazil, Romania, and Japan. "These translations were literally born of the amusement of my pen in idle moments. Not a single poem was translated on request, nor for any other preestablished reason. I had no goal in translating them—only the pleasure of rendering them in Japanese. . . . From the moment I became acquainted with Gourmont's poetry, without anyone guiding me I selected, read, and translated the works in keeping with my feel for language" (*Gekka no Ichigun no koro*, in *Horiguchi Daigaku Zenshū*, 6:365–67). This anthology, which had a notable influence on Japanese poets and writers of the time, was also an excellent exercise in language for Daigaku. He distanced himself from contemporary Japanese literary tendencies, shunning the authoritative precedent of Ueda Bin (*Kaichōon*, 1905) in the field of poetic translation. Free from the traditional poetic koine, he sought to "choose Japanese words that would render 'illusions' most adequately and transmit directly the author's gift" (Preface to *Gekka no Ichigun*, in *Horiguchi Daigaku Zenshū*, 2:7). At the cost of violating original text forms, he succeeded in obtaining a ductile, melodious, supple, and refined poetic language. His own poems of this period clearly reflect his immersion in French sources, both for themes and for language. They parallel the change of his own inclinations, from the melancholy of his first collection, *Gekkō to Piero*, which reflects mainly Symbolist influence, to the more lucid, leaner lyricism of the "Esprit Nouveau" poets. The process culminates in the fourth collection, *Suna no Makura* (1926), in which themes are treated with irony and wit and are grounded in rhythmic and concise language.

The clarity and essentiality of his language, as well as the irony and the disenchantment that marked this period of his life, accompanied him throughout his poetic career, making possible a sublimation of the erotic, a theme in which his familiarity with French poetry played a considerable role. *Kyōen ni Erosu o maneite* (1947) is a short excursus on eroticism in modern French poetry. One of Daigaku's major literary contributions is, in fact, his creation of a sensual lyricism sustained by concrete expressions and far removed from sentimentalism or the dictates of conventional decency. His translations of French literature often go beyond simple linguistic transposition and produce a felicitous dialogue between the original and the Japanese version.

SURVEY OF CRITICISM

The poet Hagiwara Sakutarō (1929) defined Horiguchi Daigaku as "a modern and happy Parisian poet whose philosophy embraces a passion for the decadence of eroticism" (630). Attempting to identify in his artistic personality the same spirit as that of the art of the Edo period, Hagiwara Sakutarō writes: "His poetry, despite its fashionable Western style, is a 'modern ukiyoe.' It is Utamaro's painting reimported by the French, interpreted with comments in the Latin alphabet, and hung on the wall of a Western building" (630). Yano Mineto (1952) sees as the substance of Daigaku's poetry "eroticism and witticism" and outlines the distinctive features of his language—"Japanese detached from tradition" (394–95). The special issue of the review *Hon no Techō* (April 1966) devoted to Daigaku gathers articles by various authors, ranging in scope from biography to analysis of his artistic personality. Kokai Eiji (1971) carefully studies Daigaku's translations by comparing them with the original texts.

SELECTIVE BIBLIOGRAPHY

Works by Horiguchi Daigaku

Horiguchi Daigaku Zenshū. 13 vols. Ed. Andō Motoo, Iijima Kōichi, Kubota Han'ya, and Hirata Bunya. Tokyo: Ozawa shoten, 1981–1988.

Rainbows: Selected Poetry of Horiguchi Daigaku. Trans. Robert Epp. Stanwood, Wash.: Yakusha, 1994.

Selective Studies of Horiguchi Daigaku

Hagiwara Sakutarō. "Horiguchi Daigaku kun no shi ni tsuite." *Orfeon* (April 1929). Now in *Hagiwara Sakutarō Zenshū*, vol. 8, 629–33. Tokyo: Chikuma shobō, 1987.

Kokai Eiji. *"Gekka no Ichigun", shō.* In *Nihon Kindai Bungaku Taikei*, vol. 52, *Meiji Taishō Yakushi Shū*, 329–414. Tokyo: Kadokawa shoten, 1971.

Thunman, Noriko. *Gathering in Moonlight: Horiguchi Daigaku and a Crossroads in Modern Japanese Poetry.* Stockholm: Stockholms Universitet, 1991.

Tokushū Horiguchi Daigaku. Hon no Techō (April 1966). (Entire issue dedicated to Horiguchi Daigaku.)

Yano Mineto. "Kaisetsu." In *Nihon Gendaishi Taikei*, vol. 7, 394–96. Tokyo: Kawade shobō, 1952.

ALDOUS LEONARD HUXLEY
(1894–1963)

James Sexton

BIOGRAPHY

Aldous Huxley was early exposed to Europe through travel and books, and although he took a brilliant first-class degree in English literature from Balliol College, Oxford, the polymath Huxley was well versed in other European languages and literatures, beginning formal study of German and music in Marburg during the spring of 1912. In France he studied French poetry and composed imitations of Mallarmé and Baudelaire. He married a francophone Belgian in 1919; the couple took up permanent residence in Florence in 1921 and vacationed often on the Italian Riviera at Forte dei Marmi. Although they returned to England frequently, they remained based in southern Europe, first in Tuscany, then in Paris, and finally in Sanary, a coastal village situated between Toulon and Marseille. In 1937 they left Europe permanently, eventually settling in California. Maria died in 1955, and in the following year Huxley married the Italian violinist Laura Archera. He was fluent in French and adept in Italian, maintaining, not surprisingly, a lively interest in these two Romance languages and cultures until the end of his life. Indeed, in the *Memorial Volume* to Huxley (1965), André Maurois recalled that when Huxley wrote about French poetry, "it was as though written by Paul Valéry," adding that Huxley was "as much a man of French as of English culture." In the poem "Italy" Huxley reveals a deep fondness for that country, "Full of an all but human grace" (*Collected Poetry*, 59).

Huxley was an inveterate traveler and published two volumes of travel diaries, *Jesting Pilate* (1926) and *Beyond the Mexique Bay* (1934), recounting his travels in the Orient and Central America. As Jerome Meckier observes, "Huxley continues to be a cross-cultural spokesperson whose influence is worldwide" (1996, 3).

MAJOR MULTICULTURAL THEMES

Huxley had a solid grounding in French utopian thought. The influence of Voltaire's *Candide* and *L'Ingénu* can be seen in *Brave New World* (1932) and *Island* (1962); and in *Ends and Means* (1937) he criticizes the misuse of reason in the Marquis de Sade's perverse utopias *Justine* and *Juliette*. Moreover, in a little-known essay, "Utopias, Positive and Negative" (1963), he discusses Louis-Sébastien Mercier's *L'An 2440*, as well as Fourier and Cabet, and also refers to Helvétius, Condorcet, Babeuf, Renouvier, and Sorel.

Huxley announced in 1919 that he was rereading all of Balzac's works and in 1920 produced two insightful articles on his political conservatism for *Athenæum*. *Do What You Will* (1929) contains two long essays critical of Pascal and Baudelaire. In addition to writing his own poetic version of "Femmes damnées," he embodies elements of Baudelaire in the dandy Spandrell in *Point Counter Point* (1928). Huxley quotes Baudelaire in *Texts and Pretexts* (1932): "Et le printemps et la verdure / Ont tant humilié mon coeur, / Que j'ai puni sur une fleur / L'insolence de la nature" (And Spring and greenery / Have so humiliated my heart / That I avenged on a flower / The insolence of nature). In the novel Spandrell punishes the insolence of nature by slashing the petals from wildflowers with his walking stick.

Mallarmé, whom Huxley knew by heart, deeply influenced his poetic technique and content, and he translated "L'Après-midi d'un faune" in an early verse collection. Other nineteenth-century French influences were Rimbaud and Laforgue, both of whom he translated in his own verse.

A fit and appreciative reader of Dante in the original ("And Wanton Optics Roll the Melting Eye" [*Music at Night*, 1931]), Huxley not infrequently refers to Italian literary figures. One major influence on his early, somewhat elitist political thought was the Italian economist and sociologist Vilfredo Pareto (1848–1923), from whose monumental *Trattato di sociologia generale* (1916) he borrowed while composing *Proper Studies* (1927). Pareto's influence can also be seen in chapter 3 of *Brave New World* and in the full-length play *Now More Than Ever* (written 1932, published 2000). Its protagonist, the industrial rationalist and swindler Lidgate, is recognizably a Paretan type, whose "instinct for combinations" is dominant and who challenges the economy of the day dominated by men of the "persistence of aggregates" type, unable to adapt to new conditions and susceptible to economic stagnation (*Between the Wars*, 144, 146).

Arguably, some of Huxley's greatest writing deals with Italian art and Italian touring. In *Along the Road* (1925) his zest for the painting and architecture of Italy is obvious, and his eye for vivid detail, unerring. He considers Piero della Francesca's *The Resurrection* at San Sepolcro to be the best picture in the world. He knowledgeably discusses other Italian masters such as Giotto, Botticelli, and Caravaggio and, in the same volume, Malatesta's and Alberti's architecture. He was also a gifted music critic and wrote perceptively about Palestrina and, in

Adonis and the Alphabet (1956), about Carlo Gesualdo (c. 1560–1613), the aristocratic madrigalist also known as the murderer of his unfaithful first wife. Moreover, Huxley's appreciation of the Italian countryside and Italian manners is deftly portrayed in richly detailed essays such as "A Night at Pietramala" and "The Palio at Siena" and in the novel *Those Barren Leaves* (1925), set in Tuscany. "Holy Face" is a fascinating account of Huxley's visit to the shrine at Lucca (*Do What You Will*).

His knowledge of Russian literature and politics was by no means inconsiderable. Twenty-six of his *Hearst Essays* (1931–1935) deal with some aspect of Russian culture, mainly politics, education, and literature. The real-life utopian laboratory of the Communist state greatly interested him, and in 1931 he agreed to travel to Russia with his brother Julian, but, because of difficulties in the writing of *Brave New World*, he reluctantly canceled the trip. In that novel he satirized Pavlov's experiments in operant conditioning and derived inspiration for his depiction of the promiscuous brave new world not only from his encounters with sexually advanced flappers on the streets of Los Angeles in 1926, but also from P.S. Romanov's fictional portraits of "amorous flat racing"—the official Soviet policy of sexual promiscuity as outlined in the essay "Obstacle Race" (*Music at Night*).

Like his friends D.H. Lawrence and John Middleton Murry, he was impressed by Dostoevsky's "Legend of the Grand Inquisitor" in *The Brothers Karamazov*. Indeed, Mustapha Mond, the World Controller in *Brave New World*, is modeled directly on the Grand Inquisitor, and the final debate between John the Savage and Mond owes much to the triple temptation of miracle, mystery, and authority that Dostoevsky appropriated from the Gospels. Although *Brave New World* satirizes some aspects of Russian policy, Huxley—at least in the early 1930s—looked to the USSR as a source of potentially beneficial economic thinking, and although he deplored the Communists' materialism and their abuse of propaganda, he praised their systematic economic planning in his essay "Abroad in England" (1931), urging the Tory government to adopt planning as an antidote to the great economic slump.

Undoubtedly Huxley's horror of the modern idolatry known as nationalism—perhaps his main multicultural theme—receives much attention in *Beyond the Mexique Bay, Eyeless in Gaza* (1936), and *Ends and Means* (1937). The historical biography of Father Joseph, aide to Cardinal Richelieu, *Grey Eminence: A Study in Religion and Politics* (1941), points to the paradox of a mystic so bent on national aggrandizement that his foreign policy helped prolong the Thirty Years' War.

SURVEY OF CRITICISM

Derek P. Scales (1969) demonstrates Huxley's broad knowledge of French literature from the seventeenth to the twentieth centuries, and R.Z. Temple provides a useful supplement (1939). Jerome Meckier (1971) has an interesting chapter on Huxley's critique in *Brave New World* of the kind of primitivism described in the fictional Mexico of D.H. Lawrence's *The Plumed Serpent* (1926). His 1996 edited volume collects critical essays on Huxley published in America, Canada, England, Germany, Israel, India, New Zealand, and Australia.

David Bradshaw (1994) develops the influence of Pareto, and Peter Firchow (1972) examines that of Dostoevsky. He provides (1984) some contemporary Smithsonian source documents for the New Mexican pueblo chapters of *Brave New World*. Robert Baker (1982) examines Huxley's antihistoricism, especially his distaste for Hegel, noting that Huxley blamed him "for the modern tendency to view the state as an animate being" (23).

The proceedings of the 1994 Aldous Huxley Centenary Symposium under the editorship of Bernfried Nugel were published in 1995. In "The Nightmare of the Frankfurt School" Robert Baker explores Huxley's parallel lines of inquiry to those of Adorno and Horkheimer in *Dialectic of Enlightenment* (1947), particularly with regard to the Marquis de Sade. Other multicultural approaches in the symposium volume are Kirpal Singh's "Aldous Huxley through Asian Eyes," which emphasizes the importance of Huxley the metaphysician as opposed to the satirist, so esteemed in the West. Kulwant S. Gill traces Huxley's progress from materialistic empiricist to nonattached mystic in "Crisis of Double Consciousness in the Huxley Canon," noting Huxley's spiritual affirmation through Vedanta and Buddhism.

SELECTIVE BIBLIOGRAPHY

Works by Huxley

Huxley's British publisher was Chatto and Windus; from 1933, his U.S. publisher was Harper.

Those Barren Leaves. London, 1925.
Jesting Pilate. London, 1926.
Brave New World. London, 1932.
Texts and Pretexts. London, 1932; New York, 1933.
Beyond the Mexique Bay. London, 1934.
Eyeless in Gaza. London, 1936.
Grey Eminence: A Study in Religion and Politics. London, 1941.
Island. London, 1962.
The Collected Poetry of Aldous Huxley. Ed. Donald Watt. Intro. Richard Church. London, 1971.
Between the Wars. Ed. David Bradshaw. Chicago: Ivan R. Dee, 1994.
Aldous Huxley's Hearst Essays. Ed. James Sexton. New York: Garland, 1994.
Now More Than Ever. Ed. David Bradshaw and James Sexton. Austin: University of Texas Press, 2000.
Aldous Huxley Complete Essays. 2 vols. (of projected 6 vols.) Ed. Robert Baker and James Sexton. Chicago: Ivan R. Dee, 2000. [Reprint the unpublished journalism and music and art criticism, as well as the essays previously published as separate volumes.]

Selective Studies of Huxley

Baker, Robert. *The Dark Historic Page*. Madison: University of Wisconsin Press, 1982.

Bradshaw, David, ed. *Aldous Huxley Between the Wars*. Chicago: Ivan R. Dee, 1994. [Published in U.K. as *The Hidden Huxley: Contempt and Compassion for the Masses*. London: Faber, 1994.]

Firchow, Peter. *Aldous Huxley: Satirist and Novelist*. Minneapolis: University of Minnesota Press, 1972.

—————. *The End of Utopia: A Study of Aldous Huxley's Brave New World*. Lewisburg, Pa.: Bucknell University Press, 1984.

Huxley, Julian, ed. *Aldous Huxley, 1894–1963: A Memorial Volume*. London: Chatto and Windus, 1965.

Meckier, Jerome. *Aldous Huxley: Satire and Structure*. New York: Barnes and Noble, 1971.

—————, ed. *Critical Essays on Aldous Huxley*. New York: G.K. Hall, 1996.

Nugel, Bernfried, ed. *Now More Than Ever: Proceedings of the Aldous Huxley Centenary Symposium, Munster, 1994*. Frankfurt and New York: Peter Lang, 1995.

Scales, Derek. *Aldous Huxley and French Literature*. Sydney: Sydney University Press, 1969.

Temple, R.Z. "Aldous Huxley et la littérature française." *Revue de littérature comparée* 19 (January–March 1939): 65–110.

IBN BATTUTA
(1304–1369?)

Marlène Barsoum

BIOGRAPHY

Abu ʿAbdallah ibn Battuta, the famous Moroccan traveler, was born in Tangier, Morocco, in 1304, into a family of Muslim scholars of Berber origin. He studied law as a young man and in 1325, at the age of twenty-one, set out alone from his native city to make the pilgrimage, or *hajj*, to the sacred city of Mecca, in Arabia. This was the start of a career of adventurous journeying spanning almost thirty years, during which he allegedly traveled approximately 73,000 miles visiting territories equivalent to forty-four modern countries. He visited North Africa, Palestine, and Syria along the way; then Baghdad and southwestern Iran; Yemen, East Africa, Oman, and the Gulf; Asia Minor, the Caucasus, and southern Russia; India, the Maldive Islands, and China; then back to his native Maghreb, from there to Andalusia, and thence to the Sahara. He married several times during his peregrinations and fathered a number of children.

His travels remained within the cultural boundaries of Dar al-Islam, or the Abode of Islam. This expression included the lands where Muslims predominated, where Muslim kings or princes ruled, and where the *sharīʿa*, or Sacred Law of Islam, was the foundation of the social order. He moved within a world of Muslim princes, scholars, holy men, and merchants and succeeded in disarming people with his piety, good breeding, and charm. He was offered hospitality and generous gifts in the course of his career on the road. He sought out those with whom he shared a common thought expressed in the Arabic language, for although he was Berber in ethnic origin, he was Arab in culture. Wishing to deepen his learning and piety, he visited great mosques, *zawiyas* (Sufi lodges), and *madrasas* (schools or colleges teaching the Islamic sciences, especially law). He was appointed to the office of *qadi*, or judge, in the Maldive Islands and in Delhi by Sultan Muhammad Tughluq. The honor conferred upon him is testimony to the respect accorded to persons of religious learning expressed in the Arabic language.

Ibn Battuta, who believed himself to have the sensibilities of a Sufi, was catapulted into his life of wanderings because he heeded the suggestion of Burhan al-Din the Lame, a venerated Sufi ascetic living in Egypt who had the gift of foretelling the future. The holy man, perceiving the wanderlust in the young pilgrim, suggested that he visit three of his fellow Sufis, two in India, the third in China. Ibn Battuta related the incident: "I was amazed at his prediction, and the idea of going to these countries having been cast into my mind, my wanderings never ceased until I had met these three that he named and conveyed his greetings to him" (Dunn, 43–44). He experienced spiritual crises at several points in his life and entertained thoughts of abandoning his life of travel and adventure in order to devote himself to the self-denying, God-seeking life of a Sufi disciple. In the end, his passion for travel won out.

When he returned to Fez in 1354, at the end of his travel career, Sultan Abu 'Inan requested that he write a narrative of his journeys. Like Marco Polo, the other famous traveler of the Middle Ages (1254–1324), Ibn Battuta did not write his own travel book. The sultan commissioned Ibn Juzayy, a scholar of Andalusian origin, to give literary form to Ibn Battuta's experiences and observations. They collaborated for two years and produced, in December 1355, the most elaborate *rihla*, or book of travels, written in North Africa in the Middle Ages, to which they gave the title *A Gift to the Observers Concerning the Curiosities of the Cities and Marvels Encountered in Travels*. Ibn Battuta and Ibn Juzayy complemented each other in the task: the former wished to project the persona of a pious, erudite, Muslim gentleman with a Sufi's sensibilities; the latter intended that their *rihla* be a representation of the Muslim world in the second quarter of the fourteenth century. Once the *rihla* was completed, Ibn Battuta retired to a Moroccan provincial town where he occupied a judicial post. The date of his death is not certain—he is reported to have died in 1368, 1369, or 1377. No one knows where his grave lies.

MAJOR MULTICULTURAL THEMES

Ibn Battuta considered himself a citizen not only of Morocco but of Dar al-Islam; his allegiance was to its universalist, spiritual, and social values. Wherever he went, he sought the company of cosmopolitan gentlemen for whom the universalist values of Islam were deemed more important than indigenous customs. Whenever Ibn Battuta traveled beyond Arabic-speaking territories, he encountered no difficulties as long as he moved within the world of the learned, where bilingualism—Arabic and Persian—was common. Unlike Marco Polo, who was a "stranger in a strange land," Ibn Battuta remained within familiar territory with the exception of China and Constantinople, where he claims not to have felt at home. His life and career underline a remarkable phenomenon of

Afro-Eurasian history at that point in time when, as Marshall Hodgson writes, Islam "came closer than any other medieval society to establishing a common world order of social and even cultural standards" (cited by Dunn, 12).

Although Ibn Battuta had no professional background as a writer of geography, he turned out to be, as Gibb puts it, "the supreme example of *le géographe malgré lui*" ("the geographer in spite of himself"; Dunn, 5). But the *rihla* he produced is also a survey of the governments, personalities, rulers, and holy men of the Muslim world in the second quarter of the fourteenth century, making it a valuable historical source.

SURVEY OF CRITICISM

Ross E. Dunn's *The Adventures of Ibn Battuta: A Muslim Traveler of the 14th Century* (1989), a vivid interpretation of Ibn Battuta's life and times, offers a glimpse of the Moroccan traveler's extraordinary personality against a rich tapestry of his contemporary Muslim world. Dunn gives a detailed account of the journey based on Ibn Battuta's own writings, provides historical, sociological, and religious explanations, and discusses the making of the *rihla* by Ibn Battuta and his editor. Albert Hourani, in *A History of the Arab Peoples* (1991), provides a concise and very informative segment on Ibn Battuta's life and travels. He points out that the value of the traveler's narrative lies in its description of the variety of human societies and experiences within the world of Islam. Herman F. Janssens, in *Ibn Batoutah, le voyageur de l'Islam (1304–1369)* (1948), shows the influence of Islam on Ibn Battuta and his narrative. He describes the intricacies of the journey, analyzes the writing style of the *rihla*, discusses its different translations, and presents the debates among scholars about the veracity of certain episodes such as the visit to the ancient city of Bulghar on the middle Volga and to China. This study also includes an interesting section on Arab geographers of the eleventh and twelfth centuries.

SELECTIVE BIBLIOGRAPHY

Works by Ibn Battuta

Ibn Battuta's *rihla* was unknown outside the Islamic countries until the mid-nineteenth century. The following is a list of translations:

Défrémery, C., and B.R. Sanguinetti, trans. and eds. *Voyages d'Ibn Batoutah*. 4 vols. Paris: Imprimerie nationale, 1854–1874. Reprint, 4 vols., ed. Vincent Monteil. Paris: Editions Anthropos, 1968–1969.

Gabrieli, Francesco, trans. and ed. *I viaggi di Ibn Battuta*. Firenze: Sansoni, 1961.

Gibb, H.A.R. *The Travels of Ibn Battuta, A.D. 1325–1354, Translated with Revisions and Notes from the Arabic Text Edited by C. Défrémery and B.R. Sanguinetti*. 3 vols. Cambridge: for the Hakluyt Society, 1958 (vol. 1); 1962 (vol. 2); 1971 (vol. 3).

Gibb, H.A.R., and C.F. Beckingham, trans. and ed. *The Travels of Ibn Batutta*, vol. 4. London: Hakluyt Society, 1994.

Hamdun, Said, and Noel King, trans. and eds. *Ibn Battuta in Black Africa*. London: Collings, 1975.

Husain, Agha Mahdi, trans. and ed. *The Rehla of Ibn Battuta*. Baroda, India: Oriental Institute, 1976.

Lee, Samuel, trans. and ed. *The Travels of Ibn Batuta* (1829). Reprint. New York: B. Franklin, 1971.

Selective Studies of Ibn Battuta

Dunn, Ross E. *The Adventures of Ibn Battuta: A Muslim Traveler of the 14th Century* (1986). Reprint. Berkeley and Los Angeles: University of California Press, 1989.

Hourani, Albert. *A History of the Arab Peoples*. Cambridge, Mass.: Belknap Press of Harvard University Press, 1991.

Janssens, Herman F. *Ibn Batoutah, le voyageur de l'Islam (1304–1369)*. Bruxelles: Office de Publicité, 1948.

IBN KHALDUN
(1332–1406)

Abdellatif Attafi

BIOGRAPHY

Abdurahman Ibn Khaldun was a product of the Muslim expansion from Saudi Arabia to North Africa to Spain. Though he was born at the beginning of the decline of the Muslim empire, his life reflected the growth of a people and their ideas. His ancestors were among the first Yemenites to emigrate to Spain during the era of Muslim civilization in al-Andalus (711 to 1492). People of ideas and action, this upper-class family first settled in Seville at the beginning of the thirteenth century, then left Spain and relocated in Tunis, where Ibn Khaldun was born. His schooling consisted of the learning of the Koran, the sayings of the Prophet, after which he was initiated into literature, poetry, philosophy, logic, and mathematics. Drawn to the power center of Fez, capital of Morocco's Marinid dynasty, he spent eight years studying at the Karouiine University. Great scholars such as Ibn Khatib introduced him to Abu Abdellah Beni Al-Ahmar, the third sultan of Granada, who was temporarily in Morocco looking for support. Later the sultan sent Ibn Khaldun to Seville to negotiate a peace treaty with the king of Castile and Granada. For his services, he received an irrigated parcel of land in Granada, where he moved with his family. Spain's instability—the Christians were engaged in the reconquest of their land—forced him to relocate at Qalat Ibn Salama, near Oran in Algeria, where he wrote the first draft of the *Muqaddimah*. This work outlining his view of world history gained the respect of Muslim scholars. It was not until 1851 that his *Histoire des Berbères*, extracted from his universal history *Kitab al-'Ibar* (published in 1867), was translated into French, thus making his work accessible to Western society. Later *Muqaddimah* was translated as well under the title *Prolégomènes d'Ibn Khaldoun* (1862–1868).

After his pilgrimage to Mecca he settled in Egypt, where he spent his last twenty-four years serving as a judge (*qadi*) and giving lectures at Al-Azhar

University. From Tunisia to Morocco to Andalusia to Algeria to Egypt, this multicultural author played a major role in politics, law, and teaching. He died in Egypt in 1406.

MAJOR MULTICULTURAL THEMES

The multicultural experiences of Ibn Khaldun are reflected in the *Muqaddimah*, for which he is best known. In this pluridisciplinary work he sought the economic, psychological, social, and geographical factors that explain, through a cause/effect chain, the developmental stages reached in the history of human civilization. In order to explain the existing nature of power, the formation of states, and their rise and fall, he compared past societies to the ones of his time, looking at specific environments and their relationship to economic factors.

His method of analysis of human history integrated classical economic concepts such as "production," "supply," and "cost" with modern concepts of "consumption," "demand," and "utility." He distinguished two kinds of earnings: "ribh," from work done by an individual who sells his products to others, and "kasb," from work done for the individual alone. Long before the economist Adam Smith, to whom Western society attributes the foundation of economics, Ibn Khaldun stated that labor is the source of value, considering this cause/effect necessary for all earnings, capital accumulation, and the wealth of nations. During his travels he noticed that for the same profession earnings were different from one place to another. The greater the affluence and the higher the standard of living within a community, he argued, the better the earnings and the settlement of highly skilled and productive workers. The opposite situation stirs people to leave or to revolt, leading to the decline of nations. He was ahead of his time in pointing to the importance of the treatment of labor as an element in fostering prosperity. He noticed that labor was a factor in increasing productivity and that the exchange of products in large markets was the main reason for a nation's wealth and prosperity. When demand was high, sales grew, prices increased, and the demand for craftsmen became stronger. Comparing the fertile land of North Africa to the arid regions in al-Andalus that were unfit for agriculture, he observed that the cost of foodstuffs was cheaper in North Africa. The cost of production, he concluded, is taken into account in fixing prices, and that cost includes raw materials, natural resources, and the labor time used in production. He explained the stages of economic development—from nomadic conditions to agricultural stages and to the birth of the cooperative. He was aware of the importance of trade between nations and believed that the people's satisfaction, the merchants' profits, and the countries' wealth would be increased through international trade.

Ibn Khaldun advocated reform in schools. He argued that since individuals interact with the world according to laws and rules, they learn through personal experience, and that Koranic teachings alone were insufficient to further society's needs. He further supported the reforms of Ibn Arabi from al-Andalus, who proposed that schools should first teach Arabic, poetry, and mathematics rather than the Koran and religion. Ibn Khaldun's pedagogical theories are based on the concept of "habitus," a stable disposition of values, culture, norms, traditions, and so forth, acquired at an early age through learning, with the help of teachers and without excessive authority. "Habitus" could be positive or negative and thus enlighten or bewilder students, in keeping with the teaching method and the socioeconomic level of the society in question. His focus on science rather than on educational institutions reflects the precariousness of the school system in the Islamic societies of his time.

In his historical works Ibn Khaldun not only dated social, cultural, political, and natural occurrences, but included as well the names of those involved. He rooted his studies in the creation of the world, basing them in "the genealogies of the world." He focused on Berber/Arab activities, omitting China and India, and gave primary importance to political events. His innovative method embraced "specific history," that of a king, family, or tribe, and "global history," that of nations, the rationale being the interaction of the two and their connection to civilization as a whole. He also distinguished between nations such as Arab, Persian, Jewish, Roman, Turk, and Berber, linking physical environment to the dynamic role of individuals in the growth of nations. He did not attempt to explain the world. He did, however, write exhaustively about Islamic societies and those close to them. Therefore, one cannot categorize Ibn Khaldun's historical writings in terms of "universal history" as defined by Western societies. When he was writing about history, he gave primacy to the human factor, believing that people are not created by history, but create their own history in keeping with their specific environment. As a multicultural writer and a freethinking philosopher, Ibn Khaldun brought into being a liberating concept of human civilization.

SURVEY OF CRITICISM

The merit of Franz Rosenthal's 1967 translation of the *Muqaddimah* is to have combined Ibn Khaldun's three-volume work in an abridged edition that summarizes repetitive citations in a more concise form and makes the author's ideas more readily accessible. Ahmed Sadik (1992) offers valuable and extensive biographical information. Ibrahim M. Oweiss (1988) sees Ibn Khaldun as the "father of economics" and focuses on his economic observations and theories. Abdeslam Cheddadi (1999) analyzes Ibn Khaldun's literary work in sociology and history. Walter J. Fischel (1967) studies Ibn Khaldun's public functions and his historical research from 1382 until his death.

SELECTIVE BIBLIOGRAPHY

Works by Ibn Khaldun

Discours sur l'histoire universelle (al-Muqaddima). 3 vols. Beirut: Collection UNESCO d'Oeuvres Représentatives, Série Arabe, 1967.

Ibn Khaldûn, The Muqaddimah: An Introduction to History. Trans. Franz Rosenthal. Bollingen Series. Princeton: Princeton University Press, 1967.

Selective Studies of Ibn Khaldun

Cheddadi, Abdeslam. *Ibn Khaldoun revisité.* Casablanca: Editions Toubkal, 1999.

Fischel, Walter J. *Ibn Khaldûn in Egypt.* Berkeley and Los Angeles: University of California Press, 1967.

Gellner, Ernest. *Nations and Nationalism.* Oxford: Basil Blackwell, 1983.

Makdisi, George. *The Rise of Colleges.* Edinburgh: Edinburgh University Press, 1981.

Oweiss, Ibrahim M., ed. *Arab Civilization: Challenges and Responses.* Albany: State University of New York Press, 1988.

Sacy, Sylvestre de. "Ibn Khaldûn." In *Biographie universelle ancienne et moderne,* vol. 20, 270. Paris, 1858.

Sadik, Ahmed. *Ibn Khaldun.* Rabat: Editions la Porte, 1992.

HENRIK JOHAN IBSEN
(1828–1906)

Barry Jacobs

BIOGRAPHY

Born in the small town of Skien in southern Norway, Henrik Ibsen was only seven years old when his once-affluent father first went bankrupt, then sank into alcoholism; only his mother held the family together. The poor, withdrawn, and introspective child took refuge in reading, painting, and creating puppets for the tiny theater he constructed in a shed at home. Lacking funds for a better education, he apprenticed himself during seven years to an apothecary in the small town of Grimstad. The spirit of the 1848 French revolution inspired him, and his study of Latin through reading of Cicero's orations against Catiline led to his first play, the unsuccessful verse tragedy *Catilina*, which treats its protagonist not as a traitor to Rome, but as an idealistic reformer.

Leaving Grimstad for Christiania (now Oslo) in 1850, he worked as a journalist. His second play, *Kjæmpehöjen* (1850), was performed three times at the Christiania Theater, but his other projects failed. Unable to realize his dream of studying at the university, in 1851 he accepted the position of "dramatic author" in the Norwegian National Theater in Bergen, Norway, to encourage Norwegian playwrights to develop an independent dramatic tradition. In his new position he was sent abroad to study current theatrical methods, spending time at Copenhagen's Royal Theater and in Dresden. Returning to Bergen, he signed a five-year contract as "scene instructor," concerning himself with everything connected with theatrical productions. He was also obliged to write a new play each year to celebrate the anniversary of the theater's opening. Two of the four plays he wrote in Bergen, *Fru Inger til Østraat* (1855) and *Gildet på Solhaug* (1856)—his first theatrical triumph—show growing mastery of the art of drama.

In Bergen he met Magdalene Thoresen, later one of Norway's first important woman authors; in 1856 her avant-garde stepdaughter, Suzannah, accepted Ibsen's marriage proposal. In 1857 he assumed the post of artistic director of the

Norwegian Theater in Christiania. Though his next play, *Hærmændene på Helgeland* (1858), proved to be a great success, it could not solve the financial difficulties of the theater, which finally closed in 1862. The controversial Ibsen emerges in *Kjælighedens Komedie* (1862), which stirred up a storm of protest because of its attack on conventional views of marriage. By 1863 he was barely able to eke out a living by serving as aesthetic adviser to another theater, the Christiania Theater. Not even the success of *Kongsemnerne* (1863), a historical drama in the manner of Shakespeare, could remedy his desperate financial situation. In 1864, supported by a state grant for foreign travel, he left Norway with his wife and son for almost three decades of self-imposed exile with only two short visits to Norway during that time.

Ibsen settled in Rome, where he began work on *Brand* (1866), which established his reputation as an important poet and a progressive thinker and made him financially independent for the first time in his life. *Brand* is more a philosophical dramatic poem than a stageable play—the premiere performance in Stockholm (1885) lasted six and a half hours. Yet it still enjoys a respectable stage history, particularly in Germany and Russia. Its companion piece, *Peer Gynt* (1867), about a shiftless but charming ne'er-do-well brought to the brink of moral annihilation, has a much richer stage history. First produced in 1876 with a musical suite by Edvard Grieg, it continues to enjoy the status of a classical theater piece. In 1868 Ibsen moved his family to Dresden, where he wrote *De unges forbund* (1869) and *Kejser og Galilæer* (1873). Popular in its day, the former play satirizing liberal politicians perished, as did the stylized and declamatory *Kejser og Galilæer*, about Julian the Apostate.

Moving his family to Munich in 1875, Ibsen embarked upon a new phase of writing. The play *Samfundets støtter* (1877), like the eleven that followed, all deal with problems in contemporary life, and these fascinating, controversial "modern" plays brought him international fame. The first three, *Et dukkehjem* (1879), *Gengangere* (1881), and *En folkefiende* (1882), all focus primarily on social problems. In his next four plays, *Vildanden* (1884), *Rosmersholm* (1886), *Fruen fra havet* (1888), and *Hedda Gabler* (1890), he delves ever farther into the psychological depths of his protagonists, creating complex characters who still provoke fresh interpretations.

By now the world's most famous living playwright, he returned to Christiania, where he spent the remaining years of his life. His last four plays, *Bygmester Solness* (1892), *Lille Eyolf* (1894), *John Gabriel Borkman* (1896), and *Når vi døde vågner* (1899), are profound poetic meditations on the relation between art and life. Ibsen's health began to fail in 1900. The next year he suffered his first stroke; a second stroke in 1903 left him bedfast until his death in 1906.

MAJOR MULTICULTURAL THEMES

As a basis for *Catilina*, Ibsen used a common literary paradigm—a male protagonist flanked by two women, his gentle, forgiving wife Aurelia and the passionate and forceful Furia, who represent the two sides of his inner conflict. But by making "the powerful woman the hero's conscience and the gentle woman the representative of moral cowardice," he rings a startling change on this paradigm (Templeton, 27–28). His Catiline, a dedicated idealist, is at odds with the prevailing ideas, institutions, and laws in the corrupt society in which he lives, but though he battles the forces of reaction in the name of truth and freedom, his efforts are undermined by his own past misdeeds—he has seduced a Vestal Virgin who in despair drowned herself in the Tiber. In *Kejser og Galilæer*, in which the Emperor Julian dreams of effecting a synthesis between Christian asceticism and pagan hedonism by establishing a "third empire," Ibsen places the opposition between Brand's self-denial and Peer Gynt's self-indulgence in a historical context. Though the dream that some such synthesis may provide a path to happiness and self-fulfillment recurs in subsequent dramas by Ibsen, after *Samfundets støtter* he abandoned historical and verse drama and reshaped the popular French "well-made play" (in the manner of Scribe) into a powerful dramatic form. To insure that all conflicts can be resolved in the final act, the "well-made play" tends to trivialize dramatic situation; Ibsen, by contrast, adds psychological depth and social significance by making the gradual revelation of past misdeeds the source of dramatic tension.

Although he lived for long years abroad, all of Ibsen's "modern" plays are set in Norway. He seemed, like James Joyce, to need to live outside his native land in order to gain the proper perspective on it. In most of his "modern" plays the protagonists, forced to confront a problem from the past, face the questions he poses: Are we capable of change? Can we break with the past? In *Samfundets støtter, Et dukkehjem, Fruen fra havet,* and *Lille Eyolf* the answer is "yes." In most of the other plays, however, the answer is "no," and his protagonists must face the tragic consequences of their past actions. His powerful impact on foreign cultures may be illustrated by the fact that around the turn of the century in China, plays like *Et dukkehjem* became rallying points for young radicals who were bent on social reforms, such as one finds in the novel *Family* by Pa Chin.

SURVEY OF CRITICISM

Meyer's biography (1971) overshadows others. The most comprehensive analysis of Ibsen's conception of tragedy is to be found in Van Laan's introduction to his translations of *Catilina* and *Kjæmpehöjen*. McFarlane's *The Cambridge Companion to Ibsen* contains interpretative essays by leading contemporary authorities. Rüdiger Bernhardt (1989) studies Ibsen's long exile from Norway.

SELECTIVE BIBLIOGRAPHY

Works by Ibsen

The Oxford Ibsen. 8 vols. Oxford: Oxford University Press, 1960–1977.
Catiline and The Burial Mound. Trans. and intro. T. Van Laan. New York: Garland, 1992.

Selective Studies of Ibsen

Bernhardt, Rüdiger. *Henrik Ibsen und die Deutschen.* Berlin: Henschelverlag Kunst und Gesellschaft, 1989.
McFarlane, J.W., ed. *The Cambridge Companion to Ibsen.* Cambridge: Cambridge University Press, 1994.
Meyer, Michael. *Ibsen: A Biography.* Garden City, N.Y.: Doubleday, 1971.
Northam, John. *Ibsen: A Critical Study.* Cambridge: Cambridge University Press, 1973.
Templeton, Joan. *Ibsen's Women.* Cambridge: Cambridge University Press, 1997.

WASHINGTON IRVING

(1783–1859)

Jane Benardete

BIOGRAPHY

A member of the generation that came of age after the American Revolution, Washington Irving admiringly recorded European scenes and traditional society in England and Spain for an American (as well as a European) audience. His writing may be characterized by the title of one of his own works: *Tales of a Traveller* (1824). Born in New York City to a commercial family (his father was a hardware merchant and deacon in the Episcopal Church), Irving was indulged by his parents and six older brothers and sisters, who took pride in the "sensibility" that he would successfully exploit in his literary life. Instead of following his brothers to Columbia College, he chose to travel in Europe (1804–6), thus establishing the pattern of gentlemanly, nonprofessional self-cultivation reflected in his best-known literary productions. Although he read law and passed the New York State bar examination (March 24, 1806), Irving never devoted himself to the profession of the law.

His early writings were written for his own amusement and that of his friends and were published pseudonymously. With his brother William Irving and James K. Paulding he produced a comic periodical, *Salmagundi* (1807–8), and in 1809 he published "Diedrich Knickerbocker's" *History of New York*, a satiric history of Dutch colonial settlement that was admired by Sir Walter Scott. Between 1812 and 1815 he edited the *Analectic Magazine*, which contained original materials as well as reviews and articles reprinted from British periodicals. In May 1815 he sailed to England, intending to work for his family's import firm in Liverpool. When the firm went bankrupt in 1818, Irving became, for the first time, a professional author. *The Sketch-Book of Geoffrey Crayon, Gent.*, published serially in the United States (1819–1820) and as a book in England (1820), established him as the first American author since the American Revolution to be applauded in England. Writing as "Geoffrey Crayon," a sauntering, "humble" lover of the "picturesque," he compiled a sentimental portfolio that included admiring sketches of Westminster Abbey and Stratford-upon-Avon, jovial descriptions of a traditional English Christmas, maudlin treatments of rural funerals in England, two largely laudatory studies of American Indians, and, above all, two perennially popular short stories, "Rip Van Winkle" and "The Legend of Sleepy Hollow."

In 1822 Irving left England to travel in France and Germany. From 1826 to 1829 he served as a temporary attaché to the American Embassy in Madrid and returned there as U.S. minister between 1842 and 1846. His residence in Spain inspired three further works: *Life and Voyages of Christopher Columbus* (1828), *A Chronicle of the Conquest of Granada* (1829), and *The Alhambra* (1832), which by its richly exotic treatment of the Spanish scene is credited with inspiring a vogue for "Alhambraism" in American literature and architecture. In 1829 he was appointed secretary to the American Legation in London, where, according to *Fraser's Magazine*, he was regarded as "a standard writer among British men of genius." Oxford conferred the degree of doctor of civil laws upon him in 1831, and he received a Royal Society of Literature medal in 1832. In that year he returned to the United States. After 1836, except for the time as minister in Madrid, he was settled at Sunnyside, in Tarrytown, New York. His late years were marked by many honors and personal tributes, including his election as president of the first Board of Trustees of the Astor Library (later combined with the Lenox Library and the Tilden Trust to become the New York Public Library). A village near his home was named Irvington. Indisputably, his comic writings left their mark upon his native New York City, which, quoting *Salmagundi*, is often called "Gotham" (after the English town whose wise men speak nonsense) and whose reigning spirit is named "Father Knickerbocker."

MAJOR MULTICULTURAL THEMES

In *The Sketchbook of Geoffrey Crayon, Gent.* and *Bracebridge Hall* (1822) Irving presented himself as an antiquarian and conservative admirer of English customs and traditions. A Federalist in spirit, he was one of those postrevolutionary Americans who remained culturally attached to England, especially its arts and letters. English readers found in him a stylist formed in imitation of such eighteenth-century writers as Oliver Goldsmith, of whom he published a study in 1849. His grace and suavity, more old-fashioned and English than new-fashioned or "American," won the admiration of both English and American readers, for whom his persona, Geoffrey Crayon, created the model of an American gentleman of the "old style." Borrowings from German legends and folktales provided the basis for some of his most enduring works (such as "Rip Van Winkle," "The Legend of Sleepy Hollow," and "The Robber Bridegroom") and demonstrate Irving's familiarity with European literary materials. In later works his romantic treatment of Spain, based upon seven years of Spanish residence, attracted thousands of Americans to the Alhambra. As one of America's first cultural ambassadors to Europe, he helped to establish a cultivated, if sentimental, appreciation of America's European heritage.

SURVEY OF CRITICISM

The multivolume Modern Language Association–approved edition of *The Complete Works of Washington Irving* provides scholarly texts. The standard life of Washington Irving is by Stanley T. Williams (1935).

In almost two centuries since his debut as a popular writer, Irving's work and achievement have often been reevaluated. Admired during his lifetime, his work became the subject of scholarly study in the later nineteenth and twentieth centuries. Excerpts from many studies of Irving and his work may be found in Andrew B. Myers, ed., *A Century of Commentary on the Works of Washington Irving, 1860–1974* (1976). Those interested in Irving's multicultural writings will want to consult Claude G. Bowers, *The Spanish Adventures of Washington Irving* (1940), and Walter A. Reichart, *Washington Irving and Germany* (1957).

SELECTIVE BIBLIOGRAPHY

Works by Irving

Notes While Preparing "Sketch Book" etc., 1817. Ed. Stanley Williams. New Haven: Yale University Press, 1927.
Rip Van Winkle and The Legend of Sleepy Hollow. Ed. Haskell Springer. Tarrytown, N.Y.: Sleepy Hollow Restorations, 1974.
The Complete Works of Washington Irving. 29 vols. Madison: Wisconsin University Press, 1969–1970 (vols. 1–3); Boston: Twayne, 1976–1986 (vols. 4–29).

Selective Studies of Irving

Aderman, Ralph M., ed. *Critical Essays on Washington Irving*. Boston: G.K. Hall, 1990.
Bowden, Mary Weatherspoon. *Washington Irving*. Boston: Twayne, 1981.
Bowers, Claude G. *The Spanish Adventures of Washington Irving*. Boston: Houghton Mifflin, 1940.
Hedges, William L. *Washington Irving: An American Study, 1802–1832*. Baltimore: Johns Hopkins Press, 1965.
Leary, Lewis. *Washington Irving*. Minneapolis: University of Minnesota Press, 1963.
Myers, Andrew B., ed. *A Century of Commentary on the Works of Washington Irving, 1860–1974*. Tarrytown, N.Y.: Sleepy Hollow Restorations, 1976.
Reichart, Walter A. *Washington Irving and Germany*. Ann Arbor: University of Michigan Press, 1957.
Springer, Haskell. *Washington Irving: A Reference Guide*. Boston: G.K. Hall, 1976.
Wagenknecht, Edward. *Washington Irving: Moderation Displayed*. New York: Oxford University Press, 1962.

VIACHESLAV IVANOVICH IVANOV

(1866–1949)

Robert Bird

BIOGRAPHY

Viacheslav Ivanov's contemporaries called him "Viacheslav the Magnificent," borrowing a Renaissance-era epithet to denote the unlikely Renaissance man in their midst. Born in Moscow of humble stock, Ivanov cultivated an erudite and cosmopolitan intellectual persona, enrolling at the University of Berlin to study ancient history with Theodor Mommsen and Otto Hirschfeld. He immersed himself in German culture, writing poems both in Russian and in German and planning a work that has been called "a Russian *Faust*." In 1891 he moved to Paris and in 1892 undertook a fateful trip to Italy. Although he was well prepared for what he would find in Italy, he felt trepidation at having his bookish passion take on concrete form. In 1895, in Florence, he met Lidia Zinovyeva, with whom he fell in love. Divorce from his first wife and marriage to Lidia inspired (or compelled) Ivanov to forsake his academic studies for the bohemian life of a poet and thinker. From 1896 to 1902 he and Lidia wandered throughout Europe, staying variously in Italy, France, England, Greece, and Palestine. In 1902–5 they settled near Geneva, where he completed a series of lectures on the Dionysian mystery religion, the tragedy *Tantal* (in stylized trimeters), and his first book of lyric poetry, *Kormchie zvezdy*. In 1905 the Ivanovs moved to Petersburg, preceded by his growing literary reputation. Their turret-like apartment hosted a leading salon for the artistic elite, and Ivanov's reputation was cemented by the poetry collections *Prozrachnost'* (1904) and *Eros* (1907) and the book of essays *Po zvezdam* (1909).

After Lidia's sudden death in 1907, Ivanov entered upon an extended bereavement, reflected in the voluminous and intricate poetry of *Cor ardens* (1911), and he began traveling again to Italy. It was in Rome in 1910 that he realized that his late wife was, so to speak, reincarnated in her daughter from her first marriage, Vera. In 1912, shortly after she gave birth to a son, Ivanov quietly married Vera at the same Greek church in Livorno where he had married her mother. In 1913 the Ivanovs moved to Moscow, where they remained until Vera's death in August 1920. In the autumn of 1920 he secured a professorship at the University of Baku, which exposed him to Turkic and Persian culture. In 1924 he left Russia for Italy, where he remained for the final twenty-five years of his life. Upon reaching Rome he penned his "Roman Sonnets," in which he likens his exile to that of Aeneas, who forsook Troy only to rediscover it in Rome. In 1926 he converted to Roman Catholicism and received a teaching position in Pavia, where he remained until 1936. Thereafter he lived in Rome, where he taught at the Pontifical Oriental Institute and kept a poetic journal (1944) entitled *Rimskii dnevnik 1944 goda*, in which the spiritual influence of Rome is explored at the juncture of multiple chronologies, from the church calendar to anniversaries of significant events in Ivanov's own life.

MAJOR MULTICULTURAL THEMES

All of Ivanov's writings display his fascination with the fundamental unity of cultural and spiritual forms, a unity of the highest common denominator, illumined by transcendent light. His studies of religion explicated the psychology of mystical experience common to all great religions. His lyrical poetry exploited a vast array of genres and styles of various national cultures, demonstrating an underlying belief in their mutual comprehensibility. His essays utilized his erudition and capacity for synthesis in order to present his theory of Symbolism as a universally and eternally valid account of art. Through all of his works, and also through his masterful if idiosyncratic translations of writers from Sappho and Aeschylus to Byron and Baudelaire, he provided a passage to Russia for ancient and Western European culture. At the same time he subscribed to a romantic notion of nationhood, identifying elements of Russian culture that he felt could present its "universal" face to the world.

After emigrating to Italy he presented an eloquent argument for Russia's place in the cultural and spiritual history (and future) of Europe. This cause was furthered by his 1926 conversion to Eastern-rite Catholicism, which he motivated by his desire as a Christian to "breathe with both lungs" (an image adopted, although in a slightly different sense, by Pope John Paul II in many ecumenical statements). The *Perepiska iz dvukh uglov* (written with Mikhail Gershenzon in 1920 and published in 1921), a defense of traditional cultural values, was translated into all the major European languages, and his letters on "Christian humanism" to Charles Du Bos (1930) and Alessandro Pellegrini (1934), along with his 1933 "Discorso sugli orientamenti dello spirito moderno," further established his reputation as a sage advocate of universal cultural values. From the early "Ital'ianskie sonety" to the later "Rimskie sonety" and the *Rimskii dnevnik 1944 goda*, Rome (and, by extension, Italy) both symbolizes and concretizes the locus of transcendent unity: even Ivanov's Russian nationalism stems from the theory of "Moscow, the third Rome."

SURVEY OF CRITICISM

The best overviews of Ivanov's life (especially in emigration) remain the memoirs of his children Lidiia (1990) and Dimitri (pseudonym Jean Neuvecelle, 1996), the long essay by Olga Deschartes in Ivanov's *Sobranie sochinenii*, and Fedor Stepun's *Mystische Weltschau* (1964). Ivanov's work on ancient Rome and Greece has been the subject of articles by Vasily Rudich (1986, 1988). His life in Italy and connections with Italian culture have been the subject of studies by Alexis Klimoff (1972) and Andrei Shishkin (1997). Klimoff (1972, 1986) and Cazzolla (1988) examine Ivanov's "Rimskie sonety" and *Rimskii dnevnik 1944 goda*. An important resource is the issue of the Italian journal *Il Convegno* (1933) devoted to Ivanov.

Robert Bird (1997) examines the connection between Ivanov's sojourns outside Russia (particularly in Italy) and his experience of the transcendent. While Ivanov's trips "abroad" often led to experiences of the transcendent, it was always necessary for him to return to Russia (even if in a purely spiritual sense) to give them form.

Ivanov's translations from modern European languages have been the subject of monographs by Pamela Davidson (1989) and Michael Wachtel (1994). Both show Ivanov to have been a master of literary translation, even as he transformed the original texts in accordance with his theoretical views. Wachtel (1995) has also collected Ivanov's correspondence with German intellectuals from the 1920s and 1930s.

SELECTIVE BIBLIOGRAPHY

Works by Ivanov

Ellinskaia religiia stradaiushchego boga (1904–1905). *The Hellenic Religion of the Suffering God*. Trans. Carol Anschuetz. New Haven: Yale University Press, forthcoming.

De societatibus vectigalium publicorum populi romani. Zapiski Klassicheskogo Otdeleniia Imperatorskogo Arkheologicheskogo Obshchestva, 6. Prilozhenie. St. Petersburg: Tipografiia M. A. Aleksandrova, 1910; Roma: "L'Erma" di Bretschneider, 1971.

With M.O. Gershenzon. *Perepiska iz dvukh uglov* (1921). *Correspondence across a Room*. Trans. Lisa Sergio. Marlboro, Vt.: Marlboro, 1984.

Die russische Idee. Trans. J. Schor. Tübingen: J.C.B. Mohr, 1930.

Il Convegno 14, no. 8 (1933). (Includes "Discorso sugli orientamenti dello spirito moderno" and Ivanov's letter to Alessandro Pellegrini, translations of Ivanov, and articles on him.)

Das alte Wahre. Afterword Victor Wittkowski. Berlin and Frankfurt: Suhrkamp Verlag, [1955]. (Ivanov's German-language essays on culture and religion.)

Sobranie sochinenii. 4 vols. Brussels: Foyer oriental chrétien, 1971–1984.

Liriche, teatro, saggi. Ed. and trans. Donata Gelli Mureddu. Preface Michele Colucci. Roma: Libreria dello Stato, 1993.

Dichtung und Briefwechsel aus dem deutschsprachigen Nachlass. Ed. Michael Wachtel. Mainz: Liber-Verlag, 1995.

Selected Essays. Trans. and annot. Robert Bird. Ed. and intro. Michael Wachtel. Evanston, Ill.: Northwestern University Press, forthcoming.

Selective Studies of Ivanov

Bird, Robert. "Viacheslav Ivanov za rubezhom." In *Kul'tura russkoi diaspory: Samorefleksiia i samoidentifikatsiia*, 69–86. Tartu: Tartu ülikooli kirjastus, 1997.

Cazzola, Piero. "L'idea di Roma nei 'Rimskie sonety' di Vjaceslav Ivanov (con richiami a Gogol' e a Herzen)." In *Cultura e memoria: Atti del terzo simposio internazionale dedicato a Vjaceslav Ivanov*, vol. 1, 81–95. Ed. Fausto Malcovati. 2 vols. Firenze: La Nuova Italia, 1988.

Davidson, Pamela. *The Poetic Imagination of Vyacheslav Ivanov: A Russian Symbolist's Perception of Dante*. Cambridge Studies in Russian Literature. Cambridge: Cambridge University Press, 1989.

Ivanova, Lidiia. *Vospominaniia: Kniga ob ottse*. Paris: Atheneum, 1990; Moscow: Kul'tura, 1992.

John Paul II. "L'anima slava, radicata nella fede in Cristo, appartiene all'Oriente e all'Occidente." *L'Osservatore Romano* no. 123 (37,313) (29 May 1983): 1, 3.

Klimoff, Alexis. "The First Sonnet in Vyacheslav Ivanov's Roman Cycle." In *Vyacheslav Ivanov: Poet, Critic, and Philosopher*, 122–33. Ed. Robert L. Jackson and Lowry Nelson, Jr. New Haven: Yale Center for International and Area Studies, 1986.

———. "Viacheslav Ivanov v Italii (1924–1949)." In *Russkaia literatura v emigratsii: Sbornik statei*, 151–65. Ed. N.P. Poltoratzky [Poltoratskii]. Pittsburgh: Department of Slavic Languages and Literatures, University of Pittsburgh, 1972.

Malcovati, Fausto, ed. *Vjaceslav Ivanov a Pavia*. N.p.: 1986.

Neuvecelle, Jean (Dimitri Ivanov). *D'Ivanov à Neuvecelle: Entretiens avec Jean Neuvecelle*. Ed. Raphaël Aubert and Urs Gfeller. Preface by Georges Nivat. Montricher: Les editions noir sur blanc, 1996.

Nivat, George, ed. *Un Maître de sagesse au XXe siècle: Vjaceslav Ivanov et son temps*. Cahiers du monde russe 35, 1–2. Paris: Centre d' études sur la Russie, l'Europe orientale et le domaine turc de l'Ecole des hautes études en sciences sociales, 1995.

Rudich, Vasily. "Viacheslav Ivanov i antichnyi Rim." In *Cultura e memoria: Atti del terzo simposio internazionale dedicato a Vjaceslav Ivanov*, vol. 2, 131–41. Ed. Fausto Malcovati. 2 vols. Firenze: La Nuova Italia, 1988.

———. "Vyacheslav Ivanov and Classical Antiquity." In *Vyacheslav Ivanov: Poet, Critic, and Philosopher*, 275–89. Ed. Robert L. Jackson and Lowry Nelson, Jr. New Haven: Yale Center for International and Area Studies, 1986.

Shishkin, A.B. "Viacheslav Ivanov i Italiia." In *Archivio italo-russo/Russko-ital'ianskii arkhiv*, 503–62. Ed. Daniela Rizzi and Andrei Shishkin. Trento: Editrice Università degli Studi di Trento, Dipartimento di Scienze Filologiche e Storiche, 1997.

Stepun, Fedor. *Mystische Weltschau: Fünf Gestalten des russischen Symbolismus*, 201–78. Munich: Carl Hanser, 1964.

Vjaceslav Ivanov: Russischer Dichter—europäischer Kulturphilosoph. Beiträge des IV.

Internationalen Vjaceslav Ivanov Symposiums. Ed. Wilfried Potthoff. Heidelberg: Universitätsverlag C. Winter, 1993.
Wachtel, Michael. *Russian Symbolism and Literary Tradition: Goethe, Novalis, and the Poetics of Vyacheslav Ivanov*. Madison: University of Wisconsin Press, 1994.

HENRY JAMES
(1843–1916)

Jane Benardete

BIOGRAPHY

Born in New York City, into a family that in regard to "its literary and intellectual accomplishments" is "perhaps the most remarkable" the United States has ever known (Lewis, i), Henry James was named for his father, an eccentric Swedenborgian philosopher and intellectual gadabout, friend of Ralph Waldo Emerson and many other philosphers, writers, and journalists of his time. (Accordingly, James published as "Henry James, Jr." until his father's death in 1882.) His older brother, William (1842–1910), would become America's best-known philosopher, a professor at Harvard, and author of *The Principles of Psychology* (1890), *The Varieties of Religious Experience* (1902), and *Pragmatism* (1907). Two other sons, Garth Wilkinson and Robertson, and a daughter, Alice, composed the lively family unit.

After receiving a sizeable inheritance, the elder Henry declared himself "leisured for life!" and, eschewing a conventional career, repeatedly took his young family for long stays in Europe—the first time in 1843—where they traveled through England, France, Germany, Switzerland, and Italy and were given an eclectic education in London, Paris, and Geneva. Returning to the United States in 1859, the James family lived in Newport, Rhode Island, during the Civil War, in which both younger sons served as officers with black regiments. Due to what he describes in his autobiographical *Notes of a Son and Brother* (1914) as an "obscure" back injury, Henry, Jr., spent the war years as a civilian, establishing himself as a writer and literary journalist. From the late 1860s on he traveled frequently to Europe; by 1875 he was living abroad, first in Paris and then in London, with frequent trips to France and Italy. He was in the United States in January 1881 (when his mother died) and again the following December, arriving just after his father's death. He returned to London in August 1882, where he moved easily in London's stimulating literary and intellectual society. He did not revisit the United States until 1904. In July 1915 he became a British citizen to protest the reluctance of his native country to enter World War I in support of the British cause. He was, by this time, widely acknowledged as a dominant figure in English as well as American letters. A member of the American Institute and Academy of Arts and Letters, he received the British Order of Merit on New Year's Day, 1916, and died in London a few weeks later.

MAJOR MULTICULTURAL THEMES

From his youth James was one of a group of well-to-do, well-traveled, well-connected Americans—for example, Washington Irving, William Wetmore Story, James Russell Lowell, Charles Eliot Norton, and Edith Wharton—who composed a literary "mid-Atlantic" group of persons equally at home in Europe and the United States. James's fiction often treats this world, especially the late-nineteenth-century phenomenon of transatlantic marriages between newly rich Americans and titled, though impoverished, Europeans, a theme that also addresses the contrast between an immature American culture and a formalized, but desiccated European tradition. In his prolific career, in numerous short stories and novels—from *The American* (1877) and *The Portrait of a Lady* (1881) to *The Wings of the Dove* (1902), *The Ambassadors* (1903), and *The Golden Bowl* (1904)—he drew openhearted, often-impetuous Americans confronting worldly, often-unscrupulous Europeans. James's best-known work, the early tale *Daisy Miller* (1878), treats this theme ambiguously, depicting the crude manners of an outspoken, unsophisticated American girl who is seen through the eyes of a Europeanized young American who fears that he has lived abroad "too long" to understand his beautiful compatriot. Yet Daisy, like James's other fictional Americans, is treated sympathetically. Although he displays their unsophisticated manners, often comically, the Americans in James's fiction are, time after time, redeemed by their hopefulness, generosity, and moral decency.

At the same time James's critical writing asserted his attachment to Europe. In *French Poets and Novelists* (1878) he praised the work of such writers as Balzac, Flaubert, and Turgenev and set the stage for a debate on literary realism that engaged him (and his American editor William Dean Howells) in the early 1880s. James's *Hawthorne* (1879), published in Macmillan's English Men of Letters series, develops the shortcomings of American society for the man of letters, whose art thrives on a "high civilization," since the United States, unlike Europe, offers the novelist "no sovereign, no court, no aristocracy, no church, no clergy, no army, no diplomatic service . . . no cathedrals, nor abbeys, nor little Norman churches . . . no Oxford, nor Eton, nor Harrow; no literature, no novels, no museums, no political life" (cited in Edmund Wilson, ed., *The Shock of Recognition*, 460). This not entirely accurate account of America's impoverished social scene suggests James's interest as a novelist of manners in the interplay of established classes and interests he found in England and Europe. His travel writing (e.g., *A Little Tour in France*, 1884) often reveals nostalgic admiration of the aristocratic European past. His trip to America in 1904–5 is the subject of *The American Scene* (1907). Whitmanesque in its density of detail and enumeration of characteristic American sights, it records, often with wonder, the growth and urbanization of the country he had left more than a generation before.

SURVEY OF CRITICISM

James's prefaces to the monumental New York edition of *The Novels and Tales of Henry James* (1907–1917) record a lifetime of literary effort, noting the inspiration and literary intention of each narrative, the author's situation when writing, and his sense of his achievement. (These prefaces are collected in R.P. Blackmur, *The Art of the Novel*, 1934.) This record of his literary career and intentions is complemented by three autobiographical volumes, *A Small Boy and Others* (1913), *Notes of a Son and Brother* (1914), and *The Middle Years* (1917), which pay tribute to James's extraordinary family, especially his brother William, and the cultural impact of his peripatetic youth.

Students of Henry James's work benefit from a long tradition of serious readership, both English and American, from Percy Lubbock's early study *The Craft of Fiction* (1921) on. Especially noteworthy are F.O. Matthiessen, *Henry James: The Major Phase* (1944); F.R. Leavis, *The Great Tradition: George Eliot, Henry James, Joseph Conrad* (1948); Dorothea Krook, *The Ordeal of Consciousness in Henry James* (1962); and Millicent Bell, *Meaning in Henry James* (1993).

Leon Edel's massive *Henry James: A Life* (1985) and Leon Edel and Lyall H. Powers's edition of *The Complete Notebooks of Henry James* (1987) provide groundwork for many later studies. Some of James's early work as an American writer abroad is the subject of *Parisian Sketches: Letters to the New York Tribune, 1875–1876*, edited by Leon Edel and Ilse Dusoir Lind (1957).

SELECTIVE BIBLIOGRAPHY

Works by James

Hawthorne (1879). In Edmund Wilson, ed. *The Shock of Recognition*. New York: Doubleday, Doran & Co., 1943.

The Novels and Tales of Henry James. 26 vols. New York: Charles Scribner's Sons, 1907–1917.

The Art of the Novel. Critical Prefaces by Henry James. Ed. Richard P. Blackmur. New York: Charles Scribner's Sons, and London: Charles Scribner's Sons, Ltd., 1950.

Parisian Sketches: Letters to the New York Tribune, 1875–1876. Ed. Leon Edel and Ilse Dusoir Lind. New York: New York University Press, 1957.

The Complete Notebooks of Henry James. Ed. Leon Edel and Lyall H. Powers. Oxford and New York: Oxford University Press, 1987.

Selective Studies of James

Bell, Millicent. *Meaning in Henry James*. Cambridge, Mass.: Harvard University Press, 1993.

Edel, Leon. *Henry James: A Life*. New York: Harper and Row, 1985.

Krook, Dorothea. *The Ordeal of Consciousness in Henry James*. Cambridge: Cambridge University Press, 1962.

Leavis, F.R. *The Great Tradition: George Eliot, Henry James, Joseph Conrad*. New York: G.W. Stewart, and London: Chatto and Windus, 1948.

Lewis, R.W.B. *The Jameses: A Family Narrative*. New York: Farrar, Straus, and Giroux, 1991.

Lubbock, Percy. *The Craft of Fiction*. London: Jonathan Cape, 1921.

Matthiessen, F.O. *Henry James: The Major Phase*. London and New York: Oxford University Press, 1944.

JIANG GUANGCI
(1901–1931)

M. Cristina Pisciotta

BIOGRAPHY

The "Chinese Blok," the "Bard of the Russian Revolution," Jiang Guangci was born in Liu An, a small village in the province of An Wei. He left his family and traditional studies early on and went to live in Shanghai, where the urgent demands of the May Fourth Movement for profound cultural, political, and social renewal were to make a great impression on his impulsive and impressionable nature.

Life in the southern metropolis with the harsh presence of imperialist powers aroused in Jiang a violent hatred of the Western nations that were placing in crisis the values of freedom and democracy. His growing admiration of Russia—with its October Revolution in particular—made it the only nation capable of both breaking with the past and dismembering the imperialist coalition in eastern Asia. Jiang joined the League of Socialist Youth early in 1920 and was sent to Moscow with a group of young students to "learn the revolution" and live in direct contact with the new reality.

Young Chinese intellectuals at that time knew little about the ideas and historical development of European Marxism (whose theories reached China mainly filtered through Japan) and were interested above all in the cultures of Europe, America, and Japan rather than that of Russia. The continuing civil war, the hunger, and the many difficulties in no way prevented Jiang from seeing in Russia "the land of new hopes." From 1920 to 1924, during Russia's revolutionary struggle, rebirth, and reconstruction, he led a very intense cultural life, studying in depth the political, philosophical, and literary ideas of the Soviets. Returning to China full of enthusiasm, he conveyed the ideal of the October Revolution and the emerging Soviet society in his first collection of poems, *Xin meng* (1925). From that moment until his premature death he wrote constantly and prolifically: he was a poet (*Zai fenmu jin*, 1925; *Ai Zhongguo*, 1926; *Zhan gu*, 1928); a novelist (*Shaonian piaobozhe*, 1926; *Duangu dang*, 1927; *Ju Fen* and *Zuihoude wei xiao*, 1928; *Lishade aiyuan*, 1929; *Zhong chu yun wei de yue liang*, 1930; *Dianyede feng*, 1932); a literary critic ("Xiandai zhongguo shehui gemin wenxue" [Modern Chinese society and the literature of revolution], 1924; "Shiyue gemin yu eguo wenxue" [The October Revolution and Russian literature], 1926; "Guanyu gemin wenxue" [On the literature of revolution], 1928); chief editor of various magazines (*Chun lei, Taiyang yuekan, Tuohuangzhe*); and an indefatigable translator from Russian. Images and characters from Russia and China are interwoven in all his works and blend into the vision of a future society modeled on the Soviet experience. Jiang anticipated (though not always successfully or in depth) themes, styles, and literary theories that would not become dominant in China until the 1940s and 1950s. A lecturer in social sciences at the University of Shanghai and a member of the Chinese Communist Party in those years, he exercised a strong influence on Chinese youth, though he was disliked by the intellectuals because of his solitary and arrogant nature.

He fled Shanghai following the massacre of the Communists by Chiang Kaishek in 1927 and returned only under the protection of foreign concessions, suffering from tuberculosis and sadly discouraged. He resumed his literary activity in 1928, founding the Sun Society and its magazine (in whose pages some of the most important literary debates of the time took place). He also opened a bookshop specializing in Russian literature. A trip to Japan in 1929 and collaboration with Kurahara Korehito (1902–1985), champion of proletarian realism, gave new life to his work, and in 1929–30 he enjoyed a final period of creative success. Expelled from the Chinese Communist Party because he had never managed to reconcile his theories, dreams, and intellectual activity with concrete revolutionary practice, he died alone and disillusioned at just thirty years of age.

MAJOR MULTICULTURAL THEMES

The time Jiang spent in Russia was crucial not only for the emergence of his literary vocation, but in terms of defining his creative output as a whole. While the other students who arrived in Moscow with him were destined in the main for a future in politics, Jiang translated the ideals of Soviet Russia and the enthusiasm and intoxication of this nascent society into literature. Russian and Chinese history in those years appears as the protagonist in all his novels, with the central theme being the ideological journey toward revolution. Often the realities and histories of the two countries are interwoven and become fused in a single theme. Thus in *Lishade aiyuan* the beautiful Russian aristocrat married to a general in the czarist army escapes to China when her privileges are at risk, but there too she watches, powerless, as the aristocracy falls. Similarly, in *Duangu dang* the adventures of the Shanghai revolutionaries in 1926 and 1927 become at times the same as those of the revolutionaries in Moscow, in the giant fresco of what was an extraordinary moment in history. The peasant revolutionary of *Shaonian piaobozhe* is different from the tormented, contradiction-ridden revolutionary of 1920s Chinese literature: he is the Soviet hero, positive and forward-looking, with no ties to the old world.

In the poetry collection titled *Xin meng*, not only do the themes echo Soviet reality ("Mosike yin," "Ku Liening," and so on) and the images refer to Russian cultural tradition (the worker-soldier, for instance, exterminates the evil demons with his sword), but the language of the poems also seems unusual in the context of the new Chinese poetry, notwithstanding the strong Western tendencies of the latter. In effect, the language brings together the fluid colloquialism of Chinese prose and the violence of Russian proletarian poetry (the "Cosmists" and the "Source" poets of the postrevolutionary era).

Jiang was also among the first to introduce Soviet literary theories to China. He did not investigate them deeply and systematically, but he managed ingeniously to capture their originality, novelty, and vitality at a time of profound transformation in Chinese culture. For him, socialist literature, the first to succeed in offering new content and reflecting a different society, could not be compared to the European or prerevolutionary Russian cultural tradition used as a reference point by the other Chinese intellectuals. In his articles he discussed and anticipated first and foremost the concept of revolutionary literature, and later the theory of proletarian realism essentially linked to the ideas of Alexander Zonin. "I cannot stay any longer" he wrote in *Yu Anna* (1924), "I must leave Soviet Moscow, but now I am able to return to the greyness of China to work" (*Xin meng*, 32).

SURVEY OF CRITICISM

In his examination of Jiang's poetry, Leonid E. Cherkassky (1972) illustrates the deep fusion of elements of Russian proletarian poetry and Chinese poetry of the same period in the choice of poetic images, the rhythm, and the language. This analysis also looks at the use of messages directed to humanity as a whole, the "cosmic" nature of the call to battle, and the type of metaphors chosen in order to demonstrate Jiang's references not only to contemporary literature but also to the cultural traditions of the two countries. Leo Ou-fan Lee in his biography of Jiang (1973) gives a wonderfully rich account of the Soviet experience of Jiang the writer, analyzing his feelings of admiration for the country and the emergence of the romantic ideals that were to play such a significant part in his writing.

Marian Galik (1972) and Douwe W. Fokkema and Elrud Kunne-Ibsch (1977) analyze Jiang's contribution to literary criticism in his country, demonstrating his synthesis of Soviet theories and those of contemporary China and his ability to anticipate time, which was the result of intuition but also of a profound knowledge of Russian literary debate and cultural movements in those years. Hsia Tsi-an (1968) adds to this picture the important role Jiang played in the Chinese Left movements with the foundation of the Sun Society and its focus on the Soviet experience. Qu Guangci (1962) devotes a section to Jiang's translations of Russian literary works, emphasizing the popularity and wide circulation they enjoyed in China during the 1920s and 1930s.

SELECTIVE BIBLIOGRAPHY

Works by Jiang Guangci

Xin meng. 1st ed. Shanghai: Shanghai shudian, 1925.
Jiang Guangci quanji (Complete works). Shanghai: Shanghai xin wenji shudian, 1932.
Schyns, Joseph. *1500 Modern Chinese Novels and Plays.* Peiping: Catholic University Press, 1948. (Reprint, Hong Kong: Lung Men Bookstore, 1966.)
Jiang Guangci xuanji (Selective works by Jiang Guangci). Ed. Huang Yaomian. Beijing: Wenhua shenghuo, 1951.
"Hassan" ("Laotaipo yu Asan"). In *Straw Sandals,* 170–83. Trans. and ed. Kai-yu Hsü. Cambridge, Mass.: MIT Press, 1974.
Berninghausen, John, and Theodore Huters, eds. *Revolutionary Literature in China: An Anthology.* White Plains, N.Y.: M.E. Sharpe, 1976.

Selective Studies of Jiang Guangci

Cherkassky, Leonid E. "Chiang Kuang-tz'u." In *Novaya kitaiskaya poezia 20–30 gody,* 276–307. Moscow: Nauka, 1972.
Fokkema, Douwe W., and Elrud Kunne-Ibsch. "Marxist Theories of Literature." In *Theories of Literature in the Twentieth Century,* 81–135. London: Macmillan, 1977.
Galik, Marian. "Studies in Modern Chinese Literary Criticism VI: Chiang Kuang-tz'u's Concept of Revolutionary Literature." *Asian and African Studies* 8 (1972): 43–70.
Hsia Tsi-an. "The Phenomenon of Chiang Kuang-tz'u." In *The Gate of Darkness: Studies on the Leftist Literary Movement in China,* 55–100. Seattle: University of Washington Press, 1968.
Lee, Leo Ou-fan. *The Romantic Generation of Modern Chinese Writers.* Cambridge, Mass.: Harvard University Press, 1973.
McDougall, Bonnie. *The Introduction of Western Literary Theories into Modern China, 1919–1925.* Tokyo: Centre for East Asian Cultural Studies, 1971.
Qu Guangci. "Jiang Guangci zhu yi xinian mulu." In *Zhongguo xiandai wenyi ziliao, diyi chi,* 167–84. Shanghai: Shanghai shudian, 1962.

JEAN DE JOINVILLE
(1224–1317)

Paul Archambault

BIOGRAPHY

Jean de Joinville was born about ten years after King Louis IX, whom he was later to immortalize in his *Vie de Saint Louis*. He refers to himself as a "chevalier" in 1248 when he took the cross to accompany the king on the Seventh Crusade, the most important event of his life. He landed with King Louis at Damietta, in Egypt, where the French encountered fierce resistance from the Saracens. He and the king were captured, remained in captivity for about a year, and were released after payment of a large ransom. He then accompanied Louis to Syria (June 1250) and remained with him until the king's departure for France. In the spring of 1254 Joinville returned to his native Champagne. He brought back to France many indelible memories of the king, but he nonetheless refused to take up the cross again in 1267 when Louis IX was preparing his ill-fated Eighth Crusade, arguing that the previous crusade had greatly impoverished both him and his people of Champagne. King Louis died at Tunis in 1270. "Of his expedition to Tunis," Joinville wrote later, "I do not wish . . . to say anything since, thank God, I was not there" (*Life*, trans. René Hague, 145.738). A quarter century after his death, however, the king had become a legend, and the movement toward his canonization was gaining momentum. Joinville was asked by Queen Jeanne of Navarre, wife of Philippe le Bel, for "a book written of the holy sayings and good deeds of our King Saint Louis" (*Life*, trans. René Hague, 1.2), which he finished in 1309. He died in 1317 at the age of ninety-three.

MAJOR MULTICULTURAL THEMES

Joinville's *Vie de Saint Louis* is a great historical war novel, with most of its chapters being dedicated to the Seventh Crusade. This crusade is a narrative of seasickness, shipwreck, savage combat, imprisonment, ransom, liberation, dispute, and dissension—in short, an experience Joinville never wished to repeat. Had he not gone abroad from 1248 to 1254, he would have remained a culture-bound, provincial Frenchman. Because he fought in the same rivers and swamps as Saint Louis, he was able to see himself and the king as the "poor, bare, forked animals" they both were.

His war experience exposed him to the Muslim culture of the Orient. He was curious about the human makeup of the enemy: the Saracens of his account are as easily able to slit the throats of their prisoners as to take pity on their condition. Joinville, who came within a hair's width of decapitation, also experienced the Saracens' humanity, even citing to them the teaching of Saladin "that you should kill no man when once you have given him of your bread and salt to eat" (65.330). To the sanctimonious Parisian who reproaches him for eating meat on a Friday while he was in captivity, Joinville cites his more broad-minded emir captor who tells him that God will not hold it against him, "because I had done it unknowingly" (65.327). Joinville is skeptical about religious conversion, realizing that, in dangerous times especially, it is too opportune a step not to appear suspect. He and the emir both concur with Saladin's saying "that you never saw a good Saracen made of a bad Christian, nor a good Christian of a bad Saracen" (65.331). More than Saint Louis himself, Joinville is able to see that moral substance is indifferent to religious labels. Saracens are as able to make and respect their oaths as are Christians: a Saracen who goes on a pilgrimage to Mecca with his head uncovered or eats pig's flesh is as dishonorable as a Christian who blasphemes or eats meat on Friday (65.360–61). Whereas Saint Louis will not even speak to the renegade Christian who has become a "finely dressed Saracen," Joinville draws the man aside, asks to hear his story, gives him "good advice," warns him that he "may be damned the day of Judgment," but never dares pronounce his damnation (65.396). This is a far cry from the opinion of Saint Louis, who once said that a Christian layman should never discuss theological matters with a Jew, but "should defend [the faith] only by the sword, with a good thrust in the belly, as far as the sword will go" (65.53).

If this sense of humanistic tolerance toward other faiths made Joinville appear lukewarm to himself, it certainly draws him closer to us today. I would not argue, as I did many years ago in *Seven French Chroniclers* (1974), that Joinville's *Vie de Saint Louis* contains implicit condemnations of the king's failures toward the code of the *preud'home*, but I am convinced that he had a more experientially oriented cast of mind than the king, and that is what, from our perspective today, makes Joinville appear always a humanist and Saint Louis appear at times a prig.

"Il y a de l'Amyot dans Joinville," wrote Sainte-Beuve, "sinon du Plutarque" (*Causeries* 8:496). He might have added, "Il y a aussi de l'Hérodote." In his observation of other lands and cultures Joinville is as curious as the father of history. Let us consider the attention he pays to the Nile River. Can one imagine any other French historian of Joinville's time allotting a full chapter to the Nile, especially in "a book written of the holy sayings and good deeds of our King Saint Louis"? The most endearing part of Joinville's description of the Nile is that it is the product of an intensely curious mind, even if some of the information is a product of hearsay:

> The river is always muddy; when the inhabitants wish to drink it they draw it in the evening and crush three or four almonds or beans in it, and the next morning you could not drink better water. . . . Before the river reaches Egypt there are people whose practice it is to set nets in it in the evening. When the morning comes they find in them the produce which is imported into this country, ginger, that is, and rhubarb, wood of aloes and cinnamon. (188–89)

Joinville's digression on the Bedouins also looks like a leaf out of Herodotus's *Historiai*:

> They do not live in towns or cities or castles, but always lie out in the open country. In the evening they set up house for the night—or in the daytime if the weather is bad—with their wives and children, in a sort of shelter made of barrel-hoops tied to poles, like the carriages in which ladies ride. Over the hoops they throw sheepskins, prepared with alum, called Damascus skins. They themselves wear big sheepskin cloaks, which cover them completely, right down to their legs and feet. If it rains in the evening and the weather is wild during the night, they wrap themselves up in their cloaks, unbridle their horses and leave them to graze beside them. In the morning they spread the cloaks out in the sun and rub them with a dressing to keep them supple, and afterwards there is nothing to show that they have been soaked all night. (250–51)

He shows an equal curiosity toward the Mamluks (280–86), the Tartars (487–92), and the Norwegians (493). In each case his curiosity as to what makes cultures different, his attraction toward the Other as Other, is remarkable. He has all the trappings of a great ethnographer, and his *Vie de Saint Louis*, allowing for differences in mentalities, might be called, with a slight stretch of the imagination, a thirteenth-century version of Claude Levi-Strauss's *Tristes tropiques*.

SURVEY OF CRITICISM

In the first of his two *Causeries du lundi* on Joinville (12 September 1853) Sainte-Beuve, while admitting that Joinville had always been a part of French folklore, deplored the fact that it had taken so long for French scholars to establish a reliable critical text of Joinville's work and praised the 1874 critical edition by Natalis de Wailly for making Joinville accessible to the French public (8:498). In the second *Causerie* (19 September 1853) Sainte-Beuve affectionately referred to Joinville as "le plus gracieux et le plus souriant des *prud'hommes* d'alors" (the most gracious and the most smiling of the courtly men of that time) (8:532). That affectionate praise has extended almost without exception to the present day.

In his monumental thousand-page study *Saint Louis* (1996) Jacques Le Goff calls Joinville a "témoin exceptionnel" and cites his testimony more than 150 times. In her 1985 study *Myth, Man, and Sovereign Saint* Maureen Slattery distinguishes between what she calls "oral," "eye-witness," and "written" sources in Joinville's biography and attempts to analyze the distinct mythological layers surrounding each of these "source-types," concluding that there is a "plurality of social meanings surrounding King Louis." Slattery's study is a valiant attempt to read both Saint Louis and Joinville in a "different" way, but one closes the book wondering whether the author's imposition of sociological, psychological, and anthropological grids on Joinville's "source-types" yields results as radical as she claims.

SELECTIVE BIBLIOGRAPHY

Works by Joinville

The Life of Saint Louis. Trans. René Hague from the text edited by Natalis de Wailly. New York: Sheed and Ward, 1955.

Joinville and Geoffrey de Villehardouin. *Chronicles of the Crusades.* Trans. and intro. M.R.B. Shaw. Harmondsworth: Penguin Books, 1963; rpt., 1984.

Histoire de Saint Louis. Ed. Natalis de Wailly. Paris: Firmin Didot, 1874; New York: Johnson Reprint Corp., 1965.

Vie de Saint Louis. Ed. and trans. Jacques Monfrin. Paris: Dunod, 1995.

Selective Studies of Joinville

Archambault, Paul. *Seven French Chroniclers: Witnesses to History*, 41–57. Syracuse, N.Y.: Syracuse University Press, 1974.

Friedman, Lionel J. *Text and Iconography for Joinville's Credo.* Cambridge, Mass.: Medieval Academy of America, 1958.

Le Goff, Jacques. *Saint Louis.* Paris: Gallimard, 1996.

Pauphilet, Albert, and Edmond Pognon, eds. *Historiens et chroniqueurs du moyen âge: Robert de Clari, Villehardouin, Joinville, Froissart, Commynes.* Paris: Gallimard (Bibliothéque de la Pléiade), 1952.

Sainte-Beuve, C.-A. *Causeries du lundi.* 3rd ed. Vol. 8, 494–532. Paris: Garnier, n.d.

Slattery, Maureen. *Myth, Man, and Sovereign Saint: King Louis IX in Jean de Joinville's Sources.* New York: Peter Lang, 1985.

FLAVIUS JOSEPHUS
(37 C.E.–c. 100)

Paul Archambault

BIOGRAPHY

The details of Josephus's youth are related in the opening pages of his autobiography (*Bios*), written in his advanced years. He was born Josephus Ben Matthias in Jerusalem in 37 C.E., the year of Caligula's accession to the Roman imperial throne. "My family is no ignoble one," he writes, exuding a remarkable self-confidence, "tracing its descent back to priestly ancestors. . . . With us a connexion to the priesthood is the hallmark of an illustrious line. Not only . . . were my ancestors priests, but they belonged to the first of the twenty-four courses—a peculiar distinction—and to the most eminent of its constituent clans. Moreover, on my mother's side I am of royal blood" (*Bios*, 1–2). Educated with his brother Matthias, Josephus, the son of one of the most noteworthy men in Jerusalem, was soon known throughout the city as an outstanding student, remarkable for both his memory and his understanding. When he was fourteen, the chief priests and the leading men of the city could consult him on some particular detail of the city ordinances. Between sixteen and nineteen he studied with the Pharisees, the Sadducees, and the Essenes, successively, looking for a disciplined rule of life. Not satisfied with this experience, he spent three years with a certain Bannus, living an ascetic life in the wilderness, after which he decided to govern his life according to the rule of the Pharisees.

In the year 64, at the end of his twenty-sixth year, he was sent to Rome to obtain the liberation of some Jewish priests who had "on some trifling charge" been arrested and taken to Rome to render an account to Emperor Nero. Shipwrecked in the middle of the Adriatic, Josephus, with a company of six hundred, had to swim all night before being rescued. Having arrived safely in Rome, he obtained an audience with Poppea, Nero's wife. Josephus pleaded the case of the Jewish priests successfully and secured their liberation, as well as unspecified "other large gifts" from Poppea. He returned to his homeland convinced of the invincibility of Roman power, only to find his countrymen in Jerusalem fomenting revolutionary movements against Rome (*Bios*, 13–16).

Josephus's efforts to persuade his countrymen that they were inviting disaster merely attracted odium and suspicion on him. Fearing arrest and execution, he took refuge in the inner court of the Temple, hoping secretly that Cestius, the Roman governor of Syria, would come from the north and crush the sedition. Cestius, sent by Nero, did come, only to be defeated by the Jerusalem rebels, leaving many of his soldiers dead. The Syrians retaliated by killing many thousands of Jewish men, women, and children living in Syrian cities and even forced them to kill their own (*Bios*, 25–27).

After Cestius's defeat Josephus was sent on a mission to Galilee to persuade the inhabitants of the Galilean cities not to revolt against Rome. This mission was to be the turning point of his life, and most of his *Bios* is dedicated to the telling of the circuitous course of events in Galilee during a six-month period between the autumn of 66 and the spring of 67. Josephus spent much of his time attempting to pacify the warring factions, only to find himself drafted into being the commander of the Galilean rebels. This time they were facing the Roman general Vespasian, a more formidable adversary than Cestius, whom Nero had sent to "pacify" the revolt in Galilee. Josephus commanded the Jewish forces at Jotapata, the last of the Galilean cities to fall into Vespasian's hands after a forty-seven-day siege. He later recounted the details of this siege in his *Peri tou Ioudaikou polemou*, written in Rome and published about a decade later (c. 78 C.E.), telling how he hid in a cave while Jotapata was being pillaged by the Romans, refused to participate in a suicide pact with the other remaining Jews, and finally surrendered to Vespasian, who had already heard of his prophetic gifts. Taken in chains into Vespasian's presence, Josephus begged the Roman general to "keep me for yourself" and predicted that Vespasian would one day be emperor, "master not of me only, but of land and sea and the whole human race" (*Peri tou Ioudaikou polemou*, trans. H. St.J. Thackeray, III.402).

Vespasian was clearly impressed. As Josephus tells it, "While he did not release Josephus from his custody or chains, he presented him with a raiment and other precious gifts, and continued to treat him with kindness and solicitude, being warmly supported by Titus [Vespasian's son] in these courtesies" (*Peri tou Ioudaikou polemou*, III.408). Nero died within a year of these events, and Vespasian, on his way to Alexandria, was declared emperor by his armies. During the siege of Alexandria, which followed the crushing of Jotapata, Vespasian, remembering Josephus's prophecy, freed him from his bondage, severing his chains with an axe as an apology for having kept him bound for so long. It was presumably at this time that Josephus acquired Vespasian's family name, Flavius.

While Vespasian was sailing back to a triumphal acclaim in Rome, Josephus accompanied Titus in the Roman siege of Jerusalem (May–September 70). In vain did he address his countrymen from the Roman earthworks outside the walls, urging them to surrender to overwhelming Roman superiority. After a five-month siege Titus's legions sacked the city, destroyed its great Temple, and killed most of its starving inhabitants, but not before Josephus had managed to secure from Titus the liberation of 190 Jewish acquaintances. After the destruction of Jerusalem he accompanied Titus to Rome, where both Vespasian and Titus showed him every mark of respect. Vespasian lodged him in a house he had occupied before becoming emperor and gave him a considerable tract of land in Judea. After Vespasian's death in 79 Josephus continued to be shown the same esteem by Titus (79–81) and by Domitian (81–96). He wrote his major works in Rome during the final years of the first century and died during the reign of Trajan, some time after 100 C.E.

MAJOR MULTICULTURAL THEMES

For the first thirty years of his life (37–67) Josephus knew exactly which culture he belonged to. He seems to have spent the next three decades wondering whether he was a Roman or a Jew, ever a source of suspicion to many Romans, who considered him a sycophant, and of loathing to the Jews, who considered him a traitor. He unquestionably possessed great subtlety of mind and intellectual brilliance. He spoke and wrote in Aramaic, Latin, and Greek, although the Greek version of his *Peri tou Ioudaikou polemou*, originally written in Aramaic, was published in 78 C.E. with some assistance from Greek-speaking tutors during the early part of his sojourn at the Flavian court. He seems to have improved his Greek during the succeeding years in Rome and wrote his massive *Ioudaike archaiologia* (93 or 94 C.E.) in Greek directly.

Whatever else Josephus believed in, he did not believe in the symbolic power of a lost cause. The only superior capacity he was willing to attribute to his own people, in the *Peri tou Ioudaikou polemou*, at least, was their capacity for suffering: "In my opinion," he wrote, "the misfortunes of all nations since the world began fall short of those of the Jews" (I.5). When he was drafted into commanding the Jewish army of Galilee at the siege of Jotapata, he writes that he did so along Roman lines, for "he understood that the Romans owed their invincible strength above all to discipline and military training" (II.577). In his account of the Jewish War he digresses at length from his narrative to study the organization of the Roman army, convinced that "this vast empire of theirs has come to them as the prize of valour, and not as a gift of fortune" (III.71). The Romans' strength lies, he writes, in their preparation for war even during peacetime, and "it would not be wrong to describe their manoeuvres as bloodless combats and their combats as sanguinary manoeuvres" (III.75–76). With an awed reverence that was clearly meant to flatter the Flavians in whose court *Peri tou Ioudaikou polemou* was written, Josephus praises that great empire whose boundaries extended from the Atlantic to the Euphrates and from the Libyan desert to the Danube, adding "without exaggeration that, great as are their possessions, the people that won them are greater still" (III.107). Judgments like these, frequent in the *Peri tou Ioudaikou polemou*, could only endear Josephus to his Flavian patrons and make him loathsome to his Jewish readers for whom the crushing of Jerusalem was a recent, searing memory.

While Josephus was easily ingratiating himself at the Roman court, he knew that history would not so easily clear him of the charge of being a traitor to his people. That is perhaps why he undertook his magnum opus, the multivolume *Ioudaike archaiologia*, to explain the history of the Jews to a largely non-Jewish audience. The design of this massive work, written during the reign of Domitian (81–96), was "to magnify the Jewish race in the eyes of the Graeco-Roman world by a record of its ancient and glorious history" (*Ioudaike archaiologia*, IV.vii). About half the work is a rephrasing of the Hebrew Bible, while much of the rest draws on previous historians.

In his final years Josephus wrote two smaller works, the autobiography (*Bios*) and *Kata Apionos*. In the latter work he defended "the extreme antiquity of our Jewish race, the purity of the original stock and the manner in which it established itself in the country which we occupy today" (I.1). Considered "the most attractive" of Josephus's works by his finest English-language translator, H. St. J. Thackeray, the *Kata Apionos* provides interesting insights into the anti-Semitism of the first century by demonstrating the antiquity of the Jewish nation while challenging the extreme antiquity of the Greeks claimed by some Greek historians. After arguing so flatteringly for the material and military superiority of the Romans in his earlier works, Josephus seems to have become more fully convinced of the historical "superiority" of his own ancient culture. He risked nothing when he wrote these final pro-Jewish works, as his great patrons, Vespasian and Titus, were now dead.

SURVEY OF CRITICISM

G.J. Goldberg, *Flavius Josephus Home Page* (1998) (http://user.aol.com/fljosephus/home.htm, pp. 1–5), provides a great deal of critical bibliography, especially in English, and especially for the period 1980–1998.

The abundance of critical and editorial commentary on Josephus's work since the early 1900s in Germany, England, France, and America (to mention only these countries) can best be summarized by breaking it down into three controversial questions. These are admirably summarized by André Pelletier (1959) in the introduction to his excellent French translation of Josephus's *Bios* (*Autobiographie*, xvi–xxvii).

The first question, a purely philological one, was debated especially among French and English scholars in the 1920s and 1930s. It dealt with determining whether Josephus had incorporated into his *Bios* a "report" he would have written for the Sanhedrin in an attempt to justify his pro-Roman position before the defeat of the Jews at the hands of Vespesian at Jotapata (67 C.E.). Some scholars concluded that such a report never existed. Richard Laqueur argued in *Der jüdischer Historiker Fl. Josephus* (1920) that Josephus had written such a report in Greek, while Henry St. John Thackeray (1926) thought Josephus had written a previous report in Aramaic. In a masterful summary of the debate, André Pelletier concludes that there is insufficient evidence for the existence of a "report" written before the battle of Jotapata, and that if Josephus did write such a report, he did so in his old age, during the reign of Domitian (81–96), when he wrote most of his major works. In any case it is impossible to prove that Josephus incorporated the substance of a previous report into the text of his *Bios* (Pelletier, xvi–xxi).

A second critical question—or set of questions—deals with the extent to which Josephus, a Jewish historian, was "christianized" by some writers of the early Church: St. Jerome called Josephus the "Christian Livy," and Eusebius credited him with the authorship of the Fourth Book of Maccabees (Pelletier, xx). While the latter is an opinion "no one takes seriously today" (Pelletier, xx), scholarly controversy still rages over the authenticity of a passage in Josephus's *Jewish Antiquities* (18.3.3), usually referred to as the *Testimonium de Christo*, or *Testimonium Flavianum*, in which Josephus recounts the life, death, and resurrection of Jesus, whom he calls "Messiah" (Goldberg, 4). Critics since the seventeenth century have argued over this text, the prevailing opinion being until recently that it "could not have been written by a Jewish man . . . because it sounds too Christian" (Goldberg, 4). In 1930 Theodor Reinach, a French translator of the complete works of Josephus, dismissed the *Testimonium Flavianum* without the benefit of argument, as "surely an interpolation" (cited in Pelletier, 22). Goldberg writes that a 1995 discovery brought new evidence to the debate over the *Testimonium Flavianum* and points to the conclusion that Josephus's account cannot have been a complete forgery. The most recent details about the *Testimonium Flavianum* debate are published in *The Journal for the Study of the Pseudepigrapha* 13 (1995): 59–77 (cited in Goldberg, 5).

The third and final debated question among critics of Josephus's work deals with their "value." Understandably, but not always fairly, critics have allowed their opinion of Josephus's character to color their evaluation of his work, since so much of his work is autobiographical and "apologetic." Was Josephus a flatterer of the Flavian emperors, Vespasian, Titus, and Domitian? Was he a traitor to the Jewish cause? Can one be a turncoat and remain a good historian? On this question, André Pelletier seems to concur with the harsh but mitigated opinion of Theodor Reinach:

Josephus is neither a great mind, nor a great character, but a singular composite of Jewish patriotism, of Hellenic culture, and of vanity. . . . One must nevertheless credit him . . . with the qualities of a fearsome polemicist, of a facile, profuse, sometimes pathetic and . . . elegant writer, in spite of his concessions to traditional rhetoric . . . [C]onsidering the disaster of almost the entirety of Hellenistic and Roman historical literature, the documentary value of his works . . . is incomparable. (xxii–xxiii)

SELECTIVE BIBLIOGRAPHY

Works by Josephus

I. *The Life; Against Apion.* Trans. H. St. J. Thackeray. London: William Heinemann; New York: G.P. Putnam's Sons, 1926.
II. *The Jewish War, Books I–III.* 1927.
III. *The Jewish War, Books IV–VII.* 1928.
IV. *Jewish Antiquities, Books I–IV.* 1930.
Oeuvres complètes de Flavius Josèphe. Ed. and trans. Theodor Reinach. Paris: Leroux, 1900–1930.
Autobiographie. Ed. and trans. André Pelletier, S.J. Paris: Les Belles Lettres, 1959.
Guerre de Juifs. 3 vols. Ed. and trans. André Pelletier, S. J. Paris: Les Belles Lettres, 1975–1982.

Selective Studies of Josephus

Laqueur, Richard. *Der jüdischer Historiker Fl. Josephus.* Darmstadt: Wissenschaftliche Buchgesellschaft, 1920.
Thackeray, Henry St. John. *Josephus.* London: Heinemann, 1926; New York: Putnam, 1981.

JAMES JOYCE
(1882–1941)

Mary Hudson

BIOGRAPHY

James Augustine Joyce was born in Dublin and died in Zürich. His relatively small literary output became one of the most influential in European and American literature of the twentieth century. His works include *A Portrait of the Artist as a Young Man* (1916), a novelized account of his childhood and education; *Dubliners* (1914), a collection of short stories detailing the life of Dublin's petty bourgeoisie at the turn of the century; his monumental comic epic *Ulysses* (1922); and, lastly, *Finnegans Wake* (1939), the inscrutable, multilingual novel that he jokingly boasted would keep scholars guessing for three hundred years. His major writings were revolutionary in their relentless and minute examination of the mundane things of life and the celebration of ordinariness through art. He popularized the "stream-of-consciousness" technique used to such astonishing and humorous effect in the Molly Bloom soliloquy at the end of *Ulysses*. In all of his novels laughter bubbles right beneath the surface, occasionally bursting forth in mirthful affirmations of life.

Spending most of his life in Italy and France and possessing a wide appreciation of other cultures and languages, Joyce was the very embodiment of multiculturalism at a time before it became perceived as a good; indeed, this was at a period of history—between the two world wars—when it could be positively dangerous. The first child of a lower-middle-class Catholic family of ten children, Joyce from an early age studied foreign languages and music, two fields for which he would retain a passionate interest until the end of his life. He received an excellent education and soon evinced an uncommon confidence in his own exceptional abilities, but he was not to follow a common path to success. Totally disregarding matters of financial security, he led a nomadic adult life, with long periods of poverty in which he and his own family lived largely on the handouts given them by various family members, friends, and admirers. His first concern being for his art, he single-mindedly pursued his literary calling despite constant upheavals from dwelling to dwelling, city to city, and country to country, and through two world wars. Although his works deal almost exclusively with Dublin, he returned to the city of his birth only once in the thirty-seven years that separated his departure from it in 1904 and his death in 1941. This fledgling genius soon outgrew the social strictures of his provincial birthplace and the oppressive moral constraints imposed by a powerful Jansenistic form of Catholicism that dominated life in Ireland almost to the end of the twentieth century.

Fleeing Ireland shortly after meeting his future wife, Nora Barnacle, the penniless Joyce spent a number of weeks in Zürich before going on to Pola, a town on the Adriatic coast then part of the Austro-Hungarian Empire, where he managed to land a teaching job with the Berlitz school. Soon, however, the discovery by the authorities of a spy ring caused all foreigners in the city to be expelled. He and Nora were forced to go to Trieste, their home for the next ten years and the birthplace of their son Giorgio and daughter Lucia. Here Joyce perfected his Italian (not to mention Triestine dialect) to such an extent that he was able to write articles for the local newspaper *Il piccolo della sera* and give lectures at the University of Trieste on topics ranging from Irish politics to Daniel Defoe. He also made lifelong friendships, most notably with Ettore Schmitz, more familiar to lovers of literature as Italo Svevo, the Italian Jewish novelist who hired Joyce to give him English lessons and later confessed to him that he had published two novels. Joyce thought that they deserved more attention than they had received and encouraged him to write more. He in turn encouraged Joyce, giving him the inspiration he needed to take up an abandoned chapter of *A Portrait of the Artist as a Young Man*, which was finally published in book form in the United States in 1916. Svevo would become for him, according to Joyce's biographer Richard Ellmann, "with humorous reluctance, one of Joyce's chief sources for the Jewish lore of *Ulysses*" as well as a model for the novel's hero, Leopold Bloom (Ellmann, 272).

The outbreak of World War I found the Joyce family forced to flee this disputed territory and go back to Zürich to await the end of the war and their eventual return to Trieste. The homecoming was to be short-lived, however, for the family lived in too-crowded circumstances with other Joyce relations and left, at Ezra Pound's behest, for a "vacation" in Paris that was to last for twenty years. It was here that *Ulysses* was completed and published, bringing Joyce, if not wealth, at least the world acclaim that his work has enjoyed ever since.

His identification with Jews was so complete that when the Joyces needed a safe haven from Nazi-occupied Paris, they were at first refused entry into Switzerland on the basis of being Jewish. The family was finally granted permission to settle once again in Zürich, to which they had fled more than once before, but their refuge was short-lived. Joyce died of peritonitis shortly after his arrival there and was laid to rest in its Fluntern Cemetery.

MAJOR MULTICULTURAL THEMES

No other author comes close to Joyce in his openness to other cultures and languages, nor in his capacity to be influenced by them, even to the point of making borrowings from other languages an integral part of his works. His mastery of foreign languages and keen interest in European literature have already been noted. Dante was perhaps his favorite author, but no literature was beyond his interest. Not only his novels, but his home life as well must have been a multilingual extravaganza. Even after leaving Italy, his children continued to converse with each other only in Italian. (Carrying on their father's love for punning, they referred to Ezra Pound, for instance, as "Signor Sterlina"—Mister Sterling). His Triestine friendship with Ettore Schmitz/Italo Svevo had contributed to his fascination and love for Jewish culture. It became a distinguishing mark of *Ulysses*, which he envisaged as "the epic of two races (Israel-Ireland) and at the same time the cycle of the human body as well as a little story about a single day (life)," (*Letters*, I:75). Joyce also admired the Jews' warm sense of family. "Look at them," his friend Frank Budgen quoted him as saying, "They are better husbands than we are, better fathers and better sons" (Ellmann, 373). Leopold Bloom, the Jewish hero of *Ulysses*, exhibits these familial qualities in Joyce's effort to make of him the perfect expression of the common, decent man, the ordinary man who demonstrates all the frailty yet all the nobility of which each of us is capable.

SURVEY OF CRITICISM

Criticism of Joyce's works is vast. Indeed, a veritable industry has sprung up, much as Joyce himself predicted, whose task it is to decipher and "deconstruct" his epic genius. Most major writers and critics of the century, from T.S. Eliot to Jacques Derrida to Umberto Eco, have contributed to the enormous body of Joycean criticism. Richard Ellmann (1959) must be credited, however, with the most exhaustive and estimable scholarship on Joyce and his writings. In *Joyce and the Jews* (1989) Ira Nadel traces Joyce's affinity for the Jews to the "parallel conditions of exile, education and displacement" of the Jews and the Irish (1). He points out that Joyce also found similarity between himself and the Jews in their approach to the word. The Jews had remained faithful to their sacred texts through constant migrations as though they were a "portable homeland." Like his, theirs was a devotion to the word—"not made flesh, nor reified into a symbol—but only as text" (Nadel, 4–6). In *The French Joyce* (1990) Geert Lernout traces the fascination Joyce holds for French-inspired poststructuralism and deconstructionist movements, devoting a chapter, for instance, to Joyce studies in the influential avant-garde French periodical *Tel quel*.

SELECTIVE BIBLIOGRAPHY

Works by Joyce

Dubliners: The Corrected Text (1914). Ed. Robert Scholes. London: Cape, 1967.

A Portrait of the Artist as a Young Man (1916). New York: B.W. Huebach, 1916.

Exiles (1918). Harmondsworth: Penguin Books, 1973.

Ulysses (1922). Ed. Hans Walter Gabler with Wolfhard Steppe and Claus Melchior. New York and London: Garland, 1984.

Pomes Penyeach (1927) *and Other Verses*. London: Faber and Faber, 1966.

Finnegans Wake. London: Faber and Faber; New York: Viking, 1939.

Letters, Vols. I, II, III. Ed. Stuart Gilbert and Richard Ellmann. New York: Viking, 1966.

James Joyce in Padua. Ed., trans., and intro. Louis Berrone. New York: Random House, 1977.

Selective Studies of Joyce

Cixous, Hélène. *L'Exil de James Joyce*. Paris: Bernard Grasset, 1968. [English trans. *The Exile of James Joyce*. New York: David Lewis, 1972.]

Cope, Jackson I. *Joyce's Cities: Archaeologies of the Soul*. Baltimore: Johns Hopkins University Press, 1981.

Ellmann, Richard. *James Joyce*. Oxford: Oxford University Press, 1959.

Gaiser, Gottlieb, ed. *International Perspectives on James Joyce*. Troy, N.Y.: Whitston Publishing Company, 1986.

Lernout, Geert. *The French Joyce*. Ann Arbor: University of Michigan Press, 1990.

Lobner, Corinna del Greco. *James Joyce's Italian Connection*. Iowa City: University of Iowa Press, 1989.

Melchiori, Giorgio, ed. *Joyce in Rome*. Roma: Bulzoni, 1984.

Nadel, Ira B. *Joyce and the Jews*. Iowa City: University of Iowa Press, 1989.

Pinguentini, Gianni. *James Joyce in Italia*. Verona: Ghidini e Fiorini, 1963.

Svevo, Italo. *James Joyce*. Trans. Stanislaus Joyce. San Francisco: City Lights Books, 1969.

Tuoni, Dario de. *Ricordo di Joyce a Trieste*. Milan: All'insegna del Pesce d'Oro, 1966.

KABIR
(1398?–1448?)

Alessandro Monti

BIOGRAPHY

Very little is known about the life of Kabir if we exclude the huge corpus of legendary biography of either Muslim or Hindu origin. He was born in Varanasi (Benares) around the end of the fourteenth century into a family of weavers recently converted to Islam. He probably joined a Hindu guru (Ramananda, according to tradition), who instructed him as a *bhakti* (devotee) to the god Ram, not the popular divine hero of the *Ramayana*, actually an avatar of Vishnu, but the sacred sound (mantra) that consists of the two syllables (one short, one long) "Râ-ma." Although he became a guru himself, he still practiced weaving, and many metaphors or figures of speech in his poetry are obviously taken from this craft. He imparted his teaching exclusively by word of mouth, given his alleged illiteracy: "I don't touch ink or paper" (*Bijak*, trans. Hess and Singh, 111).

There are many legends concerning Kabir's life. It is said that he was generated by a Brahmin widow (or by a Brahmin woman of immaculate condition) who placed him in a basket set afloat on a pond, where a Muslim couple discovered and adopted him. Different versions of the legend narrate that he was born as the miraculous result of the words spoken by Ramananda to his virgin widowed mother. His supposed birth from the palm of his mother's hand suggests the fanciful etymology of his name, from the Hindi words *kar* (hand) and *bir* (the Sanskrit *vir*, meaning hero). However, the name Kabir is clearly of Muslim origin. In the biographical text *Kabir Kasaut*, a *Qazi* (judge) was summoned to give a name to the child. Four names (Kabir, Akbar, Kubra, and Kibriya) were found on opening the Koran, all these being titles of God. All were deemed unsuitable for a low-caste Muslim, and fresh attempts were made, with the same result. Thus the *Qazi* insisted that the child be killed forthwith, but the baby Kabir spoke:

I was bodiless: I took body and I came: in this body
I am called Kabir. . . .
With all my body I belong to the Sat-lok. I dwell
in every heart. Kabir says, Hear, O brother sadhus: I have
manifested the true name. (*Bijak*, trans. Shah, 3)

Although the *sadhus* (the Hindu wandering ascetics devoted to celibacy) claim Kabir as one of their fold, it is highly credible that he was a "householder," that is, a married man with sons and daughters. The legends about his death basically revolve around two recurrent themes, his decision to die at Magahar instead of choosing the most holy city of Kashi (the Sanskrit name of Benares) and the quarrel of the Hindus and the Muslims over Kabir's corpse. In fact, it is traditionally said that whoever dies at Magahar will become an ass in his next life, whereas to die in Benares leads to salvation. However, Kabir says that if "Rama lives in one's heart," there is no difference at all between Kashi and Magahar. After Kabir's death his Hindu and his Muslim followers quarreled over his body: the former wanted to burn it, the latter to bury it. They finally agreed to cover his body with flowers, and after doing so, they were astonished to discover that only the flowers remained. Kabir was in heaven, where the gods met and greeted him.

To Kabir has been attributed the authorship of several thousand *bhajanas* (devotional songs) and *dohas* (sapient couplets) that he uttered by word of mouth and that were successively sung by his followers. His works have been collected in the *Kabir Dohe* and in the *Bijak*, an "account book" composed of his verses and observations, which was completed by a disciple about 1570. Several hundred songs attributed to him are collected in the holy book of the Sikhs. The corpus of the Kabir legends has been collected in the *Kabir Parachai* (Lorenzen, 1991).

MAJOR MULTICULTURAL THEMES

Kabir persistently escapes judgment. He was of low birth and status, either as a weaver or as a recent convert to Islam. Both *jati* (class group) and religion should have made him a Hindu outcaste. In spite of that, he was initiated into the *hatha-yoga* of Gorakhnath, whose teaching strongly influenced the figure of the medieval *sant nirgun*, a mystic devoted to a god who is *nirgun*, literally, "without attributions," and consequently not subject to definition. As a holy man, the *sant* is strongly related to the *bhakti*, a movement both devotional and literary that strove to achieve an intimate feeling of reciprocal and perfect love between the god and the devotee. Ramananda, Kabir's supposed guru, shifted the focus of the *bhakti* from Vishnu to one of his avatars, either Rama or Krishna. Perhaps in his wake, Kabir operated a mystical synthesis, one that tried to "confuse" the teachings of traditional Brahmanic Hinduism with the less ritualistic inspiration of the Muslim Sufi mystics, who nurtured intimations of an austere godhead, akin to the devotional love typical of the *bhakti* movement, but also deeply imbued, or rather mingled, with Islamic and Hebrew concepts. We must not forget the peculiar situation of North India at that time—under the Mogul rule there was no sharp distinction in the mass of the population between Hindus and Muslims, since many low-caste Hindus found it convenient to convert to the religion of the conquerors, although they adhered more or less secretly to their former beliefs. However, we cannot speak of Kabir, the religious reformer, as a synthesizer of Hinduism and Islam. He transcended both religions in his quest for ultimate truth. His world view was dominated by an over-whelming "love for the Lord" (*Kabir Dohe*, trans. Das, xviii). Truth (the term *sant* may be translated as "seeker of truth," from the Sanskrit root *sat*, truth) comes forth in his verses through flashes and leaps of momentary recognition. His key terms are *sabda* (the Word), *sahaja* (spontaneity), and *rama*, the name of Ram. One of his standard formulaic phrases is "ghata ghata me," or in every body, meaning that truth is within all of us.

SURVEY OF CRITICISM

In his 1977 volume Ram Kumar Verma summarizes Kabir's place in world poetry by quoting from the *Kabir Dohe* (trans. Das): "Kabir has been acknowl-edged as one of the greatest poets who has given the minutest details of the whole history of human thought. . . . The poet does not *write* but *utters* and his speech scores much above the authority of all scholarship of written thought. In short Kabir was 'not of an age, but for all times' " (xix–xx).

Linda Hess, who edited *The Bijak of Kabir* (1983), highlights the Platonic quality of Kabir's oral discourse and characterizes him as a good "dialectician" rather than a "rhetorician." She also stresses Kabir's attacks against the kingpins of Hindu society and the religious earnestness of the Muslim emperor, who "crows 'God' like a cock" (20).

G.N. Das, the editor of the *Kabir Dohe* (1991), foregrounds the devotional side in Kabir's verses, which cast a bridge between Hinduism and Islam. David Lorenzen, the editor of the *Kabir Legends* (1991), gives a structural reading of this material: Kabir is seen as a trickster, the Hindu underdog who antagonizes the upper-caste orthodox Brahmans and the king himself; he tricks all of them into giving him what he needs, or humbles them. The Italian scholar Pinuccia Caracchi (1999) puts emphasis on Kabir's Hindu heritage. In her opinion, Ka-bir's monotheism is rooted in the teachings of the Vedanta rather than in the Islamic movement of the Sufis.

SELECTIVE BIBLIOGRAPHY

Works by Kabir

The Bijak of Kabir. Trans. Ahmad Shah. Delhi: D.K. Publishers Distributors, 1994 (1917).

The Bijak of Kabir. Trans. Linda Hess and Shukdev Singh. Delhi: Motilal Banarsidass, 1986 (1983).

Kabir Dohe. [*Couplets from Kabir.* Ed. and trans. G.N. Das. Delhi: Motilal Banarsidass, 1991.]

Selective Studies of Kabir

Caracchi, Pinuccia. *Ramananda e lo yoga dei sant.* Alessandria: Edizioni dell'Orso, 1999.

Lorenzen, David N., ed. *Kabir Legends and Ananta-Das's Kabir Parachai.* Albany: State University of New York Press, 1991.

Verma, Ram Kumar. *Kabir: Biography and Philosophy.* New Delhi: Prints India, 1977.

NIKOLAI MIKHAILOVICH KARAMZIN
(1766–1826)

Robert Bird

BIOGRAPHY

At the crossroads of his creative life Nikolai Karamzin described himself in 1803 as a man "who has aided the development of [Russian] language and taste, earned the flattering attention of the Russian public, and whose trifles, published in the various languages of Europe, have received positive reviews from renowned foreign authors" (Cross, 1971, 218). He viewed literature as a major conduit for Russia's legitimate entry into Europe and became the first Russian writer to achieve renown in Europe as a symbol of the new Russia. His profound understanding of cultural mechanisms later led him to concentrate on Russian literary language and Russian historiography, fields in which he laid the groundwork for the flowering of Russian culture.

Born into the family of a retired officer, he studied at a school run by a Frenchman in the provincial capital Simbirsk and at a Moscow boarding school run by a German. In 1781–84 he served in the Guards, and before his retirement he translated several minor pieces from the German. His literary career began in earnest during his five years in the Masonic Friendly Learned Society in Moscow, led by Nikolai Novikov and aimed at disseminating "wisdom," largely through ambitious publishing projects. Here Karamzin met numerous prominent cultural figures, including the poet Vasily Petrov and A.M. Kutuzov, to whom he addressed his *Pis'ma russkogo puteshestvennika*. He also entered into correspondence with Johann Kaspar Lavater, a Swiss sentimentalist. In 1787 he published a prose translation of Shakespeare's *Julius Caesar*, which "marks an epoch as the first faithful translation into Russian" of Shakespeare (Cross, 1964, 93); in a preface Karamzin defended Shakespeare's nonclassical drama along the lines of contemporary German views. He also published a translation of Lessing's *Emilia Galotti*, several translations for the society's journal *Detskoe chtenie dlia serdtsa i razuma* (which he edited in 1787–1789), and several sentimentalist poems, including a long poetic manifesto that praises mainly English and German poets and expresses the hope that geniuses of comparable rank will one day appear in Russia. His fellow Masons introduced him to issues that would preoccupy him in future years, such as the relationship between heart and reason, the Enlightenment, and the role of foreign loan words and calques in the Russian literary language. He emerged from Novikov's society as a confirmed sentimentalist, and even in his final masterpiece, the multivolume *Istoriia gosudarstva rossiiskogo*, he continued to privilege feeling over intellect as the basis of moral being.

In May 1789 he left Russia for a fourteen-month excursion to Germany (where he met prominent cultural figures such as Kant and Herder), Switzerland, France (where he witnessed revolutionary events and personages), and England. Although the trip may have been conceived as an effort to cement contacts between Russian and other European Freemasons, he used it primarily to enrich his own knowledge of contemporary cultural trends. Upon his return he founded the *Moskovskii zhurnal*, in which he began to publish his *Pis'ma russkogo puteshestvennika*, the first literary record of a Russian's impressions of Western Europe. The journal propagandized contemporary European literature, especially writers of a sentimentalist or pre-Romantic hue (from Sterne to Herder and Goethe), and also Karamzin's growing interest in making the Russian literary language sound more modern. Of his prose tales of the 1790s the most renowned is "Bednaia Liza," but almost all of them exerted a powerful influence on the development of Russian prose and engendered numerous imitators.

He founded a new journal in 1802, *Vestnik Evropy*, in which, although remaining true to the ideal of the Western European Enlightenment, he took pains to stress the growing achievements of Russian culture. Here he also outlined his views on literary language, stressing the need for written Russian to be based on the spoken language (although the gentry to whom he addressed himself largely spoke French). After 1803 he devoted himself almost completely to his *Istoriia gosudarstva rossiiskogo*, the first eight volumes of which appeared in 1818. In addition to retaining his position as the grand old man of Russian letters, Karamzin became the Russian historian laureate and furthered the cause of Russian cultural self-awareness by granting it a history worthy of a European power.

MAJOR MULTICULTURAL THEMES

Karamzin strove to integrate the achievements of the European Enlightenment with Russian culture in order to facilitate Russia's entry into the family of European nations as a distinctive and equal partner. His *Pis'ma russkogo puteshestvennika* provided a much-imitated model for Russians' pilgrimages to the West and their literary presentation, concentrating on the latest European trends and personages and setting these novelties into a Russian context, making them relevant to readers. The *Pis'ma* is filled with observations about national character and customs, historical and cultural landmarks, intellectual trends, and current gossip. Intellectually Karamzin was most impressed by the Germany of Kant, Herder, and Wieland, although Rousseau's Switzerland had a special claim to his affections; on a more personal level he preferred the French, whom he characterized as "fire and air" and whose level of civilization he viewed as ideal (*Pis'ma russkogo puteshestvennika*, 320). Influenced by the Enlightenment, however, he judged all nationalities and individualities against an abstract ideal of "humanity": finding a pile of bones left after a fifteenth-century battle, Karamzin exclaims, "While taking pride in being Swiss, don't forget your most noble name—that of man!" (*Pis'ma russkogo puteshestvennika*, 147). Accordingly, while he expressed homesickness and even national pride, he was always alert to customs or novelties that he felt would help to raise Russian civilization to the abstract norm. Defending Peter the Great, he claims, "It was necessary, in a manner of speaking, to break the neck of deeply-rooted Russian obstinacy in order to make us flexible, capable of learning and adopting [foreign novelties]. . . . Being born in Europe, where the Arts and Sciences had already blossomed in all countries except Russia, [Peter] had only to tear down the curtain that hid from us the achievements of human reason" (*Pis'ma russkogo puteshestvennika*, 253–54). He repeatedly expresses regret that educated Russians often neglect their mother tongue, while pointing out all the merits of modern Russian to his readers and to the foreigners he meets; he claims that Russian can change without sacrificing its purity, like English, with foreign words.

His story "Ostrov Borngol'm," if it were not for its fantastic plot, could well be the story of the "Russian traveler's" return voyage from London to Petersburg. After hearing in London a Dane singing of Bornholm, the narrator visits the barren island off the Danish coast, where in a dream he discovers a captive maiden and learns the secret meaning of the song (which, however, he does not tell the reader). In the unfinished "Liodor" a Russian hero studies in Germany and travels to France and Spain. Other stories by Karamzin set in foreign locales are "Sierra-Morena" (Spain) and "Afinskaia zhizn' " (Athens).

SURVEY OF CRITICISM

In his study of Karamzin's life and works A.G. Cross (1971) highlights Karamzin's "Europeanness" as a constant inspiration in the writer's changing ideological orientation. Lotman (1987) provides the classic overall study of Karamzin in Russian. In addition to Rothe's magisterial study (1968) there are several works of note on *Pis'ma russkogo puteshestvennika*: by the Russian critics Bulich, Buslaev, and Lavrovskii in *Nikolai Mikhailovich Karamzin: Ego zhizn' i sochineniia* (1912), and by R.B. Anderson (1975), who argues that "the great value of *Letters of a Russian Traveler* lies in Karamzin's talented summing up of a whole era in the West . . . in the countries where cultural taste played such a formative role in Russia's growth into a member of the European community" (38). B.A. Uspenskii (1985) provides a detailed and informative discussion of Karamzin's role in formulating the modern Russian literary language.

Konrad Bittner (1960) explores Karamzin's German contacts of his early period (1786–90). Karamzin's enthusiasm for English culture, which waned somewhat after he made firsthand acquaintance with the country, is examined by A.G. Cross (1964).

SELECTIVE BIBLIOGRAPHY

Works by Karamzin

Pis'ma russkogo puteshestvennika. Ed. Iu. M. Lotman, N.A. Marchenko, and B.A. Uspenskii. Leningrad: Nauka, 1984; *Letters of a Russian Traveler, 1789–1790: An Account of a Young Russian Gentleman's Tour through Germany, Switzerland, France, and England.* Trans. and abridged Florence Jonas. Intro. Leon Stilman. New York: Columbia University Press, 1957.

"Ostrov Borngol'm" (1794). "The Island of Bornholm." In *Selected Prose of N.M. Karamzin.* Trans. and intro. Henry M. Nebel, Jr. Evanston, Ill.: Northwestern University Press, 1969.

Sochineniia. 3rd ed. 9 vols. Moscow: V tipografii S. Selivanovskogo, 1820.

Izbrannye sochineniia. 2 vols. Leningrad: Khudozhestvennaia literatura, 1964.

Selective Studies of Karamzin

Anderson, R.B. "Karamzin's Letters of a Russian Traveller." In *Essays on Karamzin: Russian Man-of-Letters, Political Thinker, Historian, 1766–1826,* 22–39. Ed. J.L. Black. Slavistic printings and reprintings, 309. The Hague: Mouton, 1975.

Bittner, Konrad. "Der junge Nikolaj Michajlovic Karamzin und Deutschland." *Herder Studien* (Würzburg) 10 (1960): 81–94.

Cross, A.G. "Karamzin and England." *Slavonic and East European Review* 43, n. 100 (1964): 91–114.

―――. *N.M. Karamzin: A Study of His Literary Career, 1783–1803.* Carbondale: Southern Illinois University Press, 1971.

Garrard, J.G. "Poor East, or Point of View of Karamzin." *Essays on Karamzin: Russian Man-of-Letters, Political Thinker, Historian, 1766–1826.* Ed. J.L. Black. Slavistic printings and reprintings, 309. The Hague: Mouton, 1975.

Lotman, Iu. M. *Sotvorenie Karamzina.* Moscow: Kniga, 1987.

Nikolai Mikhailovich Karamzin: Ego zhizn' i sochineniia. Sbornik istoriko-literaturnykh statei. Ed. V.I. Pokrovskii. 3rd ed. Moscow: V. Spiridonova i A. Mikhailova, 1912.

Rothe, Hans. *N.M. Karamzins europäische Reise: Der Beginn des russischen Romans: Philologische Untersuchungen.* Bad Homburg: Verlag Gehlen, 1968.

Uspenskii, B.A. *Iz istorii russkogo literaturnogo iazyka XVIII–nachala XIX veka: Iazykovaia programma Karamzina i ee istoricheskie korni.* Moscow: Izdatel'stvo Moskovskogo universiteta, 1985.

KIM SOWŎL
(1902–1934)

Maurizio Riotto

BIOGRAPHY

Kim Sowŏl's biography, like that of other writers of his period, combines foreign influences, traditional forms, and a spirit of nationalism. One of the most beloved poets of his country even though his literary production is quite sparse, Kim Sowŏl, whose real name was Kim Chŏngsik, was born in the region of north P'yŏng'an, today the Democratic People's Republic of Korea. Brought up in straitened circumstances, he could attend school only intermittently. At a young age he began writing poetry, publishing his early works in the literary reviews *Ch'angjo* and *Kaebyŏk*.

He moved to Japan in 1923 or 1924, intending to go into business and improve his economic situation, but he failed in his objectives and went back to Korea. Nothing is known about his Japanese sojourn, from which he returned poorer than ever, but it must have been a determining influence on his poetry, the bulk of which was composed during the years 1920–25.

Doubt subsists as to whether or not he was a poet of resistance against the Japanese invader and a standard-bearer of nationalism and Korean cultural identity. What is certain is that he made a happy compromise between Eastern tradition on the one hand, in which the human being, far from being the "measure of all things," becomes painfully aware of the impossibility of overcoming the limitations imposed by marvelous, ineffable, and sovereign nature; and, on the other hand, the mature knowledge, understanding, and judgment that followed his readings of foreign works, mainly during his sojourn in Japan. He certainly must have read the French poets, some of whom (Baudelaire, Verlaine, Rimbaud) had been translated by Kim Ŏk (1893–?, also called Anso), who had been Sowŏl's teacher in secondary school.

Kim Sowŏl did not adhere to any particular intellectual current, even if certain of his themes are similar to those adopted by the literary figures grouped around the review *Paekcho*. One of its collaborators, Pak Yŏnghŭi, later referred to the period of publication of *Paekcho* as one characterized by Oscar Wilde's extravagance, Paul Verlaine's "decadence," Edgar Allan Poe's mysteriousness, and Baudelaire's "dissoluteness." To these authors known to the Korean literati of the period may be added Arthur Rimbaud, T.S. Eliot, and other Western authors.

Kim's entire production (about 170 poems) written during 1920–25 is gathered in the volume *Chindallae kkot* (1925), which contains his three "series" of verses: *Chindallae kkot* (Azalea flowers), *Ch'ohon* (Twilight), and *Sanyuhwa* (Flowers of the mountain, in Eastern symbolist repertory the image of woman in the fullness of her youth). Mention must also be made of his essay on literary criticism entitled *Sihon*, published in May 1925 in the review *Kaebyŏk*.

Unable to make his name as a poet, he lived the last years of his short life amid all sorts of difficulties (including accusations of usury), which he often drowned in alcohol. Finally, despairing and disillusioned, he committed suicide by an overdose of opium.

MAJOR MULTICULTURAL THEMES

At first glance one may perhaps not easily grasp the multicultural aspects of Kim Sowŏl, but it suffices to observe the environment in which he developed as an individual and as a poet to recognize all those elements, foreign to traditional Korean culture, that would inevitably be reflected in his work. He has been compared to William Butler Yeats, to Robert Frost, and, because of his dramatic life, to the "cursed" nineteenth-century French poets, such as Baudelaire and Verlaine.

His epoch was one of the most tragic, yet culturally productive, of all Korean history. Practically every author of the time was a multicultural. Korea had only recently opened up to the West (the end of the feudal period had been officially sanctioned by the 1894 *Kabo* reform). Immediately the great powers of the East (China, Russia, and Japan) looked covetingly at the peninsula, which was politically and economically backward but was possessed of an excellent strategic position. In the end, Japan won out: after establishing a protectorate that began in 1905, it annexed Korea in 1910, reducing the country to the status of a Japanese colony.

A burdensome feudal heritage, a sudden opening to the West, foreign oppression, a curiosity about artistic and literary experiences different from their own—these are the elements that we encounter in the Korean authors of this period, the period of Japanese domination, which continued until 1945. Modern Korean literature was literally invented in the space of a few years by these very young poets and writers who had taken as their point of reference whatever Western works they could find, which they read for the most part in Japanese translation, and usually without any critical sense, so anxious were they to emancipate themselves at any cost from the deeply entrenched traditional narrative and poetic conventions of the past.

Kim Sowŏl's poetic language is made up of shaded tones and a simple, modest lexicon that can easily be defined as "crepuscular" (in the sense of the post-D'Annunzian Italian crepuscular poets of a disenchanted Italian twilight). In his essay *Sihon* Kim Sowŏl himself dwells upon the concept of *umyong* (suffused shade) that is at the very heart of his poetry. The symbolist language of the poet is exemplified by his approach to Eternity—the very soul of poetry and the essence of all things—through psychological introspection, in his encounter with "obscurity," or sorrow and solitude.

The poet is moved by nature, but this means that he is also stirred by death, love, sorrow, and meetings and separations, all situations in which personal experience is inevitably accompanied by sensations and universal aspirations. Time and space, or the living out of life, lead to a change in the concept of the poetic soul: no longer universal and eternal but linked to the taste and the condition of the poet. In other words, spatial-temporal conditions limit and "personalize" poetry and, in the case of Kim Sowŏl, force him to seek relief from the pain of existence by transcending his consciousness, as, for example, in a poem addressed to the smoke of his cigarette, which exorcises his pain and sorrow ("Tambae," in *Kim Sowŏl sijip*, 96). The inner torment of the artist, which springs from his lost hopes, from the infiniteness of his desire and the impossibility of its realization, emerges clearly in "Sanyuhwa," which gives its name to the third "series" in the collection of his poems.

Kim Sowŏl and his contemporaries were inspired by not one but many writers. They were all more or less influenced by different Western authors, whose themes were reworked in the light of Korean poetic tradition. Yet, paradoxically, this is the most "multicultural" period of Korean literature. Never as much as in this period did Korean authors try to keep in step with the West and learn its modes and literary tendencies for the purpose of making themselves known in turn as an ethnic group and as a politically and culturally autonomous nation, despite the historic iniquity represented by the Japanese domination.

SELECTIVE BIBLIOGRAPHY

Work by Kim Sowŏl

Kim Sowŏl sijip (Collection of poetry). Seoul: Pŏmusa, 1985.

Selective Studies of Kim Sowŏl

Kim, Yongjik, et al. *Han'guk hyŏndaesisa yŏn'gu* (Studies of the history of contemporary Korean poetry). Seoul: Ilchisa, 1987.
Maurus, Patrick. "Statisme et dynamisme chez Kim Sowŏl." *Revue de Corée* 23, no. 1 (1991): 41–66.
Riotto, Maurizio. *Storia della letteratura coreana*. Palermo: Novecento Editrice, 1996.
Yi, Sŭnghun. *Han'guk hyŏndaesironsa, 1910–1980*. (History of the criticism of contemporary Korean poetry). Seoul: Koryŏwŏn, 1993.

RUDYARD KIPLING
(1865–1936)

Maria Antonietta Saracino

BIOGRAPHY

"England is the most wonderful foreign land I have ever been in," Rudyard Kipling wrote to his friend and colleague Henry Rider Haggard in 1902, and perhaps this was not meant as a joke. Indeed, the man who, at the turn of the nineteenth century and at least for the first two decades of the twentieth, was the most popular writer in English, in both prose and verse, was the first English writer to win the Nobel Prize for Literature, in 1907, and was the recipient of honorary degrees from the Universities of Oxford, Cambridge, Edinburgh, Durham, McGill, Strasbourg, and the Sorbonne, during his entire life regarded India as his real home.

Kipling was born in Bombay on December 30, 1865, the first child of English parents who had gone out to India early that same year. His father, John Lockwood Kipling, was a teacher of architectural sculpture at the government-sponsored Bombay School of Art. His mother, Alice Macdonald, was, like her husband, the child of a Methodist minister in England.

As was customary among the British living in India, Kipling was sent to England at the age of six to receive his education at a private school. His parents placed him for five and a half years in Southsea, a district of Portsmouth, with a certain Mrs. Holloway. These early years in a new environment, in the care of a woman he disliked, would later be remembered as years of hell, marked by a sense of maternal betrayal. References to what he later described as "the House of Desolation" may be found in his autobiographical writing, *Something of Myself* (1937), as well as in *The Light That Failed* (1890) and in the story "Baa Baa, Black Sheep" (1888).

In 1878, aged twelve, he was sent to North Devon to attend a public school that had been founded by Indian army officers to offer a suitable education for their sons. Unlike his previous school experience, this one proved all joy and satisfaction to young Kipling, who, at the end of a five-year period, left England and returned to his family in India. In Lahore (Punjab), where his father had in the meantime become the head of the new School of Art and the curator of the Lahore Museum, he found a job as a journalist and assistant editor for a small English newspaper, the *Civil and Military Gazette*. After his training had been completed and his professional reputation had been established, he moved in 1887 to a more prestigious paper, the *Pioneer*, of Allahabad. The very special viewpoint that his position as a journalist granted him gave him the opportunity to see the British Empire at work at all levels. Dedicated and hardworking, he reported on the daily routine of army men, as well as the life and customs of remote Indian villages. During these fruitful years he wrote *Plain Tales from the Hills*, *Soldiers Three*, *The Story of the Gadsbys*, *In Black and White*, *Under the Deodars*, *The Phantom Rickshaw*, and *Wee Willie Winkie*—all during 1888 and 1889.

But the so-called Indian period came to an end in 1889 when Kipling, who had already made a name for himself as a writer, left the subcontinent to return to England and try his fortune on the London literary scene. During the follow-ing triumphant ten years he wrote successful novels and collections of short stories, most of them set against the background of India: *The Light That Failed*, *Life's Handicap* (1891), *Many Inventions* (1893), *The Jungle Books* (1894 and 1895), *The Seven Seas* (1896), *The Day's Work* (1898), *Stalky & Co* (1899), and *Kim* (1901). He also traveled extensively, visiting countries such as Italy, Australia, and New Zealand, with only one short visit to India.

He had married a young American, Caroline Balestier, in 1892, and settled in Vermont; after five years the family moved to England. Restless, incapable of finding a place which he could really call his own, he returned to the United States. Excited by the Boer War (1899–1902) and deeply committed to the side of the British, he moved to South Africa, where he spent eight years just outside Cape Town in a little house that his friend Cecil Rhodes had built for him. In 1908, a year after he had received the Nobel Prize for Literature, he returned to England, where he died. He was buried in Westminster Abbey.

MAJOR MULTICULTURAL THEMES

In spite of his having spent fewer than fifteen years in India, in spite of his having traveled ceaselessly from the United States to New Zealand, from South Africa to Japan, almost all of Kipling's art fed on the memories of his early Indian years: from his stories and poems to his collection of travel writings (*From Sea to Sea*, 1899) and the most famous of his works, *Kim*. Kipling's India is deeply marked by the presence of British imperialism, against which he does not take much of a critical stand, rather assuming a basically uncontested empire. To him, the British presence in India is not something to apologize for, but simply the reality he was born into and loved. For him, the British had a greater aptitude for ruling than other people, not for reasons of racial superiority, but of competence. Talented and gifted as he was, he managed to translate, in the words of T.S. Eliot, "the imperial . . . into the historical imagination," as is the case with *The Jungle Books*, two collections of tales in which animals play an important role. *Plain Tales from the Hills* (1888) is a collection of stories drawn mainly from the articles he published in the Anglo-Indian, Lahore-based newspaper, the *Civil and Military Gazette*.

Kim, regarded as his finest literary achievement, is marked by skillful craftsmanship and keen insight. Faintly rooted in Kipling's early childhood memories, *Kim* is the story of a young Irish-born boy who grows up among Indians, and whose knowledge of native culture and languages earns him a place in the imperial spy network. Bringing together a multiplicity of cross-cultural themes and a variety of literary heritages, *Kim* is regarded by Indian scholar and critic Nirad C. Chaudhuri not only as the best novel ever written on India, but also one of the best novels in English.

SURVEY OF CRITICISM

Kipling was admired and respected by many prominent authors of the time, including Henry James, Joseph Conrad, and T.S. Eliot, the latter writing a long introductory essay to Kipling's poetry: "In his Indian tales it is on the whole the Indian characters who have the greater reality, because they are treated with the understanding of love. . . Kipling is of India in a different way from any other Englishman who has written, and in a different way from that of any particular Indian, who has a race, a creed, a local habitation and, if a Hindu, a caste. He might almost be called the first citizen of India" ("Rudyard Kipling," 242). Eliot's opinion of Kipling's art is shared by H.G. Wells, for whom his writings "opened like window shutters to reveal the dusty sun-glare and blazing colours of the East" ("Kipling," 305).

In recent years multicultural studies have devoted critical attention to the imperial themes in Kipling's literary production. For Palestinian critic and scholar Edward Said, to speak of Kipling's representation of India "as if the India he wrote about was a timeless, unchanging, and 'essential' locale . . . [would be] a radical misreading of his work. If Kipling's India has essential and unchanging qualities, this was because he deliberately saw India that way" (*Culture and Imperialism*, 1993, 161–62). For Indo-Pakistani novelist Salman Rushdie, "There will always be plenty in Kipling that I will find difficult to forgive, but there is also enough truth in these stories to make them impossible to ignore." Kipling's stories, in Rushdie's opinion, are "packed with information about a lost world. It used to be said that one read in order to learn something— and nobody can teach you British India better than Rudyard Kipling" ("Kipling," 75, 80).

SELECTIVE BIBLIOGRAPHY

Works by Kipling

Departmental Ditties. Lahore, 1886.
Kipling's India: Uncollected Sketches, 1884–88. Ed. Thomas Pinney. Basingstoke: Macmillan, 1986.
Plain Tales from the Hills (1888). Ed. H.R. Woudhuysen. Intro. and notes David Trotter. London: Penguin, 1990.
The Jungle Book and *The Second Jungle Book* (1894–1895). Ed., intro., and notes W.W. Robson. Oxford: Oxford University Press, 1987.
From Sea to Sea (1899). In James McG. Stewart, *Rudyard Kipling: A Bibliographical Catalogue,* ed. A. Yeats. Toronto: Dalhousie University Press and University of Toronto Press, 1959.
Kim (1901). Garden City, N.Y.: Doubleday, Doran, 1941.
Something of Myself and Other Autobiographical Writings. Ed. and intro. Thomas Pinney. Cambridge: Cambridge University Press, 1990.

Selective Studies of Kipling

Bloom, Harold. *Rudyard Kipling.* New York: Chelsea House, 1987.
Eliot, T.S. "Rudyard Kipling." In *On Poetry and Poets,* 228–51. London: Faber & Faber, 1957.
Green, Roger Lancelyn, ed. *Kipling: The Critical Heritage.* London: Routledge & Kegan Paul, 1971.
Gross, John. *Rudyard Kipling: The Man, His Work, and His World.* London: Weidenfeld & Nicolson, 1972.
McClure, John. *Kipling and Conrad.* Cambridge, Mass.: Harvard University Press, 1981.
Mason, Philip. *Kipling: The Glass, the Shadow, and the Fire.* London: Cape, 1975.
Rushdie, Salman. "Kipling." In *Imaginary Homelands,* 74–80. London: Granta, 1991.
Rutherford, Andrew. *Kipling's Mind and Art.* London: Oliver & Boyd, 1964.
Said, Edward. *Culture and Imperialism.* London: Chatto & Windus, 1993.
Wells, H.G. "Kipling." In *Kipling: The Critical Heritage.* Ed. Roger Lancelyn Green. London: Routledge & Kegan Paul, 1971.
Wurgaft, Lewis. *The Imperial Imagination: Magic and Myth in Kipling's India.* Middletown, Conn.: Wesleyan University Press, 1983.

ADAMANTIOS KORAÍS
(1748–1833)

Bruce Merry

BIOGRAPHY

A Gallicized intellectual of the Greek Enlightenment, Adamantios Koraís was born in Smyrna, the city with the largest Greek population in Anatolia (Asia Minor), where he was introduced to classical literature by a Dutch Protestant pastor. From 1771 to 1778 he worked as a merchant in Amsterdam; from 1782 to 1786 he studied medicine at Montpellier, France; then he lived in Paris as a medical doctor and scholar from 1788 until his death in 1833. He experienced the French Revolution and the campaigns of Napoleon, whom he censured as a despot. This was a little ungrateful, as Napoleon had awarded him a 3,000-franc pension for his translation of the geographer Strabo.

In 1805 a wealthy Greek merchant and philanthropist living in Europe, Michael Zosimas, agreed to publish (Paris, 1807–1826) the *Helliniki Vivliothíki*, a series of classical texts with extensive prefaces drafted by Koraís himself, presenting classical Greek texts to a modern Greek readership. These were to be distributed by Zosimas and circulated all over Europe and Greek Asia Minor, the eastern Mediterranean, and the Greek-speaking communities of Romania and Russia. Several supplementary books, *Hellinikìs Vivliothíkis Párerga*, were also published in Paris (1809–1827).

Perhaps influenced by the English historian Edward Gibbon, Koraís developed an aversion to the Church and the Middle Ages. He knew and quoted from the French translation (Paris, 1819) of Gibbon's *History of the Decline and Fall of the Roman Empire* (1776–1788). The holdings in his personal library show a predilection for the Enlightenment and for scientific authors, as well as for James Fenimore Cooper, Pierre Bayle, David Hume, Marie Josephe de Lafayette, Claude Henri de Saint-Simon, Jacques Bénigne Bossuet, Claude Fleury, and others.

In 1798 a Greek in Paris published an anticlerical pamphlet, *Adelphikì di-*

daskalía. Appearing anonymously, but certainly by Koraís, it is an attack on an encyclical supposedly signed by Patriarch Anthimos of Jerusalem, stigmatizing the atheism that underpins the French Revolution and blending Holy Scripture with contemporary social thinking to prove the legitimacy of Ottoman rule as a salvation for Greeks. Koraís had reacted with fury to the encyclical. At this time freedom was in the air. The new French republic was preparing military action against Egypt. Rigas Velestinlís and other Greek independence figures had just been arrested in Vienna. Expressing solidarity with the conspirators and with a view to incite them, Koraís subtitled his pamphlet "to all Greeks found throughout the Ottoman Empire, a Refutation of the pseudonymously produced teaching recently published at Constantinople, falsely issued in the name of the Most Blessed Patriarch." He summoned his compatriots to show the "inhabited world" (that telltale Hellenocentric phrase, *I Oikouméni*) how the patriarchal document was nonsense. Though he was residing in France, he now stepped up his work on Greek patriotic themes, issuing a war hymn, *Âsma polemistírion* (1800), and the nationalist manifesto *Sálpisma polemistírion* (1801), the frontispiece of which showed a Turk with sword threatening a woman in rags, symbol of contemporary enslaved Greece. He deplored the Turks' sack of Chios, but rejoiced that his collaborator, Neophytos Vambas (1770–1856), "teacher of the race," had been saved. He expressed the hope that Vambas would found a national school in the Peloponnese, and, in fact, Vambas was involved in the founding of modern Greece's first university (1837), in Athens. As for the Turkocracy, Koraís thought that the Greek people needed a longer intellectual preparation before national revolution. In an 1827 letter he maintained that the uprising was "still untimely since it did not leave us sufficient time to learn how our teachers might be changed." He even regarded Ioannis Kapodistrias (1776–1831), the first president of Greece (1828–31), as a tyrant.

MAJOR MULTICULTURAL THEMES

The Greek Enlightenment was really a string of educational initiatives. Traveling or exiled teachers composed grammars, compiled dictionaries, wrote commentaries, appealed to foreign princes or tutored their children (in Russia, France, Romania, and Austria), and gathered disciples (*mathetés*) whom they dispatched to the four winds. Scholars like Koraís, who lived in Western cities, and *paidagogoí* (educators) in the Ionian Islands or in areas of the Ottoman Empire with a strong Phanariot tradition (Constantinople, the Danubian principalities), traveled to found schools and promote education, which they saw as the key to Greek freedom from Turkey.

Koraís gave a moral example from Paris, even while contributing to the language debate by developing an eclectic solution (in essays and prefaces written from 1805). He accommodated parts of the radical position of the Vulgarizers (supporters of a simple, plebeian Neohellenic language) and also accepted views held by conservatives, who wanted the Greek language to favor Atticism or remain "pure." He considered the artificial idiom he espoused for his distant countrymen as a *koinì miloumḗni* (shared community language), which he believed should be the national mother tongue. He favored the rejection of foreign loan words, especially Turkish, by a process of gradual purification. Despite his call for a new dictionary of Greek to record current usage, and his rejection of Attic forms, he is the one nineteenth-century intellectual most responsible for *Katharevousa* (the purified language). His *Átakta* (5 volumes, 1828–1835) incorporates the first dictionary of modern Greek.

His prefaces to the first four books of Homer's *Iliad* are known as *Papatréchas*, in which he uses more dialogue than narrative, thus distancing himself from the narrative forms of the Romantic manifestos of northern Italy, as well as of writers of Germany and France (Goethe, Friedrich von Schiller, Chateaubriand, Benjamin Constant, Madame de Staël). He demonstrates how education can be brought to the people, how islanders can be proud that Homer once lived in a parish on Chios, and how Greeks can save their antiquities from being exported to London.

Koraís despised the Byzantine past and even disliked the early demotic Cretan masterpiece, *Erotókritos*. He was too stern a neoclassicist to recommend *Erotókritos*, but he covered his censure with a neat ambiguity, confusing many readers when he gave it the appellation "a Homer from Vulgar literature." He saw Byzantine history as Hellenism in decline. For him, the Hellenic inheritance was taken "from the paralyzed hands of despots, the Graeco-Roman emperors." He once remarked that reading a page by a Byzantine author could give a man an attack of gout, and he reckoned that when the sultan assaulted Byzantium in 1453, "instead of an army on the alert he found monasteries and monks squabbling over points of dogma, and learned men dabbling with paper and inkpots" (Fassoulakis, 173).

SURVEY OF CRITICISM

Dionysios Solomós, who studied in Italy and breathed the progressive air of the Ionian Islands, refuted Koraís in *Pezà kaì italiká* (1955): "The writer does not teach the language; he learns it from the people." So the "corrections" by Koraís to contemporary diction were as ridiculous as trying to upgrade the first line of Dante's *Divina Commedia* from "Nel mezzo del cammin di nostra vita" to "In medio camini nostrae vitae." Konstantinos Dimaras, in *A History of Modern Greek Literature* (1974), Bruno Lavagnini, in *La letteratura neo-ellenica* (1969), and Linos Politis, in *A History of Modern Greek Literature* (1973), all consider Koraís as the key Greek intellectual of his period though he did not live in Greece.

SELECTIVE BIBLIOGRAPHY

Works by Koraís

Koray's Letters Written from Paris. 1788–1792. Trans. and ed. P. Ralli. London: Hatchards, 1898.

Mémoire sur l'état actuel de la civilisation dans la Grèce. Paris: Firmin Didot, 1803. [Also trans. Elie Kedourie in Elie Kedourie, *Nationalism in Asia and Africa.* London: Weidenfeld & Nicolson, 1970.]

Pródromos Hellinikìs Vivliothíkis. Paris: Firmin Didot, 1805.

Hellinikì Vivliothíki. 16 vols. Paris: variously I.M. Everard, T. Barrois, Firmin Didot, 1807–1826.

Hellinikìs Vivliothíkis Párerga. 9 vols. Paris: I.M. Everard, T. Barrois, 1809–1827.

Átakta. 5 vols. Paris: K. Everard, 1828–1835.

Selective Studies of Koraís

Chaconas, Stephen George. "The Jefferson-Korais Correspondence." *Journal of Modern History* 14, nos. 1 and 2 (March and December 1942): 64–70, 593–96.

Clogg, Richard. "The Correspondence of Adhamantios Korais with the British and Foreign Bible Society (1808)." *Greek Orthodox Theological Review* 14, no. 1 (Spring 1969): 65–84.

Dimaras, Konstantinos. *A History of Modern Greek Literature.* London: University of London Press, 1974.

Fassoulakis, S. "Gibbon's Influence on Koraes." In *The Making of Byzantine History: Studies Dedicated to Donald M. Nicol,* 169–73. Ed. R. Beaton, and C. Roueché. Aldershot: Variorum, 1993.

Lavagnini, Bruno. *La letteratura neo-ellenica.* Firenze: Sansoni, 1969.

Politis, Linos. *A History of Modern Greek Literature.* Oxford: Clarendon Press, 1973.

Solomós, Dionysios. *Ápanta.* Vol. 2, *Pezà kaì italiká.* Athens: Ikaros, 1955.

BARTOLOMÉ DE LAS CASAS
(1484–1566)

Carlos R. Hortas

BIOGRAPHY

More than three hundred years after the death of Bartolomé de Las Casas, his monumental *Historia de las Indias*, written from 1527 to 1565, was finally published in 1875. Las Casas had wanted this important work to be published after his death, but the question remains: why was publication delayed for over three centuries?

The answer is to be found in the publication of his *Brevísima relación de la destrucción de las Indias* (1552), a virulent attack on the injustices perpetrated against the Indians of the New World. His attack on the system under which Indians were apportioned to landowners made him many enemies among those with vested interests in the system. When it was translated and reprinted abroad, many of his own countrymen criticized the author for exaggeration and hyperbole; they saw the publication of the *Brevísima relación* as a disservice to Spain and as a weapon in the hands of its enemies. It is true that his tone was accusative, that his rhetoric was not evenhanded, and that his main purpose as a writer was to make evident the need for urgent reform in the treatment of the Indians. In fact, although his constant enumeration of atrocities served to gain him many supporters, his accusations also alienated and made enemies of powerful and influential men in the Indies and in Spain. Those in power believed that his writings had led to much of the anti-Spanish feeling in Europe; thus they were banned in Spain. The controversy spawned by the *Brevísima relación* may have led him to ask that his longer *Historia de las Indias* not be published during his lifetime.

Bartolomé de Las Casas was born in Seville, Spain, in 1484. His father, Pedro, and three uncles accompanied Christopher Columbus on his second voyage to the Indies in 1493 and returned to Spain in 1498 on one of five ships loaded with slaves. Pedro presented his son with a little Indian boy, whom Bartolomé kept as a companion until 1500, when the Indian boy was repatriated. Since he lived in Seville, Las Casas spoke with men who had returned from the new lands, and on the Seville docks he saw flora, fauna, and artifacts brought back from the New World. When Pedro decided that he would sign on for a second trip in 1502, his son accompanied him. Having recently become a priest, Bartolomé went on this expedition to Hispaniola as a *doctrinero*, to help spread the Christian faith among the Indians. He dedicated the rest of his life to reforming the system that assigned Indians to Spanish landowners for the performance of hard labor. He petitioned the king for the passage of more humane laws and declared that, as subjects of the Spanish Crown, Indians had certain inalienable rights, including the right to be free and the right to defend their lands from those who would take them by force. Perhaps from the time his father had brought him a little Indian boy to be his companion, he had begun to develop sympathy for the Indians' plight, and as he worked among them and sought to Christianize them, he became aware of the contradictions between the ethics of the Christian doctrine he was asking the Indians to accept and the decidedly unethical behavior of the Spanish overseers. In his nineties, close to death, he continued to write letters to the king on behalf of the Indians.

MAJOR MULTICULTURAL THEMES

Bartolomé de Las Casas was one of the first defenders of human rights in the Americas. The *Brevísima relación* accused the Spanish of expropriating Indian lands and of subjecting the Indians to forced labor and hardships; it lists repeated instances of torture, executions, and massacres of the New World Indians at the hands of the Spanish. His advocacy of Indian rights and his writings were particularly influential in the development in Spain of a body of laws that called for humane treatment of New World Indians.

From 1502 to 1514 he witnessed the massacre of Indians and the death of many from disease and from forced labor. Yet his conversion into an active agent on their behalf did not come until 1514, when, from the pulpit, he renounced both the lands that had been apportioned to him and the Indians that had been assigned to work for him and declared that henceforth he would dedicate his life to defending the Indians. He claimed that this conversion came about through his reading of Holy Scripture, but it is also certain that his personal contact with the Indians and their inhuman treatment at the hands of the Spanish inspired his final decision to come out in their defense. He lived the life of a religious "activist" well into his ninety-first year of age. In his seventies, after he was named bishop of Chiapas, Mexico, he startled the Catholic Church by proclaiming that he would deny absolution to those who had profited through forced Indian labor or to those who "owned" Indians until such individuals reimbursed the Indians justly for their labor or gave them their freedom.

In his seventy-fifth year he entered the Colegio de San Gregorio in Valladolid, Spain, and devoted the rest of his life to a continued defense of the Indians both through his writings and by helping to organize missions to convert and to catechize the Indians of the New World. During this period he maintained an extensive correspondence with Amerindian communities that sought his help and empowered him to act in their defense.

In *Los tesoros del Perú* he maintained that the Spanish had no right to loot the treasures of the Incas, and he called for the restitution of all treasure that had already been removed from Peru by the Spanish. By extension, everything that belonged rightfully to the inhabitants of the new lands, including the land itself, was to be protected from the depredations of the Spanish and all other Europeans. For its time, this was a revolutionary demand, and it remains pertinent to matters relating to Indian claims even to the present day.

SURVEY OF CRITICISM

Juan Friede (1952) relates Las Casas's work to the wider "indigenista" movement of those times. Eloy G. Merino Brito (1966) shows how Lascasian thought has influenced later revolutionary thought and revolutionary movements in Latin America. In addition to his excellent introduction to Las Casas's *Historia de las Indias* (1951), Lewis Hanke has studied many aspects of Las Casas's work; in his *Bartolomé de Las Casas, Bookman, Scholar, and Propagandist* (1952) he explains the name Las Casas made for himself during his lifetime and his posthumous fame. Silvio Zavala (1966) has put together three of his valuable studies on the work of Las Casas; and a number of collections of articles have been published over the years, including those of Marcel Bataillon (1966) and Juan Friede and Benjamin Keen (1971).

SELECTIVE BIBLIOGRAPHY

Works by Las Casas

Brevísima relación de la destrucción de las Indias (1552). Madrid: Cátedra, 1992.

Historia de las Indias (1875). Mexico: Fondo de Cultura Económica, 1951.

Apologética historia. Biblioteca de Autores Españoles, vol. 105. Madrid: Ediciones Atlas, 1958.

Del único modo de atraer a todos los pueblos a la verdadera religión. Mexico: Fondo de Cultura Económica, 1942.

De thesauris in Perú (*Los Tesoros del Perú*). Madrid: Consejo Superior de Investigaciones Científicas, 1958.

Selective Studies of Las Casas

Adorno, Rolena. *The Intellectual Life of Bartolomé de las Casas*. New Orleans: Graduate School of Tulane University, 1992.

Bataillon, Marcel, and Raymond Marcus, ed. *Études sur Bartolomé de las Casas*. Paris: Centre de Recherches de l'Institut d'Études Hispaniques, 1966.

Friede, Juan. "Las Casas y el movimiento indigenista en España y América en la primera mitad del siglo XVI." *Revista de Historia de América* 33–34 (1952): 339–411.

Friede, Juan, and Benjamin Keen, eds. *Bartolomé de las Casas in History*. De Kalb: Northern Illinois University Press, 1971.

Hanke, Lewis. *Bartolomé de las Casas, Bookman, Scholar, and Propagandist*. Philadelphia: University of Pennsylvania Press, 1952.

Hanke, Lewis, and Manuel Giménez Fernández. *Bartolomé de las Casas, 1474–1566: Bibliografía crítica y cuerpo de materiales para el estudio de su vida, escritos, actuación, y polémicas que suscitaron durante cuatro siglos*. Santiago de Chile: Fondo Histórico y Bibliográfico José Toribio Medina, 1954.

Mahn-Lot, Marianne. *Bartolomé de Las Casas et le droit des Indiens*. Paris: Payot, 1982.

Merino Brito, Eloy G. "Fray Bartolomé de las Casas y la guerra justa." *Revista de la Biblioteca Nacional "José Martí"* (La Habana) 8, no. 4 (October–December 1966): 5–17.

Parish, Helen Rand, with Harold E. Weidman, S.J. *Las Casas en México: Historia y obra desconocidas*. Mexico: Fondo de Cultura Económica, 1992.

Saint-Lu, André. *Las Casas indigéniste: Études sur la vie et l'oeuvre du défenseur des Indiens*. Paris: L'Harmattan, 1982.

Zavala, Silvio. *Recuerdo de Bartolomé de las Casas*. Guadalajara, Jalisco: Librería Font, 1966.

D(AVID) H(ERBERT) LAWRENCE
(1885–1930)

Robert E. Clark

BIOGRAPHY

One of the best-traveled writers of his day, D.H. Lawrence was even more fully connected to the European landscape than to the spare American desert: important works are set in English mining villages, sleepy resorts in the Mediterranean, and Prussian military camps. Whatever continent he found himself on, he combined a romantic but unsentimental view of nature, sexuality, and human passion with the European Modernist challenge. Like other Modernists, he sought to overturn the literary forms, prudery, and intellectual slightness of ordinary nineteenth-century fiction, although as his career progressed, he increasingly separated himself from all formal literary movements. His works draw on biblical literature as well as legend and myths of Greece, Rome, Scandinavia, and Germany, superimposing ancient symbols and allegories onto modern life and enjoining debates encompassing Freud, Nietzsche, Darwin, Wagner, and avant-garde art, morality, theology, and politics.

Born in 1885 in the mining town of Eastwood, he knew the soot and squalor of coal country well. At the same time he was enchanted by the beauty of nearby Sherwood Forest, the setting of the Robin Hood legends, and became a masterful nature writer who later described Sicily, New Mexico, Tuscany, and the Australian bush unforgettably.

Around the period 1910–24 Lawrence met the larger world of British letters as well as world literary culture; he embraced Modernist openness to the fiction of Russia and America and shared Yeats's and Pound's interest in Asia. He was championed by London editor and man of letters Edward Garnett, who also worked closely with Conrad and Galsworthy. Ford Madox Hueffer (later famous as the novelist Ford Madox Ford) accepted Lawrence's stories and essays for the *English Review*, a seedbed for writers seeking a new literary realism. Lawrence's apprentice years brought brushes with German psychoanalytic circles and Yeats's and Pound's coteries and acquaintance within the Bloomsbury group. By 1912 he had eloped with Frieda Weekly, the German-born wife of a professor of French, to Italy and Germany. While his international literary acquaintance broadened, he finished two versions of his first great novel, *Sons and Lovers* (1913).

The two major groupings of Lawrence's later novels span cultures in a more obvious way and were composed on what the writer called his "savage pilgrimage" of globe-trotting to Germany, Italy, France, Ceylon, Australia, the United States, and elsewhere. *Kangaroo* (1923), set in Australia, and *The Plumed Serpent* (1926), set in Mexico, contain his controversial ideas about authority and leadership. Bertrand Russell found them fascistic. But sympathetic readers point out that though his late work is antidemocratic and marred by ethnic prejudice, it extends Lawrence's lifelong radical individualism and his attacks on ersatz tolerance and brotherhood. Undeniably his work has always attracted admirers in the camp of freedom and tolerance; they admit misanthropy and other flaws in his work, but see equal blindness in his critics, including Aldous Huxley, Ford Madox Ford, E.M. Forster, Katherine Mansfield, Rebecca West, Anaïs Nin, Anthony Burgess, and Steven Spender among writers, and, among critics, F.R. Leavis, Harry Moore, Frank Kermode, and David Lodge, the novelist and scholar.

His late essay "Pornography and Obscenity" (1929) makes clear the idealism and purity of his ambitions for the novel, which he called "the one bright book of life." He freed later writers to treat love, sex, and human psychology more honestly. His friend Aldous Huxley, who was with him in Vence, France, near his death in 1930, said, "Tuberculosis undoubtedly sharpened his sense of imminent extinction, but also heightened—in his works on the resurrection theme—his appreciation of physical sensations and the beauty of the body" (in Nehls, vol. 3:172). His widow established a shrine to his memory in Taos, New Mexico, at the ranch where they lived while Lawrence wrote his novels and stories of the Southwest and Mexico. The ranch is well known from a picture of the "Lawrence tree" by Georgia O'Keeffe depicting his beloved pine from the ground up, looking skyward through branches and lacy needles. The image suggests Lawrence's gift for creating literature both rooted and soaring, earthy and intricate.

MAJOR MULTICULTURAL THEMES

Exploring mystical connections between humans and particular landscapes, vividly rendered, is the first principle Lawrence brought to all his encounters with Europe, Australia, and America. Indeed, many of his metaphysical ideas are clearest in his fine travel literature, *Twilight in Italy* (1916), *Sea and Sardinia* (1921), *Mornings in Mexico* (1927), and *Etruscan Places* (1932) (although they are also stated in the expository books *Psychoanalysis and the Unconscious* [1921] and *Fantasia of the Unconscious* [1922]). But the sensuality with which

Lawrence connects his heroes to particular landscapes is rare in prose writers before him and owes much to his skill as a poet.

The short story "Sun," for instance, written in Spotorno, Italy, in December 1925, and set in Taormina, Sicily, presents the sun as a mythic god (Helios, Apollo), but also a human lover. Juliet, the protagonist, leaves her pale life in New York for a Mediterranean rest to revive her health, taking her child with her. Lying naked in the sun, she finds the beams "alive" and pulsing; she can "feel the sun penetrating even into her bones; nay farther, into her emotions and her thoughts."

Kicking over the traces of civilization and continuity, in Lawrence's second multicultural insight, was valid only when a new age, union of cultures, or experience was promised. Otherwise, he feared, only sterile renunciation of tradition would result.

Among the earliest major British writers to take American literature seriously enough to venture a broad and coherent review of it, Lawrence published *Studies in Classic American Literature* in 1923. An early version of one chapter, "Spirit of Place," remarks, "The world doesn't fear a new idea. It can pigeonhole any idea. But it can't pigeonhole a new experience." The new American experience, he argues, is not one of freedom: the lynching of America's powerless and dissidents proves that. Lawrence instead claims that the experience of Americans is "getting away from everything they are and have been. That's why most people have come to America, and still come" (cited in Kermode, 75).

Typically contrarian, he skewers leaders of the "American experiment" such as Franklin, Crèvecoeur, Cooper, and Poe; qualified praise is saved for Whitman and Hawthorne. Much earlier than most observers, American or otherwise, Lawrence boldly proclaims that the center of American experience is the conflict of the races. He hopes that America will be resurrected through such conflict, bearing a truly new idea. Cross-cultural transformation—although he did not know where it would lead—was his one hope for America.

SURVEY OF CRITICISM

John Worthen, director of the University of Nottingham Center for Lawrence Studies, wrote the first part of a comprehensive biography (1991), followed by the second volume (1996) by Mark Kincaid-Weekes and the third (1998) by David Ellis. Book-length studies that address Lawrence's work and life in each of the major settings are the works of Joseph Foster (1972), Taos; Leo Hamalian (1982) and Jeffrey Meyers (1982), Italy; and David J. Cavitch (1969), the New World. John Poplawski (1996) offers a current guide to the secondary literature as a whole.

SELECTIVE BIBLIOGRAPHY

Works by Lawrence

Sons and Lovers (1913). Cambridge: Cambridge University Press, 1992.
Sea and Sardinia (1921). London: Heinemann, 1923.
Kangaroo. Harmondsworth, Middlesex: Penguin, 1923.
Studies in Classic American Literature. New York: Seltzer, 1923.
The Plumed Serpent. New York: A.A. Knopf, 1926.
Mornings in Mexico (1927) *and Etruscan Places* (1932). London: Heinemann, 1956.

Selective Studies of Lawrence

Burgess, Anthony. *Flame into Being*. New York: Arbor House, 1985.
Cavitch, David J. *D.H. Lawrence and the New World*. New York: Oxford University Press, 1969.
Draper, R.P., ed. *D.H. Lawrence: The Critical Heritage*. New York: Routledge & Kegan Paul, 1970.
Ellis, David. *D.H. Lawrence: Dying Game, 1922–1930*. Cambridge: Cambridge University Press, 1998.
Foster, Joseph. *D.H. Lawrence in Taos*. Albuquerque: University of New Mexico Press, 1972.
Hamalian, Leo. *D.H. Lawrence in Italy*. New York: Taplinger, 1982.
Kermode, Frank. *D.H. Lawrence*. New York: Viking, 1973.
Kincaid-Weekes, Mark. *D.H. Lawrence: Triumph to Exile, 1912–1922*. Cambridge: Cambridge University Press, 1996.
Leavis, F.R. *D.H. Lawrence, Novelist*. New York: Knopf, 1956.
Meyers, Jeffrey. *D.H. Lawrence and the Experience of Italy*. Philadelphia: University of Pennsylvania Press, 1982.
Moore, Harry T. *The Intelligent Heart*. London: Penguin, 1960.
Nehls, Edward. *D.H. Lawrence: A Composite Biography*. 3 vols. Madison: University of Wisconsin Press, 1957–1959.
Poplawski, John. *D.H. Lawrence: A Reference Companion*. Westport, Conn.: Greenwood Press, 1996.
Worthen, John. *D.H. Lawrence: The Early Years, 1885–1912*. Cambridge: Cambridge University Press, 1991.

FANNY LEWALD
(1811–1889)

Elisabeth Plessen

BIOGRAPHY

Fanny Lewald, the "German George Sand," was the most important female German writer of her time. Although she published more than thirty pragmatic novels, most of them today are largely forgotten. She was born the eldest of eight children of an assimilated, liberal Jewish merchant in Prussian Königsberg, the town of Immanuel Kant. She attended private school for seven years, but when the school closed down, Fanny was constricted to the female role at home. She envied the education of boys, which demonstrated to her the injury done to women. A second experience of being different was the persecution of Jews in Germany in 1819, sparked by economic failure and national disillusionment after the Napoleonic Wars and the Congress of Vienna. Her father, too, went bankrupt, but his business gradually recovered. She converted to Protestantism and was christened à la Heinrich Heine, who later became her friend and her "entrebillet to European culture." "Trinity for me was the harmony of art, poetry, and thought," she wrote in her autobiography, *Meine Lebensgeschichte* (1861–1862). Her religion was Spinoza's philosophy of nature.

Accompanying her dominating father on a business tour, she met Ludwig Börne, whom she regarded highly for his *Briefe aus Paris*, through which he brought the ideas of the French revolution of 1830 to Germany. After two unhappy love affairs she opposed her father's wish of a marriage of convenience and began her career as a writer in 1840 with a report on celebrations in Königsberg for King Friedrich Wilhelm IV's accession. She at first published anonymously, on her father's orders, but with the success of her second novel, *Jenny*, in which she vindicates equality of rights and gender, she gave up her anonymity. She traveled to Italy for the first time in 1845, rented a flat in Rome, and frequented the city's colony of German artists. She met the Gymnasialprofessor and art historian Adolf Stahr, six years her elder, in poor health, married, and father of five children. They married in 1855. With Stahr she tried to combine independence and her ideal of a marriage of love. She published her first travel book, *Italienisches Bilderbuch* (1847), and, after the February 1848 revolution, traveled to Paris, where she met Heine. Back in Berlin, where she settled, she recorded her experiences in *Erinnerungen aus dem Jahre 1848*. In the autumn of that year she attended meetings in Frankfurt to fight for national unity (it must be recalled that Germany at the time was a patchwork of more than thirty principalities or states). She envied England and France, which were conscious of their national identity, and saw the possibility of German national identification, if only through literature: the classical authors—Goethe and Schiller—were the "true enlargers of the empire, this empire, where we Germans . . . hold together whilst the saddest political disunion separates us from each other" (128), she wrote in *Ein Winter in Rom* (1869).

She traveled to England and Scotland and again to Paris in 1850. In 1855 she and Stahr visited the international exhibition in Paris, "the work of the most modern Bonapartist politics," as Stahr sarcastically remarked. She met Heine for the last time before his death in February 1856, as well as many German democrats and former revolutionaries still living in exile. ("It's bad enough," she exclaimed, "that you have to leave your fatherland in order to see your best friends again.") At the salon of Marie d'Agoult she met Daniele Manin, who was fighting for Italy's liberation—experiences that found their place in *Benvenuto* (1876). She traveled to Switzerland in 1856 and to Italy again in 1858. During the 1860s and 1870s Lewald and Stahr were the leaders of a salon in Berlin similar to those of Rahel Varnhagen and Henriette Herz in their time. Guests at their weekly *jour fixe* were prominent figures of progressive, left-wing tendency: Theodor Fontane, Gottfried Keller, Friedrich Spielhagen, George Eliot, Levin Schücking, Fürst Pückler von Muskau, Paul Heyse, Franz Liszt, Ferdinand Lassalle, Johann Jacoby, Heinrich Simon, and other revolutionaries of 1848, as well as Grand Duke Carl-Alexander von Sachsen-Weimar, grandson of the duke who had once summoned Goethe, Lewald's literary idol, to his court in Weimar.

The couple spent 1866–67 in their "beloved Rome," witnesses of the country's change after unification in 1861 as reported by "das 4-beinige zweigeschlechtliche Tintentier" (the four-legged, two-sexed ink-animal), as Gottfried Keller characterized the coauthors of *Ein Winter in Rom*, a collection of letters to friends from Lewald and Stahr. In Switzerland she was excluded from participation in the 1867 peace congress at Geneva, but she succeeded in having her ten articles against the war, *Zehn Artikel wider den Krieg*, read and approved. At the congress she met Giuseppe Garibaldi, whom she venerated—a meeting reported in *Sommer und Winter am Genfersee: Ein Tagebuch von Fanny Lewald* (published in 1869 and 1872). She set high hopes on Bismarck, although he was "no gonfaloniere of freedom" (*Ein Winter in Rom*, 5). If her political views seesawed, it was because she was limited by Stahr, whose authority she accepted and who had never been a revolutionary like herself in her early days; and now the Paris Commune frightened her: "From the Commune, where the genius has to dig potatoes to gain the necessary motivation, nothing can rise but brutishness," she noted in her diary *Gefühltes und Gedachtes (1838–1888)*, published in 1900. Because of the Franco-Prussian War she became a patriot and enemy of France. She deplored, in *Reisebriefe aus Deutschland, Italien, und Frankreich (1877–1878)* (published in 1880), the two (unsuccessful) attempts on the life of Emperor Wilhelm I—"crimes against our old emperor"—allegedly by labor leaders. (She was, perhaps, in the heart of her so very contradictory heart, always a monarchist.)

Stahr having died in 1876, she traveled to Rome, lonesome and in poor health. After seventeen months she returned to Berlin suffering heart trouble. Her last trip to Rome was in 1880; she took yearly cures in Bad Ragaz in Switzerland and died traveling, in Dresden.

MAJOR MULTICULTURAL THEMES

A chronicler of her times, Lewald wrote about Italy following the tradition of critical reports of a Goethe, a Seume, a Heine. But hers is a woman's view. She contrasts the wealth and poverty of Italy with that of other European countries; her view of the splendor and decline of Rome sweeps through history, from an Egyptian obelisk to St. Peter's to the city under French occupation since 1849; from railways to telegraph wires, different from those in Berlin, Paris, and London. Rome, with all its trade and businesses, had never lost contact with country life and nature.

Switzerland, politically on a higher level, offers hope for moving humankind toward true brotherliness and serves as the "introduction to Italy's symphony of joy" (*Italienisches Bilderbuch*, 6). As a northerner from a "pensive country where . . . so many people forget enjoyment," her obvious desire is to relish Italian sociability, love of pleasure, and dolce far niente. She enjoys herself among Italians "who lack self-tormenting grief and lamentation" (154) and "laugh heartily" at matters over which Germans would weep. Lewald the pantheist criticizes the Protestant's theory of renunciation in the north, describing with pleasure and in great detail Roman popular life, the "theater season" of folk festivals, whether of lay or religious origin, from spring to late summer, their collective culture, games and feasts in Villa Borghese and outside the gates, and the Carnival. She compares domestic arrangements, cleanliness of lodgings, prizes, working conditions, and Catholic and Protestant divine worship. She depicts the behavior of English, Russian, French, German, and Scandinavian tourists in contact with the international community of artists on the occasion of the promotion of French artists at Villa Medici (the French Academy at the time). She comments on political Germany and German artists. France was a nation; Germany was divided into thirty-two "monarchies." Traveling Britons are ill spoken of in her travel books and journals: she caricatures them in the fashion of her time.

As for her art criticism, the cathedral of Florence, instead of "raising her to the ideal," "humiliates" her. "You despair and you become sad, the doctrine of original sin, the nullity of human endeavors hover over those rooms" (79). She dislikes the Medici Venus and rejects Michelangelo's *Last Judgment* in the Sistine Chapel as "too powerful for the comprehending faculties of my mind. Every saint is gigantic and wild, like Hercules, and I feel positive fear of his greatness. With these sentiments it is impossible to derive any pleasure from a contemplation of the works of Michel Angelo, and I am sure it is the same with many women who cannot understand this sublime genius" (202).

The Protestant northerner takes offense at the pomp and endless ceremonies of the papal household and criticizes the Catholic Church, and the Jesuits above all, for oppressing the mind's critical activity, for deforming humans, seizing their souls, their lives, their money. Papal Rome is a supervisory state. The pope, "very unhappy in his papal capacity . . . must know what a structure of superstition the Church has raised on the ideal of true Christianity" (204). On the occasion of a christening, she criticizes "the rigid system of exclusion" of the Jews, the breaking of their family ties, and the revenge taken on their confessors.

Rome is the city of two faces, the eternal one of history and art and the permanently changing, open, modern one. Naples is the vital, sparkling town under the red clouds of Vesuvius. Palermo preserves the tombs of the Capuchins and the spectacular five-day feast of Santa Rosalia that unfolds in the presence of the king in his double role as Sicily's spiritual leader. Venice is a "poetic miracle" where she could not live, as nature is lacking, with no tree between stones and canals; the city is in decay, languishing under Austrian control since 1804. She loves the visionary power of the Venetian painters of independent republican times: Veronese, Piombo, Titian.

Lewald likes the childlike nature of the Italians, yet considers it as a weakness of intellect, or at least the lack of an intellectual approach to matters, a childlike stiffening into conventionality. She praises the French, who utter their political, religious, and literary thoughts freely, signifying, for Lewald the evolutionist, progress.

SURVEY OF CRITICISM

Ulrike Helmer, in her epilogue (1992) to the *Italienisches Bilderbuch*, emphasizes the triumph of Lewald's liberation and completes the "triumph" with quotations from the private diary, *Römisches Tagebuch, 1845/46*, not printed until 1927. Gerhard Wolf asks, in his critical epilogue (1992) to Lewald's *Lebensgeschichte, Briefe, Erinnerungen*, why the author today is almost forgotten, and he brings into sharper focus her contradictory sides. Who is she: the pretentious (trivial) poet, the reporter of a journey, the ambitious writer of memoirs, the unconstrained composer of letters and diaries? He traces her way from a "Vormäz" (radical) author to a follower of Bismarck. Gabriele Schneider, in her biography *Fanny Lewald* (1996), characterizes Lewald as a young lady of Jewish origin who became Protestant and fought for the emancipation of the bourgeoisie, Jews, and women. She sees Lewald's life and work as that of an influential woman who disdained traditions and conventions—exemplary for bourgeois intellectuals of her time.

SELECTIVE BIBLIOGRAPHY

Works by Lewald

Römisches Tagebuch 1845/46. Leipzig: Klinkhardt & Biermann, 1927.
Italienisches Bilderbuch (1847). Ed. Ulrike Helmer. Frankfurt am Main: Ulrike Helmer Publishers, 1992.
Erinnerungen aus dem Jahre 1848. In *Freiheit des Herzens.* Ed. Günter de Bruyn and Gerhard Wolf. Frankfurt am Main and Berlin: Ullstein, 1992.
Meine Lebensgeschichte (1861–1862). In *Freiheit des Herzens.* Ed. Günter de Bruyn and Gerhard Wolf. Frankfurt am Main and Berlin: Ullstein, 1992.
Stahr, Adolf, and Fanny Lewald. *Ein Winter in Rom.* Berlin: J. Guttentag, 1869.
Reisebriefe aus Deutschland, Italien, und Frankreich (1877–1878). Berlin: Otto Janke, 1880.

Selective Studies of Lewald

Maio, Irene S. di. "Reclamation of the French Revolution: Fanny Lewald's Literary Response of the Nachmärz in *Der Seehof.*" In *Geist und Gesellschaft: Zur deutschen Rezeption der Französischen Revolution.* Ed. Eitel Timm. Munich: Fink, 1990.
Mortier, Roland. "Une romancière spectatrice de la Révolution française de 1848." In *Littérature et culture allemandes: Hommages à Henri Plard.* Ed. Roger Goffin, Michel Vanhelleputte, and Monique Weyembergh-Boussart. Bruxelles: Editions de l'Université de Bruxelles, 1985.
Schneider, Gabriele. *Fanny Lewald.* Rowohlts Monographien, 553. Reinbek bei Hamburg: Rowohlt Taschenbuch Verlag, 1996.

LIN YUTANG
(1895–1976)

Qian Suoqiao

BIOGRAPHY

Lin Yutang was born in the mountain village of Banzai, in Fujian Province, China, to a not-well-to-do, third-generation Chinese Christian family of many children. The year of his birth, 1895, was a significant turning point in China's history, marking the beginning of its modern period. It was in 1895 that China lost the first Sino-Japanese War, which sent a shock wave throughout the country and especially to the intelligentsia. The general consensus was that the "old traditional" system had to go. China ushered in a period of so-called Cultural Renaissance, which culminated in the 1919 May Fourth Movement. Unlike most leading intellectuals of the movement, whose early education had been in the traditional Chinese classics and then were sent abroad, returning to denounce the "old feudal system," Lin Yutang grew up quite detached from the national sentiment. After an exclusively Christian childhood education, he entered St. John's University in Shanghai, an American Presbyterian mission school, where all classes were taught in English with textbooks imported from the West. However, precisely due to the epistemic change under way in China at the time, Lin's Christian/English education became most desirable. After graduating in 1916, he became an instructor of English at Qinghua College. He then won a government scholarship for graduate study at Harvard University, receiving his master of arts degree in comparative literature in 1922. In Europe he earned his Ph.D. in philology from Leipzig University in 1924, then returned to China until 1936, when he left for the United States. These were the formative years during which he established himself as one of China's leading intellectuals and a popular and controversial writer/critic.

Lin taught English at Peking University (1924–27) and became dean of educational affairs at Peking Women's Normal University. He started his writing career as a member of the *yusi* literary group headed by the Zhou (Chou) brothers, Lu Xun and Zhou Zuoren, perhaps the best-known modern Chinese writers. He also became a "radical professor," going to the streets together with students to throw rocks at the police, and was eventually blacklisted by the then Beiyang government. He was forced to flee Beijing in 1926. After moving to Shanghai in 1927, though he was sometimes still fiercely critical of the new Nanjing government, he mellowed somewhat his political passion and focused more on "pure" writing as a profession, advocating "humor" both as a modern life attitude and a means for political critique. He launched three literary periodicals, *Lunyu* (Analects), *Renjianshi* (This human world), and *Yuzhoufeng* (Cosmic wind), which became so successful that Lin was nicknamed "Master of Humor." Little known to the Chinese reading public, however, was the fact that Lin had first started out in 1928 as a columnist, "Little Critic," for the English-language journal *China Critic*. In fact, many of his Chinese essays first appeared in English. Although these English writings had a much smaller readership, they did attract the attention of Pearl S. Buck, whose introduction of Lin to Richard Walsh, the publisher of the John Day Company, brought Lin to a new career in the United States and in the world.

Although Lin traveled and moved frequently to China, France, and Singapore (1936–66), his main "home base" was New York, and he wrote exclusively in English. Amicably called "Y.T." in New York's intellectual circles, he became a self-styled cultural ambassador, the wise "Chinese philosopher," introducing Chinese culture to Western audiences with a series of best-sellers, including *My Country and My People, The Importance of Living, Moment in Peking, The Wisdom of China and India,* and *Between Tears and Laughter*. After World War II, however, his popularity in America declined. He moved again in 1966, this time to Taiwan, where the Kuomintang government had fled after its defeat by the mainland Chinese Communists in 1949. He spent his last ten years between Taiwan and Hong Kong, resumed writing essays in Chinese, and completed the compilation of a *Chinese-English Dictionary of Modern Usage*. Even as his fame reached another high in the Chinese world outside the mainland during the postwar period, his name was banned in mainland China, where now, however, after he has long been forgotten in America, his "little essays" are again enjoying great popularity.

MAJOR MULTICULTURAL THEMES

Lin Yutang at the age of eighty called his life "a bundle of contradictions." In fact, the twentieth century in China can also be characterized as a century of contradictions, resulting from the West's enclosure of China and the necessity for China to engage the West. Therefore, Lin Yutang's cross-cultural conflicts are characteristic of Chinese modernity. The combination of his Christian educational background and his thirty years of diaspora existence provided him with a unique approach to East-West cross-cultural mediation.

In Shanghai's intellectual circles in the 1930s, as leader of the "Analects school" (or society), he was seen as a "most Westernized gentleman," having been to Harvard and Europe and speaking and writing eloquent English. When George Bernard Shaw visited Shanghai in 1933, which was a big event in Chinese literary circles, it was Lin, dressed in traditional long gown, who hosted, translated, and humored him during his visit. Lin spent much time and effort delving into the study of Chinese classical literature and culture at a time when such learning was denounced by Nationalists and Communists alike. It is true that his immersion in the classical world was already tinged with his Western training, which may arouse scorn in certain classicists, but what he attempted to do was to find sources within the Chinese tradition that could be incorporated into modernity. For instance, he rediscovered Yuan Zhonglang and the "*xingling* school," promoting them enthusiastically because he believed that he found a modern affinity between this school and the Crocean aesthetics of expression.

However, when he moved to the United States, his original approach to East-West mediation took on a rather different dimension. He was the first Asian writer ever to establish himself in American intellectual circles as well as the reading public. His popularity in America rests on both the hybrid nature of the East-West combination within him and his own "familiar style" of writing in the English language. But the popular and respected role for this "Oriental gentleman" was appropriate only for introducing "Oriental wisdom" to the Americans. This was the role of an amicable Other, the success of which could only be transitory, as shown, for instance, in the failure of *On the Wisdom of America* (1950), where he shifts his role to comment on American culture by asserting his own modern identity.

SURVEY OF CRITICISM

Criticism on Lin Yutang remains quite slim and is mostly in the form of biographical commentary, the most comprehensive of which, in Chinese, is by Wan Pingjin (1996), a mainland Marxist critic. The biography by Lin's daughter Lin Taiyi (1989) offers a colorful look at Lin's family life, while Diran Sohigian's dissertation (1991) is the most comprehensive biography in English. The present author is engaged in a sustained (cross-)cultural critique on the discourses and practices of Lin Yutang in the context of twentieth-century China and the West.

SELECTIVE BIBLIOGRAPHY

Works by Lin Yutang

My Country and My People. New York: John Day, 1935.
The Importance of Living. New York: John Day, 1937.
Moment in Peking. New York: John Day, 1939.
Leaf in the Storm. New York: John Day, 1941.

LIN YUTANG 269

The Wisdom of China and India. New York: Random House, 1942.
Between Tears and Laughter. New York: John Day, 1943.
The Vigil of a Nation. New York: John Day, 1944.
Chinatown Family. New York: John Day, 1948.
On the Wisdom of America. New York: John Day, 1950.
From Pagan to Christian. Cleveland: World Publishing, 1959.

Selective Studies of Lin Yutang

Lin Taiyi. *Lin yutang zhuane.* Taipei: Lianjing, 1989.
Qian Jun. "Lin Yutang: Negotiating Modernity between East and West." Ph.D. Dissertation, University of California, Berkeley, 1996.
Shi Jianwei. *Lin yutang zai dalu.* Beijing: Beijing shiyue wenyi, 1991.
Sohigian Diran John. "The Life and Times of Lin Yutang." Ph.D. Dissertation, Columbia University, 1991.
Wan Pingjin. *Lin yutang pingzhuan.* Chongqing: Chongqing, 1996.
Zhang Shizhen. *Lunyu shiqi de Lin yutang yanjiu.* Taipei: Wenshizhe, 1993.

PIERRE LOTI
(1850–1923)

Michael Bishop

BIOGRAPHY

Born in Rochefort on the Atlantic coast north of Bordeaux, Julien Viaud adopted the pseudonym of Pierre Loti with the publication in 1879 of his first novel, *Aziyadé*. His childhood was comfortable, coddled among the many women of his larger family, yet perhaps torn eventually between a nostalgic fondness for such tender ideality and a growing youthful desire to take to the sea, as had his ancestors. Even though his brother had died while returning from Indochina, Loti, seventeen, nevertheless felt compelled to pursue naval studies and, two years later, set sail on the *Jean Bart*, launching a professional naval career that would take him around the globe. The year 1891 saw him elected to the still-prestigious Académie française ahead of the claims of Zola, Loti's literary success having been considerable and rapid and in distinct contrast both in mode and subject matter with the "naturalism" of the period. His 1886 marriage to Jeanne Blanche Franc de Ferrière offered them, after one miscarriage, the potential happiness of a son, but Loti seems to have found marriage unsuited to his instincts and professional life, and Jeanne chose largely to live apart, with occasional visits to son and husband. (Loti also recognized two sons born of a love for a Basque woman, Crucita Gainza.) Having published almost forty books—initially novels, increasingly travel diaries, journals, even polemical pieces such as *Turquie agonisante* (1913) and *La Mort de notre chère France en Orient* (1920), and memoirs of his childhood and youth—Loti died, ironically paralyzed, in Hendaye (Basses-Pyrénées) in 1923 and was buried with full national honors.

MAJOR MULTICULTURAL THEMES

Almost all of Loti's work derives from his extensive travel as a French naval officer to Turkey, Polynesia, Japan and the Far East, Morocco, Senegal and elsewhere on the African continent, the Middle East, Persia, and India. The more culturally remote and distinctive regions of France also held great fascination for him: the Basque country and Brittany. If it is true that his work plunges deep into the cultural identity of the other, of many others, it is equally important to appreciate that the images shown in the many mirrors of his various writings also reveal his own difference, a self ironically ever diverging from its avatars. New identities are precarious, ephemeral, and disorienting, even though they may enrich, expand, and deeply appeal, revealing truly felt affinities as barriers crumble. While such divertissements—the ironical notion is Loti's—can, then, authentically fascinate and the depths of difference and specificity can be cease-lessly explored (for Loti's work offers no casual, silly, or scintillating "exoti-cism"), they also may be said, paradoxically, to divert the self away from a quest for the self's identity that unquestionably lies at the heart of an oeuvre endlessly dealing with the experience of convergence/dissociation and sameness/distinction.

Chateaubriand, Baudelaire, and Rimbaud, in radically divergent yet linked ways, wrestle with issues that Loti examines at once more concretely yet in both a psychological and cultural perspective. The pointillist, somewhat kaleidoscopic art of Loti—one that may frustrate certain aestheticizing stylists but one, equally, that charms in its unpretentious directness—generates both a discreet and yet insistent caress of the cultural othernesses his writing explores. If, as Bachelard argues, Loti is indeed a "great writer of visual quality" (85), a sharp observer of surface, shape, and color, his power as a transcultural sensitive yet stems probably far more, on the one hand, from a constant insertion into the observed "object's" presence of psychological, emotional, and, in the broadest sense, spir-itual meditation and mood, and, on the other hand, from a sense given off paradoxically by this very insertion, of the impossibility of truly penetrating the mask of the other, truly penetrating to the heart of being—and thus one's own being. This, of course, is no small calamity—for this is, indeed, how Loti ex-periences it, how his protagonists and narrators often experience it—and it accounts for the tirelessly resurgent themes of nonaccomplishment and unfini-shedness of the transcultural dream or experiment. The woman-as-other, often further transfigured by her cultural—and therefore physical, mental, moral, and spiritual—difference, is commonly the emblem, the lived and mortal emblem (for very much in Loti's novels is near the autobiographical mark) of a quest for primal, primitive, original purity and shared simplicity. Such idealization, such "absolutism" is certainly caught up in the frustrations of his sense of the crumbling, mortal brittleness of the ancient civilizations thoughtlessly (mis)handled by a colonial intrusion and dominance whose atrocities or simple blundering he will not hesitate to document.

Aziyadé (1879), from the outset, distills fascination with and enthusiasm for the other, yet tenderness is beset with loss, the menace of reciprocal exile, and cultural alienation, so that self-other encounter shimmers almost as an illusion, as does, consequently, the simultaneous, one could even say synonymous, encounter of self with self. *Le Mariage de Loti* (1880), appearing fast on the heels of *Aziyadé*, evokes the natural splendors as well as the social, psychological, and intercultural climate of late-nineteenth-century Tahiti. What is perhaps most striking is Loti's sense of all that language cannot conceivably document or speak adequately of: the deeper meanings and quasi-primordial beauties of a land and a civilization barely conceivable, let alone spiritually penetrable, to Europeans.

Le Roman d'un spahi (1881) picks up once more the thematics of disorientation and adventure, anguish and an "amusement" that transforms alternately into pleasure, adaptation, and loving attachment to West African mores and circumstance, and, more violently, into a sense of absurd contradiction, of a mutually wasteful noncoincidence that prevents self and other from attaining completeness together while disabling any feasible return to earlier idealized states. *Pêcheur d'Islande* (1886) speaks of the joys and boldly defied terrors of the sailors and fishermen of Brittany journeying to China or to the far North and Iceland, ostensibly to earn a living. Traditional colonial attitudes are exposed and mingle with a characteristic Lotian discourse on the sheer strangeness of intercultural, indeed general, human exchange, leading to fundamental questions as to the existential purpose and meaning of impulse, need, and "destiny" that have us commune, both simply, innocently, and carrying the baggage of our cultural bias, with "the other side of the Earth."

Madame Chrysanthème (1887) constitutes and narrates another bold gesture of exploration, this time of Japanese difference. Marriage, as often elsewhere, is emblematic of this self-other fusion and separation: its success is relative, never fully consummated, even though the body and mind of the other, the other's space, sense of time, language, art, religion, and myth may truly obsess, slowly seeping into the pores of the colonial self (who is often equally "other" to himself—it always is a "him," even though woman is at the center of Loti's otherness). Cultural "divorce" in Loti seems implacable, but then the "marriage" is always somewhat unreal: sought, but not with the absolute energy of undying, blind passion. "As I leave [Japan]," writes the ambivalent, half-ironic, half-seduced narrator, "I can only find within myself a lightly sardonic smile thinking of this teeming small race with its bowings, its laboring, its industriousness, its keenness to profit, a constitutional finicalness that slightly sullies it, as do its tradition of cheap goods and its incurable grimacing" (247–48).

Ramuntcho (1897) offers a subtle, sensitive, even audacious exploration of fin de siècle Basque culture, its specificities and its betweenness, its un-Frenchness and its un-Spanishness. Here there is no outside, colonial narrator-protagonist, as usually is the case, and the portrayal lacks therefore the direct ironies and cynicism associated with colonial—even if strongly empathetic—voice. The tone and the deep fascination are, however, still psychological, implicitly ontological, never banally didactic. For all that, loss, exile, and difference still dominate thematically, turning endlessly about the complexities of cultural marks, whether delightful, troubling, or simply enigmatic, irreducible, like "the *irrintzina*, the great Basque cry, which has been transmitted faithfully from the depths of the abyss of time to the men of today, and which constitutes one of the strangenesses of this race with its origins wrapped in mystery" (77). A certain number of books by Loti had, by the time *Ramuntcho* appeared, turned into unambiguous travel journals—*Au Maroc* (1890) or *Jérusalem* (1895), for example—or else equally unambivalent autobiography, as in the 1890 *Roman d'un enfant*. Nonetheless, he remains always a keen, darting observer, fascinated by and strangely enamored of difference. Books like *L'Inde (sans les Anglais)* (1903) or *Turquie agonisante* (1913) testify to this, as do his three journals, two appearing posthumously (*Journal intime, 1878–1881* and *Journal intime, 1882–1885*), all of which shed light on his at once colonial and culturally available, even liberated fascinations and conceptions.

SURVEY OF CRITICISM

Michael Lerner's study of Loti's poetics (1974) is articulate and thoughtful and carefully though not abusively woven into a subtle sense of Loti's personal life. It is wide-ranging yet concise in its intelligent treatment of Loti's teeming inter- and transcultural preoccupations. Clive Wake's study of Loti's novelistic universe (1974) is informed and probing and again digs deeply into the logic of Loti's experience of otherness, both its inevitable colonial trappings and the authentic desire for self-redemption via such experience and the creativity it unleashes. Pierre Briquet's analysis of Loti's orientalist poetics (1945) is extremely useful: the Islamic world is at the core of Loti's exploration here. Lesley Blanch gives an excellent biography of Loti (1983), inescapably interwoven with a sense of his imaginative world. K.G. Millward's study (1955) centers on the fin de siècle poetics felt to be at the heart of an oeuvre and a life that modernity (and soon postmodernity) would seem—but only seem—to outdistance. It would be useful to rethink this good study in the light of postcolonial writing and criticism.

SELECTIVE BIBLIOGRAPHY

Works by Loti

Aziyadé (1879). Paris: Calmann-Lévy, 1949.
Le Mariage de Loti (1880). Paris: Calmann-Lévy, 1950.
Le Roman d'un spahi (1881). Paris: Calmann-Lévy, 1947.
Mon frère Yves (1883). Paris: Calmann-Lévy, 1950.
Pêcheur d'Islande (1886). Paris: Calmann-Lévy, 1968.
Madame Chrysanthème (1887). Paris: Calmann-Lévy, 1948.
Japoneries d'automne. Paris: Calmann-Lévy, 1889.
Au Maroc. Paris: Calmann-Lévy, 1890.
Le Roman d'un enfant (1890). Paris: Calmann-Lévy, 1927.
Jérusalem. Paris: Calmann-Lévy, 1895.

Ramuntcho (1897). Paris: Calmann-Lévy, 1941.
L'Inde (sans les Anglais). Paris: Calmann-Lévy, 1903.
Vers Ispahan. Paris: Calmann-Lévy, 1904.
Les Désenchantées (1906). Paris: Calmann-Lévy, 1952.
Un pélerin d'Angkor. Paris: Calmann-Lévy, 1912.
Turquie agonisante. Paris: Calmann-Lévy, 1913.
Prime jeunesse. Paris: Calmann-Lévy, 1919.
La mort de notre chère France en Orient. Paris: Calmann-Lévy, 1920.
Un jeune officier pauvre. Paris: Calmann-Lévy, 1923.
Journal intime, 1878–1881. Paris: Calmann-Lévy, 1925.
Journal intime, 1882–1885. Paris: Calmann-Lévy, 1929.

Selective Studies of Loti

Auvergne, E.B. d'. *Pierre Loti: The Romance of a Great Writer*. London: Werner Laurie, 1926.

Bachelard, Gaston *La Terre et les rêveries du repos*. Paris: Corti, 1948.

Barthes, Roland. "Le Nom d'Aziyadé." *Critique* 297 (February 1972): 103–17.

Blanch, Lesley. *Pierre Loti: The Legendary Romantic*. New York: Harcourt Brace Jovanovich, 1983.

Briquet, Pierre-E. *Pierre Loti et l'Orient*. Neuchâtel: La Baconnière, 1945.

Brodin, Pierre. *Loti*. Montreal: Parizeau, 1945.

Lerner, Michael G. *Pierre Loti*. New York: Twayne, 1974.

Le Targat, François. *A la recherche de Pierre Loti*. Paris: Seghers, 1974.

Millward, K.G. *L'Oeuvre de Pierre Loti et l'esprit "fin de siècle."* Paris: Nizet, 1955.

Traz, R. de. *Pierre Loti*. Paris: Hachette, 1948.

Wake, Clive. *The Novels of Pierre Loti*. The Hague: Mouton, 1974.

ANDRÉ MALRAUX
(1901–1976)

Domnica Radulescu

BIOGRAPHY

Born in Paris in 1901, Georges André Malraux was raised, after the separation of his parents in 1905, by his mother, grandmother, and an aunt, who at times exposed him to Parisian opera and theater, but he spent his summers with his father in Normandy in another cultural and ethnic ambiance. He failed to gain admission to the Lycée Condorcet, which caused him to give up his secondary education altogether. During his adolescence he devoured French and foreign literatures, from classical Greek to medieval French, *The Arabian Nights*, Tolstoy, Flaubert, Balzac, Dostoevsky, Baudelaire, Verlaine, and Cubist poetry. He educated himself through secondhand books sold along the Seine and visits to the Louvre. He sporadically attended classes at the School for Oriental Languages and became a "habitué" of the Museum of Oriental Art Guimet, learning much of Western and Oriental art.

In the 1920s he traveled to many European cities as well as to exotic Indochina, where he spent two years (1923–24). The Indochinese experience determined, to a large extent, the direction of his career. He joined an archeological expedition from Phnom Penh in search of the famous Khmer temple of Banteaï-Srey, some of whose artifacts he took to study, to offer to the Guimet Museum, or to sell to finance the expedition. The result was a prison sentence, from which he extricated himself and returned to France. Returning to Indochina in 1925, he was largely responsible for the launching of the journal *Indochine* that denounced French injustices toward the Annamite population.

In 1929 he traveled to Persia (where he was particularly enchanted by Isfahan), visiting Iraq and Syria on his return. This was as much an intense period of discovering worlds, cultures, and modes of thinking other than French and European as one of self-discovery and intellectual effervescence.

Echoes of his adventures and travels resound in the works of the first part of his career: *La Tentation de l'Occident* (1926), an epistolary philosophical meditation on East and West, the novel *Les Conquérants* and the fantastic tale *Royaume-Farfelu* (1928), and the novels *La Voie royale* (1930) and *La Condition humaine* (1933). The last develops philosophical problems, such as the confrontation between man and his destiny, man and death, and the nature of heroic action, on the canvas of the Chinese Revolution in Shanghai under the leadership of the Kuomintang.

On the track of ancient Rome's Egyptian prefect Aelius Gallus, he took a risky flight (1934) over the Arabian desert of Yemen in search of the lost kingdom of the legendary queen of Sheba, which attracted much publicity and added to his image as a Romantic hero. As his contacts with other cultures became more steeped in politics, he leaned to the Left and became a fighter against Fascism. Four months spent in the USSR in 1934 cooled his enthusiasm for Communism as he discovered its system of lies and terror. His short novel *Le Temps du mépris* (1935) is aimed against Nazism.

In the Spanish Civil War (1936–37) he fought on the Republican side. He immersed himself both in the war and the spirit of Spanish culture, the outgrowth of which was the novel *L'Espoir* (1937). His last novel, *Les Noyers de l'Altenburg* (1943), is both a philosophical and largely autobiographical work in which Alsace's mixture of French and German culture plays a significant role. During World War II he served as a leader of the partisans (the "maquis"), escaped from a Gestapo prison, and became the commander of the Brigade Alsace-Lorraine (1944–45). The period between 1950 and 1970 saw the publication of three major works, *Les Voix du silence* (1951), *La Métamorphose des dieux* (1957), and the *Antimémoires* (1967), in which he emphasized the dialogue that, according to Malraux, the arts and literatures of different cultures and centuries silently carry on with each other.

As France's minister of cultural affairs (1959–69) he encountered political personalities of the world, from the Kennedys to Nasser and Mao Tse-tung. Three years before his death he visited India, met with Indira Gandhi, delivered speeches at Dacca and Chittagong, and was awarded an honorary degree at the University of Rajshahi. *Hôtes de passage* (1975) is a collection of dialogues and stories of famous encounters. His literary and political career was posthumously crowned in November 1996 when his remains were placed in the vaults of the Pantheon.

MAJOR MULTICULTURAL THEMES

Malraux's exploration of foreign cultures reveals (1) a curiosity about, and fascination with, the "Other" and the unknown, in ontological terms; (2) a desire to probe the specific means by which a given culture grasps the basic existential problem of the meaning of life and death and by which it leaves its trace in the world; (3) a consistent shift from the "Other" back to the "Self" for reconsideration and reinterpretation of his own culture.

1. *La Tentation de l'Occident* is a dialogue revolving around the philosophical differences between East and West. It contrasts the Eastern serene acceptance of the insignificance of the individual in a universal context and the Western feverish struggle to affirm individual conscience as a significant force in the universe. The dialogue between East and West has profound echoes also in *La Condition humaine, La Voie royale, Les Conquérants,* and *Les Noyers de l'Altenburg,* in which he connects it with the idea of resignation in the face of death and destiny versus the ambition to defy them through heroism or creativity, and with the search for an answer to the fundamental existential question "what is man?" *La Voie royale* in particular bears upon the dialectical confrontation between the colonizer's attempt to possess and subjugate the "Other" and the Hegelian recognition of the basic irony of the master-slave relation.

2. Malraux gathers art of all countries and epochs in his famous imaginary space that he liked to call his *musée imaginaire.* He tries to penetrate the mysterious balance of thoughts, forms, and colors that has established their survival over time, as well as the silent voice that unites them all in the human attempt to defy eternity. Malraux the agnostic always respected the religious manifestations of every culture. He defined the "sacred" as an attempt to establish a connection with that which transcends the human. He penetrated the essence of a culture by analyzing its cultural artifacts, as well as by intense and often-rapid exchanges with people of that culture, from peasants and soldiers (as during the Spanish war) to intellectuals and politicians. The *Antimémoires* offers a rich array of these encounters, from Nehru to the imaginary dialogue with the legendary Sheba over the expanse of the Arabian desert.

3. Malraux is first and foremost French. His dialogue with other cultures reverts inevitably to his attempt to understand French culture in more profound ways by comparison with others. In his charismatic speeches delivered in many parts of the world he invariably returned to the same metaphysical questions that haunted him his entire life, and to his attempts to define the essence of national cultures and the interactions among them. In Athens in 1959 he stated that "there is a secret Greece at the heart of all Westerners," giving impetus to his generous wish of showing the world that "the spirit knows no minor nations, it knows only fraternal nations" ("Hommage à la Grèce," in *Oeuvres complètes,* 3:923). The many cultural relations that he established with the world during the period of his ministry are overwhelming; his multiculturalism brought a new dimension to French twentieth-century literature and gave a new flair to France's cultural politics.

SURVEY OF CRITICISM

Walter Langlois's *André Malraux: The Indochina Adventure* (1966) remains the most complete and authoritative source on Malraux's early travels and experiences in Indochina, exploring the many ways in which they were fundamental in shaping his life and career. Langlois offers a wealth of information on the case of the Khmer statues and its legal complications and analyzes as well the many social, political, and philosophical ramifications of Malraux's publication of the journal *Indochine* and his complex interactions with the Annamite population and culture. Langlois's article "Malraux and the Greek Ideal" (1971) is an eloquent analysis of Malraux's appreciation and interpretation of the art and philosophy of classical Greece.

Robert Thornberry's *André Malraux et l'Espagne* (1977) does for Malraux's Spanish experience what Walter Langlois has done for the Indochinese experience. Malraux's direct involvement in the war, his many roles in the fight against the Nationalists, the historicopolitical panorama and background of the war, and the metamorphosis of this experience into art are discussed in detail and supported by rich data and information. *André Malraux and Cultural Diversity* (1992–1993), edited by Françoise Dorenlot and Robert Thornberry, contains an excellent collection of articles that deal precisely with Malraux's multicultural experiences. Curtis Cate's *André Malraux: A Biography* (1955) offers an excellent panorama and analysis of Malraux's travels, adventures, contacts with other cultures, and political roles in the larger context of both his personal life and his literary career. Axel Madsen's *Silk Roads: The Asian Adventures of Clara and André Malraux* (1989) is a captivating account of Malraux's first experience with Asia and its culture and of the literary, political, and personal aspects of the couple's voyages.

SELECTIVE BIBLIOGRAPHY

Work by Malraux

Oeuvres complètes. 3 vols. Paris: Gallimard, 1989.

Selective Studies of Malraux

Cate, Curtis. *André Malraux: A Biography.* London: Hutchinson, 1955.
Dorenlot, Françoise E., and Robert Thornberry, eds. *André Malraux and Cultural Diversity. Revue André Malraux Review* 24, nos. 1/2, Edmonton, Alberta, 1992–1993.
Langlois, Walter. *André Malraux: The Indochina Adventure.* New York: Praeger, 1966.
———. "Malraux and the Greek Ideal." In *The Persistent Voice*, 195–212. Ed. Walter Langlois. New York: New York University Press, 1971.
Madsen, Axel. *Silk Roads: The Asian Adventures of Clara and André Malraux.* New York: Pharos Books, 1989.
Radulescu, Domnica. *André Malraux: The "Farfelu" as Expression of the Feminine and the Erotic.* New York: Peter Lang, 1994.
Thornberry, Robert. *André Malraux et l'Espagne.* Geneva: Droz, 1977.

THOMAS MANN
(1875–1955)

Ingeborg Baumgartner

BIOGRAPHY

Multicultural heritage, extensive travel, and exile shape Thomas Mann's life and work. Born in the free city of Lübeck to Thomas Johann Heinrich Mann, a German patrician merchant, and his wife, Julia da Silva Bruhns, native of Brazil and daughter of a German and a Portuguese-Creole, Mann stayed on in Lübeck long enough to complete his secondary education before his move to Munich in 1894. Supported by a modest inheritance, he devoted his time to writing. His early novellas are collected in *Der kleine Herr Friedemann* (1898). In the late 1890s he resided with his brother Heinrich (1871–1950), a writer and essayist, in Italy (Venice, Naples, Rome, and Palestrina) while writing his first novel, *Buddenbrooks: Verfall einer Familie* (1901), autobiographical in nature and pessimistic in tone. Subsequently he turned again to short pieces, exemplified by *Tonio Kröger* (1903), elaborating on the theme of the artist as a "lost" burgher, one who needs to reconcile himself to his fate.

His happy marriage (1905) to Katja Pringsheim, daughter of a prominent Munich family, inspired *Königliche Hoheit* (1910), a fairy-tale-like love story between an impoverished, sensitive German prince and a rich, independent-minded, intelligent American heiress of mixed parentage. Italian history figures in his only drama, *Fiorenza* (1906), which examines the intellectual and political conflict between Lorenzo de' Medici and Savonarola. *Der Tod in Venedig* (1912) tells of the degrading surrender of Gustav von Aschenbach, a middle-aged, self-disciplined, successful writer, to the beauty of the fourteen-year-old Tadzio, son of a Polish family vacationing in Venice. Influenced by Friedrich Nietzsche, this novella's classical form clashes with the baroque descriptions of homoerotic passion, obsession, and decadence.

The advent of World War I marked a turn away from "aesthetic self-absorption" (Reed, 222) and a shift in Mann's political thinking to a painstakingly introspective examination of his own time and his place in it. A number of essays, especially *Betrachtungen eines Unpolitischen* (1918), expose his gradual metamorphosis from patriotic monarchist to unambiguous advocate of democratic government. This arduous process is symbolically and ironically represented in *Der Zauberberg* (1924) as the reeducation of Hans Castorp, the naïve hero who spends seven years in a Swiss sanatorium with an Italian representing faith in rational, progressive ideas and a Polish Jew converted to Catholicism, advocating Communism. Castorp falls in love with a Russian married to a Frenchman, mistress of a Dutch planter from Indonesia, by virtue of whose personality Castorp, in the end, turns against "sympathy with death" and chooses life. This novel, as well as *Buddenbrooks*, earned Thomas Mann the Nobel Prize for Literature in 1929. A year later appeared *Mario und der Zauberer* (1930), set in Italy and describing how an "illusionist" subjugates the will of his audience, only to be shot to death by Mario, one of the spectators. This political allegory with its penetrating analysis of "political mass hypnosis" (Feuerlicht, 129) uncannily presages Germany's torpor in the face of rising Fascism.

In 1925 Mann began preparations for a novel about the biblical story of Joseph by reading sources and traveling in Egypt. After completion of the first volume, *Die Geschichten Jaakobs* (1933), his life changed radically when Hitler became chancellor in January 1933. Having left Munich in February with his wife Katja for a lecture tour in Amsterdam and vacation in Arosa, Switzerland, Mann feared to return to Germany (he was accused of "intellectual high treason" against the new state, *Briefe* 1:328). He became an exile, first in Switzerland, then in the United States. When the status of émigrés was most precarious, he and his family accepted citizenship of Czechoslovakia (1936) while continuing to reside in Switzerland. After the dismemberment of Czechoslovakia in 1938 he emigrated to the United States and was granted citizenship in 1944.

Despite these upheavals he continued his prolific output of novels, essays, articles, and radio addresses in tireless criticism of Third Reich policies and passionate advocacy of democracy. He found respite in writing the sequels of the tetralogy *Joseph und seine Brüder* (1933–1943), perhaps the finest testimony to his multiculturalism: he immersed himself in the ancient myths of the Jews at a time when their descendants suffered unspeakable horror in Germany. The resulting volumes, *Der junge Joseph* (1934), *Joseph in Ägypten* (1936), and *Joseph der Ernährer* (1943), offer a vast panorama of psychology, mythology, and biblical history. As was his custom, Mann interrupted the production of long works with the writing of shorter pieces: a novel about Charlotte Buff's visit to Goethe, *Lotte in Weimar* (1939), and narratives dealing with distant times, *Die vertauschten Köpfe: Eine indische Legende* (1940) and *Das Gesetz* (1944).

Universally considered Mann's greatest novel, *Doktor Faustus: Das Leben des deutschen Tonsetzers Adrian Leverkühn, erzählt von einem Freunde* (1947) becomes his attempt to understand the Third Reich catastrophe. By using the Faust legend together with Nietzsche's biography, he gives a penetrating assessment of German culture and history. Finally, in the incestuous background of Pope Gregorius (*Der Erwählte*, 1951) he finds solace in and some reconciliation to his European heritage in ironic humor, wit, and lightness of tone. In his last novella, *Die Betrogene* (1953), a parodistic reversal of *Königliche Hoheit*, he again gives the outsider an American identity: a German falls in love with a war veteran from Detroit. Cold War tensions and longing for his beloved Europe persuaded Mann to emigrate once again, seeking a home not in divided Germany, but in Switzerland. He died of thrombosis in Zürich in 1955.

MAJOR MULTICULTURAL THEMES

Thomas Mann's immense oeuvre is rich with multicultural themes. First, he thematized his dual heritage by making it the wellspring of his early short novellas. Imbued with the aestheticism of the 1890s (Ohl, 1995), they focus on the creative artist as an outsider who suffers from the dichotomy of "health, normality" on the one hand and "disease, abnormality" on the other. While the setting of *Buddenbrooks* is confined to Germany, the "influence came from everywhere: France, England, Russia, the Scandinavian countries" (Mann, *Rede und Antwort*, 9) to inspire a family saga of "Westeuropean type."

Second, Mann's major works were influenced and enriched by journeys to foreign countries: Denmark (*Tonio Kröger*), Italy (*Fiorenza, Der Tod in Venedig, Mario und der Zauberer*), Egypt (*Josef und seine Brüder*), and Switzerland (*Der Zauberberg*). Many protagonists leave their native home, travel abroad, and experience their otherness in the form of national difference but also in artistic sensibilities as opposed to those of the "normal burgher." Familiarity with the foreign country makes for convincing treatment of characters from the European milieu.

Third, intimate with the Western canon and steeped in the Hellenic, Judeo-Christian traditions, Mann exploited these in imaginative ways. He alludes to motifs in Roman history (*Mario und der Zauberer*), weaves in Hellenic myths (*Der Tod in Venedig*), and reinterprets Jewish mythology (the *Joseph* novels, *Das Gesetz*). Furthermore, he explores different worlds in his works: for example, the Catholic medieval world in *Der Erwählte* and ancient India in *Die vertauschten Köpfe*. Profoundly influenced by Russian literature (Tolstoy, Turgenev), Mann created a panoply of figures of Slavic origin representing a ubiquitous code for artistic inclinations, a tendency to irrationalism, and "sympathy with death," for example, Lizaveta Ivanovna in *Tonio Kröger*, Tadzio in *Der Tod in Venedig*, and Clawdia and Naphta in *Der Zauberberg*. But in all of his works he uses his multiculturalism not as access to a particular foreign culture, but as a mirror of his own personal experience.

SURVEY OF CRITICISM

The most recent biographies of Mann are unique in focus, long in number of pages: Hayman (1995) and Prater (1995) offer psychological insights; Heilbut (1996) interprets sexuality; Kurzke (1999), the artistry. Older biographies such as Richard Winston's (1981) or Peter de Mendelssohn's (1975) focus on the artist's development. More succinct literary analyses of the works are by Henry Hatfield (1951), Ignace Feuerlicht (1968), Martin Swales (1980), and above all, the perceptive study by T.J. Reed (1974). Examining Mann's relationship to other nationalities are comprehensive works by Jonas (1969), Mádl and Györi (1977), Sumichrast (1970), and especially essays assembled in Helmut Koopmann's *Handbuch* (1990) (e.g., Guy Stern on Mann's knowledge of Jews, Hans Rudolf Vaget of America, Thomas Sprecher of Switzerland).

SELECTIVE BIBLIOGRAPHY

Works by Mann

Gesammelte Werke in zwölf Bänden. Frankfurt am Main: S. Fischer Verlag, 1960.
Briefe, 1889–1936. Ed. Erika Mann. Frankfurt am Main: Fischer Verlag, 1961.
Gesammelte Werke in Einzelbänden. Frankfurter Ausgabe, 20 vols. Frankfurt am Main: S. Fischer Verlag, 1981–1985.
Rede und Antwort. Frankfurt am Main: S. Fischer Verlag, 1984.

Selective Studies of Mann

Feuerlicht, Ignace. *Thomas Mann.* New York: Twayne Publishers, 1968.
Hatfield, Henry. *Thomas Mann.* Norfolk, Conn.: New Directions Books, 1951.
Hayman, Ronald. *Thomas Mann: A Biography.* New York: Scribner, 1995.
Heilbut, Anthony. *Thomas Mann: Eros and Literature.* New York: Alfred A. Knopf, 1996.
Jonas, Ilsedore. *Thomas Mann und Italien.* Heidelberg: Carl Winter Universitätsverlag, 1969.
Koopmann, Helmut, ed. *Thomas-Mann-Handbuch.* Stuttgart: Alfred Kröner Verlag, 1990.
Kurzke, Hermann. *Thomas Mann: Das Leben als Kunstwerk: Eine Biographie.* Munich: C.H. Beck, 1999.
Mádl, Antal, and Györi, Judit, eds. *Thomas Mann und Ungarn: Essays, Dokumente, Bibliographie.* Budapest: Akademiai, 1977.
Mendelssohn, Peter de. *Der Zauberer: Das Leben des deutschen Schrifstellers Thomas Mann, Erster Teil, 1875–1918.* Frankfurt am Main: S. Fischer, 1975.
Ohl, Hubert. *Ethos und Spiel: Thomas Manns Frühwerk und die Wiener Moderne.* Freiburg im Breisgau: Rombach Verlag, 1995.
Prater, Donald. *Thomas Mann: A Life.* Oxford: Oxford University Press, 1995.
Reed, T.J. *Thomas Mann: The Uses of Tradition.* Oxford: Clarendon Press, 1974.
Sprecher, Thomas. *Thomas Mann in Zürich.* Zürich: Verlag Neue Zürcher Zeitung, 1992.
Sumichrast, Marika Elisabeth. "Thomas Mann and Czechoslovakia." Ph.D. dissertation, Ohio State University, 1970.
Swales, Martin. *Thomas Mann: A Study.* Totowa, N.J.: Rowman and Littlefield, 1980.
Winston, Richard. *Thomas Mann: The Making of an Artist, 1875–1911.* New York: Alfred A. Knopf, 1981.

W[ILLIAM] SOMERSET MAUGHAM
(1874–1965)

Marina MacKay

BIOGRAPHY

Somerset Maugham was born in the British Embassy in Paris to English parents, and thus his multicultural status was ensured from his earliest moments of life. After the death of his father, a legal attaché, and his mother, the daughter of a writer of French novels, the French-speaking, ten-year-old Maugham was removed to his alien, yet paradoxically native, England. Marginalized by both his manifest foreignness and the debilitating stammer that was perhaps exacerbated by the demands of his new language, English, Maugham commenced an unhappy stay in his uncle's Kent vicarage, and his misery eventually found articulation in his most famous novel, *Of Human Bondage* (1915). The adolescent Maugham found escape in travel and in 1890 moved to Heidelberg, where he spent over a year, learning German and falling under the influence of Schopenhauer's bleakly atheistic philosophy and Ibsen's stagecraft. Returning to London, Maugham was unable to reveal his literary ambitions, but his new experiences in the London slums as an obstetric clerk proved invaluable as source material for his first novel, *Liza of Lambeth* (1897), written in the naturalistic tradition of slum writing. While he was still a medical student at St. Thomas's Hospital, he found time for a six-week visit to Italy in 1894, and he was to put his Italian research to use in his second novel, *The Making of a Saint* (1898). This novel is based, like *Then and Now* (1946), on aspects of the biography and writings of Machiavelli. In 1897 Maugham visited Spain for the first time, and the visit inspired a lifelong passion for the country: its people, its landscapes, and its artistic achievements.

The first decade of the new century was punctuated by European travels, and Italy received particular attention, not least because the Italian island of Capri was swiftly proving a welcome sanctuary for rich British homosexuals, for whom the scandalous trial of Oscar Wilde had provided a harsh reminder of

English intolerance. Driving an ambulance in Flanders in 1914, Maugham met the gregarious American Gerald Haxton, who was to become not only a longtime secretary and lover, but also a dynamic and intelligent traveling companion. It was with Haxton that Maugham turned his back temporarily on Europe and made his first trip to the South Sea island groups in 1916. This journey proved a turning point in his career, and *The Moon and Sixpence* (1919), loosely based on Paul Gauguin's escape to Tahiti, remains one of his most widely read novels. In the years between 1922 and 1926 he pursued travels in the Far East, through Burma, Indochina, and Siam, which culminated in two books of travel writings and sketches: *On a Chinese Screen* (1922) and *The Gentleman in the Parlour* (1930). Although he was always a keen traveler, he had, by the end of the 1920s, bought the Villa Mauresque in Cap Ferrat on the French Riviera. Although he was forced to leave his French home at the outbreak of World War II, for the duration of which he lived in the United States, Maugham continued to occupy the Villa Mauresque until the end of his long life.

MAJOR MULTICULTURAL THEMES

Of all the European nations, it was Spain that most inspired Maugham's admiration and awe, and his enormous enthusiasm perhaps explains why his books on Spain leap so indiscriminately across the conventional boundaries of fact and fiction, reportage and invention, history and the present. This tendency is most apparent in his first book on Spain, *The Land of the Blessed Virgin* (1905), which, although it glances at the conventions of the travelogue genre, conveys a strong flavor of self-conscious literariness through its Pateresque prose. In *The Summing Up* (1938), an autobiographical work, he described the early book as merely "an exercise in style . . . wistful, allusive and elaborate" (26). In contrast, the more mature *Don Fernando; or, Variations on Some Spanish Themes* (1935), a collection of essays on the art, religion, and literature of Spain's sixteenth-century Golden Age, gives a more representative illustration of Maugham's intellectual calibre, and his account of El Greco's homosexuality is especially intriguing. It was to Spain that Maugham returned with his final novel, *Catalina* (1948), an eccentrically fantastical tale of a miracle at the time of the Inquisition. Although Maugham was himself an agnostic from an early age, he repeatedly uses religious tropes when writing of other cultures, and by setting novels in Roman Catholic Spain and Italy, he perhaps earned himself a respite from the stolid materialism of his "English" stories.

Equally, one of his South Seas stories, "Honolulu," ends with a murder executed by indigenous magic. Most of the South Seas stories, however, are concerned, not with the lives of the native peoples, but with the effects that such a life has on white colonial settlers, missionaries, and administrators. In some instances, such as in the ironically titled "The Fall of Edward Barnard," in which the eponymous hero renounces his initial intention to make his fortune by exploiting Tahitian resources and adopts instead a more passive Tahitian lifestyle, the cultural collisions are ultimately a catalyst for spiritual and moral growth. Alternatively, in "The Pool" both the English protagonist and his Samoan wife are destroyed by their irreconcilable cultural differences. In what, thanks to numerous stage and screen adaptations, has become Maugham's most famous short story, "Rain," he satirizes the missionaries for their attempts to efface such cultural divisions entirely through the propagation of their own values. Although, we are told, the Davidsons have managed to eradicate "immoral" native dances and the "indecent" *lava-lava*, they still struggle with natives "so naturally depraved that they couldn't be brought to see their wickedness" (*East and West*, 4, 5, 12). Mr. Davidson tells the Macphails that he "had to make sins out of what they [the natives] thought were natural actions" (12). Describing his own initial encounter with South Sea islanders, Maugham wrote of "heterogeneous creatures thrown into a life that had preserved a great deal of its primitiveness . . . nearer to the elementals of human nature than any of the people I had been living with for so long" (*The Summing Up*, 202–3). Thus, while Maugham's stories generally reveal a profound pessimism about the possibility of reconciling cultural differences, and his landscapes divide clearly along colored lines, his distaste for the missionary mindset rather unexpectedly anticipates a later, post-colonial, consciousness.

SURVEY OF CRITICISM

John Whitehead (1987) divides Maugham's oeuvre into chronological and geographical sections, and chapters 3 and 5, "Between the Wars: Far East" and "Between the Wars: Europe," juxtapose biographical detail and textual analysis to assess the success of Maugham's literary uses of his many multicultural interests. Calder's chapter (1972) on Maugham's cosmopolitanism (chapter 8) locates him within a wider tradition of European literary modernism and, unusually, pays close attention to Maugham's spy stories, collected under the title of *Ashenden; or, The British Agent* (1928). Brander's overview (1963) of Maugham's career has a chapter (chapter 8) on Maugham's travel writing in which he systematically and enthusiastically assesses the merits of each travel book, even the less highly thought-of *The Land of the Blessed Virgin*. Archer (1993) identifies character as the main preoccupation of the "exotic" short stories. He argues that Maugham's theme is a naturalistic one: the effects on the Western character of the foreign environment, with its enervating climate and stultifying passivity. Menard (1965) offers a detailed and informed biographical reconstruction of Maugham's fruitful 1916 journey to the islands in the Pacific. Morgan's biography (1980) is a highly anecdotal version of Maugham's life, but, perhaps consequently, gives invaluable social context for his travels and provides lively accounts of, in particular, his life in France.

SELECTIVE BIBLIOGRAPHY

Works by Maugham

The Land of the Blessed Virgin. London: Heinemann, 1905.
The Moon and Sixpence. London: Heinemann, 1919.
On a Chinese Screen. New York: George H. Doran, 1922.
Ashenden; or, The British Agent. London: Heinemann, 1928.
The Gentleman in the Parlour. London: Heinemann, 1930.
East and West: The Collected Short Stories of Somerset Maugham. Garden City, N.Y.: Garden City Publishing Company, 1934. [Contains "Honolulu," "The Pool," "The Fall of Edward Barnard."]
Don Fernando; or, Variations on Some Spanish Themes. London: Heinemann, 1935.
The Summing Up (1938). London and Toronto: Heinemann, 1940.
Catalina. London: Heinemann, 1948.

Selective Studies of Maugham

Archer, Stanley. *W. Somerset Maugham: A Study of the Short Fiction.* New York: Twayne, 1993.
Brander, L. *Somerset Maugham: A Guide.* Edinburgh and London: Oliver & Boyd, 1963.
Calder, Robert Lorin. *W. Somerset Maugham and the Quest for Freedom.* London: Heinemann, 1972.
Menard, Wilmon. *The Two Worlds of Somerset Maugham.* Los Angeles: Sherbourne Press, 1965.
Morgan, Ted. *Somerset Maugham.* London: Jonathan Cape, 1980.
Whitehead, John. *Maugham: A Reappraisal.* London: Vision; Totowa, N.J.: Barnes & Noble, 1987.

ADAM MICKIEWICZ
(1798–1855)

Kinga Eminowicz Galica

BIOGRAPHY

In typically Central European fashion Adam Mickiewicz, the greatest poet of the Polish language, might be claimed by three adjoining nations as one of their own. Though he was born in the Grand Duchy of Lithuania and called it his motherland, the village of his birth, Nowogrodek (or nearby Zaosie), is located in present-day Byelorussia, and the folklore of the Byelorussian-speaking local population enriches his poetry. His father was a small-town lawyer, and although the family lived modestly, the poet had a happy childhood. The first significant event in his adolescence was the entry of Napoleon's army into his village (1812) on its way to Moscow, stirring high hopes for the rebirth of the dismembered Polish state—hopes that hinged on France. A Polish Legion had been created in Napoleon's army in 1797 and remained with it until his fall. In 1807 Napoleon had created the so-called Duchy of Warsaw, whose army marched with him to Moscow in 1812. Mickiewicz witnessed the triumphant march eastward and the humiliating defeat—events that help in understanding the poet's lifelong devotion to Napoleon and his descendants. In 1815 Mickiewicz entered the University of Wilno, where he concentrated on the field of languages and literature. The intellectual atmosphere in Wilno being permeated by the spirit of the Enlightenment, he read the writings of Diderot, Rousseau, Condillac, and Helvétius, as well as the works of Voltaire, which he translated and imitated.

His first book of poems, *Ballady i romanse* (1822), drawn from local folklore, appeared at the beginning of Romanticism in Poland. The originality of the poems lies in the fact that, unlike classical poetry, they could be understood even by uncultivated people. The second volume (1823) contains parts of the *Dziady (Forefathers' Eve)*, a major Romantic drama recalling the old Lithuanian folk ritual of conjuring the dead and offering them food on All Saints' Day.

Despite czarist officials' efforts to suppress them, clandestine and semiclandestine groups of Polish students flourished; some had contacts with Freemasons and promoted patriotic and progressive ideas. Mickiewicz and his friends were arrested in 1823; he was sentenced to exile in Russia. On arrival in St. Petersburg, he was greeted by the young Russian intelligentsia as one of their own. Although his exile in the European part of Russia cannot be compared with the plight of some Lithuanian schoolboys sentenced to serve in the Russian army as common soldiers, he deplored the loss of his homeland, which he was never to see again. He reached Russia at the time of the Decembrist conspiracy, two of whose leaders, the poet Kondraty Ryleyev and the novelist Alexander Beztuzhev (pseudonym Marlinsky), became his close friends. In 1825 he traveled through the Crimea, bringing from his trip a collection of *Sonety krymskie*, published in Moscow in 1826 and immediately translated into Russian. Influential friends procured him permission to leave Russia. En route to Rome, where he lived among the colony of Polish, Russian, French, and American artists, he paid homage to Goethe in Weimar. Upon the 1830 Polish uprising he left for Poznan, then under Prussian control. By the time of his arrival in Poland via Paris and Dresden, the uprising had already been crushed; Mickiewicz was remorseful for having missed the action. He joined the Polish émigrés in Dresden, where he published the third part of the *Dziady* (1832), marked by strong Illuminist and cabalistic accents. The hero of the drama changes from a Romantic lover to a fighter for his nation and even humanity at large.

Mickiewicz settled in Paris in 1832, where he published *Księgi narodu i pielgrzymstwa polskiego* (1832), in which he develops his theory of "messianism," assigning to the Polish nation a role in the rebirth of Europe similar to that of the Jews in the Roman Empire. *Pan Tadeusz* (1834) is a reminiscence of his Lithuanian childhood. He abandoned poetry for revolutionary action after 1834. As the spiritual leader of the Polish nation, he united its cause with that of all humanity, never narrowing his ideals to intolerant nationalism. He was a success in Lausanne, where he taught Latin in 1839–40 and was popular among his students. Thence he was appointed to the first chair of Slavic literatures at the Collège de France (1840–44). His lectures having become the gathering place of the Parisian intellectual and artistic worlds, the suspicion of the French authorities was aroused, and he was deprived of his chair. In Italy in 1848 he formed a Polish Legion to fight against Austria for the liberation of Italy. The legion was greeted enthusiastically in Rome and Florence, where he addressed the crowds. Returning to Paris to recruit more volunteers for the legion, he founded the republican socialist newspaper *La Tribune des peuples* in 1849. It was an international newspaper with editors of diverse nationalities and representing various political orientations.

At the outbreak of the Crimean War he left for Constantinople, where he proposed, in addition to the Polish and Cossack legions being formed in Turkey to fight against Russia, the creation of a Jewish Legion. Having applied to the Turkish authorities for permission to enlist not only Russian Jewish prisoners of war but also Jews from Palestine, he even established and equipped a synagogue in the camp, and the Sabbath was made the day of rest for Jewish soldiers, a unique occurrence in those days. He died of cholera in Constantinople in 1855 and was buried at the Polish Cemetery near Paris, but his remains were reburied in the Cathedral of Cracow in 1890.

MAJOR MULTICULTURAL THEMES

Mickiewicz's poetry and ideas reverberated outside the Polish émigré circles. He was one of the leaders of the new Europe. He felt at home in Italy, addressing students of Florence on April 21, 1848, and calling their country "your and our Italy." The Polish Legion in Italy, created personally by Mickiewicz, fought in the Battle of Lonato (Brescia) and during the defense of Rome. The poet was admired by Italian independence leaders Giuseppe Mazzini and Camillo Cavour: Mazzini attempted to translate Mickiewicz's poetry using French and English translations, and Cavour called him the greatest poet of the century.

His lectures in France attracted liberal and artistic Paris. George Sand came out of seclusion in order to attend them. He warned the Western nations that supported czarist Russia of a despotism that would subjugate all Europe if it were not stopped. He tried to introduce Slavic literatures to Western audiences. He influenced the socialist religious ideas of Félicité Robert de Lamennais, as expressed in his *Paroles d'un croyant*. The three friends—Edgar Quinet, Jules Michelet, and Mickiewicz—were called the "triumvirate" at the Collège de France. A large group of Polish political émigrés had settled in Paris, and Mickiewicz was their leader. His undying loyalty to Napoleon, seen with suspicion by the French authorities, was a mixture of nostalgia for 1812 and admiration for Bonaparte's genius and progressive ideas.

Although Mickiewicz fought against the Russian czarist government all his life, he was at one with the people. His enormously popular poems had to be translated into Russian anonymously, at a time when it was forbidden by the censorship to mention the very name of the poet. He spent five years in exile in Russia, becoming friendly with leading Russian liberals, poets, and artists. He and Pushkin felt mutual admiration and translated each other's poetry, despite the latter's subsequent conservatism and nationalism.

Mickiewicz had strong pro-Jewish feelings and equated the history of the Jewish and the Polish peoples. He believed that a rebirth of Europe would come through these two chosen nations. In his "Exposition of Principles," prepared for the recruiting for the Polish Legion in Italy, he promised in Principle 10 respect, brotherhood, and equal rights to "the Jew, our brother." He was admired, particularly outside Polish émigré circles, as a political and spiritual leader. He was not, however, a political theorist and is remembered today, first and foremost, as a poet. His poetry, written in Polish, can enjoy only a limited popularity. He had a somewhat utopian vision of a united Europe led by a class of extraordinary individuals, the aristocrats of the spirit.

SURVEY OF CRITICISM

Mickiewicz's reception by other European nations, the Russians, French, Germans, Italians, and Czechs, is discussed in the proceedings of a symposium, *Adam Mickiewicz, Poet of Poland* (1951), edited by Manfred Kridl. Czesław Miłosz, in *The History of Polish Literature* (1969), discusses Mickiewicz's activity in the service of the Polish cause, as well as his contacts with other European leaders of the day.

SELECTIVE BIBLIOGRAPHY

Works by Mickiewicz

Forefathers' Eve [*Dziady*, 1823–1833]. Trans. Count Potocki of Montauk. London: Polish Cultural Foundation, 1968.

Konrad Wallenrod (1828) *and Other Writings*. Trans. Jewell Parish, ed. George R. Noyes. Westport, Conn.: Greenwood Press, 1975.

Pan Tadeusz: or, The Last Foray in Lithuania (1834). Trans. Watson Kirkconnell, annot. Harold B. Segel. New York: Polish Institute of Arts and Sciences in America, 1962.

Adam Mickiewicz, 1798–1855: Selected Poems. Ed. Clark Mills. New York: Noonday Press, 1956.

Selective Studies of Mickiewicz

Kridl, Manfred, ed. *Adam Mickiewicz, Poet of Poland: A Symposium*. Columbia Slavic Studies. New York: Columbia University Press, 1951.

Miłosz, Czesław. *The History of Polish Literature*. New York: Macmillan, 1969. 2nd ed., Berkeley: University of California Press, 1983.

Weintraub, Wiktor. *Literature as Prophecy: Scholarship and Martinist Poetics in Mickiewicz's Parisian Lectures*. The Hague: Mouton, 1959.

HENRY MILLER

(1891–1980)

William Wolf

BIOGRAPHY

Grandson of German immigrants, the son of a tailor and a tailor's wife, Henry Valentine Miller, one of the world's most exasperating and controversial writers, was born in Manhattan on December 26, 1891. The family soon moved to Brooklyn, New York, whose streets were flooded with new immigrants from Germany, Ireland, Italy, Poland, Syria, and elsewhere. This atmosphere helped to shape the nascent writer's gritty personality and infused in him a delightful acceptance of raw experience and an exuberant fascination for all strata of humanity.

Miller lived an American middle-class life with his domineering mother, his ineffectual but kindly father, and his disabled, feebleminded sister. After graduating from the Eastern District High School in 1909, he enrolled at City College in New York; disillusioned and dejected, he left after one semester. During the following years he fell in and out of love, discovered sex, toyed with writing, and worked part-time in his father's tailor shop. On June 17, 1917, he began his unhappy and disastrous marriage to Beatrice Wickens; from 1920 to 1924 he worked full-time for the "Cosmodemonic Telegraph Company" (Western Union); and in the summer of 1923 he met and fell head over heels in love with June Mansfield, a local taxi dancer. Divorcing Beatrice in 1923, he married June in 1924. His early years in America, his Western Union employment, and his divorce and remarriage are mythically recounted in *Tropic of Capricorn* (1939) and *Sexus* (1949). *Tropic of Cancer* (1934) and *Quiet Days in Clichy* (1956) recount his Paris years.

Miller and June took a brief trip to France in 1929. Soon after, June, insisting that he was to become a great writer and needed the experience of Europe to expand his outlook and grow as an artist, raised money for a second trip—but this time Miller would go alone. He set foot in Paris on March 4, 1930, where he met and wooed Anaïs Nin. June visited and established the infamous and torrid triangle, June, Henry, Anaïs: a boon for romantics and literary gossips. More important, Miller began to write in earnest and was published in France.

He left Paris in 1939 and, before returning to America, visited Greece for five months, the outgrowth of which was his autobiographical novel cum travelogue, *The Colossus of Maroussi* (1941). By the time of his death on June 7, 1980, Miller had taken several excursions, both in America and back to Europe, had settled in California, had married three more times (Janina Lepska, Eve McClure, and Hiroko Tokuda), and, eventually, had achieved fame and recognition—although, because of the pornographic flavor of most of his work, the major novels were not published in his homeland until the early 1960s.

MAJOR MULTICULTURAL THEMES

Throughout both the American and European years Miller's influences came from two major sources: a broad, eclectic devouring of books—Balzac, Dostoevsky, Durrell, Hamsun (Miller's favorite), Joyce, Lawrence, Melville, Rilke, and many others—and an ongoing, perhaps compulsively excessive, examination of himself. The second influence may be the more difficult to consider; it could be argued that because of Miller's egotistical viewpoint—the vast majority of his writing is a first-person, fictionalized account of his physical, spiritual, and intellectual life—he could be living and writing anywhere, and it would make no difference whatsoever. Upon reflection, however, it becomes clear that it was Paris that finally liberated him; his liberation becomes the thematic element of his work. To risk a tired but useful cliché, he was liberated through wine, women, and song.

It was in the streets of Paris, after scraping together a few francs from friends or strangers, that the hours spent with a glass of wine at an outside café, watching and absorbing Parisian life flowing by, imbued him with a curious mixture of excitement and serenity. It was his hunger and thirst for life, relieved and renewed by the wine-fueled, long, circuitous walks throughout the city, that inspired him to spend the rest of the afternoon at the typewriter, pounding out his version of his life in Paris and the adventures of those he met and hated and loved, all intertwined and refracted through his voracious sensibilities. Miller absorbed Paris, made it his own, and it was Paris, in collaboration with Miller, that soon churned out what many consider his best work, *Tropic of Cancer*.

The women he met in Paris helped to set his prose afire, bursting aflame with the language of the street and of the night, illuminating the raw sexual encounters—creating, as it were, the essential style and commitment of all the work that followed. Fascinated with the whores of Paris, he found in them the freedom and the harsh romanticism that saturate his autobiographical fiction. In an apartment he shared with his friend Alfred Perlés he befriended and sexually engaged—sharing her also with Perlés—the underage waif Colette. This sordid adventure is at the heart of *Quiet Days in Clichy* (1956). Miller and his pal, after the girl's parents and the police became involved, were not indicted because, according to Miller, of his status as a fringe American celebrity. It is in passages such as this that his dark side emerges. He becomes controversial and, to some, abhorrent because of his treatment of women as found in his literature. Even admirers often find his views concerning women difficult to appreciate or defend.

Wine, women, and song—liberties will be taken with the last of these. It is the song of Paris that refreshed and stole his heart; but it is his song, brash, bold, loud, and obscene, that finally found voice during the Paris years. In the early 1930s, through friends like Michael Fraenkel, Walter Lowenfels, and Wambly Bald, Miller was becoming known, and his work was slowly becoming accepted in various magazines and the *Paris Tribune*. It was Jack Kahane, an Englishman living in Paris, who brought out *Tropic of Cancer* (the first of the novels to be published). It was the liberating, less puritanical climate of Paris that finally allowed the world to really hear Henry Miller sing.

SURVEY OF CRITICISM

In the preface to his revised edition of *Henry Miller* (1990), Kingsley Widmer writes that he had been told "by an apparently reliable source that Miller intensely disliked [Widmer's] study but nonetheless granted that it might be the enduring scholarly-critical view of him" (vii). This is indeed the case. Ihab Hassan's quite rewarding study (1967) teams Samuel Beckett with Miller and deals with the absurd. *Henry Miller and the Critics* (1966), edited by George Wickes, is invaluable; Lawrence Durrell, Aldous Huxley, and George Orwell are among those represented, and this book also includes transcripts from Miller's 1960s obscenity trials. Two biographies stand out: Mary V. Dearborn's (1991)—although there are times when Dearborn cannot conceal her disdain for Miller—and Robert Ferguson's (1991), which shows solid scholarship and achieves an excellent balanced view. Nin's *Henry and June: From the Unexpurgated Diary of Anaïs Nin* (1986) is essential for a study of the Paris years, as is *A Literate Passion: Letters of Anaïs Nin and Henry Miller, 1932–1953* (1987).

SELECTIVE BIBLIOGRAPHY

Works by Miller

Tropic of Cancer (1934). New York: Grove Press, 1961.
The Colossus of Maroussi (1941). New York: New Directions, 1958.
Sexus (1949). New York: Grove Press, 1965.
Quiet Days in Clichy (1956). New York: Grove Press, 1987.
My Life and Times. New York: Gemini Smith (Playboy Press), 1971.
A Henry Miller Reader. Ed. John Calder. London: Picador, 1985.

Nin, Anaïs, and Henry Miller. *A Literate Passion: Letters of Anaïs Nin and Henry Miller,
1932–1953*. Ed. Gunther Stuhlman. San Diego: Harcourt Brace Jovanovich, 1987.
Durell, Lawrence, and Henry Miller. *The Durrell-Miller Letters, 1935–1980*. Ed. Ian S.
MacNiven. New York: New Directions, 1988.

Selective Studies of Miller

Dearborn, Mary V. *The Happiest Man Alive: A Biography of Henry Miller*. New York:
Simon & Schuster, 1991.
Ferguson, Robert. *Henry Miller: A Life*. New York: W.W. Norton & Co., 1991.
Hassan, Ihab. *The Literature of Silence: Henry Miller and Samuel Beckett*. New York:
Alfred A. Knopf, 1967.
Nin, Anaïs. *Henry and June: From the Unexpurgated Diary of Anaïs Nin*. San Diego:
Harcourt Brace Jovanovich, 1986.
Perlés, Alfred. *My Friend Henry Miller: An Intimate Biography*. New York: John Day
Co., 1956.
Wickes, George, ed. *Henry Miller and the Critics*. Carbondale: Southern Illinois University Press, 1966.
Widmer, Kingsley. *Henry Miller*. Rev. ed. Boston: Twayne, 1990.

LADY MARY WORTLEY MONTAGU
(1689–1762)

Patricia Owen

BIOGRAPHY

Mary Pierrepont was the first child of parents from families distinguished for rank, wealth, and intelligence. The loss, by the age of nine, of both her mother and her grandmother, and consequent changes of home, gave her little security in childhood. She next passed into the care of her father, the earl of Kingston, where she had the run of a well-stocked library, glutting herself on French and English romances, but later "stealing" some skill in Latin, the gateway to higher education at that time reserved to males. The education provided by her father covered the usual domestic and social skills, as well as Italian. All her life, her beauty or her talents claimed admiration and flattery, which she admitted to enjoying. Poems, essays, and novels survive from her thirteenth year onwards. She wrote in many genres throughout her life, for private circulation or anonymously: a woman of her rank could not present herself as a professional author. Her husband, Edward Wortley, was rich, a member of Parliament, and the friend of men of letters. He encouraged his wife to continue writing; she urged him to push his career with the Whig administration of the new Hanoverian king, George I. Their son was born in 1713. In London she became close to court circles and made friends who were to be of great influence on her life, especially the poets Alexander Pope and John Gay. Then she became dangerously ill with smallpox, the disease that had already killed her only brother. Her beauty was marred.

In 1716 Wortley was appointed ambassador to the Turkish court, charged with brokering a peace between the sultan and the Austrian emperor. Their train of coaches set out for the East via Cologne and Frankfurt to Vienna. King George summoned them north to Hanover; they returned to Vienna via Dresden. Thence they passed through devastation in war-torn Hungary to enter the Ottoman Empire. For the three weeks that they were held up in Belgrade she learned about Arabic poetry and the religion, customs, and language of the empire from her scholarly Turkish host. In Sofia she visited the ladies' public baths, the best-known episode in *The Turkish Embassy Letters* (1763); this passage inspired Ingres's painting *Le Bain Turc*. They reached the sultan's court at Adrianople, where Lady Mary was received in the harems of noble Turkish ladies. In May 1717 they moved to Pera, the foreigners' quarter opposite Constantinople. Here her daughter was born in January 1718. The embassy surgeon, Charles Maitland, and Lady Mary had been finding out about the Turkish practice of inoculation with a weak strain of smallpox as a preventive against a severe infection. She had her own son successfully inoculated. On her return to London doctors were vigorously disputing about treatment, but had no idea of prevention. During the epidemic of 1721 she asked Maitland to inoculate her daughter. Three observers from the College of Physicians monitored the child's rapid recovery. Inoculation aroused furious partisanship, for and against; Lady Mary was fortunate to secure the support of Princess Caroline, wife of the heir to the throne. Lady Mary's only writing intended for print in her lifetime, "A Plain Account of the Inoculating of the Small Pox," appeared in the *Flying Post* in September 1722.

Wortley was recalled on the fall of Walpole's ministry. The return was by sea via the isles of Greece to Malta, North Africa, and Genoa, then over the Alps and on to Paris. In London, always the subject of gossip and innuendo, she suffered from the breach with Pope; his attacks in print, presenting her as "Lewd Lesbia" and "furious Sappho," culminated in the portrait of Flavia in "Of the Characters of Women." The relationship with her husband had become progressively cool, her son was a disappointment, and her daughter, married to the future Lord Bute, George III's prime minister, found her mother's public image an embarrassment. At the age of forty-seven she fell passionately in love with a much younger Italian visitor, Francesco Algarotti. Three years later she left England in the vain hope of living with him. She lived in Italy and the south of France, visited by Englishmen as one of the sights of the Grand Tour, admired and ridiculed, returning to England only in the year of her death.

MAJOR MULTICULTURAL THEMES

Lady Mary had worked up her journals and letters written during the embassy, ready for publication. The manuscript, complete with preface by Mary Astell, had been left in Rotterdam before she embarked for England; it was thus saved from the fire to which her daughter gave her diary. In 1763 the *Letters of the Right Honourable Lady M—y W—y M—e, Written during her travels in Europe, Asia, and Africa* . . . were published posthumously. Diplomatic status had given her access that no private traveler could enjoy. Her sex opened to her the unseen half of Turkish life, and, as a woman, she saw Oriental women without the sexual frisson of male travelers; they appeared to her handsome (unmarked by smallpox), companionable, and free from the competitive backbiting she had suffered at home. Though secluded, they were not immured; the harem was their important sphere of activity. She had learned enough Turkish to converse and, throughout her eighteen months in the Ottoman Empire, continued the studies begun in Belgrade. Though she was horrified by the cruelty of the soldiery, she regarded the religion, mores, and lifestyle that she observed with respect. Her own country could learn from them: Turkish hans were preferable to Western inns; Sinan's Great Mosque at Adrianople outshone any church in England. In Tunis, by contrast, her comparison of the people to baboons was crudely racist. In her "Plain Account" Lady Mary deplored the way in which English doctors, with their regimes of purging and bloodletting, had failed to follow the best, Turkish, practice of inoculation. Other Westerners had been inoculated in the East; she was the first to arrange for it to be done in England. Her campaign was beset by medical-faction fighting and sexism; nevertheless, preventive control of smallpox was shown to be possible.

SURVEY OF CRITICISM

Mary Astell's preface to the early editions of the *Letters of the Right Honourable Lady M—y W—y M—e* claims that they surpass male travelers' writing and asks women to be "pleased that a *woman* triumphs" (x–xi). Later feminists have not all been as favorable: while her contemporaries were shocked, or titillated, by her description of nudity, in the twentieth century she is blamed for not shedding her corsets and joining in (Leeks, 1986) or for distancing herself by describing the bathers in terms of famous paintings. Bohls (1994), however, considers that she thus "neutralizes orientalist stereotypes" and notes her use of the newly emerged aesthetic approach throughout the *Letters*. She seized from men the privileged viewpoint of the aesthetic subject (Bohls; Pratt 1992; and, especially, Pointon, 1993). Fernea (1985) finds her "remarkably free of ethnocentrism," and Hourani (1991) places her among those who wrote before the shift of power to the West, when "a European traveller in the Ottoman lands . . . could still find much to admire," even to prefer (137). While Dervla Murphy, the travel writer, thinks that she was "born too soon. Essentially she was a career woman" (introduction, *Embassy to Constantinople*, 1988, 28), Anita Desai, herself a multicultural writer, places her among those early travelers who were freed by travel from their cultural preconceptions, "exceptionally open to new impressions and points of view," with "a rare ability to see herself through the eyes of others" (introduction, *The Turkish Embassy Letters*, 1994, xvii, xxix).

SELECTIVE BIBLIOGRAPHY

Works by Montagu

"A Plain Account of the Inoculating of the Small Pox." *Flying Post* (London), September 11–13, 1722. [Also in *Essays and Poems and Simplicity, A Comedy*, 95–97. Ed. Robert Halsband and Isobel Grundy. Oxford: Clarendon Press, 1977.]

Letters of the Right Honourable Lady M—y W—y M—e, Written during her travels in Europe, Asia, and Africa. . . . With a "Preface, by a Lady," signed M.A., [i.e., Mary Astell]. 3 vols. London: T. Beckett and P.A. De Hondt, 1763; Dublin: P. Wilson, 1763.

Halsband, Robert, ed. *The Complete Letters of Lady Mary Wortley Montagu.* 3 vols. Oxford: Clarendon Press, 1965–1967.

Pick, Christopher, ed. *Embassy to Constantinople: The Travels of Lady Mary Wortley Montagu.* Intro. Dervla Murphy. London: Century, 1988.

The Turkish Embassy Letters. Ed. Malcolm Jack. Intro. Anita Desai. London: Virago, 1994.

Selective Studies of Montagu

Bohls, Elizabeth A. "Aesthetics and Orientalism in Lady Mary Wortley Montagu's Letters." In *Studies in Eighteenth-Century Culture*, 179–205. Ed. Carla H. Hay and Syndy M. Conger. East Lansing, Mich.: Colleagues Press, 1994.

Fernea, Elizabeth Warnock, ed. *Women and the Family in the Middle East: New Voices of Change.* Austin: University of Texas Press, 1985.

Grundy, Isobel. *Lady Mary Wortley Montagu: Comet of the Enlightenment.* Oxford: Oxford University Press, 1999.

Hourani, Albert. *Islam in European Thought.* Cambridge: Cambridge University Press, 1991.

Leeks, Wendy. "Ingres Other-Wise." *Oxford Art Journal* 9 (1986): 29–37.

Melman, Billie. *Women's Orients: English Women and the Middle East, 1718–1918.* London: Macmillan, 1992.

Pointon, Marcia. *Hanging the Head: Portraiture and Social Formation in Eighteenth-Century England.* New Haven: Yale University Press, 1993.

Pratt, Mary Louise. *Imperial Eyes: Travel Writing and Transculturation.* New York: Routledge, 1992.

MONTAIGNE (MICHEL EYQUEM, SEIGNEUR DE)
(1533–1592)

Marcel Gutwirth

BIOGRAPHY

The château de Montaigne in the Bordeaux region saw the birth in 1533 of Michel, the eldest living son of Pierre Eyquem and Antoinette de Louppes. The Eyquems were an old Périgord family; Antoinette de Louppes was of recent Spanish immigrant stock, of almost certain (though remote) Jewish origins. Michel Eyquem, whose father, by fighting in the Italian wars, had fully consolidated the family's standing as small provincial nobility, was the first to drop the Eyquem family name, taking the surname he was to make world-famous from the château of his birth. While he did, at least on two occasions, bear arms in the king's cause, it was as a magistrate that he spent the years of his prime. He studied law in Toulouse or perhaps in Paris before taking up a seat purchased for him by his father on the Tax Court of Périgueux, soon melded into the Bordeaux Parliament (a body with mixed judicial, legislative, and administrative duties).

Montaigne's early schooling, however, is as incontrovertible as it is distinctive. Pierre Eyquem clearly wanted the best for his heir presumptive, and he put his heart and mind into the method of his upbringing. "The best father who ever was" had him roused from sleep to the sound of music to spare him the pain of waking with a start, and he consulted local authorities on the best way to inculcate a knowledge of Latin, gateway at the time to all further learning. Hence that remarkable early experiment in "Latin without tears": the hiring of a German tutor who knew no French and could communicate with his infant charge in Latin only. Father, mother, servants, and neighboring farmers were all drawn into the scholarly charade. Armed with Latin as his mother tongue, when he was admitted at the age of seven to the Collège de Guyenne, whose cosmopolitan faculty included the Scottish humanist George Buchanan and the Portuguese headmaster André de Gouvêa, young Michel rather intimidated his masters, not "native" like him to an ancient tongue. Erasmus was the fountain-head of the pedagogical spirit of that newly created institution, just as he had been the spirit of Pierre Eyquem's tenderhearted experimentalism. Thus we may add the Dutch humanist to the international medley of formative influences.

In his self-portrayal Montaigne leaves unspoken the sixteen years he sat in court and other highly significant aspects of his political life. While his *Essais* touch on many sides of his personal experience, they nowhere purport to be an autobiography. If you had asked him, however, what he prized in his career in the judiciary, he would have spoken of one thing, and one thing only, the passionate friendship that bound him to his beloved and admired colleague Etienne de La Boétie, which he chronicled movingly in his chapter "On Friendship." It was the early death of La Boétie, followed by the death of the equally beloved Pierre Eyquem in 1568, that brought on the uncharacteristic bout of melancholy that returned Montaigne to the library tower of his château, having resigned judicial office in 1570 to take up his abode the following year "in the bosom of the Muses." From 1572 to 1580 he was to annotate his vast, mostly classical readings, slowly building up the first two books of his life's work, the *Essais*, which came out in 1580 to European acclaim. Upon his return from a great journey through Germany and Italy (1580–81), he took up his duties as mayor of Bordeaux, all the while preparing the augmented edition of the *Essais* in three books (1588). They are the systematic probings of a mind that was curious about its own workings and even more so about the whole planet and beyond. His motto was "Que sçais-je?" (what ever do I know?), and he was at pains to set out his observations as tentative and inconclusive: "I don't teach, I tell" (III, 2, "On Repentance," in *The Complete Essays of Montaigne*, trans. Donald Frame, 612). Mistrusting all assurance, and especially his own, he looked to the Greeks and Romans for models of how to live and die, but found even more to admire in the quiet resignation of the humble folk around him caught in a time of plague. The *Essais* are presented as a self-portrait, but it is a self that manages to embrace whole worlds; hence their enduring hold on readers of every age and clime.

MAJOR MULTICULTURAL THEMES

We find in Montaigne a prefiguration of the notion of culture taken in its anthropological sense. Mixed parentage, a foot in two social classes with a benign regard for the laboring third, and a propensity to dispraise himself (recorded in the chapter "On Presumption") all gave him a facility for looking at his own place and time as from the outside. He derided our tendency to think that the truth is lodged in our own bailiwick. He saw in the ways of the so-called savages of the New World less savagery than in the conduct of their conquerors. He had the audacity to disbelieve the supernatural powers of witches, and he coolly remarked that "we are Christians as we are natives of Périgord, by accident of birth." He accumulated examples of the bizarre customs of others, only to conclude that none outdid our own. As an antidote to parochialism, he recommended foreign travel "to rub and polish our brains by contact with those of others." He traveled to Rome (returning to France by way of Germany and Switzerland) ostensibly to take the waters for the hereditary kidney stones that would eventually lead to his death. The journey is described in the *Journal de voyage en Italie* (first published in 1774), which he dictated to a secretary at first in French, then in Italian as an exercise in the language. The *Journal* was written without literary intent, but it serves as a sourcebook for many of the reflections contained in the *Essais*. His visit to Torquato Tasso, confined to an institution at Ferrara, which is recorded in the essay "Apologie de Raimond Sebond," deeply moved him, for somehow he saw in the disturbed mind of the Italian a reflection of his own ductile and melancholy spirit. The chapter "On Vanity" in Book III of the *Essais* makes clear, however, the almost sensuous love of travel that took him on horseback to foreign lands.

History books were his favorite readings, and the *Essais* are replete with examples drawn from Francisco López de Gómara's history of the West Indies, Pedro González de Mendoza's history of China, and Jerónimo Osório's history of the kings of Lusitania, to say nothing of Plutarch's ubiquitous *Lives*. Montaigne's celebrated admiration for the naked cannibals of Brazil, who ate their enemies dead while we torture ours alive, and his lament for the fall of the civilizations of Mexico and Peru solely because they lacked firearms and bad faith, give full notice of his repudiation of all ethnocentricity, as well as of his disposition to look upon so-called primitives as models we neglected—to our loss.

SURVEY OF CRITICISM

The fullest account of Montaigne's life is to be found in Donald Frame's *Montaigne: A Biography*, updated but not superseded by Madeleine Lazard's *Michel de Montaigne*. In Géralde Nakam's *Les "Essais" de Montaigne, miroir et procès de leur temps*, Montaigne's critique of his own age is set out in a detailed account of its contemporary relevance, with, in chapter V, an exposition of his views on the Other (Indians, Jews, Turks). Gérard Defaux's "Un Cannibale en haut de chausses: Montaigne, la différence, et la logique de l'identité" goes into Montaigne's canny utilization of the cosmographers he feigns to ignore and repudiate. René Etiemble's "Sens et structure dans un *Essai* de Montaigne" construes the chapter "On Coaches" as a thoroughgoing political indictment of the monarchy's mismanagement of state finances (under the cover of his praise of Aztec and Inca magnificence), and of Christendom's calamitous imperialism. Malcolm Smith's *Citizen of the World: Montaigne's Travels* combs the *Journal de voyage en Italie* for a conspectus of Montaigne's observations on the minds and the manners of those he encountered abroad on his way to Rome and back. Frank Lestringant, in "Le cannibalisme des 'Cannibales,' " goes deeply into the issues raised by that theme and provides an important bibliography. *Montaigne, espace, voyage, écriture: Actes du congrès international de Thessalonique* offers chapters on Montaigne's views on Germany and Italy, among other topics.

SELECTIVE BIBLIOGRAPHY

Works by Montaigne

Les Essais de Michel de Montaigne. Ed. Pierre Villey and Verdun-Louis Saulnier. Paris: Presses Universitaires de France, 1965.
The Complete Essays of Montaigne. Trans. Donald Frame. Stanford: Stanford University Press, 1965.
Le Journal de voyage de Michel de Montaigne. Ed. François Rigolot. Paris: Presses Universitaires de France, 1992.

Selective Studies of Montaigne

Defaux, Gérard. "Un Cannibale en haut de chausses: Montaigne, la différence, et la logique de l'identité." *Modern Language Notes* 97, no. 4 (May 1982): 919–57.
Etiemble, René. "Sens et structure dans un *Essai* de Montaigne." *Cahiers de l'Association Internationale des Etudes Françaises* 14 (1962): 263–74.
Frame, Donald M. *Montaigne: A Biography*. New York: Harcourt, Brace, 1965.
Lazard, Madeleine. *Michel de Montaigne*. Paris: Fayard, 1992.
Lestringant, Frank. "Le cannibalisme des 'Cannibales.' " *Bulletin de la Société des Amis de Montaigne* 6, nos. 9–10 (1982): 27–40; nos. 11–12 (1982): 19–38.
Montaigne: Espace, voyage, écriture: Actes du congrès international de Thessalonique, 23–25 septembre 1992. Paris: Champion, 1995.
Nakam, Géralde. *Les "Essais" de Montaigne, miroir et procès de leur temps*. Paris: Nizet, 1984.
Smith, Malcolm. *Citizen of the World: Montaigne's Travels*. Egham, Surrey, England: Runnymede Books, 1989.

CHARLES-LOUIS DE SECONDAT DE MONTESQUIEU
(1689-1755)

Richard A. Brooks

BIOGRAPHY

Charles-Louis de Secondat de Montesquieu was born at La Brède near Bordeaux; his early education was conducted by priests of the Oratory at the Collège de Juilly, near Paris. He received his law degree at the Faculty of Law at Bordeaux at the age of nineteen and immediately became a lawyer in the Parlement of Bordeaux. In 1715 he married Jeanne de Lartigue, a wealthy Protestant, and a year later his uncle, Jean-Baptiste de Montesquieu, died, leaving him his estates, the barony of Montesquieu, and the position of president of the Parlement of Bordeaux. Montesquieu was already studying Roman law and, as a member of the recently established Academy of Bordeaux, devoting himself to broader interests such as the sciences of physics, biology, and geology.

In the 1720s in Paris he frequented the scintillating court of the duc d'Orléans and there met the British politician, Viscount Bolingbroke, exiled in France, whose views on the English constitution were later reflected in Montesquieu's *De l'esprit des lois* (1748). Selling his position at the Parlement of Bordeaux, Montesquieu, through contacts in Paris, particularly through the salon of Madame de Lambert, was successful in getting himself elected to the Académie française (1728). He continued to broaden his horizons through foreign travel, setting off for Vienna with a British companion, Lord Waldegrave, former British ambassador in Paris, and continuing on to Hungary, Italy, Germany, and Holland. Subsequently, accompanied by Lord Chesterfield, he went to England in 1729, was presented at court, and became acquainted with such Englishmen as the dukes of Richmond and Montagu and the Prince of Wales. He became a fellow of the Royal Society and studied the British political system as a spectator at some of the parliamentary debates and through contemporary journals. It is generally agreed that his stay in England was one of the most important periods in his career as a source for much of his future work in political theory.

After a number of essays on scientific subjects (1717–1720), his first important multicultural work, the *Lettres persanes*, appeared anonymously in 1721. Its authorship, however, soon became known, and the work was an immediate literary sensation. Montesquieu here uses the literary device of an epistolary exchange between two travelers from the Orient transplanted into the Paris of the Regency period, who present their observations of contemporary French institutions and mores from a comparative and completely fresh point of view. Montesquieu exploited a contemporary vogue of interest in France in things Oriental but went beyond mere exotic curiosity to provide a witty, biting, and bold commentary on French mores and institutions, ranging from the Church, the Académie française, and the university to the contemporary theater and cafés. The parochialism of the French was satirized in passages describing their capriciousness, exemplified by the oddities of fashion and by the idea that anything that was not French was perforce ridiculous to Frenchmen. Perhaps the most memorable line from the work is the question "How is it possible to be Persian?"

Although the *Lettres persanes* is a work of fiction, it refers critically and freely to important historical events of the times, including the religious persecution of Jansenists in France, the revocation of the Edict of Nantes, the death of Louis XIV, the subsequent establishment of the regency of Philippe d'Orléans, and the crash of the French financial system during the speculative frenzy of John Law. Adding a sufficient dose of eroticism and licentiousness, Montesquieu was able to attract the interest of a large reading public to his serious political and moral analyses that were based on the author's erudition and extensive readings of serious works on travel, philosophy, history, and politics. His method was multicultural and comparative and included analysis of the French monarchy vis-à-vis Oriental despotism, a moral and pragmatic analysis of the importance of arts, sciences, and industry, and an examination of an economy that encouraged the consumption of luxuries. Discussions of the true functions of the legislator and of the importance of religious toleration and religious pluralism were among other subjects grounded in comparative analysis.

Travel and travel books played an important role in the dissemination of liberal ideas during the French Enlightenment. Among the bolder aspects of the work were the author's criticism of the monarchy and the papacy, his attack on the Catholic Church as an institution, and his attempt to puncture the moral claims of Christianity as a religion of peace. He used the example of the English political system to emphasize the importance of limited governmental powers and to define the best system of government as that which reaches its goal with the least amount of force. Through a discussion of the comparative attitudes toward women in Europe and Asia, Montesquieu re-created the sensual atmosphere of Oriental harems from the feminine point of view.

In his *Considérations sur les causes de la grandeur des Romains et de leur décadence* (1734), published in Amsterdam, he was not interested in considering the immediate causes of historical events, which were often due to chance, but the deeper underlying bases and their truly general causes. He presented Roman history in an entirely new light. Historians have found that the many multicultural sources cited by Montesquieu—Plutarch, Cicero, Dionysius of Halicarnassus, Machiavelli, and others—were generally accurate. This work stands as one of the important histories of Rome along with Saint-Evremond's *Réflexions sur les divers génies du peuple romain* and Gibbon's *History of the Decline and Fall of the Roman Empire.* For the Enlightenment, the work was important as a work of secular historical interpretation, comprehensible in terms of logical cause and effect and minimizing the role of divine intervention.

De l'esprit des lois (1748) is a seminal work of political theory that is highly comparative in its guiding principles; it is based on Montesquieu's vast multicultural knowledge in the fields of politics, economics, religion, history, and social studies in general. Apart from his close knowledge of the political philosophies of antiquity, he was thoroughly conversant with the laws and customs of Greece and the legal and historical heritage of Rome, as well as with more recent literature on Persia and China for his references to the political systems of Asia. He was indebted to his study of the histories of Poland and Venice for his knowledge of aristocratic forms of government. In general, he was much more concerned with the underlying bases of laws or their *spirit* than with a narration or discussion of particular laws. It is in this work that the British influence on Montesquieu is most apparent, particularly the principle of the separation of powers as a guarantee of political freedom; it is this concept emphasized by Montesquieu that was influential in the development of modern democracies. As he writes in his preface, "Each nation will find here the reasons for its maxims." For the student of multiculturalism, Montesquieu's emphasis on the principle of relativity, based on his broad knowledge of different cultures, their histories, and their customs, is of singular importance. It was his genius to be able to reduce this vast knowledge to the following general principle: "Several things govern man: climate, religion, laws, maxims of government, the examples of things past, customs and manners, from which, as a result, there is formed a general spirit."

While this work, now universally considered as one of the basic works in the entire field of political theory, was acclaimed internationally in Montesquieu's own time, it was attacked in his own country in the Sorbonne and in French ecclesiastical circles, and eventually *De l'esprit des lois* was placed on the Vatican's *Index* of prohibited works (1751). In his later years he was asked by the liberal editors of the *Encyclopédie* to contribute articles to that work on the subjects of democracy and despotism. He had, however, expressed his views on those subjects at length in his previously published works and chose, instead, to write the essay on taste. His funeral on February 11, 1755, was attended by his fellow *philosophe*, Diderot.

SURVEY OF CRITICISM

The standard biography of Montesquieu in English is Robert Shackleton's (1961). Joseph Dedieu's 1909 work, which lacks a bibliography, is still a standard but dated treatment of Montesquieu and English political tradition in France. Paul Spurlin's presentation of Montesquieu in America (1940) is from the point of view of literary history rather than political science. Paola Berselli Ambri (1960) focuses particularly on Montesquieu's reputation at the Vatican between 1748 and the French Revolution. Cecil Patrick Courtney (1963) offers a concise presentation with emphasis on the British statesman Edmund Burke. Fritz Schalk's 1964 article is an interesting consideration of Montesquieu's contributions to French political thought alongside those of Rousseau and Jean Bodin. Other critics who discuss the multicultural aspects of Montesquieu's work include Jeannette Geffriaud Rosso (1977) and Alain Grosrichard (1979).

SELECTIVE BIBLIOGRAPHY

Works by Montesquieu

Lettres persanes (1721). [*Persian Letters*. Trans. C.J. Betts. Harmondsworth, Middlesex: Penguin, 1977 (reprint edition).]
Considérations sur les causes de la grandeur des Romains et de leur décadence (1734). [*Considerations on the Causes of the Greatness of the Romans and Their Decline*. Trans. David Lowenthal. Indianapolis, Ind.: Hackett Publishing Co., 1999.]
De l'esprit des lois (1748). [*The Spirit of the Laws*. Trans. and ed. Anne M. Cohler, Basia Carolyn Miller, and Harold Samuel Stone. Cambridge: Cambridge University Press, 1989.]

Selective Studies of Montesquieu

Berselli Ambri, Paola. *L'opera di Montesquieu nel settecento italiano*. Firenze: Olschki, 1960.
Courtney, Cecil Patrick. *Montesquieu and Burke*. Oxford: Blackwell, 1963.
Dedieu, Joseph. *Montesquieu et la tradition politique anglaise en France*. Paris: Gabalda, 1909.
Geffriaud Rosso, Jeannette. *Montesquieu et la féminité*. Pisa: Goliardica, 1977.
Grosrichard, Alain. *Structure du sérail*. Paris: Seuil, 1979.
Schalk, Fritz. "Montesquieu und die europäische Traditionen." In *Studien zur französischen Aufklärung*, 107–26. Munich: Hueber, 1964.
Shackleton, Robert. *Montesquieu: A Critical Biography*. London: Oxford University Press, 1961.
Spurlin, Paul. *Montesquieu in America, 1760–1801*. University: Louisiana State University Press, 1940.

MORI (RINTARŌ) ŌGAI
(1862–1922)

Matilde Mastrangelo

BIOGRAPHY

The period Mori Ōgai spent in Germany (spanning almost four years, from October 1884 to July 1888) was to determine the direction of the rest of his life as a man of letters and man of science. He had been sent to Germany by the Japanese government, charged with broadening research in the health area, with particular reference to the provision of health services to the military. From birth he had been destined for a career in medicine: for thirteen generations the Mori family had constituted the medical class of the fief of Tsuwano, where the writer was born. In tandem with his research he studied art and literature, not only in Germany but in Europe as a whole. His cultural baggage was formed mainly through the German language, which he began studying at the age of ten. His language skills allowed him to read a wide range of literature, from Ibsen to Shakespeare to D'Annunzio. He proved himself proficient in German translation even before going to Germany, and during his stay there he seems to have read collections of poetry in German nightly in order to improve his literary knowledge and devote himself to scholarly practice in the language. Active in both the scientific and cultural fields, he not only delivered speeches at health conferences in German, but as a representative of Japan carried on a newspaper debate with the geologist Edmund Naumann in defense of Japanese culture as well.

On his return to Japan he used what was by now his second language to edit *Omokage* (1899), a collection of poetic works by Goethe, Hoffmann, and others. He made his first appearance as a prose writer with the publication of three stories described as a "German trilogy"—*Maihime* and *Fumitsukai* (both 1890), and *Utakata no ki* (1891), inspired by his stay in Germany and set in Berlin, Munich, and Dresden and Leipzig, respectively.

It is interesting to note the extent of the German influence in Ōgai's private life. He chose German-sounding names for his children: Otto, Mari (Marie), Furitsu (Fritz), Annu (Anne), and Rui (from the abbreviated form of Ludwig). His second daughter thought he looked like a German as he worked in the garden where he had planted seeds brought from Germany.

In March 1922 he saw his two eldest children off to Europe and was not to see them again: for some time he had been concealing the fact that he was ill, and on 9 July that year he died. His last wish was to be remembered by his birth name, Mori Rintarō, as an ordinary person and not for the official posts he had held.

MAJOR MULTICULTURAL THEMES

When the main character in the story *Maihime* first encounters Berlin and the German culture, he remarks, "My eyes were dazzled by such splendor and my heart confused by the variety of colors" (*Mori Ōgai zenshū*, 1:4). A few lines further on: "Now, at the age of twenty-five, after experiencing for a time the freedom of the university environment, something in my soul refused to let me rest. My true self, relegated to the depths, gradually began to come to the surface, as though battling the part that until yesterday I thought was the real me" (Ibid., 5). Thus for him the European city represented fascination and splendor but also the possibility of moving away from the cultural ties that can inhibit full self-realization. From the moment his journey begins, the hero of *Maihime* takes note of everything, marveling at each detail as though his senses had acquired special powers of perception. In the same way the character in *Fumitsukai* is excited at the idea of a "real-life" experience living with a noble family in Saxony.

In the "German trilogy" Ōgai describes, in three different settings, a deep desire to know, which is superimposed on a more superficial curiosity and becomes a common factor in the encounters between Japanese and German characters. The Japanese characters in the "trilogy" have no frustrations when faced with the rhythms and lifestyle of the West because they are prepared both culturally and linguistically, but they cannot help but be embarrassed by the curiosity aroused by their "yellow" faces and different appearance, and by the fact that they come from a distant, unknown land.

But encounters between Japanese and foreigners are the subject of stories set in the Japanese archipelago itself as well. Two significant examples are *Fushinchu* (1910) and *Sakai jiken* (1913). In the first, which is seen almost as a continuation of *Maihime*, the Japanese official Zatanae meets a German woman with whom he had an affair during an earlier stay in Germany; the coldness he shows is explained by the need to follow the rules of behavior in his own country, which is still going through a "reconstruction" phase (*Fushinchu* being translated as "under reconstruction"). The second example belongs to the genre of *rekishi shōsetsu* (historical novels) and takes as its starting point an actual incident in which Japanese border guards at the port of Sakai, misinterpreting orders from above, killed a number of French soldiers. The clash of the two cultures is well depicted in the discomfort and agitation of the French minister who, for diplomatic reasons, is obliged to watch the ritual suicide of the Japanese soldiers responsible for the incident.

The many translations through which Ōgai presented European authors to Japan provided a further opportunity for encounters with other cultures. This rich legacy of translations contributed to the development of Japan's modern literary idiom and had a substantial influence on Japanese culture. Worthy of mention are his translations of Tolstoy, Turgenev, Hans Christian Andersen, Schnitzler, Rilke, Goethe, Shakespeare, Edgar Allan Poe, Anatole France, Prévost, Ibsen, Oscar Wilde, and Gabriele D'Annunzio—an enviable repertoire.

Approaching another culture through literature was a frequent theme for Ōgai: he also included explanations in his stories, sometimes—as in *Maihime*—addressed to Japanese readers, sometimes to an eventual foreign readership. An example of the latter is found at the beginning of *Hyaku monogatari* (1911): "A novel should not contain explanations, but everyone has his pride, and should this story be translated into the language of any European country, or should the opportunity arise for it to be part of a repertoire of world literature, foreign readers would understand nothing of it. To avoid giving them the impression that it is a series of unconnected ideas, I shall begin the story with an unusual explanation" (*Hyaku monogatari, Mori Ōgai zenshū*, 2:162).

Ōgai's last literary efforts, from 1912 onwards, were dedicated to *rekishi shōsetsu*, in which he wrote about often-unknown episodes and characters in history. The period spent in Germany and the comparisons with foreign literatures were determining factors in his decision to address the Japanese tradition with greater understanding.

SURVEY OF CRITICISM

The writer Kinoshita Mokutarō (1971) likened Ōgai to "the great city of Thebes with its hundred gates. If you tackle him from the approach facing east you cannot control the roads to the west. If a hundred scholars were each to watch one or two portals they would still lose sight of the others" (*Mori Ōgai zenshū*, Appendix, 26). Ōgai was in fact involved in numerous cultural and institutional areas, and consequently the starting points for an analysis of his work are many.

His narrative debut with *Maihime* led to a critical stream concerned first and foremost with the biographical details identifiable in the text, the search for figures who could have been the models for his characters, and in particular the analogies between the figure of Elise and the German girl of the same name who, according to Ōgai's sister Koganei Kimiko, followed him to Japan. Miyoshi Yukio (1966) has described Ōgai's body of work as *jikayō bungaku*, writing addressed to his own family, because given his institutional roles it was often the only way he had of communicating his thoughts in a context other than the official one. Only since the 1980s has a substantial critical corpus appeared that analyzes the style and structure of Ōgai's work, as far as possible maintaining a separation between text and author.

Ōgai's severe classical style has been identified by Mishima Yukio (1971) as his inspiration. What makes Ōgai's prose in the short novels effective, said this writer, is "the deliberate omission of subjects, frequent adoption of the present tense and sparing use of onomatopoeia" (*Mori Ōgai zenshū*, Appendix, 132). "Like the taste of water, the flavor of Ōgai's short novels remains; perhaps this is because of his excellent intellectually dry style and a narrative mode that is free of construction" (Ibid., 131–32). Thus Mishima emphasized the way Ōgai's stories seem to prepare the reader for something that will happen only at the very end of the story through the use of details and descriptions that apparently have nothing to do with the plot. In the opinion of the critic Katō Shuichi (1995), no other Japanese writer has distinguished himself with such excellence in such a wide range of writing (covering narrative, poetry, drama, and essays), successfully developing new forms and original theories in each area.

SELECTIVE BIBLIOGRAPHY

Works by Mori Ōgai

Mori Ōgai zenshū. 9 vols. Tokyo: Chikuma, 1971.
Historical Literature of Mori Ōgai. 2 vols. *The Incident at Sakai and Other Stories* (1), *Saiki Koi and Other Stories* (2). Ed. David Dilworth and J. Thomas Rimer. Honolulu: University Press of Hawaii, 1977.
Youth and Other Stories. Ed. J. Thomas Rimer. Honolulu: University of Hawaii Press, 1994.

Selective Studies of Mori Ōgai

Bowring, Richard. *Mori Ōgai and the Modernization of Japanese Culture*. Cambridge: Cambridge University Press, 1979.
Hirakawa Sukehiro, Hiraoka Toshio, and Takemori Tenyū, eds. *Kōza Mori Ōgai*. Vol. 1, *Ōgai no hito to shuhen*; vol. 2, *Ōgai no sakuhin*; vol. 3, *Ōgai noam chiteki kūkan*. Tokyo: Shinyōsha, 1997.
Katō Shuichi. *Ōgai Mokichi Mokutarō*. Tokyo: NHK, 1995.
Kinoshita Mokutarō. "Mori Ōgai." In *Mori Ōgai zenshū*, vol. 9, Appendix, 3–28. Tokyo: Chikuma, 1971.
Koganei Kimiko. "Ani no kichō." In *Mori Ōgai zenshū*, vol. 9, Appendix, 195–98. Tokyo: Chikuma, 1971.
Mastrangelo, Matilde. "Ritratti femminili e vendetta nei racconti storici di Mori Ōgai: *Gojiingahara no katakiuchi*, la creatività che necessita un punto di partenza." *Il Giappone* 32 (1992): 87–128.
——— " 'Il viaggio sentimentale' di Mori Ōgai: La trilogia tedesca." *Il Giappone* 36, (1998): 81–101.

Mishima Yukio. "Mori Ōgai no tanpen shosetsu." In *Mori Ōgai zenshū*, vol. 9, Appendix, 129–32. Tokyo: Chikuma, 1971.

Miyoshi Yukio. *Mori Ōgai*. Tokyo: Yuseido, 1966.

Mori Ōgai wo yomu tame no kenkyūjiten. Special issue of *Kokubungaku: Kaishaku to kyōzai no kenkyū* 43, no. 1 (1998).

NAGAI KAFŪ
(1879–1959)

Luisa Bienati

BIOGRAPHY

Nagai Kafū is the nom de plume of Nagai Sōkichi, a Japanese writer of short fiction, diaries, and essays. The literal translation of Kafū is "Lotus breeze," inspired by the name of a young lady, Ohasu (Lotus flower), the protagonist of his first (unpublished) short story.

Kafū was born in Tokyo at the beginning of the Meiji era (1868–1912), and his aesthetic development reflects the cultural trauma caused by the sudden modernization of his country. The attraction for the West that permeated his youth was compounded by nostalgia for the past and for his traditional cultural heritage. He personally lived out the modern dilemma in all its disruptive clash between progress and conservatism. His early attraction to the popular arts and to the literature of Edo (the name of Tokyo until 1868) marked his mature aesthetic vision. Looking to past literary tradition, he found a precious source of inspiration in the *ninjōbon* (books of sentiment) of Tamenaga Shunsui, a writer of popular narrative in the preceding era, but his first short stories, *Oboroyo* and *Hanakago*, are conscious imitations of the *hisan shōsetsu* (tragic novels) of the master, Hirotsu Ryūrō (1861–1928). His readings of Emile Zola, Guy de Maupassant, Henri de Régnier, and French literature in general prompted him to acquaint Japanese readers with French Naturalism through his essays. This phase of his production, exemplified by *Yashin* and *Jigoku no hana* (both 1902) and *Yume no onna* (1903), has been called *zoraizumu*: in these texts Kafū himself recognized an unusual cross between the *ninjōbon* and the works of Maupassant.

His father, a high official of the new Japanese bureaucracy, loved to travel, which allowed his son to take a prolonged trip abroad (1903–8) and thereby escape Tokyo's demimonde. He spent four years in the United States, first studying, then working in the Japanese Embassy in Washington and the Yokohama

Specie Bank in New York. In 1907 he succeeded in getting himself transferred to France, a long-cherished goal. His foreign experience helped him to evaluate Japanese society more critically and more severely and made his return trip all the more bitter. His publications based on his foreign experience are the American stories, *Amerika monogatari* (1908), the French stories, *Furansu monogatari* (1910), and a diary of his Western voyage, *Saiyū nisshishō* (1917).

Having returned to his native land, he felt more and more an "exile," disillusioned by what he saw and critical of Japan's superficial modernization. He withdrew from society, finding an escape in art and in past traditions and cocooning himself in aesthetic experiences that revived for contemporary Tokyo whatever was left of the recent past. His Naturalist standards gave way to a lyrical, romantic, nostalgic vision that inspired his best-known works: *Sumidagawa* (1909) and *Udekurabe* (1917). Geishas and prostitutes are the characters in his stories, but the settings, the atmosphere, and the quarters of old Tokyo are the real protagonists.

He isolated himself even more from the literary world by leaving his prestigious teaching post in French literature at Tokyo's Keiō University in 1916. After the publication of his essays *Henkikan manroku* (1918) and *Shōsetsu sahō* (1921), he wrote a short masterpiece, *Ame shōshō* (1921), in a discursive style closer to the narrative mode of classical tradition than to the model of the Western novel. Two tales, *Tsuyu no atosaki* (1931) and *Bokuto kitan* (1937), in which modern content and setting contrast with recherché prose of the past, reconfirmed his success as a novelist.

Faithful to his lifestyle, during World War II he maintained a position of noninvolvement, and perhaps for this reason his works attained even greater and unexpected success after the war. Meticulous annotations in his diary, *Danchōtei nichijō* (1917–1959), furnish information on his last decades of activity up to his death in 1959.

MAJOR MULTICULTURAL THEMES

Kafū played an important role in introducing Western literature to Japan at the beginning of the twentieth century. With his essays on Zola he spread knowledge of the theoretic principles of French Naturalism, and in the following decades, even after he had changed his literary inspiration, he never refuted what he had learned from Zola, Maupassant, Baudelaire, Flaubert, and Loti. His well-known collection of translations, *Sangoshū* (1913), introduced Symbolist poetry to Japan. For young people of his generation, he was a myth: an artist abroad who could delight in the sensual and intellectual joys offered by the West and be free from the oppressive bonds of his own society. From the pages of *Amerika monogatari* emerges an idealization of the West, the product of Kafū's literary imagination. The stories in this collection are closely related in both form and content to his "French readings"; the subject is that of the Japanese emigrant in a foreign land, but the places described are mythical rather than actual. The

West, for Kafū, is "elsewhere"—another world on which to project his desires
and his dreams. His experience in France has been compared to Pierre Loti's in
Japan: the latter's *Madame Chrysanthème* describes a fictitious world that reflects an image of Japonaiserie in vogue in France. Kafū's descriptions in his
French stories often become quotations superimposed on his lyricism: the words
of the "masters" are continually juxtaposed to the reality before his eyes. For
Kafū, Paris symbolizes a perfect modernization, thanks to its harmonious fusion
of past and present. His European experience reinforced his scorn of Japan of
the Meiji period, during which Japan imitated the West without any critical
sense, obliterating its own past and cultural identity. The East was the antimyth,
the reality that clashed with the dream. This reverse Orientalism arose from a
need for compensation, as a projection outward of an inner search. After his
return to his native land the dimensions of Kafū's longing for the "elsewhere"
shifted from spatial to temporal. His search now was for old Tokyo's past, but
he proceeded by superimposing his recollections of the literature of Edo onto
the little that remained for him to observe.

SURVEY OF CRITICISM

The most complete critical biography of Kafū in Japanese is Isoda Koichi's
(1989). In English Edward Seidensticker's (1965) is the most credited. Akase
Masako's comparative study (1986) focuses on themes gleaned by Kafū from
his readings of Maupassant, which flow together in the stories of *Amerika monogatari*. The essays on *Amerika monogatari* by Amino Yoshihiro (1984) and
Iriye Mitsuko (1992) focus on these parallelisms. The influence of French literature on Kafū's writing has been studied by Egashira Hikozō (1984), while
Kawachi Kiyoshi (1971) concentrates on Kafū and Zola. Stephen Snyder (2000)
distinguishes the formal elements of Kafū's writings as related to both French
influences and the canons of modern Japanese literature. Ching-mao Cheng
(1970) studies the links between Kafū's writings and Chinese literary tradition.

SELECTIVE BIBLIOGRAPHY

Work by Nagai Kafū

Kafū zenshū. 29 vols. Ed. Iwanami Yujiro. Tokyo: Iwanami shoten, 1962–1974.

Selective Studies of Nagai Kafū

Akase Masako. *Nagai Kafū: Hikaku bungakuteki kenkyū.* Tokyo: Aratake shuppan, 1986.
Amino Yoshihiro. "Amerika monogatari." *Kokubungaku kaishaku to kanshō* 49, no. 3
    (1984): 51–58.
Cheng, Ching-mao. *Nagai Kafū and Chinese Tradition.* Doctoral dissertation. Ann Arbor:
    University Microfilms International, 1970.

Egashira Hikozō. "Kafū to furansu bungaku." *Kokubungaku kaishaku to kanshō* 49, no. 3 (1984): 118–24.

Iriye Mitsuko. "*Amerika monogatari* no yoyaku ni miru Kafū." *Bungaku* 3, no. 3 (1992): 5–15.

Isoda Koichi. *Nagai Kafū*. Tokyo: Kodansha bungei bunko, 1989.

Kawachi Kiyoshi. "Nagai Kafū to Zola." In *Nihon kindai bungaku no hikaku bungakuteki kenkyū*, 151–71. Ed. Yoshida Seiichi. Tokyo: Shimizu kōbundō shobō, 1971.

Nihon bungaku kenkyū shiryō kankōkai. *Nagai Kafū*. Nihon bungaku kenkyū shiryō sōsho. Tokyo: Yuseido, 1971.

Seidensticker, Edward. *Kafū the Scribbler: The Life and Writings of Nagai Kafū, 1879–1959*. Stanford: Stanford University Press, 1965.

Snyder, Stephen. *Fictions of Desire: Narrative Form in the Novels of Nagai Kafū*. Honolulu: University of Hawaii Press, 2000.

GÉRARD DE NERVAL
(GÉRARD LABRUNIE)
(1808–1855)

John W. Kneller

BIOGRAPHY

Gérard Labrunie, as he was known before he adopted his pseudonym, was born in Paris in 1808. The day after his baptism his parents sent him to nurse in Loisy, just outside Paris. His father, Dr. Étienne Labrunie, an adjutant doctor and later physician ordinary, had been assigned to Napoleon's Grande Armée in Germany. His mother, who accompanied her husband, died in 1810 in Silesia (then a Prussian province) at Gross-Glogau. Dr. Labrunie received a medical discharge from active service in 1814. Gérard, who had been living with his granduncle Antoine Boucher in the Valois town of Mortefontaine, returned to Paris to live with his father.

From 1822 to 1826 he attended the Collège Charlemagne, where he met Théophile Gautier. They would become lifelong friends. Having received the baccalaureate with mediocre grades, he enrolled in the Collège de Médecine de Paris (1832–33), but never finished his studies. He had other, more compelling interests. Germany—the Germany of Goethe, Schiller, Klopstock, and Bürger and the country of his mother's grave—had become his second homeland. In 1827 he had published a translation of Goethe's *Faust*, which delighted its author and became its standard French translation for many decades. He also completed a volume of translations of German poetry. His preoccupation with Germany was rooted in the loss of his mother and deepened by his absorption in the German poets. His maternal grandfather, Pierre-Charles Laurent, died in 1834, leaving him a substantial inheritance. In the fall of the same year he fell in love with Jenny Colon, an unexceptional actress. With his newly acquired money he took a trip to the south of France and Italy. On his return he settled into a bohemian existence with other artists and founded in 1835 *Le Monde dramatique*, a review that boasted a team of brillant collaborators including Alexandre Dumas and Théophile Gautier. The review permitted him to heap praise on Jenny Colon, but it folded in 1838 and left him swamped in debt, and Jenny Colon married a flutist by the name of Louis-Marie-Gabriel Leplus.

From 1836 on Nerval became a full-time drama critic for *Figaro*, the *Charte de 1830*, *La Revue de Paris*, and other periodicals. Their editors gave him advances with the understanding that he write accounts of his trips. The articles, as well as the letters he wrote to his friends, provide much of what we know about the importance of travel for Nerval. Apart from brief visits to Italy in 1834 and to London with Gautier in 1849, his destinations were either symbolically north to Germany, Belgium, Holland, and Austria or symbolically east to Egypt, Lebanon, and Turkey. At the end of the journey to the symbolic north was the sealed grave of his mother. Somewhere to the east was the eternal goddess Isis. Both these trips inspired him to publish separate articles mostly contemporaneous with the trips themselves. Each culminated in a masterpiece.

Nerval and Alexandre Dumas went to Germany in 1838 to compile documents on German secret societies and on the assassination of the dramatist and politician August von Kotzebue by the student Karl Sand. These researches led to articles appearing in diverse periodicals in 1839 and 1840 and to the play *Léo Burckart*, based on that assassination and produced in April 1839 at the Porte Saint-Martin theater in Paris. His first mental breakdown (1841) and his journey to the Middle East (1843) ushered in the masterpieces that we now associate with his name: *Voyage en Orient* (1851), *Lorely*, *Les Nuits d'octobre*, *Contes et facéties*, *Les Illuminés*, *La Bohême galante* (all in 1852), *Petits châteaux de Bohême* (1853), *Les Filles du feu* and *Les Chimères* (both in 1854), and *Aurélia* (posthumous).

A key year for Nerval was 1850. Newspapers announced a festival in honor of Herder and Goethe. His friend Franz Liszt was to be the master of ceremonies. Nerval learned that Goethe had praised his translation in his *Gespräche mit Eckermann*. In poor health when he set out, he went first to Goethe's Weimar, but details of this trip remain obscure. We know that he was in close contact with Liszt, that he had to interrupt his stay in Germany to return to Paris on business, and that he suffered another mental breakdown.

In early 1854 Nerval's friends wanted to secure for him a paid trip to hasten his recovery. They remembered the beneficial effects of the 1843 Middle East journey. His doctor urged him not to go to the Middle East but rather to Germany, which he did—to Strasbourg, Stuttgart, Munich, Donauwörth, Nuremburg, Bamberg, Leipzig, Weimar, Frankfurt, Bar-le-Duc, and back to Paris. His last letter was to his aunt Madame Alexandre Labrunie: "Don't wait for me this evening, for the night will be black and white." During the night of the 25th and the 26th of January 1855, he was found hanging in a sordid street of Paris.

MAJOR MULTICULTURAL THEMES

The play *Léo Burckart* and all the articles written contemporaneously with the trips to the north found their way into *Lorely: Souvenirs d'Allemagne* (1852), heterogeneous memories of his four trips. The main sections as they appear in the final work reflect its scope: *Sensations d'un voyageur enthousiaste, Scènes de la vie allemande, Rhin et Flandre,* and *Les Fêtes de Hollande.* As was his wont, he read a lot to supplement his impressions. But *Lorely* is more than the summation of all these trips previously described in various journals. Through the filter of time and enhanced by his travels to the east, he depicts a German universe perpetuated and mythologized by Goethe, Schiller, Herder, Spohr, Liszt, and Wagner. German exoticism, symbolized by the Lorelei, found its way into the final version.

The journey to the Middle East resulted in *Scènes de la vie orientale: Les Femmes du Caire* (1848), *Scènes de la vie orientale: Les Femmes du Liban* (1850), and a serial, *Les Nuits du Ramazan,* before culminating in the definitive 1851 *Voyage en Orient.* If we look at his actual itinerary (reconstituted according to his correspondence), we find that he sometimes describes places that he did not visit and neglects to mention the places he did visit. He borrows heavily from written sources, not only to enrich his actual observations, but also to be able to provide copy and be paid for his contributions. These facts have led critics to complain that he "read more than he saw."

Nerval did everything he could to become part of the people whose country he was visiting and to experience deeply the places, the buildings, and the events he was describing. His accounts were never aimed at mere description. In the part entitled "Druses et Maronites" he gives a complete study of the life of the Lebanese people. In Turkey "Les Nuits de Ramazan" presents lively pictures of the bazaars, the theaters, and the people of Stambul. He also produced two outstanding stories, "Histoire du Calife Hakem" and "Histoire de la Reine du Matin et de Soliman, prince des génies." In the first he sees in the theme of the *ferouër* the equivalent of the Germanic *Doppelgänger* (double), which would recur later in "Sylvie" and "Aurélia." In the second Adoniram is the prototype of the artist-creator whose posterity would include the sons of Cain, the disinherited, like "El Desdichado" and "Anteros" of *Les Chimères* (1854). Always the poet, he wrote as a poet. We do not read *Lorely* or the *Voyage en Orient* as tour guides. Nerval's major works, like Marcel Proust's, owe their unmatched beauty to the fact that they are filtered through memory and reminiscence.

SURVEY OF CRITICISM

Charles Dédéyan's three volumes (1957–1959) focus on the influence of Germany on Nerval, on the one hand, and Nerval's judgments on German literature and culture, on the other. Jean-Marie Carré (1932) was one of the first to study the art and composition of the *Voyage en Orient.* He observed that "there is in Nerval's narration more poetry than truth." Hassan el Nouty (1958) points out that with Nerval travel literature becomes a recognized literary genre, rather than "a hybrid tributary of other genres." Ross Chambers, in a book significantly entitled *Gérard de Nerval et la poétique du voyage* (1969), delves more deeply into the artistic and lyric qualities of the poet's travel accounts. Bettina Knapp's 1980 work is the best book in English on the subject; she devotes two chapters in Part I to German elements in Nerval and the entire Part II to the *Voyage en Orient*. The magisterial three-volume Pléiade edition of Nerval's *Oeuvres complètes* (1984, 1989, 1993) contains not only a presentation of "Nerval, tout Nerval, seulement Nerval" but the present state of scholarship on the works.

SELECTIVE BIBLIOGRAPHY

Works by Nerval

Oeuvres complètes. 3 vols. Bibliothèque de la Pléiade. Paris: Gallimard, 1984, 1989, 1993.
Voyage en Orient. Ed. Jacques Huré. Paris: Imprimerie Nationale, 1997.

Selective Studies of Nerval

Aubaude, Camille. *Le Voyage en Égypte de Gérard de Nerval*. Paris: Kimé, 1997.
Bowman, Frank Paul. *Gérard de Nerval: La conquête de soi par l'écriture*. Orléans: Paradigme, 1997.
Carré, Jean-Marie. *Voyageurs et écrivains français en Egypte*. Vol. 2. Le Caire: Institut Français d'Archeólogie orientale, 1932.
Chamarat-Malandain, Gabrielle. *Nerval, réalisme et invention*. Orléans: Paradigme, 1997.
Chambers, Ross. *Gérard de Nerval et la poétique du voyage*. Paris: J. Corti, 1969.
Daunais, Isabelle. *L'Art de la mesure; ou, L'invention de l'espace dans les récits d'Orient (XIXe siècle)*. Saint Denis: Presses Universitaires de Vincennes, 1996.
Dédéyan, Charles. *Gerard de Nerval et l'Allemagne*. 3 vols. Paris: Société d'édition d'enseignement supérieur, 1957–1959.
Guers, Simone. *Nerval et la patrie perdue*. New York: Peter Lang, 1989.
Illouz, Jean-Nicolas. *Nerval, le "rêveur en prose": Imaginaire et écriture*. Paris: Presses Universitaires de France, 1997.
Knapp, Bettina. *Gérard de Nerval: The Mystic's Dilemma*. University: University of Alabama Press, 1980.
Nouty, Hassan el. *Le Proche-Orient dans la littérature française de Nerval à Barrès*. Paris: Nizet, 1958.
Pichois, Claude, and Michel Brix. *Gérard de Nerval*. Paris: Fayard, 1995.
Richer, Jean. *Nerval, expérience et création*. 2nd ed. Paris: Hachette, 1970.
Schaeffer, Gérald. *Le Voyage en Orient de Nerval: Étude des structures*. Neuchâtel: La Baconnière, 1967.

ANAÏS NIN
(1903–1977)

Bettina L. Knapp

BIOGRAPHY

The *Diary of Anaïs Nin*, which spans a lifetime, details Nin's early and glamorous years in Paris, her birthplace. Despite a philandering composer and concert-pianist father, Joaquin Nin, she, her two younger brothers, and her French-Danish mother, Rosa Culmell, seemed to be a well-knit family. In 1913, however, the whirlwind tours and the travels throughout Europe to meet influential and fascinating people ended abruptly when Nin's father deserted the family. A sense of harrowing loss impacted on her. Deprived of her confidant and of the one she loved most, she began writing her diary, through which she sought to make the past manifest, the dream reality, and which accompanied her wherever she went.

Mother and children settled in New York City in 1914. Anaïs felt constrained by her parochial school, went on to high school, but dropped out. Humiliation followed as a result of her mother's renting out rooms in their home. Meanwhile, Anaïs had grown into a slender, regal young lady with an oval face and haunting almond-shaped eyes. Her aunt invited her to Cuba, where in 1923 she married Hugh P. Guiler, a banker, later known as an engraver and filmmaker under the name of Ian Hugo. They left Cuba a year later for Paris, where she started creative writing, beginning in 1923 *Waste of Timelessness*, a series of vignette-novellas describing Parisian life.

The entire family moved in 1931 to Louvenciennes outside Paris, where Nin entertained, among others, Henry Miller and his wife, June. While Nin's oblique and indirect world of subtle emotions was closed to the realistic Miller, the writings of D.H. Lawrence and Proust influenced her profoundly. Her *D.H. Lawrence: An Unprofessional Study* was published in 1932.

Her growing interest in fragmented personalities and their image equivalents drew her to Picasso and Braque. Dreams, automatic writing, archetypal images, and the poetic and artistic innovations of André Breton, the father of Surrealism, fascinated her. Her emotional problems encouraged her to seek psychiatric help from René Allendy, but his scientific and reductive method blocked her. She tried analysis with Otto Rank, who understood the mysteries of dreams and myths and the creative instinct. He invited Nin to join him in his thriving practice in New York, which she accepted, but the artist in Nin remained unfulfilled. The Jungian analyst Esther Harding explained to her the need of integrating the shadow factor into her whole personality. Still later, Nin continued therapy with Inge Bogner, who empathized with the artist's anguish.

In Paris and New York Nin's expanding vision drew her to Antonin Artaud, Ossip Zadkine, Joseph Delteil, Jean Cocteau, Chana Orloff, Constantin Brancusi, Jules Supervielle, Lawrence Durrell, Theodore Dreiser, and Waldo Frank, to mention but a few. At the outbreak of World War II she left Paris, moved to New York's Greenwich Village, set up her own printing press, and developed a circle of friends that included Frances Steloff, Dorothy Norman, Yves Tanguy, Sherwood Anderson, Salvador Dali, Luise Rainer, Clifford Odets, and Jacques Lipschitz. Her breakthrough into international fame occurred with the publication of the seven-volume *Diary of Anaïs Nin* and *The Early Diary of Anaïs Nin* (1920–1931). Letters and all types of essays—*Henry and June, Incest: From "A Journal of Love," In Favor of the Sensitive Man and Other Essays*—saw the light of day. During those exciting years when fame had finally become hers, Nin embarked on lecture tours throughout the world. She died of cancer in 1977.

MAJOR MULTICULTURAL THEMES

The Diary of Anaïs Nin is a quest—a woman's journey of self-discovery— that Henry Miller placed beside the revelations of Saint Augustine, Petronius, Abélard, Rousseau, and Proust. Having rejected the systems and formulas of conventional criticism with their cerebral approach to art and life, Nin chose intuitive forays to guide her through her novels, critical works, and her *Diary*, which best expresses the universality of her subjectively French/American cross-cultural life experience. Her insight into peoples of the many lands that she visited or in which she lived, and the cultural riches they offered her, were a source of nourishment for her own creative instinct. Her extensive travels—to Africa, Europe, North, Central, and South America, and Asia—opened her up to other cultures. Her visual world—descriptions of a chess game, a Greenwich Village café in New York, exotic Mexican greenery, a tea ceremony in Japan, the Tibetan Bardo (limbo between death and rebirth), or the spirals and circumambulations of a Spanish dance—is invested with transcendent reality. From the Irish James Joyce to the English Virginia Woolf and the French Marcel Proust and André Breton, she bonded in her own way with their synesthetic poetics, interior monologues, stream of consciousness, involuntary memory events, and dreams in the artistic process.

SURVEY OF CRITICISM

Sharon Spencer's highly informative and sensitive *Collage of Dreams* (1977) assesses most significantly Nin's life and literary contributions. Important as well is *The Mirror and the Garden* (1973) by Evelyn Hinz. Richard Centing's quarterly *Under the Sign of Pisces: Anaïs Nin and Her Circle* (1970–1981), now called *The Seahorse*, is invaluable for the researcher. Extremely useful and aesthetically beautiful is *Anaïs Nin: A Book of Mirrors* (1996) edited by Paul Herron. *Recollections of Anaïs Nin by Her Contemporaries* (1996), edited by Benjamin Franklin V, is a fascinating work that brings together twenty-six contributions by those who knew Nin. Gunther Stuhlmann, editor of the yearly *Anaïs: An International Journal*, publishes not only articles on Nin's writings but also translations, stories, and articles by authors the world over.

SELECTIVE BIBLIOGRAPHY

Works by Nin

The Early Diary of Anaïs Nin. 4 vols: vol. 1, 1914–1920; vol. 2, 1920–1923; vol. 3, 1923–1927; vol. 4, 1927–1931. New York: Harcourt Brace Jovanovich, 1978–1985.
D.H. Lawrence: An Unprofessional Study. Paris: Edward W. Titus, 1932.
Winter of Artifice. Paris: Obelisk Press, 1939. Reprint: Denver: Alan Swallow, 1966.
The Diary of Anaïs Nin, 1931–1934. New York: Harcourt, Brace & World, 1966.
The Diary of Anaïs Nin, 1934–1939. New York: Harcourt, Brace & World, 1967.
The Diary of Anaïs Nin, 1939–1944. New York: Harcourt, Brace & World, 1969.
The Diary of Anaïs Nin, 1944–1947. New York: Harcourt Brace Jovanovich, 1971.
The Diary of Anaïs Nin, 1947–1955. New York: Harcourt Brace Jovanovich, 1974.
The Diary of Anaïs Nin, 1955–1966. New York: Harcourt Brace Jovanovich, 1976.
Waste of Timelessness; and Other Early Stories. Weston, Conn.: Magic Circle Press, 1977.
The Diary of Anaïs Nin, 1966–1974. New York: Harcourt Brace Jovanovich, 1980.

Selective Studies of Nin

Centing, Richard, ed. *Under the Sign of Pisces: Anaïs Nin and Her Circle* (quarterly). Vols. 1–12, 1970–1981; now published as *The Sea Horse*.
Evans, Oliver. *Anaïs Nin*. Carbondale: Southern Illinois University Press, 1968.
Fitch, Noel Riley. *The Erotic Life of Anaïs Nin*. Boston: Little, Brown, 1993.
Franklin, Benjamin, V, ed. *Recollections of Anaïs Nin by Her Contemporaries*. Athens: Ohio University Press, 1996.
Herron, Paul, ed. *Anaïs Nin: A Book of Mirrors*. Huntington Woods, Mich.: Sky Blue Press, 1996.
Hinz, Evelyn. *The Mirror and the Garden*. New York: Harcourt Brace Jovanovich, 1973.
Jason, Philip K., ed. *Anaïs Nin Reader*. Intro. Anna Balakian. Chicago: Swallow Press, 1973.

————, ed. *The Critical Response to Anaïs Nin*. Westport, Conn.: Greenwood Press,
    1996.
Knapp, Bettina. *Anaïs Nin*. New York: Frederick Ungar, 1978.
Richard-Allerdyce, Diane. *Anaïs Nin and the Remaking of Self: Gender, Modernism, and
    Narrative Identity*. De Kalb: Northern Illinois University Press, 1998.
Spencer, Sharon. *Collage of Dreams*. Chicago: Swallow Press, 1977.

GEORGE ORWELL
(1903–1950)

Mary Hudson

BIOGRAPHY

Eric Blair, better known to the world as George Orwell, was a curious figure altogether. Born into the lower echelons of the British imperial civil service, he grew up to repudiate the values of the empire, to lay his life on the line in the struggle against European Fascism, and to win worldwide acclaim for warning the world of the danger of totalitarianism in his most famous works, *Animal Farm* (1946) and *Nineteen Eighty-Four* (1949). He was an unlikely candidate for the job. His heritage was that of the "Little Englander," embodying values of patriotism, thrift, and conservatism. Although he would reject none of these values, he went beyond them to explore other cultures and political ideas out of which grew his great contributions to Western literature.

He was born in Bengal, where his father worked in the Opium Department of the Government of India. Like many English boys born overseas, he was taken back to his homeland to be educated. Working hard at what he called (with the Britons' superb sensitivity to class hierarchy) a "lower-upper-middle-class" prep school, he won a scholarship to England's most prestigious grammar school, Eton. That he did not take the usual route to Oxford afterwards was as much a consequence of his family's genteel penury as of his own disinclination. Instead, he joined the Imperial Indian Police and was stationed for five years in Burma. He returned to England in 1927, not able to bear police work any longer. There he found that he could not fit back comfortably into his class. Thus began a stretch of his life when his long-suffering family tolerated its peculiar son's aspirations to become a writer. But too proud to live on others' handouts, he began the life of a tramp, roaming throughout the English countryside and as far away as Paris, inhabiting the underworld of the dispossessed, discovering the futureless life of those whose energy is entirely consumed by their search for food and shelter. Out of this experience came *Down and Out in Paris and*

London (1933), which was the first in a series of books mixing novelistic techniques with eyewitness accounts of experiences ranging from the most commonplace to the most historically relevant. Perhaps even more important than these full-length books, however, were his innumerable articles, seventy-six of them written for the socialist weekly *Tribune*, in which an inveterate good sense and common man's decency were his guiding principles. By 1936, though he was still living a marginal existence, he was publishing enough to afford to marry Eileen O'Shaughnessy, who was content to share his subsistence living and agreed with his left-leaning political outlook.

For a while he saw action on the Republican side of the Spanish Civil War, where he incurred the wrath of many on the Left by strongly criticizing the role of the Communist Party in double-crossing its allies in their failed struggle against Franco's fascists. He proved to be a brave soldier and was shot in the neck, but luckily survived the war. When his prediction proved true that Italy and Germany's support of Franco would be the first step toward a second world war, he tried to enlist in the British army but was refused on medical grounds and instead joined the Home Guard, which he saw, characteristically, as a potential workers' militia. He worked steadfastly throughout the war years broadcasting to India for the BBC, careful to word his talks to defend the government anti-Hitler stance while avoiding giving support to whatever imperial aims it might have on the subcontinent.

His marriage to Eileen ended tragically in 1945 when she died during what was meant to be a minor operation. The end of World War II found him a widower with a newly adopted son to care for, and a war correspondent for the *Observer*, as he finished his famous allegory of totalitarianism, *Animal Farm*. Upon its publication he became an overnight sensation. A very private man, he took no advantage of his celebrity status, instead moving to a remote island off the coast of Scotland. But his increasingly debilitating tuberculosis forced him to give up his rural idyll. Despite severe illness he wrote what would be his literary-political testament, *Nineteen Eighty-Four*, and shortly before his untimely death he married for a second time. He left behind a legacy of simple, lucid prose, untainted by ideological jargon, and some of the most influential novels and essays written in English in the twentieth cenury. Most important, he left the world a standard of integrity and common decency to live up to in public intercourse and discourse.

MAJOR MULTICULTURAL THEMES

Orwell was an internationalist of a decidedly political bent. He rejected nationalism, which he defined as one group's conviction of superiority over others, but saw it as quite distinct from normal, healthy patriotism. This stance was solidified by his early experiences in Burma, where he suffered intensely from the consequences of colonialism and his own role in it. In *The Road to Wigan Pier* (1937) he wrote that he wanted to escape not only from imperialism but from all forms of man's dominion over other men, and to live among the oppressed and take up their battle against all forms of tyranny. There is nothing sentimental about his identification with the suffering masses, however:

You hear your Oriental friends called "greasy little babus", and you admit, dutifully, that they *are* greasy little babus. You see louts fresh from school kicking greyhaired servants. The time comes when you burn with hatred of your own countrymen, when you long for a native rising to drown their Empire in blood. And in this there is nothing honourable, hardly even any sincerity.... You are a creature of the despotism, a pukka sahib, tied tighter than a monk or a savage by an unbreakable system of tabus. (*Burmese Days*, 69)

After Burma Orwell's travels were restricted to his tour of duty in Spain and short trips to the Continent and North Africa. What cultural lines he crossed were mostly within his own country, but they were no less distinct for all that. He rejected class prejudice as much as he did colonialism and was unusual among English writers in actually living the everyday existence of workers, farmers, and even tramps. In *Down and Out* he wrote of the discovery of the great redeeming feature of poverty: the fact that it annihilates the future. Orwell believed that what human beings of all races, cultures, and classes have in common far outweighs their differences, that social responsibility is more important than individual gratification, and that if socialism could not perfect humanity, it could go a long way toward improving the lot of all.

Perhaps his most lasting contribution to twentieth-century thought, however, was his analysis of the role of language in the political sphere. He was appalled by Stalin's show trials and remained a staunch opponent of the hypocrisy of the European Communist parties. He exposed and analyzed "doublespeak":

[T]he decline of a language must ultimately have political and economic causes.... But an effect can become a cause, reinforcing the original cause and producing the same effect in an intensified form.... [The English language] becomes ugly and inaccurate because our thoughts are foolish, but the slovenliness of our language makes it easier to have foolish thoughts.... Modern English, especially written English, is full of bad habits which spread by imitation and which can be avoided if one is willing to take the necessary trouble. If one gets rid of these habits one can think more clearly, and to think more clearly is a necessary first step towards political regeneration. (*The Collected Essays, Journalism, and Letters of George Orwell*, 4:156).

SURVEY OF CRITICISM

Although Orwell wished no biography ever to be written about him, this wish was not to be fulfilled. Mention must be made of the excellent critical biography (1980) by Bernard Crick, which benefited from the support of Sonia Orwell and access to all of the author's papers.

Critics tend to agree that despite the enormous influence of some of his fictional works, Orwell's essays remain his great legacy to the world of letters. What Peter Davison states in *George Orwell: A Literary Life* (1996) is representative: "It is remarkable that so many of Orwell's essays, especially those on the politics of his time, which might be expected to be limited by temporality, and those on popular culture, the techniques for the analysis of which have become infinitely more sophisticated since he wrote, still speak to us directly, informedly and polemically" (110). Two collections of articles, Miriam Gross's (1971) and Harold Bloom's (1987), offer interesting insights from a variety of critics. The latter includes pieces by such preeminent Orwell scholars as Lionel Trilling, Malcolm Muggeridge, Philip Rieff, and Jeffrey Meyers.

Orwell and the Left (1974) by Alex Zwerdling is a comprehensive analysis of Orwell's long evolution as a socialist who remained a freethinker and did not shy away from excoriating the Left for its own failings. This kind of contradiction is also explored by Richard J. Voorhees in *The Paradox of George Orwell* (1961).

SELECTIVE BIBLIOGRAPHY

Works by Orwell

Down and Out in Paris and London (1933). New York: Harcourt, Brace and Company, 1950.
Burmese Days (1934). New York: Harcourt, Brace and Company, 1950.
The Road to Wigan Pier (1937). New York: Harcourt, Brace and Company, 1958.
Homage to Catalonia (1938). New York: Harcourt, Brace and Company, 1952.
Animal Farm. New York: Harcourt, Brace and Company, 1946.
Nineteen Eighty-Four. New York: Harcourt, Brace and Company, 1949.
Shooting an Elephant. New York: Harcourt, Brace and Company, 1950.
The Collected Essays, Journalism, and Letters of George Orwell. 4 vols. London: Penguin Books, 1970.

Selective Studies of Orwell

Bloom, Harold, ed. *George Orwell*. Modern Critical Views. New York: Chelsea House, 1987.
Crick, Bernard. *George Orwell, a Life*. Boston: Little, Brown, 1980.
Davison, Peter H. *George Orwell, a Literary Life*. Basingstoke: Macmillan, 1996.
Forster, E.M. "George Orwell." In *Two Cheers for Democracy*, 60–63. New York: Harvest, 1951.
Gross, Miriam, ed. *The World of George Orwell*. London: Weidenfeld and Nicolson, 1971.
Hoggart, Richard. "George Orwell and the 'Road to Wigan Pier.'" *Critical Quarterly* 7 (1965): 72–85.
Htin Aung, Maung. "George Orwell and Burma." *Asian Affairs* 57 (1970): 19–28.
———. "Orwell of the Burmese Police." *Asian Affairs* 60 (1973): 181–86.

Jain, Jasbir. "Orwell and Gandhi." *Thought* (Delhi) 19 (14 March 1967): 11–12.

———. "Orwell and Imperialism." *Banasthali Patrika* 16 (1971): 1–7.

Lewis, Robin. "Orwell's *Burmese Days* and Forster's *A Passage to India*: Two Novels of Human Relations in the British Empire." *Massachusetts Studies in English* 4, no. 3 (1974): 1–36.

Meyers, Jeffrey. "Orwell in Burma." *American Notes and Queries* 11 (1972): 52–54.

New, Melvyn. "Orwell and Antisemitism: Toward 1984." *Modern Fiction Studies* 21 (1975): 81–105.

Odle, Francis. "Orwell in Burma." *Twentieth Century* 179 (1972): 38–39.

Voorhees, Richard J. *The Paradox of George Orwell*. Lafayette, Ind.: Purdue University Press, 1961.

Zwerdling, Alex. *Orwell and the Left*. New Haven: Yale University Press, 1974.

PAUSANIAS
(Second Century C.E.)

Domizia Lanzetta

BIOGRAPHY

Little or nothing is known of the origins and identity of the traveler-geographer Pausanias. Some claim that he was a native of Asia Minor or of Cappadocia; others identify him with a certain Pausanias of Stephanos, born in Damascus. So closely is his work modeled on Herodotus's writings that some believe that he was born, like his predecessor, in Halicarnassus. Nor does he speak of himself in his description of Greece, *Hellados Periegesis*—ten books of cold, minimalist prose that today are an invaluable guide to ancient Greek ruins. He failed to interest his contemporaries, perhaps because he focused on the remotest, most archaic traditions of Hellas. Yet he apparently lived during the emperorship of Hadrian, when Atticism was at its peak. Some scholars, however, place him later, in the era of the Antonines, and even during the reign of Marcus Aurelius, when interest in the Greek world was less intense, which would explain the lack of enthusiasm that greeted the descriptions of his journey. But these are only deductive attempts to explain why no one took the trouble of handing down Pausanias's biographical data.

MAJOR MULTICULTURAL THEMES

Before visiting Greece, Pausanias had traveled widely in Asia Minor, Syria, Palestine, Egypt, Macedonia, Epirus, and parts of Italy. But it is the description of the trip to Hellas that is of prime importance and gives us a clue to his identity. Taking the form of a tour starting in Attica, it is presented as a sort of "guidebook" to the regions of Greece, but it is a strange account, suggesting perhaps another reason for that apparent lack of interest in him and his work: he seems purposely to have sought anonymity, and for purely spiritual reasons. Gradually the reader senses that he is describing not a physical world but a spiritual landscape.

The *Periegesis* is often criticized as lacking sufficient comment on the artistic importance and beauty of Athens's monuments. Evidently the author was not interested in the external aspect of the city, but rather in the spiritual reasons for the monuments' existence. He was more concerned with mythology and religion, and his travels unfold in time rather than in space. His search is for the roots of the Greek soul and, accordingly, for the essence of himself. He tells, in fact, of Attica's successive generations and its line of rulers, and he attributes a particular relief to the Lagides (the dynasty founded by Alexander's general, Ptolemy) as though, for personal reasons, he felt himself linked to the Greeks of Egypt. He justifies himself by asserting that it was the Lagides who had produced the eponymous statues of the ten new tribes of Athens.

His most intimate convictions in matters of faith are linked to a remote past. Reflecting on the myth of Pandion, he asserts that it is impossible for mortals to escape the fate assigned them by divinity. Probably because he felt that his own roots lay in most ancient Greece, his trip begins with a vision of the temple of Athena at Cape Sunium, quickly followed by a recollection of Phalerum, the ancient port from which mythical heroes of yore set sail, and whence Theseus set forth to free Athens from the terrible tribute it owed to the Minotaur. Ideally, this seems to be the spot from which Pausanias will set out toward a dimension beyond space and time in his search for himself. Through Attica he will approach the marvelous world of gods and myth, and his will be a voyage into the secret of things divine.

He reveals something of himself and of his deep religious convictions when he stands before the temples of Triptolemus, of Demeter, and of Kore. As he contemplates them, he names the peoples that, in his opinion, are most favored by the gods: the Egyptians, the Phrygians, the Athenians, and the Argives. If we consider these four ancient civilizations, we perceive that they were commonly linked by important mystery cults dedicated to analogous gods: Egypt, the cult of Isis; Phrygia, of the Great Mother of the Gods, Cybele; and Athens and Argos, of Demeter and Kore. Pausanias goes on to speak of the myth of these two goddesses of Eleusis, but suddenly interrupts himself, to the disconcertment of the reader, because a sudden vision prevents him from "describing something" connected with the Eleusinium of Athens, which must not be revealed to the uninitiated. Thus he discloses his own knowledge of the most secret aspects of the cult of Demeter and Kore, which may be known and seen by the priests and the initiated only.

In a second episode, having left Athens behind, he reaches Eleusis, only to stop suddenly in his description of the sanctuary of the two goddesses. He refers to a premonitory dream reminding him that the profane must know nothing about what is preserved within the walls of the *telesterion* (the hall of initiation at Eleusis). Since we know that only those who had been initiated into the mysteries of Demeter and Kore were allowed to penetrate into the *peribolos* (the enclosed sacred space around the temple), the implication here again is that Pausanias was an adept in the mysteries of Eleusis.

Thus we may consider his voyage to Attica as signifying a trajectory toward the focal point of his own soul. In the spiritual vision of the ancient Hellenes, the return voyage to one's native land—for example, the homeward journey of the epic hero—was of highly symbolic value. Pausanias may have chosen to begin his wanderings through the regions of Hellas precisely from the point in which his spiritual rebirth had occurred: that is, at the point where he had been initiated into the mysteries of the two goddesses.

Athens represented the place of two births: one civil, the other spiritual. He could not but start his voyage from Athens, as though the city were the gate to the center, the essence of Hellas. He can no longer be considered a foreigner inasmuch as initiation into the Eleusinian mysteries was granted only to citizens of Attica and especially to those of Athens. The only recourse for others in the Greek empire who sought this privilege was to allow themselves to be adopted by a citizen of Athens. Not even Emperor Hadrian was exempted from this rule. Recourse to adoption, then, probably had allowed Pausanias to become a *telestes* (initiate) and, as such, to enter into contact with the most arcane aspects of Greek sacredness, closed to the masses. Nor can we exclude the intention on Pausanias's part of communicating, through his writings, with other initiates.

In fact, his work strangely presents two faces: a physical one, which lies in the past and the future, and a metaphysical one, which shares in the eternal present. To the latter belong the myths of the two goddesses in the ritual transposition of the Eleusinian cult, as well as those strange, remote images of the Minoan-Cretan world that surface in the myths that Pausanias narrates: Theseus and the Minotaur, Epimenides of Crete, that very Iakchos whose sacred image led the processions from Athens to Eleusis. What Heracles is for the Argives, Theseus is for the Athenians, that is, a hero of his lineage as well as a liberator who can transmute the bond of death into a promise of life. Against the background of these stories Pausanias places the enigmatic images of Minos and of the primordial children of Mother Earth. He names the sanctuaries, wrapped in silence and secrecy, of Cecrops and Erichthonius, Athena and Demeter, Dionysius and Theseus, recalling the myths revolving around them and alluding to the rites dedicated to them.

The sometimes almost invisible lines that Pausanias traces for us contour the sacred Ilissus and Cefissus rivers; the former flows near the spot where Kore's lesser mysteries were celebrated, the latter near Eleusis, where Demeter's great and solemn mysteries were performed. Here the pilgrim treads on sanctuary ground where the *Rheitoi*, strange brackish streams, run underground for certain distances, disappearing and reappearing.

Pausanias passes continuously from events firmly fixed in space and time into projections of symbolic and mythical dimension. For example, even while recalling the conflict between the Macedonians and the Athenians, he speaks of the Erechtheum and of the house of the Arrephoria (for initiation rites), as though he wished to impress on the reader the particular truth of the faith of the Hellenes. Availing themselves of the myth, they conceived the world of humans as verging on that of the gods—for the ancient Greeks, the only true "reality."

The "Greek soul" moves outward toward border territories and continually undertakes the "return" voyage toward Mnemosyne, that is, toward itself, or toward the font of "ancient memory." Pausanias's journey contemporaneously includes the workaday world and transcendence, chronicle and history, what is visible and what is invisible.

SURVEY OF CRITICISM

James George Frazer, in *Pausanias and Other Greek Sketches*, offers a series of comparative descriptions of the most significant places in Greece as they appeared to Pausanias in the second century and to his own eyes at the end of the nineteenth. The most exhaustive study on the subject of Pausanias's still-unknown identity is Aubrey Diller's "The Authors Named Pausanias" (1955). *Pausanias historien* (1994), edited by Jean Bingen, contains eight enlightening articles by Domenico Musti and others on Pausanias's historical method, on various interpretations of his descriptions, on his "landscapes of memory," and on his responses to the Greek past and his Graeco-Roman present.

SELECTIVE BIBLIOGRAPHY

Works by Pausanias

Pausanias's Description of Greece. Translated with a commentary by James George Frazer. 6 vols. London: Macmillan, 1898.

Pausanias: Ellados Periegesis. Ed. Luigi Beschi and Domenico Musti. Fondazione Lorenzo Valla. 1st ed. Milano: Mondadori, 1982.

Selective Studies of Pausanias

Bassi, Domenico. *Pausania come fonte mitologica*. Milano: Ulrico Hoepli, 1939.

Bingen, Jean, ed. *Pausanias historien*. Entretiens sur l'antiquité classique 41. Vandouvres-Genève, 15–19 August 1994. Genève: Fondation Hardt, 1996.

Diller, Aubrey. "The Authors Named Pausanias." *Transactions and Proceedings of the American Philological Association* 86 (1955): 268–79.

Frazer, James George. *Pausanias and Other Greek Sketches*. London and New York: Macmillan, 1900.

———. *Sulle tracce di Pausania*. (Translation by Raul Montanari of *Pausanias and Other Greek Sketches*.) Milano: Adelphi, 1994.

Habicht, Christian. *Pausanias' Guide to Ancient Greece*. Berkeley: University of California Press, 1985.

Hejnic, Josef. *Pausanias the Perieget and the Archaic History of Arcadia*. Prague: Nakladatelství Ceskoslovenske Akademie Ved, 1961.

Strid, Ove. *Über Sprache und Stil des Periegeten Pausanias*. Stockholm: Almqvist & Wiksell, 1976.

FERNANDO PESSOA
(1888–1935)

Maria José de Lancastre

BIOGRAPHY

Octavio Paz's aphorism applies more aptly to Fernando Pessoa than to any other twentieth-century poet: "Poets have no biography; their work is their biography." Accordingly, the most authoritative Pessoa biographies, from Simões's pioneering work (1950) to the most recent and sharpest ones by Angel Crespo (1988) and Robert Bréchon (1996), are based mainly on Pessoa's works in order to extract his life. Thus his life, except for a few verifiable and easily summarized facts, is essentially an exegesis (or conjecture) educed from his texts. We must distinguish between his external, anagraphic life and his true life of emotions, passions, and strictly personal vicissitudes, about which Pessoa was always very reserved (nay, parsimonious), both in his letters that are available today and in his autobiographical notes or diary jottings written for himself alone and not intended for publication. Between Pessoa and his life stands an impenetrable wall, which leads us to understand that "la vraie vie est ailleurs" (real life is elsewhere), in Rimbaud's words.

As stereotypic biography, we may say that Pessoa was born in Lisbon to a middle-class family on June 13, 1888. His father, Joaquim, a dilettante musician, was a freelance music critic for a Lisbon evening paper. The boy saw his little magic world collapse at the age of six with the death of his tubercular father and of his infant brother, as well as the confinement of his demented paternal grandmother to a psychiatric hospital. His mother then married by proxy Colonel João Miguel Rosa, Portuguese consul at Durban during the British colonial era, resulting in the boy's uprooting from Lisbon to spend the rest of his childhood, adolescence, and youth in an English-speaking land, where he obtained his schooling in an Anglo-Saxon cultural environment. A voracious reader, he excelled in his studies, undergoing at Durban High School the deep influence of his headmaster, W.H. Nicholas, professor of English literature and classical culture. At the age of fifteen (1903) he enrolled at Cape Town University, where he obtained a good knowledge of classical literature and philosophy (the Greek dramatists, Plato, Aristotle, and the pre-Socratics) and an excellent knowledge of English literature. He preferred readings in the baroque (Milton and Shakespeare) and the Romantics (Keats, Shelley, Tennyson, and others) and was particularly fascinated by Edgar Allan Poe (life's events presented as detective-story problems, or existence seen as a metaphysical crossword puzzle). Having chosen not to continue his studies in an English university, despite the fact that he won the Queen Victoria Prize for English style, he returned alone to Portugal. Repudiating Lisbon University's cultural narrow-mindedness of the time, he sought openings in commercial life, formed a close friendship with the poet Mário de Sá-Carneiro, who would commit suicide in Paris in 1916, and fell deeply in love with Ophélia Queirós. The rest—invention of artistic movements such as Paulism, Intersectionism, or Sensationism, avant-garde adventures, the founding of important reviews such as *Orpheu* or *Athena*—is no longer biography. Rather, it is text, it is literature.

His death at the age of forty-seven is ascribed to a now-mythical "hepatic crisis" caused by alcohol abuse (perhaps only a hypothesis offered by his first biographer, it remains to be proven). He left a body of work that, aside from three small volumes, is unpublished or scattered in magazines. Systematic publication, begun in 1942, is still incomplete and still presents problems of a philological nature.

MAJOR MULTICULTURAL THEMES

After his return to Portugal from South Africa, Pessoa never left his native country again. In fact, with the exception of a single trip to nearby Portalegre, he remained in Lisbon. "Lisboa, meu lar!" (Lisbon, my hearth!)—the affectionate invocation that the semiheteronymous Bernardo Soares pronounces in *Livro do Desassossego*—could be attributed to Pessoa himself because of the similarity of his own life to that of his personage: a methodic routine of time schedules, offices, modest restaurants, trips to the Baixa (the center of the city, reconstructed by the marquis de Pombal after the 1755 earthquake). The Baixa is a bit of the city where streets retain the names of ancient trades or craftsmen's corporations: Rua dos Douradores (Gilders' Street), Rua dos Fanqueiros (Haberdashers' Street), and so forth—a "little city" that would lead one to imagine a narrow, provincial panorama. Nothing could be more misleading in Pessoa's case. Lisbon, both hearth and village of his literary make-believe (the "church-bells of my village," in one of his famous poems), in his abstract vision, estranged from the world, takes on the metaphysical dimension of a "circular and eternal place," a sort of metaphor of the Cosmos (Lancastre, 1977), just as the heteronymous Bernardo Soares intuits that the All, the absolute dimension of the universe, can be sought (and this far before Borges invented his Aleph) in the workaday world of a barber shop or a humble street: "Também há um

Universo na Rua dos Douradores" (There is a Universe even in Gilders' Street), as Pessoa writes in *O Livro do Desassossego por Bernardo Soares* (2:124).

If these are some of the many themes that Pessoa absorbed from the pre-Socratics, from the English Metaphysicals, or from a certain German philosophy (Schopenhauer), many other multicultural elements line the fabric of his work. Life as theater (or the play within the play) that sustains his entire heteronymous construct has its roots in his beloved Shakespeare. The feeling of time's evanescence, the melancholy pleasures of the senses, and the "sad Epicureanism" of his pseudonymous Ricardo Reis obviously refer back to the Greek philosophers and lyric poets and to Horace, but also to Omar Khayyam, whose exquisite translator he became through Edward FitzGerald. The weariness of existence and the enigma of the world are a Leopardi revisited with the measure of an existentialist phenomenology (Tabucchi, 1998).

The ease with which Pessoa moves in a multicultural dimension was certainly favored by his virtual bilingualism (cf. *35 Sonnets* [1918] and *English Poems*. I. *Antinous*. II. *Inscriptions*. III. *Epithalamium* [1921], all in English). According to some reliable critics, his bilingualism makes him a sort of curious alloglot, in the sense that his spontaneous language (or "mother tongue") seems to be English, and that Portuguese is a voluntary language (or "vice-mother"), that is, the result of a choice or rational assent. His Portuguese is, in fact, a syntactically extravagant language that follows a linguistic logic all its own and is not that of the established language. This endows Pessoa's Portuguese with an extraordinary personality marked by an inimitable aesthetic linguistic space. Perhaps it is for this reason too that his real literary interests—as witnessed by his pages on aesthetics and his theoretic writings—with some rare exceptions (Camões, Antero de Quental, Pessanha, Cesário Verde), were English. He translated Poe, Hawthorne, Elizabeth Barrett Browning, and others and introduced to Portugal the neoclassicism of Walter Pater and Ruskin's aesthetics, and his interests and comparisons almost always transcend national boundaries. From Homer to Dante, Milton (whose *Paradise Lost* was a referentiality for the architecture of his poem *Mensagem*), Goethe, the French Symbolists, and the European avantgarde movements (Cubism, Futurism, and others), Pessoa moves transversally across the great European literature of all times. "Eu não evolvo, viajo" (I do not evolve, I travel) is the emblematic side of this intellectual adventure that makes of Pessoa, without his ever leaving his city, one of the greatest cosmopolitans of modern thought.

SURVEY OF CRITICISM

Maria da Encarnaçâo Monteiro (1956) and Jorge de Sena (1982) focus on English themes in Pessoa's work; Alexandrino Severino (1983) studies the influence of English literature on his work and language. Georges Güntert (1971) offers a Freudian analysis with references to Heidegger, Nietzsche, and Bachelard's oneiric. José Gil (1988) offers comparisons with Maurice Merleau-

Ponty's phenomenology, Heidegger, and contemporary philosophy. Esoteric themes are focused on by Dalila Pereira da Costa (1971), with reference to Hofmannsthal, Mircea Eliade, and Kerényi. On the subject of foreign authors and literary movements, Maria Teresa Rita Lopes (1977) studies Pessoa's theatrical works in the perspective of European Symbolism; Antonio Tabucchi (1998) draws comparisons with Leopardi, Mallarmé, and historical European avant-garde movements. Joaquim-Francisco Coelho (1987) discusses the "melancholy" of the ancients, Aristotle, Dürer, Spinoza, and Eugenio d'Ors. Eduardo Lourenço (1986) focuses on "dandy" literature, Hoffmann, Dostoevsky, and Browning's masks.

SELECTIVE BIBLIOGRAPHY

Works by Pessoa

Obras Completas de Fernando Pessoa. Lisboa: Edições Ática (11 vols. of poetry, 1942–1974, and 9 vols. of prose, 1966–1982); Rio de Janeiro: Edições José Aguilar, 2 vols., 1960, 1974.
O Livro do Desassossego por Bernardo Soares. 2 vols. Ed. Jacinto do Prado Coelho. Lisboa: Edições Ática, 1982.
Edição Crítica de Fernando Pessoa. 4 vols. Lisboa: Imprensa Nacional–Casa da Moeda, 1990–1997.
Obras de Fernando Pessoa. Lisboa: Edições Assírio e Alvim, forthcoming.

Selective Studies of Pessoa

Bréchon, Robert. *Etrange étranger: Une biographie de Fernando Pessoa*. Paris: Christian Bourgois Editeur, 1996.
Coelho, Jacinto do Prado. *Diversidade e unidade em Fernando Pessoa*. Lisboa: Editorial Verbo, 1949.
Coelho, Joaquim-Francisco. *Microleituras de Álvaro de Campos*. Lisboa: Dom Quixote, 1987.
Crespo, Angel. *La vida plural de Fernando Pessoa*. Barcelona: Seix-Barral, 1988.
Gil, José. *Fernando Pessoa, ou, La métaphysique des sensations*. Paris: La Différence, 1988.
Güntert, Georges. *Das fremde Ich: Fernando Pessoa*. Berlin and New York: Walter de Gruyter, 1971.
Lancastre, Maria José de. *Fernando Pessoa: Uma fotobiografia*. Lisboa: Imprensa Nacional, 1981; Lisboa: Quetzal, 1996; 2nd ed., 2000.
———. *Peregrinatio ad loca fernandina: La Lisbona di Pessoa*. In "Quaderni Portoghesi," 117–35. Pisa: Giardini, 1977.
Lopes, Maria Teresa Rita. *Fernando Pessoa et le drame symboliste*. Paris: Fondation Calouste Gulbenkian, 1977.
Lourenço, Eduardo. *Fernando Pessoa revisitado: Leitura estruturante do drama em gente*. Porto: Inova, 1973; 2nd ed., Lisboa: Moraes, 1981.

————. *Fernando, rei da nossa Baviera*. Lisboa: Imprensa Nacional–Casa da Moeda, 1986.

Monteiro, Maria da Encarnaçao. *Incidências inglesas na poesia de Fernando Pessoa*. Coimbra: Atlântida, 1956.

Pereira da Costa, Dalila. *O esoterismo de Fernando Pessoa*. Porto: Lello, 1971.

Sena, Jorge de. *Fernando Pessoa & Cª Heterónima*. 2 vols. Lisboa: Edições 70, 1982.

Severino, Alexandrino. *Fernando Pessoa na África do Sul: A formação inglesa de Fernando Pessoa*. Lisboa: Dom Quixote, 1983.

Simões, João Gaspar. *Vida e obra de Fernando Pessoa: Historia de uma geração*. Lisboa: Bertrand, n.d. [1950].

Tabucchi, Antonio. *Un Baule pieno di gente*. Milano: Feltrinelli, 1990.

————. *La Nostalgie, l'automobile, et l'infini*. Paris: Editions du Seuil, 1998.

PETRARCH (FRANCESCO PETRARCA)

(1304–1374)

Carla Scognamiglio

BIOGRAPHY

Because Petrarch undertook to provide detailed written information about himself—his subjectivity being unusual during medieval times—readers can become familiar with an abundance of facts about him. Mainly in the letters of his *Familiarium rerum libri* (written from 1345 to 1366) do his personality and individuality show through, but they are recognizable in all of his works.

Petrarch was born on July 20, 1304, in Arezzo, where his father, Ser Petracco (after 1312 referred to as Petrarca), having been expelled from Florence with Dante and the Whites (Guelphs), sought refuge. In the *Familiarium rerum libri* Petrarch wrote that he was conceived and born in exile; that the midwife and doctors in charge of his mother's risky and protracted labor assumed the child to be dead; that his life was thus endangered even before he was born; and that an omen of death accompanied him from the very outset of his existence.

His family took him, aged seven months, away from Arezzo to spend the first seven years of his life at Incisa in Valdarno near Florence. When he was seven years old, he was taken to Pisa, after which the family sailed to France and settled in Avignon and Carpentras in Provence. Here he began his studies in grammar, rhetoric, and dialectics, attending the University of Montpellier (1318) and then the University of Bologna, where, in accordance with his father's wishes, he studied law. But long fascinated by his readings of classical Greek and Latin authors, he soon balked at the arid language of law and decided to devote himself entirely to research in the classics. He would help to spread humanism through the realization that Greek authors and Platonic thought offered Europe new cultural concepts. Although he wrote several important works in Latin (*De viris illustribus*, *Africa*, and others), he is best known for his sonnet sequences in Italian in the medieval courtly love tradition. The poems, in praise of Laura, the lady of his *Canzoniere* (definitive collection, 1360), made him a force in the history of the European lyric.

Having become well known as a love poet, Petrarch caught the attention of Bishop Giacomo Colonna, who presented him to his circle at Avignon. Here his writings awarded him a prestige that took him throughout Europe as well as to Rome (1337), whose classical civilization fulfilled him. Returning to Avignon toward the end of that year, he withdrew to nearby Vaucluse, where he lived in a modest home at the fountainhead of the Sorgue River, a place he immortalized in his verses. He held Vaucluse dear for its peace and beauty, where he could at last indulge in amorous daydreams and pursue his studies. But his obligations toward Cardinal Giovanni Colonna (Bishop Giacomo meanwhile had died) required his return to Avignon.

On another visit to Rome he was crowned with laurel in a ceremony on the Capitoline hill on Easter Day of 1341—a sensational event, inasmuch as no poet had ever been crowned on Rome's sacred hill since ancient times. Rich, honored, and admired by all, he might have considered himself a happy man were it not for his melancholy nature and deep dissatisfaction with himself. Things of this world repulsed him to the point of increasing his innate restlessness and ceaseless search for peace and tranquility.

Having left Milan in 1361, he settled in Venice for two years and then moved to Padua, often sojourning in Arquà, in the Euganean Hills, where he lived with his illegitimate daughter, Francesca, from 1370 on. On the morning of July 19, 1374, he was found dead in his study, his head resting on a book.

MAJOR MULTICULTURAL THEMES

Petrarch sought to reconcile the classical and Christian worlds. In *De viris illustribus* he presents biographies of famous people of all times since Adam, underscoring his intent of linking the ideals of the Old Testament, of classical antiquity, and of Christianity. His epic poem *Africa*, relating the Second Punic War, though based on Cicero's *De republica* and Livy's *Ab urba condita libri*, is sprinkled with what he saw as Christian moral truths. Fired with enthusiasm for new learning, he followed in the footsteps of Varro, Pliny, and Livy as he traveled through Europe to Paris, Gand, Liège, Aix-la-Chapelle, Cologne, the Ardennes, Lyons, and Rome. In the introductory letter to his *Familiarium rerum libri*, he gave his readers a picture of his adventurous life, comparing Ulysses' voyages to his own and maintaining that, the Greek hero's name and exploits aside, his own wanderings were equally long and far.

His life with its risky onset continued through his dangerous peregrinations. He wrote to Doge Andrea Dandolo on February 26, 1352, that he was being tossed here and there, that he knew well that no place on earth was peaceful, but that throughout his many hardships he never ceased to yearn for tranquility. But side by side with this figure that Petrarch presents of himself as a strong man who knows how to face life's adversities courageously, there is another—

that of a free-spirited and independent traveler. His numerous trips were not business affairs but rather unique occasions to know and learn from contacts with diverse societies. It is his specificity as a foreigner—"peregrinus ubique" (*Epistole* III, 19, 16)—with respect to his beloved native land (not limited to any of the numerous Italian city-states) that lends him the aspect of a cosmopolitan intellectual. He was one of the great figures of the Renaissance in Italy and a luminary in the development of European culture. His extraneousness from communal situations removed him from every cultural particularism, and his sophisticated bearing made him both international and modern.

SURVEY OF CRITICISM

In the introduction to his chapter on Petrarch (1995) Marco Ariani succinctly explains his modernism and originality with respect to his times and his contemporaries. Petrarch's sojourns in Avignon and his presence at the ecclesiastical circle of the Colonna family were basic to the construction of his persona as a cosmopolitan intellectual. In Avignon he learned how to "think big" and gain a general and universal view of the world: no longer the urban reality of the commercial middle class (as it would be for Boccaccio), but rather that of a sovereign "transnational" state—the Church. According to Ariani, Petrarch was among the very first to incarnate the figure of the uprooted intellectual constantly seeking strong protection to guarantee him reasonable freedom of cultural action and allow him to produce works of wide scope—that is, works that look to the past and future rather than dwell on the present, his "secolo noioso" (tiresome century). Similarly, Aldo Scaglione in his chapter "A Sketch for a Portrait" (1975) insists on Petrarch's modernism: "Modern for his curiosity toward the world and peoples, since he did not only travel for practical reasons and to seek out forgotten codices, but while travelling he kept his observing eyes well open on things and men" (5–6).

SELECTIVE BIBLIOGRAPHY

Works by Petrarch

Opere: Canzoniere, Trionfi, Familiarium rerum libri. Ed. Mario Martelli. Firenze: Sansoni, 1975.
Epistole. Ed. Ugo Dotti. Torino: Unione Tipografico-editrice torinese, 1978.

Selective Studies of Petrarch

Ariani, Marco. "Francesco Petrarca." In *Storia della letteratura italiana*, vol. 2, 601–726. Ed. Enrico Malato. Roma: Salerno, 1995.
Bernardo, Aldo S., ed. *Francesco Petrarca Citizen of the World*. Padova: Antenore, 1980.
Dotti, Ugo. *Petrarca e la scoperta della coscienza moderna*. Milano: Feltrinelli, 1978.

Preveggenze umanistiche di Petrarca: Atti delle giornate petrarchesche di Tor Vergata, Roma-Cortona, 1–2 giugno 1992. Pisa: Ets, 1993.

Scaglione, Aldo. "A Sketch for a Portrait." In *Francis Petrarch, Six Centuries Later: A Symposium*, 1–24. Chapel Hill, Department of Romance Languages, University of North Carolina. Ed. Aldo Scaglione. Chicago: Newberry Library, 1975.

Trinkaus, Charles. *The Poet as Philosopher: Petrarch and the Formation of Renaissance Consciousness*. New Haven: Yale University Press, 1979.

MARCO POLO

(1254–1324)

Marcello Ricci

BIOGRAPHY

Marco Polo, the merchant, traveler, and author of the famous *Il Milione*, which contributed significantly to knowledge of a part of the world almost entirely unknown to Europeans up to his time, was probably born in Venice in 1254, if we can rely on his information that he was fifteen years old when his father returned in 1269 from his first trip to Asia. Marco's family, merchants for many generations and probably originating in Dalmatia (perhaps in Sebenico), had moved to Venice in the early years of the eleventh century, even though the name Polo appears for the first time only in the following century, in some state documents. It is also believed that in the second half of the twelfth century the Polos had so expanded their merchant activities as to own commercial subsidiaries in Constantinople and the Crimea.

Archival research has revealed that Marco's grandfather, Andrea, had three sons, Marco, Nicolò, and Matteo. The senior Marco had expanded the Polos' maritime business to ports on the Black Sea. To promote the business, Nicolò and Matteo undertook a nine-year journey in 1261 from the Crimea to Sarai and Bolgar on the lower and middle course of the Volga River; then, tacking on the Caspian Sea, to Bokhara, the most "distinguished and grand" city of Persia, where they were obliged to stay for three years. Continuing on, along unidentifiable itineraries, they reached China and were welcomed at the court of the great Kublai Khan, where they were entrusted with diplomatic missions to the pope in Rome.

Having returned to Venice in 1269, they left again for China in 1271 with the young Marco, going along the "silk route" through the most important commercial centers. Traveling across Turkmenia, Lesser and Greater Armenia, the kingdom of Baghdad, the Persian kingdom, the Pamir, and the Mongolian steppes, the three travelers reached Cambaluc, the summer residence of the great

Kublai Khan. In *Il Milione* Marco Polo details his journey and the seventeen years spent in the service of the emperor Kublai Khan, whose esteem he earned and for whom he even completed three missions in the provinces of the empire. To add to his luster, it has been claimed, although not confirmed by Chinese sources, that he administered for three years the region whose capital was the city of Yangju, located northeast of present-day Nanking.

At the beginning of 1292 a princess of the imperial court was to be taken to the harem of Argun Khan, king of Persia. Kublai Khan assigned the Polos to escort her, thus allowing them to begin their journey home. Traveling by sea, they touched the northern coast of Sumatra, the island of Ceylon, and the southwestern part of India and reached the Persian court, where, having completed their mission for Kublai Khan, they remained for nine months. Then, in 1295, after having crossed western Persia and Armenia, having reached Trebizond and Constantinople, and having crossed the eastern Mediterranean Sea, Marco, Nicolò, and Matteo were finally able to set foot again in Venice.

It may be reasonable to assume that Polo's life from then on was comfortable, thanks to the riches accumulated during the journey and to the fact that, as some documents show, he profitably resumed his commercial activities. What is certain is that he was made a prisoner of the Genoese in the Ligurian capital in 1298, but it is unknown whether he had been captured during the naval battle of Curzola (September 1298) against Genoa or on the waters of Lajazzo in a fight between the merchant galleys of the two maritime republics.

His time in captivity was of great importance because he was able to dictate his travel experiences to Rustichello da Pisa, not an eminent prose writer but an expert in the art of handwriting. The title of the work that took shape, written in a French full of Italianisms, is in fact *Livre des merveilles du monde*, but it took on the better-known name of *Il Milione*, a nickname of the Polo family.

Freed from captivity to return to his native Venice in September 1299 after the peace treaty between Genoa and Venice (July 1, 1299), Marco at once married Donata Badoèr, with whom he had three daughters. Although the date of his death is also uncertain, January 8, 1324, seems to be the most plausible. According to his testamentary wishes, his body was buried in the Church of San Lorenzo; but when, at the end of the sixteenth century, the building was renovated, the crypts were removed and the remains therein preserved were lost.

MAJOR MULTICULTURAL THEMES

If what we call today the multicultural approach denotes a willingness to know what is "different," to compare oneself with the "other," and to dialogue with dissimilar cultural worlds not simply for the purpose of exchanging material goods, then Marco Polo, because of his openness and intellectual curiosity for the variety of cultures, customs, and traditions he came to know, was clearly a man well ahead of his times. In the sixteenth chapter of *Il Milione* it is written that not long after reaching the court of the great Kublai Khan, Marco had learned four languages and their respective alphabets and scripts, and that he also had appropriated, in an admirable way, Tatar customs.

In his work he stressed religious cults, even if he was not always able to distinguish between different aspects of Asian beliefs, which range from animism to the most evolved intellectual systems of metaphysical knowledge. Consequently he confused, for example, Brahmanism and Buddhism with the lowest idolatry. For this reason, some scholars have accused him of superficiality, of not being able to understand the deeper meaning of spiritual manifestations. But he scarcely could have been capable of understanding spiritual dimensions so different from his own, having been raised in a medieval Europe locked in pride of its Christian and Catholic credo. Others argue that although Marco Polo lived in a culture whose approach to other civilizations meant Christianizing them, he was able to recognize the high moral value and the contribution of Buddhism and Taoism to Far Eastern civilization. It might be added that he missed no opportunity to deny or to refashion the fantastic images and the prejudices of his contemporaries, who were accustomed to biblical and evangelical symbols and allegories adopted over the centuries without critical scrutiny. He debunked legends, as, for example, in his description of the island of Madagascar (1299), where he verified the factual existence of the mythological bird *rukh* of Sinbad the Sailor lore.

He was a careful observer of popular traditions, giving much space in his book to the day-to-day life of the Eastern world. With the help of short anecdotes and ethnographic details, he describes peoples and tribes, clothing and hairstyles, rituals and ceremonies, food, drink, and erotic practices. He was an innovator of his age. His description of Asia was absolutely original for Europeans: namely the information he supplied about the climate of the regions he visited, their natural products (petroleum, pit coal, asbestos), the manufactured articles of Chinese industries, completely unknown on the Old Continent, and so forth.

He was the first European to present China in all its richness and vastness, describing the characteristics of its physical and human geography: its large rivers, the urbanistic and architectural aspects of its beautiful cities, its active people, its incredibly numerous fleets; he was the first to mention some completely unknown countries such as Tibet, Burma, Laos, Siam, Japan, and the island of Ceylon. He gave information, albeit secondhand, about not only East Africa, but also Siberia and the lands washed by the Arctic's polar sea, reporting on white bears, dog-dragged sleds, and people mounted on reindeer. The rich mass of information he furnished greatly influenced fourteenth- and fifteenth-century cartography; it was used to update both the drawings and the inscriptions inserted on maps.

Marco Polo was the first to have joined, in his travel and life experience, the two continents with the oldest civilizations. Always accurate and moderate, he rarely fell into bias or prejudice, managing to be sharp without being trivial; though he was conscious of his own value and sure of his judgments, he never was haughty; although he was a member of the court of the winners (the Mongolians), he was able to bow to the civilization of the vanquished (the Chinese), just as he was able to respect other people's values, without distinction of race or religion.

SURVEY OF CRITICISM

Only in the twentieth century has Marco Polo's importance been fully acknowledged. His work is now considered the most powerful laical and worldly synthesis that the Middle Ages have left us and has been compared to the theological and philosophical syntheses formulated by Dante and Thomas Aquinas. In the past *Il Milione* was considered a legendary report; its author was suspected of exaggeration and swaggering, sometimes even of untruth. With the acknowledgment of Marco Polo's objectivity and realism, the book nonetheless continued to be deprived of its poetic significance and was considered mainly as a compendium of notations of economic interest.

Despite the good fortune of *Il Milione* throughout the centuries, it has reached us in an altered form, having undergone mistakes of handwritten transcriptions and also misunderstanding of meanings. Only after the philological reconstruction of the text in the early twentieth century, mainly through the efforts of Luigi Foscolo Benedetto, has the inquisitive and open spirit of Polo been fully understood. It has also been recognized that from the point of view of geographic and historic knowledge, Marco Polo permitted the Western world to take a giant step foward, substituting reliable data for the hodgepodge of fairy tales and legends that used to be associated with the unexplored East. For Giotto Dainelli (1941, 1954), Polo represents a milestone in the history of exploration.

SELECTIVE BIBLIOGRAPHY

Editions of *Il Milione*

The Book of Ser Marco Polo, the Venetian, Concerning the Kingdoms and Marvels of the East. Ed. Henry Yule and Henri Cordier. London: J. Murray, 1903.

Il Milione. Ed. Luigi Foscolo Benedetto. Firenze: L.S. Olschki, 1928.

Il Milione di Marco Polo. Ed. Dante Olivieri. Bari: Laterza, 1928.

The Description of the World. Trans. and ed. A.C. Moule and Paul Pelliot. London: G. Routledge, 1938.

La description du monde. Trans. (modern French) and ed. Louis Hambis. Paris: C. Klincksieck, 1955.

Il Milione. Ed. Ruggero M. Ruggieri. Firenze: Olschki, 1986.

The Book of Marco Polo. Trans. and ed. Juan Gil. Madrid: Testimonio, 1986.

The Travels of Marco Polo and Ibn Battuta. Ed. Richard Scheuerman and Arthur Ellis. Madison, Wis.: Demco, 1998.

Selective Studies of Polo

Alulli, Ranieri. *Marco Polo*. Torino: Paravia, 1953.

Collis, Maurice. *Marco Polo*. London: Faber and Faber, 1950.

Dainelli, Giotto. *Marco Polo*. Torino: Unione Tipografico-editrice torinese, 1941.

———. *Marco Polo. Celebration of the VII Centenary of His Birth, 1254–1954*. Venezia: Municipalità di Venezia, 1954.

Gabrielli, Aldo. *La vita di Marco Polo*. Firenze: Marzocco, 1959.

Larner, John. *Marco Polo and the Discovery of the World*. New Haven: Yale University Press, 1999.

Zorzi, Alvise. *Vita di Marco Polo veneziano*. Milano: Rusconi, 1982.

JAN POTOCKI
(1761–1815)

Kinga Eminowicz Galica

BIOGRAPHY

At the time of the birth of Jan Potocki to one of the most influential aristocratic families of Poland, the province of Podolia, where he spent his earliest child-hood, was a land of a rich mixture of traditions. Here the historical kingdom of Poland met with the Ottoman Empire and presented a unique mosaic of cultures where Poles, Ruthenians, Jews, Muslims, and Gypsies lived together. Potocki was educated in Lausanne, traveled tirelessly, and learned various languages, but wrote only in French, the common language of the aristocracy of his time.

After his schooling he joined the Knights of Malta in 1779, fought with pirate ships in the Mediterranean, and witnessed the slave trade. His career as a soldier quickly gave way to the concerns of an assiduous and irreverent mind. He was a true polyhistor, interested in mathematics, history, geography, anthropology, and linguistics. His astonishing breadth of knowledge produced works on the principles of chronology for the times prior to the olympiads, a description of a new machine to coin money, and an archeological atlas of European Russia. Among his scientific works, many are devoted to the study of exotic peoples and cultures (histories of Sarmatia and the peoples of Russia). He was particu-larly attracted by Islam, perhaps a reminiscence of his native Podolia impreg-nated by the Orient, where bilingual Koran books were circulated for the benefit of Polish Muslims. A passionate traveler, in addition to most European countries he reached such distant lands as Mongolia, Turkey, Egypt, and Morocco. Be-tween 1785 and 1787 he lived in Paris, coming under the influence of the philosophy of the Enlightenment. He frequented Madame Helvétius and Count Volney, whose work he greatly admired, and was hailed by the Jacobins as "citizen Count."

Returning to Poland in 1787, he became convinced of the Prussian danger for his native Poland in the face of the revolt against the Stathouder in the

Netherlands and the ensuing retaliation of the Prussian army. He was elected to the Polish Sejm (lower chamber of the Parliament), where he remained but a short time. With his own money he created the Free Press, which published many of his unorthodox political texts. In 1788 he created a sensation by flying over Warsaw with the French aeronaut Jean-Pierre Blanchard in a hot-air balloon. After the partition of Poland between Russia, Prussia, and Austria in 1795, Potocki lost interest in politics and even entered the service of the czar. In 1805 he was named chief scientist accompanying the official Russian mission to China. The mission was a diplomatic fiasco (reaching only present-day Ulan Bator in Mongolia), due in large part to a lack of understanding of the Chinese culture on the part of the Europeans. Potocki knew that more sensitivity to Chinese traditions and culture would have facilitated communication, and he was disappointed by the lack of success of a unique scientific opportunity. The behavior of the Russian diplomats may in fact have provoked his early withdrawal from active life.

He had begun writing his gigantic novel *Manuscrit trouvé à Saragosse* in 1797, during a trip to the Caucasus, and continued working on it until his death. (The *Manuscrit* was never published in its entirety during his lifetime.) He spent his last years in Uladovka in Podolia and took his own life in 1815. According to the legend, he killed himself with a bullet he had been polishing for quite some time.

MAJOR MULTICULTURAL THEMES

Potocki carefully documented his travel volumes, devoted to his trips to Turkey and Egypt, to Morocco, and to the steppes of Astrakhan and the Caucasus. A polyglot and an accomplished etymologist and linguist, he studied even the sacred languages, customs, and rites of the tribes of the Caucasus. He was fluent in Arabic and Turkish, and his linguistic interests coincide with the realization in Europe of the importance of the study of Oriental languages. He believed it important to know the "notions" of a people as much as or even more than its language. He attempted a sympathetic understanding of the Muslim world, believing that Arabs were the people who loved equality most of all and who hated despotism. In his opinion, the peoples of Asia had a naturally sweet and quiet temperament, and he yearned for a peaceful Asia, whose peoples lived closer to nature in quiet resignation, in contrast to the "arrogant pretensions" of Europeans.

Unlike most European travelers of his day, during his trips to Turkey and Egypt he focused almost exclusively on the Islamic aspects of the civilization, of which he was a great connoisseur, ignoring antiquity for the most part. His style is sober, as he strives at all times to avoid "exaltation." Each "voyage" ends with a fiction piece in the "Oriental" style, and the author seems very anxious to imitate that style faithfully. Spain occupied a special place in Potocki's work, serving as a background for his masterpiece *Manuscrit trouvé à*

Saragosse. He makes many valuable observations about the Sierra Morena mountains, their history, and their legends. The *Manuscrit* reflects the author's fascination with the rich culture of Andalusia, where various religions and cultures had coexisted and enriched each other. He visited Spain twice, in 1779 on his way back from Tunisia, when he journeyed through Andalusia and fell under its spell, and again in 1791, on his way to Morocco (through Gibraltar), whose ambassador to Spain he befriended in Madrid. He was given official permission to take back to Poland antiquities destined for the Polish king Stanislas August Poniatowski. In Tangier, where he was received by the sultan, he witnessed a retaliatory attack by Spain for an earlier Arab raid into Andalusia. Interested as much in everyday life in the streets as in court intrigues, he was often critical of the Arab ruling class, which allowed the population to live in poverty or starve while officials lived in wasteful opulence.

In Potocki's tolerant universe Jews, Arabs, Christians, and Gypsies live together more or less peacefully, and even the Inquisition, as described in the *Manuscrit* in his typically ironic manner, is somehow less menacing. This general coexistence allows him to paint a canvas of all the major religions and political systems of his time. The story begins during Napoleon's campaign in Spain, when an anonymous French officer discovers the manuscript during the siege of Saragossa. In this new *Decameron* characters tell each other their stories, each story opening up a new one, told by its characters. The link between the stories is loosely provided by Alphonse Van Worden, a young Walloon officer in the Spanish army who travels to Madrid in 1739. His typical Catholic upbringing is soon challenged by two Muslim sisters who appear in an abandoned inn at the stroke of midnight. No less intriguing are the sheikh des Gomelez, the rabbi Zadok ben Mamoun and his beautiful and learned daughter Rebecca, the Gypsy chief Pandesowna, the mathematician Velasquez, the Wandering Jew, and hundreds of other characters whose life stories illustrate all aspects of morality and bring forth all the knowledge of the day.

Potocki was fascinated with Judaism and during his visit to Morocco met with a local rabbi with whom he had a discussion about Talmudic commentaries made by Jews living in Poland, who, as he acknowledged with pride, were renowned the world over. A typical son of the Enlightenment, Potocki believed that writers and philosophers could change the world and that better understanding among various cultures would create a better world. During his trip to Morocco he commented that travelers ordinarily observe only with the lenses they bring from their own country and that they neglect entirely to readjust them in the countries they visit, a deplorable omission resulting in much poor observation.

SURVEY OF CRITICISM

Daniel Beauvois, in his introduction (1980) to Jan Potocki's *Voyages*, observes that his travel diaries are a marvelous disorder in which literature, politics, archeology, and ethnology mingle with the very life of the author. Gabriela Makowiecka in *On Polish-Spanish Roads* (1984, in Polish) underlines the fact that the *Manuscrit* serves as an example for many later stories and novels set in Spain, whose Romantic landscapes and fascinating history are an ideal background for Romantic literature. Larry Wolff in his review of the new English translation of the *Manuscrit*, "Love Beneath the Gallows," remarks that it testifies to a European vision whose cultural breadth and passionate intellectual inquiry have everything to offer to readers in Europe and America today.

SELECTIVE BIBLIOGRAPHY

Works by Potocki

Voyages. Ed. Daniel Beauvois. 2 vols. Paris: Fayard, 1980.
Manuscrit trouvé à Saragosse. Ed. René Radrizzani. Paris: José Corti, 1989.

Selective Studies of Potocki

Krakowski, Edouard. *Un Témoin de l'Europe des lumières, le comte Jean Potocki*. Paris: Gallimard, 1963.
Makowiecka, Gabriela. *On Polish-Spanish Roads* (in Polish). Kraków-Wroctaw: Wyd. Literackie, 1984.
Rosset, François. *Le Théâtre du romanesque: "Manuscrit trouvé à Saragosse" entre construction et maçonnerie*. Lausanne: L'Age d'Homme, 1991.
Triaire, Dominique. *Potocki: Essai*. Arles: Actes Sud, 1991.
Wolff, Larry. "Love Beneath the Gallows." *The New York Times Book Review*, January 14, 1996.

AMEEN F. RIHANI
(1876–1940)

Ameen Albert Rihani

BIOGRAPHY

Born in Freike, Lebanon, Ameen Rihani was one of six children and the oldest son of Ferris Rihani, who was engaged in raw-silk manufacturing. The father's commercial ambitions attracted him to America, where he sent his brother and Ameen first and then followed a year later. The twelve-year-old immigrant was placed in a school outside New York City, where he learned the rudiments of English. His father and uncle set up shop in a small cellar in lower Manhattan, using the boy's indispensable knowledge of English for the family business. His first readings in the cellar introduced him to William Shakespeare and Victor Hugo, but in time he became familiar with many of Europe's greatest writers. Endowed with a natural talent for eloquent speaking, in 1895 the stagestruck teenager joined a touring stock company headed by Henry Jewet (who later opened a theater in Boston), but during the summer of that year the troupe became stranded in Kansas City, Missouri, and the prodigal son returned to his father. He was determined, however, not to rejoin the business but to insist on following a regular course of study that would lead to a professional career. The choice having fallen on law, Rihani attended night school for a year, then entered law school in 1897. But a lung infection soon interrupted his studies, requiring his return to Lebanon to recover.

Back in his homeland he taught English in a clerical school in exchange for lessons in his native Arabic tongue. He read Arab and other Eastern poets and especially the forerunner of Omar Khayyam, Abul-ʿAlaʾ, some of whose quatrains he would translate into English and publish in 1903. Returning to New York in 1899, he joined several literary and artistic societies and contributed regularly to the Arabic weekly *Al-Huda*, published in New York. His first published work in Arabic was a treatise on the French Revolution entitled *Nubtha fith-thowra-t-Faranciya* (1902).

Back once again in his native mountains (1905), he spent the next six years writing two volumes of essays, a book of allegories, and a few short stories and plays in Arabic. He also lectured at the American University of Beirut and other institutions in Lebanon, as well as in the Syrian cities of Homs and Damascus, even while working along with other patriots for the liberation of his country from Turkish rule. *Ar-Rihaniyat* (1910) established him as a forward thinker and visionary, and the Egyptian media hailed him as "the Philosopher of Freike." *The Book of Khalid* (1911, illustrated by Kahlil Gibran) was the first English novel ever authored by a Lebanese Arab and was crowned by the New York Pleiades Club.

After his return to New York via Paris and London, where he met with artists and fellow writers, Rihani married an American artist, Bertha Case, in 1916. She was associated with the Matisse, Picasso, Cézanne, and Derain group that frequently worked together in Paris and the Midi.

Rihani met with Theodore Roosevelt in 1917 in connection with the Palestinian problem and two years later was invited to represent Arab interests at the Hague Peace Conference. He served as the only Near Eastern member at the Reduction of Armaments Conference in Washington, D.C., in 1921. Although he was intensely involved politically, he continued writing and publishing novels, essays, and poetry in both English and Arabic.

In 1922 he was then the only traveler, European or Arab, to have covered the whole Arabian territory in one trip. His encounters with the rulers of Arabia are described in *Muluk-ul 'arab* (1924), and between 1924 and 1932 he published no fewer than six best-selling works in English and Arabic related to three Arabian trips. During the last eight years of his life he continued to be active in his literary, political, and philosophical endeavors. He died at the age of sixty-four from multiple skull fractures sustained in a bicycle fall and was laid to rest in the Rihani family mausoleum at Freike.

MAJOR MULTICULTURAL THEMES

Upon once being asked the school from which he graduated, Rihani replied that he had been "a vagabond on the highway of education." Considered to be the founder of "Adab al-Mahjar" (emigrant literature), he was the first Arab to write and publish complete literary works in the United States, and his writings pioneered the movement of modern Arabic literature that played a leading role in the Arab Renaissance. He is also the founding father of Arab-American literature, his early writings marking the beginning of a body of literature that is Arab in its concerns, culture, and characteristics, English in language, and American in spirit and platform. His extensive writings about social traditions, religion, national politics, and philosophy bridged two different worlds. Influenced by the American poet Walt Whitman, Rihani introduced free verse into Arab poetry as early as 1905. His book of free verse, *Hutaf-ul Awdiya*, was published posthumously in 1955. The new verse form flourished in the Arab world and still maintains itself at the beginning of the twenty-first century.

On the political front, Rihani advocated and worked tirelessly toward East-West rapprochement, the liberation of Syria and Lebanon from the rule of the Ottoman Empire, and the countering of the rising influence of Zionism that sought to establish a state in Palestine. His travels throughout Arabia were for the purpose of meeting and becoming better acquainted with its rulers. Acquiring invaluable firsthand accounts of the character, vision, and belief of each of these rulers, he was able to present an alternative perspective to the Orientalist movement. He gave the world for the first time an objective and analytical description of all Arabia from an Arab point of view.

His major novel, *The Book of Khalid*, is, according to some scholars, the foundation of a new trend in Lebanese-American literature in particular and in Arab-American literature in general. The trend is toward wisdom and prophecy, which seeks to reconcile matter and soul, reason and faith, and East and West in an attempt to explicate the unity of religions and to represent the unity of the universe.

SURVEY OF CRITICISM

Kamal Yousuf el-Hajj, in his original and in-depth study of *The Philosophy of Ameen Rihani* (1963), sees in Rihani's writings reflections of Kant, James, Averrhoës, Comte, and Spinoza and attempts to map out the author's thought along the lines of rationalism and pragmatism, mysticism and idealism, agnosticism and existentialism. Rihani's severe criticism of the implementation of democracy in the New World is the subject of Raif Khoury's *Rihani and the Truth of American Democracy* (1948)—criticism that began in Rihani's *The Book of Khalid* and is studied in Elias Naddaf's "Sintesi culturali e strutture narrative in 'The Book of Khalid' di Amin Rihani" (1996). Naddaf highlights the multicultural theme of *The Book of Khalid*, in which narration is subordinated to Rihani's concept of the superman of East and West.

Carmen Ruiz Bravo-Villasante, in her book *Un testigo arabe del siglo XX: Amin al-Rihani en Marruecos y en España* (1993), studies the notion of travel as the author's personal quest to rediscover himself, his background, and the cultural and social orgins of his nation. Maria Tkhinvaleli, in "Travel in Modern Arabic Literature: The Example of Ameen Rihani (1991), considers the author to be the most representative figure in twentieth-century travel literature, extending the medieval tradition of Ibn Battuta and Ibn Jubayr while at the same time making a futuristic attempt to analyze the modern Arab citizen and his concerns. Walter E. Dunnavent III, in his 1991 doctoral dissertation "Ameen Rihani: Transcendentalism in an Arab-American Writer," demonstrates the relationship between Rihani's mysticism and love of nature and American Transcendentalism as manifested in the works of Emerson and Thoreau.

SELECTIVE BIBLIOGRAPHY

Works by Rihani

Nubtha fith-thowra-t-Faranciya. New York: Al-Huda Printing Press, 1902.
The Quatrains of Abu'l-'Ala'. New York: Doubleday, Page and Co., 1903.
Ar-Rihaniyat. Beirut: Scientific Printing Press, 1910.
The Book of Khalid. New York: Dodd, Mead and Co., 1911.
Muluk-ul 'arab. Beirut: Scientific Printing Press, 1924.
Qualb-ul 'Iraq. Beirut: Sader Printing Press, 1935.
Al-Maghreb-ul 'Aqsa (posthumous). Cairo: Al-Ma'aref, 1952.
Hutaf-ul Awdiya (posthumous). Beirut: Rihani Printing and Publishing House, 1955.
The Fate of Palestine (posthumous). Beirut: Rihani Printing and Publishing House, 1967.

Selective Studies of Rihani

Batti, Raphael. *Ameen Rihani in Iraq.* Baghdad: Dar As-Salam Press, 1923.
Bravo-Villasante, Carmen Ruiz. *Un testigo arabe del siglo XX: Amin al-Rihani en Marruecos y en España. 1939.* Madrid: Editorial CantArabia, Universidad Autónoma de Madrid, 1993.
Dunnavent, Walter Edward, III. "Ameen Rihani in America: Transcendentalism in an Arab-American Writer." Ph.D. dissertation, Indiana University, 1991.
El-Hajj, Kamal Yousuf. *The Philosophy of Ameen Rihani.* Beirut: Lebanese College Press, 1963.
Hussein, Husni Mahmoud. *Arab Travel Literature and the Model of Ameen Rihani.* Amman, Jordan: Arab Publishing and Distribution Agency, 1995.
Khatib, Hikmat Sabbagh. *Ameen Rihani: The Traveler of the Arabs.* Beirut: Beit Al-Hikma, 1970.
Khoury, Raif. *Rihani and the Truth of American Democracy.* Beirut: Dar Al-Kari' Al-Arabi, 1948.
Naddaf, Elias. "Sintesi culturale e strutture narrative in 'The Book of Khalid' di Amin Rihani." Master's thesis, University of Sassari, Sardinia, Italy, 1996.
Rafi'i, Toufik. *Ameen Rihani in Egypt: The Introducer of the Philosophy of the East to the West.* Cairo: Dar Al-Hilal, 1922.
Tkhinvaleli, Maria. "Travel in Modern Arabic Literature: The Example of Ameen Rihani." Doctoral dissertation, Tiblisi University, The Republic of Georgia, 1991.
Zeitouni, Latif. *Sémiologie du récit de voyage.* Beirut: Lebanese University Press, 1997.

RAINER MARIA RILKE
(1875–1926)

Luanne Frank

BIOGRAPHY

René Karl Wilhelm Johann Josef Maria Rilke was the only son of poorly matched parents who separated in little more than a decade, not soon enough to spare him the need to accomplish through writing the childhood that their difficulties and his mother's peculiarities denied him. His father, forced to retire early from a military career, became a minor railroad official and anticipated his military dreams' fulfillment by his son. The family was kept in circumstances inadequate to the expensive tastes of his merchant-class mother, who had been reared in a palace. Overextended social hopes, ostentatious religiosity, and desire for the daughter she had lost before Rilke's birth characterized her life with her young son. She took him on her frequent visits to shrines and churches and reared him partly as a girl, keeping him in long curls and lace-trimmed dresses—unsurprising for the time—but also giving him dolls to play with and playing games with him in which he took the role of a daughter. Two of the defining parental tendencies, his father's militarism and his mother's Christianity, he soon abandoned, rejecting both as forms of institutionalized authoritarianism. His mother's pretensions and her false coding of him did not diminish his love for women or erase his ideal of sublime femininity and motherhood; nor did his turn from the Christian God dissolve his yearnings toward divinity in some form.

He was sent to a military school (1886), which he compared with a Siberian prison from Dostoevsky's reminiscences of life in the death house, declaring that he would have been unable to achieve his life had he not suppressed all memories of those five brutal years at school. Writing and reading became a refuge and escape. His health possibly affected, he left in 1891 to study business in Linz. In 1895 he entered Prague's Karl Ferdinand University to read philosophy, changing shortly to law and leaving in the fall of 1896 to study art history in Munich. The Prague years saw him go from invisibility to prominence in the

provincial city. He published poems, essays, and stories in newspapers and journals, wrote plays (two were performed), and published three issues of a journal
and three volumes of poetry, winning supporters such as the poet Detlev von
Liliencron, the university professor August Sauer, and Valerie von David-
Rhonfeld, the fiancée who paid for publication of his first book and was the
first of a succession of women to provide friendship and financial assistance.

Rilke's multiculturalism could be said to have begun in Munich, where he
encountered literary models that challenged him. He became friends with fellow
writers, among them Jakob Wassermann, who introduced him to the work of
Turgenev (he had read Tolstoy in Linz) and the Dane Jens Peter Jacobsen. He
met and became inseparable from his most transformative personal influence,
Lou Andreas-Salomé, sometime beloved of Nietzsche and wife of Persianist
Karl Andreas. Born in St. Petersburg to a czarist general of French Huguenot
ancestry and a German mother, Lou was fourteen years Rilke's senior and for
the next three years occupied for him the roles of mistress, surrogate mother,
teacher, and relentless critic, and of dedicated counselor thereafter. With Lou
his work came of age; at her behest his name became Rainer; with her he began
the unceasingly renewed encounters with other cultures without which his works
as we know them are inconceivable.

After taking up residence in Berlin in the fall of 1897 to be near her, Rilke
embarked at her urging on the first of his ongoing travels: Italy became a never-
ending love affair. There he developed his early "seeing," laying the groundwork
for his "thing poems," a major departure from Western culture's 2,000-year-old
modes of relating to the world and a major poetic achievement. Opposed to
mere looking at, seeing takes place inside the world it apprehends and registers
its entities in their terms. In Florence in April and May 1889 he wrote the
important *Florenzer Tagebuch*.

In Munich with Lou, Rilke also embraced Russian culture, one of his most
pervasive experiences and an influence on all his major works. In the spring of
1899 Lou, Andreas, and Rilke visited Moscow and St. Petersburg; in May–
August Rilke and Lou returned, traveled the countryside to Kiev and the river
Volga to Kazan, Nizhny-Novgorod, and Yaroslavl, stayed with peasants, visited
Tolstoy at Yasnaya Polyana, visited monasteries and museums, met artists and
writers, and bought books and icons.

With this trip the affair cooled, the two parted, and Rilke visited painter
Heinrich Vogeler at the artists' colony at Worpswede, near Bremen, where he
investigated the artists' visual techniques and developed his seeing further. There
he met the sculptress Clara Westhoff, whom he married in April 1901. Without
income and unwilling to take commercial posts offered, he secured a commission to write on Worpswede artists (*Worpswede*, 1902). In August 1902 he moved
to Paris, another of his definitive cultural experiences, where Clara returned to
her studies with Rodin. Rilke, impressed by the old artist's resolute concentra-
tion on his art, completed a work on him (*Auguste Rodin*, 1903), perfected his
own seeing, and was engulfed by the enormous, frenetic, uncaring city, an in-

delible experience reflected most strongly in *Das Stundenbuch* (1905) and in *Die Aufzeichnungen des Malte Laurids Brigge* (1910).

In Italy Rilke was struck in Viareggio by one of the unpredictable, intensely creative periods punctuating his life, writing part 3 of the *Stundenbuch* in eight days. In 1904 he and Clara were in Rome, she with a sculpture stipend. There he began *Malte* and, inspired by classical culture, wrote "Orpheus. Eurydike. Hermes." He studied Danish to read Jacobsen and Kierkegaard and traveled to Scandinavia, another crucial cultural influence whose scenes appear in *Malte* and a number of poems. Taking up residence in Paris again, he completed there *Neue Gedichte* (1907–1908) and *Malte*, and met Princess Marie von Thurn und Taxis, one of his most generous patronesses. She introduced him to her powerful friends and opened to him her castles at Lautschin and Duino, the latter the site in early 1912 of the first *Duineser Elegien* (1923). In the same year he befriended the aging Eleonora Duse.

During the years 1910–11 he traveled in Germany, Italy, Czechoslovakia, and North Africa (Algiers, Tunis, and Egypt). In the winter of 1912–13 he went to the Toledo of El Greco, whose angels leave their un-Christian mark on the angels of the *Elegien*, and there, drawn to Islam by his North African travels, began reading the Koran. On a brief visit to Germany (July 1914) he was caught by the war; he was inducted into the Austrian army in 1916, was eventually mustered out with friends' assistance, and lived out the war in Munich.

Rilke left Germany for the last time in 1919 to give readings in Switzerland. Establishing himself in a diminutive thirteenth-century castle at Muzot, bought for him by a friend, he completed the elegies and a whole new work, *Die Sonette an Orpheus*, in 1922. In 1924 French poems flooded from his pen (*Vergers*, 1926; *Quatrains valaisans*, 1926), and he spent eight months in Paris. Returning to Muzot, he wrote his will and made burial arrangements. The year 1926 marked two important Russian friendships by correspondence: with Marina Cvetaeva, a poet in exile, and Boris Pasternak. On December 29 Rilke died of leukemia.

MAJOR MULTICULTURAL THEMES

Often considered the greatest poet writing in Germany since Goethe, Rilke was born in Prague to Austrian Catholics inhabiting the socially dominant but minority German community. He did not consider German-speaking lands his real or spiritual homes and for the most part did not regard German-Austrian culture of his time as an object of special interest, though its militaristic, authoritarian aspects marked him deeply as a child and adolescent. The culture and history of his Czech birthland interested him briefly, but his most intense inspirations were Russia, Italy and France, and Scandinavia. He traveled also in North Africa and Spain and embraced ancient classical and Eastern cultures that had affected Europe. He was a citizen of many lands, visiting, being inspired by, and then entering into the way of life and language of first one and then another culture, returning often, and retaining from each contents, moods, tones, attitudes, and ways of being, speaking, and seeing that recur in his work to the end. He achieved himself in the terms of the languages of the cultures that most absorbed him, publishing poems in the French he loved, writing them in Italian, translating voluminously from both these languages, and reading in Russian and Danish. His was a quintessential European multiculturalism that, though possessed of precedents in late Renaissance and Enlightenment aspirations, stands out, in a time of fortresslike nationalisms, as a remarkable individual achievement, one not yet normalized by widespread theories valorizing the embrace of Otherness.

His multiculturalism exhibits other dimensions than the supranational and supraethnic as well. He literally steps out of his times' paradigms for living and being, its conditions of possibility for thought and perception, into other worlds and ways of being, thinking, and seeing, which he both borrows and creates (though seldom theorizes), ways in which the subject, accomplishing its own deacculturizations, no longer dominates the object, and constricting cultural patterns are breached, allowing individuals new, unauthorized forms of individuality. One's ownmost ownness becomes for Rilke an integration of aspects of diverse cultures and of diverse conditions of possibility for being, and an absorption of and suffusion by them.

His chief themes are God and the nature of divinity; the artist and the nature of the artistic work; the nature of seeing; childhood lost and recovered; the rarified femininity of young girls; love and love unrequited; animals; nature and landscape; the past; and death. In his mature work these themes are suffused by his multicultural experiences. This work in fact begins only with his intense experiences of other cultures.

SURVEY OF CRITICISM

Anna Tavis (1994) surveys Rilke's Russian travels, Lou's "Russian" influence, and Rilke's relation to Russian writers of the time. Patricia Brodsky (1984) traces Russia throughout the oeuvre, and Constanze Schäfer (1996) examines the meaning of Russia and Germany for his life and work. Jean Gebser (1946) evaluates Spain's meaning for Rilke.

SELECTIVE BIBLIOGRAPHY

Works by Rilke

Tagebücher aus der Frühzeit (1898–1903). Frankfurt: Insel, 1973. [Contains *Florenzer Tagebuch.*]
Sämtliche Werke. 7 vols. Ed. Ernst Zinn. Frankfurt: Insel, 1955–1997.

Selective Studies of Rilke

Astrom, Paul. "Rilke in Schweden: Borgeby und Jonsered." *Blätter der Rilke-Gesellschaft* 16–17 (1989–1990): 129–39.

Brodsky, Patricia Pollock. *Russia in the Works of Rainer Maria Rilke*. Detroit: Wayne State University Press, 1984.

Dédéyan, Charles. *Rilke et la France*. 4 vols. Paris: SEDES, 1961–1963.

Fülleborn, Ulrich. "Rilkes schwedische Gedichte." *Blätter der Rilke-Gesellschaft* 16–17 (1989–1990): 156–66.

Gebser, Jean. *Rilke und Spanien*. Zürich: Oprecht, 1946.

Naumann, Helmut. "Rilke und Toledo." *Blätter der Rilke-Gesellschaft* 18 (1991): 111–32.

Schäfer, Constanze. *Projizierte Sehnsucht und schöpferische Begegnung*. Frankfurt: Peter Lang, 1996.

Storck, Joachim W. "Frankreich und die 'Latinität' in Rilkes Geschichtsbild." *Blätter der Rilke-Gesellschaft* 19 (1992): 11–23.

Tavis, Anna A. *Rilke's Russia: A Cultural Encounter*. Evanston, Ill.: Northwestern University Press, 1994.

Unglaub, Erich. "Rilke und das Dänemark seiner Zeit." *Blätter der Rilke-Gesellschaft* 16–17 (1989–1990): 92–118.

GEORGE SAND (AMANDINE AURORE LUCILE DUPIN)
(1804–1876)

Nadine Dormoy

BIOGRAPHY

The most important French woman writer of the nineteenth century, George Sand, is better known for her adventurous life and her friends and lovers than for her fifty-odd literary works, her voluminous autobiography, and the most extensive correspondence of her century, all of which make her one of the most prolific writers ever. During her lifetime she was acclaimed as a poet, as a Romantic, as a utopist, as a feminist, and as a socialist, but posterity remembers her first of all as a scandalous woman.

Born in Paris as Amandine Aurore Lucile Dupin, at the age of four she was taken by her father to Madrid, which was then occupied by the French army. It was an unforgettable experience for the young girl. But her father died shortly after returning to France, and she found herself in the uncomfortable position of being a one-woman melting pot, torn between her loving but unpredictable "low-class" mother and her domineering grandmother of German descent, who decided to supervise her education herself.

As a child, the future George Sand shared the life of the peasant children on her grandmother's estate at Nohant, in the central province of Berry, while receiving a fine education—a boy's education—under private tutors. As an adolescent she attended the "Couvent des Anglaises," an English-style Parisian boarding school.

Settling in Paris in 1831, she published her sensational first novel, *Indiana* (1832), under her new pen name, George Sand. In Henry James's words: "She wrote as a bird sings; but unlike most birds, she found it unnecessary to indulge, by way of prelude, in twitterings and vocal exercises; she broke out at once with her full volume of expression" ("George Sand," in *Literary Criticism*, 705–6).

The following year she produced her most innovative and controversial novel,

Lélia (1833). A philosophical and poetic discourse centered on the role of the intellectual woman in society, it was condemned by the Catholic Church as indecent and heretical and is still the cause of Sand's "scandalous" reputation.

Her philosophical search and metaphysical longings were best expressed in her next two novels, *Spiridion* (1838) and a second version of *Lélia* (1839). Most of her books explore the individual's dilemma in the face of authority and argue in defense of the weak, among whom women appear as particularly vulnerable, but often psychologically strong. Her peculiar sensitivity to nature and to the world of country folk, truly unique in French literature, was hailed by Dostoevsky, who saw in her social involvement the most fundamental message of Christ: "She identified herself, through her thinking and through her feelings, with one of the most fundamental ideas of Christianity, the respect of the human personality and of liberty. . . . Perhaps no other philosopher or writer in France at that time understood as deeply as she did that 'man does not live by bread alone' " (*Polnoe sobranie hudozestvennyh proizvedenii* [Leningrad: Izdatelstvo Akademii Nauk SSR, 1926–1930], II:311). By the end of the 1850s Sand had become known as "la Bonne Dame de Nohant," a hospitable and "bon vivant" old lady who received the visits of her many friends, such as Gustave Flaubert, Eugène Delacroix, Ivan Turgenev, Marie d'Agoult, and Franz Liszt, even while continuing to produce approximately two books per year.

Critics usually agree that *Lélia* and *Consuelo* (1842) are Sand's masterworks, but many consider her fabulous *Correspondance* and her remarkable *Histoire de ma vie* (1854–1855) to be her true masterpieces. The *Correspondance* is unique in volume, content, and time span of over fifty years. It includes letters to Eugène Delacroix, Giuseppe Mazzini, Louis Blanc, Pauline Viardot, Mikhail Bakunin, Sainte-Beuve, Lamartine, Balzac, Flaubert, Heinrich Heine, and even a very harsh letter to Karl Marx in defense of Bakunin. As early as 1835 Heine had expressed his admiration and had encouraged her to continue writing because he felt that she would "always do better than the others."

She died of intestinal obstruction at the age of seventy-two in Nohant and was buried there under a tree. Her house has recently been turned into a museum, and both grave and house receive numerous visitors each year.

MAJOR MULTICULTURAL THEMES

Sand's German and Swedish ancestry, her English educational experience, and her attachment to the rural life of the Berry countryside, combined with a passionate interest in music and art and attraction to Spain and Italy, produced a truly international frame of reference for all her works. The setting for *Lélia* is an unidentified, imaginary location strongly reminiscent of northern Italy, which she adored for its landscapes, its art, and its people. It is also to Italy, more precisely to Venice, that she traveled in the company of the poet Alfred de Musset, with whom she had a long, passionate, and stormy love affair. It was the Venice countryside that inspired the delightful series of semifunctional narratives known as *Lettres d'un voyageur* (1830–1836), one of the best examples of what she called the "wonderful harvest" that she had brought back from Venice and the Vicentine mountains.

The novel *Spiridion*, a long meditation on civilization, Christianity, and the French Revolution, was also set in northern Italy during the period of the Napoleonic Wars. *Spiridion* was completed in Majorca, where Sand and Frédéric Chopin spent the winter of 1838–39, at the beginning of their long liaison, during which both produced some of their finest works.

Sand admired and defended Garibaldi, proclaiming the sisterhood of the Italians and the French in their struggles and in their shared love of liberty. She did not like the Rome of her time, considering it a "hideous city," superposed on the "august ruins" of antiquity and making its own claim to fame through buildings "of uncommon dimension" that she deprecatingly calls "masterpieces of architectural science." She objected especially to carryovers of pagan idolatry into the "stupid faith" of the general populace and to the "vices of the cloister," especially "hatred and vengeance" (quoted in Poli, 332, 335).

In *Consuelo* and its sequel, *La Comtesse de Rudolstadt* (1843), both characters embody a long European tradition of philosophy and art. Consuelo is a young street singer from Venice who travels from Italy to Bohemia in search of her true love and her true vocation. She is confronted with the timeless enigmas of History, Faith, and Love in much the same way as would a wandering medieval knight.

Worthy of mention for their multicultural overtones are two later novels: *L'Homme des neiges* (1858), which is set in Sweden, and *Monsieur Sylvestre* (1865), which may be seen as a defense of interracial marriage in that it includes black and Jewish characters. Her own complex talent and personality was best analyzed by herself in *Histoire de ma vie*, of which the first 450 pages are devoted to the multicultural trajectory of her family: "Histoire d'une famille de Fontenoy à Marengo." Although it does not account for every event in her life, it gives her own interpretation of what she saw and did in many parts of the world in the course of 1,500 fascinating pages.

SURVEY OF CRITICISM

The most complete and most objective of the many biographies of George Sand remains the four-volume tour de force by Wladimir Karénine (a Russian woman's pseudonym), *George Sand: Sa vie et ses oeuvres* (1899–1926). She places her examination of Sand's life and works within a large European framework. The second-best biography in French is *George Sand* (1976) by Francine Mallet. Many other biographies, particularly Joseph Barry's *Infamous Woman: The Life of George Sand* (1976), discuss her travels and friendships.

In recent years the most interesting study of George Sand's works is Isabelle Hoog Naginski's *George Sand: Writing for Her Life* (1991). In chapter 5 Naginski explains fully the influences that came into play in *Consuelo*, and in chapter 9 she sees Sand's "Ars Poetica" as inspired by her multiple intellectual experiences. In a different vein, Annarosa Poli surveys the Italian influences in the life and works of Sand in *L'Italie dans la vie et dans l'oeuvre de George Sand* (1960). Basing her work on the most complete list of manuscripts available at the time from the Collection Spoelberch de Lovenjoul, from the French Bibliothèque nationale, and from libraries in Venice, Treviso, Florence, Rome, Genoa, Spoleto, and London, Poli sees in Italy Sand's "nostalgie de la seconde patrie," both in terms of art and in terms of politics.

The *Colloque de Cerisy* (1983) edited by Simone Vierne includes a study by Marie-Jacques Hoog of *Lettres d'un voyageur* as a "texte initiatique." The special issue of *Europe. Revue littéraire mensuelle* (March 1978) is devoted entirely to Sand and contains various contributors' discussions of Sand and Franco-Spanish relations, and Bakunin and Sand, as well as the text of a long, political letter from Bakunin to Sand dated 10 December 1848. Volume 31/32 of *Présence de George Sand* (March 1988) is titled "La Russie et George Sand" and is devoted to her reception in Russia.

SELECTIVE BIBLIOGRAPHY

Works by Sand

Lettres d'un voyageur (1830–1836). Paris: Garnier-Flammarion, 1971.

Lélia (1833). Paris: Garnier, 1986.

Spiridion (1838). Plan de la Tour, Var: Editions d'Aujourd'hui, 1976; Paris: Editions Champion, 1999.

Consuelo (1842); *La Comtesse de Rudolstadt* (1843). 3 vols. Meylan: Editions de l'Aurore, 1983.

Oeuvres autobiographiques. 2 vols. [Contains *Histoire de ma vie* (1854–1855), *Voyage en Espagne, Mon grand-oncle, Voyage en Auvergne, La blonde Phoebe, Nuit d'hiver, Voyage chez M. Blaise, Les couperies, Sketches and hints, Lettres d'un voyageur, Journal intime, Entretiens journaliers, Fragment d'une lettre écrite de Fontainebleau, Un hiver à Majorque, Souvenirs de mars-avril 1848.*] Ed. Georges Lubin. Editions de la Pléiade. Paris: Gallimard, 1970–1971.

Un hiver à Majorque. Palma de Mallorca: Editorial Clumba, 1951.

Correspondance. Ed. Georges Lubin. 26 vols. Paris: Garnier, 1964–1992.

Selective Studies of Sand

Barry, Joseph. *Infamous Woman: The Life of George Sand.* Garden City, N.Y.: Doubleday, 1976.

Cate, Curtis. *George Sand: A Biography.* New York: Avon, 1975.

Europe. Revue littéraire mensuelle. Paris. Special issue devoted to George Sand. March 1978.

James, Henry. *Literary Criticism.* New York: Literary Classics of the United States; distrubuted by Viking Press, 1984.

Karénine, Wladimir. *George Sand: Sa vie et ses oeuvres.* 4 vols. Paris: Librairie Plon, 1899–1926.

Mallet, Francine. *George Sand.* Paris: Grasset, 1976.

Naginski, Isabelle Hoog. *George Sand: Writing for Her Life.* New Brunswick, N.J.: Rutgers University Press, 1991.

Poli, Annarosa. *L'Italie dans la vie et dans l'oeuvre de George Sand.* Paris: Armand Colin, 1960.

Présence de George Sand: Bulletin de l'Association pour l'étude et la diffusion de l'oeuvre de George Sand (Echirolles) 31/32 (March 1988).

Vierne, Simone, ed. *Colloque de Cerisy.* Paris: SEDES, 1983.

DOMINGO FAUSTINO SARMIENTO
(1811–1888)

James O. Pellicer

BIOGRAPHY

Domingo Sarmiento's birthplace, San Juan de Cuyo, typical in its colonial atmosphere, had more churches than public buildings; friars and priests dominated all thought. It was one of the smallest villages in the Argentine territory that acquired independence under the name of the United Provinces of the South. Those of Sarmiento's relatives who were priests took control of his early education in a place where no school yet existed. One of his priest-uncles taught him to read and write and also trained him in the religious duties of a good altar boy.

Designated for the priesthood, the young Sarmiento failed to win a scholarship for entry into the Loreto Seminary. His needy family tried for one of the two presidential scholarships instituted in each province to foster liberal education and the propagation of new ideas in the country. Failing again, he decided to accompany another of his priest-uncles, José de Oro Albarracín, into exile. This priest, together with other clergy, had organized an armed revolution against the provincial governor but, suffering defeat, was deported from San Juan Province to a remote village in a neighboring state. With him went his protégé, the young Sarmiento.

For the next ten years Sarmiento stumbled through odd jobs in various places, including Chile. He struck up friendships with the fortunate young men from his province who had won the presidential scholarships and had completed their studies in Buenos Aires. Through them he came into contact with French thinking: the ideas of Victor Cousin and of the early French socialists, Saint-Simon and Pierre Leroux. Distant South America was invaded by French thought through journals, especially the *Revue encyclopédique*, which President Bernardino Rivadavia backed in order to reduce the power of priests and Scholastic philosophy throughout the United Provinces.

Manuel Quiroga Rosas and Vicente Fidel López, young lawyers of the so-called Generation of '37, were both close friends of Sarmiento and key influences in the evolution of his thought. Their graduation dissertations clearly revealed two well-defined stages of the incoming flow of French ideas. The first was embodied in Rosas's dissertation, "The Philosophical Nature of Right," in which he declared that individual right is the basis for society and cited Victor Hugo as a leader in the Romantic/liberal movement. The second stage was marked by the growing influence of Victor Cousin through articles in the *Revue encyclopédique*, as well as through his *Cours de l'histoire de la philosophie*, which found reflection in López's dissertation, "Memoria." Like López, Sarmiento thought that Civilization, whose center is the city, marches against Barbarism, emanating from the spirit of the "pampas." Accordingly, he battled the Argentinean government backed by the masses—a product, in his opinion, of the barbaric country lands.

Sarmiento dedicated himself not only to innumerable writings, but also to education, creating schools in Santiago, Chile (one with López as his codirector), as well as teaching language and reading skills at the local university. López's radical ideas, inspired by Voltaire, Hegel, and Montesquieu and espoused by Sarmiento and his friends, soon transcended the limits of academic discussion and entered the public domain. A popular uprising led to the closing of their school, as parents, horrified by the ideas expounded by the teachers' radicalism, withdrew their children. An article written by one of the radicals was burned in the public square by order of the Court of Justice. Sarmiento's violent anti-Argentine stance moved the Chilean government to silence him: he was sent to Europe with the task of studying school administration and teaching methodologies.

In England he heard of a famous American educator, Horace Mann. He changed his itinerary to make room for a country about which he knew very little and had never considered important in the development of Western education. The American experience (1845–48) shocked him and forever altered his way of thinking, especially after he made the acquaintance of Mann and his wife, Mary Peabody, in Boston. The result was his "Schools, Basis for the Prosperity and the Republic in the United States."

Argentinean political conditions allowed his return in 1852, and from Buenos Aires he propagated his new ideas through tireless journalism and book writing, the creation of newspapers and schools, and the holding of key political and government positions. In 1865 he was named ambassador to the United States, where he renewed his friendship with Horace Mann's widow, who translated into English his main work, *Facundo* (1845), a sociological interpretation of Argentine dictatorship. The University of Michigan conferred on him a doctorate *honoris causa* in June 1868. While he was still in the United States, he received the news of his election to the presidency of the Argentine nation. In his acceptance speech he declared his intention to convert the whole country into a school, and during his four years of tenure (1868–72) he worked with this purpose in mind. He was a national senator in 1875 and later accepted the position of superintendent of schools in the state of Buenos Aires. Returning to journalism, he became director of the newspaper *El Nacional* in 1878. He died in Paraguay in 1888 during the course of a scientific expedition.

MAJOR MULTICULTURAL THEMES

Thanks to Sarmiento's acquaintance with French culture, new ideas flowed into Argentina, bringing progress to the entire Southern Cone, achieved especially by the breakaway from the Church's domination of minds and the religious monopoly that characterized Hispanic-American life. Spanish-speaking intellectuals reacted bitterly against the subjection attempted by Pope Pius IX through his encyclical *Quanta cura* (1864), which declared all education as his domain and all disagreement devilish.

Through the French writers, German and Italian authors also became known in the Latin American countries. Victor Cousin introduced the ideas of the German philosopher Hegel both to France and to South America, while the French writer Jules Michelet introduced those of the Italian philosopher Giambattista Vico. The march of History toward Civilization and the "new science" were the subjects of daily discussion among the young Argentinean intellectuals. Of course, the theme of those who were less adapted to the march toward the light of civilization also came into focus, and the concepts of "superior" and "inferior" races were born. The step to a thesis favoring suppression of less fit groups was short and was taken before Darwin appeared in the history of ideas. In 1844 Sarmiento wrote in Santiago's daily newspaper, *El Progreso*:

There is no possible amalgam between a savage people and a civilized one; where this one puts his foot . . . , the other one must abandon existence. . . . Instead of America remaining abandoned to the savages, incapable of progress, She is occupied today by the Caucasian race, the most perfect, the most intelligent, the most beautiful that populate the earth; . . . the strong races exterminate the weak ones; the civilized peoples supplant the savages in the possession of the land. This is providential and useful, sublime and great. (*Obras completas*, 2:218).

Nevertheless, during the last stage in the evolution of his ideas, when he was in America with Horace Mann, he corrected his original French/German synthesis. Although he never entirely ceased being a racist, believing that the Bible forbade any relationship with the children of Canaan (in this case meaning Indians, gauchos, Africans, and so on), henceforth he was convinced that education was the key to the correction of social ills and the opening of the way to progress in all nations. He dedicated himself to developing the education of every Argentinean and to attracting valuable immigrants, professionals, and scientific scholars for the betterment of the country.

SURVEY OF CRITICISM

Dithyrambic critics, naïvely accepting the autobiographies as infallible, omit the fact that Sarmiento was on one side of the Argentine civil war and thus was responsible for the death of numerous persons, many of whom were summarily executed, and that he wrote his two autobiographies in order to justify his own actions and those of his allies. The best North American work on Sarmiento is Allison W. Bunkley's excellent *The Life of Sarmiento*, which nonetheless depicts Argentina as a backward country, composed on the one hand of a very small number of valuable people, and on the other hand of immense nothingness— the violent hordes of wanton gauchos. Bunkley also bases his work on the historical position adopted by Sarmiento and his political group to justify their actions. Numerous scholarly works appeared on the occasion of the 1988 centennial of Sarmiento's death. Paul Verdevoye published a Spanish version of his French classic in 1988: *Domingo Faustino Sarmiento, educar y escribir opinando (1839–1852)*. The best biography remains that of Manuel Gálvez, *Vida de Sarmiento* (1952), while the honesty of Alberto Palcos in his various works is highly appreciable: harsh utterances by Sarmiento, quietly omitted from the edition of his *Obras completas*, find a place in Palcos's writings (*Sarmiento: La vida, la obra, las ideas, el genio*, 1929, and *El "Facundo": Rasgos de Sarmiento*, 1934), thus protecting for scholars texts that otherwise would have been difficult to find. Raúl A. Orgaz's thorough studies on Sarmiento and his epoch (e.g., *Sarmiento y el naturalismo histórico*, 1940) are indispensable.

SELECTIVE BIBLIOGRAPHY

Works by Sarmiento

Obras completas de Sarmiento. 52 vols. Buenos Aires: Editorial Luz del Día, 1948– 1956.

Facundo. Ed. Alberto Palcos. Buenos Aires: Ediciones Culturales Argentinas, 1962.

Selective Studies of Sarmiento

Bunkley, Allison W. *The Life of Sarmiento* (1952). New York: Greenwich Press, 1969.
Gálvez, Manuel. *Vida de Sarmiento*. Buenos Aires: Editorial Tor, 1952.
Orgaz, Raúl A. *Sarmiento y el naturalismo histórico*. Córdoba, Argentina: Imprenta Argentina, 1940.
Palcos, Alberto. *El "Facundo": Rasgos de Sarmiento*. Buenos Aires: El Ateneo, 1934.
———. *Sarmiento: La vida, la obra, las ideas, el genio*. Buenos Aires: El Ateneo, 1929.
Pellicer, Jaime O. *El "Facundo," significante y significado*. Buenos Aires: Editorial Trilce, 1990.
Verdevoye, Paul. *Domingo Faustino Sarmiento, educar y escribir opinando (1839–1852)*. Buenos Aires: Editorial Plus Ultra, 1988.

VICTOR SEGALEN
(1878–1919)

Michael Bishop

BIOGRAPHY

Born in the great Breton naval center of Brest, Victor Segalen pursued medical studies in Bordeaux and became a naval doctor whose missions took him to Tahiti (where he acquired the sculptures that had adorned the cabin of the just-deceased Gauguin) and, repeatedly, to China (1909–13, 1914–15, 1917–18). His medical thesis bore upon neurosis in contemporary literature and appeared in 1902, the same year in which his exploration of symbolist poetics resulted in the publication of his compact essay *Les Synesthésies et l'école symboliste*. These early years led to relations with Huysmans, Saint-Pol Roux, and Remy de Gourmont and contact with Debussy (via the latter's noticing one of his short stories, *Dans un monde sonore*, 1907), for whom Segalen wrote a dramatic libretto, *Orphée roi*, never set to music and not published until two years after Segalen's death.

The 1907 *Les Immémoriaux*, along with the 1912 *Stèles* and the 1916 *Peintures*, constitutes one of the few major writings appearing in his short lifetime. Like the posthumous *Hommages à Gauguin* and a 1904 piece also on Gauguin, *Les Immémoriaux* (published under the pseudonym Max Anély) stems from his Polynesian experience (1902–4). The Chinese experience was even more powerful and enduring, however, though psychologically somewhat differently centered. He traveled extensively throughout China and into Tibet and took part in archeological expeditions with Gilbert de Voisins and Jean Lartigue. He did wartime service as a doctor on the Belgian front and in Brest in 1915–16 before being sent back to China in 1917. His deep affinitary fascination for the "land" of China and Tibet, as well as their art, their spirituality, the debate he feels constantly at the center of his meditation on them between the real and the imaginary, existence and essence—all of this is reflected in posthumous works such as *René Leys* (1922), *Odes* (1926), *Equipée* (1929), *L'Art funéraire à l'époque des Han* (1935), *Le Fils du ciel* (1975), and *Thibet* (1979). He returned to Brest in 1918. His death, in the Breton forest of Huelgoat, is varyingly attributed to accident and suicide, both possibly related to a mysterious illness recently contracted.

MAJOR MULTICULTURAL THEMES

Neither Segalen's writing inspired by his early Polynesian stay and discovery of the threatened enchantments of Maori culture, nor his major works arising from the long fascination with the China and Tibet physically encountered and spiritually meditated from 1909 on, reveal an inclination to offer documentary realism, somewhat stereotypical touristic impression, on a certain manifestly colonial "exoticism" for a wide Parisian and French readership. His oeuvre as a whole—even *Les Immémoriaux*, which does provide a more stable ethnographic portrait, a text of wilful conservation of Polynesian myths and spiritual and psychological modes of being—tends to the hermetic, the idiosyncratic, an esotericism that is not aesthetically coquettish or merely intellectualizing but deeply engaged in a search, through the contact of self with the other, otherness, diversity, difference, of what lies still further beyond (but deeply within) them both: the intuitable, yet unsayable Other.

For Segalen, the ascetic, mental, psychic, "religious" path of "essential exoticism" must orient itself toward some "Attaining high and . . . / Being" (*Thibet*, 67), and neither realism nor symbolism suffices. The influence of the Chinese Tao, Hinduism's Brahman and atman, even (as one critic has suggested) of Parmenides' unitary philosophy, is likely, and certainly broad affinities exist. The early *Synesthésies et l'école symboliste* appropriates for science and medicine the sensory experience and ontological intuitions of symbolist poets such as Baudelaire and Rimbaud while contesting them also in some measure, but it is not until *Les Immémoriaux* appears that the writing of Segalen begins to find its true mission and orientation in the exploration of an "aesthetics of the diverse" and yet a further budding sense of Baudelaire's "tenebrous and profound unity" beyond (yet, most essentially, through) the mystery of honored difference.

His central work, *Stèles*, offers a set of ritualized, lapidary, austerely lyrical poems inspired both concretely and symbolically by the many stelae of China with their dense though often-limpid inscriptions cut into stone, offering "body and soul, total being." Each stela/poem constitutes a celebratory monument, at once to itself and beyond itself, to the ineffable, the "yet-to-come." Dedicated to Paul Claudel, whom he had already met in China and who had published *Connaissance de l'Est* in 1900, *Stèles*, like the stelae scattered across the land in the various "directions" that structure the volume, at once revels in the cultural specificities of place, custom, belief, and perception and leaps beyond them, exploring the serene tensions of "Here" and "There," of self and that enigmatic yet spiritually emblematic *She*, whose felt presence and dreamed, meditated essence permeate Segalen's consciousness. "I owe to her out of nature and destiny the strict relation of distance, extremeness and diversity" (73). *Stèles* thus is a book whose experience and intentions penetrate the land of the other that he seems strangely to have loved almost for itself, and reaches through to a radiance of the nonutilitarian, the nonpresent, an elsewhere beyond self and other, a "Forbidden Violet City" where, beyond knowledge, "the devastating torrent" might be experienced.

The model of *Stèles*, at once profoundly acculturated and acultural, persists in his underrated 1916 *Peintures*, which offers a wonderful series of antidescriptive meditations cum commentaries on very largely imaginary Chinese art works. *René Leys*—like most of the rest of Segalen's work, appearing posthumously—is a book centered upon ambiguity, the tensions of truth and falsehood, being and appearance, and constitutes also a reflection on its own creation. Set in the China of his first visit, it is the book that incited the sinophile Simon Leys to attribute to himself the name of its hero.

The other two most celebrated books are *Odes* and the remarkable *Thibet*. The rhythm of the Chinese five- or seven-syllable line is used for *Odes*, which also continues to be inspired by ancient and, at the time, still-continuing myth and spirituality. Like his stelae/poems, Segalen sees his *Odes* as "temporary, perishable surgings," yet, via their very mortal precariousness, as articulations or "songs" looking out through a "mystical screen" upon the "unsayable." Elegy, rooted in the ephemeral and the relative, thus combines with an energy that sings of "something infinitely Other." The "commentary" that accompanies each ode may offer cultural and conceptual contextualization of a sort, but it cannot pretend, any more than the ode itself, to speak the "Upper Place," to attain to the esoteric (if also "real," truly intuited) heart of being's otherness, filtered though it may be through the Chinese cultural, spiritual sieve.

Thibet certainly offers a poetry of place, of other cultural, spiritual space; the high peaks of this already intrinsically extraordinary land are escalated, physically gazed upon; its inhabitants, peasants and mystics alike, are seen as immersed in an atmosphere of desirable difference. Yet Tibet's diverseness, its alterity, its exotic though available "beyondness" still remain for Segalen secondary to their emblematicalness. The Tibetan, like the Chinese, experience, sensory, emotional, and spiritual, powerful as it is, thus leads Segalen to a larger sense still of "paradise without apostle," a diversity cum unity "not of outside but of inside." The mystical, unifying feminine force Segalen projects through his Tibetan/Chinese experience is, ultimately, "divine beyond the world and more diverse than your peaks" (62).

The unfinished *Le Fils du ciel*, finally, is a narrative cum chronicle, fueled both by history and imagination, centered on the life of the early-twentieth-century Chinese emperor Kuang-Hsu. It is a tale of dispossession and nostalgia, passion, violence, and madness, but treats too of a search for ideality, for secret, inner truth.

SURVEY OF CRITICISM

Jean-Louis Bédouin's critical introduction (1963) to a personal choice of texts offers a global sense of both the multicultural and extracultural factors at play in Segalen's work. Simon Leys (1989) gives an interesting and lively assessment of Segalen's "aesthetic of the diverse" and the particularities of his "exoticism." Kenneth White (1979) evaluates the logic of "travel," of the movement from self to "other"—here to "there." Michael Taylor (1983) also seeks to present a coherent assessment of Segalen's journeys and analyze the motivation essential to them. Anne-Marie Grand's compact but elegant study (1990) offers many insights into Segalen's Oriental explorations, erudition, and creative exploitation, while centering much of her book upon a poetics of absence, desire, void, and a strictly inner quest for the self's otherness.

SELECTIVE BIBLIOGRAPHY

Works by Segalen

Les Synesthésies et l'école symboliste (1902). Montpellier: Fata Morgana, 1981.
Les Immémoriaux (1907). Paris: Plon, 1956.
Stèles (1912). Collection Poésie. Paris: Gallimard, 1973.
Peintures (1916). Paris: Gallimard, 1983.
René Leys (1922). Paris: Gallimard, 1971.
Odes (1926). Collection Poésie. Paris: Gallimard, 1986.
Le Fils du ciel. Paris: Flammarion, 1975.
Thibet. Paris: Mercure de France, 1979.

Selective Studies of Segalen

Bédouin, Jean-Louis. *Victor Segalen.* Collection Poètes d'Aujourd'hui. Paris: Seghers, 1963.
Bouillier, Henry. *Victor Segalen.* Paris: Mercure de France, 1961.
Courtot, Claude. *Victor Segalen.* Paris: Henry Veyrier, 1984.
Germain, Gabriel. *Victor Segalen: Le voyageur des deux routes.* Mortemart: Rougerie, 1982.
Grand, Anne-Marie. *Victor Segalen: Le moi et l'expérience du vide.* Paris: Méridiens Klincksieck, 1990.
Jouve, Pierre Jean. "Avant-Propos." In Victor Segalen, *Stèles, Peintures, Équipée.* Paris: Plon, 1970.
Leys, Simon. "L'Exotisme de Segalen." In Victor Segalen, *Stèles.* Paris: La Différence, 1989.
Manceron, Gilles. *Segalen.* Paris: Lattès, 1991.
Taylor, Michael. *Vent des royaumes; ou, Les voyages de Victor Segalen.* Paris: Seghers, 1983.
White, Kenneth. *Segalen: Théorie et pratique du voyage.* Lausanne: Eibel, 1979.

PERCY BYSSHE SHELLEY
(1792–1822)

A.L. Rogers II

BIOGRAPHY

Percy Shelley was indeed a multicultural writer. Following expulsion from Oxford for his part in writing *The Necessity of Atheism* (1811), he traveled constantly throughout his native Britain and the European continent, living as a virtual nomad in Italy from 1818 until his death in 1822 and reading widely in English, Greek, Latin, French, Spanish, German, and Italian. He was keenly sensitive to his environment, and his greatest works were inspired by specific experiences in his travels. Excepting *Queen Mab* (1813), *Alastor* (1816), and *Laon and Cythna* (1817), all of his major poems were written abroad.

Shelley was raised in Sussex, the son of a member of Parliament and grandson of a baronet. The habitual nomadic roaming began in earnest when Shelley eloped to Scotland in 1811 with sixteen-year-old Harriet Westbrook. After brief stays in Edinburgh, York, and Keswick, the couple visited Dublin in 1812, where Shelley distributed pamphlets urging Catholic emancipation and Irish independence, and where he tried unsuccessfully to establish a society of radical philanthropists. The impact of this Irish visit was profound: after witnessing the misery of the Dublin poor, Shelley dedicated himself to warring against political, economic, and religious tyranny worldwide. He visited Wales twice in 1812–13, intending to reside there, but financial difficulties prevented his staying permanently. At Tremadoc he canvassed support for a land-reclamation project, and after a (possibly imagined) attempt on his life the Shelleys returned to Ireland and then for a year to England.

His second elopement, with Mary Wollstonecraft Godwin in 1814, excited outrage in England that was heightened by Harriet's 1816 suicide and a failed Chancery suit for custody of their two children in 1817. Specious accusations of romantic involvement with Mary's stepsister, Claire Clairmont, and others followed Shelley all his life, which, together with harsh reactions against his radical politics and opposition to formal religion, made him feel himself the object of "social hatred" in England. This second elopement spurred a journey through France, Switzerland, Germany, and Holland, recounted in his and Mary's *History of a Six Weeks' Tour* (1817). Shelley's response to the destruction he saw in the wake of Napoleon's defeat in France is related in the preface to *Laon and Cythna*, which was catalyzed by a later visit to Versailles. The 1814 trip to the Continent and a three-month stay in 1816 with Lord Byron in Switzerland impressed upon Shelley the beauty and power of nature, and from the magnificence of the Alps he drew the belief in an elusive spiritual presence in Nature described in "Hymn to Intellectual Beauty" and "Mont Blanc" (1817).

Though he had hoped to establish a home in England, harassing debts and poor health led Shelley and Mary, now his wife legally, to move in March 1818 to Italy, which he calls in *Julian and Maddalo* (1818) the "paradise of exiles." Here more than ever the Shelleys traveled incessantly between Bagni di Lucca, Venice, Este, Rome, Livorno, Florence, and Naples. Their restlessness was increased by the deaths of two of their children. In this Italian period, marked by sadness though it was, Shelley produced his most important poems: *The Mask of Anarchy* (1819), *Prometheus Unbound* (1820), *Epipsychidion* (1821), and *Adonais* (1821), among others. From 1820 to 1822 the Shelleys settled in and around Pisa. Though he was contemplating a move to India, Spain, or Greece, San Terenzo was his final place of residence. He died at age twenty-nine in a sailing accident.

MAJOR MULTICULTURAL THEMES

While abroad Shelley interacted mainly with a small circle of English compatriots. In truth, he often found Europeans "gross and uncultured." Typically, though, he considered shortcomings in people of other cultures a product of their political oppression, and in his writing he is clearly the outspoken champion of the oppressed in all cultures. Some of his works focus on the oppression of the individual. Beatrice murders her father in *The Cenci* (1819) to save her family from the evil Count Francesco, who rapes his daughter and exults in the deaths of his sons. *Epipsychidion* (1821), inspired by Emilia Viviani, a friend of the Shelleys kept by her father in a Pisan convent and forced to marry against her wishes, laments the restrictive conventional morality that "enslaves" marriage partners and prohibits their pursuit of love outside marriage. More often Shelley's work encourages the liberation of whole cultures from systematic oppression. *A Philosophical View of Reform* (first published in 1920) and *A Defence of Poetry* (1821) describe poets as the "unacknowledged legislators of the world," suggesting that innovative, "poetic" thinkers effect progressive reform in religious, political, social, and personal thought. Laon speaks for Shelley the poet-legislator in *Laon and Cythna*: "I will arise and waken / The multitude" (784–85) . . . "and / Fill the world with cleansing fire" (787–88) using "words which [are] weapons" (842) drawn from a "mine of magic store" (841). That he meant to rouse "the world" literally is evident from the outset of his public career. As he says in *An Address to the Irish People* (1812), "Those are my brothers and my countrymen, who are unfortunate" (215), and he declares that reform in Ireland is merely a starting point, that his ultimate goal is "universal emancipation" (237), an ideal for which he wrote and fought all his life.

A Philosophical View of Reform traces the overthrow of tyrannical rule throughout history in India, China, Egypt, and the European continent, a pattern echoed and expanded in the 1820 "Ode to Liberty." "Lines Written among the Euganean Hills" (1818) describes the symbolic death of Italy, which lies "mouldering" under Austrian rule, the light of its once-great culture "Trampled out by Tyranny." Revolution in Naples and rumors of Austrian armies gathering to quell it prompted "Ode to Naples" (1820), conveying Shelley's hope that the Neapolitans would "henceforth ever . . . be, free, / If Hope, and Truth, and Justice can avail," and urging other Italian states to rebel as well (62–63). "An Ode, Written October, 1819" encourages rebellion in Spain, and after the Spanish did revolt, "Ode to Liberty" (1820) calls upon all Europeans to follow Spain's example in liberating itself from tyranny. News of the Greek war for independence in 1821 inspired the last work published in Shelley's lifetime, *Hellas* (1822), which depicts the crumbling Turkish dominion over the Greeks and predicts the rebirth of Greece's ancient greatness in liberty.

While Shelley did recognize specific differences between cultures, ultimately he believed that the differences were superficial, that common bonds of humanity united people of all cultures in more significant kinship. The 1812 *Proposals for an Association* declares that the greatest occasions for philanthropy are those that "make the hearts of individuals vibrate not merely for themselves, their families, and their friends, but for posterity, for a people; till their country becomes the world, and their family the sensitive creation" (253). To this end, he prays in "Ode to the West Wind" (1820) that his poetry will spread his "thoughts over the universe / Like withered leaves to quicken a new birth" (63–64), sounding "The trumpet of a prophecy!" (69). He enjoyed little popularity during his lifetime, but as recognition of his poetic genius grew over the nineteenth and twentieth centuries, and as one after another of his ideas for "radical" reform have been historically borne out, it is clear that his prayers to the West Wind were answered. Shelley was indeed one of the "unacknowledged legislators of the world" (*A Defence of Poetry*, 140).

SURVEY OF CRITICISM

P.M.S. Dawson (1980) examines Shelley's Irish experiences, while Alan Weinberg (1991) offers a thorough study of Shelley's absorption of Italian history, literature, and culture. Mark Kipperman (1991) mediates between views of *Hellas* as purely utopian idealism and as historically grounded propaganda. Shelley's treatment of Egypt and India is examined by Michael Rossington (1991). Betty Bennett and Stuart Curran (1996) have edited papers from nine nations presented at the Keats-Shelley Association of America's international conference celebrating the two-hundredth anniversary of Shelley's birth, addressing such multicultural concerns as Shelley's assimilation of Greek cultural history, the role of the poet in the "ideology of the nation," Shelley's impact on Italian literature, his Eurocentric views on Eastern thought, and the viability of Shelleyan radicalism in twentieth-century India, East Germany, and South Africa.

SELECTIVE BIBLIOGRAPHY

Works by Shelley

An Address to the Irish People (1812). *Proposals for an Association* (1812). In *The Complete Works of Percy Bysshe Shelley*, vol. 5, 215–47; 253–68. Ed. Roger Ingpen and Walter E. Peck. New York: Gordian, 1965.

Laon and Cythna (1817). In *The Complete Poetical Works of Percy Bysshe Shelley*, vol. 2, 97–273. Ed. Neville Rogers. Oxford: Clarendon Press, 1972.

"Ode to Liberty" (1820), "Ode to Naples" (1820), and *Hellas* (1822). In *Shelley: Poetical Works*, 603–10, 616–20, 446–82. Ed. Thomas Hutchinson. London: Oxford University Press, 1967.

A Defence of Poetry (1840). In *The Complete Works of Percy Bysshe Shelley*, vol. 7, 109–40. Ed. Roger Ingpen and Walter E. Peck. New York Gordian, 1965.

A Philosophical View of Reform (first published 1920). In *The Complete Works of Percy Bysshe Shelley*, vol. 7, 3–55. Ed. Roger Ingpen and Walter E. Peck. New York: Gordian, 1965.

Selective Studies of Shelley

Bennett, Betty T., and Stuart Curran, eds. *Shelley: Poet and Legislator of the World.* Baltimore: Johns Hopkins University Press, 1996.

Dawson, P.M.S. "Shelley in Ireland." In *The Unacknowledged Legislator: Shelley and Politics*, 134–65. Oxford: Clarendon Press, 1980.

Kipperman, Mark. "History and Ideality: The Politics of Shelley's *Hellas*." *Studies in Romanticism* 30, no. 2 (1991): 147–68.

Rossington, Michael. "Shelley and the Orient." *Keats-Shelley Review* 6 (1991): 18–36.

Weinberg, Alan M. *Shelley's Italian Experience.* London: Macmillan, 1991.

GEORGES SIMENON
(1903–1989)

Lucille Frackman Becker

BIOGRAPHY

Georges Simenon, the most widely published author of the twentieth century, was born in Liège, Belgium, the older son of petit bourgeois parents. His mother, of mixed German and Dutch parentage, came from an unstable family undermined by alcoholism, a form of self-destruction ubiquitous in his work. His mother was the major influence on his life and work; she was at the heart of his fear of loss of identity through female domination. Her psychological inheritance determined his anxiety and his lifelong search for equilibrium. Writing was to be a way of purging these inner demons. While he revolted against his mother, he revered his father, the youngest child of a large Walloon family, who inspired his famous detective hero, Maigret.

Simenon's novels are inseparable from his biography. Even as a small child he listened, observed, and absorbed everything around him, particularly fascinated by the dark side of life. He perceived from the very beginning that the human condition was characterized by dishonesty, fear, and guilt, and these were to lie at the heart of his fictional universe. He used his prodigious memory as an encyclopedia, borrowing from it a name, a tic, a gesture, an atmosphere. Taking this as a starting point, he went beyond it, integrating it into a new reality, the novel.

He became a reporter in 1919 on the *Gazette de Liège*, a conservative Catholic newspaper, where he remained until December 1922. While his childhood provided the themes and characters and many of the plots of his novels, his experience as a journalist broadened his knowledge of people and different social milieux; the situations he encountered provided material for his novels. Journalism was also an excellent apprenticeship for the future novelist in other ways; it taught him to grasp the essential detail and to write quickly.

Determined to achieve success as a writer, he left Liège for Paris in 1922.

Paradoxically, the city he fought to escape became the past to which he kept returning, reconstituting it through sensory evocations. But even more than Liège in and of itself, it is the original experience of provincial insularity, of a stifling and unbearable milieu that he acquired there and internalized in a universally applicable model.

In Paris in the early 1920s he began submitting stories to the newspaper *Le Matin*, while also writing pulp fiction. The 190 popular novels that he wrote under seventeen pseudonyms from 1921 to 1934 can be divided into three basic categories—crime, love, and adventure. These potboilers were, for Simenon, an apprenticeship in his craft. They were followed by a series of detective novels featuring the Parisian policeman Commissaire Maigret, which were designed to serve as a bridge between the potboilers and the more serious literary efforts to which he aspired and for which he did not consider himself ready. Yet throughout his career he always returned to Maigret in one hundred novels and short stories, often trying out in them themes and situations he would use later in his more serious works. In the so-called Maigrets he used the conventions of the detective novel to create a new type of fiction, transforming its rules and techniques to express some of the most important themes of the twentieth-century novel: guilt and innocence, solitude and alienation. In working toward what he would later define as the "pure" or quintessential novel, Simenon brought a crucial innovation to the detective novel—he sought not so much to unmask and punish the criminal as to understand him.

In all, he wrote under his own name a total of 358 novels and short stories, both detective ("Maigrets") and hard, problem novels ("romans durs"), 25 autobiographical works, 30 series of articles for the French press, and a ballet scenario. The constant subject of his "romans durs," the novels on which his literary reputation is based, like that of the "Maigrets," is the violent nature of aberrant human behavior. Like the prototypal crime novel, the "romans durs" are novels of deviance. The deviant individual is one who differs markedly, for example, in social, adjustment or sexual behavior, from what is considered normal or acceptable to the group of which he is a member. Simenon's modernity lies in his recognition that the deviant, the criminal of one sort or another, is an appropriate and even representative man for our age.

Until the outbreak of World War II he traveled in France and northern and eastern Europe, gathering material for articles and novels. He had traveled throughout Africa in 1932 and three years later took an extended trip to Panama, Colombia, Ecuador, Tahiti, the Galapagos, Fiji, the New Hebrides, Turkey, and Egypt. He used a few of these landscapes as background for several of his novels, *Les Clients d'Avrenos* (Turkey), *Quartier nègre* (Panama), *Le Coup de lune* (Gabon), *45° à l'ombre* (sea route from Matadi to Bordeaux), *L'Aîné des Ferchaux* (Congo, Panama), *Ceux de la soif* (the Galapagos), *Touriste de bananes* (Tahiti), *Long cours* (Panama and Tahiti), *Le Passager clandestin* (Tahiti), and *Le Blanc à lunettes* (Belgian Congo). Rather than exotic adventures, they just became settings for the presentation of his usual characters and themes. He remarked that local color exists only for people who are passing through and that he hated being a tourist, that he was not seeking the sense of being abroad. On the contrary, he was looking for what was similar in men, the constant.

During the German occupation of France during World War II he continued to write, enjoy his family, and fraternize with members of influential Franco-German society. Eight of his novels were adapted for the cinema during these years. Concerned with the risk of being tried as a collaborator after the war, he left France for North America in 1945. He traveled throughout the United States and wrote several novels based on his travels as well as a series of articles, "L'Amérique en auto." In 1950 he settled in Connecticut. The nine novels situated on the East Coast of the United States—*Un nouveau dans la ville, La Mort de Belle, L'Horloger d'Everton, La Boule noire, La Main, Maigret à New York, Trois chambres à Manhattan, Feux rouges, Les Frères Rico*—contain his major themes of solitude and alienation, but introduce a new one that he found to be distinctly American, the overwhelming need to belong. He returned to Europe in 1955 and, in 1957, settled in Switzerland, where he lived until his death.

MAJOR MULTICULTURAL THEMES

In 1932 Simenon took a long trip in Africa from Cairo to Matadi financed by the weekly paper *Voilà*. In several articles inspired by this trip he set forth the philosophical and political reflections that he did not want to put into his novels. These articles, titled "L'Heure du nègre" and "Les Ratés de l'aventure," were a crushing indictment of colonialism in Gabon and the Belgian Congo. A campaign seeking to recruit young men to emigrate to the colonies had popularized the slogan "L'Afrique vous parle." Simenon adapted this slogan to read "L'Afrique vous dit merde" and used it as a scathing conclusion to his six articles. Alcoholism, forced labor, slave trade, and routine sadism make up the picture of French or Belgian colonization. Africa drives the colonizer mad, while the colonized make out a little better thanks to their bovine passivity.

"Exotic novels" is the name given to a group of Simenon's "romans durs" situated in Africa, South America, Tahiti, and the Galapagos, but all of his novels, whatever their locale, delve into the heart of human experience—the easy slide into depression, or unbridled sexuality, or drugs, or alcohol; the hard, if not impossible, struggle back out. He used these tropical landscapes as background in these novels, but he is not a writer like Joseph Conrad or Somerset Maugham for whom the exoticism of foreign places allows for a heightened or different existence and for the illusion of liberation. On the contrary, he underlines the fact that wherever one travels, one takes oneself along, and that always limits the possibilities for transcendence. The exotic decors in his novels became, in effect, his own inner landscapes, settings for the presentation of his usual characters and themes. The deterioration of his characters takes place in all surroundings, but the unmerciful rain, heat, insects, and diseases of the tropics destroy them more quickly and relentlessly.

Eschewing any of the exotic attractions of the tropics, he chose only those elements that confirmed his assertion that "there is no such thing as exoticism. When you are *over there*, whether in Africa, Asia or in the equatorial forest, you immediately become accustomed to the landscape and a tree is a tree, whether it is called an oak, a mango, or a coconut tree; a passer-by is a passer-by, white or black, dressed in cloth or simply in a few strands of dried grass. Man becomes accustomed to everything" (*La mauvaise étoile*, 31). According to Simenon, if you do away with picturesque elements, most tropical adventures assume a tragic aspect, "a day-to-day tragedy, heavy as the sky, thick as the forest, a nightmarish tragedy, an oppression, the emptiness of the mind and the soul before a landscape that is always the same, that remains forever alien and where, nonetheless, you must die, knowing that there is in France, a village, a city in which . . . " (*La mauvaise étoile*, 68).

This ubiquitous "everyday tragedy" and this "emptiness of the mind and the soul" that he discerns in the tropics reflect his weltanschauung and exist to the same degree within all of the characters in all of his works. Mythical exotic paradises become, in Simenon's oeuvre, morasses of unrelenting rain and intolerable heat, of decay, deterioration, tropical diseases, filth, cannibalism, poisonous snakes, and myriads of "swarming insects, strange flies, flying scorpions, hairy spiders" (*Le Coup de lune*, 10–11). His tropics are worse than anything to be found in the works of Graham Greene, since there are no saving expressions or theological lifelines attached.

SURVEY OF CRITICISM

Jacques Lacarme (1989) writes that Panama in Simenon's novel *Quartier nègre*, with its well-named city of Colón (colonizer), although not in Africa, presents an archetypal African colonial society with its caste system and its pariahs. Jean-Louis Dumortier (1997) finds that the articles of "L'Heure du nègre" are filled with racist stereotypes; that while they ridicule colonialism in general, they nonetheless preserve the myth of the solitary hero who offsets his exploitation of the natives by a paternalism appropriate to their infantile mentality. Lucille F. Becker (1997) writes that Simenon's tropics reflect his personal vision, one that ignores all of the splendor of the tropics and sets forth only the dismal, hostile aspects.

SELECTIVE BIBLIOGRAPHY

Works by Simenon

Le Coup de lune. Paris: Fayard, 1933.
Quartier nègre. Paris: Gallimard, 1935.

Long cours. Paris: Gallimard, 1936.
Le Blanc à lunettes. Paris: Gallimard, 1937.
Ceux de la soif. Paris: Gallimard, 1938.
La mauvaise étoile. Paris: Gallimard, 1938.
Touriste de bananes; ou, Les dimanches de Tahiti. Paris: Gallimard, 1938.

Selective Studies of Simenon

Assouline, Pierre. *Simenon, biographie*. Paris: Julliard, 1992.
Becker, Lucille F. " 'L'Exotisme n'existe pas': Paysages intérieurs de Georges Simenon."
    In *Traces 9: Georges Simenon et l'exotisme*, 289–95. Liège: Centre d'Etudes
    Georges Simenon, 1997.
———. *Georges Simenon Revisited*. New York: Twayne, 1999.
Deligny, Pierre. Preface to *Le Drame mystérieux des îles Galapagos*, by Georges Si-
    menon. Brussels. Les Amis de Georges Simenon, 1991.
Dumortier, Jean-Louis. "Anticolonialisme patent et racisme larvé: L'effet idéologique de
    'L'heure du Nègre.' " In *Traces 9: Georges Simenon et l'exotisme*, 229–61. Li-
    ège: Centre d'Etudes Georges Simenon, 1997.
Lacarme, Jacques. "Les Romans coloniaux de Georges Simenon." *Textyles: Revue des
    lettres belges de langue française*, no. 6 (November 1989): 179–89. Bruxelles:
    Textyles Editions.
Traces 9: Georges Simenon et l'exotisme (articles on Simenon and exoticism). Liège:
    Centre d'Etudes Georges Simenon, 1997.

MADAME DE STAËL (ANNE-LOUISE-GERMAINE NECKER)
(1766–1817)

Nadine Dormoy

BIOGRAPHY

One of the very few women in French literature who enjoyed international recognition from the start, Madame de Staël was born Anne-Louise-Germaine Necker, daughter of Jacques Necker, the famous Swiss banker of Geneva who served as minister to King Louis XVI during the last years of the French monarchy. She was initiated into the life of the eighteenth-century Parisian salons by her mother, Suzanne Curchod, who attracted to her home such intellectuals as Marmontel, d'Alembert, Diderot, Grimm, Buffon, and Bernardin de Saint-Pierre. In 1786 Germaine Necker married Baron Erik-Magnus de Staël-Holstein, Swedish ambassador to France. The French Revolution forced him to return to Sweden and his wife to emigrate. After a brief stay in London she settled in Switzerland at the château de Coppet, on the banks of Lake Geneva. She divorced her husband in 1798.

She returned to Paris in 1795, where her "subversive" opinions displeased Bonaparte, who forced her into exile. She published an essay, *De la littérature considérée dans ses rapports avec les institutions sociales*, in 1800, and a novel, *Delphine*, in 1802. At Coppet her vast circle of friends included Madame Récamier and Benjamin Constant. She had a long and passionate love affair with the latter that is echoed in his famous novel *Adolphe* (1816). During the ten-year period of the Consulate and the Empire she traveled throughout Europe. In 1804 she met Goethe in Weimar, and Schiller, and Queen Louise of Prussia received her in Berlin. The same year she visited Italy, which inspired her most famous novel, *Corinne*, published in 1807. Back in Germany she worked on her remarkable essay *De l'Allemagne* (1810). After returning to Coppet, she secretly married a young officer, Jean Rocca.

From 1812 to 1813 she traveled through Austria, Russia, Sweden, and England, where she met the future Louis XVIII. After the Restoration in France

Louis became king, and she returned to Paris in 1814 to reopen her salon. She died two years later, leaving some of her works unpublished.

MAJOR MULTICULTURAL THEMES

In *De la littérature* Staël offers a historical survey of Western literature, beginning with that of Greece and Rome. She develops a theory based on the influence of climate and art on society. She sees Homer as the classical model for southern Europe, and Ossian as the Romantic model for northern Europe. While a bright and sunny climate leads to the perfection and clarity of classical forms, fog, cold, and long winters encourage sentimental, poetic, and mystical relationships. The latter culture, conducive to modernity in that it excites the imagination, dreams, and artistic and literary aspirations, transformed her into an early and major propagandist of the Romantic movement in France. While the Romantic movement emphasized self-expression, for women as well as for men, it cannot be dissociated from the principle of political and human rights, nor from its early support of nationalist movements in Europe. Staël, who placed liberty and happiness above all, was Romanticism's ideal—and idealistic—spokesperson. In *De l'Allemagne* she emphasizes the role accorded to sentiment and feeling in shaping the human spirit, as opposed to the rational heritage of Roman law and philosophy.

The protagonist in *Corinne ou l'Italie*, her masterpiece, is named after the Greek poetess Corinna, who lived in Thebes at the end of the sixth century B.C.E. and was a well-known rival to Pindar. Corinne, an Italian poetess honored at the Capitol for her splendid poems, enjoys fame and personal independence. Her bliss-filled love affair with the English dandy Oswald, Lord Nelvil, ends with his return to England to attend to the management of his estate. For Corinne to leave Italy would reduce her to ordinary stature. Shorn of her inspiration and of a zest for life, she would, and does, seal her fate. After her lover's departure, Corinne dies of a broken heart. The conflict between Italy, the country of art, and England, the country of civil rights, albeit Corinne's dilemma, was also that of Madame de Staël.

SURVEY OF CRITICISM

Although Staël is one of the most European authors of all time, she was also a nomad, a rebel, a woman "born for opposition," as *Lord Byron and Madame de Staël: Born for Opposition* by Joanne Wilkes (1999) demonstrates. Another telling title, *Germaine de Staël: Crossing the Borders* (1991), involves the Swiss-born Parisian hostess in constant pursuit of a suitable home and never really finding it. The volume, edited by Madelyn Gutwirth, Avriel H. Goldberger, and Karyna Szmurlo, shows Staël in a singularly modern light. Another study devoted to Staël's cosmopolitan upbringing is *The Birth of European Romanticism: Truth and Propaganda in Staël's "De l'Allemagne," 1810–1813*

(1994) by John Claiborne Isbell. This study attempts to prove Staël's selective and therefore highly subjective view of Germany. Staël's affinity for Germany has been exhaustively and convincingly argued by the Austrian scholar Georges Solovieff in his *Madame de Staël, ses amis, ses correspondants* (1970) and, more recently, *L'Allemagne et Madame de Staël: En marge d'un évènement* (1990), in which he uses the manuscript of *De l'Allemagne*, her *Journal sur l'Allemagne*, and *Les Carnets de Voyage*, as well as her private correspondence, to survey the wealth of cultural events in literature, philosophy, politics, art, and science that formed the terrain from which sprang the oeuvre of the gracious and forceful author of *De l'Allemagne*.

Suzanne Balayé, the major contemporary French specialist on Staël's works, indicated in her preface to the 1985 edition of *Corinne* that while Germany's sensibility and philosophy are the novel's constant leitmotif (Préface, 19), one of its most remarkable aspects is its focus on three countries: France, England, and Italy. The dichotomy expressed in *Corinne* reflects the inner contradictions of its author, both as a woman and as an artist.

SELECTIVE BIBLIOGRAPHY

Works by Staël

De la littérature considérée dans ses rapports avec les institutions sociales (1800). Ed. Gérard Gengembre et Jean Goldzink. Paris: Garnier-Flammarion, 1991.
Corinne ou l'Italie (1807). Ed. Simone Balayé. Folio-classique. Paris: Gallimard, 1985. [*Corinne or Italy*. Trans. and ed. Avriel Goldberger. New Brunswick, N.J.: Rutgers University Press, 1987.]
De l'Allemagne (1810). Préface de Simone Balayé. 2 vols. Paris: Garnier-Flammarion, 1968.
Dix années d'exil (1820). Ed. Simone Balayé et Mariella Vianello Bonifacio. Paris: Librairie Fayard, 1996.

Selective Studies of Staël

Balayé, Simone. *Les Carnets de voyage de Madame de Staël: Contribution à la genèse de ses oeuvres*, suivi de *Le Séjour en Angleterre, 1813–1814*, une étude de Norman King. Genève: Droz, 1967.
———. "Corinne et la ville italienne." In *Mélanges à la mémoire de Franco Simone: France et Italie dans la culture européenne*, vol. 3, *XIXe et XXe siècles*. Genève: Slatkine, 1984.
———. *Madame de Staël: Lumières et liberté*. Paris: Klincksieck, 1979.
———, ed. *Corinne et Rome ou le Chant du cygne (Thèmes et figures du siècle des Lumières)*. Mélanges offerts à Roland Mortier. Genève: Droz, 1980.
Besser, Gretchen Rous. *Germaine de Staël Revisited*. New York: Twayne, 1994.
Gennari, Geneviève. *Le premier voyage de Madame de Staël en Italie et la genèse de "Corinne."* Paris: Boivin, 1947.

Gutwirth, Madelyn, Avriel H. Goldberger, and Karyna Szmurlo, eds. *Germaine de Staël: Crossing the Borders*. New Brunswick, N.J.: Rutgers University Press, 1991.

Hawkins, Richmond L. "Madame de Staël and the United States." *Harvard Studies in Romance Languages* 7 (1930).

Herold, J. Christopher. *Mistress to an Age: A Life of Madame de Staël*. Westport, Conn.: Greenwood Press, 1975.

Isbell, John Claiborne. *The Birth of European Romanticism: Truth and Propaganda in Staël's "De l'Allemagne," 1810–1813*. Cambridge: Cambridge University Press, 1994.

Madame de Staël et la Suède: Cahiers Staëliens No. 39. Paris: Jean Touzot, 1988.

Madame de Staël et l'Europe: Colloque de Coppet (juillet 1969). Paris: Klincksieck, 1971.

Solovieff, Georges. *L'Allemagne et Madame de Staël: En marge d'un évènement*. Paris: Klincksieck, 1990.

———. *Madame de Staël, ses amis, ses correspondants*. Paris: Klincksieck, 1970.

Szmurlo, Karyna, ed. *The Novel's Seduction: Staël's "Corinne" in Critical Inquiry*. London: Associated University Presses, 1998.

Walleborn, Melitta. *Deutschland und die Deutschen in Mme de Staëls "De l'Allemagne": Staaten, Landschaften, und Menschen*. Frankfurt am Main and New York: Peter Lang, 1998.

Wilkes, Joanne. *Lord Byron and Madame de Staël: Born for Opposition*. Aldershot: Ashgate, 1999.

STENDHAL (MARIE-HENRI BEYLE)
(1783–1842)

Alba Amoia

BIOGRAPHY

The Frenchman known as Stendhal whose Montmartre Cemetery epitaph epitomizes him as "Milanese," who is also identified as "Enricus Beyle, Romanus," and who spent more than one-third of his entire life in Italy was born in Grenoble, the elder son of rich bourgeois parents. A royalist father, a mean aunt, and a tyrannical tutor dominated the lad's world following the death of his "beloved" mother in 1790. He came to despise his birthplace (a "mudhole") and declared himself an atheist and Jacobin. As an adolescent he read the works of Corneille, Molière, Rousseau, Prévost, and Laclos, but also of Cervantes, Shakespeare, Milton, Jonson, Dryden, and Addison. At the age of seventeen he entered Bonaparte's army, eventually finding himself in Italy, the country that became his spiritual homeland. He claimed to be of Italian descent on the side of his mother, using his heritage as an explanation of his contradictory nature, and was equally enthusiastic over his great-aunt's "espagnolisme." He flourished in Italy, visiting Parma several times and molding the city to fit his politico-literary purposes. Italy inspired him to write a history of Italian painting as well as lives of the librettist Pietro Metastasio and Gioacchino Rossini; in the Piedmontese city of Novara he discovered the works of Domenico Cimarosa, one of Italy's principal composers of comic operas; in Milan he was overwhelmed by La Scala, the home of great opera, which "intoxicated" him; and in Venice he admired initially (though later criticized) Carlo Goldoni's comedies written in Italian, Venetian dialect, and French.

Following the Napoleonic army's retreat from Russia in 1812, Beyle lived chiefly in Milan from 1814 to 1821, where he began writing works on the lives of German and Italian composers and the history of Italian painting. Milan was also the home of his mistress, Angela Pietragrua, whose animating influence is seen in several of his heroines. After Napoleon's fall and Beyle's self-imposed exile during the Bourbon Restoration, he wrote the travel book *Rome, Naples, et Florence* (1817). This was his first work signed "Stendhal," one of his in-numerable pseudonyms that themselves hint at his own multiculturalism. (The name was borrowed from the small Prussian town of Stendal, the birthplace of the famous German art critic J.J. Winckelmann.) Two other Italian travel books followed: *L'Italie en 1818* and *Promenades dans Rome* (1829), much of whose material came from secondary sources but which nonetheless display his own loving and detailed descriptions of things Italian. After the publication in France of *Le Rouge et le noir* (1830), which ranks among the world's great novels, he returned to Italy as consul at Trieste. The Austrian police having earlier sus-pected him of espionage in Milan, Beyle was denied permission by Metternich to exercise his official duties in Trieste. From 1831 until his death in 1842 he served as consul in Civitavecchia, the Papal States' seaport town, from whose dullness he escaped for long stays in Rome. The year 1838 saw the publication of *Mémoires d'un touriste*; the following year of *La Chartreuse de Parme* and of a volume of *nouvelles, Chroniques italiennes*. His posthumous works include *Lucien Leuwen* (1855), *Lamiel* (1889), and *Vie de Henri Brulard* (1890), parts of which were written during the author's 1834–36 sojourn in Rome's Palazzo Conti behind the Pantheon. *Souvenirs d'égotisme* (1892) contains some engag-ing accounts of his visits to England, the country that helped him lessen his "spleen" thanks to "the works of Shakespeare and [the performances of] the actor [Edmund] Kean."

MAJOR MULTICULTURAL THEMES

Stendhal's hectic life was marked by military and political assignments abroad, as well as by pleasurable travel throughout Europe. But it was "sublime" Italy that catalyzed his writings. If common sources of inspiration and reflection gave rise to both the renderings of Michelangelo and the creation of the hero of *Le Rouge et le noir* (V. del Litto, Préface, *Voyages en Italie*, xix–xx), it is surely Stendhal's love of Italy that lends his novel *La Chartreuse de Parme* its youthfulness and bravura. Against a backdrop of Milanese institutions and Parma's *palazzi*, Lake Como, and the Italian Alps, a young and ambitious hero, the *italianissimo* Fabrice del Dongo, thirsts for glory and happiness with all the egoism, energy, and passion typical of the Stendhalian hero.

The author's Italian journals provided him with a vehicle for his confessions and for the recording of his own strong sensations. *Promenades dans Rome* contains his expression of faith: to travel, to learn how Romans and Neapolitans plot their search for happiness. In Rome he might find a cure for the "bad taste" that unfortunately he would reacquire on his return to Paris; he even hazards such "blasphemies" as "it is the [inferior] paintings one sees in Paris that prevent one from admiring the frescoes of Rome" (*Promenades dans Rome*, August 3, 1827).

His first visit to Italy in 1811 gave him the confirmation that this land of love, of the fine arts, and of the marionette theater that delighted him was indeed his perfect homeland. In the cynical yet sensitive Italian commedia dell'arte he found that ever-intriguing admixture of the grotesque and the beautiful. His ardent, positive, and singularly original brand of romanticism, known as "beylisme," advocated an individualistic, utilitarian, analytical, critical, and cynical morality imbued with adventure and energy in the "pursuit of happiness."

During his travels he sought to penetrate the nature of governments and of papal power and to analyze the character of the inhabitants of the cities where he sojourned, both for purposes of comparison with France and to "complete, extend, and verify what we think we know about humankind in general" (Stendhal, *Journal*, cited in V. del Litto, Préface, *Voyages en Italie*, xvi). In *Promenades dans Rome* he depicts Italy as a vast museum, giving "an idea of the customs of the Italians and their manner of feeling. . . . It is from the core of this manner of feeling that have sprung the Correggios, the Raphaels, and the Cimarosas . . . to whom I surely owe the most agreeable moments and the greatest gratitude." Italy is a land of ebullience, savory customs, and dolce far niente, which he paints in contrast to the "colors" of France and England. He eschews comparisons between Italy and Germany: "[I]f I never compare the manners of behaving of Italy to the usages of Germany it is because that country . . . has only artificial and passing social usages. . . . I could not use [the manners and social habits of Germany] as a point of comparison [for] better knowledge of the country from which Paris, for three hundred years, has brought the Rossinis, the Piccinis [sic], the Leonardo da Vincis, the Primatices and the Benvenuto Cellinis" (*Voyages en Italie*, 899, 901).

SURVEY OF CRITICISM

Victor del Litto, in his preface (1973) to Stendhal's *Voyages en Italie*, demonstrates the Stendhalian notion of travel as the author's quest for his own self. Michel Crouzet (1982) provides an in-depth study of myths and realities in Stendhal's approach to Italy's people, history, politics, religion, and art and concludes that Italian and Stendhalian paradoxicalness are mutually transferable. Massimo Colesanti (1985) analyzes the author's inner feelings of indignation and admiration, of attraction and detachment during his Roman sojourns, and explains how the author's Italian experience helped to sustain his own myths and ideas. The physical and moral superiority, in Stendhal's view, of the ancient Romans as contrasted with his contemporaries is the object of study by both Lucien Jansse (1975) and James G. Shields (1985). Jonathan Keates's biography (1997) vividly evokes the author's entry into and fascination with Italy, as well as his rise and fall with Napoleon across the entire European scene. Amoia and Bruschini (1997) survey the places that aroused his enthusiasm and, in the light of more recent historical and archeological research, point to his errors and misconception of the Roman scene.

SELECTIVE BIBLIOGRAPHY

Works by Stendhal

Voyages en Italie. Ed. V. del Litto. NRF, Bibliothèque de la Pléiade. Paris: Gallimard, 1973. [Contains *Rome, Naples, et Florence en 1817; L'Italie en 1818; Rome, Naples, et Florence* (1826); *Promenades dans Rome* (1829).]

La Chartreuse de Parme (1839). Paris: Gallimard, 1972.

Souvenirs d'égotisme (1892). Ed. Henri Martineau. Paris: Le Divan, 1950. [*Memoirs of an Egotist.* Trans. D. Ellis. London: Chatto and Windus, 1975.]

A Roman Journal. Ed. and trans. Haakon Chevalier. London: Orion, 1959.

Selective Studies of Stendhal

Amoia, Alba, and Enrico Bruschini. *Stendhal's Rome: Then and Now.* Roma: Edizioni di Storia e Letteratura, 1997.

Boyer, Ferdinand. "Logements de Stendhal à Rome (1831–1842)." *Editions du Stendhal-Club,* no. 5 (1924): 3–5.

Colesanti, Massimo. "La Roma di Stendhal." In *Stendhal, Roma, l'Italia,* 19–28. Ed. Massimo Colesanti, Anna Jeronimidis, Letizia Norci Cagiano, and Anna Maria Scaiola. Roma: Edizioni di Storia e Letteratura, 1985.

Colesanti, Massimo, Anna Jeronimidis, Letizia Norci Cagiano, and Anna Maria Scaiola, eds. *Stendhal, Roma, l'Italia: Atti del Congresso Internazionale, Roma, 7–10 novembre 1983.* Roma: Edizioni di Storia e Letteratura, 1985.

Crouzet, Michel. *Stendhal et l'italianité.* Paris: José Corti, 1982.

Jansse, Lucien. "Stendhal et la Rome antique." *Stendhal Club* 69 (1975): 56–69.

Keates, Jonathan. *Stendhal.* New York: Carroll & Graf, 1997.

Shields, James G. "Enricus Beyle, Romanus: Le classicisme d'un romantique." In *Stendhal, Roma, l'Italia,* 63–82. Ed. Massimo Colesanti, Anna Jeronimidis, Letizia Norci Cagiano, and Anna Maria Scaiola, eds. Roma: Edizioni di Storia e Letteratura, 1985.

ROBERT LOUIS STEVENSON
(1850–1894)

Timothy L. Carens

BIOGRAPHY

Until Robert Louis Stevenson was twenty-five, he lived in his parents' home in Edinburgh, Scotland. Suffering from chronic bronchial infections, he was often too ill as a child and adolescent to leave his bed. As an adult, however, he traveled and lived in many different locations in Europe, the United States, and the South Pacific. Indeed, he died on Upolu, the principal island of Samoa, halfway round the world from his birthplace. While his travels were often prompted by ill health, they also indicate his espousal of an artistic and personal identity unrestricted by regional and national borders. Stevenson chose the vantage point of the exile, a perspective from which he could view his native land from a distance and explore new cultural contexts as well.

He entered Edinburgh University in 1867, but found his course of study, designed to prepare him for a career in the family engineering firm, to be uninspiring. He preferred to spend his time conversing with friends in taverns and developing his writing style. In 1875, having sparked a painful rift with his parents by confessing his religious doubts, he began to visit an artist cousin at various artist colonies in France, the bohemian atmosphere of which struck a welcome contrast to his parents' respectable home. On one such trip he met Fanny Osbourne, an American woman whom he eventually married.

Stevenson's professional writing career began with works that reflect the emergence of a wide-ranging intellect and a multicultural sensibility. His first two books are, significantly, narratives of travel in foreign countries. *An Inland Voyage* (1878) describes a canoe trip taken with a friend through Belgium and France. In *Travels with a Donkey in the Cévennes* (1879), he narrates a solitary walking tour in the French mountains. *Familiar Studies of Men and Books* (1882) includes essays on writers as diverse as Victor Hugo, Charles of Orléans,

François Villon, Walt Whitman, Henry David Thoreau, and Yoshida Torahiro, a Japanese reformer.

In 1879 Stevenson left Edinburgh to join Fanny in California, traveling by ship and train along with poor European emigrants. *The Amateur Emigrant* (1895) records the exacting journey. The trip to America also provided material for *The Silverado Squatters* (1883), which describes the unconventional honeymoon Stevenson and Fanny spent in an abandoned mining camp in California. Returning to Europe in 1880, he and his family lived for extended periods in Switzerland, the south of France, and Bournemouth, on the English Channel coast. In this last place he wrote *The Strange Case of Dr Jekyll and Mr Hyde* (1886), an immediate success, particularly in the United States, and still his most widely read work.

When his father died in 1887, Stevenson and his extended family sailed for the United States in pursuit of a more congenial climate. He never returned to Scotland. After spending a frigid winter in upper New York State, he and his entourage chartered a yacht and departed for tropical seas. Stevenson found the sea voyage invigorating and discovered in the cross-cultural milieu of the Polynesian islands a rich topic for nonfictional and fictional writing. For one who roved as much as he, the fact that he chose to settle in Upolu testifies to the strength of his commitment to Samoa, where he died in 1894.

MAJOR MULTICULTURAL THEMES

In his early writing Stevenson upholds travel in foreign parts as an exciting alternative to a comfortable life of bourgeois respectability at home. The fast-paced adventure plot of his first novel, *Treasure Island* (1883), in which the young British protagonist proves himself in battle with pirates on an exotic West Indian island, certainly reflects this contrast. *An Inland Voyage* narrates a canoe trip on the Oise, while *Travels with a Donkey in the Cévennes* features camping in foul weather and encounters with local people who as often derided or ignored as befriended him. In *The Amateur Emigrant* Stevenson tells of the grueling conditions under which poor emigrants from northern Europe make their way to America. The pleasures of detached observation give place, in this darker volume, to an acute consciousness of injustice, deprivation, and bigotry. In the American West he deplores the treatment of Native Americans and Chinese by European emigrants, contemplating the irony that those despised for their poverty in turn despise others for their race.

As he explores the impact of colonialism on the island world of the South Pacific, he reveals a growing sensitivity to racial and cultural discrimination. At the beginning of *In the South Seas* (1896) he observes that the imperial power that enables such discrimination is arbitrary and unstable. Just as the "polite Englishman comes to-day to the Marquesans and is amazed to find the men tattooed, polite Italians came not long ago to England and found our fathers stained with woad . . . so insecure, so much a matter of the day and hour, is the pre-eminence of race" (13). In *A Footnote to History* (1892) Stevenson offers a historical account of the contemporary political crisis in Samoa that is deeply critical of European colonial governments.

A skeptical distrust of the imperialist notion that European contact effects "civilizing" development informs two of his finest short works of fiction, *The Beach of Falesà* (1893) and *The Ebb-Tide* (1894). Wiltshire, the narrator of the former work, is a trader who cheats the islanders and dupes Uma, an indigenous woman, into "marrying" him for a single night. A murderous conflict with an even less scrupulous trader triggers a partial moral reform, but Wiltshire never becomes anything like the upstanding representative of civilization he professes to be. Although he eventually marries Uma in good faith, the fact of his inter-racial family does not fundamentally alter his contempt for Polynesians.

In *The Ebb-Tide* a dissolute Oxford graduate named Herrick faces a dilemma when his two disreputable associates, Davis and Huish, devise a plot to murder Attwater, a successful colonist who has amassed a fortune in pearls. Although indigenous characters are marginal to the plot, they help to gauge the varieties of colonial corruption between which Herrick must choose. The drunken excess and selfish greed of his companions strikes a shameful contrast to the Polynesian ship crew. Attwater, an evangelical Christian who murders a disobedient native worker without remorse, offers a repellent authoritarian alternative to their degradation. That Herrick ultimately throws in his lot with Attwater triggers a conclusion as fraught with moral ambiguity as that of *The Beach of Falesà*.

SURVEY OF CRITICISM

James Wilson (1983) argues that the genre of travel writing provides Stevenson with a forum in which he displays his talent for capturing the telling detail, for developing morally rich portraits of individuals and social conventions, and for exploring his own responses to experience. Alex Clunas (1996) shows that Stevenson's early travel writing reflects the influence of French aestheticism. As he pursues "travel for travel's sake," Stevenson constructs what Clunas calls a "disencumbered self" (61), an identity liberated both from his native culture and the unfamiliar scene that rapidly changes before him. J.C. Furnas (1981) discusses Stevenson's romantic attitude to life at sea and in Samoa, noting that the experience in the South Pacific exposed the author to a cross-cultural environment that "did much to jar his talent into maturity" (138). In his full-length biography (1951) Furnas, like Jenni Calder (1980), gives much attention to the years that Stevenson spent in the South Pacific. Robert Kiely (1965) shows that as Stevenson matured as a writer and moral philosopher, his work began to register a disenchantment with the heroic adventure plot set in exotic locales. In his survey of the fictional and nonfictional works on Polynesia Robert Hillier (1989) contends that Stevenson provides a more complex and realistic alternative to the "archetypal" view of the South Seas as an exotic realm beyond the restrictive laws of civilization.

Evaluating the series of letters eventually published as *In the South Seas*, Barry Menikoff (1992) argues that Stevenson explores in the volume the difficulty of appropriating the strangeness of another culture, a philosophical concern that leads him to subvert certain conventions of travel writing and to question the politics of imperialism. Roslyn Jolly (1996) interprets *A Footnote to History* as a historical account that subverts the imperialist assumption that colonial conquest marks historical progress. Peter Gilmour (1983) departs from the generally positive response to *The Beach of Falesà* and *The Ebb-Tide*, holding that Stevenson represents the Polynesians as passive victims and fails to condemn imperialism conclusively.

SELECTIVE BIBLIOGRAPHY

Works by Stevenson

An Inland Voyage. London: Kegan Paul, 1878.
Travels with a Donkey in the Cévennes. London: Kegan Paul, 1879.
A Footnote to History. London: Cassell, 1892.
The Beach of Falesà (1893). In *Dr. Jekyll and Mr. Hyde and Other Stories*. Ed. Jenni Calder. New York: Penguin, 1979.
The Ebb-Tide (1894). In *Dr. Jekyll and Mr. Hyde and Other Stories*. Ed. Jenni Calder. New York: Penguin, 1979.
The Amateur Emigrant (1895). In *From Scotland to Silverado*. Ed. James D. Hart. Cambridge, Mass.: Balknap Press of Harvard University Press, 1966.
In the South Seas (1896). New York: Penguin, 1998.

Selective Studies of Stevenson

Calder, Jenni. *Robert Louis Stevenson: A Life Study*. New York: Oxford University Press, 1980.
Clunas, Alex. " 'Out of My Country and Myself I Go': Identity and Writing in Stevenson's Early Travel Books." *Nineteenth-Century Prose* 23, no. 1 (1996): 54–73.
Furnas, J.C. "Stevenson and Exile." In *Stevenson and Victorian Scotland*, 126–41. Edinburgh: Edinburgh University Press, 1981.
———. *Voyage to Windward*. New York: William Sloane, 1951.
Gilmour, Peter. "Robert Louis Stevenson: Forms of Evasion." In *Robert Louis Stevenson*, 188–201. Ed. Andrew Noble. Totowa, N.J.: Barnes and Noble, 1983.
Hillier, Robert Irwin. *The South Seas Fiction of Robert Louis Stevenson*. New York: Peter Lang, 1989.
Jolly, Roslyn. "Robert Louis Stevenson and Samoan History: Crossing the Roman Wall." In *Crossing Cultures: Essays on Literature and Culture of the Asia-Pacific*, 113–20. Ed. Bruce Bennett, Jeff Doyle, Satendra P. Nandan, and Loes Baker. London: Skoob, 1996.
Kiely, Robert. *Robert Louis Stevenson and the Fiction of Adventure*. Cambridge, Mass.: Harvard University Press, 1965.
Menikoff, Barry. " 'These Problematic Shores': Robert Louis Stevenson in the South

Seas." In *The Ends of the Earth, 1876–1918*, 141–56. Ed. Simon Gatrell. Atlantic Highlands, N.J.: Ashfield Press, 1992.

Wilson, James. "Landscape with Figures." In *Robert Louis Stevenson*, 73–95. Ed. Andrew Noble. Totowa, N.J.: Barnes and Noble, 1983.

CORNELIUS TACITUS

(c. 56–c. 120)

Domizia Lanzetta

BIOGRAPHY

Cornelius Tacitus probably was of Gallic origin, in view of the frequent occurrence of his cognomen among the inhabitants of Gallia Narbonensis and Cispadane Gaul. Yet he wrote unflatteringly about the Gauls, whom he compared unfavorably with the Germanic peoples in *De origine, situ, moribus, ac populis Germanorum* (28, 29).

What emerges from his writings is his conservative, aristocratic mentality. He approves the priests' having decisional power in the assemblies of the Germanic peoples. He cherishes Rome's archaic values and the decemvirate that drafted laws and plebiscites. (Later, Rome's Olgunian Law [300 B.C.E.] allowed plebeians to accede to positions of pontiffs and augurs in the religious college.)

Son of a high government official in Gallia Belgica and in the two Germanias, he himself held the important positions of quaestor under Emperor Vespasian (69–79) and praetor under Emperor Domitian (81–96). Then, having married the daughter of Julius Agricola, conqueror of Britannia, he became imperial legate for the northwestern regions of the empire, which probably offered occasion for encounter with the Germanic peoples.

He was free to write only at the end of the Julio-Claudian and Flavian dynasties, an era marked by mad emperors accompanied by evil women scheming at their side. Perhaps this was why he sang the praises of Germanic women who, even though they were wives of princes and kings, wore simple dresses of unbleached fabric, accompanied their men to the edge of the field of battle, and inspired them to valiant action.

After the death of Emperor Domitian Tacitus gained the consulship and from 112 to 113 was proconsul of Asia. He died in the early years of Emperor Hadrian's reign.

MAJOR MULTICULTURAL THEMES

Tacitus is one of the most surprising figures of imperial Rome, as attested by his funeral oration in praise of Arminius, Rome's bitterest enemy. This German chief of the Cherusci tribe had fought to free his land from Roman dominion and inflicted a major defeat on the enemy legions in the battle of the Teutoburg Forest. Tacitus judged him to be "unquestionably the liberator of Germania" (*Annalium*, II, 88). Why did he praise the enemy? A natural question, to which the historian himself seemingly wished to provide the answer by describing the enemy's valor. Behind his aristocratic equanimity one glimpses Tacitus's atavistic intolerance of Roman tyranny, which offended his principles of civic virtue. For him, Arminius is a personification of the pride of an indomitable tribe that refuses subjugation to Rome. The regions beyond the Rhine, in Tacitus's day, were inhabited by peoples who, though conquered, could never be kept in bondage. *Virtus*—that is, warlike bravery—ranked highest among Latin civilization's archaic ideals. Thus the enemy was worthy of Tacitus's admiration.

De origine, situ, moribus, ac populis Germanorum (98), generally known as the *Germania*, is Tacitus's second and best-known work. Not accepting Rome's new mores, he felt that they distorted the spirit of the ancient Latin peoples. He rejected Rome's dominant cosmopolitanism and emphasized instead Germanic compactness. He had discerned in the Germanians common physical traits: height, red hair, a bold and untamed look in their steely blue eyes. But he was no racist: these homogeneous physiognomic characteristics were not a positive element to his mind. It was a question rather of a "virgin" people who preserved within their original physical characteristics that inner purity of which he thought the ancients were possessed.

What probably prompted him to write the *Germania* was his personal interest in "cultural anthropology," but what especially engaged him was the spirit of the tribes settled on the right bank of the Rhine—a disquieting, mysterious land, beyond which lay the unknown. To a Roman, the landscape must have appeared sinister, but fascinating. Beyond the Rhine one entered the kingdom of thick mists, deadly swamps, and deep forests—not that there were not mists and forests on the left bank as well, but in the collective imagination of the Romans the left bank apparently seemed somewhat more accessible.

To Tacitus's mind, the fierce and proud Germanic tribes, whose chiefs were chosen for their prowess and their kings for their noble lineage, were emblematic of Rome's lost past. The Rome of his own day rested on tyrannical power and was estranged from its traditions and from its gods. Rome would, according to the gloomy prognostication of the poet Propertius (c. 50–c. 15 B.C.E.), be crushed by its arrogance and wealth. By contrast, the Germanic peoples' vision of the simple life, shorn of false glitter, offered Tacitus a way of life that would never be his.

Despite the dark cold of the northern region, he was nonetheless seduced by its grandiosity and a mysterious sacredness pervading its rivers, lakes, and forests. He had a strong sense of the divine: not for nothing was he one of the Quindecemviri Sacris Faciundis, the priestly college that read and interpreted the Sibylline Books. He delved into the domain of the gods and goddesses of Germania. Like other Latin authors before him, he too tried to homologize Germanic divinities with those of the Greek and Latin worlds. Although he failed to transmit the names under which the Germanic tribes invoked a triad to whom blood sacrifices were made (perhaps the three idols of which Adam of Brema caught a glimpse in the sanctuary of Uppsala in the eleventh century), he nonetheless identified it with the Roman triad of Hercules, Mars, and Mercury. For Tacitus, even if the Germanic gods were similar to those worshiped by the Greeks and Romans, the essence of the former was contained in a fundamentally different form of nature, whose gloominess and mystery were reflected in their warriors' fear-inspiring singing that emanated from behind their immense shields.

Some of the religious practices of the Germanic tribes surprised Tacitus—as, for example, the casting of sticks incised with strange symbols that allowed them to interpret omens—but what aroused his stupefaction was the arcane relationship that they held with their gods. At times one has the impression that he sensed the presence of a divine Nemesis whose powers would descend through these peoples onto Rome and onto a great part of the civilized world. In addition to being fascinated by the Germanic tribes' indifference to wealth, fidelity to their leaders, scorn of danger, and furor in battle, Tacitus was continuously disconcerted by that subtle link existing between them and their mysteriously terrifying divinities. With marked admiration and surprise he wrote of the Swabian Semnones who not only sensed the presence of their divinities in their sacred woods, but bound themselves with cords and dragged themselves on the moss-covered ground in submission to the highest god in their pantheon. They considered one of their primeval forest sanctuaries to be the "original" birthplace of their people. These rituals may have brought to mind, for Tacitus, his recollections of mystical legends accompanying the genesis of the Latin race.

He may also have seen similarities between the Germanic women whom he praised and the ancient Italic heroines. Were the ancient queens of Rome incarnated in the prophetesses deified by the tribes beyond the Rhine? He does not consider Germanic worship of Velleda and Albruna and other prophetesses as though they were divine to be superstition, but rather accepts the fact with seriousness and respect.

Tacitus describes the Harii (dwellers west of the Vistula River) who went to war with shield and body painted black, preferring to do battle in the darkness of night and appearing suddenly like an army of specters. He tells of a fabulous people living in a place reached by very few—the Finns, who live by hunting and fishing, who dwell in tree branches, and who sleep on the naked ground. Nonetheless they consider themselves happy because they are not constrained to toil in the fields nor to make laborious efforts to build dwellings. Nor do they oscillate between hope and fear. For this reason, their lives are serene in the presence of both men and gods, because they have divested themselves of the need to desire anything. As to what lay beyond the region of the magical Finns, Tacitus did not wish to concern himself because, he explained, it would mean overstepping the confines of the historian and entering into legend.

SURVEY OF CRITICISM

Ronald Syme (1970) goes far in detailing the nature of the Gallic problem in the early Principate and Tacitus's awareness of it. He explains the necessary ambiguity of Tacitus's views on men and government as a reflection of the situation at that time. Pierpaolo Fornaro (1980) compares Flavius Josephus, the historian of the Jews, and his contemporary, Tacitus, historian of the Germanic tribes, concluding that the greatness of the two lies not only in what they documented but also in what they intuited and revealed. In Georges Dumézil's comprehensive study of the Germanic gods (1959), the author assimilates the Hercules-Mercury-Mars triad mentioned by Tacitus to Tyr, Thor, and Odin (63–64 and passim).

SELECTIVE BIBLIOGRAPHY

Works by Tacitus

Annalium ab excessu Divi Augusti libri: The Annals of Tacitus. Ed. and intro. H. Furneaux. 2 vols. Oxford: Clarendon Press, 1884–1891.

De origine, situ, moribus, ac populis Germanorum liber. Ed. Bruno Zanco. Roma: Società editrice Dante Alighieri, 1984. (*The "Germania" of Tacitus*. Ed. R.G. Latham. London: Taylor, Walton, and Maberly, 1851.)

Selective Studies of Tacitus

Arnaldi, Francesco. *Tacito*. Napoli: Macchiaroli, 1973.

Dorey, Thomas Allen, ed. *Tacitus*. London: Routledge and Kegan Paul, 1969.

Dumézil, Georges. *Gli Dèi dei Germani*. Trans. Bianca Candian. Milano: Adelphi, 1974. (*Les dieux des Germains*. Paris: Presses Universitaires de France, 1959.)

Fornaro, Pierpaolo. *Flavio Giuseppe, Tacito, e l'Impero*. Torino: Giappichelli, 1980.

Grant, Michael. *The Ancient Historians*. New York: Barnes & Noble, 1994, 271–305.

Mendell, Clarence Whittlesey. *Tacitus, the Man and His Work*. Hamden, Conn.: Archon Books, 1970.

Michel, Alain. *Tacite et le destin de l'empire*. Paris: Arthaud, 1966.

Syme, Ronald. *Ten Studies in Tacitus*. Oxford: Clarendon Press, 1970.

Vielberg, Meinolf. *Pflichten, Werte, Ideale: Eine Untersuchung zu den Wertvorstellungen des Tacitus*. Stuttgart: F. Steiner Verlag Wiesbaden, 1987.

RABINDRANATH TAGORE
(1861–1941)

Alessandro Monti

BIOGRAPHY

Rabindranath Tagore was the son of the Great Sage (Maharishi) Devendranath Tagore, a well-known Hindu philosopher and religious reformer active in the Brahmo Samaj sect (Society of Brahma or Society of God). His father tried to eradicate Hindu idolatry and casteism, eventually drifting toward Christianity. His grandfather was a friend of the Bengali social and cultural reformer Rammohan Roy. Rabindranath was born to a Bengali landed family and had no regular schooling or academic grounding. He was fifteen when he started writing lyrics, in the tradition of Hindu devotional poetry and of the Bengali Vaishnava singers in particular. The Jesuit fathers of St. Xavier's College (Calcutta) also contributed to shaping his mysticism. He early visited England, where he imbibed (although he was not a voracious or systematic reader) the English Romantic poets and Shakespeare. He was involved for a brief time in the nationalist struggle, but soon retired to Shantiketan and nearby Sriniketan, where he founded an ashram for retirement and meditation. These two places became the center for a new experiment in living in which the East-West dichotomy was to be transmuted into harmony, as well as for the foundation of Visvabharati University. The award of the Nobel Prize for Literature in 1913 gave Tagore wider international fame, and he grew into an itinerant and unofficial ambassador of the new and independent India. As the years passed, his identity merged with that of the Upanishadic "rishis," seeing the way and showing it to others.

MAJOR MULTICULTURAL THEMES

Tagore's art highlights the rich and versatile heritage of the so-called Bengali Renaissance, a cultural movement that started in the first quarter of the nineteenth century and received its primary impulse from Rammohan Roy's letter

(1823) to the British authorities. The writer advocated for Indian subjects the redeeming benefits of Western culture and science so as to counteract the long centuries of stifling Muslim rule. The earnest plea for the full renewal (or "renaissance") of a stagnant society brought about "a deep association," to quote Tagore himself, between the West and the East, the latter not to be considered the beggar of the former. The introduction of Standard English as a literary and communal medium of expression not only modified the Bengali language structurally, but also helped to shape a new literary consciousness: novels were written (after Sir Walter Scott's historical romances), and Shakespeare and the Romantic poets were widely read and appreciated.

If Rammohan Roy's letter gave the necessary impetus to a policy of social and religious reforms within the pale of traditional Hindu society, the eminent Bengali novelist and essayist Bankimchandra Chatterjee anticipated Tagore's masterly bilingual skill in Bengali and English. Tagore acknowledged the mixed soil out of which his complex cultural identity had grown. He believed not only that India must recognize the West's arrival in his subcontinent as providential, but that the East must show and convince the West of its great contribution to the history of civilization. His full-length novels (he approved the English translation of three of them, including *Gora* [1910], translated as *Gora* [1924], and *Ghare-Baire* [1916], translated as *The Home and the World* [1919]) continue and refine Bankimchandra's themes of conflict and tension between the English and Indian populations, their orthodox beliefs and the need for emancipation. The novel *Gora* has been equated to a modern epic like *War and Peace*. A historical piece of fiction set in the 1857 Mutiny of the sepoys against the English, *Gora* anticipates the loaded question of hybridization, featuring as it does the life of a "half-caste," part Irish (as Kim in Kipling was), part Indian. In the end the character becomes completely integrated into the great Indian patchwork.

The modernity of Tagore is better viewed in his plays or in his fiction, rather than in his poetical output. However, the songs of *Gitanjali* (1912, with an introduction by W.B. Yeats) are in the great *bhakti* tradition. They view the phenomenal world as the "lila" (or divine play) of the God and devoutly sing out the means by which humans may partake of the sublime glory of the infinite. In his best-known poem Tagore seeks the redemption of India in the wake of Kabir's passionate plea for a spiritual rebirth, but also in the high patriotic tones sounded by Bankimchandra.

The spiritual heritage of India emerges in Tagore's Bengali plays, which deal with issues of asceticism (*Sanyasi*, 1917), kingship (*Raja o Rani*, 1884, translated as *The King and the Queen*, 1917), and political struggle (*Visjaran*, 1890, translated as *Sacrifice*, 1917). In his plays he develops a new national drama, one that mingles the psychological turmoil and torment learned from Ibsen with the great epics and philosophical notions of the East: the lure of maya (the world as illusion) as against the redemptive act of devotional love, the "dark room" inside the heart of humans as against the Divine Self. By doing so, he hybridizes the Sanskrit approaches of Kalidasa with the psychism of modern eras. He partakes of the timeless heritage of Hinduism while remaining a keen and effective explorer of the modern inner being.

SURVEY OF CRITICISM

The so-called Bengali Renaissance is the obligatory starting point for a serious assessment of Tagore's works. The cultural and historical background out of which his art emerges is cogently outlined by Subhas Chandras Saha (1998) and M.L. Pandit (1996). Both emphasize the cross-cultural aspects of Tagore's writing, at the turn of the colonial period and at the dawn of the national and postcolonial experience. His deep absorption of Western culture and literature has been unique and has vastly expanded both Indian and Western sensibilities. K.R. Srinivasa Iyengar, in his now-classic work (1962), sheds light on how the modern and contemporary Bengali language has been a flexible medium of literary communication, imbued as it is with the spirit of "deshi" (autochthonic) India. However, it is also the communal language of a sensibility that underwent deep modifications in order to be able to express the discursive identity of the reborn Hindu nation.

SELECTIVE BIBLIOGRAPHY

Works by Tagore

Gora (1910). London: Macmillan, 1924.
Ghare-Baire (1916). London: Macmillan, 1919. [*The Home and the World*. Trans. Surendranath Tagore. Intro. Anita Desai. Harmondsworth, Middlesex: Penguin, 1985; New York: Viking, 1985.]
Poems. 2nd ed. Ed. Krishna Kripalani. Calcutta: Visva-Bharati, 1943.
Nationalism. 2nd ed. London: Macmillan, 1950.
Collected Poems and Plays of Rabindranath Tagore. London: Macmillan, 1961.
A Tagore Reader. Ed. Amiya Chakravarty. New York: Macmillan, 1961.
One Hundred and One: Poems. Ed. Humayun Kabir. New York: Asia, 1966.

Selective Studies of Tagore

Kopf, David. *British Orientalism and the Bengal Renaissance*. Berkeley: University of California Press, 1969.
Kripalani, Krishna. *Rabindranath Tagore*. London: Oxford University Press, 1962.
Pandit, M.L. *New Commonwealth Writing*. New Delhi: Prestige, 1996.
Saha, Subhas Chandras. *Indian Renaissance and Indian English Poetry*. New Delhi: Prestige, 1998.
Srinivasa Iyengar, K.R. *Indian Writing in English*. New Delhi: Sterling, 1962, reprinted 1989.

Thompson, Edward J. *Rabindranath Tagore: His Life and Work.* London: Oxford University Press, 1921.

———. *Rabindranath Tagore: Poet and Dramatist.* Bombay: Oxford University Press, 1948, reprinted 1976.

TERENCE (PUBLIUS TERENTIUS AFER)

(early second century–159 B.C.E.)

Jeffrey S. Carnes

BIOGRAPHY

Donatus, a fourth-century C.E. commentator, has preserved a brief *Life* of Terence (derived from the imperial biographer Suetonius's *Lives of the Poets*), according to which Terence was born in Carthage and came to Rome as a slave in the household of a senator named Terentius Lucanus, who treated him well and eventually manumitted him *ob ingenium et formam* (because of his talent and beauty). His first play, *Andria*, was produced in 166, his last, *Adelphoe*, in 160, and he died on a journey to Greece, barely over the age of thirty. Recent scholarship, however, has demonstrated what many had long suspected: that ancient literary biographies are often not based on independent historical sources, but consist rather of educated guesses and inferences from the author's works. In the case of Terence, the details seem plausible enough: a freedman would often take the name of his former master, and *Afer* (African) as a cognomen might well indicate geographic origin. Yet there is no independent confirmation of the existence of a Terentius Lucanus, and Roman cognomina were both extremely flexible and heritable; thus *Afer* could indicate some connection with Africa other than origin (e.g., military service there) or could be a family name not unique to the author. Moreover, the various speculations about his relations to important Roman political figures seem to derive entirely from his comments in the prologue to the *Adelphoe*, which are too general to permit the sorts of conclusions sometimes derived from them.

Yet even if the literal truth of his biography is in doubt, it is plausible enough as an expression of important trends in Roman society in the days when Rome was becoming the dominant power in the Mediterranean world. Long known for its provincialism and relative lack of high culture, Rome in the course of the third and second centuries B.C.E. was on the way to becoming the most cosmopolitan city the world had ever known. If Terence was not actually born in Carthage, many inhabitants of Rome were. The struggle between the two great empires had effectively ended with Rome's victory in the Second Punic War (201). (The Third Punic War, 149–46, eliminated an annoying but relatively insignificant rival.) Thus a certain number of Carthaginians would have come to Rome either as free traders and craftspeople or as slaves (the taking of slaves from conquered populations was a common feature of ancient warfare). Nor was it unusual for slaves to be educated: many were highly trained for specialized professions such as architecture and accounting. In addition, poets in early Rome were often of low status or foreign birth (Livius Andronicus was said to be a slave; Caecilius was a Gaul).

The suggestion of a sexual element in Terence's relationship with his master is similarly in accord with the context and mores of second-century Rome. Among the many cultural changes brought in from contact with other civilizations (Greece in particular) was an attitude toward sexuality that considered attraction between adult and adolescent males to be commonplace and unobjectionable (and also no bar to marriage and family life). Slaves, in particular, were desirable insofar as they were at the absolute disposal of their masters, and indeed jokes about the sexual use of slaves show up in Roman comedy, particularly in the work of Terence's great predecessor Plautus.

MULTICULTURAL ELEMENTS

As tempting as it might be to speculate on the African nature of Terence's work, in truth we lack sufficient information to do so; nor is there any element in his plays that could rightly be called Carthaginian. This stands in contrast, oddly enough, to the native Italian Plautus, whose play *Poenulus* features characters of Carthaginian extraction (thus the title, a diminutive form of *Poenus*, the Latin word for Carthaginian), and in which the characters sometimes speak what is meant to be Punic. (Although the authenticity of these passages is uncertain, it is generally believed that Plautus, anticipating the presence of Punic speakers in the audience, wrote at least a plausible simulacrum of that language.)

For Terence, however—as for most Roman authors, and for most Greek authors under Roman rule—the one significant component of multiculturalism was the blending of Greek and Roman elements. The Roman conquest of Greece, begun in the late third century, was nearing completion in Terence's lifetime. Yet Roman political dominance was balanced by a Greek cultural dominance of the emerging empire. In Horace's famous phrase, "Graecia capta ferum victorem cepit et artis intulit agresti Latio" (captured Greece captured the savage victor and brought the arts to rustic Latium), an oversimplification, obviously, yet a useful and not altogether inaccurate one. To be sure, the process of cultural blending was not an entirely smooth one: traditional Roman attitudes included hostility to and suspicion of foreign influences, and even 250 years after Terence's death the satirist Juvenal could play on his audience's prejudices with the figure of the hustling, inquisitive, morally suspect Greek. Yet Roman adoption of Greek culture, especially in the arts, was a foregone conclusion by Terence's time. Already by the mid-third century B.C.E. the importation of Greek literary forms had forever changed the Roman literary landscape. On the stage native Roman farces gave way to what came to be called *fabulae palliatae* (tales in Greek dress, from the Greek cloak known as the *pallium*). The plays of Plautus are adaptations of Greek originals, with the models being the fourth- and third-century New Comedy writers Menander, Philemon, and Diphilus. In addition to using Greek forms and adapting Greek plots, Plautus often left intact the original Greek settings of the plays, and the outlandishness of Greek legal and social customs taken over from the originals was sometimes used for comic effect. Yet Plautus introduced Roman institutions as well, and the whole was a sort of pastiche, a cultural never-never land where improbabilities were tolerated and cultural mixing was comic fodder.

Terence, by contrast, exhibited a purer form of Hellenism in his plays. This had to do with form—he had fewer freestanding musical elements and less obvious farce than did Plautus—as well as content; his imitations of the more thoughtful, character-based dramas of Menander produced a depth of insight and characterization that were new to the Roman stage. Rather than combining Greek and Roman elements and using their inconcinnity for comic purposes, Terence created instead a group of comedies almost entirely devoid of topical allusions and shorn of the specific references to Greek places and institutions found in the originals. The political and cultural import of this purer Hellenism is still uncertain. For a long time the standard opinion was that Terence was part of the "Scipionic Circle," a group of philhellenic aristocrats and literati associated with P. Cornelius Scipio Aemilianus. This circle was thought to be characterized by its self-conscious claims to a universalizing, cross-cultural *humanitas* and by its opposition to the backward-looking and insular chauvinism of nobles such as Cato the Elder. Unfortunately, scholars now agree that the evidence for a Scipionic Circle is tenuous at best, and even Terence's oft-quoted paean to *humanitas*, "Homo sum: humani nil a me alienum puto" (I am human, and consider nothing human foreign to me), is now recognized as the utterance of a self-interested, meddling character rather than the author's own sentiment.

Yet Terence's return to a purer Hellenism, even if devoid of overt political content, serves as a reminder of how entrenched Greek culture had become in Rome. His six plays—*Andria, Heauton Timorumenos, Eunuchus, Phormio, Hecyra*, and *Adelphoe*—enjoyed tremendous success despite the relative absence of farce and stand with those of Plautus as having a tremendous influence not only on subsequent Roman literature, but on the entire Western comic tradition.

SURVEY OF CRITICISM

To understand Terence, it is necessary to understand Plautus; and to understand either, it is necessary to consider their models. The discovery in the nineteenth and twentieth centuries of numerous papyrus fragments of Greek New

Comedy, including a virtually complete play by Menander, has caused a revolution in studies on Roman comedy. Particularly valuable on Plautine adaptations of Greek models are Friedrich Leo's 1912 study and that of Eduard Fraenkel (1922). Traditional views of Terence's relation to Plautus are found in Gilbert Norwood's works (1923 and 1965); a more nuanced and modern approach, along with a solid appreciation of the playwright's aesthetics, can be found in Sander M. Goldberg (1986). For the unreliability of the ancient biographical traditions, see Mary R. Lefkowitz (1981).

SELECTIVE BIBLIOGRAPHY

Works by Terence

Comediae. Ed. Robert Kaver and W.M. Lindsay. Oxford Classical Texts. Oxford: Clarendon Press, 1926.
Terence. Ed. and trans. John Sargeaunt. Loeb Classical Library. Cambridge, Mass.: Harvard University Press, 1947–1953.
Phormio, and Other Plays. Trans. and intro. Betty Radice. Harmondsworth: Penguin, 1967.
The Complete Comedies of Terence. Trans. Palmer Bovie, Constance Carrier, and Douglas Parker. New Brunswick, N.J.: Rutgers University Press, 1974.

Selective Studies of Terence

Büchner, Karl. *Das Theater des Terenz*. Heidelberg: C. Winter, 1974.
Fantham, Elaine. "Adaptation and Survival: A Genre Study of Roman Comedy in Relation to Its Greek Sources." In *Versions of Medieval Comedy*, 19–49. Ed. Paul G. Ruggiers. Norman: University of Oklahoma Press, 1977.
Fraenkel, Eduard. *Plautinisches im Plautus*. Berlin: Weidmann, 1922.
Goldberg, Sander M. *Understanding Terence*. Princeton: Princeton University Press, 1986.
Lefkowitz, Mary R. *The Lives of the Greek Poets*. Baltimore: Johns Hopkins University Press, 1981.
Leo, Friedrich. *Plautinische Forschungen*. 2nd ed. Berlin: Weidmann, 1912.
Norwood, Gilbert. *The Art of Terence*. Oxford: B. Blackwell, 1923; New York: Russell & Russell, 1965.
———. *Plautus and Terence*. New York: Cooper Square Publishers, 1963.

ALEXIS DE TOCQUEVILLE
(1805–1859)

Melvin Richter

BIOGRAPHY

Alexis de Tocqueville came from an ancient Norman noble family. Through his mother he was related to Chrétien Guillaume de Lamoignon de Malesherbes, once minister under Louis XVI, whom he defended as his attorney when the king was tried and condemned to death. Malesherbes was also guillotined, a fate barely avoided by Tocqueville's parents. Alexis was trained and served briefly as a magistrate. In 1831 he went to the United States, ostensibly on a mission to write an official report on American prisons, but his real purpose was to study democracy firsthand. The first part of *De la démocratie en Amérique* appeared in 1835; the second, in 1840. The volume's success enabled him to begin his political career as a member of the Chamber of Deputies, where he served as head of the commission reporting on Algeria, recently conquered by France. Although he rejected the racial theories of Joseph Arthur Gobineau, his positions on the French treatment of Algerians differed from his criticism in *De la démocratie en Amérique* of how native Americans were dealt with by the United States. But Tocqueville championed both the abolition of slavery in the French colonies and reform of the French prison system.

After the 1848 revolution Louis-Napoléon was elected the first president of the Second Republic. Although Tocqueville served briefly as his foreign minister, following the coup d'état and plebiscite that made Louis-Napoléon emperor, he withdrew from political life and wrote two important works on the level of the *Démocratie*, his *Souvenirs* and *L'Ancien Régime et la Révolution*, the one completed volume of the three he intended on the origins of the French Revolution, the Revolution itself, and the seizure of power by Napoleon Bonaparte and his establishment of a martial empire. His search for the origin and nature of Bonapartist plebiscitary dictatorship in democracy, revolution, and war was among the most powerful sources of his later work.

MAJOR MULTICULTURAL THEMES

Tocqueville ranks high as one of the most penetrating, prophetic, and least deceived political thinkers of his century. The concepts with which he concerned himself, important in his time and ours, were democracy, despotism, revolution, centralization, liberty, equality, and history—its interpretation, significance, and effects upon political choices. He was a great practitioner of the comparative method he had learned from Montesquieu: "Although I seldom mentioned France, I did not write a page without thinking of her, and placing her before me, as it were. And what I especially tried to draw out and explain about the United States [were] . . . the points in which it differs from or resembles our own. I believe that this perpetual silent reference to France was a principal cause of the book's success" (*Correspondance d'Alexis de Tocqueville et de Louis de Kergolay*, in *Oeuvres complètes* [Gallimard edition] 13, tome 2, 209).

Because he cared so much for freedom, Tocqueville devoted much of his attention to its endangerment in the age of democracy: the tyranny of majority opinion, of elected legislatures, of democratic armies and their Bonapartist leaders, and the unprecedented "democratic despotism," beneficent to citizens, but allowing them neither a place in government nor opportunities to participate in self-government in order to develop the qualities essential to citizenship. He diagnosed dangers to liberty created by previous violent revolutions and by the great changes in the structures of politics and society, as well as in ideas, all of which had made inevitable the end of the ancien régime in Europe. To study the prototype of the democratic and egalitarian society he believed would dominate Europe as well as the United States, he had traveled to the New World in 1831. From that visit came his great *De la démocratie en Amérique*.

He contrasted the democracy he had seen in Jacksonian America to the political practices developed in France during the Terror, Consulate, and Empire. He himself considered the aspirations of the French Revolution's first period to have been noble and disinterested—the attempt to realize in political life the ideals of freedom and equality for all. What he condemned was the destruction of political and religious liberties during the more radical phases of the Revolution and the ensuing Bonapartist regime. In his view, the French Revolution had left an ambiguous heritage: two traditions of democracy, one compatible with citizens ruling themselves, while enjoying liberty, the rule of law, and individual rights; the other, rule in the name of the people by individuals, groups, or parties openly contemptuous of any limits upon popular sovereignty, the ostensible source of the power they themselves wielded in the name of the people. Worst of all among those who regarded themselves as revolutionaries was their scornful disdain for constitutional procedures and individual rights.

As evidenced in *De la démocratie en Amérique*, his concerns there were not limited to the United States. American success in creating a democracy that combined liberty and equality was due to the self-limiting restraint citizens imposed on themselves, acknowledging the laws to which they had consented and that they had helped frame. Tocqueville distrusted centralized bureaucracies that gave no scope to local governments. Administered from the center, they neither recognize the advantages of voluntary groups nor concede the rights to free expression of its citizens. He ultimately incorporated into his political theory his analysis of the French Revolution and his comparison of it to the English and American revolutions. For, in his view, the ultimate causes of the French Revolution came from long-standing policies of the Crown and from failures of his own class, the aristocracy. The Crown had long divided social classes and excluded subjects from government. Unlike its British opposite numbers, the French aristocracy made itself into a caste closed to new talents; it ceased to perform the functions that had once justified its privileges. Yet he believed that France, too, could combine equality with liberty. To do so, the French would have to follow Tocqueville's example in taking seriously the political cultures of the United States and Great Britain, the practices and political institutions of which would have to be adapted to France's own unique heritage.

SURVEY OF CRITICISM

The single best book on Tocqueville's life and political career is by André Jardin (1988). Classic works on *De la démocratie en Amérique* include those of G.W. Pierson (1938, reprinted 1996), for its reconstruction of the journey; and James Schleifer (1980), for its analysis of how the book was written. The two critical editions of the *Démocratie* (Nolla, 1990; Lamberti and Schleifer, 1992) although indispensable, do not altogether agree. A disputed issue—whether Tocqueville changed his views while writing the 1840 part of the *Démocratie*—is argued by Lamberti in *Tocqueville and the Two Democracies* (1989) and by Drescher and Schleifer in the Eisenstadt (1988) and Nolla (1992) collections. Tocqueville's intellectual debts are treated by Richter (1969) and by Raymond Aron (1968), who contrasts Tocqueville to Marx and Comte. Tocqueville's views on French colonial and foreign policy, particularly the conquest of Algeria, are studied by Richter (1963) and Todorov (1989).

SELECTIVE BIBLIOGRAPHY

Works by Tocqueville

Oeuvres complètes d'Alexis de Tocqueville. Ed. Gustave de Beaumont. 9 vols. Paris: Michel Lévy, 1864–1866.

Democracy in America. Ed. and trans. Phillips Bradley. 2 vols. New York: Random House, 1945.

Oeuvres complètes d'Alexis de Tocqueville. 18 vols. Paris: Gallimard, 1951–.

Recollections. Trans. George Lawrence. Ed. J.P. Mayer and A.P. Kerr. Garden City, N.Y.: Doubleday, 1970.

De la démocratie en Amérique. Ed. Eduardo Nolla. 2 vols. Paris: Vrin, 1990.

Oeuvres. 2 vols. *Voyages; Ecrits et discours politiques: Écrits sur L'Algérie, les colonies, l'abolition, et l'esclavage* (vol. 1). Ed. André Jardin, Françoise Mélonio, and Lise Queffélec. Bibliothèque de la Pléiade. Paris: Gallimard, 1991.

De la démocratie en Amérique. Ed. Jean-Claude Lamberti et James Schleifer. Bibliothèque de la Pléiade. Paris: Gallimard, 1992.

Selective Studies of Tocqueville

Aron, Raymond. *Main Currents in Sociological Thought.* 2 vols. Garden City, N.Y.: Anchor Books, 1968.

Drescher, Seymour. *Dilemmas of Democracy.* Pittsburgh: University of Pittsburgh Press, 1968.

———. *Tocqueville and England.* Cambridge, Mass.: Harvard University Press, 1964.

Eisenstadt, Abraham S., ed. *Reconsidering Tocqueville's Democracy in America.* New Brunswick, N.J.: Rutgers University Press, 1988.

Jardin, André. *Tocqueville: A Biography.* Trans. Lydia Davis and Robert Hemenway. New York: Farrar Straus Giroux, 1988.

Lamberti, Jean-Claude. *Tocqueville and the Two Democracies.* Cambridge, Mass.: Harvard University Press, 1989.

Nolla, Eduardo, ed. *Liberty, Equality, Democracy.* New York: New York University Press, 1992.

Pierson, G.W. *Tocqueville and Beaumont in America* (1938). Reprinted as *Tocqueville in America.* Baltimore: Johns Hopkins University Press, 1996.

Richter, Melvin. "A Debate on Race: The Tocqueville-Gobineau Correspondence." *Commentary* 25 (1958): 151–60.

———. "Tocqueville on Algeria." *Review of Politics* 25 (1963): 362–98.

———. "Comparative Political Analysis in Montesquieu and Tocqueville." *Comparative Politics* 1 (1969): 129–60.

Schleifer, James. *The Making of Tocqueville's* Democracy in America. Chapel Hill: University of North Carolina Press, 1980.

Todorov, Tzvetan. *Nous et les autres: La réflexion française sur la diversité humaine.* Paris: Editions du Seuil, 1989.

LEV NIKOLAEVICH TOLSTOY
(1828–1910)

Robert Bird

BIOGRAPHY

Lev Tolstoy's life was one long search for truth and an equally tortuous process of constant metamorphosis. Born into one of the most ancient and renowned families of the Russian landed aristocracy, he suffered from a perfectionism that saw him by turns try his hand at being officer, celebrated writer, pedagogue, novelist, and then universal moral teacher, without ever achieving inward contentment.

Tolstoy grew up at the family estate of Yasnaya Polyana. His mother died before his second birthday, and his fondest memories were of his German tutor Friedrich (Fedor) Rössel. After his father's death in 1837 he was shunted among relatives and ended up in Kazan, where in 1844 he enrolled at the university, but left without obtaining a degree. He then spent a few years at Yasnaya Polyana and in 1851 traveled to the Caucasus, becoming a commissioned officer in the army and serving in Romania and Moldavia. Concurrently he began publishing stories from military life and a series of autobiographical novels, *Detstvo*, *Otrochestvo*, and *Iunost'* (1852–1857). His service in the Crimean War was reflected in the three Sevastopol sketches (1855–1856), in which his unique narrative mode was widely noted. Leaving the army, he settled in St. Petersburg and in 1857 toured Paris, Switzerland, Italy, and Germany—experiences that inspired him to social critique. His penchant for moral allegory and protest marks stories such as "Liutserna" (1857) and "Tri smerti" (1859).

Up to this time his life presents a series of dissipated sprees and ensuing self-recriminations, minutely chronicled in his diary. Although he never resolved all the contradictions of his private life, he finally gathered the strength to break with the most egregious forms of womanizing, gambling, and carousing. The year 1859 marks the first of many breaks in his writing career, as he returned to his estate to devote himself to educating his peasants and developing popular pedagogy. In 1860 he traveled to Germany and London (with visits to France, Italy, and Belgium) expressly to gather information on contemporary pedagogical theory, about which he then published a journal, *Iasnaia Poliana* (1862–1863). In 1862 he fulfilled one of the major conditions of his moral reform by marrying Sofia Bers, after which he returned wholeheartedly to literature, rarely abandoning the family nest and only then for destinations inside Russia, although at his estates in Samara Province he came into close contact with national minorities. In *Kazaki* (1863) he presents a kind of synthesis of his military and moral stories, extended into an epic narrative that prepared the way for his next and most celebrated work, *Voina i mir* (finished in 1869).

After another bout of pedagogy (1870–75), during which he wrote a popular grammar and several readers of traditional and original tales, he completed *Anna Karenina* (1877). He then underwent a comprehensive spiritual crisis that he recounted in *Ispoved'* (1882) and other religious books. His syncretic religious creed and social engagement, especially during the famine of the early 1890s, attracted both disciples and derision: pilgrims to Yasnaya Polyana included people of many nationalities and walks of life, but his works were often banned, and in 1901 he was solemnly excommunicated from the Russian Orthodox Church. His disavowal of literature was frequently breached, most notably by the stories "Smert' Ivana Il'icha" (1886), "Kreitserova sonata" (1889), and "Khoziain i rabotnik" (1895) and by the novels *Voskresenie* (1899; banned in England due to its explicit treatment of sex) and *Khadzhi Murat* (1904). He continued to publish (often outside of Russia) religious and moral tracts, pedagogical books, and collections of morally instructive tales. He took up the cause of various religious minorities and dissenters in Russia, eventually gaining them the right to emigrate. The last decades of his life were plagued by ill health and mutual suspicions between himself, his wife, and his followers, so much so that he eventually ran away from home and died, at the age of eighty-two, at a train station in the small town of Astapovo.

MAJOR MULTICULTURAL THEMES

Many of Tolstoy's earliest works, his small gem "Kavkazskii plennik" (1872), and his final masterpiece *Khadzhi Murat* were set in the Caucasus and touched upon the relations between the colonizing Russians and the colonized native populations, who were typically portrayed as noble, but as quite amoral in their warfare and human relationships. A similarly ambivalent attitude prevailed in his depiction of Gypsies, as in "Dva gusara" (1856) and the play *Zhivoi trup* (1900). This realistic portrayal of "savage" Oriental character, calculated to clash with reigning romantic clichés, was combined with an equally realistic assessment of the shortcomings of the "civilized" Russians; Tolstoy always relished the clash of human imperfections, which for him underscored a universal ideal of human brotherhood and self-abnegation.

In diary entries written during the Crimean War he showed respect for the efficiency and dignity of the English and French troops, and in 1872 a run-in with the local authorities drove him to contemplate emigrating to England for its civil liberties. However, his travels in Europe left little trace in his works and letters; a negative aspect of his attitude toward the West was foregrounded in "Liutserna," where the Russian protagonist finds a poor Italian street musician of infinitely greater human value than the mass of diffident English tourists at his hotel. A similar attitude, however, is expressed in the story "Al'bert" (1858) concerning the superficial Russian aristocracy's inability to understand a German musician in Petersburg. Thus Tolstoy's use of cultural stereotypes is most often a means of highlighting authentic and inauthentic attitudes toward life.

Nowhere is this as prominent as in *Voina i mir*, which opens in a Russian aristocratic salon where the conversation is mostly in French: the negative connotations of this scene have less to do with any inherent deficiency of the French language than with the artificiality of Russians discussing their national fate in a foreign tongue. Similarly, the negative portrayal of Napoleon and of the German generals in the Russian army is directed mostly at their mistaken and hubristic belief that through their personal greatness or calculation they are able to direct historical events. All the positive characters in the novel are Russian, but it is only those Russians who are in harmony with their own national character and, therefore, in harmony with the uncontrollable flow of nature and history that merit Tolstoy's approval.

A similar situation obtains in *Anna Karenina*. The title heroine is shown reading an "English novel" on a train, which implies that she lives in an illusionary reality where ethical standards are suspended. Her lover Vronsky, who races horses and aspires to be a model English squire, is trapped in a similar predicament. Only Levin, who engages in an untiring search for an authentic lifestyle (which, however, is pointedly not that of a Russian peasant), is felt to be capable of personal salvation. Tolstoy may have seen Russians as somewhat closer to achieving authenticity than Western Europeans, for whom he rarely had an unequivocally good word in his works, but in the end he was an individualist and saw this as the personal quest of every conscientious human. This was also reflected in his writings on pedagogy, where he opposed the systematic approach of German pedagogical theory and advocated an approach based on the teacher answering the concrete needs of his or her pupils; Tolstoy saw popular education as more promising in Russia than in the West precisely because it had not yet been spoiled by rote learning and inhumane discipline.

In his ethical-religious writings he tended to erase differences between nationalities. He undertook a study of ancient languages in order to read the Scriptures in the original and then composed a universal gospel, a kind of religious Esperanto marked by pacifism, nonresistance, vegetarianism, temperance, and physical labor. Tolstoy's four *Russkie knigi dlia chteniia* (1875) include numerous tales and anecdotes set in locales as distinct as Algeria and Rome, but these settings are mostly conventional and dispensable. In his *Krug chteniia* he collected parables and moralizing sayings from all national traditions into an edifying calendar. His syncretic religion thus attracted disciples throughout the world, from England to India (e.g., Mahatma Gandhi).

SURVEY OF CRITICISM

The best Tolstoy biographies are by his friend and translator Aylmer Maude (1987) and by Ernest J. Simmons (1946). Richard Gustafson (1986) offers a convenient scheme for considering Tolstoy's relations to other cultures. Gustafson writes that Tolstoy, pursued by a constant sense of alienation from those around him, forever sought to be at home somewhere, and that this formed the basic tension in many of his works. Moreover, Tolstoy was profoundly suspicious of people who seemed themselves to feel at home, such as the English in "Lucerne" with their staid self-satisfaction or even the Caucasian warriors and Cossacks of his military tales.

Tolstoi i zarubezhnyi mir (1965) provides a vast array of materials on Tolstoy's personal relations with representatives of various national cultures. The volume *Tolstoi and Britain* (1995), edited by W. Gareth Jones, presents a collection of contemporary writings and later criticism on Tolstoy's links to British literature and society, while Thaïs Lindstrom's *Tolstoi en France, 1886–1910* (1952) studies his connections to French contemporaries. Robert Kenneth Schulz (1969) summarizes the role of Germans in Tolstoy's works. Judith Kornblatt (1992) discusses Tolstoy's portrayal of the Cossacks compared to the tradition established by Gogol and other Russian writers. Andrew Donskov and John Woodsworth's edited volume (1996) includes several chapters that address the writer's understanding of how brotherly relations could be established among peoples.

SELECTIVE BIBLIOGRAPHY

Works by Tolstoy

Polnoe sobranie sochinenii. 90 vols. Moscow: Gosudarstvennoe izdatel'stvo "Khudozhestvennaia literatura," 1928–1958.

Nine Stories. Trans. Louise and Aylmer Maude. London: Oxford University Press, 1934. (Includes "Liutserna" and "Al'bert.")

Sobranie sochinenii v dvadtsati tomakh. 20 vols. Moscow: Gosudarstvennoe izdatel'stvo khudozhestvennoi literatury, 1960–1965.

Voina i mir (1869). *War and Peace.* Trans. Louise and Aylmer Maude. Ed. George Gibian. New York: W.W. Norton, 1966.

Great Short Works of Leo Tolstoy. Trans. Louise and Aylmer Maude. Intro. John Bayley. New York: Harper and Row, 1967. (Includes *Kazaki* and *Khadzhi Murat.*)

Selective Studies of Tolstoy

Donskov, Andrew, and John Woodsworth, eds. *Lev Tolstoy and the Concept of Brotherhood.* Ottawa: Legas, 1996.

Gustafson, Richard F. *Leo Tolstoy, Resident and Stranger: A Study in Fiction and Theology*. Princeton: Princeton University Press, 1986.

Jones, W. Gareth, ed. *Tolstoi and Britain*. Oxford and Washington, D.C.: Berg, 1995.

Kornblatt, Judith Deutsch. *The Cossack Hero in Russian Literature: A Study in Cultural Mythology*. Madison: University of Wisconsin Press, 1992.

Lindstrom, Thaïs S. *Tolstoi en France, 1886–1910*. Paris: Institut d'études slaves de l'Université de Paris, 1952.

Maude, Aylmer. *The Life of Tolstoy*. Oxford and New York: Oxford University Press, 1987.

Schulz, Robert Kenneth. *The Portrayal of the German in Russian Novels: Goncarov, Turgenev, Dostoevskij, Tolstoj*. Slavistische Beiträge, Bd. 42. Munich: O. Sagner, 1969.

Simmons, Ernest J. *Leo Tolstoy*. Boston: Little, Brown, 1946.

Tolstoi i zarubezhnyi mir. Literaturnoe nasledstvo, tom 75. 2 vols. Moscow: Nauka, 1965.

Zinner, E.P. *Tvorchestvo L.N. Tolstogo i angliiskaia realisticheskaia literatura kontsa XIX i nachala XX stoletiia*. Irkutsk: Irkutskii gos. pedagog. inst., 1961.

CRISTINA TRIVULZIO BARBIANO DI BELGIOIOSO
(1808–1871)

Rinaldina Russell

BIOGRAPHY

Princess Barbiano di Belgioioso, née Countess Cristina Trivulzio, described by some as a "romantic princess," was a historian, a pragmatic politician, and an indefatigable activist. Born into an illustrious Milanese family, she learned Italian, French, English, and Latin and became multicultural at an early age. After a failed marriage she traveled in Italy and France, eventually settling in Paris, where she adopted the French language. Her progressive ideas, her aversion to the Austrian domination of Lombardy, and her backing of political conspirators placed her under the surveillance of the Milanese police, who, in order to force her return, blocked any transfer of her funds. Introduced by Adolphe Thierry to François Auguste Mignet and General Lafayette, the men who had promoted the constitutional monarchy of Louis Philippe, Trivulzio maintained a friendship with them that strongly influenced her political convictions and social outlook. Her salon was the meeting place for intellectuals and artists from many parts of Europe, as well as for Italian expatriates. To gain support for Italian unity and independence, she began a lifelong career as a political journalist, contributing articles to French and Italian newspapers and journals, some of which she founded, directed, or financed.

Back in Italy in 1840, partly inspired by the ideas of Saint-Simon and Charles Fourier, she transformed her country estate at Locate into a community for rural workers, equipped with schools and workshops for women and men, and produced contemporarily two volumes on Catholic dogma, a translation of Giambattista Vico's *Scienza nuova*, and a lengthy *Étude sur l'histoire de la Lombardie dans les trente dernières années* (1846). When the 1848 Milanese uprising against Austria failed, Trivulzio, who had entered Milan at the head of a volunteer battalion she had herself financed, returned to Paris, explaining to the French the reasons for the failure through a series of articles in *La Revue des deux mondes*. In 1849, at the time of the short-lived Roman Republic, she was in Rome, appointed by Giuseppe Mazzini as the director of all field hospitals. After the fall of the Republic she went into exile, sailing for Malta, Greece, and, finally, Istanbul, writing letters all the while to her friend Madame Jaubert in Paris, which appeared serially in the Parisian *Le National* ("Souvenirs dans l'exil," 1850). After purchasing Turkish property in the valley of Ciaq-Maq-Oglou, she embarked on a year's journey to Jerusalem, crossing Turkey, Syria, and Lebanon, then all parts of the Ottoman Empire, writing articles that appeared in *La Revue des deux mondes* (1855) and were then edited for the volume *Asie Mineure et Syrie: Souvenirs de voyage* (1858). In 1858 she returned to Italy, where she died thirteen years later.

MAJOR MULTICULTURAL THEMES

Trivulzio drew from both Italian and French intellectual life, her early belief in progress becoming strengthened by close friendship with François Mignet. His philosophy of history posited a continuous advance toward freedom and justice, which she associated with the spirit of equality found in evangelical Christianity. Yet she advocated the separation of church and state, a notion that was at the core of the political principles of such Italian liberals as Bettino Ricasoli and Gino Capponi. In her introduction to *La Science Nouvelle par Vico* (1844) she disputed the cyclical theory of history, maintaining that human events move relentlessly toward their final goal, which is the reconstruction of national identities and the abolition of social inequality.

Her awareness of how the hegemonic culture is at work in a given society, and how important customs and institutions are in understanding the way different people behave, helped to develop her exploration of the Austrian domination in northern Italy into a study of the critical role played by the educational system and cultural institutions in the systematic corrosion of the Italian spirit and identity. Pervasive in her work also is the persuasion that the education and improved economic conditions of the masses would redound to the benefit of the whole nation; its corollary was her lifelong belief in the effectiveness of newspapers for the political emancipation of the public, as well as for promoting understanding between nations. The marks of a multicultural writer become more obvious in her works on Italy's economic situation and potential for economic development, in which she makes constant reference to other countries in Europe and to neighboring Islamic nations.

The intercultural dialogue intensifies in *Asie Mineure et Syrie*—not travel writing limited to a description of landscapes, sites, and historical background, but a lively study of the life that unfolds in the villages of the poor, in the residences of the powerful, and in the tents of nomadic tribes. She inquires about the use of thoroughfares (and those who control them), about local agriculture, and about mining profits; she discusses local moral values and the logic of the economic life of the different ethnic and religious groups, as well as the reasons for the hatred that divides them. We find detailed descriptions of the harems and of the difference of Turkish peasant households, which, she states, should be held up as a model to European peasants. Scattered throughout are astute psychological observations on the motivations of both women and men and on the effects of strong respect for tradition. The reader is also apprised of Christian institutions in the Middle East, in their Greek, Armenian, Catholic, and Protestant variations, as well as of the attempts by the Anglican clergy to convert the native population—attempts she calls naïve. She is aware of her own cultural bias, declaring that her observations are those of a European Christian whose cultural standards, morality, and taste are diametrically opposed to those of the countries observed. Even so, she believes in the necessity of studying the conditions of the local people through "the traditions that have influenced them and the institutions growing out of them." The questions that she asks are still relevant today and could be extended to other parts of the globe: "What are the principles of the Turkish government? What germs of vitality and basis for reform does it contain? What relationship can subsist between it and Christian Europe?" (*Asie Mineure et Syrie*, 232–33).

SURVEY OF CRITICISM

Trivulzio's many-sided personality, her mixture of aristocratic background, wealth, intellectual interests, and arresting good looks, and her friendships with intellectuals, politicians, writers, and artists of her day have intrigued contemporaries and modern biographers alike, often leading them toward gossipy and sensational depictions of her personal life. Both Beth Archer Brombert (1977) and Arrigo Petacco (1993) offer insightful evocations of Trivulzio's private life. Raffaello Barbiera (1902) was the first to consider her contribution to the Risorgimento struggle. Luigi Severgnini (1972) and Emilio Guicciardi (1973) underline the progressive beliefs motivating her activism. In his long preface to *Il 1848 a Milano e Venezia* (1977), Sandro Bortone analyzes the various domestic and foreign influences on Trivulzio's political and social conduct, while Ludovico Incisa and Alberica Trivulzio (1984) stress the leading part she played in constructing the character and morality of the nation, as well as the international outlook permeating her political ideas and social projects. Feminist studies, two of which adopt a multicultural approach, have focused on Trivulzio's representation of women's condition in the Middle East and on her proposal for the emancipation of women in Italy: Claire Marrone (1997) studies Trivulzio's fiction with an eye to her representation of gender oppression in different cultures; Paola Giuli (1991) links Trivulzio's observations of Muslim reality to her subsequent understanding of patriarchal society.

SELECTIVE BIBLIOGRAPHY

Works by Trivulzio

La Science Nouvelle par Vico, traduite par l'auteur de l'Essai sur la formation du dogme catholique. Paris: J. Renouard, 1844.

Étude sur l'histoire de la Lombardie dans les trente dernières années. Paris: Jules Laisné, 1846. (Published also as *Studi intorno alla storia della Lombardia negli ultimi trent'anni e delle cagioni del difetto d'energia dei Lombardi.* Paris: Jules Laisné, 1847.)

"L'insurrection milanaise. Le gouvernement provisoire. Les corps auxiliaires" and "La guerre de Lombardie, le siège et la capitulation de Milan." *Revue des deux mondes,* September 15 and October 1, 1848. (Both published as *L'Italia e la rivoluzione italiana nel 1848.* Lugano: Tipografia della Svizzera italiana, 1849; now to be found as *Il 1848 a Milano e a Venezia: Con uno scritto sulla condizione delle donne.* Ed. Sandro Bortone. Milano: Feltrinelli, 1977.)

"Souvenirs dans l'exil." *Le National,* September 5–October 12, 1850. (These letters were republished in book form by the Istituto Editoriale Italiano of Milan in 1946 and were translated into Italian by Luigi Severgnini with the title *Ricordi dell'esilio,* Roma: Edizioni Paoline, 1978.)

Asie Mineure et Syrie: Souvenirs de voyage. Paris: Michel Lévy, 1858. (*Oriental Harems and Scenery.* New York: Carleton, 1962.)

Scènes de la vie turque. Paris: Michel Lévy, 1858. (This volume contains three stories: "Emina," "Un prince Kurde," and "Les deux femmes d'Ismail-Bey.")

"Zobeydeh." *Revue des deux mondes.* April 1 and 15, 1858.

Selective Studies of Trivulzio

Barbiera, Raffaello. *La principessa di Belgioioso, i suoi amici, i suoi nemici e il suo tempo.* Milano: Treves, 1902.

Brombert, Beth Archer. *Cristina: Portraits of a Princess.* New York: Knopf, 1977.

Giuli, Paola. "Cristina di Belgioioso's Orient." *NEMLA Italian Studies* 15 (1991): 129–50.

Guicciardi, Emilio. *Cristina di Belgiojoso Trivulzio cento anni dopo.* Milano: La Martinella di Milano, 1973.

Incisa, Ludovico, and Alberica Trivulzio. *Cristina di Belgioioso: La principessa romantica.* Milano: Rusconi, 1984.

Marrone, Claire. "Cristina Trivulzio di Belgiojoso's Western Feminism: The Poetics of a Nineteenth-Century Nomad." *Italian Quarterly* 34 (Summer–Fall 1997): 21–32.

Petacco, Arrigo. *La principessa del Nord: La misteriosa vita della dama del Risorgimento.* Milano: Mondadori, 1993.

Severgnini, Luigi. *La principessa di Belgiojoso.* Milano: Edizioni Virgilio, 1972.

IVAN SERGEEVICH TURGENEV
(1818–1883)

Robert Bird

BIOGRAPHY

Ivan Turgenev, the preeminent Russian European, maintained in his private life a precarious balance between aristocratic tradition and bohemian rootlessness. His father was of the landed gentry in Orel Province and encouraged his sons in their education, especially in their command of their native tongue. This paternal sense of historical roots was an important counterpoint to the overwhelming influence of Turgenev's mother, a ruthless landowner who preferred all things French. In 1833 he entered Moscow University, transferring to St. Petersburg University a year later. He soon gained entrance to the literary world of Petersburg, brushing shoulders with such luminaries as Pushkin and Gogol. In 1838 he traveled to Europe to continue his studies at the University of Berlin, where he became close to Russian thinkers of a liberal or socialist persuasion, and also to tour Germany and Italy. He spent 1841–45 in Russia, expanding his contacts with "Westernizer" circles, debating representatives of the nascent Slavophile movement, considering an academic or bureaucratic career, and fathering a daughter with one of his mother's serfs.

In 1845 he left Russia again, this time in order to be near the singer Pauline Garcia-Viardot, whom he had met in St. Petersburg in 1843; his strange, lifelong attachment to Viardot, who was married to the writer and director Louis Viardot, meant that for the rest of his life Turgenev was unable to remain in Russia for long, traveling home mostly to deal with publishing or financial matters. Through the Viardots he became active in French artistic circles. He was abroad again in 1847–50, witnessing the tumult of 1848 at close quarters in Paris, as he later described in memoir sketches. Returning to Russia in 1850, he experienced a painful break with his mother, who died shortly thereafter, but also a meteoric ascent to the summit of Russian literature after the publication of his *Zapiski okhotnika* (1852), which received more acclaim than any of his previous writings. After several months under house arrest at his estate (ostensibly for publishing an obituary of Gogol), he moved to St. Petersburg (1853–56), establishing a tense relationship with Lev Tolstoy and participating wholeheartedly in the life of the capital.

His 1855 *Rudin* was the first of several novels that did the most to secure his international reputation, including *Dvorianskoe gnezdo* (1858), *Nakanune* (1859), *Ottsy i deti* (1862), *Dym* (1867), and *Nov'* (1877). He resided mainly in Europe (1856–61), maintaining contact with Russians in Europe, broadening his circle of European acquaintances, and meeting such figures as Carlyle and Thackeray. Inspired by the emancipation of the Russian serfs in 1861, he returned with the intention of participating in Russia's renewal, but, finding the economic and ideological situation disappointingly ambivalent, in 1863 he retired to Baden-Baden to join the Viardots. He lived mostly in Germany until 1870, when in the aftermath of the Franco-Prussian War (which he reported on for a Russian periodical) the Viardots moved to London, where in 1871 Turgenev met George Eliot and Tennyson, and then France, where he entered into close and lasting contact with leading French writers and struck up a close friendship with Henry James. Periodic visits to Russia continued, giving rise to intermittent love affairs and gradually restoring his credibility as a voice in Russian society. In the final years of his life, encumbered with a series of serious illnesses, he wrote several stories with unusually supernatural elements and a book of "poems in prose," published under the title *Senilia*. In 1879 he traveled to Oxford to receive an honorary degree. He died of cancer of the spine at the Viardots' residence near Paris.

MAJOR MULTICULTURAL THEMES

Turgenev was an important mediator between Russian and Western European literatures. For the Russian reader, he translated Flaubert and several poets and popularized writers from Shakespeare and Calderón to George Sand. For the Western reader, he translated or aided others (Louis Viardot, Prosper Mérimée) in translating Russian writers such as Pushkin, Lermontov, Gogol, and Tolstoy.

He often held Western civilization up as a model for his compatriots. In the travelogue "Iz-za granitsy" (1857) he complained of the lack of curiosity of Russians in Europe, who were oblivious to "the joy that comes from staying in a country whose past you know well, from the personal verification of historical memories and facts, and from that special feeling that overcomes a man when he sees the traces or monuments of a great national life" (*Polnoe sobranie sochinenii*, 15:8–9). However, both here and in a famous late "poem in prose" entitled "Russkii iazyk" he was also calling on Russians to cultivate a consciousness of their own "great national life," founded on the Russian tongue. Russia's misfortune was to be muddling along without being able to express its own character: "Foreign influences are liable to knock from their path only those who in any case were not going anywhere" (*Polnoe sobranie sochinenii*, 15:11).

There was an inner tension in his efforts to synthesize Russian cultural energy and the forms of Western civilization, which contributed to his reputation as a "gentle barbarian" or lyric tragedian. His works do not yield a simplistic opposition between Russia and the West; it is possible to view the two cultures as representing the principles of Don Quixote and Hamlet, which he set forth in 1860. Russians (together perhaps with Italians) match the idealistic principle of Don Quixote, while Western civilization is represented by the realistic but reflective and indecisive Hamlet. In some of his stories ("Faust," "Veshnie vody") the purity of the Russian's Quixotic ideal is corrupted by the unsteady moral compass of a reflective attitude gained from the West. The heroes of Turgenev's novels are often either foreigners (e.g., the Bulgarian Insarov in *Nakanune*) or too divorced from reality (e.g., the superfluous Lavretsky in *Dvorianskoe gnezdo*) to act on their ideals. Positive heroes seem most likely to arise from those elements of Russian society that remain close to tradition: the peasantry and noble women (e.g., Liza in *Dvorianskoe gnezdo* and Elena in *Nakanune*). In *Zapiski okhotnika* Turgenev lent an artistic and human voice to the Russian peasantry, a feat often compared to Harriet Beecher Stowe's *Uncle Tom's Cabin*. He is also notable for presenting national minorities first and foremost as human beings (e.g., in "Zhid"). Many of his multicultural works are tied to the theme of emigration, featuring either non-Russians in Russia (e.g., Lemm in *Dvorianskoe gnezdo*) or Russians abroad (e.g., "Vecher v Sorrento," *Dym*).

SURVEY OF CRITICISM

Essays and notes on Turgenev's life abroad and connections with various foreign cultures are collected in *I.S. Turgenev: Novye materialy i issledovaniia* (1967) and in *I.S. Turgenev und Deutschland*, edited by Gerhard Ziegengeist (1965), which covers the writer's manifold ties to Germany and contains detailed studies of his life in Baden (by G. Schwirtz) and Karlsruhe (by E. Th. Hock). Schulz (1969) provides a catalogue of things German in Turgenev's works. Grevs's *Turgenev i Italiia* (1925) and the chapters by Calmaev, Cazzola, and Risaliti in the volume *Turgenev e l'Italia* edited by Alessandro Ivanov (1987) explore Turgenev's connections to Italy as well as the role of Italy in his works. Kauchtschischwili's "Turgenev europeista" (1980) gives an informative overview of Turgenev's position within and between various national cultures. Pumpianskii (1940) places Turgenev's novels in the context of contemporary European literature. Turgenev's relations with Britain are the subject of Waddington's *Turgenev and England* (1981) and his edited volume *Ivan Turgenev and Britain* (1995), which includes as well a bibliography of sources on Turgenev and England.

SELECTIVE BIBLIOGRAPHY

Works by Turgenev

Zapiski okhotnika (1852). *Sketches from a Hunter's Album.* Trans. Richard Freeborn. London: Penguin, 1990.

Dym (1867). *Smoke.* Trans. Constance Garnett. London: Heinemann, 1906.

"Veshnie vody" (1872). *Spring Torrents.* Trans. Leonard Schapiro. London: Eyre Methuen, 1972.

Literaturnye i zhiteiskie vospominaniia (1874). *Literary Reminiscences and Autobiographical Fragments.* Trans. David Magarshack. With an essay on Turgenev by Edmund Wilson. New York: Farrar, Straus and Cudahy, 1958.

Polnoe sobranie sochinenii i pisem v dvadtsati vos'mi tomakh. 28 vols. Moskva and Leningrad: Nauka, 1960–1968.

Sochineniia v dvenadtsati tomakh. 12 vols. 2nd ed. Moskva: Nauka, 1978–1986.

Flaubert and Turgenev: A Friendship in Letters: The Complete Correspondence. Ed. Barbara Beaumont. New York: Norton, 1985.

Selective Studies of Turgenev

Calmaev, Viktor. "Le immagini dell'Italia nel mondo artistico di I.S. Turgenev." In *Turgenev e l'Italia*, 25–36. Ed. Alessandro Ivanov. Biblioteca del viaggio in Italia. Genève: Slatkine, Centro interuniversitario di ricerche sul "Viaggio in Italia," 1987.

Cazzola, Piero. "Personaggi e paesaggi italiani nell'opera di I.S. Turgenev." In *Turgenev e l'Italia*, 49–61. Ed. Alessandro Ivanov. Biblioteca del viaggio in Italia. Genève: Slatkine, Centro interuniversitario di ricerche sul "Viaggio in Italia," 1987.

Freeborn, Richard. "Turgenev at Ventnor." In *Ivan Turgenev and Britain*, 173–93. Ed. Patrick Waddington. Oxford and Providence, R.I.: Berg, 1995.

Grevs, I.M. *Turgenev i Italiia: Kul'turno-istoricheskii etiud.* Leningrad: Brokgauz-Efron, 1925.

Halperine-Kaminsky, E., ed. *Tourguéneff and His French Circle.* Trans. Ethel M. Arnold. London: T. Fischer Unwin, 1898.

Hock, E. Th. "Turgenev in Karlsruhe." In *I.S. Turgenev und Deutschland: Materialen und Untersuchungen*, vol. 1, 270–87. Ed. Gerhard Ziegengeist. Berlin: Akademie-Verlag, 1965.

I.S. Turgenev: Novye materialy i issledovaniia. Ed. V.P. Shcherbina. Literaturnoe nasledstvo. Tom 76. Moskva: Nauka, 1967.

Ivanov, Alessandro, ed. *Turgenev e l'Italia.* Biblioteca del viaggio in Italia. Genève: Slatkine, Centro interuniversitario di ricerche sul "Viaggio in Italia," 1987.

Kauchtschischwili, Nina. "Turgenev europeista." In *Turgenev e la sua opera*, 105–28. Roma: Accademia nazionale dei Lincei, 1980.

Pumpianskii, L.V. "Turgenev i Zapad." In *I.S. Turgenev: Materialy i issledovaniia*, 90–107. Ed. N.L. Brodskii. Orel: Izdatel'stvo Orlovskogo Oblastnogo Soveta deputatov trudiashchikhsia, 1940.

Risaliti, Renato. "Turgenev e l'Italia: Natura, storia, arte e amicizie italiane in I. S. Turgenev." In *Turgenev e l'Italia*, 81–89. Ed. Alessandro Ivanov. Biblioteca del viaggio in Italia. Genève: Slatkine, Centro interuniversitario di ricerche sul "Viaggio in Italia," 1987.

Schulz, Robert Kenneth. *The Portrayal of the German in Russian Novels: Goncarov, Turgenev, Dostoevskij, Tolstoj.* Slavistiche Beiträge, Bd. 42. Munich: O. Sagner, 1969.

Schwirtz, G. "Baden im Leben und Schaffen Turgenevs." In *I.S. Turgenev und Deutschland: Materialen und Untersuchungen,* vol. 1, 247–69. Ed. Gerhard Ziegengeist. Berlin: Akademie-Verlag, 1965.

Simmons, J.S.G. "Turgenev and Oxford." In *Ivan Turgenev and Britain,* 208–12. Ed. Patrick Waddington. Oxford and Providence, R.I.: Berg, 1995.

Toman, I.B. "I.S. Turgenev i nemetskaia kul'tura." In *Turgenevskii sbornik.* Vypusk 1, 31–70. Moskva: Russkii put', 1998.

Waddington, Patrick, ed. *Ivan Turgenev and Britain.* Oxford and Providence, R.I.: Berg, 1995.

———. *Turgenev and England.* New York: New York University Press, 1981.

Ziegengeist, Gerhard, ed. *I.S. Turgenev und Deutschland: Materialen und Untersuchungen.* Vol. 1. Berlin: Akademie-Verlag, 1965.

GIAMBATTISTA VICO
(1668–1744)

Paul Archambault

BIOGRAPHY

Born in Naples in 1668, Giambattista Vico, in his autobiographical *Vita* (1725), describes his temperament as a "concourse" between his father's cheerful ("allegro") and his mother's melancholic ("malinconica") temper. At age seven he fell from a ladder, and it was predicted that he would either die of the cranial concussion he had suffered or become an idiot. Neither prediction came true, but he later attributed to this accident his "melancholy and irritable temperament such as belongs to men of ingenuity and depth" (*Autobiography*, translated by Fisch and Bergin [henceforth abbreviated A], 111).

Between his tenth and his eighteenth year his mind was shaped by his Jesuit education at the Collegio Massimo in Naples, where he studied Latin and Greek grammar before proceeding to the study of rhetoric, philosophy, and canon law. Among the books that shaped his thinking were the *Disputationes metaphysicae* of Francisco Suárez and the *Institutiones iuris civilis a Justiniano compositas commentarius* of Hermann Vulteius; he also took courses in canon law given by Francesco Verde. His health was delicate, his financial means were limited, and he had "an ardent desire for leisure to continue his studies," coupled with "a deep abhorrence for the clamor of the law courts" (A118). He was fortunate when he met the jurist Monsignor Geronimo Rocca, bishop of Ischia, who hired him to tutor his nephews in the castle of Vatollá in the Cilento region south of Naples. Vico spent most of the next nine years in that castle (1686–95), studying canon law and writing poetry in the manner of Boccaccio, Petrarch, and Dante (A119–20). Upon his return to Naples in 1695, trained as he was in the Greek philosophical tradition, he found himself "a stranger in his own land," since the geometrically based philosophy of Descartes was very much in fashion and Aristotle had been relegated to the rank of fable (A132). Rejecting an invitation to become a Theatine monk, he was appointed to a chair of rhetoric at the Royal University of Naples in 1699, a post he maintained for nearly forty years.

Between 1699 and 1708 he delivered a series of inaugural orations at the university, all of which reflected his conviction that a complete education needed to combine the scientifically based curriculum of a Descartes with the humanistic wisdom of the ancients. His conviction had been confirmed in the late 1690s by his discovery of Francis Bacon (1561–1626), who "did justice to all the sciences, and always with the design that each should make its special contribution to that *summa* which the universal republic of letters constitutes" (A139). Each of Vico's inaugural lectures set forth a course of liberal studies that follows a "true, easy, and unvarying order" based on "the knowledge of the corrupt nature of man" (A144). Eschewing Descartes's insistence on the training of mathematical reasoning to the exclusion of memory and imagination, Vico reasserts the conviction of ancient wisdom that memory is "marvelously strong" in childhood (A144). Memory and imagination must be developed first: hence the importance of languages, of poetry, of history "both fabulous and true," of quantitative science, then of progressively abstract sciences leading to metaphysics, then to ethics, revealed theology, Christian ethics, and Christian jurisprudence. Vico's ideal curriculum stresses a progression in scientific abstraction, then a "descent" based on ethical experience and "humbled intellect" back to theologically based studies of ethics and jurisprudence (A144–45).

One of the greatest setbacks of his life came in 1723 when he lost his bid for the chair of "the head morning lectures in law," which carried a stipend of six hundred ducats a year, six times what Vico was then earning (A160), but he showed his capacity to rebound from adversity and to keep working. Two years later, with the publication of the *Scienza nuova*, he became one of the most celebrated—and misunderstood—minds in all of Europe. The 1725 edition of that work was so overwhelmingly popular that a second, revised edition was requested of him in 1731, and a third version in 1744.

In spite of his fame and the controversy surrounding the meaning and importance of the *Scienza nuova*, the final years of his life were plagued by financial woes, domestic problems, and ill health. Appointment to the rank of royal historiographer by Charles of Bourbon in 1735 brought some financial relief, but his failing health forced him to retire as professor of rhetoric at the Royal University of Naples that same year. During his last eight years he suffered from what now appear to be symptoms of Alzheimer's disease, and according to the Marquis de Villarosa, his biographer, at the end he "did not recognize his own children" (A206).

MAJOR MULTICULTURAL THEMES

The chief problem of Vico's intellectual life he best formulated in the *Vita*, his intellectual autobiography: "Vico . . . came to perceive that there was not yet in the world of letters a system so devised as to bring the best philosophy, that of Plato made subordinate to the Christian faith, into harmony with a philology exhibiting scientific necessity in both its branches, . . . that of languages and that of things; to give certainty to the history of languages by reference to the history of things; and to bring into accord the maxims of the academic sages and the practices of the political sages" (A155). Although his judges failed to recognize the breadth and originality of his oration delivered in 1723, he fleshed out these ideas in his *Scienza nuova* two years later. In this, his magnum opus, he said that he had finally discovered "that principle which in his previous works he had as yet understood only in a confused and indirect way" (A166). Whereas previous research into the founders of nations had focused on their earliest written texts, Vico realized that these written texts "came thousands of years after these founders" and focused his own research on the popular traditions of the nations (A167). He took the division of history into three ages—gods, heroes, and men—and also adopted the threefold classification of language, coeval with the three ages: divine (hieroglyphics), symbolic (metaphors), and epistolographic (or demotic) (A167).

What he called the "master key" of his new science was that "the first gentile peoples were poets who spoke in poetic characters." This discovery had cost him twenty years of laborious research, forced as he was to "grope his way back from these humane and refined natures of ours to those wild and savage natures which we cannot really imagine and can only apprehend with great toil" (A56). Vico's mature intellectual life, one remembers, coincided with the Quarrel of the Ancients and the Moderns, which began in France but extended to all of Europe (1687–1715). He realized that the Quarrel, formulated in historically provincial terms, centered around Homer: to determine whether he had been equalled or surpassed in modern times. Vico dedicates the entire third book of his *Scienza nuova* to the "Homeric Question." His "master" intuition was that Homer, and what Western humanism since the Renaissance had called "antiquity," far from being ancient, was but the culmination of thousands of years of previous civilization (Levine, 73–75).

Vico anticipates the transition from rationalism to historicism, which was to become a commonplace of European thought in the century that followed him (A56). His impact on European thought was powerful. He exploded the European sense of time and history, forcing historians to look back thousands of years to the roots of European thought. While he gave impetus to fields such as Egyptology and the study of ancient Near Eastern civilizations, he is also considered the forefather of German historicism, especially as articulated in the works of Hegel, Marx, and Wilhelm Dilthey. While he has been hailed by some intellectual historians such as Benedetto Croce and Isaiah Berlin as the greatest modern philosopher of history, his influence extends to fields such as archeology, philology, and law, in which disciplines as well he argued for a historicist rather than a static view of natural law. The French historian Jules Michelet, who rediscovered Vico in the early nineteenth century after he had remained ignored for nearly a hundred years, paid tribute to "this solitary genius, from whom I have learned everything" (Introduction to *Oeuvres choisies de Vico*, vol. 1).

SURVEY OF CRITICISM

Vico's importance, since Michelet, has been clarified by Benedetto Croce, Isaiah Berlin, R.G. Collingwood, Edmund Wilson, and many others. William Butler Yeats wrote in 1938: "Vico was the first modern philosopher to discover in his own mind, and in the European past, all human destiny: 'We can know nothing,' he said, 'that we have not made' " (A99). The best statement concerning Vico's influence appears in Max Fisch and Thomas Bergin's introduction to their translation of Vico's *Autobiography* (61–107). For the original I have used the edition of Vico's *Opere*, edited by Fausto Nicolini. For more recent studies of Vico's impact on American academic historical scholarship, one should consult the books of Patrick Hutton and Philip Verene and a most illuminating article by Joseph Levine, "Vico and the Quarrel between the Ancients and the Moderns" (1991).

SELECTIVE BIBLIOGRAPHY

Works by Vico

La Science nouvelle (1725). Trans. Christina Trivulzio Princesse de Belgiojoso. Paris: Gallimard, 1993.

Oeuvres choisies de Vico, contenant ses Mémoires écrits par lui-même, la Science nouvelle, les opuscules, lettres, etc., précédées d'une introduction sur sa vie et ses ouvrages par M. Michelet. 2 vols. Paris: Hachette, 1835.

The Autobiography of Giambattista Vico. Trans. Max Harold Fisch and Thomas Goddard Bergin. Ithaca: Cornell University Press, 1944.

Opere. Ed. Fausto Nicolini. Milan and Naples: R. Ricciardi, 1953.

Vie de Giambattista Vico écrite par lui-même. Trans. Alain Pons. Paris: B. Grasset, 1981.

Selective Studies of Vico

Berlin, Isaiah. *Vico and Herder: Two Studies in the History of Ideas*. New York: Viking Press, 1976.

Croce, Benedetto. *Bibliografia Vichiana*. Napoli: Stab. Tip. della R. Università, 1904.

Hutton, Patrick. *History as an Art of Memory*. Hanover, N.H.: University Press of New England, 1993.

Levine, Joseph. "Giambattista Vico and the Quarrel between the Ancients and the Moderns." *Journal of the History of Ideas* (1991): 55–79.

Michelet, Jules. *Oeuvres complètes*. Ed. Paul Viallaneix. Vol. I, 1798–1827. Paris: Flammarion, 1971.

Verene, Donald Philip. *The New Art of Autobiography: An Essay on the Life of Giambattista Vico Written by Himself*. Oxford: Clarendon Press, 1991.

GEOFFROY DE VILLEHARDOUIN

(c. 1150–c. 1213)

Paul Archambault

BIOGRAPHY

Historians have differed widely as to the year and even the decade of Geoffroy de Villehardouin's birth. Older historians (Du Cange, Buchon) long stated that he was born around 1164, although the more recent opinion is that he was born around 1150 at the château de Villehardouin, near Troyes, and that he was named marshal of Champagne around 1185 (Zink, 193). All historians agree that he died around 1213 and no later than 1218.

More certain details about his life are those provided in his famous chronicle of the Fourth Crusade, the *Conquête de Constantinople*, written, presumably, between 1207 and the year of his death. He lists himself among those French barons who took the cross in 1199. He was one of six French envoys sent to Venice in April 1201 to arrange with the Venetians for the transport of the French crusaders to Egypt. The Venetians, led by an aging, blind doge, Enrico Dandolo, agreed to build transports to carry 4,500 horses and 9,000 squires, and other ships to accommodate 4,500 knights and 20,000 foot sergeants, plus a nine months' supply of rations for all these men, for a total cost of 85,000 marks (*Chronicles*, trans. Shaw, 32–33). Villehardouin repeatedly bewails the failure of that contingent of French soldiers and barons—"those who sailed from other ports"—to meet at Venice at the appointed time (summer 1202), which precipitated a chain of events that led ultimately to the capture and plunder of Constantinople by the French and the Venetians combined on 13 April 1204. His view is that the Venetians, seeing that the French who did congregate at Venice were unable to meet their contractual obligations, agreed to transport them, but with conditions of their own. When the fleet sailed from Venice in October 1202, Doge Enrico Dandolo persuaded a divided French army to aid the Venetians to recapture the port of Zara (Zadar), further down the Dalmatian coast, which had been taken from them by the king of Hungary (*Chronicles*, 43). The

French agreed, despite strong protests from many within the French ranks and a decree of excommunication from Pope Innocent III against those participating in the capture of a Roman Catholic city (*Chronicles*, 45–49). After the conquest of Zara the Venetians were visited by the young Alexius Angelos, son of Isaac, the emperor of Constantinople, who had been deposed by his brother. Crown Prince Alexius Angelos had escaped from prison in Constantinople and, in league with Boniface de Montferrat, had appealed, first to King Philip of Swabia, his brother-in-law, and then to the Venetians, to help restore him to the throne (*Chronicles*, 44–45). He arrived at Zara to tell the French and the Venetians assembled that if they helped him reconquer his throne, he would place his whole empire under the authority of Rome, pay them 200,000 silver marks, and accompany them to Egypt with an army of 10,000 men (*Chronicles*, 50). "There was great discord in the army," records Villehardouin; but after Pope Innocent III, calming his anger over the capture of Zara, gave the plan his blessing, Villehardouin could only agree that the most important thing was to keep the crusading army together (*Chronicles*, 51–56).

The conquest of Constantinople tells but roughly half the story of Villehardouin's chronicle. The other half tells of the French attempt to retain the city and the adjoining lands of "Romania" in the face of fierce Greek and Bulgarian counterattacks. It is a complex, vividly written account of wars against "the Greeks" in "Romania," highlighted by Villehardouin's several attempts to intervene in the strained relations between Emperor Baudoin (who held Constantinople) and Marquis Boniface de Montferrat (who held Salonika). Their common danger? The fierce counterattacks by the Greek armies, led by Murzuphlus in Thessaly and Macedonia and by Theodoros Lascaris in Nicomedia. In Villehardouin's chronicle the brilliant strategist who inflicts grievous disasters upon the French in Romania is King Johanitza of "Wallachia" (Bulgaria). Villehardouin probably remained in Romania until his death, since his chronicle is then immediately continued by the *Histoire de l'Empereur Henri* of Henri de Valenciennes, suggesting that death was the reason for the abrupt end to his chronicle (*Chronicles*, 14).

MAJOR MULTICULTURAL THEMES

Nearing Constantinople on 23 June 1203, Villehardouin records how he and the whole army were stunned, "having never imagined there could be so fine a place in all the world." Like an awestruck tourist he notes "the high walls and lofty towers encircling it, and its rich palaces and tall churches, . . . and viewed the length and breadth of that city which reigns supreme over all the others" (*Chronicles*, 59). He never questions the aesthetic and cultural supremacy of this, the greatest of Greek cities. After the first siege and the restoration of Crown Prince Alexius, believing perhaps in the imminent reunification of the Byzantine Empire with Rome, he speaks of "French and Greeks" as sharing a common Christian culture. French soldiers stroll peacefully through the streets of Constantinople, viewing its "many splendid palaces and tall churches," as well as "relics . . . beyond description." The Greeks and the French are "on friendly terms with each other in all respects, including trade and other matters" (76).

He is disillusioned with the Greeks, however. Alexius and Murzuphlus, both former usurpers now evicted from Constantinople by the French, meet at Mosynopolis, where Alexius invites Murzuphlus to the baths and has him blinded. To justify the recent French rape and plunder of the city, Villehardouin writes, "Judge for yourselves, after hearing of this treachery, whether people who could treat each other with such savage cruelty would be fit to hold hands or would deserve to lose them?" (99).

In the first half of his chronicle he refers to himself as "Marshal of Champagne" (*Chronicles*, 30 and passim). After the conquest he calls himself "Marshal of Champagne and Romania" (117, 149, and passim). Otherwise stated, the *Conquête de Constantinople* tells only half his story. The second half might be entitled "The Greek Wars," or "The Wars in Romania," recounting the Franks' desperate attempt to cling to their conquest against a vigorous Greek and Bulgarian counteroffensive throughout Thrace and Macedonia. "Romania," to Villehardouin and contemporaries of the conquest, refers to the Byzantine Empire in Europe, as opposed to "Anatolia," which designates the empire in Asia Minor (Lurier, 69). He records that Marquis Boniface de Montferrat, holding Salonika, offered him "the choice of two cities" in Macedonia, Mosynopolis or Serrès, but he does not specify which he chose as the city in which he presumably wrote his chronicle and spent his last years.

He considers the conquest of Constantinople perfectly justified, as was the French attempt to keep Constantinople and all of Romania in the face of a ferocious Greek counteroffensive. Unlike the Greek historian Niketas Choniates, who does not hesitate to call the Franks "barbarians," Villehardouin not only never insults the Greeks, but seems even to admire that fierce and determined enemy King Johanitza of Bulgaria.

SURVEY OF CRITICISM

Criticism of Villehardouin's chronicle in the past century and a half has focused not on the multiculturalism of his vision but on its selectivity and has been sometimes called the problem of Villehardouin's "sincerity." Unlike Sainte-Beuve, who called Villehardouin one of the most "honorable and complete" historians of his time (*Causeries*, 354), European and American historians of the nineteenth and twentieth centuries have usually argued that Villehardouin knew a great deal more than he admits and that he must be considered an accomplice to one of the most ignominious acts ever perpetrated by the Latin West against the Byzantine East, with Innocent III's benediction (see Pears, 1885, and Queller and Stratton, 1964). Influenced by Pears's account, I once argued that Villehardouin's text itself is by nature selective and "Manichean"

(*Seven French Chroniclers*, 1974, 25–39), but I would be less harsh toward Villehardouin today. Like many scholars, I have tended to read history retrospectively and upbraid Villehardouin for an outcome for which he cannot be held responsible, that is, the ultimate fall of Constantinople to the Turks in 1453. Eyewitnesses to an event cannot be read in this way. Though their own prejudices are inevitable, one cannot forget that they were living these events in their incremental progression, not in retrospection. What I would retract most willingly in my harsh criticism of Villehardouin in 1974 is my too-easy dismissal of the second half of his chronicle as "tedious." I now believe that Villehardouin's account of the wars in Romania is the finest part of his chronicle and one of the finest pieces of military reporting in all medieval literature.

SELECTIVE BIBLIOGRAPHY

Work by Villehardouin

Joinville, Jean de, and Villehardouin. *Chronicles of the Crusades*. Trans. and intro. M.R.B. Shaw. Harmondsworth: Penguin Books, 1963; rpt., 1984.

Selective Studies of Villehardouin

Archambault, Paul. *Seven French Chroniclers: Witnesses to History*, 25–39. Syracuse, N.Y.: Syracuse University Press, 1974.

Buchon, J.-A.-C. *Recherches et matériaux pour servir à une histoire de la domination française aux XIIIe, XIVe, et XVe siècles dans les provinces démembrées de l'Empire grec à la suite de la Quatrième Croisade*. Paris: Auguste Desrez, 1841.

Du Cange, Du Fresne. *Histoire de l'empire de Constantinople: Sous les empereurs français jusqu'à la conquête des turcs*. 2 vols. Paris: Veridière, 1926.

Choniates, Niketas. *O City of Byzantium: Annals of Niketas Choniates*. Trans. Harry J. Magoulias. Detroit: Wayne State University Press, 1984.

Lurier, Harold E., ed. and trans. *Crusaders as Conquerors: The Chronicle of Morea*. New York: Columbia University Press, 1964.

Pears, Edwin. *The Fall of Constantinople*. London: Longmans, 1885.

Queller, D.E., and S.J. Stratton. "A Century of Controversy on the Fourth Crusade." In *Studies in Medieval and Renaissance History*, 235–77. Ed. William M. Bowsky. Lincoln: University of Nebraska Press, 1964.

Sainte-Beuve, C.A. "G. de Villehardouin." *Causeries du lundi*. Vol. 9. 3rd ed., 381–412. Paris: Garnier, 1857.

Zink, Michel. *Littérature française du moyen âge*. Paris: Presses Universitaires de France, 1992.

VOLTAIRE (FRANÇOIS-MARIE AROUET)
(1694–1778)

Richard A. Brooks

BIOGRAPHY

François-Marie Arouet, known as Voltaire (a pseudonym he adopted in his early twenties), was a philosopher, playwright, essayist, historian, poet, and writer of fiction. At age twenty-one he was incarcerated in the Bastille after being wrongly accused of slandering the regent, Philippe d'Orléans. During his imprisonment he wrote his first tragedy, *Oedipe* (after the Greek dramatist Sophocles' *Oedipus the King*) and the beginnings of his epic poem on Henry IV entitled *La Henriade*. Nine years later he found himself once again in the Bastille, this time having quarreled with a member of the powerful de Rohan family, and was released only on the stipulation that he go into exile in England. Here he spent the next two years mastering English, writing two essays in that language, and becoming acquainted with British literary figures of the period. His stay in England provided him with a model for religious and political ideas that shaped his thought for the rest of his life. The spirit of religious toleration and the scientific and philosophical ideas of Locke and Newton became the basis of his intellectual outlook. Indeed, his *Lettres philosophiques*, published in French in 1734, following an English version of the same work entitled *Letters Concerning the English Nation* a year earlier, was a catalyst for the popularity of English philosophical and scientific thought throughout the French Enlightenment. It was during his English stay that he also wrote his first historical work, *Histoire de Charles XII*.

He took up residence in 1734 at the Château de Cirey in the duchy of Lorraine with his companion, the marquise du Châtelet, who exerted a strong intellectual influence over him. It was there that he wrote his *Eléments de la philosophie de Newton* and engaged in physical and chemical experiments with Madame du Châtelet. During this same period Voltaire became historiographer of France and a "gentleman of the king's bedchamber" through the influence of Madame de Pompadour, mistress of King Louis XV. His *Poème de Fontenoy*, which gave an account of the French victory over the English during the War of the Austrian Succession, was published in 1745. For a number of years he had been engaged in correspondence with Crown Prince Frederick of Prussia (the future Frederick the Great), and after Madame du Châtelet's death in 1749 he accepted the invitation of the "enlightened despot" to take up residence at the Prussian court. During his Prussian residence he completed his innovative historical masterpiece, *Le Siècle de Louis XIV*, in which he departed from a Christian interpretation of history and emphasized the importance of cultural history and the study of civilization as a whole. Not surprisingly, the autocratic character of the Prussian monarch and the sharp wit and the spirit of independence of the French *philosophe* clashed, and Voltaire left the Prussian court in 1753.

The owner of property in Geneva and near Lausanne purchased in 1755, Voltaire soon came into conflict with the Genevese authorities for having inspired the writing of the article "Genève" by d'Alembert in Diderot's *Encyclopédie*, a piece considered heretical by the religious patriarchs of the city of Calvin both because of its defense of the theater as an institution and the accusation of Socinianism launched against them. Because of the volatility of his relationship with the French authorities, Voltaire lived a somewhat nomadic existence, but in 1758 he finally settled in Ferney, a village near the Swiss border, where he lived for the last twenty years of his life.

MAJOR MULTICULTURAL THEMES

Voltaire was one of the great storytellers of eighteenth-century French literature, and it is largely his *contes* that have guaranteed his literary posterity. Most of them demonstrate his interest in other cultures and, indeed, other planets: *Zadig* (1747), a philosophical tale with an Oriental setting, on the subject of destiny; *Micromégas* (1752), an example of eighteenth-century science fiction with interplanetary travelers used to develop the theme of relativity and to destroy the Christian notion of an anthropomorphic universe; and *L'Ingénu* (1767), a tale having as its principal character an uncorrupted American Indian to question the absurdity of conventional religious rites and to demonstrate the perpetration of political injustice in eighteenth-century France. His literary masterpiece, *Candide* (1759), a gem of irony and caustic wisdom, presents an overview of the absurdities and inequities of eighteenth-century society, politics, and religion while attempting to deal with the philosophical question of evil. All this is done in a multicultural context by a devastating satire of the works of the great German rationalistic philosopher Gottfried Leibniz, whose *Essais de théodicée sur la bonté de Dieu, la liberté de l'homme, et l'origine du mal* (1710) provided the philosophical grounding for the philosophy of optimism. Candide, through his travels in quest of his beloved Cunégonde, witnessed the pomposity of Prussian institutions, the cruelties of the Inquisition in Portugal, the corruption of Parisian society, the power-hungry Jesuit presence in the New World under the guise of a civilizing mission, the venality of the Catholic Church in Italy, and the cruelties of Islam in Turkey.

Perhaps Voltaire's most ambitious contribution to the field of multicultural studies was his *Essai sur l'histoire générale et sur les moeurs et l'esprit des nations*, which he completed in 1756. It is an expansion of *Le Siècle de Louis XIV*, which became volumes VI, VII, and VIII of the broader work in which he attempted a history of the world from the time of Charlemagne to the reign of Louis XIV. A dominating idea of the work is the importance of studying world history and not merely focusing on Europe alone. Even going beyond the borders of France and reducing the study of history to Western civilization meant neglecting the civilizations of the Hindus, Chinese, Japanese, and others; to Voltaire's mind this represented a total distortion of the field of historiography. The *Essai* is at one and the same time a broad sketch of philosophical history and an expansion of historiography to the study of humanity itself.

SURVEY OF CRITICISM

Studies on Voltaire and the Eighteenth Century (over 300 volumes), published by the Voltaire Foundation at Oxford, is a serial publication that covers every imaginable topic concerning Voltaire. The standard introduction to Voltaire and his career remains Gustave Lanson's *Voltaire*, originally published in 1906 and since updated (1960) by René Pomeau. An excellent volume on Voltaire's engagement in political and social issues of his time and an analysis of some of his works is Peter Gay's *Voltaire's Politics: The Poet as Realist* (1988). More specifically on Voltaire as a "multicultural" writer, Norman Torrey (1967) deals with his religious ideas and their British origins; and Charles Dédéyan (1988) covers the general connection between Voltaire amd England.

SELECTIVE BIBLIOGRAPHY

Works by Voltaire

The Complete Works of Voltaire. Ed. Theodore Besterman et al. Geneva and Toronto: Institut et Musée Voltaire and University of Toronto Press, 1968.
The Selected Letters of Voltaire. Ed. and trans. Richard A. Brooks. New York: New York University Press, 1973.
Letters Concerning the English Nation. Ed. and intro. Nicholas Cronk. Oxford: Oxford University Press, 1994.

Selective Studies of Voltaire

Badir, Magdy Gavriel. *Voltaire et l'Islam*. Banbury: Voltaire Foundation, 1974.
Dédéyan, Charles. *Le Retour de Salente; ou, Voltaire et l'Angleterre*. Paris: Nizet, 1988.

Gay, Peter. *Voltaire's Politics: The Poet as Realist*. New Haven: Yale University Press, 1988.

Gunny, Ahmad. *Voltaire and English Literature: A Study of English Literary Influences on Voltaire*. Oxford: Voltaire Foundation, 1979.

Lanson, Gustave. *Voltaire*. Ed. René Pomeau. Paris: Hachette, 1960.

Magnan, André. *Dossier Voltaire en Prusse: 1750–1753*. Oxford: Voltaire Foundation, 1986.

Mervaud, Christiane. *Voltaire et Frédéric II: Une dramaturgie des lumières, 1736–1778*. Oxford: Voltaire Foundation, 1985.

Song, Shun-Ching. *Voltaire et la Chine*. Aix-en-Provence: Université de Provence, 1989.

Torrey, Norman L. *Voltaire and the English Deists*. Hamden, Conn.: Archon Books, 1967.

Wilberger, Carolyn H. *Voltaire's Russia: Window on the East*. Oxford: Voltaire Foundation, 1976.

EDITH WHARTON
(1862–1937)

Jane Benardete

BIOGRAPHY

Although Edith Wharton is usually identified with the upper-class New York society into which she was born and that she satirized in her best-known novels (e.g., *The House of Mirth*, 1905; *The Custom of the Country*, 1913; and *The Age of Innocence*, 1920), she was an enthusiastic, lifelong traveler and, after 1910, a resident of France. Overall, she lived more than half of her life in Europe. She was born among well-to-do New Yorkers who, she said, were happiest when boarding an ocean liner to carry them to new lands. She is America's preeminent literary "lady," who did not need to write for a living and came of a class opposed to all work for women. Although she felt marginalized by both gender and class, she became a prolific author with an international circle of friends active in literature and the arts, most notably Henry James.

Between 1866 and 1872 young Edith traveled with her parents in Italy, France, Spain, and Germany, with long stays in Rome, Florence, and Paris. This sojourn marked her emergence as a writer: in her autobiography, *A Backward Glance*, she recalled that she first felt the "ecstasy" of "making up" stories as a four-year-old, not yet able to read, alone in Paris, on a winter day, holding Washington Irving's *Alhambra* in her hands and talking to herself. She would, in fact, become an inheritor of Irving's romantic style of travel writing.

She was again in Europe from 1880 until 1882, when her father died at Cannes. The family then returned to New York; ultimately, her mother and both of her brothers settled in Europe. In 1885 she married Edward Wharton, a well-to-do Bostonian, with whom she made annual trips to France and Italy, educating herself as a connoisseur. She also read and wrote voluminously, so that, before middle age, she was "able to write fiction in French, to translate (for publication) into English, and to speak both these languages, as well as Italian with complete facility" (Auchincloss, 52). Her first novel, *The Valley of Decision*, a tale set in Italy, appeared in 1902. Her first best-selling novel, *The House of Mirth*, appeared in 1905. About the same time she published two works based on her European travels: *Italian Villas and Their Gardens* (1904) and *Italian Backgrounds* (1905).

In 1901 she initiated the construction of her great house, the Mount, in Lenox, Massachusetts, where she summered and entertained lavishly, yet she never failed to spend part of each year in Europe, often as an enthusiastic tourist. *A Motor-Flight through France* (1908) begins, "The motor-car has restored the romance of travel," and celebrates journeys through the French countryside with visits to such towns as Amiens, Rouen, and Beauvais.

Beginning in 1906, she was introduced to Paris salons by the French writer Paul Bourget. In 1907 she leased an apartment in the Faubourg St. Germain, and in 1909, prompted by growing alienation from her husband, who, after 1902, suffered from recurrent bouts of mental instability, she determined to live in Europe. In 1910 she moved permanently to France, where she obtained a divorce in 1913.

World War I roused her to passionate support of the French cause. In *Fighting France: From Dunkerque to Belfort* (1915) and *French Ways and Their Meaning* (1919) she praised French valor and culture and rallied her admiring American readers to support her adopted nation. She also organized, administered, and raised money for several wartime relief efforts. For her wartime achievements France made her a chevalier of the Legion of Honor in 1916.

Two later novels, *The Marne* (1918) and *A Son at the Front* (1924), reflect the strong emotions aroused by Wharton's wartime activities, especially her visits to the front. An interesting outgrowth of this experience is *The Spark: (the 'Sixties)* (1924), a short novel set in America in the 1860s that draws upon Wharton's memories of the post–Civil War era, her admiration for Walt Whitman, and her idealized view of personal moral improvement achieved through wartime sacrifice.

Post–Civil War America also provides the setting for *The Age of Innocence*, for which she received a Pulitzer Prize in 1921. Ironically nostalgic, it treats the provincialism of New York's "brownstone society" in the 1870s—her parents' generation—a world whose clannish peace is almost shattered by the sudden appearance of a Europeanized cousin and would-be divorcée, the beautiful, somewhat bohemian Ellen Olenska, who might be read as a fantasized version of the worldly, long-divorced, Parisian woman that Wharton had become.

In the years after the war she spent summers at the Pavillon Colombe, a villa north of Paris, and winters at Hyères on the Riviera. In both houses she maintained elegant gardens, entertained widely, and wrote productively. On her last trip to the United States in the spring of 1923 she received an honorary doctorate from Yale University. She died at Pavillon Colombe in August 1937 and was buried at Versailles, attended by an honor guard of French war veterans.

MAJOR MULTICULTURAL THEMES

Many of Wharton's narratives have multicultural themes. Among the best known are *The House of Mirth*, "Madame de Treymes" (1906), *The Custom of the Country*, *The Marne*, *A Son at the Front*, and *The Age of Innocence*. Her travel writings, influenced by John Ruskin and Bernard Berenson, offered her an alternate mode in which to develop the contrast of cultures and her ironic eye. The travel writing reflects her studious appreciation of European art and cultural artifacts. Wharton's tribute to France, *French Ways and Their Meaning*, admiringly notes the independence and social power of French women. In contrast, her portraits of well-to-do American women, the staple heroines of her novels, suggest that they are victims of a materialistic society, forced to trade spiritual freedom for financial and social security. Some of Wharton's most successful fictions treat Americans engaged in hardheaded transatlantic marital negotiations: for example, *The Custom of the Country* and *The Buccaneers*. Her thoroughly American, "local-color" novels, for example, *Ethan Frome* and *Summer*, also show women constrained by a harsh environment and a limited, moralistic culture. For Wharton, Europe, especially France, represented a standard of taste, intellectual development, and moral honesty that she did not find in the "gros public" of the United States. Despite her disdain, she was a popular, financially successful author whose writing appealed to the tastes of her largely female American readership. For them, she described the elegant transatlantic world she inhabited and communicated her admiration of the European culture she esteemed.

SURVEY OF CRITICISM

Different biographers offer different views of Wharton's remarkable life and productive career. A friend, Percy Lubbock, reproduces impressions of Wharton by her contemporaries and offers an admiring personal view in *Portrait of Edith Wharton* (1947). Drawing upon a collection of Wharton's letters, as well as a special affinity for her "brownstone society," Louis Auchincloss (1971) gives a convincing, handsomely illustrated account of her life. Students will want to consult two more recent works: *Wretched Exotic* (1993), edited by Katherine Joslin and Alan Price; and Eleanor Dwight's *Edith Wharton: An Extraordinary Life* (1994). Wharton's autobiography, *A Backward Glance* (1934), includes two insightful chapters on her relationship with Henry James.

SELECTIVE BIBLIOGRAPHY

Works by Wharton

Italian Villas and Their Gardens. New York: Scribner's 1904.
House of Mirth. New York: Scribner's, 1905.

Italian Backgrounds. New York: Scribner's, 1905.
"Madame de Treymes." New York: Scribner's, 1906.
A Motor-Flight through France. New York: Scribner's, 1908.
The Custom of the Country. New York: Scribner's, 1913.
Fighting France: From Dunkerque to Belfort. New York: Scribner's, 1915.
The Marne. New York: Appleton, 1918.
French Ways and Their Meaning. New York: Appleton, 1919.
The Age of Innocence. New York: D. Appleton & Co., 1920.
In Morocco. London: Macmillan, 1920.
A Son at the Front. New York: Scribner's, 1924.
A Backward Glance. New York: Appleton-Century, 1934.

Selective Studies of Wharton

Auchincloss, Louis. *Edith Wharton: A Woman in Her Time*. New York: Viking Press, 1971.
Dwight, Eleanor. *Edith Wharton: An Extraordinary Life*. New York: Harry N. Abrams, 1994.
Joslin, Katherine, and Alan Price, eds. *Wretched Exotic*. New York: Peter Lang, 1993.
Lewis, R.W.B. *Edith Wharton: A Biography*. New York: Harper and Row, 1975.
Lubbock, Percy. *Portrait of Edith Wharton*. New York and London: D. Appleton-Century, 1947.
Price, Alan. *The End of the Age of Innocence*. New York: St. Martin's Press, 1996.
Schriber, Mary Suzanne. Intro. to *A Motor-Flight through France*, by Edith Wharton. De Kalb: Northern Illinois University Press, 1991.
Wolff, Cynthia Griffin. *A Feast of Words: The Triumph of Edith Wharton*. Oxford: Oxford University Press, 1977.
Wright, Sarah Bird. *Edith Wharton's Travel Writing: The Making of a Connoisseur*. New York: St. Martin's Press, 1997.

OSCAR WILDE
(1854–1900)

Mary Hudson

BIOGRAPHY

Oscar Fingal O'Flahertie Wills Wilde was a man of the world, and, like the world, he was full of contradictions. He remained till his death an Irish nationalist, yet for most of his adult life played the role of the consummate Englishman. He was the epitome of the aesthete, yet believed that socialism was mankind's one real hope. He was lavishly generous and equally self-indulgent. He was a married man ever fond of his wife and two sons, yet enjoyed the dangerous blandishments of youthful homosexual prostitutes and eventually fell in love with a young gentleman who would prove to be his undoing. He was by all accounts extremely good-natured and the toast of London town, yet he incurred the wrath of Victorian society on two sides of the Atlantic and died a well-nigh-friendless pariah. Perhaps the fact that he embodied so many contradictions contributed to his being the greatest source in the English language of paradoxical aphorisms. For these he has become world-famous. His witticisms are still fondly quoted, and his plays and poems remain as fresh now as they were when they first appeared.

He was born into a distinguished but eccentric Dublin family: his father, Sir William Wilde, was a renowned eye and ear surgeon; his mother, Jane Francesca Agnes Elgee, the poet "Speranza," had a reputation in her own right as a fiery Irish nationalist and colorful hostess. From his father he must have inherited his profligacy—Sir William was known to have fathered more than one child out of wedlock—and from his mother his flamboyancy and generosity of spirit. With his older brother Willie he was educated at the Portora Royal School in County Fermanagh (which would also have the distinction of schooling Samuel Beckett), whence he proceeded to Trinity College, Dublin, in 1871. He was awarded the Berkeley Gold Medal for Greek at Trinity and received a scholarship to study at Magdalen College, Oxford. There he came under the influence of such great nineteenth-century minds as Walter Pater, John Henry Cardinal Newman, and John Ruskin. After a brilliant career at Oxford he moved to London, where he dabbled in journalism, published some poetry, continued to make a name for himself as a wit and aesthete, and began writing the first of his plays.

After a tour in the United States (1882) he spent three months in Paris (1883) finishing his play *The Duchess of Padua*, renewing his friendship with Sarah Bernhardt, and making the acquaintance of Edmond de Goncourt and Victor Hugo. He often returned to Paris, where he frequented the great poets and artists of the day. In 1884 he married Constance Lloyd, who remained his ally even after their marriage failed, but who died two years before her husband.

His most productive period (1888–95) was marked by contributions to numerous periodicals and the publication, among other works, of *The Happy Prince and Other Tales*, his still-acclaimed novel *The Picture of Dorian Gray*, "The Soul of Man under Socialism," and the most enduring of his plays, *Lady Windermere's Fan*, *An Ideal Husband*, and *The Importance of Being Earnest*. It was during this time that his fate became bound up with that of Lord Alfred Douglas. This beautiful young Oxford student was the son of the marquess of Queensbury, who hounded Wilde into prison and exile. Leaving prison broken and impoverished and dependent on his wife's allowance, he took refuge in France, where he spent the remainder of his short life wandering under an assumed name. Paris nursed him in his final illness, and it is fitting that Paris should have the honor of holding his remains, for it has always been a refuge for artists, freethinkers, and pleasure seekers from every corner of the globe, and Oscar Wilde was all of these in great measure. A mere two years after his release from prison, he was released from his mortal coil on November 30, 1900, after fulfilling a lifelong desire to be received into the Catholic Church.

MAJOR MULTICULTURAL THEMES

One of Wilde's abiding loves was France, and France played a central role in his life and death. His mother had early introduced him to the joys of French literature—she translated Alexandre Dumas père and Lamartine into English—and he was as much at home in literary Paris as he was in London. André Gide was a good friend, and Wilde was a frequent visitor to Stéphane Mallarmé's "Tuesdays," which brought together the artistic and intellectual elite. In 1884 Joris-Karl Huysmans's *A Rebours*, the last word of the "decadent" movement, greatly impressed him, and Wilde in turn was to exercise his fascination on French art and letters for a long time to come. He had written his play *Salomé* in French, partly because he hoped to have his dear friend Sarah Bernhardt perform the title role.

He was already a celebrity in the United States when in 1882 he went on a continentwide tour, lecturing to sometimes-bemused audiences on aestheticism. The tour was a financial success and gave Wilde the fuel for another series of lectures on his "Impressions of America" once back in the British Isles. He also traveled widely in Italy, which already in 1875 had provided the inspiration for his poem "San Miniato," and in the year of his death he made a last journey there, where in Rome he was blessed by the pope no fewer than seven times (Ellmann, 1987, 542).

Wilde's sympathies were as vast as his prejudices were scarce. He crossed many boundaries. He was the epitome of the upper-class sophisticate, yet he could charm servants and miners and tradesfolk with his generosity and lack of pretense in their company. He was the very antithesis of the puritan in the most puritanical of ages. In fact, his heedless disregard for Victorian values eventually deprived him of his freedom, his livelihood, and his health. That is because his generosity of spirit prevented him from seeing the dangers of narrow provincialism. Understandably, the circumstances of his trial and imprisonment have made of him an icon of the Gay Liberation movement. This is another Wildean paradox, as he himself would not have interpreted his own pursuit of pleasure as a defining principle, setting him off from his fellow men, labeling him as anything other than a dalliance-prone gentleman.

He was indeed an apostle, but an apostle of Art. Far from being reserved for an elite, Art, he believed, was the birthright of all. The role of Art was to liberate humanity, and this would be achieved under a socialist system that preserved individual rights.

SURVEY OF CRITICISM

Wilde's invasion of America is broadly documented. Lewis and Smith (1936, 1967), in their exhaustive guide to his travels there, note that the parody of him in William S. Gilbert's musical *Patience* was widely known by the time Wilde arrived in January 1882, and as a result, people all over the continent flocked to see him. In Denver, Colorado, we learn, the audience "sat to the end with the silence and courtesy that Wilde had learned to expect in the West, but it was obvious that the people were spectators, not listeners" (305). In an interesting study of Wilde's tour of the American West, it is written that his lecture at Leadville, Colorado, entitled "The Practical Application of the Aesthetic Theory to Exterior and Interior House Decoration with Observations on Dress and Personal Ornament," was greeted by the local miners "with great respect, since Wilde had proved that he could drink them all under the table" (Erdoes, 173).

Much has been written about Wilde's relationship with France. Ellmann (1988) refers to the influence of *A Rebours* on Wilde and his friends, pointing out that "something of the book's effect rubbed off on [his] life as well" (18). André Gide wrote about his friendship with Wilde, notably in *Si le grain ne meurt*, and Kelver Hartley (1935) documented Wilde's nineteenth-century French sources. Jacques de Langlade (1975) recounts Wilde's life in France and devotes chapters to his influence on Gide, Proust, and Cocteau. Inversely, he notes that Wilde did not hide how much his *Duchess of Padua* owed to Hugo's *Lucrèce Borgia* and his *Vera* to Sardou's *Fedora*. He also reminds us that after

Salomé was banned by the British censor, Wilde wanted to take out French citizenship in protest, and that the French writer Octave Mirbeau had wanted to present Wilde's candidature to the Académie Goncourt and only renounced the plan following the scandal over Wilde's trials.

SELECTIVE BIBLIOGRAPHY

Works by Wilde

Impressions of America. Ed. Stuart Mason. Sunderland: Keystone Press, 1906.
The Works of Oscar Wilde. Ed. and intro. G.F. Maine. New York: E.P. Dutton, 1954.

Selective Studies of Wilde

On French and Other Cultural Influence

Albeaux-Fernet, Michel. "Narcisse. Cantate à trois voix (Paul Valéry, Oscar Wilde, André Gide)." *La Nouvelle Revue des deux mondes* (December 1972): 564–71.
Benz, Ernst. "A propos de la Salomé d'Oscar Wilde." *Englische Studien* 51, no. 1 (1917): 48–70.
Ellmann, Richard. *Oscar Wilde*. London: Hamish Hamilton, 1987.
———. "The Uses of Decadence: Wilde, Yeats, Joyce." In *Studies in Anglo-French Cultural Relations: Imagining France*, 17–33. Ed. Ceri Crossley and Ian Small. London: Macmillan, 1988.
Hartley, Kelver. *Oscar Wilde: L'influence française dans son oeuvre*. Paris: Librairie du Recueil Sirey, 1935.
Langlade, Jacques de. *Oscar Wilde, écrivain français*. Paris: Editions Stock, 1975.
Lemonnnier, Léon. "Oscar Wilde en exil, d'après des documents nouveaux." *Grande revue* (January 1931): 373–98.
Mikhail, E.H. "The French Influences on Oscar Wilde's Comedies." *Revue de littérature comparée* 42, no. 2 (April–June 1968): 220–33.
Ricaumont, Jacques de. "Oscar Wilde: Ecrivain français." *Nouvelle revue des deux mondes* (October 1975): 54–58.
Roditi, Edouard. *Oscar Wilde*. Norfolk, Conn.: New Directions, 1947.
Sahai, Surendra. *English Drama, 1865–1900*. New Delhi: Orient Longman, 1970.
Schaffner, Roland. "Die Salome-Dichtungen von Flaubert, Laforgue, Wilde, und Mallarmé." Dissertation. Würzburg: Universität, 1965.
Temple, Ruth Z. *The Critic's Alchemy: A Study of the Introduction of French Symbolism into England*. New York: Twayne, 1953.

On Wilde and North America

Aslin, Elizabeth. "Oscar Wilde and America." In *The Aesthetic Movement: Prelude to Art Nouveau*, 97–111. London: Elek Books; New York: Praeger, 1969.
Boone, Joseph A., and Michael Cadden, eds. *Engendering Men: The Question of Male Feminist Criticism*. New York: Routledge, 1990.
Eckhoff, Lorentz. *The Aesthetic Movement in English Literature*. Oslo: Oslo University Press, 1959.

Erdoes, Richard. *Saloons of the Old West*. New York: Alfred A. Knopf, 1979.

Hogan, William, and William German, eds. *The San Francisco Chronicle Reader*. New York: McGraw-Hill, 1962. (Includes a reprint of a story concerning Wilde's lecture tour in California.)

Lewis, Lloyd, and Henry J. Smith. *Oscar Wilde Discovers America*. New York: Harcourt, Brace, 1936; Toronto: McLeod, 1936; New York: Benjamin Blom, 1967.

Symons, A.J.A., ed. "Oscar Wilde in America." In *Essays and Biographies*, 170–90. London: Cassell, 1969.

MARY WOLLSTONECRAFT (GODWIN)
(1759–1797)

Patricia Owen

BIOGRAPHY

Mary Wollstonecraft was one of seven children of an incompetent businessman and "gentleman farmer" and his Irish wife. Growing up in a household often moving in search of prosperity, she became painfully aware of her father's periodical wife battering and of the privileged status of her elder brother; she later supported a sister who had fled from her husband. Denied a systematic education, she read widely, beyond the narrow range expected of women. At nineteen she left home to work as a paid "lady companion"; later she went to live with the family of her close friend, Fanny Blood. Together with Wollstonecraft's sisters, they attempted to support themselves by running a school in London. Fanny Blood married and went with her husband to Lisbon; in 1785 Wollstonecraft went there to help her friend with her first childbirth, only to find her dying. The school failed, and employment as a governess to an aristocratic family in Ireland ended abruptly after their return to England.

Wollstonecraft had formed friendships within dissenting and radical circles in London; she now became a professional writer for the publisher Joseph Johnson in return for board and lodging. Her views of the oppressive nature of marriage and the damage done by the miseducation of women were expressed in *Thoughts on the Education of Daughters* (1787) and *Mary: A Fiction* (1788) with strong personal overtones. For Johnson she translated from French, German, and Dutch, reviewed, and acted as his assistant editor. He published her *Vindication of the Rights of Men* (1790), a point-by-point reply to Edmund Burke's *Reflections on the Revolution in France*. In 1792 appeared *A Vindication of the Rights of Women*, the work that made her the honored foremother of feminism, but to many of her own time a "hyena in petticoats." It was written in the hope of persuading Talleyrand to give girls, like boys, a scientific and factual curriculum in the free, secular education system proposed by the National Assembly.

Believing in partnership without marriage, she had hoped to join the household of Henry Fuseli, the Swiss painter. Disappointed, she decided at the end of 1792 to see revolutionary France for herself; in Paris she met and lived with the American Gilbert Imlay, whose daughter she bore in 1794. She gained access to Girondin political circles, which held out hopes of granting civil rights to women. With the ascendancy of Robespierre foreigners were trapped; she moved for safety to Neuilly. Back in Paris she wrote during the Terror her *Historical and Moral View of the Origin and Progress of the French Revolution; and the Effect It Has Produced in Europe.* Imlay became increasingly evasive, and she returned to London with her child, twice attempting suicide. In a final attempt to maintain relations with Imlay she spent four months in Scandinavia as his business agent. She failed, but her letters became in 1796 the book that William Godwin declared would "make a man in love with the author": *Letters Written during a Short Residence in Sweden, Norway, and Denmark.* Godwin, the author of *An Enquiry Concerning Political Justice*, was the leading radical thinker of the time. He and Mary became lovers, though each maintained their separate working quarters; their affectionate notes chart the progress of their work and of her pregnancy—their daughter, Mary, was to become the author of *Frankenstein*. Personal happiness seemed assured at last, the lovers married, the child was safely delivered, but the mother became infected and died of septicemia at the age of thirty-eight. Godwin published her remaining writings and the loving *Memoirs of Mary Wollstonecraft*, which, by its frankness about her personal life, earned her a reputation for sexual laxity with the nineteenth century.

MAJOR MULTICULTURAL THEMES

Wollstonecraft had met in London such leaders of the new France as Madame Roland and Talleyrand; she was well read in the Enlightenment writers, especially Rousseau, whose views on women's education she found deplorable. Her visit to Portugal left her with strong impressions of the poverty of the common people in "a despotic country"; these contribute to the indignation with which she describes in *A Vindication of the Rights of Men* the gap, economic and cultural, between rich and poor: "virtue can only flourish amongst equals." Her early political works hold out the hope that by the light of reason society can speedily be made just and its citizens happy; firsthand experience of the rule of the Jacobins in France led her to hope rather for a gradual equalization of wealth and improvement of education and morals in her *Historical and Moral View of the Origin and Progress of the French Revolution; and the Effect It Has Produced in Europe.* Her business in Scandinavia led her to remote villages where she observed the harshness of life and behavior with a greater sympathy and understanding; she now trusts in contacts with more advanced Europe gradually to ameliorate conditions in Sweden and warns against the well-meaning impulse to interfere; indeed, peasant frankness and straightforwardness were preferable to the "apish" middle-class manners. In Norway she found the freest community she had ever seen. She sums up her attitude to cultural strangeness: "Travellers who require that every nation should resemble their native country, had better stay at home" (*Letters*, 49).

Though it is still reason that can root out error, Wollstonecraft shows in these *Letters* a Romantic response to Nature as "the nurse of sentiment,—the true source of taste." She feels a pull between the economic need to develop the barren countryside and its present picturesque "originality of character." In the late essay "On Poetry and Our Relish for the Beauties of Nature" she explicitly values the inexplicable pleasure of a spontaneous response to nature, poetry, or art, when perception is not staled by literary convention.

SURVEY OF CRITICISM

Ralph Wardle (1951) warns against a simplified reading of the earlier works as those of a pure rationalist, brought by her experiences in France to awareness of the importance of the emotions; it was sentimentality, not true feeling, that she rejected. Kelly (1992) identifies Wollstonecraft's use of a balance between sensibility and reason as a means of representing the contradictory nature of the Revolution and denies that the political writings are formless. He sees her as knowingly combining two kinds of travel writing, the philosophical and the sentimental. Sapiro (1992) also finds a greater integration of reason and passion than do many critics. Jump (1991, 1994) also claims her as an innovator in travel writing with her use of a possibly fictive autobiographical context; had she visited the North first, she might have been less critical of French national character. Todd, in a 1994 edition of *Political Writings*, reminds readers of the letters to Johnson, which do show disillusion with what she has seen in revolutionary France; describing the first months of the Revolution, she shows awareness of the grim events to come, attributed to deficiencies in the national character resultant on despotism and to too-rapid change, while honoring revolutionary ideals. Jump (1994) regrets that she missed the chance of a lifetime to describe the Terror firsthand. Carol Poston's 1976 edition of the *Letters Written during a Short Residence in Sweden, Norway, and Denmark* praises her courage in traveling to unfrequented places with her child and her ability to write at the same time as woman, mother, and political radical. Her view of social change is evolutionary; many observations have an unexpected modernity. Holmes, in his edition (1987) of the same work, also emphasizes the unusual range of her travels; Scandinavia was then seldom visited; he likens her Romanticism to Coleridge and Dorothy Wordsworth. He publicizes the solution to the puzzle of what she was searching for in these remote fishing communities: a hijacked treasure ship.

SELECTIVE BIBLIOGRAPHY

Works by Wollstonecraft

A Vindication of the Rights of Men, in a Letter to the Right Honourable Edmund Burke. London: Joseph Johnson, 1790.

A Vindication of the Rights of Women: With Strictures on Political and Moral Subjects.
    London: Joseph Johnson, 1792.
*Historical and Moral View of the Origin and Progress of the French Revolution; and
    the Effect It Has Produced in Europe.* London: Joseph Johnson, 1794.
Letters Written during a Short Residence in Sweden, Norway, and Denmark (1796). Ed.
    Carol H. Poston. Lincoln: University of Nebraska Press, 1976.
*A Short Residence in Sweden, Norway, and Denmark and Memoirs of the Author of "The
    Rights of Woman."* Ed. Richard Holmes. Harmondsworth: Penguin, 1987.
Political Writings. Ed. Janet M. Todd. Oxford: Oxford University Press, 1994.

Selective Studies of Wollstonecraft

Jump, Harriet D. " 'The Cool Eye of Observation': Mary Wollstonecraft and the French
    Revolution." In *Revolution in Writing: British Literary Responses to the French
    Revolution,* xi, 53–57, 93, 97–98, 101–2, 112–22. Ed. Kelvin Everest. Milton
    Keynes: Open University Press, 1991.
———. *Mary Wollstonecraft: Writer.* New York and London: Harvester Wheatsheaf,
    1994.
Kelly, Gary. *Revolutionary Feminism: The Mind and Career of Mary Wollstonecraft.*
    London: Macmillan, 1992.
Sapiro, Virginia. *A Vindication of Political Virtue: The Political Theory of Mary Woll-
    stonecraft.* Chicago: University of Chicago Press, 1992.
Todd, Janet. *Mary Wollstonecraft: A Revolutionary Life.* London: Weidenfeld & Nich-
    olson, 2000.
Wardle, Ralph M. *Mary Wollstonecraft, a Critical Biography.* Lawrence: University of
    Kansas Press; London: Richards Press, 1951.

XENOPHON

(between 430 and 428–c. 359)

Paul Archambault

BIOGRAPHY

Xenophon's dates make him an almost exact contemporary of Plato (429–347), and with Plato he is the major source of our information about their common master Socrates. Xenophon's unusual name, a compound of the Greek words for foreigner (*xenos*) and voice (*phone*), was no doubt intended to call attention to his family's foreign connections, a sure mark of aristocratic pedigree. By economic circumstance and military choice Xenophon belonged to one of the four Athenian property classes, the Hippeis (cavalrymen) class.

His most ancient biographer, Diogenes Laertius (fl. early third century B.C.E.) called Xenophon "modest and most superlatively handsome" and adds the story of his first encounter with Socrates, who allegedly blocked his passage in an alleyway and asked him where he might find various products. After Xenophon had answered several queries, Socrates asked him where men might become honorable and virtuous (*kaloi kai agathoi*). When Xenophon confessed his ignorance, Socrates replied, "Then follow me and learn." "And from that time on," adds Diogenes Laertius, "Xenophon was Socrates' disciple" (*Anabase* I.16; cf. Anderson, 9).

Toward the end of the Peloponnesian War (404–403), Xenophon, then about twenty-five, served in the Athenian cavalry and was a member of Socrates' circle. He never hid his upper-class sympathies and was fundamentally hostile toward Athenian democracy. He probably supported the rule of the Thirty Oligarchs (404–403) and became unpopular in Athens after their defeat and the restoration of democracy. His unpopularity in Athens cannot be separated from his association with Socrates: several members of Socrates' circle were Oligarchs, and all were members of the upper classes and were held in suspicion by the Five Hundred, who ruled after 403.

Xenophon left Athens in 401 and enlisted as a Greek mercenary officer in the army of Cyrus the Younger, who wanted to dethrone his older brother Artaxerxes II Memnon, king of Persia, who ruled at Babylon. The march from Sardis toward Babylon of thirteen thousand Greek mercenaries enlisted by Cyrus, Cyrus's defeat and death at the Battle of Cunaxa (401), and Xenophon's taking charge of a strategic retreat by twelve thousand Greek survivors through mountainous terrain inhabited by hostile tribes over a distance of thirteen hundred miles from Cunaxa (near Babylon) to Trapezus, where the Greeks finally sighted the Black Sea ("Thalassa! Thalassa!"), are the subjects of Xenophon's best-known work, the *Anabasis*. Written some three decades after the events (around 370), that work has continued to be studied for centuries as a masterpiece of retreat tactics in hostile circumstances.

In Persia (401–399) Xenophon learned that he had been officially banished from Athens, no doubt because of his unconcealed sympathy for Sparta, victor over Athens during the Peloponnesian War, and his engagement with Persia, Athens's traditional enemy since the early fifth century. At the end of the events narrated in the *Anabasis*, usually referred to as the "March of the Ten Thousand," Xenophon found himself in Asia Minor serving with the Spartan expeditionary force led first by the Spartan king Thibro and then by his successor, King Agesilaus II, both warring for the liberation of the Greeks of Asia against Persian satraps in Asia Minor (399–94). Xenophon returned to the Greek mainland in 394 and participated on the Spartan side in their victory over the combined Theban and Athenian forces at the Battle of Coronea that year.

The Athenians considered Xenophon's defection to Sparta, or Lakonia, an act of high treason and had a term for it: *lakonismos*. For Xenophon, however, it was a highly conscious decision, as he had become friends with King Agesilaus II, whose antidemocratic, anti-Athenian politics he shared. Agesilaus rewarded Xenophon for faithful service at Coronea by granting him an estate at Scillus, in the Peloponnesian city-state of Elis, just south of Olympia. There Xenophon spent the next twenty-three years (394–371) farming, hunting, entertaining, and writing most of his major works. When Elis recovered Scillus from Sparta after the Battle of Leuctra (371), Xenophon established himself at Corinth. Athens, having allied itself with Sparta against Thebes, restored his citizenship in 367. Diogenes Laertius places Xenophon's death at Corinth "in the first year of the hundred and fiftieth Olympiad," that is, around 359 B.C.E.

MAJOR MULTICULTURAL THEMES

Xenophon, an Athenian, served as a mercenary Greek general in the Persian army and, from an Athenian viewpoint, "defected" to Sparta after 394. By his own admission he "became a Peloponnesian" (*Hellenica* VII.4.35, my translation) from that time until his death. In short, though he considered himself a Greek throughout his life, he appears to have ceased considering himself an Athenian sometime around the age of thirty-five.

Throughout the *Anabasis* he distinguished clearly between "Hellenes" and "barbaroi," a term he uses about seventy-five times in that work alone. Though he was a mercenary in the employ of a Persian prince and admired many things Persian, he refers to the Persians as "barbaroi," as he did the other "natives" inhabiting lands through which the Ten Thousand marched—the Kurds, the Armenians, and the Paphlagonians, among others. To translate "barbaroi" by the English "barbarian" is erroneous: for Xenophon the word designated non-Greek "natives," or "foreigners." When Clearchus, early in the expedition, deals with a mutiny of the Greek soldiers (after they learn that the expedition is directed not against the Pisidians, as they have been told, but against King Artaxerxes), he chides them for their change of heart but vows to stay with them wherever they go, for he does not want it to be said "that I led Greeks into a foreign country and then threw them over and chose to make friends with the natives" (*Anabasis* I.3, Warner trans., 66).

Xenophon's admiration for both Cyrus the Younger (r. 424–401) and Cyrus the Great (r. 550–530) is well known to his readers. Why Xenophon wrote *Cyropaedia* is still open to question: was it to show that Cyrus the Great, a Persian, best incarnated the Greek concept of *paideia*, the Platonic philosopher-king? Or was it to demonstrate Xenophon's admiration for the older Cyrus's grandson, Cyrus the Younger? Whatever the reason, Xenophon showed a great admiration for the autocratic Persian system, an admiration shared by Plato when he wrote in the *Laws* (694) that the Persian regime under Cyrus (the Younger) represented a "perfect mean between freedom and enslavement." *Cyropaedia* presents the Persian monarch as a model of virtue, so virtuous in fact that even the Victorian age found him somewhat dull and priggish. As for Cyrus the Younger, whom Xenophon knew and served during the expedition against Artaxerxes, he was for Xenophon a "model" of the civilized leader, who valued the beauty of his gardens (Persian *firdu*, Greek *paradeisioi*) as much as he did excellence in warfare. In his *Oeconomicus* Xenophon's Socrates recalls how Cyrus the Younger awed Lysander, the Spartan military leader, when he showed him his *paradeisos* in Sardis by telling him that he had planned the entire garden himself.

Xenophon admired Sparta as much as he did Persia, and very much for the same reasons. He opted openly for the Spartan side at Coronea (394), and the Athenians banned him officially as a deserter. Xenophon's "desertion" was due not so much to anti-Athenian sentiment as to his conservative, class-inspired contempt for Athenian democratic rule. Since his return from the Persian expedition he had become a close friend of King Agesilaus II. His treatise on Agesilaus, written at his estate at Scillus, is an encomium on a model king much like the *Cyropaedia*. This king, like Cyrus the Great, exhibited the best of "Athenian" virtues—piety, justice, self-control, courage, wisdom—and the greatest proof of his virtue is "the fact that he was judged worthy of the highest office in the most powerful state by the best of men" (*Agesilaus* 1.5, Waterfield trans., 34). Xenophon's praise of Agesilaus's mental agility in old age was an implied defense of Spartan gerontocracy (*gerousia*), a compliment to Spartan political culture that was later challenged by Aristotle (*Politics* 1270b). His short essay on the Lacedemonians, written after 381, called Sparta "the most powerful and most celebrated city in Greece" and said of the Spartan lawgiver Lycurgus that "he reached the utmost limit of wisdom" (*Scripta Minora*, Marchant trans., 137).

"I do not think well of their constitution," wrote Xenophon in his essay on the Athenians, adding that "they have chosen to let the worst people be better off than the good" (*Scripta Minora*, Marchant trans., 475). Xenophon's authorship of this text has been challenged, but the idea is Xenophontic enough. In admiring and serving the traditional enemies of Athens, Persia and Sparta, Xenophon no doubt wanted to show the Athenians that they did not have a monopoly of public or private virtue. Xenophon became a wandering cosmopolitan—or Panhellenist—but wherever he resided, he saw the foreign culture incarnating, even better than Athens, an Athenian ideal of politics and education. What Xenophon failed to realize was that his conception of Athenian *paideia*, based, as he thought, on the military, agricultural, and religious values of the fifth century, had died with the end of the Peloponnesian War.

SURVEY OF CRITICISM

J.K. Anderson's *Xenophon* (1974) is the best general introduction to the subject, profitable reading for specialist and general reader alike. H.G. Dakyns's English translation of the *Cyropaedia*, or *The Education of Cyrus*, which appeared originally in 1914, was republished in 1992, with an excellent introduction by Richard Stoneman. James Tatum (1989) attempts to revive modern interest in the masterpiece, which was considered a classic "mirror for princes" from the time of Alexander the Great to the Victorian age, arguing that it should be read as "a piece of lost fiction" that stands at the origin of the modern novel. Deborah Levine Gera's book (1993) is a detailed, academic study of the same work, an outstanding revised thesis published in the Oxford Classical Monographs series.

Rex Warner's translation of the *Anabasis*, titled *The Persian Expedition*, first appeared in 1949 and has been through eight reprintings; Warner's translation of the *History of My Times* (*Hellenica*) is an admirable 1966 sequel to his 1954 translation of Thucydides' *The Peloponnesian War*, much as Xenophon himself takes up where Thucydides left off; Hugh Tredennick and Robin Waterfield (1990) have collaborated on most readable translations of Xenophon's three Socratic dialogues; and Waterfield has translated the shorter Xenophontic treatises, *Hieron*, *Agesilaus*, *Hipparchicus*, *Hippike*, and *Poroi*, for Penguin Classics (1997). For the original Greek text of Diogenes Laertius's life of Xenophon, as well as for a close, literal translation of the *Anabasis*, Paul Masqueray's two-volume French translation, with facing Greek original (Les Belles Lettres, 1964, 1967) is invaluable.

SELECTIVE BIBLIOGRAPHY

Works by Xenophon

The Persian Expedition (*Anabasis*). Trans. Rex Warner. Intro. George Cawkwell. Harmondsworth: Penguin Books, 1949; rpt. 1975.

History of My Times (*Hellenica*). Trans. Rex Warner. Harmondsworth: Penguin Books, 1966; reprinted 1979 as *A History of My Times*. Intro. and notes George Cawkwell.

Anabase. 2 vols. Trans. Paul Masqueray. Paris: Les Belles Lettres, 1964–1967.

Scripta Minora. Trans. E.C. Marchant. Cambridge, Mass.: Harvard University Press, 1968.

Conversations of Socrates. Trans. Hugh Tredennick and Robin Waterfield. Ed. Robin Waterfield. Harmondsworth: Penguin Books, 1990.

The Education of Cyrus (*Cyropaedia*). Trans. H.G. Dakyns. Intro. and notes Richard Stoneman. London: J.M. Dent and Sons, Everyman's Library, 1992.

Hiero the Tyrant and Other Treatises. Trans. Robin Waterfield. Intro. and notes Paul Cartledge. Harmondsworth: Penguin Books, 1997.

Selective Studies of Xenophon

Anderson, J.K. *Xenophon*. New York: Charles Scribner's Sons, 1974.

Gera, Deborah Levine. *Xenophon's Cyropaedia: Style, Genre, and Literary Technique*. Oxford: Clarendon Press, 1993.

Tatum, James. *Xenophon's Imperial Fiction: On the Education of Cyrus*. Princeton: Princeton University Press, 1989.

XU ZHIMO
(1896–1931)

M. Cristina Pisciotta

BIOGRAPHY

Xu Zhimo, one of the leading figures in modern Chinese romantic poetry, has been described by Robert Payne as "the most brilliant representative in China of a culture that came out of Cambridge" (35). He was born in Chejiang to a well-off family and was considered a "wonder boy." After attending a Western-style college in Shanghai he left for America, where he studied political science and economics first at Clark University and then at Columbia. When he moved to England in 1921, he still had in mind a career in politics or finance and enrolled in the London School of Economics. Here, however, his life changed, and several meetings of fundamental importance (for example, with Thomas Hardy, Katherine Mansfield, and Bertrand Russell) led him unexpectedly into literature. It was at Cambridge that the poet emerged: the character of the town, its river, its countryside, the lively academic life, and the highly intense social and intellectual relationships were to remain the core experiences of his life. ("To spend an evening on the banks of the river . . . is a panacea for the soul . . . night after night under the bridges in a kind of enchantment," *Xu Zhimo quanji*, 3:232.) It was also at Cambridge that he began a "journey through feelings" ("Zhimo shuxin," in *Xu Zhimo quanji*, 4:358), which was for him a journey of increasing Westernization.

Returning to China in late 1922, teaching Western literature at Peking University, and studying with his great friend Liang Qichao (the last great philosopher of classical China, who marked the passage to modern thought), he won instant popularity for the poems related to his European experience and for a kind of diary of feelings written in a mixture of Chinese and English (1922). This was the period when Chinese poetry moved into free verse, signaling a definitive break with traditional fixed models, and came closer to contemporary reality with the passage from antiquated literary language to a colloquial mode of expression. However, Xu and Wen Yiduo, the other great exponent of romantic poetry, went beyond this initial iconoclastic and pioneering phase and created new set forms, as elegant as those of the past but suited to the requirements of the spoken language and sensibilities of modern times.

From 1925 Xu's cultural prestige became ever greater: he was a professor of English at the University of Kuanghua and at Taxia University in Shanghai; in 1926 he launched *Shikan* (the most prestigious modern poetry periodical) and a newspaper literary supplement. He also founded a theatrical review devoted exclusively to Western-style works. His divorce from the wife imposed on him by an arranged marriage and his new union with an open-minded woman who was also divorced caused a great stir in China and became an example for young people who wanted to rebel against their country's traditional customs.

The years 1928–29 were difficult for Xu; marital problems contributed to his increasing despondency, and his growing political consciousness filled him with anguish for the future of his country. He died tragically in an air crash following his return from a further stay in his beloved England, where he had gone in search of the "sweet enjoyment" and "gentle solitude" of the past.

Xu left four collections of poetry, which represent the pinnacle of Chinese romantic poetry. *Zhimo de shi* (1925) appears strongly influenced by Hardy in its choice of themes and its romantic and social consciousness and marks the move from free verse to the new fixed form in Chinese poetry. Already in *Feilengcuide yiye* (1926) the verses are regulated and highly complex in terms of both poetics and prosody, which are very close to those of Keats and Shelley. *Menghu* (1931) and *Yunyou* (published posthumously in 1932), by contrast, are more experimental and autobiographical in nature: here Eliot and Tagore seem to have inspired the symbolic language of the poems, a language filled with melancholy and despair.

MAJOR MULTICULTURAL THEMES

Although Xu was highly Westernized as a result of his studies and the long trips to Europe, it was only during the years at Cambridge, frequenting English circles (in particular the Bloomsbury group), that he he drew together all the elements to drastically change his life. He discovered his poetic potential and recognized his "literary mission": for him, West came increasingly to signify Love, and Love became the central manifestation of his life, the supreme moment in which all feeling is consumed. Thus Cambridge represented the long emotional journey that was to lead him directly to poetry. In those years in England life and poetry became one and the same, clothed in a dynamic power.

For Xu, the encounters with English culture were accidental, never prearranged: "I began reading Shelley only after I discovered he was divorced" ("Wo suo zhidaode Kangqiao," in *Xu Zhimo quanji*, 3:243). The protagonists of nineteenth- and twentieth-century English literature became his heroes and his gods: "Byron stood tall on the crest of the waves" (ibid., 244). Where possible he wanted to know them, touch them, bring them into his life. He was deeply attracted not only to England's culture but to its landscapes and customs and the character of its people. Far removed from the Chinese revolutionary spirit of his time, he admired the English, who were "free but not violent," who were fighting "for democracy and a generalized individualism" (Ren Zhuoxuan, 224). The serenity of English landscapes, the extraordinary gentleness of the country-side, and the comforting gurgle of the river in Cambridge are constantly present in his poems and succeed in creating an atmosphere of total harmony and mys-tical union.

Xu's independent and passionate spirit led him to experiment continually with new forms and metrics, which was to make him one of the major innovators in modern Chinese poetry. Most of his innovations are the product of a profound knowledge of English poetic techniques and of his ability to adapt Western forms to colloquial Chinese poetry. The extraordinary way in which he suc-ceeded in adapting the meters of the English poets (Keats in particular) to his verse characterizes all his work and marks an entirely original step in the de-velopment of modern Chinese poetry: the casual yet melodic colloquial idiom, the sophisticated elegance of his poetic diction, his skill in echoing the same or similar sounds.

While it is true that his task was essentially to "construct a body" for "the spirits of thought which desire to become flesh," as he wrote in *Shikan* in 1926 (no. 1, 7), it is also true that he had created a new poetics, linked to tradition, certainly, but again, and above all, to English models—Shelley ("lofty" lyricism, abstract vocabulary, ethereal and sensual symbols) and Keats (the transitory nature of love and beauty, the battle between death and time, the union with nature). A sensitive translator of poetry in English (Byron, Shelley, Keats, Hardy, Browning, Mansfield, and others), by introducing English poetry and metrics Xu Zhimo was able to point to new paths and lay the foundations of modern Chinese poetry. With his awareness and technical ability he succeeded in fusing West and East, the new and the conventional, the different and the familiar.

SURVEY OF CRITICISM

Cyril Birch (1961) gives a highly detailed metrical analysis of Xu's poems, showing his ingenious ability to adapt a specific metrical model, Keats's iambic tetrameter, to the Chinese popular idiom. More generally, however, according to Birch, the English poetic models provide Xu with the structural unity he sought, in other words, a form with balance and beauty that at the same time avoids the rigidity of the conventional metrical system. Julia Lin (1971), by contrast, analyzes the relationship in Xu's poetry between the English models (Shelley, Keats, Hardy) and the traditional Chinese models (Li Shangyin, Qu Yuan), demonstrating the admirable synthesis he achieved and his important role in the evolution of Chinese poetry. Michelle Loi (1971) looks at the "Westernism" of Xu Zhimo, showing how the introduction of Western metrical rules into his work was not to be understood as exoticism or Anglicism but rather as an innovative instrument.

Xu's education in romanticism, his years in Cambridge and London, his journey through English culture, the legendary friendship with Bertrand Russell, and other minute biographical details are the focus of attention for Leo Ou-fan Lee (1973). Finally, Lloyd Haft (1989) analyzes Xu's four poetry collections, tracing their evolution and their different relationships to English culture.

SELECTIVE BIBLIOGRAPHY

Works by Xu Zhimo

Zhimo de shi. 1st ed. Shanghai: Xinyue shudian, 1925.
Feilengcuide yiye. 1st ed. Shanghai: Xinyue shudian, 1926.
Menghu. 1st ed. Shanghai: Xinyue shudian, 1931.
Yunyou. 1st ed. Shanghai: Xinyue shudian, 1932.
Twentieth Century Chinese Poetry: An Anthology. Ed. and trans. Hsü Kai-yu. Ithaca: Cornell University Press, 1970.
Xu Zhimo quanji (Complete works). Vols. 3 and 4. Ed. Jiang Fucong and Liang Shiqiu. Taipei: Wenhua dushu gongsi, 1964.
Anthology of Modern Chinese Poetry. Ed. and trans. Michelle Yeh. New Haven: Yale University Press, 1992.

Selective Studies of Xu Zhimo

Birch, Cyril. "English and Chinese Meters in Hsü Chih-mo." *Asia Major* 8, no. 2 (1961): 258–93.
Haft, Lloyd, ed. *A Selective Guide to Chinese Literature, 1900–1949.* Vol. 3, *The Poem.* Leiden: E.J. Brill, 1989.
Lee, Leo Ou-fan. *The Romantic Generation of Modern Chinese Writers.* Cambridge, Mass.: Harvard University Press, 1973.
Lin, Julia. *Modern Chinese Poetry: An Introduction.* Seattle: University of Washington Press, 1972.
Loi, Michelle. *Roseaux sur le mur: Les poètes occidentalistes chinois, 1919–1949.* Paris: Gallimard, 1971.
Payne, Robert, ed. *Contemporary Chinese Poetry.* London: Routledge, 1947.
Ren Zhuoxuan. *Wenxue he yuwen.* Taipei: Guangwen shuju, 1966.
Yeh, Michelle. *Modern Chinese Poetry: Theory and Practice since 1917.* New Haven: Yale University Press, 1991.

Select Bibliography

Aldrich, Robert. "From *Francité* to *Créolité*: French West Indian Literature Comes Home." In *Writing across Worlds: Literature and Migration*, 101–24. Ed. Russell King, John Connell, and Paul White. London and New York: Routledge, 1995.

Anagnost, Ann. *National Past-Times: Narrative, Representation, and Power in Modern China*. Durham, N.C.: Duke University Press, 1997.

Appiah, K. Anthony. "The Multiculturalist Misunderstanding." *New York Review of Books* (October 9, 1997): 30–36.

Appiah, Kwame Anthony, and Henry Louis Gates, Jr., eds. *The Dictionary of Global Culture*. New York: Knopf, 1997.

Baetens Beardsmore, Hugo. *Bilingualism: Basic Principles*. 2nd ed. Clevedon, Avon: Multilingual Matters, 1986.

Baker, Colin. *Key Issues in Bilingualism and Bilingual Education*. Clevedon, Avon: Multilingual Matters, 1988.

Barefoot, Brian. *The English Road to Rome*. Upton-upon-Severn: Images, 1993.

Barkan, Elazar, and Marie-Denise Shelton, eds. *Borders, Exiles, Diasporas*. Stanford: Stanford University Press, 1998.

Batten, Charles L., Jr. *Pleasurable Instruction: Form and Convention in Eighteenth-Century Travel Literature*. Berkeley: University of California Press, 1978.

Brand, Michael, and Chuch Phoeurn. *The Age of Angkor: Treasures from the National Museum of Cambodia*. Canberra: Australian National Gallery, 1992.

Brilli, Attilio. *Il viaggio in Italia*. Milan: Silvana, 1987.

Cameron, Averil. "Before the Fall." *New York Review of Books* (June 22, 1995): 55–58.

Campbell, Mary Baine. *Wonder and Science: Imagining Worlds in Early Modern Europe*. Ithaca: Cornell University Press, 1999.

Cary, M., and H.H. Scullard. *A History of Rome down to the Reign of Constantine*. 3rd ed. London: Macmillan, 1979.

Certeau, Michel de. *Culture in the Plural*. Trans. Tom Conley. Minneapolis: University of Minnesota Press, 1997.

Clifford, James. *Routes: Travel and Translation in the Late Twentieth Century*. Cambridge, Mass.: Harvard University Press, 1997.

The Columbia Encyclopedia. 6th ed. New York: Columbia University Press, 2000.

Descartes, René. *Oeuvres et lettres.* Bibliothèque de la Pléiade, Paris: Gallimard, 1953.

Didier, Béatrice. *Dictionnaire universel des littératures.* 3 vols. Paris: Presses Universitaires de France, 1994.

Dodd, Philip, ed. *The Art of Travel: Essays on Travel Writing.* London: Cass, 1982.

Duffy, Patrick. "Literary Reflections on Irish Migration in the Nineteenth and Twentieth Centuries." In *Writing across Worlds: Literature and Migration,* 20–38. Ed. Russell King, John Connell, and Paul White. London and New York: Routledge, 1995.

Edwards, John. *Multilingualism.* London and New York: Routledge, 1994.

Encyclopaedia Britannica. 24 vols. Chicago: William Benton, 1967.

Fredrickson, George M. "America's Caste System: Will It Change?" *New York Review of Books* (October 23, 1997): 68–75.

Gelfant, Blanche H. *Cross-cultural Reckonings.* New York: Cambridge University Press, 1995.

Glazer, Nathan. *We Are All Multiculturalists Now.* Cambridge, Mass.: Harvard University Press, 1997.

Gnisci, Armando, ed. *La letteratura del mondo.* Roma: Sovera Multimedia, 1993.

―――. *Noialtri Europei: Saggi di letteratura comparata su identità e luoghi d'Europa.* 2nd ed. Roma: Bulzoni, 1994.

Gnisci, Armando, and Franca Sinopli, eds. *Letteratura comparata: Storia e testi.* Roma: Sovera Multimedia, 1995.

Grafton, Anthony. "The Rest vs. the West." *New York Review of Books* (April 10, 1997): 57–64.

Grosjean, François. *Life with Two Languages.* Cambridge, Mass.: Harvard University Press, 1982.

Hakuta, Kenji. *Mirror of Language.* New York: Basic Books, 1986.

Hamers, Josiane, and M. Blanc. *Bilingualité et bilinguisme.* Bruxelles: Pierre Mardaga, 1983.

Historical Atlas of Armenia. New York: Armenian National Education Committee, 1987.

Honour, Hugh. "Burma: Splendor and Miseries." *New York Review of Books* (July 13, 1995): 56–61.

Huntington, Samuel P. *The Clash of Civilizations and the Remaking of World Order.* New York: Simon and Schuster, 1997.

Ibnlfassi, Laila, and Nicki Hitchcott, eds. *African Francophone Writing: A Critical Introduction.* Washington, D.C.: Berg, 1996.

Iriye, Akira. *Cultural Internationalism and World Order.* Baltimore: Johns Hopkins University Press, 1997.

Issawi, Charles. *Cross-cultural Encounters and Conflicts.* New York: Oxford University Press, 1998.

Jackson, William T.H., and George Stade. *European Writers: The Middle Ages and the Renaissance.* 2 vols. New York: Charles Scribner's Sons, 1983.

Jenkyns, Richard. "China Is Near." *New York Review of Books* (December 3, 1998): 21–23.

Jensen, Lionel M. *Manufacturing Confucianism: Chinese Traditions and Universal Civilization.* Durham, N.C.: Duke University Press, 1997.

Jones, Rosemarie. "*Pied-noir* Literature: The Writing of a Migratory Elite." In *Writing across Worlds: Literature and Migration*, 125–40. Ed. Russell King, John Connell, and Paul White. London and New York: Routledge, 1995.

King, Russell, John Connell, and Paul White, eds. *Writing across Worlds: Literature and Migration*. London and New York: Routledge, 1995.

Krell, David Farrell, and Donald L. Bates. *The Good European: Nietzsche's Work Sites in Word and Image*. Chicago: University of Chicago Press, 1997.

Kymlicka, Will. *Multicultural Citizenship: A Liberal Theory of Minority Rights*. Oxford: Clarendon Press; New York: Oxford University Press, 1995.

Leithauser, Brad. "A Small Country's Great Book." *New York Review of Books* (May 11, 1995): 41–45.

Leonardo, Micaela di. *Exotics at Home: Anthropologies, Others, American Modernity*. Chicago: University of Chicago Press, 1998.

McDonagh, Bernard. *Turkey*. 2nd ed. London: A&C Black; New York: W.W. Norton, 1995.

McNeill, William H. "Decline of the West?" *New York Review of Books* (January 9, 1997): 18–22.

Magill, Frank N., ed. *Great Women Writers*. New York: Henry Holt, 1994.

Martinet, Marie-Madeline. *Le Voyage d'Italie dans les littératures européennes*. Paris: Presses Universitaires de France, 1996.

Maurer, Doris, and Arnold E. Maurer. *Guida letteraria dell'Italia*. Parma: Guanda, 1993.

Meillet, Antoine. *Esquisse d'une histoire de la langue latine*. Paris: Klincksieck, 1966.

Millar, Fergus. *The Roman Near East, 31 B.C.–A.D. 337*. Cambridge, Mass.: Harvard University Press, 1993.

Miller, John J. *The Unmaking of Americans: How Multiculturalism Has Undermined the Assimilation Ethic*. New York: Free Press, 1998.

Miner, Earl R. *The Japanese Tradition in British and American Literature*. Princeton: Princeton University Press, 1958.

———. "Gli studi comparati interculturali." In *Letteratura comparata: Storia e testi*, 179–204. Ed. Armando Gnisci and Franca Sinopoli. Roma: Sovera Multimedia, 1995.

Morrison, Helen Barber, ed. *The Golden Age of Travel: Literary Impressions of the Grand Tour*. London: Andrew Melrose, 1953.

Mudimbe, V.Y., ed. *Nations, Identities, Cultures*. Durham, N.C.: Duke University Press, 1997.

"Multilingualism in Europe." *International Herald Tribune* (January 26, 1998): 15.

National Museum of Korea. Seoul: Tongchon Publishing Company, 1991.

Pellegrini, Carlo, ed. *Venezia nelle letterature moderne*. Venezia: Fondazione Giorgio Cini, 1961.

Possin, Hans Joachim. *Reisen und Literatur: Das Thema des Reisens in der englischen Literatur des 18. Jahrhunderts*. Tübingen: Niemeyer, 1972.

Queneau, Raymond. *Histoire des littératures*. 3 vols. Encyclopédie de la Pléiade. Paris: Gallimard, 1958.

Ritchie, J.M. *German Exiles: British Perspectives*. New York: Peter Lang, 1997.

Rowland, Ingrid D. "The Renaissance Revealed." *New York Review of Books* (November 6, 1997): 30–35.

Saadé, Gabriel. *Ougarit: Métropole cananéenne*. Beyrouth, Liban: Imprimerie Catholique, 1979.

Said, Edward W. *Orientalism*. New York: Pantheon, 1978.

Saint-Gille, Anne-Marie, ed. *La vraie patrie, c'est la lumière! Correspondance entre Annette Kolb et Romain Rolland (1915–1936)*. Bern: Peter Lang, 1994.

Saracino, Maria Antonietta, ed. *Altri lati del mondo*. Roma: Sensibili alle foglie, 1994.

Scammell, Michael. "Loyal toward Reality." *New York Review of Books* (September 24, 1998): 36–40.

Schweizer Schriftsteller der Gegenwart/Ecrivains suisses d'aujourd'hui/Scrittori svizzeri d'oggi/Scriptuors Svizzers da noss dis. Bern: A. Francke AG (Verlag Bern), 1962.

Seta, Cesare de. *L'Italia del Grand Tour da Montaigne a Goethe*. Napoli: Electa Napoli, 1992.

7000 Years of Chinese Civilization. (Catalog of the exhibition at the Peking Museum of Chinese History.) Milano: Silvana Editoriale, 1983.

Shalem, Avinoam. *Islam Christianized*. 2nd rev. ed. Frankfurt am Main: Peter Lang, 1998.

Shepard, Odell. *The Lore of the Unicorn*. New York: Dover, 1993.

Shumsky, Neil Larry. "Return Migration in American Novels of the 1920s and 1930s." In *Writing across Worlds: Literature and Migration*, 198–215. Ed. Russell King, John Connell, and Paul White. London and New York: Routledge, 1995.

Simenon, Georges. *La mauvaise étoile*. In *Tout Simenon*, vol. 20. Paris: Presses de la Cité, 1992.

Smith, Carolyn D., ed. *Strangers at Home: Essays on the Effects of Living Overseas and Coming "Home" to a Strange Land*. New York: Aletheia, 1996.

Spence, Jonathan D. *The Chan's Great Continent: China in Western Minds*. New York: W.W. Norton, 1998.

Stam, Robert. *Tropical Multiculturalism: A Comparative History of Race in Brazilian Cinema and Culture*. Durham, N.C.: Duke University Press, 1997.

Stavans, Ilan, ed. *Mutual Impressions: Writers from the Americas Reading One Another*. Durham, N.C.: Duke University Press, 1999.

Stowe, William W. *Going Abroad: European Travel in Nineteenth-Century American Culture*. Princeton: Princeton University Press, 1994.

Stoye, John Walter. *English Travellers Abroad, 1604–1667: Their Influence in English Society and Politics*. London: Jonathan Cape, 1952.

Tanner, Tony. *Venice Desired*. Oxford: Blackwell, 1992.

Todorov, Tzvetan. *Nous et les autres: La réflexion française sur la diversité humaine*. Paris: Editions du Seuil, 1989.

Tomasch, Sylvia, and Sealy Gilles, eds. *Text and Territory: Geographical Imagination in the European Middle Ages*. Philadelphia: University of Pennsylvania Press, 1998.

Toynbee, Arnold. *The World and the West*. London: Oxford University Press, 1953.

Vance, William L. *America's Rome*. 2 vols. New Haven: Yale University Press, 1989.

Walzer, Michael. *On Toleration*. New Haven: Yale University Press, 1997.

Weightman, John. "Multicultural Mandarin." *New York Review of Books* (December 1, 1994): 41–43.

Weschler, Lawrence. *Calamities of Exile: Three Nonfiction Novellas*. Chicago: University of Chicago Press, 1998.

Williams, Robert C. *Russia Imagined: Art, Culture, and National Identity, 1840–1995*. New York: Peter Lang, 1997.

Wilpert, Gero von. *Lexikon der Weltliteratur*. 3 vols. Stuttgart: Alfred Kröner, 1968; 2nd ed., 1975; 3rd ed., 1993.

Yi-fu Tuan. *Cosmos and Hearth: A Cosmopolite's Viewpoint.* Minneapolis: University of Minnesota Press, 1996.

Zwerdling, Alex. *Improvised Europeans: American Literary Expatriates and the Siege of London.* New York: Basic Books, 1998.

Index

The main entries for writers profiled in this sourcebook are identified by boldfaced page numbers.

About the Editors and Contributors

ALBA AMOIA is Associate Professor Emerita, Department of Romance Languages, Hunter College of the City University of New York. She has published several literary biographies (Edmond Rostand, Jean Anouilh, Albert Camus, Fedor Dostoevsky) and studies of the Italian theatrical and literary scenes. Her most recent book, *No Mothers We!* (2000), analyzes the revolt of Italian women writers against maternity.

BETTINA L. KNAPP is Thomas Hunter Professor of French and Comparative Literature (Emerita) at Hunter College and the Graduate Center of the City University of New York. She is the author of over fifty books, of which the most recent (2000) are *Gambling, Game, and Psyche* and *Voltaire Revisited*. Editor of the annual review *Antemnae*, she is also a Knight in the Order of Arts and Letters.

PAUL ARCHAMBAULT is Professor of French at Syracuse University, New York, where he directs the French program. He has written many books and articles dealing with autobiography, the most recent book being *A Monk's Confession: The Memoirs of Guibert de Nogent* (1996). He delivered four lectures at the Collège de France in 1998 on the relation between autobiographical discourse and historical narrative.

ABDELLATIF ATTAFI, originally from Tangier, Morocco, completed his Ph.D. in Lille, France. He is currently Associate Professor of French at the University of Charleston in South Carolina. His research interests include the brain-drain phenomenon of North African students in France and North African literature, specifically that of Tahar Ben Jelloun.

MARLÈNE BARSOUM is Assistant Professor of French and Francophone Literature at Hunter College of the City University of New York. Her fields of interest are Egyptian francophone literature, nineteenth-century literature, travel literature, and poetry. She has published articles in poetry magazines on Théophile Gautier and Andrée Chedid.

INGEBORG BAUMGARTNER is Professor of Foreign Languages at Albion College, Michigan. Her research and publications are on nineteenth- and twentieth-century literature, particularly the novella and Thomas Mann. Recent publications include "Czechoslovakia's Beautiful Gesture: Thomas Mann as Citizen of Czechoslovakia, 1936–1944" and "Herder and Romanticism."

LUCILLE FRACKMAN BECKER is Professor Emerita of French, Drew University, Madison, New Jersey. She has lectured on modern French literature at universities throughout the world. The author of numerous articles and reviews, she has published seven books, the most recent of which is *Georges Simenon Revisited* (1999).

JANE BENARDETE, Professor Emerita of English at Hunter College of the City University of New York, is an Americanist who specializes in the literature of the nineteenth and early twentieth centuries. She is the editor of Hamlin Garland's *Crumbling Idols* (1960), author of *American Realism: A Shape for Fiction* (1972), and coeditor of *Companions of Our Youth* (1980), an edition of tales for children by well-known American women writers of the nineteenth century, as well as of numerous articles and reviews.

LUISA BIENATI teaches modern and contemporary Japanese Literature in the Department of East Asian Studies of the University of Venice. She has published translations of, and articles on, Nagai Kafū, Tanizaki Jun'ichirō, and Ibuse Masuji. Her translation and annotated edition in Italian of Nagai Kafū's tales appeared in 2000.

ROBERT BIRD is Assistant Professor of Russian at Dickinson College in Carlisle, Pennsylvania. He has published widely on Russian literature of the Silver Age, especially on Viacheslav Ivanov, and has also been active in the study of Russian religious philosophy, both as scholar and translator.

MICHAEL BISHOP is McCulloch Professor of Humanities at Dalhousie University, Halifax, Canada. He is the author of many articles and studies devoted to modern and contemporary literature and culture. His most recent publications include *Michel Deguy* (1988), *René Char, Les dernières Années* (1990), *Contemporary French Women Poets* (2 volumes, 1995), *Women's Poetry in France, 1965–1995: A Bilingual Anthology* (1997), and *Thirty Voices in the Feminine* (editor, 1996). Translations of Salah Stétié and a study of Jacques Prévert are in press.

SUSAN BRANTLY is Professor of Scandinavian Studies at the University of Wisconsin at Madison. A specialist in Scandinavian literature, she has published articles on August Strindberg, Pär Lagerkvist, Tove Ditleven, E.T.A. Hoffmann, and other topics. Author of *Understanding Isak Dinesen*, she has also written a biography of Laura Marholm, a turn-of-the-century woman writer and translator of Scandinavian literature into German.

RICHARD A. BROOKS is Professor of French at the Graduate Center of the City University of New York and Professor of Comparative Literature at the College of Staten Island of the City University of New York. His field of research interest is eighteenth-century French literature.

TIMOTHY L. CARENS is Assistant Professor of English at the College of Charleston, South Carolina. Focusing on the impact of imperialism on Victorian literature, he has published articles on the work of Charles Dickens and George Meredith.

JEFFREY S. CARNES is Associate Professor of Classics at Syracuse University, New York. His publications include "The Ends of the Earth: Fathers, Ephebes, and Wild Women in *Nemean* 4 and 5" (1996), "This Myth Which Is Not One: Construction of Discourse in Plato's *Symposium*" (1997), and *The Uses of Aiakos: Pindar and the Aiginetan Imaginary* (forthcoming).

ROBERT E. CLARK holds the Ph.D. in English and Comparative Literature from Columbia University. He is an editor and writer living in New York City.

MARLIES K. DANZIGER is Professor Emerita of English at Hunter College and the Graduate Center of the City University of New York and is currently an editor with the Boswell Papers at Yale University. She has written books and articles on Boswell, Johnson, Goldsmith, and Sheridan; has edited Boswell's last journals (*Boswell: The Great Biographer*, 1989, with Frank Brady); and is now completing the Yale research edition of Boswell's journals in Germany and Switzerland.

NADINE DORMOY, Editor-in-Chief of *Europe Plurilingue (Plurilingual Europe)* and on the faculty at the Université de Paris VIII-Saint-Denis, France, formerly was Associate Professor of French at Herbert H. Lehman College of the City University of New York. Her most recent publication, *L'Écriture ou la vie* (1999), is the translation of Isabelle Hoog Naginski's *George Sand: Writing for Her Life*.

BARBARA FOSTER, Associate Professor Emerita, Library Department, Hunter College of the City University of New York, is coauthor of *The Secret Lives of Alexandra David-Neel* (1998). She is a world traveler in the tradition of the heroic women about whom she writes and has acted as a referee for the Royal Geographical Society of London.

MICHAEL FOSTER is a novelist and historian.

LUANNE FRANK is Associate Professor, University of Texas, Arlington. She teaches literature, criticism, and theory in the English Department and Graduate

Humanities program. Her specialties are eighteenth- and twentieth- century German literature, semiotics, hermeneutics, and psychoanalysis. She has coedited *Husbanding the Golden Grain*, edited *Literature and the Occult*, and coedited, cotranslated, and introduced *Basic Concepts of Poetics by Emil Staiger*.

KINGA EMINOWICZ GALICA teaches French at Lakeland Regional High School in New Jersey. She holds a Ph.D. in French literature and has done research and published articles on women in nineteenth-century prose, writers of East Central Europe, literature, and exile.

MARCEL GUTWIRTH is Distinguished Professor Emeritus of French, Graduate Center of the City University of New York. His field of scholarship is seventeenth-century French literature. His publications include *Laughing Matter: An Essay on the Comic* (1993) and "The Lesson of Sophonisba: French Classicism and the Unloving Heroine" (1999).

JULIE E. HALL is Associate Professor of English at Sam Houston State University, Huntsville, Texas. She has published articles on Hawthorne in the *Nathaniel Hawthorne Review* and most recently authored a chapter on Sophia Hawthorne for a forthcoming volume of *The Dictionary of Literary Biography: American Women Prose Writers, 1820–1870*.

CARLOS R. HORTAS was formerly Dean of Humanities and is currently Professor of Spanish at Hunter College of the City University of New York. His field of research is colonial Latin American literature.

MARY HUDSON holds the Ph.D. in French Literature from the Graduate Center of the City University of New York. A specialist in twentieth-century literature, she is employed by the International Baccalaureate in New York.

BARRY JACOBS, who is Professor of English and Comparative Literature at Montclair State University in New Jersey, has also taught Scandinavian and comparative literature at Harvard University and Brigham Young University. He is recognized as a translator of Swedish literary and scholarly works and has published widely on Ibsen, Strindberg, and other Scandinavian writers.

JOHN W. KNELLER is President Emeritus of Brooklyn College and Professor Emeritus of French at the Graduate Center of the City University of New York. He is a former Associate Editor of *Yale French Studies* and Editor-in-Chief of the *French Review*. He is currently preparing a book on *Privileged Moments in Nerval, Baudelaire, and Rimbaud*.

MARIA JOSÉ DE LANCASTRE of Lisbon, Portugal, is Professor of Portuguese Language and Literature at the University of Pisa, Italy.

DOMIZIA LANZETTA is Director of the Department of Romanist Studies of the Accademia Tiberina, Rome, Italy. Writer, lecturer, and researcher in the field of Greek and Hellenistic religions, she is the author of two novels set in antiquity. Her latest published article is "Fato e fortuna nella visione spirituale del mondo greco e latino" (1999).

MARINA MACKAY is a tutor in English literature at the University of East Anglia, Norwich, England, where she was awarded the Ph.D. in 1999. Her dissertation was on the novels of Angus Wilson, and she has published articles on Wilson in *Pretext* and the *Journal of Modern Literature*.

MARIE-MADELEINE MARTINET is Professor at the Université de Paris IV-Sorbonne, and Co-Director of the Center for Anglophone Studies and Information Technology (Project in Humanities Computing). *Le Voyage d'Italie dans les littératures européennes* (1996) is her most recent book; "Squaring the Circle: Visual Paradoxes as an Image of Intercultural Experiences" (2000), her most recent article.

MATILDE MASTRANGELO, Adjunct Professor of Japanese Language and Literature at the University of Rome, holds degrees from the University of Tokyo and the Oriental Institute of the University of Naples. Her main fields of research are Japanese verbal arts and the works of Mori Ōgai, of whom she has translated and edited the "German trilogy" and four historical tales.

BRUCE MERRY, formerly Chairman of the Italian Department at the University of the Witwatersrand, South Africa, is presently Associate Professor in the Department of English Literature at Kuwait University. He is the author of numerous articles in the field of Italian literature. His most recent publication is *Dacia Maraini and the Written Dream of Women in Italian Literature* (1997).

ALESSANDRO MONTI is Professor of English Language and Postcolonial Literatures and Languages at the University of Torino. He is the author of studies on Indian literature in English and Associate Editor of the *Atlantic Review* (Delhi). His publications include *Durga Marga* (1995) and *The Time after Cowdust* (2000).

MAX E. NOORDHOORN is Professor of German at Albion College, Michigan. His main areas of interest are lyric poetry from the seventeenth century to the present and popular culture, ranging from Wilhelm Busch to the Wiener Volkstheater.

PATRICIA OWEN, formerly Senior Lecturer at the West London Institute of Higher Education, is Lecturer in the International Programs of Wisconsin, Stevens Point, and St. Mary's University, Minnesota. She is coauthor of *A Rebel Hand, Nicholas Delaney of 1798: From Ireland to Australia* (1999).

JAMES O. PELLICER is Professor in the Department of Romance Languages at Hunter College of the City University of New York. His most recent publication is *El "Facundo," significante y significado.* In preparation are two textbooks, *Structures of Modern Spanish* and *Advanced Spanish Writing.* His field of interest is the history of ideas in Spanish America, mainly in the nineteenth century.

M. CRISTINA PISCIOTTA is Professor of Chinese Language and Literature at the Oriental Institute of the University of Naples, Italy. She has earned degrees in modern Chinese language and literature at the University of Rome, the Ecole des Hautes Etudes Chinoises of the Sorbonne, the Language Institute, and the University of Beijing and has taught at the University of Venice and the University of Rome. Her publications include the translation and edition of Lu Wenfu, *Vita e passione di un gastronomo cinese* (1991), and "Nuove tendenze del teatro di prosa contemporaneo in Cina" (*Atti del Convegno sulla Letteratura Cinese Contemporanea*, 2000).

ELISABETH PLESSEN, a novelist, poet, and translator who resides in Lucca, Italy, and Berlin, is the author of two collections of short stories and four novels. The latest translation of one of her novels was into Italian (*Kohlhaas il ribelle*), published in 1983. She has also edited, with Michael Mann, Katja Mann's autobiography, *Meine ungeschriebenen Memoiren*.

JEANINE PARISIER PLOTTEL is Professor Emerita of Romance Languages at Hunter College and the Graduate Center of the City University of New York and a scholar of nineteenth- and twentieth-century French literature. Her recent publications deal with Victor Hugo and Rodin and with morality and literature in France during the World War II German occupation.

VALERIA POMPEJANO is Associate Professor of French Language and Literature at the University of Rome, Italy. A specialist in French literature of the seventeenth century, she has concentrated on baroque authors, themes, and literary theories, publishing books and articles since 1974. Her latest article, on Italianism in France, appeared in *Franco-Italica* 13 (1999).

ELIZABETH POWERS, Adjunct Assistant Professor of German at Drew University in Madison, New Jersey, is coeditor of *Pilgrim Souls: A Collection of Spiritual Autobiographies* (1999). Other published writings include two novels, three articles on Goethe, and literary articles and reviews for national magazines. She is currently working on a biography of young Goethe.

QIAN SUOQIAO is Assistant Professor in the Department of Comparative Literature at Hamilton College, New York. He is the author of a number of articles and a book, *Cosmopolitan Chinese: Lin Yu Tang and Crosscultural Agency*. His fields of interest are Chinese-American cross-cultural studies, modern Chinese literature, and American literature.

DOMNICA RADULESCU is Associate Professor of Romance Languages at Washington and Lee University in Lexington, Virginia. She is the author of *André Malraux: The "Farfelu" as Expression of the Feminine and the Erotic* and of scholarly articles on Camus, Malraux, Seneca, and Euripides. She has recently completed a book-length manuscript, *Sisters of Medea: The Tragic Heroine across Cultures.*

MARCELLO RICCI, Doctor of Research in Geographical-Historical Sciences, teaches cartography and geography at the University of Rome. A member of the editorial board of the *Bollettino della Società Geografica Italiana*, he is also the author of numerous works in the fields of the environment, landscape, and geographical exploration.

MELVIN RICHTER is Professor Emeritus of Political Science at Hunter College of the City University of New York. He is the author of *The Politics of Conscience: T.H. Green and His Age* and *The History of Political and Social Concepts: A Critical Introduction*; the recipient of the Chevalier de l'Ordre des Arts et Lettres and of the Triennial Prize, Conference on British Studies; and has held Fulbright Professorships in Paris and Munich.

AMEEN ALBERT RIHANI is Professor of Bilingual and Bicultural Literature and Vice-President for Academic Affairs at Notre Dame University in Zouk Mosbeh, Lebanon. He has taught Arab philosophy at the American University of Beirut and literary criticism at the Lebanese American University. He is the author of fourteen books, many articles, and has also edited volumes of conference proceedings. Among his recent books are *Water Rituals* (1999) and *Forgotten Springs* (2000).

MAURIZIO RIOTTO is Associate Professor of Korean Language and Literature at the Oriental Institute of the University of Naples, Italy. His titles include Research Fellow at Seoul National University, Visiting Scholar at Kyotō's Doshisha University, and Visiting Scholar at Seoul's Hanyang University. He is the author of numerous books, articles, and translations in the field of Korean language and literature. His most recent publication (1998) is his Italian translation and edition of two classical Korean novels.

A.L. ROGERS II is Visiting Instructor in the Department of English at the College of Charleston, South Carolina. He received the B.A. from Duke University (1985) and the M.A. from the University of North Carolina in Charlotte (1992) and is presently writing a dissertation on Charles Dickens for the Ph.D. at the University of Tennessee in Knoxville.

MARTHA L. RUBÍ is Adjunct Lecturer in Spanish at Hunter College of the City University of New York. Works in progress are *Twentieth-Century Themes in the Poetry of Hispanic American Women: A Selected Anthology* and *Spanish-American Feminist Literary Theory: An Approach through the Concept of Willing and Willingness.*

RINALDINA RUSSELL is Professor of European Languages and Literatures at Queens College of the City University of New York. She is coeditor and co-translator of Tullia d'Aragona's *Dialogue on the Infinity of Love* (1997) and editor of two volumes published by Greenwood Press: *Italian Women Writers* (1994) and *The Feminist Encyclopedia of Italian Literature* (1997).

IKUKO SAGIYAMA is Associate Professor of Japanese Language and Literature at the University of Florence, Italy. She has published numerous Italian translations of, and articles on, Japanese poetry, recently translating into Italian the complete *Kokin Waka shū*.

MARIA ANTONIETTA SARACINO is Researcher and Lecturer in Postcolonial Literature in English in the Department of English of the University of Rome, Italy. She has written extensively on themes and authors in contemporary African, Caribbean, and Indian literature in English. Her most recent publications (2000) are *Africa bambina* and *Il calypso e la Regina*.

CARLA SCOGNAMIGLIO is Librarian at the Istituto Enciclopedia Italiana in Rome, Italy. She collaborates with the Library of the Società Geografica Italiana as well as with the Consortium Biblioteche e Archivi Istituti Culturali di Roma.

JAMES SEXTON, Professor in the English Department of Camosun College, Victoria, British Columbia, is the editor of *Aldous Huxley's Hearst Essays* (1994), coeditor (with David Bradshaw) of Huxley's *Now More Than Ever* (2000), and coeditor (with Robert Baker) of *Aldous Huxley Complete Essays* in a projected six volumes. Volumes 1 and 2 were published in 2000.

BRITA STENDAHL, a native of Sweden, has lived and taught Scandinavian literature in Cambridge, Massachusetts, since 1954. She is particularly interested in Sweden's foremost nineteenth-century feminist, Fredrika Bremer. Her biography, *The Education of a Self-made Woman: Fredrika Bremer, 1801–1865*, was published in 1994.

BEATRICE STIGLITZ, Professor of French at the University of Charleston in South Carolina, was educated in Romania, France, and the United States. In research, as in teaching, she specializes in French language and literature, intellectual history, Eastern European politics and culture, Jewish studies, women's studies, film, and popular culture.

VALERIA TOCCO is Researcher in Portuguese Language and Literature at the University of Pisa and temporary Professor at the University of Bergamo, Italy. Specializing in Portuguese literature of the sixteenth century, she has published critical editions (1997 and 1999) of the poets of the *Cancioneiro Geral de Resende*, as well as essays on various aspects of Renaissance-baroque culture. Her recent research on Luís de Camões has resulted in the publication of her critical notes for the Italian edition of the *Lusíadas* (2000).

JOAN VON MEHREN, author of *Minerva and the Muse: A Life of Margaret Fuller* (1994), is an independent scholar who has lived for many years in Europe and Asia. Her field of interest is nineteenth-century American cultural interaction with Europe.

ROBERT J. WHITE is Professor in the Department of Classical and Oriental Studies at Hunter College of the City University of New York. His *Interpretation of Dreams: The Oneirocritica of Artemidorus* (1975; revised and enlarged, 1990) is the first English translation of the earliest complete manual on dream interpretation that survives from classical antiquity. He has also written *An Avalanche of Anoraks* (1994) and coauthored *The Key to the Name of the Rose* (1987; revised, 1999).

WILLIAM WOLF earned his M.A. in Literature at Montclair State University. He is a published poet and a Sunday painter. He teaches English at Livingston Alternative High School in Livingston, New Jersey.